Space-Time Perspectives on
Early Colonial Moquegua

Space-Time Perspectives on Early Colonial Moquegua

Prudence M. Rice

UNIVERSITY PRESS OF COLORADO
Boulder

© 2013 by University Press of Colorado

Published by University Press of Colorado
1580 Market Street, Suite 660
PMB 39883
Denver, Colorado 80203

All rights reserved
First paperback edition 2024

 The University Press of Colorado is a proud member of
Association of University Presses.

The University Press of Colorado is a cooperative publishing enterprise supported, in part, by Adams State University, Colorado State University, Fort Lewis College, Metropolitan State University of Denver, University of Alaska Fairbanks, University of Colorado, University of Denver, University of Northern Colorado, University of Wyoming, Utah State University, and Western Colorado University..

Library of Congress Cataloging-in-Publication Data

Rice, Prudence M.
  Space-time perspectives on early colonial Moquegua / Prudence M. Rice.
     pages cm
  Includes bibliographical references and index.
  ISBN 978-1-60732-275-7 (hardcover : alk. paper) — ISBN 978-1-64642-650-8 (paperback) — ISBN 978-1-60732-276-4 (ebook)
 1. Indians of South America—Colonization—Peru—Moquegua (Department) 2. Indians of South America—First contact with Europeans—Peru—Moquegua (Department) 3. Indians of South America—Peru—Moquegua (Department)—Antiquities. 4. Landscape archaeology—Peru—Moquegua (Department) 5. Cultural landscapes—Peru—Moquegua (Department) 6. Political ecology—Peru—Moquegua (Department) 7. Encomiendas (Latin America) 8. Names, Geographical—Peru—Moquegua (Department) 9. Spain—Colonies—America—Administration. 10. Moquegua (Peru : Department)—History. 11. Moquegua (Peru : Department)—Colonization. 12. Moquegua (Peru : Department)—Antiquities. I. Title.
  F3429.1.M65R53 2013
  985'.34—dc23

                    2013018794

Cover illustration: Detail from plate painted by Domingo Punter of Teruel, Aragón, Spain (from the author's collection; computer rendering by Don S. Rice).

Contents

List of Illustrations	ix
List of Tables	xiii
Preface	xv
Acknowledgments	xix

PART I. INTRODUCTION TO MOQUEGUA AND ITS ENVIRONMENT — 1

1. Moquegua: A Landscape Perspective	3
Spatiality and Spatialization: Landscape, Space, and Place	4
Cultural Environment	7
The Moquegua Bodegas Project	9
Early Colonial Moquegua and the Emerging World System	15
2. The "Natural" Landscape of Moquegua	19
Geology: Mountains and Minerals	20
River Systems: Low Flow	22
Soils: Rich but Limited	24
Weather: Sunny and Dry	27
Vegetation and Agriculture	29

PART II. INDIGENOUS SPACES AND PLACES — 31

3. Late Pre-Hispanic Colonization and Re-spatialization	35
Late Intermediate Period: Multiple Sites and Ethnicities	37
The Late Horizon	40

    Landscape and Order: The Inka Heartland   42
    Imperial Expansion: The Lake Titicaca Basin and
        the Aymara   47
    Inka Re-spatialization   52

4. Inka Spaces and Places: The Inkas in Moquegua   55
    Interrogating the Account   56
    Inka Sites in the Osmore Drainage   61
    Inka Re-spatialization in Moquegua   65

5. Language and Toponyms   69
    Toponymy   69
    Indigenous Toponymy in Moquegua: Pre-Hispanic
        Multivocality   71
    Toponymy in Spanish-Colonial Moquegua   78
    The Region and the Legacy of Indigenous Provinces   82

PART III. SPANISH-COLONIAL SPACES AND PLACES   89

6. Spanish Order and Re-spatializations   91
    New World Conquest and Agendas   93
    Space-Related Spanish Institutions   94
    Spanish (Re-)Spatialization and
        (Re-)Politicization in Moquegua: Contestation   100
    Economic Re-spatialization: Moquegua's Wine
        Heredades   103
    Four Excavated Bodega Sites in Moquegua   109

7. Encomiendas in Moquegua   117
    Encomiendas in Peru   117
    The Buenos and Carumas   120
    Lucas Martínez Vegaso and Cochuna   124
    Discussion   127

8. Torata Alta: From Inka Administrative Center to Spanish Congregación   129

Reducción *in Moquegua*	129
Torata Alta: Layout and Structures	131
Material Culture and Economy	152
Colonial (Re-)Spatialization and (Re-)Politicization	159
Abandonment	165

9. Locumbilla: A Colonial Wine Heredad — 169
   - *Yaravico and Locumbilla: The Buenos and Estradas* — 170
   - *Locumbilla Bodega: The Industrial Sector* — 176
   - *Residential Sector* — 189
   - *Specialized Analyses* — 191
   - *Later History of Yaravico and Locumbilla* — 195

10. Religion ... and Resistance? — 199
    - *Local Catholicism in Pre-Modern Spain* — 200
    - *Catholicism in Early Peru: Formal and Local* — 203
    - *Religion in Early Moquegua* — 207
    - *Inscriptions on* Tinajas — 211
    - *Reducción and Resistance at Torata Alta?* — 217

PART IV. DECORATIVE SPACES AND DECORATING PLACES: ANDEAN "MAJOLICA" POTTERY — 223

11. Transcending Worlds — 227
    - *Historical Background* — 227
    - *Mudéjar Style* — 230
    - *Christian Persecutions and Restrictions on Trade* — 237
    - *From the Old World to the New* — 239
    - *Myths and Voices* — 242

12. Technological Spaces and Transfers — 249
    - *Spanish Majolica: Resources and Production Technologies* — 251
    - *Majolica and Loza in the Americas* — 255
    - *Two Ibero-American Loza Spheres* — 267

Morisco Wares and Influences in Spanish American Pottery	272
Travel, Trade, and Technology	276

13. **Ceramic Spatialization: Southern Styles** *(Prudence M. Rice and Wendy L. Natt)* — 281

Moquegua's Bodegas and Loza	281
Space and Style: Hierarchical Design-Structure Analysis	283
Vessel Forms	285
Color Use and Application	287
Levels of Design Structure	291
Summary of Comparisons: Tin-Enameled Ware in Colonial Peru and Aragón	299
Interpretations	302

PART V. CONCLUSIONS — 309

14. **Moquegua's Landscapes, Spaces, and Places through Time** — 311

Glossary	321
References	325
Index	367

Illustrations

1.1. The modern Department of Moquegua — 2
1.2. The middle Osmore valley showing bodega site locations — 10
2.1. Tributaries of the Río Osmore — 23
2.2. The upper Moquegua valley — 26
3.1. Late pre-Hispanic sites in the tributaries of the Río Osmore — 36
3.2 Approximate extent of the Inka empire and the four *suyus* — 41
4.1. Garcilaso de la Vega's family tree — 57
4.2. Core area of the site of Sabaya — 63
5.1. The Collao and adjacent Aymara territory — 74
5.2. The Contisuyu quarter of Tawantinsuyu — 75
5.3. Southern Contisuyu and Colesuyu — 76
5.4. Southwestern Peru and nested moieties — 83
5.5. Provinces in the modern Department of Moquegua — 85
6.1. Map of the Iberian Peninsula — 92
6.2. *Capitulaciones* and *audiencias* in South America — 95
6.3. The upper Moquegua valley (confluence area) showing bodega site locations relative to soils — 104
6.4. Toponymic zones in the confluence area of the Río Osmore — 105
6.5. Chincha bodega site plan — 110
6.6. Features at Chincha bodega — 111
6.7. Yaravico Viejo bodega site plan — 113
6.8. Yahuay bodega site plan — 114
8.1. Location of San Antonio, Torata Alta, and modern Torata — 131

8.2. The Torata valley, looking west-southwest	132
8.3. The site of Torata Alta	134
8.4. Plan of the Torata Alta church	138
8.5. Profile of the southeast wall of Trench 1 through the church nave, Torata Alta	140
8.6. Composite profile of the northwest wall of Trench 1 and part of Trench 4, Torata Alta	141
8.7. Lower center wall of the church apse, Trench 2, Torata Alta	142
8.8. Profile of the northeast wall of Trench 2 in the church apse, Torata Alta	143
8.9. Modern shrine in the Torata Alta church ruins	144
8.10. Northwestern half of Str. 161 (Kancha 17), Torata Alta	145
8.11. Str. 156 (Kancha 17), Level 2, Torata Alta	146
8.12. Pottery recovered in excavations at Torata Alta	147
8.13. Str. 229 (Kancha 23), Torata Alta	148
8.14. Str. 150 (Kancha 16), Torata Alta	150
8.15. Str. 210 (Kancha 20), Torata Alta	151
8.16. West profile of Str. 250 (Kancha 24), Torata Alta	151
8.17. Indigenous decorated pottery from Torata Alta	154
9.1. The Yaravico toponymic zone	170
9.2. The Locumbilla bodega site plan	175
9.3. Standing remains at Locumbilla	176
9.4. Locumbilla bodega site, view to the southwest	177
9.5. Profile of foundation trench, Lagar 1, Locumbilla	179
9.6. Profile of Str. 6 excavation, Locumbilla	181
9.7. Falca complex at Locumbilla	184

9.8. Southeastern corner of the Locumbilla site   187

9.9. Profile of interior of excavated lagar in Str. Y, Locumbilla   189

11.1. Baptismal font from Teruel, Spain   232

11.2. The Iberian Peninsula in the late sixteenth century   233

11.3. Modern verde y morado plate from Teruel   234

12.1. Fragments of Mas Alla Polychrome type from the Moquegua valley   264

12.2. Late-twentieth-century tin-enameled *chúa* from the Titicaca basin   265

12.3. Tin-enameled footed dish from Cusco   266

12.4. The two spheres of tin-enameled ware circulation   268

12.5. Tin-enameled chamber pot–like vessel from Cusco   274

12.6. Tin-enameled pitcher from Cusco   275

13.1. Schematic diagram of the design layouts on loza forms   286

13.2. Elements and motifs on loza from Moquegua   288

13.3. Intra- and inter-regional loza design comparisons   294

Tables

1.1. Chronological periods in the southern Peruvian Andes and the Osmore drainage	8
1.2. Radiocarbon dates from the Late Horizon and Colonial Period in the Osmore drainage	13
2.1. Classification of agricultural capacity of soils in the valleys of southwestern Peru	27
3.1. Comparison of various Spanish accounts of Inka conquest of the Collao	49
5.1. Proposed moiety nesting and sixteenth-century populations in Moquegua	84
6.1. Archdioceses and dioceses in early colonial South America	101
6.2. Names of *kurakas* in Torata and Moquegua	103
7.1. Sixteenth-century population of Carumas	123
8.1. Approximate chronology of Torata Alta	133
8.2. Internal area of nineteen excavated structures at Torata Alta	137
8.3. Textile-related implements at Torata Alta	153
8.4. Non-Chucuito-Inka decorated bowl sherds from Torata Alta	155
8.5. Non-ceramic European goods recovered at Torata Alta	157
8.6. Botanical remains from Torata Alta	158
8.7. MNI and EMW of pre-1600 fauna at Torata Alta	159
9.1. Bodegas in the Yaravico zone and their industrial facilities	171
9.2. Dimensions of fermentation bodegas in the Yaravico zone	180

9.3. Dimensions of adobes used in constructions — 180

9.4. Occurrence of "YB" and variant inscriptions by toponymic zone — 183

9.5. Botanical remains at Locumbilla bodega — 193

9.6. Owners of the Yaravico/Locumbilla estate in the sixteenth through early eighteenth centuries — 196

10.1. Saints and religious themes referenced in Moquegua — 213

10.2. Co-occurrence of hearths and horseshoe recovery at Torata Alta — 219

11.1. Muslim dynasties in Spain and their capitals — 230

11.2. Spanish decrees related to Muslims — 238

12.1. Variable composition of white tin glazes in Zaragoza, Spain — 254

12.2. Tin-enameled loza types produced at Panamá La Vieja — 259

12.3. Production of glazed wares in Colonial-period and later Peru — 260

13.1. Loza analyzed in Natt's HDSA — 284

13.2. Decorated wares at Baños de la Reina Mora, Sevilla — 290

13.3. Comparative occurrence of primary design configurations, motifs, and elements — 296

13.4. Comparative occurrence of boundary markers and central medallions — 306

Preface

Since the early 1990s I've fretted about not meeting my responsibilities for full and timely publication of the data from the Moquegua Bodegas Project. I can trot out the usual excuses: increasing administrative duties, a return to fieldwork in the Maya area, supervision of graduate students, and so on. In 2009, however, with the good fortune of both a sabbatical leave and growing interest in historical archaeology in the Andes, I was able to synthesize the findings of the Moquegua Bodegas Project into a monograph entitled *Vintage Moquegua: History, Wine, and Archaeology on a Peruvian Periphery* (Rice 2011b). *Vintage Moquegua* is a history of the introduction of wine-based agrarian capitalism into this tiny valley on the periphery of the European world system. But because of limits on the length of the volume, I was unable to include raw data from project excavations, especially at Locumbilla, the most intensively investigated winery site, and at the *congregación* site of Torata Alta.

So I began writing half a dozen articles presenting these data and interpretations. While developing these analyses, however, I grew increasingly frustrated with the sclerotic processes of peer review and publication in scholarly journals and the need for repetition of basic background information in each manuscript: field operations, Moquegua's environment, various maps, references, and so on. Mindful of a frequent critique of academicians—that we publish the same information over and over, but in different journals—as well as the waste of trees in devoting repeated pages to the same information (even in this electronic world), I concluded that the most appropriate solution to both dilemmas was to bring everything together in a single volume.

The sense of "unfinished business" had another component. After leading a graduate seminar on "Space and Place" focused on the Maya, I grew more interested in the production of space in settings of in-migration and colonization. I was particularly concerned with the "*espacio Moqueguano*" as part of what Carlos Sempat Assadourian (1972) calls the "*espacio Peruano*." Specifically, I wanted to explore what Moquegua's experience might tell us about landscape, space, and place and their meanings and orderings in colonial encounters, as well as what the orderings and meanings of landscape, space, and place—the spatializations—in such encounters might tell us about Moquegua. I drafted a paper about some of my ideas and asked the seminar participants to read it, and one student responded that she thought it contained too many ideas for a single article. So I decided to prepare the present book, the completion of which has been greatly furthered by my retirement from academia.

With respect to the meanings of spaces and places, I am intrigued by the observation that "places come into being through praxis . . . places produce meaning . . . [and] control over the meanings of place [should be returned] to the rightful producers" of it (Rodman 1992: 642, 643, 644). One way to investigate the processes of colonialism and layering of spatial meanings is through toponyms: their linguistic sources (i.e., the colonized or the colonizers) and patterns of retention, loss, and renaming. In the Moquegua landscape, for example, some ancient Indigenous toponyms were lost, and others were appropriated into the Spanish-colonial wine-based political economy. I also look at the spaces and spatializations embodied in tin-enameled ("majolica") pottery: this beautiful ware has a history of more than a millennium that spans the globe. The details of its production—especially the colorful decoration carefully painted onto its surface spaces—its trade, and its use provide insights into cultural interactions not otherwise easily obtained.

The result of my explorations is the present volume, a compilation of essays about various aspects of the history and archaeology of Moquegua from the perspective of spaces and their ordering. This volume lacks the narrative arc of *Vintage Moquegua* because it treats disparate topics that are not strictly organized chronologically, although they are thematically linked. The focus is primarily on a "moment" in Moquegua's history: Spanish contact, which appears to have begun around AD 1534–35. Archaeologically (and even historically), of course, it is impossible to define this literally as a single moment in clock-time or calendar-time. Indeed, to try to do so would be a pointless exercise: Spanish contacts with, and colonization of, the valley occurred over several decades, and Moquegua's initial experience with the Europeans was significantly contoured by its incorporation into the Inka empire little more than a half century earlier.

Indeed, Moquegua was the focus of repeated contacts with, and colonization by, outsiders in pre-Hispanic times. So, for the present purposes I consider "contact" loosely as a centuries-long process, roughly defined by complex multiethnic and multivocal interactions and transformations that included coloniz*ation* and ended with the entanglements of Spanish colonial*ism* (see Silliman 2005).

The findings of my project in Moquegua can be situated in the movement, beginning in the late 1970s, to shift colonial Andean historiography from a focus on "political elites revolving around the opulent viceregal court and the European legacy" of Lima and Cuzco and instead to investigate rural landscapes and peoples (Campbell 1986: 193). In this "historical reconquest of 'Peruvian space'" (see also Sempat Assadourian 1972; Glave 1986), colonial Andean history is being reclaimed to include Indigenous peoples, rural economies (Quiroz Paz Soldán 1991b), and Andeans' various strategies of negotiating the alien canons of Catholicism and capitalism. Similarly, Andean archaeology has been undergoing a "neo-historicist" paradigm shift, inspired in part by Mesoamerican studies, that is giving greater credence to native traditions and oral histories (Hiltunen and McEwan 2004: 237–38).

But scholarly critique works both ways: archaeologists interested in Andean civilizations typically write their histories up to the Spanish conquest and then end abruptly, as if pre- and post-conquest societies were totally disjunctive. Despite the catastrophic epidemiological and demographic "Columbian consequences" of European contact, elements of Indigenous civilizations, some elite and some commoner, survived throughout the Americas. The artifice of assigning pre- and post-1534 events to different scholarly disciplines, archaeology and (ethno-) history, often contributes to a failure to recognize and integrate the perduring influences of Indigenous voices, structures, institutions, material/technological influences, cosmologies, and what can be broadly termed "worldview" into post-1534 Andean histories. It diminishes and dishonors the survivorship. Further, as I try to show, historical documentation can contribute insights into the late pre-Hispanic period (see also Wernke 2007a, 2007b).

I use the terms *Peru* and *southwestern Peru* here to refer to the modern nation-state, strictly as a matter of convenience (recognizing Sempat Assadourian's [1972: 11] critique). In early Spanish-colonial times, of course, Peru referred to the viceroyalty that was centered on the Inka empire of Birú along the Andean spine and encompassed nearly the entire continent of South America. When I refer to the viceroyalty, I specify it as such.

Acknowledgments

The data reported here were obtained in the late 1980s as part of the Moquegua Bodegas Project. The Bodegas Project operated under the umbrella of Programa Contisuyo, a multidisciplinary, multi-institutional program initiated by Michael E. Moseley and sponsored by the Museo Peruano de Ciencias de la Salud, Fernando Cabieses, then-director. Permits for excavation and artifact export were authorized by the Comisión Nacional de Arqueología and the Instituto Nacional de Cultura in Lima, under Resoluciones Supremas nos. 176-86 ED, 322-88 ED, 236-88 ED, and 34-89 ED. Fieldwork was supported by National Endowment for the Humanities grant no. RO-21477-87 and National Geographic Society research grants nos. 3566-87 and 4065-89 to Prudence M. Rice, Principal Investigator. Parts of chapters 4, 8, and 10 are reprinted (from Rice 2012) from *Latin American Antiquity* (vol. 23, no. 1, 2012) by permission of the Society for American Archaeology. I acknowledge with appreciation the support of these institutions.

I am grateful to many people for their contributions to this study. My deepest thanks go to Mike for inviting me to join his project and experience the excitement of interdisciplinary research in a new culture area. I owe an extended debt to Luis (Lucho) Watanabe for his steady guidance and advice. My project could not have been successful without the support of the Southern Peru Copper Corporation.

At the time of Bodegas Project excavations, the Locumbilla site was the property of the regional Centro de Investigaciones y Promoción Agropecuario of Moquegua (CIPA IX), part of the Instituto Nacional de Investigación y Promoción Agropecuaria (INIPA).

This group began studies in Moquegua in 1986 to plan for future planting of vines in the valley, with a goal of 400 ha of vineyards by 1990. I thank them for allowing us access to the site for the entire period of fieldwork.

I particularly acknowledge my debt to Greg Smith for supervising the excavations and artifact analyses; without his experience in Spanish-colonial archaeology, the project would not have succeeded. In addition, then-graduate students Mary Van Buren and Peter Bürgi jointly and ably supervised the Torata Alta excavations in 1988 and 1989. Additional funding for Mary was provided by the Tinker Foundation, Sigma Xi, and the University of Arizona. Mary and Peter very generously granted me permission to publish data from their field notes and drawings.

Kathleen Deagan graciously allowed me access to tin-enameled pottery from Panamá La Vieja in the collections of the Florida Museum of Natural History. I thank David Goldstein for his most thoughtful gift of Teresa Cañedo-Argüelles's two recent books on Moquegua. And as always, I am grateful to Don Rice for his patient labor in preparing the illustrations, especially the many Google™-based maps.

Space-Time Perspectives on
Early Colonial Moquegua

Part I

Introduction to Moquegua and Its Environment

The interactions and exchanges that transpire in extended intercultural encounters typically occur in places that are familiar to one party and alien to the other. Familiarity of place derives from the way it is experienced by its occupants and the meaning(s) assigned to it. Places and their meanings, in turn, are inextricably entangled in power relations, and the places in which encounters of colonization are played out are especially deeply entrained in the asymmetrical relations of identity negotiation, politicization, and contestation.

In the following chapters, I explore such encounters as they transpired in a specific place—Moquegua, in far southern Peru—through an implicit political-ecology approach. My interests are political in terms of examining power relations and their exercise with respect to the ecological: the kind, quality, distribution of, and access to resources. One key resource is productive agricultural soil, which is limited in Moquegua's mountainous desert environment. More broadly, the concern is to understand a "region," which can be defined by unique, historically contingent processes of social construction and, more specifically, by the contested political-economics of commodity production: "conflict over resource access, appropriation, and extraction" (Neumann 2010: 371). Varied data, reviewed herein, indicate that the Pacific watershed of the southwestern part of the modern nation-state of Peru, extending from around Arequipa south to northern Chile and west from the Lake Titicaca basin, constituted a discrete region in late pre-Hispanic and early Spanish-colonial times. The region was produced, reproduced, and negotiated through human agency

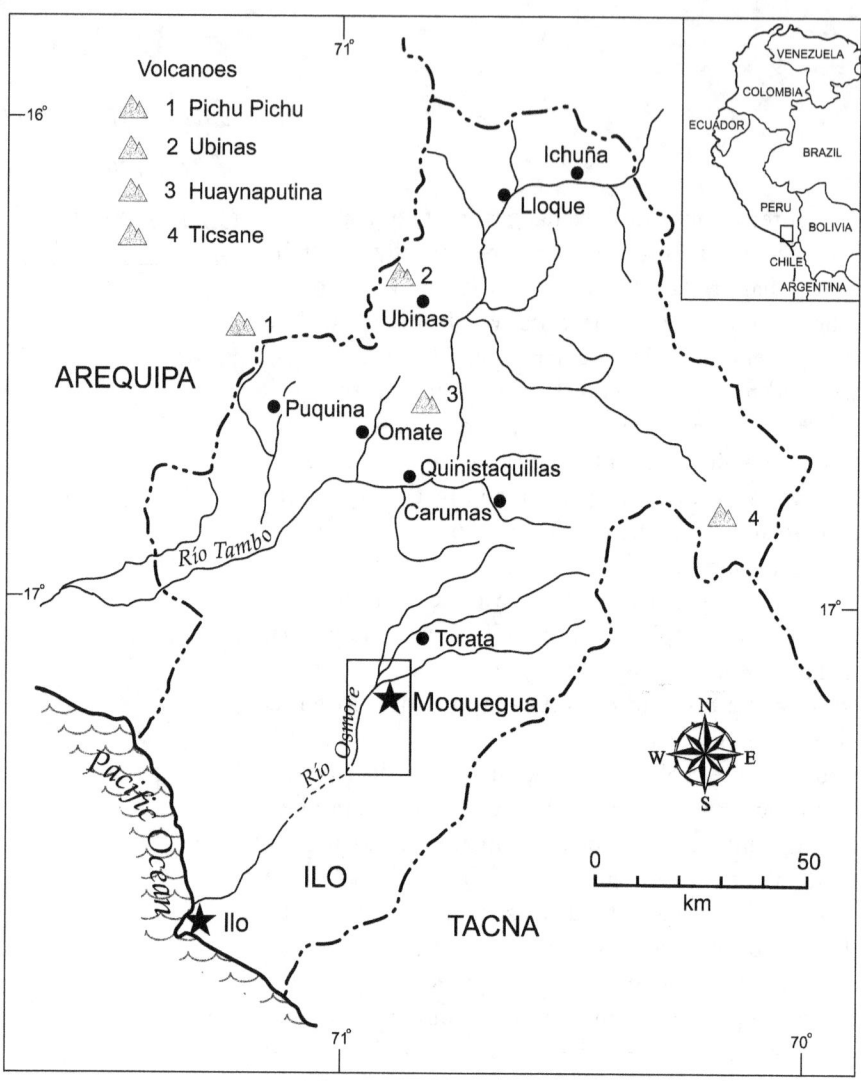

FIGURE 1.1 *The modern Department of Moquegua, showing the Tambo and Osmore River systems, modern towns, and volcanoes. Rectangle shows the "middle valley" illustrated in figure 1.2.*

over the centuries, but nonetheless it maintained a surprising integrity. I use as a case study a small slice of this region: the space now known as the Department of Moquegua in far southern Peru (figure 1.1).

1

Moquegua

A Landscape Perspective

> An anthropology whose objects are no longer conceived as automatically and naturally anchored in space will need to pay particular attention to the way spaces and places are made, imagined, contested, and enforced.
> —Akhil Gupta and James Ferguson (1997a: 47)

Moquegua—more specifically, the valley of the Río Osmore and its tributary streams—has a long history of contacts with, and colonization by, expansionist states. Colonization begins at least as early as the middle of the first millennium of the Common Era, with settlers from hundreds of kilometers distant: Wari to the north and Tiwanaku to the southeast. Later, in the late fifteenth century, the Inkas from Cusco, midway between these earlier centers, made their presence felt in Moquegua. Finally, in the sixteenth century, the Osmore drainage came to be occupied by an alien culture—the rapacious, emergent-capitalist, rabidly evangelical Spaniards. Subsequent centuries of growing settlement left an indelible imprint on the landscape, particularly with respect to agricultural production as evidenced by small plots on valley flatland demarcated by walls, trees, irrigation canals, and roads. Today, the Panamerican Highway streaks along the east side of the river course before veering southeast and disappearing into the barren hills. The growing city of Moquegua and its urban services dominate the upper mid-valley, whereas to the south the landscape is rural, its built environment consisting of the adobe ruins of Colonial and later wine haciendas dotting the margins.

DOI: 10.5876/9781607322764:c01

All these waves of colonists, despite having different traditions and speaking different languages, shared similar economies—agro-pastoral, with metallurgy and vast trading networks—and valued similar resources. They all contributed to the layers of imbricated places and meanings in the landscape of today's Moquegua. How did they "learn the new landscape" (Rockman and Steele 2003) of the southwestern region? How were landscape, space, and place variably defined, bounded, named, and otherwise cognitively structured by the participants in these emplaced interactions? My interest is in both "contact" and "colonialism" (see Silliman 2005), especially in one aspect of the power relations and negotiations inherent in the latter: How was the Osmore valley "re-spatialized," particularly with the entry of the Spaniards and subsequent entanglements with Catholicism, capitalist market forces, and nascent globalization? The area's multi-ethnicity and multivocality are of special interest, given evidence of considerable ethno-linguistic diversity.

SPATIALITY AND SPATIALIZATION: LANDSCAPE, SPACE, AND PLACE

Spaces, both built and "natural," are constitutive of social actions and relations, while at the same time those actions and relations structure and order spaces (Keith and Pile 1993a). My interest is in the various spatialities and spatializations constructed in the Andean environment of Moquegua as they can be accessed through archaeological and documentary evidence.

Spatiality refers to the perceived qualities or conditions that define socially produced spaces and their functions. These qualities and conditions order a landscape and its places. Dictionary definitions of the term *spatiality* do not begin to approach the nuances of its meanings in anthropology and geography, which emphasize both social and physical spaces and individuals' and groups' interactions with them. Social groups create unique definitions of space, its use, and its meaning based on their values, economic activities, myths, and histories. Spatialities exist at multiple levels or scales, and because they may be variably perceived and defined, they are almost invariably contested (Keith and Pile 1993b: 26).

Spatialization refers to *how*—the recursive processes by which—such structuring spatialities are created and recreated (see Martin and Ringham 2006: 190). These processes include defining, naming, bounding, and cognitively ordering spaces, not all of which are detectable archaeologically. Similarly, geographers might analyze the creation and use of space on the basis of processes of their appropriation, environment, exploitation, and management). In the topographically diverse Andes region, spaces are not only horizontally defined, but their vertical dimensions are also significant structuring elements, both physically and cognitively.

A landscape[1] is generally considered a particular segment of a holistically perceived/construed/experienced environment as shaped by both natural and cultural processes (see, e.g., Naveh and Lieberman 1993: 3–5). A landscape may be considered a "cognitive or symbolic ordering of space" (Ingold 1993: 152) or, more epigrammatically, a "network of places" (Chapman 2008: 188), a "layered artifact" (Dunning et al. 1999: 650), or an "additive amalgam" (Fisher and Feinman 2005: 64) that is "simultaneously place, process, and time" (Silverman 2004: 4). Landscapes are at once "real and imagined, objective and subjective, past and present, space and place, nature and culture" (Fowles 2010: 461). Most salient, landscapes are not static: they are ever-changing, as natural processes and human activities transform them at the same time as they contour human behavior. Landscapes have been studied by geographers with various specializations but also—and increasingly—by archaeologists interested in how centuries and millennia of human activity influenced landscapes' production and perception (David and Thomas 2008).

Certain kinds of socially constructed spaces are "places." Places are "politicized, culturally relative, historically specific" spaces that "come into being through praxis" (Rodman 1992: 641–42). That is, they are lived and experienced spaces, which makes them "meaning-full." Places have socially assigned meanings—spatialities—that can change over time, that can be multiple, that can differ among actors, and that can shape and be shaped by memory (ibid.; Van Dyke 2008; Whitridge 2004).

Spaces and places may or may not have boundaries, and such boundaries can be conceptual/symbolic, socio-political, physical/spatial, or some combination thereof. Symbolic boundaries separate conceptual classes that allow actors to categorize components of their realities and to establish "us-them" identity distinctions (Lamont and Molnár 2002: 168). Social boundaries are closely linked to, and often reconfigurations of, symbolic boundaries: they establish patterns of relations among groups of individuals (e.g., by class, sex, ethnicity) as well as access to resources (ibid.: 168–69, 186). Physical or spatial boundaries (see Jones 2010) may be "natural" (e.g., oceans, rivers, mountain ranges, deserts) or human constructions, the latter typically reifying social boundaries. The crossing of physical boundaries—entering a church, passing through gates in walls, checking passports at national borders—is often ritualized and accompanied by some degree of transformation of the actor's identity.

How can archaeologists begin to approach perceptions of a landscape or concepts of space and place in ancient times, especially those of non-literate societies? The process is fraught with incertitude, as efforts to define landscape and the related concepts of space and place have resulted in little agreement for either operations or heuristics. Because scholars frequently decry the application of strict binaries (e.g., nature vs. culture; "Cartesian dualism") in establishing and clarifying the distinctions, the terms overlap and appear to be fuzzy sets or elements of fuzzy sets.

Varied approaches to investigating relations between society and the built environment (Hillier 2008; Hillier and Hanson 1984; Upton 1991) are applicable more generally to relations between the built and natural environments. "Society-first" approaches begin by analyzing the spatial dimensions of social processes to understand the (built) environment, whereas "environment-first" analysis begins by looking at the spatial forms of the (built) environment for evidence of social processes. Archaeologists may adopt either, although the latter is more amenable to development of testable hypotheses about design (Hillier 2008). My approach is similar to that of vernacular architectural historian Dell Upton (1991: 198), who describes "cultural landscapes" as constructions that fuse the physical with the inhabitants' imaginations: they are the "product of powerful yet diffuse imaginations, fractured by the faultlines of class, culture, and personality" of both their builders and those who study them. Here I am interested in the historical trajectory of spatializations of landscape, space, and place—built and natural—in the Moquegua area and how they were variably defined, bounded, named, and otherwise cognitively and physically (re)structured by its succession of colonists and continuing residents.

Fortunately, numerous scholars have preceded me in analyzing these phenomena in the Andes (e.g., Acuto 2005; Bouysse-Cassagne 1986; Gade 1992; Kaulicke et al. 2003; Moore 2004, 2005; Scott 2009; Silverman 2004; van de Guchte 1999; Wernke 2007b), particularly with respect to the Inkas. The Moquegua rural, vernacular landscape and its spaces and places have not been explicitly investigated, however, at least as they might have been perceived by Indigenous peoples and interlopers alike, which establishes my goal here: to explore the different layers of spatialities through time and at the time of contact, and how they structured power relations.

A landscape can be the starting point of an analysis, beginning with describing it as a whole and moving to identify its constituent spaces and places. Alternatively, the process can begin with identification of particular spaces and places and how they fit together to constitute a landscape. I make use of both approaches here, as they are appropriate to the task. I am especially interested in places, both natural and human-made, and, in particular, I give weight to Moquegua's toponyms (chapter 5). If a geographic locus, large or small, is given a specific name, it has been, by that very action, cognitively (or emically) identified as a place that is significant in some way to some group of people. That significance may be social, political, economic, religio-ritual, or based on some other dimension of experience and acknowledged or unrecognized by others who come into contact with the place.

The Department of Moquegua in general, and the Osmore drainage in particular, constituted a distinct kind of space in pre-Hispanic and Spanish-colonial times: a periphery (Rice 2011b). For at least a millennium and a half, Moquegua—as landscape, space, and place—represented a social, economic, and political periphery, particularly a frontier of agricultural colonization by expansionist states. Throughout the late history of human occupation of the Andes, the Osmore valley and its rich but limited arable existed on the margins of larger, more powerful societies whose centers lay well beyond. This peripheral status had a deep imprint on constructions of space and place in the department.

CULTURAL ENVIRONMENT

Because of its high-quality soils and temperate climate (chapter 2), the Osmore drainage was for centuries a favored destination for agricultural colonists sent from empires centered in higher elevations in the Andean sierra and altiplano. Thus a brief overview of late Andean chronology and the ethno-linguistico-political affiliations of the peoples impacting the history of the Osmore basin is useful before delving into the details of these cultures.

Archaeologists divide the late pre-Hispanic occupation of Andean Peru into alternating horizons and periods (table 1.1): horizons are intervals of broad quasi-imperial domination, and periods are intervals of political decentralization and regionalization. During the Middle Horizon (MH), two large states—Wari (Huari) and Tiwanaku (Tiahuanaco)—dominated southern Peru and established colonies in Moquegua. Of greater interest here are the succeeding Late Intermediate Period (LIP) and Late Horizon (LH). The LIP in Moquegua saw the withdrawal of Wari and Tiwanaku influence and abandonment of their colonies. The relatively brief LH is marked by Inka expansion throughout the Andes, which was truncated by Spanish conquest.

Analyses of Andeans' cognitive organization of their social and spatial environments emphasize various dualities, including high-low, male-female, dry-wet, and left-right (Bouysse-Cassagne 1986; Dean 2007). During the LH and likely earlier, dual organization was manifest socially, economically, and politically in the organization of the *ayllu* (Quechua; Aymara *hatha*). Ayllus are kin-based residential and landholding collectivities of various sizes, sometimes

TABLE 1.1 Chronological periods in the southern Peruvian Andes and the Osmore drainage

General periodization	Local phase	Dates AD	Where
Middle Horizon (MH)	Omo, Chenchen	500/600–1000/1150	
Late Intermediate Period (LIP)		1000–1450	
	Tumilaca	900/1000–1200	Middle valley
	Chiribaya	900/1000–1300/1350	Coast, lower mid-valley
	Estuquiña	1350–1450	Upper mid-valley
	Otora	1200–1300/1350	Tributaries
Late Horizon (LH)		1450–1535	
	Estuquiña-Inka	1450/1475–1500	Tributaries
Colonial Period	Early Colonial	1535–1600	
	Middle Colonial	1600–1778	
	Late Colonial	1778–1820	

Source: Modified from Stanish 1991.

spatially dispersed, whose members claim a common founding ancestor. Land is held by the ayllu as an inalienable resource for the use of its members and is not privately owned, although usufruct passes through the female line. Members of an ayllu labor together to raise crops and herds and manage resources, including lands and irrigation systems (see, e.g., Cavagnaro Orellana 1988: 109; Cushner 1980: 25; Moseley 1992: 49–52; Silverblatt 1987: 217–20; Urton 1990: 22–23).[2] Ayllus held responsibility for meeting annual labor and tax obligations to their Inka and later Spanish overlords, for example, through maize or textile production (see Urton 1990: 22–24, 76–77).

The sociopolitical reality of dual organization is seen in moieties: division into two ranked descent groups. Ayllus were nested in a series of ever-larger dyadic groups, typically exogamous, based on unilateral descent. Among the Quechua-speaking Inkas, the upper moiety was called *hanansaya* and was considered politically stronger, male, and more powerful than the lower, or *hurinsaya*, moiety (Hiltunen and McEwan 2004: 247–48). Physically, moiety organization was often expressed as different areas of a community, themselves often spatially divided. Each moiety, which the Spaniards referred to as a *parcialidad*, had its own leader, a *kuraka*, also called a *principal* or *cacique*, the latter term imported from the Caribbean.

THE MOQUEGUA BODEGAS PROJECT

Between 1985 and 1990 I directed the Moquegua Bodegas Project, an archaeological and historical investigation of Spanish-colonial settlement in the Moquegua valley and the development of its colonial wine-based economy (Rice 2011b). The Bodegas Project was part of Programa Contisuyo, directed by Michael Moseley, which began in the early 1980s after initial reconnaissance of the previously unsurveyed valley revealed more than 500 archaeological sites (Moseley, Feldman, and Pritzker 1982: 6). Since then, archaeologists with the programa have investigated sites throughout the Osmore drainage, ranging in elevation from the coast to the high sierras and in date from 10,000 years ago through modern times (e.g., Aldenderfer 1993; Marcus and Williams 2009; D. Rice, Stanish, and Scarr 1989).

Bodegas

Bodegas Project fieldwork began with pedestrian surveys to identify and inventory Moquegua's colonial heritage resources: ruins of the wineries, which we called *bodegas*, and large earthenware jars, or *tinajas*, used for fermentation and storage (see Rice 1987; Rice and Ruhl 1989; Rice and Smith 1989; Smith 1991). The term *bodega* has several meanings, which makes for some confusion in reconciling historical and archaeological data. A bodega is most commonly defined as a wine cellar, a storeroom or warehouse for storing or aging wine, or a shop for selling wine. The word is generally said to derive from the Latin *apotheca*, which in turn is from the Greek *apothēkē*, relating to apothecary but more generally to a storehouse. Buenaventura Aragó (1878: 3), however, gives the etymology as the Greek *boutis*, a clay vessel to hold wine, and relates it to the French *bouteille* and Spanish *botella*, *bota*, and *botija*.

Archaeologically, the problem was to decide if "bodega" referred narrowly to an individual room or wine cellar for fermentation (*elaboración*) and storage (*conservación*) of wine in tinajas or if it should be applied more broadly to a structural complex that might include multiple such rooms. The Bodegas Project opted for the latter, glossing the term as "winery," following Jan Read's (1986: 229) definition: an "establishment where wine is made and/or blended and matured."

By the end of the field project in 1990, we had identified 130 bodega sites (figure 1.2) and 1,424 tinajas. At one point during discussions with local Moqueguanos, however, we were told there were 240 bodegas in the valley. This was puzzling until a colleague suggested that the reference might be to the existence of 240 *rooms* or cellars housing tinajas—the former definition above—rather than to the site complexes, which frequently have several rooms. As used here, "bodega"

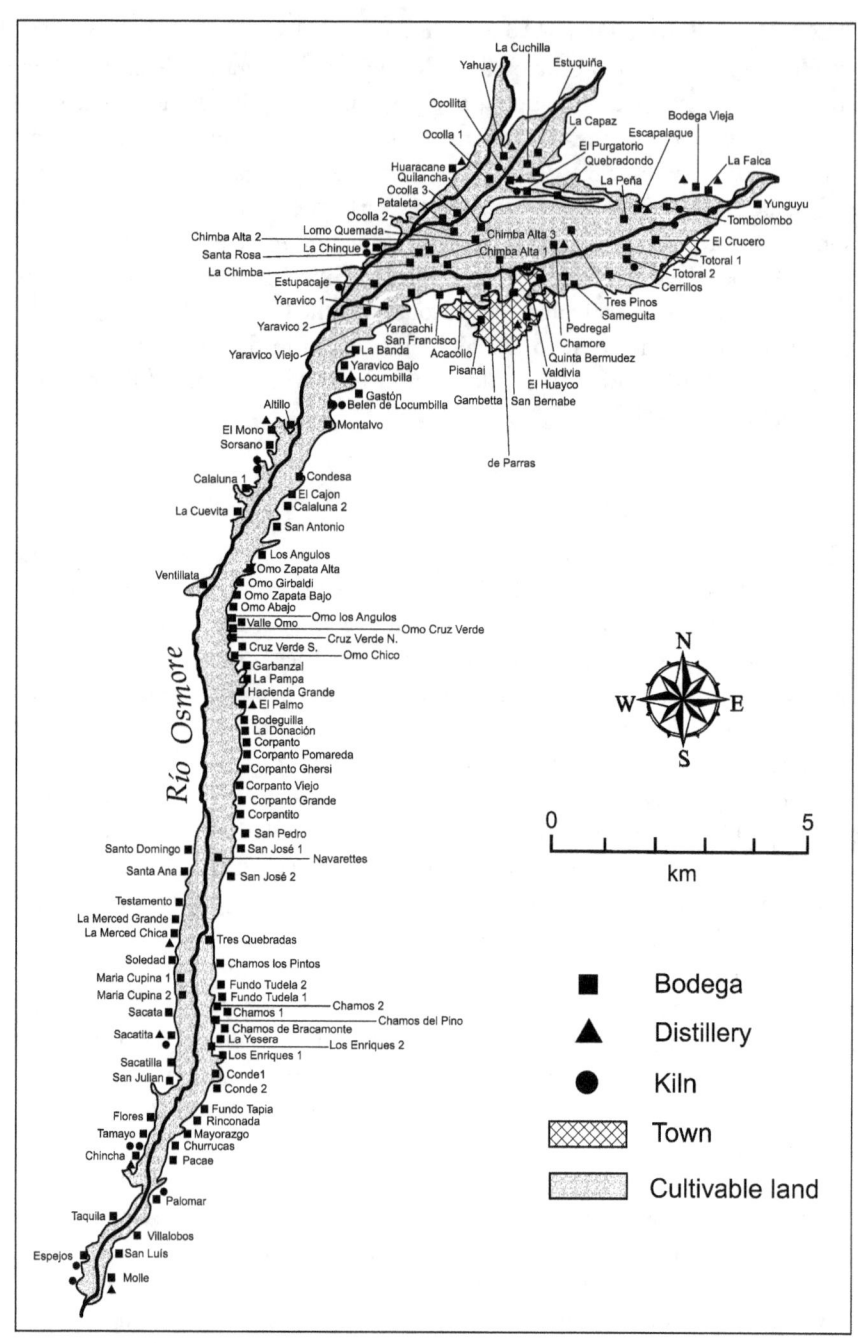

FIGURE 1.2 *The middle Moquegua (Osmore) valley showing the locations of 130 bodega sites.*

refers to a site of wine making and related activities and "bodega proper" distinguishes, where necessary, an individual storage/fermentation room or cellar.

In organizing Bodegas Project fieldwork and testing, the Moquegua valley was conceptually divided into upper/northern (confluence), middle, and lower/southern areas, and bodega sites in each area were qualitatively categorized by relative degree of preservation. Sites consist of complexes of adobe structures occasionally on fertile valley flatland or, more commonly, perched along its hilly desert margins. The former siting was common in the early-occupied confluence zone, where seventeen of fifty-four sites (31.5 percent) were so located (see figure 6.3), but rare in the more restricted arable of the middle and lower valley. Most sites were poorly preserved, a consequence of modern road and canal construction activities; many were completely destroyed, their existence interpreted from data gathered from informants and from 1970 and 1971 aerial photographs.

A program of mapping, surface collection, and shovel testing was initiated in 1987 at twenty-eight sites (21.5 percent of the total) throughout the valley, selected on the basis of the degree of preservation of standing and visible in-ground remains and owners' permission to work. Mapping was carried out using a Topcon ET-1 Totalstation and Global Information System (GIS). The shovel-testing program began with an attempt to use motorized augers to identify and delimit spaces of use, following Kathleen Deagan's (1983) exploration of the spatial limits of St. Augustine, Florida. This was an immediate failure, largely as a consequence of the valley's rocky soils. In addition, some local residents were convinced that the auger was a metal detector and that we were searching for the gold and silver the wealthy bodega owners allegedly hid in the tinajas in advance of the Chilean armies during the late-nineteenth-century Pacific Wars. (Surely our continual failure to recover such treasure helped disabuse them of this notion!) In any case, we switched to shovel-excavating small units, about 50 cm in diameter and ca. 1 m in depth, placed on a 10-m grid over as much of the site as was accessible (see Smith 1991: chapter 5),[3] plus isolated units inside structures.

Information from shovel testing helped identify sites likely to represent sixteenth-century occupation in the early history of the valley's colonial wine industry. Four sites were chosen for intensive excavations: Yahuay and Estopacaje in the upper valley, Locumbilla in the upper-middle valley (chapter 9), and Chincha in the far southern valley (Smith 1991). Excavated soils were passed through ¼-inch screen, with ⅛-inch screen used for features. Fieldwork was frequently made unpleasant by the presence of goats and sheep in the tinaja rooms, guinea pigs in the tinajas, pigs and ducks in the lagars, and chickens and vicious dogs everywhere. Because of all the animal life, past and present, at these sites, surface deposits were usually dry, powdery animal excrement—giving new meaning to George Kubler's (1948) sobriquet "guano archaeology."

Torata Alta

The Bodegas Project also investigated the site of Torata Alta, an intrusive, planned settlement in the lower reaches of the tributary Río Torata (chapter 8). The site is organized by an orthogonal grid of streets that define two dozen rectangular room blocks or compounds (*kanchas*). It was initially unclear, however, whether this distinctive gridded layout reflected strictly Inka (Stanish 2001: 224–25) or also Spanish site planning.

Torata Alta was first mapped in 1982 as part of Programa Contisuyo (Stanish and Pritzker 1983, 1990), with excavations (eight test pits) and mapping updates in the following year. Bodegas Project interest in the site was driven in part by a desire to sample Colonial-period material culture at an Indigenous site to compare with that of the bodega sites in the valley. In addition, local officials in Torata requested archaeological intervention because they were concerned about developers' plans to construct residences at the site. The Bodegas Project carried out surface collections, test excavations, and map corrections in 1987 (Rice and Smith 1990: 211–12), 1988, and 1989 (Rice et al. 1990: 246–47; Van Buren 1993, 1996; Van Buren and Bürgi 1990; Van Buren, Bürgi, and Rice 1993). Each kancha was divided into smaller areas ("quads") on the basis of internal cultural or topographic features or by arbitrary lines. In the end, around 270 structures (excluding small, attached, bin-like features) were mapped at the site and 16 kanchas were surface-collected.

The possibility that Torata Alta could be a Spanish settlement had initially been given only cursory consideration (Stanish and Pritzker 1983: 9). Interpretations of the site's role in the Moquegua valley addressed John Murra's (1972) model of Andean economy, variously known as the vertical archipelago or zonal/ecological complementarity model (Bürgi 1993; Van Buren 1993, 1996, 1997; Van Buren, Bürgi, and Rice 1993). Despite the presence of distinctive Spanish "olive jar" sherds strewn about the surface and the eventual realization that a large structure near the site center was a colonial church (Rice and Smith 1990: figure 3; Van Buren, Bürgi, and Rice 1993: 137), other confirmatory data were lacking; and "historical" (Colonial-period) archaeology was outside the interests of most Andeanists in the 1980s. Now, however, archival research carried out since Bodegas Project fieldwork has identified "Torata" as a Spanish resettlement of native populations known as a *congregación* (Cañedo-Argüelles

TABLE 1.2 Radiocarbon dates from the Late Horizon and Colonial Period in the Osmore drainage

Site	Age	Calibrated Range (1-σ)	Comment
San Antonio Beta-22437	370 ± 80	1439–60	Str. 20, with Inka artifacts
San Antonio Beta-22438	650 ± 50	1265–1365	
Porobaya[a] Teledyne		1356–1536	upper Otora valley
Torata Alta Beta-22436	380 ± 90	1431–1640	Kancha 22, Str. 213, fea.
Torata Alta Beta-22435	90 ± 100	1640–present	Kancha 20, Str. 193, hearth
Locumbilla Beta-33725	230 ± 70	1586–1726	Kiln firebox
Locumbilla Beta-22434	320 ± 60	1570–1690	SE corner
Locumbilla Beta-22433	250 ± 60	1565–1685	SE corner; Fea. 3 (pit)

a Stanish (1992: 141) gives 1446 ± 90.

Fábrega 1995: 130). Thus Torata Alta was an important locus of administrative power for both the Inkas and the Inka-Lupaqa alliance (Stanish 2001: 224–25) and also for the Spaniards (Rice 2011a, 2012).

CHRONOLOGY AND DATING

Dating the Spanish-colonial–period deposits at the Moquegua sites was difficult and was accomplished only through gross periodization into Early, Middle, and Late intervals (see Smith 1991: 87). Radiocarbon assays are generally not very useful at New World late pre-Hispanic and Colonial sites (because of a bimodal probability curve), although dates were obtained from Locumbilla bodega and Torata Alta (table 1.2). Spanish contact with Moquegua and with the southwestern region more generally is thought to have begun in 1534–35.

Early Colonial deposits stratigraphically underlay a thin stratum of white to light gray ash from the 1600 eruption of Huaynaputina volcano, 70 km to the north in the upper Río Tambo drainage. According to testimony by officials in

Arequipa, seismic activity began with three days of earthquakes, followed by an explosive eruption beginning on February 19 (see Rice 2009). Huaynaputina's plinian eruption lasted ten days, during which it ejected massive quantities of boulders, ash, and lava that caused roofs to collapse, devastated crops, dammed rivers into lakes, and killed untold scores of people and animals throughout southwestern Peru. The blast was comparable in magnitude to Krakatau in 1883, and its ash has been detected as far away as Greenland (de Silva and Zielinski 1998). Locally, the zone of major destruction was primarily west and northwest of the volcano, especially in Indigenous sierra villages, and Arequipa also suffered massive damage. In the Moquegua valley, volcanic ash was encountered at only three tested bodega sites, Locumbilla, Chincha, and Soledad (Smith 1991: 197), and in greater quantities at Torata Alta.

Late deposits in the Moquegua valley were dated by the presence of a variety of imported European goods, especially British "whitewares," and also amethyst glass and wire nails, newly available to the colonies under Spain's Bourbon rulers' declaration of *comercio libre* (free trade) in 1778. All tested bodega sites yielded late eighteenth- and nineteenth-century artifacts (ibid.: 195), supporting historical accounts of intensive production of wine and brandy during this period. The Middle Period was essentially a default category for contexts above or lacking relation to the ash layer and also lacking late European (non-Spanish) artifacts.

Relative construction sequences within and among bodega sites could be proposed by degree of weathering of adobe bricks, the older ones highly weathered with rounded corners whereas newer ones retained angular shapes. For example, it was clear from the near absence of weathering of adobes at El Mono bodega in the Calaluna zone that it was constructed recently. Bonding—or lack thereof—of adobes in corners and wall joins, and disjunctions in corners also permitted inferences of earlier versus later construction, for example, at the Locumbilla (chapter 9) and Huaracane sites. In addition, differences in construction dates could be inferred from variations in color, dimensions, and composition of adobes and mortar.[4] Informants told us of at least three bodegas in the middle and lower valley that were remodeled in the early twentieth century

Torata Alta was primarily dated by stratigraphy. The hilltop was not occupied prior to the Late Horizon: although a few Tiwanaku-related Middle Horizon sherds were reportedly recovered in early testing at Torata Alta (Van Buren 1993: 90n10), none were identified in subsequent excavations. Torata Alta appears to have been established as an Inka administrative center, probably in the last quarter of the fifteenth century, and to have been settled by Lupaqa colonists from the Titicaca basin. It was converted into a Spanish reduction settlement of native Andeans in the early 1570s. The only distinctive stratigraphic marker at Torata Alta is the volcanic ash layer from the 1600 Huaynaputina eruption, but in many structures the ash was swept out and the structure continued to be used and occupied. Thus although the site had distinct pre-Hispanic and post-conquest occupations, a clear stratigraphic sequencing that might have existed in principle—Indigenous, pre-reduction Spanish contact, sixteenth-century reduction, and seventeenth-century reduction (see table 8.1)—has remained elusive in practice.

EARLY COLONIAL MOQUEGUA AND THE EMERGING WORLD SYSTEM

As mentioned, for centuries the Osmore drainage lay on the peripheries of larger political-economic systems, the last of which was the world system that began to emerge in the sixteenth century. Moquegua's participation in the capitalism that was the driver of this early globalization began in the 1560s, when Spanish colonists from Arequipa moved into the valley, appropriated Indigenous cropland, and established a traditional agro-pastoral lifestyle (see Rice 2011b).

Briefly, Moquegua was a distant participant in a nested system of core-periphery relations: its colonial beginnings were as a frontier of expanding settlement out of Arequipa, which was peripheral to Lima and Cusco in the Viceroyalty of Peru, which in turn was peripheral to Spain in the Euro-centered world economy. Because of Spain's difficulties in providing the viceroyalty with all manner of necessary goods—difficulties that were partly a consequence of extreme distance but also of the crown's protectionist economic policies—the colonists quickly arranged their own supply-side solutions. In the case of wine for church ritual and domestic consumption, the solution was to produce their own wine: throughout the dry Pacific coastal valleys, individuals and religious houses planted vineyards. These vineyards thrived, despite boom-and-bust cycles resulting from local circumstances (such as earthquakes) and broader economic conditions (e.g., Spain's depression; threats from the popularity of *aguardiente* from sugar cane).

Moquegua's viticultural agro-industry suffered through such cycles. Moquegua was the largest of several valleys in the southwest, all of which supplied local communities but primarily consumers in the Lake Titicaca region and the mining areas of Upper Peru (modern Bolivia). A boom in the late sixteenth century, fueled by silver mining at Potosí, was abruptly ended by the Huaynaputina eruption in 1600; another boom in the eighteenth century developed with renewed mining expansion and the innovation of grape brandy (*pisco*). Unlike Arequipa, which directed its wines toward consumers in central Peru, participated to a greater degree in other sectors of the broader capitalist economy, and eventually moved out of viticulture into other areas of commodity production, Moquegua maintained its quasi-monocultural focus on regional consumers—and increasing consumption—through the destruction wrought by war with Chile and the introduction of phylloxera.

In the terms used in political ecology studies, colonial Moquegua can be considered a "business cluster" (Porter 1998; Robbins 2004). That is, the valley was a localized production system, an area where multiple independent "firms"—wineries, in this case—owned by individuals and monasteries produced "local collective competition goods" (wine, brandy, and related products) in some degree of competition with each other. Much of the coast of the viceroyalty, including south into Chile, can be seen as a "cluster region" (Whitford and Potter 2007), the individual clusters or sub-regions of which also competed with each other in targeted but overlapping zones of consumers.

Clusters and cluster regions typically develop horizontal and vertical dimensions based on innovations and specializations that provide competitive advantages. In Moquegua, the wine agro-industry's gradual development was primarily vertical, apparent as intensification (monoculture and industrial-capitalist–style reinvestment of profits in production facilities) and "upstream vertical integration" of all aspects of the industry, from owning the vineyards and harvests to making standardized containers for storing and shipping the goods (Rice 2011b: 276–77). This latter is not a consequence of capitalism per se, as similar vertical arrangements existed in Roman estates (Rice 1996b). They were convenient solutions to problems of scale and costly transport, irrespective of time or place, in earlier, pre-"global" economic systems.

These processes and their outcomes are narrated at greater length in *Vintage Moquegua* (Rice 2011b). Here, the aim is to explore in greater detail some of the human-constructed cultural contexts—social, political, and economic—of colonial encounters while situating them in their various human- and "nature"-constructed spatial contexts: the sites and spaces of Moquegua.

NOTES

1. I acknowledge, but do not dwell on, the fact that some scholars consider "landscape" to reflect Western epistemology, particularly a genre of painting, which reflects an artificial distinction between nature and culture.

2. Among the Kallawayas (Qollahuayas) of Bolivia, ayllu seems to refer to various kinds of ties within a community: territorial (*llahta ayllu*), affinal (*masi ayllu*), and work (*mitmaj ayllu*) (Bastien 1985: 609n1).

3. At two bodegas in the extreme southern end of the valley, Chincha and Sacatilla, shovel testing revealed pre-Hispanic burials (Smith 1991: 128, 232). Because these were not part of the Bodegas Project research design, excavations were halted, the remains carefully covered, and the units backfilled.

4. Perhaps relative sequences of construction of the bodegas could eventually be achieved by seriation of adobes, as at the pre-Hispanic Chimu site of Chan Chan on Peru's north coast (Kolata 1982), or mortar thickness.

2

The "Natural" Landscape of Moquegua

> The crux of the problem was temperature. Spain lies in the temperate zone. The great bulk of the Spanish empire lay [in the tropics]. No farmer would ever be able to grow the staples of an Iberian diet at sea level in the tropical latitudes. He would have to ... find a substitute for a higher latitude in a higher altitude.
>
> —Alfred Crosby (1972: 70)

The Department of Moquegua is a small and historically relatively impoverished political unit in the western Andean watershed, in the far south of the present nation-state of Peru. It is bordered by the Departments of Arequipa to the west, Puno to the northeast, and Tacna to the southeast and by the Pacific Ocean on the southwest (see figure 1.1). Moquegua's most distinctive environmental characteristics are its arid climate, sharp altitudinal zonation, and frequent tectonic activity (Rice 1989). Except for the modern cities of Moquegua and Samegua, the landscape is decidedly rural, its built structures and their distribution a function of the valley's agricultural economy and historical patterns of land division.

Examination of the components of the natural (as opposed to cultural) landscape generally begins with the physical environment. Physical environments, in turn, are typically described and analyzed in terms of their physiographic and biological components, including geology and soils, climate and weather, topography, hydrography, and floral and faunal populations.

The natural landscape of Moquegua is dominated by mountains and desert. Physiographically, the department lies on the western slopes of the Andes Mountains, its eastern edge demarcated by the towering

DOI: 10.5876/9781607322764.c02

cordillera separating that watershed from the basin of Lake Titicaca in the altiplano ("high plateau"; elevations ca. 3,500–4,000 m). Peaks reach above 6,000 m (19,500 ft) in elevation, with several small lakes tucked among them. Thermal springs and baths, with water temperatures of 72°C (162°F), are found in the higher elevations of the department (Anonymous 1998: 812).

Numerous volcanoes, dormant and active, lie in the cordillera. Three in the Department of Moquegua—Ubinas, Huaynaputina, and Ticsane—have erupted frequently. Southern Peru is active tectonically, with major destructive earthquakes—sometimes accompanied by deadly tsunamis—in 1600, 1604, 1715, 1784, 1831, 1868, 2001, and 2006 (Rice 2009). Moquegua and its wine industry also suffered economic repercussions from earthquakes occurring farther to the north, including in Cusco in 1650, south-central Peru in 1687, and Lima in 1746.

The narrow Pacific coastal region of Moquegua crosses the arid to hyper-arid Atacama Desert, which runs from northern coastal Peru through Chile. Lying at elevations below 1,000 m (3,280 ft), the coastal strip is only 3–7 km (2–4 mi) wide on the north side of the Río Osmore. South of the river it widens, reaching 30–50 km (18–30 mi) inland beyond the department's borders. This barren, hilly coastal desert is frequently fog-shrouded and lacks both rainfall and permanent vegetation except for temporary growth responding to *garúa*, a thick, drizzle-like coastal advection fog formed as air cooled by the ocean moves over land and upslope, cooling further and condensing.

The early Spaniards learning the environment of southwestern Peru faced different challenges in establishing their agro-pastoral regimes compared with earlier Indigenous Andean colonists. As noted in the epigraph, the Iberian Peninsula enjoyed a temperate climate, but Spain's empire primarily comprised tropical regions of the Americas, where many Iberian dietary staples could not be grown at sea level. Making the Andean environment productive for both plants and animals meant adapting to the mountains and exchanging latitude for altitude.

GEOLOGY: MOUNTAINS AND MINERALS

The geology of Moquegua (Barua 1961; Bellido Bravo 1979: 36–41; ONERN 1976: 89–106; Shockey et al. 2009), like that of the entire western Andean region, is complex, with sedimentary, metamorphic, and igneous/volcanic deposits dating generally from Precambrian through Quaternary times. Sedimentary and metamorphic rocks in the Osmore drainage basin include clays, sandstones, conglomerates, limestone, and quartzites. Igneous rocks comprise volcanics such as tuffs and deposits formed from lavas of andesitic, rhyolitic, and dacitic composition; intrusives are components of the Andean Batholith, including diorite, granodiorite, granite, monzonite, and dacite.

The Department of Moquegua is dominated geologically by the Moquegua Formation, a Tertiary-age deposit of continental sediments extending many hundreds of kilometers along the southern coast of Peru. The formation consists of siltstones, sandstones, and conglomerates, the latter with clayey and fine-grained sandstones and mudstones and pink ignimbrite intercalations (Shockey et al. 2009: 4). The Lower Moquegua Formation, south of the city of Moquegua, overlies Cretaceous deposits and consists of brown and gray tuffaceous and arkosic sandstones, alternating with gray to reddish clayey sandstone, locally called *moro-moro*. This is topped by a gypsiferous deposit laid down in an ancient tectonic depression occupied by lakes (Bellido Bravo 1979: 40; cf. Dregne 1968: 307), which seems to bespeak a period of major desiccation and transition to desert-like conditions.

The Upper Moquegua Formation is found in the higher elevations and is partly covered by a 15–20-m (49–66-ft)-thick bank of white dacitic or rhyolitic tuff from the late Pliocene Huaylillas volcanic formation. The lithology consists primarily of volcanics and sandy conglomerates, including tuffaceous sandstones, sandy tuffs, and some clays. These were deposited on the broad plain that resulted from the drying of the ancient lakes and were subsequently dramatically uplifted. A stratum of volcanic ash from an outcrop west-southwest of Moquegua yielded a $^{40}Ar/^{39}Ar$ age determination of 26.25 ± 0.10 million years for the lower part of the Upper Moquegua Formation (Shockey et al. 2009: 5, 19), as well as late Oligocene fossils, previously unknown in the area.

The coast is part of a broad, Quaternary-age marine terrace extending south into Chile, the sediments of which are composed of "stratified sands, gravels and clays, with frequent inclusions of strata of gypsum, lime, and indurated salts" (Dregne 1968: 307).

Moquegua is located in the "Pacific Copper Belt," which encompasses portions of both southern Peru and northern Chile. This location confers access to rich deposits of valuable metallic minerals and ores, including copper (chalcopyrite, malachite, and bornite), galena (lead ore), and iron ores (hematite, magnetite, and limonite) that were economically important in pre-Hispanic and Colonial times and into the twenty-first century (ONERN 1976: 92; also Bellido Bravo 1979: 65–71; Petersen 2010). Copper has been commercially mined for many decades at Cuajone, just outside Moquegua in the upper Department of Tacna; and a mine at Tisco, north of Arequipa, was exploited in pre-Hispanic times. A tabulation of past and present producers and possible future mining operations in southwestern Peru lists 23 mines in Moquegua, 97 mines to the north in the Department of Arequipa, and 165 to the south in Tacna (http://mineral-resources.findthedata.org/d/d/Peru/). In addition to copper, lead, and iron, the mineral resources listed for these mines include gold, silver, zinc, manganese, molybdenum, alumina, and antimony. Additional non-metallic minerals are mica, graphite, halite, magnesite, bentonite, and silica.

In the Osmore drainage specifically, useful non-metallic mineral deposits comprise gypsum, salt, limestone, and sulfur. An outcrop of high-quality gypsum (*yeso*), 15–20 cm thick, lies on the east side of the middle Moquegua valley 17 km (10.2 mi) south of the city (Bellido Bravo 1979: 37, 71; ONERN 1976: 103) and was mined into the late twentieth century at the former bodega called La Yesera. Salt deposits interlayered with tuffaceous sands and clays at Salina de Loreto on the coast, 12 km (7.2 mi) east of the port of Ilo, occur in two visible strata, one 10–12 cm (4–4.7 in) thick lying 5 m (16.4 ft) below surface and the other 40–50 cm (15.75–19.7 in) thick, at 10 m (32.8 ft) b.s. Limestone (*caliza*) outcrops in the sierra along the road between Carumas and Torata (Barua 1961: 44). Deposits of sulfur, with various uses in viniculture, are known in the volcanic regions around Ubinas and Carumas and from the flanks of volcanoes in the Department of Tacna (ibid.: 59; Chabert and Dubosc 1905: 35; ONERN 1976: 106).

RIVER SYSTEMS: LOW FLOW

The Department of Moquegua is drained by two river systems, the Tambo in the north and the Osmore in the south. The southwest-flowing Río Tambo has two main tributaries, the Ichuña and Coralaque, each with headwaters in the altiplano. The Río Ichuña, which arcs from the north and west, meets the Coralaque, flowing along the floor of the altiplano, at the edge of the cordillera near the Indigenous community of Ubinas. Together they form the Río Tambo, which is joined downstream by smaller tributaries: the Río Carumas (in Carumas) and the Vagabundo (near Omate). The lower 57 km (35 mi) of the Tambo pass through the extreme southern corner of the Department of Arequipa before debouching into the Pacific Ocean.

The Río Osmore system, which drains a smaller watershed than the Tambo, lies entirely within the Department of Moquegua and follows the Chololo geological fault for part of its flow (Clement and Moseley 1989: 439). Its three main tributaries arise in the cordillera and plunge 5,000 m (16,300 ft) over a distance of only 140 km (86 mi), joining to form the Río Osmore (sometimes called the Tambopalla) at ca. 1,450 m (ca. 4,750 ft) elevation (figure 2.1). These tributaries, from north to south, are known by several names:

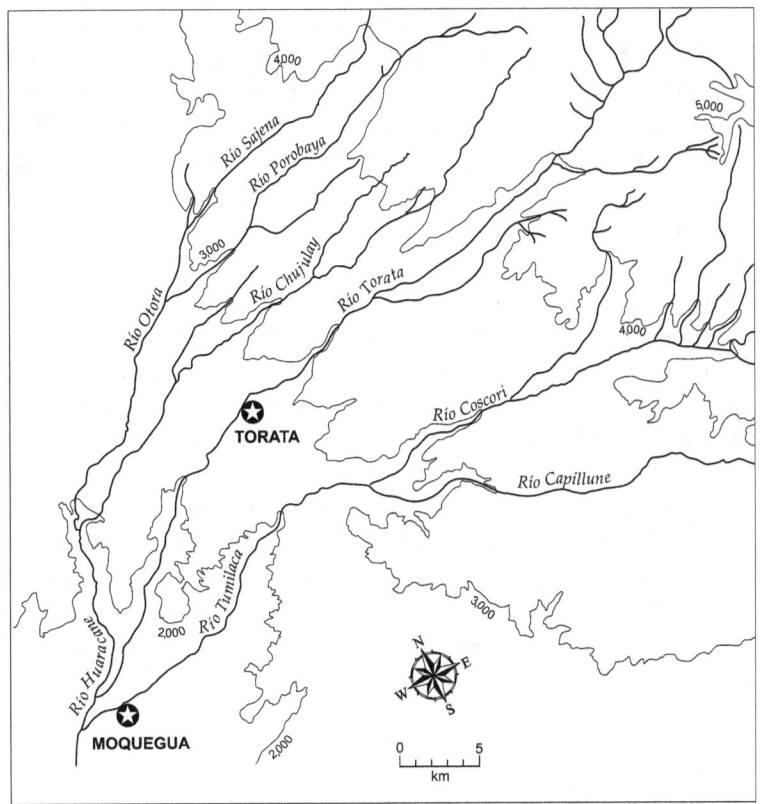

FIGURE 2.1 *Tributaries of the Río Osmore (contours in meters).*

- The Río Huaracane, also known as the Otora, has three tributaries: the Sajena and Porobaya, which form the Río Otora, and the Chujulay. Its drainage basin extends 59 km (36.6 mi) and covers 505 km² (195 mi²).
- The Río Torata was also known, particularly in Colonial times, as the Río Quilancha or Ocolla. Its basin is ca. 65 km (40.3 mi) long and drains an area of 410 km² (158 mi²).
- The Río Tumilaca's tributaries are the Río Coscori, formed from the Asana and Charaque streams, and the Capillune. This is the largest drainage basin of the three tributaries, at 625 km² (241.3 mi²) in area and 61 km (37.9 mi) long.

The "Moquegua valley" or "middle valley" comprises the arable section of the Río Osmore, extending about 25 km (15.5 mi) north-south between approximately 1,700 m and 1,100 m (5,577–3,609 ft) elevation. The upper Moquegua valley is a broad (ca. 4 km/2.5 mi) triangular area where the three tributary streams converge. The Ríó Huaracane joins the Torata, which meets the Tumilaca about 2.2 km (1.4 mi) farther downstream. The colonial and modern city of Moquegua sits on the southern (left) bank of the lower Río Tumilaca on the flank of Cerro Chenchen, at an elevation of 1,450 m. Below the city the river turns south, narrows, and flows more gently, falling only 300 m (984 ft) over 20 km (12.5 mi). This middle valley "proper" is a narrow strip of floodplain 0.5–0.75 km wide.

The middle valley ends at about 1,100 m (3,609 ft), where the stream abruptly enters an underground course for 20 km (12.4 mi), emerging 30 km (18 mi) from the coast at an elevation of ca. 300 m (1,000 ft). This lower course of the Osmore, sometimes called the Río Ilo, flows through the coastal region and is marked by a broadening southern floodplain before reaching the Pacific Ocean near the port city of Ilo.

The Osmore flows with a generally low but erratic volume, and irrigation agriculture at least since the time of the Inkas has necessitated strict water control regimes. Heavy rains in the upper sierras can bring disastrous flooding, which is occasionally noted in archaeological and historical records, along with changes in the river channel and floodplain loss (Manners, Magilligan, and Goldstein 2007).

SOILS: RICH BUT LIMITED

Surface materials—"soils" in a general sense—in the arid coastal region of Moquegua present an unpropitious picture for agriculture: 65 percent consist of lithosols (rock fragments overlying bedrock, frequently on steep slopes), 25 percent regosols (fine, unconsolidated mineral materials; sand dunes), 5 percent red desert and black clay soils, and 5 percent alluvial soils (Dregne 1968: 307). Moreover, as compared with other valleys in the Andes and even other river systems of far southern Peru, such as the larger and broader valleys of the Ríos Locumba, Sama, and Caplina, the Osmore provides only an extremely small and narrow strip for cultivation, with a total area of around 3,200 ha (7,900 acres).

Arable soils (i.e., non-lithosols and non-regosols) of the Osmore drainage, as well as those of the other southern departments, were classified by Peru's Oficina Nacional de Evaluación de Recursos Naturales (ONERN) in terms of their capacity for irrigation agriculture. The classification was based on characteristics such as depth, drainage, susceptibility to erosion, friability, moisture retention, presence of salts, and so forth. This analysis divided the Osmore drainage into two sectors: the mid-valley Moquegua sector (sometimes including land under cultivation in the Torata valley) and the coastal Ilo sector. These sectors represent 2,810 ha (ca. 6,900 acres) and 510 ha (1,260 acres), respectively, of lands potentially cultivable by irrigation.

The Osmore's arable soils were classified into four categories, Class 1 (best) through Class 4 (unsuitable), for irrigation agriculture (ONERN 1976); Classes 5 and 6 are also unsuitable for agriculture and are not discussed further here. Moquegua (MQ) Series (Class 1; 846 ha) soils occur primarily on alluvial terraces with little slope. These highly productive soils are slightly alkaline, deep to very deep, with moderate moisture retentiveness; they lack problems with drainage or salinity. Class 2 soils (714 ha) have three subdivisions: Aeropuerto (AE), Calaluna (CA), and Ladera (LD), all of which are moderately deep, with slight (to moderate: CA) alkalinity and average to good productivity. AE soils have 10 percent to 20 percent of angular gravel inclusions measuring 2–8 cm in size; CA soils occur generally on the margins of the river and have roughly 10 percent poorly sorted sub-angular gravel of 3–15 cm. LD soils occur on hillsides with slopes of 2 percent to 7 percent; containing angular and sub-angular gravel, they exhibit excessive drainage.

Poorer-quality soils include Class 3 (443 ha), the Estación (ET) and Espejos (EP) Series. ET soils are moderately deep, distributed on slopes, have gravel throughout, and have a neutral pH. EP soils, found in the extreme southern valley, are moderately to strongly alkaline, have relative high salinity, and have average to good productivity. Class 4 Talud Series (208 ha) are unsuitable for irrigation agriculture because of their low fertility and location on steep slopes.

The confluence of the Osmore's tributaries has soils in all four arable classes, with the highest-quality soils occurring in sizable areas adjacent to the Tumilaca and Torata Rivers (figure 2.2). Class 2 soils are found on the elevated area near the modern airport and on the ridge above the Río Torata's flow into the Tumilaca. Class 3 soils occupy the flat summits of the desert ridges that separate the lower tributary valleys, and the steep slopes of these ridges fall into Class 4. In the middle Moquegua valley, from the tributaries' confluence south to approximately San José, soils are primarily gravelly Class 2 immediately adjacent to the riverbed, bordered by Class 1 at slightly higher elevations. Unfortunately, many large modern constructions—the military base, airport, tourist hotel, Panamerican Highway—occupy major sections of these two highly productive agricultural zones in the upper and middle valleys. Southern valley soils are Class 2 or Class 3 (EP), limited by salinity.

A smaller area of good soils lies in the lower valley of the Río Torata. Here, between about 2,100 and 2,300 m (6,890–7,500 ft) elevation, approximately 430 ha (ca. 1,060 acres) of arable floodplain are found on either side of the riverbed,

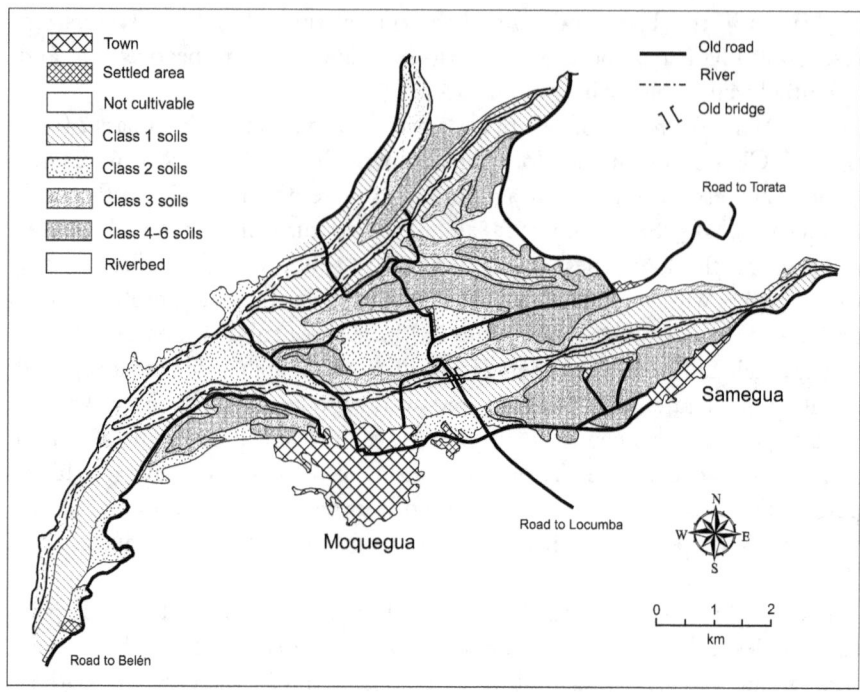

FIGURE 2.2 *The upper Moquegua valley—confluence of the Osmore's tributaries—showing modern towns, old roads, and soil classifications (see text). From ONERN 1976.*

with extensive ancient and modern irrigated terraces on the surrounding hills. In the Otora valley, fewer than 200 ha (ca. 500 acres) of land were farmed in the late twentieth century, with another 500 ha (ca. 1,200 acres) occupied by active and abandoned terraces (Stanish 1992: 106–7).

In all, of the approximately 2,800 ha of agricultural land in the Moquegua valley and its tributaries, more than 1,560 ha (ca. 3,855 acres) are of the highest-quality soils, representing the largest swath of good soils between Arequipa and the Caplina valley of Tacna (table 2.1; ONERN 1976). Most of this land lies in the broad confluence region and the narrow Moquegua valley. The second-largest area of cultivable soils lies around the mouth of the river near Ilo. Although the tributaries (except Torata) lack large areas of flat bottomland for agriculture, the steep hillsides were cultivated for centuries through systems of terraces and irrigation canals. Today, the mid-valley's sunny, warm climate is favorable for growing a variety of temperate and semitropical row and tree crops, indigenous and introduced, the lack of rainfall mitigated by irrigation systems.

TABLE 2.1 Classification of agricultural capacity of soils in the valleys of southwestern Peru

	Moquegua[a]		Locumba		Sama		Caplina	
Class[b]	ha	%	ha	%	ha	%	ha	%
1	846	30.1	—	—	—	—	—	—
2	714	25.5	1,030	23.5	1,121	25.5	4,862	54.2
3	443	15.7	1,439	32.8	1,338	30.5	3,091	34.4
4	208	7.4	605	13.8	119	2.7	—	—
Unsuitable	599	21.3	1,315	29.9	1,807	41.2	1,020	11.3
TOTAL	2,810	100.0	4,389	100.0	4,385	99.9	8,973	99.9

Source: ONERN 1976.
a Includes the tributaries but excludes 510 ha in Ilo.
b Classes 1 and 2 are best for agriculture. See text for information.

WEATHER: SUNNY AND DRY

Moquegua gets very little rainfall, not unexpected given its location in the hyper-arid Peruvian Atacama Desert. During the thirty-two years (1931–72) for which records were analyzed by ONERN, the city's recording station measured a *total* of only 228.8 mm (9.0 in) and an annual mean of 7.9 mm (0.31 in), with a range of 0.0 to 25.5 mm (1.0 in) per year. It follows, then, that the flow of the Río Osmore and its tributaries is unpredictable and not a consequence of rainfall in the lower sierras but rather a response to rain and snowfall in the upper sierra and cordillera. Most of the precipitation falls during January and February.

Moquegua's weather is pleasant virtually the entire year, with very low humidity and abundant sunshine. Total hours of sunshine, an important climatic factor in a wine-growing region, vary monthly from a high mean (316 hours) in October to a low mean (209) in February, with an annual mean of 276.6 hours. Annually, total hours of sunshine range from 3,109 to 3,557, with a mean of 3,319 hours (ONERN 1976: anexo II, p. 17), higher than in the dry wine-producing regions of southern Spain.

Temperatures are moderate, with the low seasonal variation common in the tropics and the sharp diurnal changes common in deserts: warm, sunny days and clear, often chilly nights. This pattern results from the lack of humidity and from radiational cooling; that is, because cloud cover does not form to hold in the heat of the day, that heat is rapidly radiated from the ground surface after the sun sets. The warmest months of austral summer are the "rainy season" months of January through March, and the coolest months are June through August. The mean annual temperature, calculated from records between 1932 and 1972, is 18.75°C (65.7°F) (ibid.: anexo II).

The Moquegua valley exhibits the alternating day and night patterns of air movement typical of a mountain valley. "Mountain breezes" move downslope beginning in the evening; as the sun sets, the slopes of the valley cool quickly, and the air above them cools and becomes denser, sliding down to lower elevations. Frequently, this nighttime cooling causes the heavy colder air in the lower valley to condense, producing radiation fog. This fog "grows" upward from the ground and during the course of the night moves up-valley. After daybreak, the sun begins to dissipate the fog and warm the slopes of the hills, causing the warmer air to rise and the cooler air at lower elevations to warm and move up to take its place. This produces a gentle "valley breeze" that begins by midmorning and blows upslope during the day until late afternoon.

Meteorological records did not begin to be kept in Moquegua until the twentieth century, and so they provide details of only recent variations in weather. We do not have such data for the preceding four centuries of post-conquest occupation, making it difficult to determine the kinds of climatic and weather conditions, favorable or unfavorable, to which the European settlers had to adapt. Nonetheless, several efforts have been undertaken to reconstruct general climatic conditions during the late pre-Hispanic and Colonial periods in Andean South America.

One set of data comes from cores sampling the Quelccaya ice cap, 200 km (120 mi) northwest of Lake Titicaca in the Department of Puno. These suggest that the early Colonial period was a relatively cold interval corresponding to the so-called Little Ice Age of the Northern Hemisphere (Thompson et al. 1986). Concentrations of particulate matter and changes in oxygen isotopes, among other things, indicate dry periods from AD 650 to 750 and 1250 to 1310, a wet period from 1500 to 1720, followed by an extremely dry period from 1720 to 1860; the middle of this dry interval, from 1800 to 1820, was also quite cold. Localized variations are apparent, however.

Other data come from analysis of El Niño/La Niña (combined with the Southern Oscillation; together called ENSO) events. ENSO refers to the pattern of warming of Pacific Ocean currents that brings about changing weather patterns worldwide. In the western Andes, the La Niña phase of ENSO coincides with episodes of unusually heavy rainfall and severe flooding in the river valleys in both pre-Hispanic and recent times (see, e.g., Moore 1991; Moseley 1987). In the Osmore valley, two large flooding events have been dated to AD 690/700 and AD 1300/1330 (Magilligan and Goldstein 2001).

Colonial-period ENSO episodes can also be identified in documentary records (Quinn, Neal, and Antuñez de Mayolo 1987). Between the mid-sixteenth century and 1900, thirty-six ENSO events have been categorized as strong or very strong (ibid.). Many—perhaps most—of these events likely resulted in flooding in Moquegua, yet another problem for the residents to cope with over and above the region's frequent (and far more unpredictable) earthquakes. Floods apparently occurred in the early seventeenth century, although they might have been exaggerated in the context of ongoing disputes between the residents on opposite banks of the Tumilaca. A severe flood is said to have occurred in 1750 (Kuon Cabello 1981: 377) but is not clearly associated with an ENSO event. And a disastrous flood occurred in February 1900 (Chabert and Dubosc 1905: 26) as part of a strong El Niño (Quinn, Neal, and Antuñez de Mayolo 1987), destroying vineyards in Moquegua, uprooting olive trees in Ilo, and leaving huge rocks and deposits of sandy alluvium up to 1 m thick in its wake.

VEGETATION AND AGRICULTURE

Little wild or natural plant life characterizes the arid Osmore valley today, except for grasses, canebrakes, and sparse trees along the streambed. Trees whose wood was important for construction include *algarrobo*, or mesquite (*Prosopis*), *pacay* (*Inga feuillei*), and *molle*, or pepper tree (*Schinus molle*); molle berries were used to flavor corn beer (*chicha*). Most of what grows in the valley, now and in the past, consists of domesticates—indigenous corn (*Zea mays*), chili peppers (*Capsicum spp.*), potatoes (*Solanum* spp.), and cotton (*Gossypium*)—and introduced cultigens including alfalfa (*Medicago sativa*), wheat (*Triticum* spp.), various tree fruits, and especially grapevines (*Vitis vinifera*).

The major limitation on viticulture—and agriculture in general—in Moquegua is water: low rainfall and the low flow of the river. Less than 20 percent of the Osmore drainage lies in the upper elevations that capture annual seasonal rainfall, meaning that the valley's agricultural systems, even if irrigation-based, were "highly vulnerable" to drought (Kolata 1993: 293). Nonetheless, beginning in the early Colonial period, the Spanish settlers planted grapevines and viticulture thrived in the abundant sunshine of the upper and middle valley, the products being primarily wine and pisco brandy distilled from the wine. Documentary and archaeological evidence records the spread of viticulture down-valley, with relatively large properties cultivating poorer soils.

In the early 1970s, when ONERN carried out its analysis of the department's resources and land use, 56 percent of the cultivated hectarage in the valley was in alfalfa and 13 percent, primarily in the upper valley around Samegua and the Río Tumilaca, was in tree crops—including stone-fruits (*Prunus*: peach, apricot, plum), cherimoya (*Annona cherimola*), mango (*Mangifera indica*), and avocado (*Persea americana*). Only 1.7 percent of the valley was planted in vineyards, primarily in the far southern end. Of the three cultivable soil series, only high-salinity EP soils in the southern valley were extensively cultivated in grapes at the time of the government study. This might relate to a characteristic not considered in the ONERN analysis: the possible role of gypsum in these soils. If gypsum has been eroding more or less continuously into the lower valley, it might have created sediments with some of the characteristics of southern Spain's famous gypsiferous *albariza* soils in the sherry region of Jeréz (Amerine, Berg, and Cruess 1972: 408).

Part II
Indigenous Spaces and Places

Moquegua's long history of occupation began more than 10,000 years ago, with the large Ring Site shell mound registering early exploitation of Peru's productive coastal waters (Sandweiss et al. 1989). But population sizes and densities were low, leaving little evidence of how the landscape was perceived and how (or if) significant places were constructed by its early inhabitants. The valley's status as a colonized landscape began a millennium before the arrival of Europeans, when its comparatively rich soils and temperate climate meant that it was widely perceived as an attractive agricultural space. Moquegua thus became a distant annex attached to larger, more densely settled, territorially expansionist states. The spatializations—the ordering of the valley's open agricultural spaces and the distributions of built places and boundaries—produced by these early colonists, still low in numbers, made an imprint that is still visible on the landscape.

Moquegua's occupational history before and after the arrival of the European colonists is dominated by relations with the altiplano. There, during the Late Intermediate Period (LIP), a number of petty kingdoms, or *señoríos*, developed in the Lake Titicaca basin, filling the power vacuum left by the collapse of the powerful Middle Horizon (MH) state of Tiwanaku, south of the lake in Bolivia. Moquegua's residents had particularly close ties to two rival señoríos of Aymara-speakers that emerged in the western basin: the Qolla (Colla) and the Lupaqa. The Qolla appear to have been the more powerful of the two groups in the LIP, sending agricultural colonists to cultivate maize, coca, and peppers in the temperate river valleys throughout the southwestern region of what is now Peru, from

Arequipa through northern Chile. During the Late Horizon (LH), the Inka created an alliance with the Lupaqa, deploying them as agricultural colonists in the tributaries of the Río Osmore.

A distinctive set of policies of Inka imperial administration involved the resettlement of peoples—particularly those with special skills such as pottery making, weaving, or stone working—from the conquered provinces into these new areas, often far from their homelands. This clustering was done in part to facilitate payment of tribute obligations (Julien 1983: 78). At least six other categories of resettlement can be identified (ibid.: 78–79, citing Cieza de León 1967 [1553]: 55, 73–78, 83–84, 232), including people who were relocated

- when a new territory was organized as a province, "for security reasons and to aid in the acculturation of the inhabitants to their role as subjects of the empire";
- "to frontier areas to serve as garrisons";
- "as colonies in underpopulated regions to bring them into production";
- to grow or collect "certain plants unavailable at home, like maize, coca and a variety of fruits";
- from the coast to highland administrative centers "to facilitate storage of goods"; and
- "from hilltop locations to more level ground."

These practices were part of Inka re-spatialization strategies, a set of policies and practices intended to restructure alien spaces for economic and political purposes and order them in line with imperial goals.

New communities were often strategically placed "away from local political, economic, and cultural centers, in areas that local agents experienced as peripheral, marginal, and even dangerous" (Acuto 2005: 222). As a result of this liberal resettlement policy, the cultural landscape of the Andes increasingly became a mosaic of discontinuous, inter-digitated colonies and enclaves of highlanders and coastal dwellers and northern and southern Andeans (Ramírez 2005: 37–39). Through this and related policies and practices, the Inka constructed new landscapes "embedded into the imperial ideology, [and] resignified the sense of place that these marginal regions had for local communities ... Center became periphery and periphery became centers" (Acuto 2005: 222). It is also important to remember that in the mountainous Andes, spaces and spatializations were not only horizontal but also perceptually and literally vertical, and higher elevations may be associated with higher Indigenous statuses.

A key consequence of the waxing and waning of outside political powers over the centuries in Peru is that the southwestern region in general, and the Osmore drainage in particular, was home to colonists speaking various languages and having different cultural traditions. The LIP Qolla and LH Lupaqa colonists in the sierras spoke Aymara and the Inka, if any "ethnic" Inka were actually present in the valley, spoke Quechua. It is not clear that altiplano control extended to or through the coastal zone, where farmers and fisherfolk may have spoken a now-extinct language called Koli (Coli, Cole; Rostworowski 1988). Another now-extinct language in the region was Puquina/Pukina, perhaps related to the original language of Tiwanaku and its MH settlers in the Osmore (Bouysse-Cassagne 1986: 208; Browman 1994; Galdos Rodríguez 1996: 293). This language may have continued to be spoken by people remaining in the Moquegua valley after the demise of Tiwanaku's colonies.

The chapters in part II of *Space-Time Perspectives* explore pre-Hispanic spatializations of the Osmore drainage: the intersections of the imperial with the local in short- and long-term impacts of these distant Indigenous Andean states on the Moquegua landscape. Chapter 3 begins with brief consideration of MH Wari and Tiwanaku settlement in the valley before moving to the LIP and regionalization. Of particular interest are the relations between the Moquegua valley settlements and the more powerful groups in the Lake Titicaca basin at the time of the Inka conquest. The Inka intrusion into Moquegua is discussed in chapter 4 through the only known Spanish-language account of this event, with particular concern for Inka re-spatialization of settlement and land use in the Torata valley. Chapter 5 looks at Moquegua's existing toponyms as they articulate the history of late pre-Hispanic spatializations in the Osmore drainage, especially how those spatializations are retained in the region's modern political divisions.

3

Late Pre-Hispanic Colonization and Re-spatialization

> The holy was ubiquitous in the ancient countryside of the Andes, and it could not be separated from the sights and doings of everyday life.
> —SABINE MACCORMACK (1985: 455)

The Osmore drainage was repeatedly settled by agricultural colonists from distant empires with varied ethnic and linguistic backgrounds. Colonization began in the middle of the first millennium of the Common Era, during the Middle Horizon (MH, ca. AD 500–1100), as the local Indigenous farmers (Huaracane tradition) throughout the valley were joined by newcomers from Wari and Tiwanaku (Isbell and Vranich 2004; Moseley et al. 1991; Sims 2006; Williams and Nash 2002). Why did these settlers come to Moquegua, and what imprint did they have on construction of Moquegua's landscape?

Wari (Huari), located in Ayacucho, 1,275 km (790 mi) north of Moquegua, established a small colony atop the iconic butte-like mountain known as Cerro Baúl and adjacent lower hilltops (Cerros Mejía and Petroglifo) between the Ríos Torata and Tumilaca (figure 3.1; Moseley et al. 2005; Nash and Williams 2009; Williams 2001). This settlement, representing the southernmost extent of the Wari state, appears to have had largely administrative and ceremonial functions, to judge from its architecture and use of space (Nash and Williams 2009: 263–65). Rituals were likely associated with mountain (*apu*) worship, as numerous snow-capped volcanic peaks are visible to the north and east from the summit of Cerro Baúl (Williams and Nash 2006). Various structural complexes form alignments with Picchu Picchu 75 km to the north-northwest and

DOI: 10.5876/9781607322764.c03

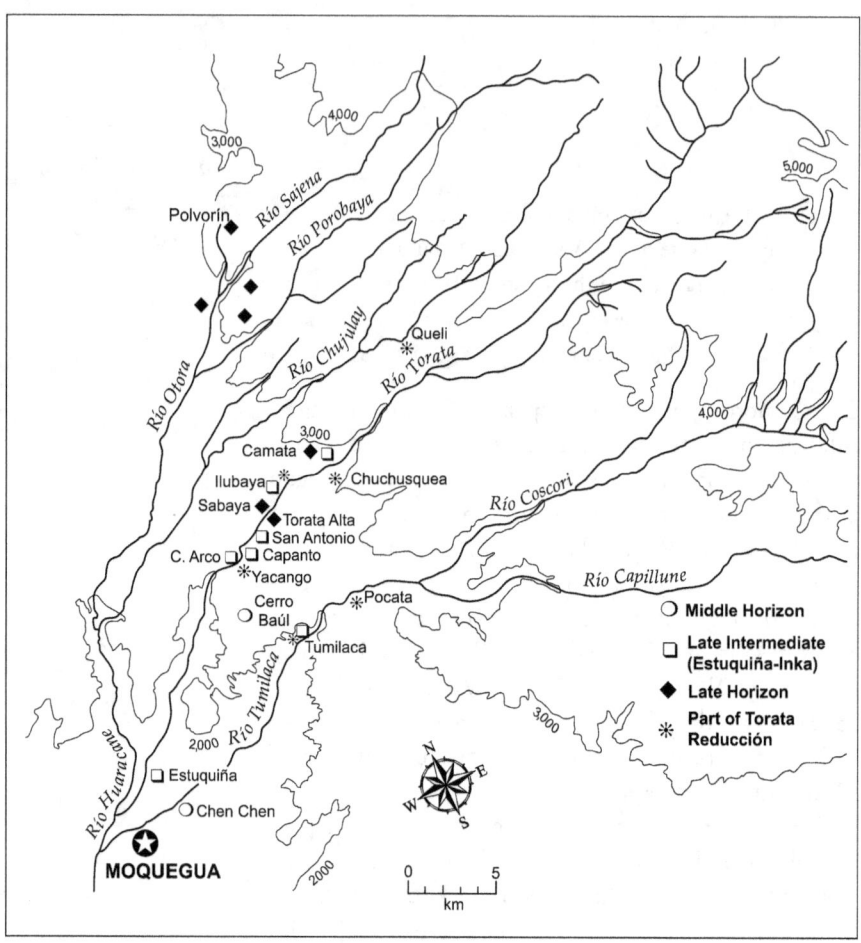

FIGURE 3.1 *Late pre-Hispanic sites and colonial reduction communities in the tributaries of the Río Osmore.*

Arundane about half that distance to the east. An enormous brewery produced chicha (beer) flavored with molle berries for feasting among residents and pilgrims participating in associated ceremonies (Goldstein and Coleman 2004; Goldstein, Coleman Goldstein, and Williams 2009; Moseley et al. 2005). Wari's reasons for establishing this colony in Moquegua are still unclear, but they may have been related to mineral extraction, including production of gold (a possible smelting location was noted at Cerro Mejía) and beads of blue stone (chrysocolla) and other materials (Nash and Williams 2009: 265–66).

Tiwanaku (Tiahuanaco), south of Lake Titicaca in what is now Bolivia, roughly 250 km (155 mi) from Moquegua, established a more significant and widespread presence farther downstream in the valley. Among the twenty-eight Tiwanaku-related sites in the Osmore drainage (Goldstein 1993a: figure 3.1, table 3.1) are a large ritual center at Omo on the east bank of the river in mid-valley and an administrative center and cemeteries at Chen Chen, near the modern city of Moquegua; the Torata Alta location also may have had some use. These sites were settlements of agriculturalists taking advantage of the valley's warm temperatures and fertile soils to cultivate corn (maize) and *ají* (chili peppers) under irrigation (Goldstein 1993a, 1993b; Janusek 2004: 239–43; Kolata 1993: 252–59, 292–94; Owen 2005). Once considered in terms of a central state-directed agricultural expansion model, the Tiwanaku presence in Moquegua and elsewhere is now seen as representing two diasporas, the earliest pastoralist colonists perhaps attracted by a well-watered environment following a strong El Niño event around AD 700 (Goldstein 2009; Owen 2005). Later, the Chen Chen immigrants established themselves adjacent to, but not among, the earlier settlements. This spatial distribution of Moquegua's Tiwanaku-related occupation appears to "represent two maximal ayllus within the Tiwanaku confederation that maintained distinctive ethnic identities in diaspora" (Goldstein 2009: 290). Outside of Moquegua, Tiwanaku's influence extended farther south into the western valleys of Chile, which supplied copper, lapis, and turquoise (Rivera 1991: 31).

Around the end of the first millennium, these powerful MH states collapsed, perhaps in response to drought. Data from core samples in the Quelccaya ice cap and sediments of Lake Titicaca suggest a dramatic decrease in precipitation (as rain or snow) and a slight rise in temperature ($1°C$) in highland southern Peru and adjacent Bolivia beginning about AD 1000 (Kolata 1993: 284–91). Tiwanaku state power diminished in Moquegua around 950, while Wari persisted for another century or so (Sims 2006).

LATE INTERMEDIATE PERIOD: MULTIPLE SITES AND ETHNICITIES

The succeeding Late Intermediate Period (LIP, ca. 1000–1450) was an interval of regionalization and mobility throughout the Andes and of adaptation to drought in southern Peru. In the Osmore valley, unaffiliated groups (*yanaconas*)[1] that remained after the MH collapse moved upstream, where they lived in small communities and were gradually joined by new agricultural colonists from outside the drainage (Moseley 1992: 227).

The post-Tiwanaku occupation in the valley, known as Tumilaca, is typically found around the lower tributary valleys and was succeeded around 1200 by the Estuquiña occupation in the same area as well as farther upstream (Stanish 1992). Settlements were commonly on fortified hilltops, which may have been located to defend access points for irrigation canals (Kolata 1993: 297).[2] Occupation of the tributary valleys increased, public architecture was limited, households may have been organized around extended families, and ceramic styles were localized, with emphasis on black-on-red decoration (Covey 2008: 313–18). The Moquegua valley lacks civic-ceremonial structures and settlement hierarchies in the LIP, thereby evidencing a decentralization similar to that noted in the Colca valley north of Arequipa (Wernke 2006: 189, 191).

LIP settlement is known from two sites in the upper mid-valley: Estuquiña and Tumilaca. In the lower Torata valley, LIP sites include San Antonio, Capanto (Bürgi 1993: 95–196), Camata, Ilubaya, Cerro Arco, and an unnamed site. These sites have variable settings, although most are on hilltops and consist of agglutinated, rectangular rooms (Bürgi 1993). An unusual type of site in Moquegua as well as other southern valleys is the *sitio de fiesta* (Zori 2011: 356–58), identified by concentrations of decorated vessel fragments—beaker-like *keros* and jars—and a lack of architecture. They appear to be sites of outdoor feasting and drinking and are located on prominent hilltops, "significant points on the landscape outside of town and temple" (Goldstein 2003: 162). These sites call to mind Cristóbal de Molina's description (in Zuidema 1994: 166) of an Inka ceremony at the June (winter) solstice, when the king, noble lords, and chosen women went out to a local hill to dance and drink.

The site of San Antonio (sometimes also called Torata Alta Viejo) is a defensively located, fortified community atop a ridge on the east side of the river. The site is difficult to access because of the steep slopes that bound it everywhere but the northeastern end (Borstel, Conrad, and Jacobi 1989: 376), and it is bordered by walls that still stand more than 2 m high in places. Archaeological investigations in the 1980s revealed that San Antonio has ninety-two structures (mostly in the south and center of the site), seventy-four primarily architectural terraces (on the northwest, north, and northeast), and thirteen narrow pedestrian corridors that lead to its central spine from the peripheries (ibid.: 379; Conrad 1993). The site's physical organization, divisible into two residential sectors, with each further divided in two, strongly suggests moiety-based dual social organization (Conrad and Webster 1989: 411–13).

Ceramics indicate that San Antonio was occupied in the late Estuquiña or Estuquiña-Inka (E/EI) phases of the LIP (Borstel, Conrad, and Jacobi 1989: 371). Parts of the community might have been briefly occupied in the Late

Horizon (LH), at the same time as nearby Torata Alta, because "Inka and Inka-related sherds" were recovered in excavations in Structure 20 in the southwest corner of the site. Str. 20 is a "special purpose building" added onto a larger household unit built over earlier tombs, and the doorway to one building was sealed (Conrad 1993: table 5.5; Conrad and Webster 1989: 414n3, n4). This household unit might have been the residence of the leader of the lower moiety at the site (Conrad and Webster: 412). The presence of Huaynaputina volcanic ash primarily over rubble, plus a radiocarbon date of AD 1439–1640 (see table 1.2), indicates that San Antonio had "been abandoned and was already in ruins" by that date (ibid.: 414n3). Other than Str. 20, there is relatively little evidence of post-abandonment activity at the community.

A question of longstanding interest among Programa Contisuyo archaeologists concerns the ethno-political affiliations of the residents of the Osmore drainage during the LIP and LH. It is generally agreed that they were Aymara-speaking colonists from the señoríos on the shores of Lake Titicaca, high in the altiplano. But the specific question was whether they were Qollas from north and northwest of the lake or Lupaqas from the western shore. Domestic architecture of three LIP sites—San Antonio, Estuquiña, and Tumilaca—was analyzed as a proxy for Qolla versus Lupaqa ethnic affiliations in the region (Bawden 1993; Conrad 1993; see also Stanish 1989). These studies suggested that San Antonio architecture shares characteristics with Qolla-affiliated sites at higher elevations in the Otora tributary of the Río Huaracane (Conrad 1993: 64–65). The Estuquiña and Tumilaca sites are distinctively different from San Antonio and may instead have ties to the middle and lower (coastal) valley (ibid.), inhabited by possible Koli-speakers. During the E/EI phase, there may have been no Lupaqa colonies in the middle valley, and any Lupaqas present might have been "interspersed among the local populations, probably by marriage" (ibid.).

These and related studies indicate that late pre-Hispanic altiplano colonial settlement in the upper Osmore began with the Qolla in the LIP (Conrad 1993; Stanish 1989, 2001: 224–25, 2003: 271–72). This archaeological evidence supports ethnohistoric data: Pedro de Sarmiento de Gamboa (2007: 114) reported that at the time of Inka conquest, the Qolla controlled a large area of the southwestern Andean watershed stretching from Arequipa along the coast to Atacama, Chile. Indeed, the Qolla appear to have expanded into the Azapa valley (near Arica) by AD 1300 (Rivera 1991: 36). Similarly, in the Osmore drainage, Qolla "influence" appears to have been felt in the Otora valley beginning in what Charles Stanish (1991: 1, 1992: figure 9) calls the Otora period (AD 1200–1300/1350) and continuing into the Late Horizon. It is not clear to what extent Qolla (versus Lupaqa) relations might be traced at lower elevations, however.

Coastal regions of the Peruvian southwest appear to have cultural and historical trajectories distinct from those of the sierras. Although the coast is bleak and barren today, during LIP times it might have been better watered, with small, spring-fed irrigation agriculture systems in the foothills and larger settlements in the valley (Clement and Moseley 1989; Reycraft 2000). Post-Tiwanaku occupation of the coast and lower mid-valley, known as Chiribaya, appears to be an autochthonous development out of Tiwanaku culture (Stanish 1992: 105–6). Chiribaya populations extended along the coast from the Río Tambo south into northern Chile (the Azapa valley), where the LIP occupation is known as Gentilar. Chiribaya and Gentilar pottery assemblages differ distinctively from those of the higher elevations in having polychrome decoration (Rivera 1991: 35). The area around Ilo was probably the Chiribaya political center (Zaro et al. 2010), although the coast and lower sierras might have been under the dominion of altiplano kingdoms (Rostworowski 1988: 140). The end of the Chiribaya culture might have been a consequence of a particularly serious pan-Andean ENSO event identified in deposits in the lower Osmore valley dated around AD 1300–50 (Magilligan and Goldstein 2001; Reycraft 2000; Satterlee et al. 2000).

THE LATE HORIZON

During the Late Horizon (LH) (ca. 1450 to 1533–35), most of western South America was dominated by the Inka empire, Tawantinsuyu. An "unfinished world-system" (Kuznar 1999; La Lone 1994, 2000) eventually incorporating an estimated 10 million–14 million people, Tawantinsuyu stretched roughly 3,300 km (2,050 mi) over the rugged Andes Mountains from present-day Ecuador into central Chile and northern Argentina (figure 3.2). Physically, this immense territory was integrated by 40,000 km (24,855 mi) of roads, with two main north-south highways, sierra and coastal, linked by east-west arteries; in some areas, way stations (*chaskiwasi*) or storage facilities (*tambos, tampu*) were spaced every 20 km (12 mi) or so (D'Altroy and Schreiber 2004: 268; Hyslop 1984). Segments of this road system might have been built earlier by the Wari (Schreiber 1991).

The methods the Inkas employed to annex and manage the different parts of their empire have been widely debated, and models posed by archaeologists and ethnohistorians vary on a continuum from territorial (direct) to hegemonic (indirect) in terms of imperial control over people and places (e.g., Acuto 2005; D'Altroy and Schreiber 2004: 259; Silverman 2004; Wernke 2006). A frequent point, perhaps most forcefully enunciated by ethnohistorian Susan Ramírez (2005), is that the Inkas placed supreme value on human capital (especially labor, service, kin ties, and generous reciprocity), as opposed to other kinds of

FIGURE 3.2 *Approximate extent of the Inka empire and its four suyus.*

politico-economic wealth resources. Inka dominance throughout the Andes, she claims (ibid.: 32), was based on human relations centered in "complicated notions of sacred duty, sanctions, reciprocity, and ritual kinship"; and the empire is "best described as divinely sanctioned and won jurisdiction over subjects, not over a delimited, bounded, and contiguous territory." Be that as it may, the Inkas unarguably desired not only the human labor in a particular territory to be annexed but also the varied resources (e.g., foodstuffs, precious metals, other minerals) extracted by that labor and delivered as tribute. Clearly, the Inkas deployed a variety of strategies and tactics—political, economic, military, ideological—along with varied infrastructural arrangements deemed appropriate for different regions, depending on the kinds and degrees of exploitation intended.

The Inkas produced various kinds of representations of their places, although none were textual in pre-Hispanic times because Andean peoples were non-literate. Among the physical representations are map-like devices—painted drawings and models of cities made of clay and pebbles. Despite lacking a writing system, the Inkas were numerate and employed a well-developed decimal system for keeping track of the people, goods, and camelid herds throughout their vast empire for purposes of tribute and exchange (see Julien 1988). A unique method of recording details of spatio-economic organization was the system of knotted strings known as *khipus* (*quipus*) (see Urton 2005; van de Guchte 1999: 158–62).

LANDSCAPE AND ORDER: THE INKA HEARTLAND

Many of the Inkas' strategies for ordering their vast mountainous empire are evident in the built environment—settlement distributions (Hyslop 1990), architecture (Gasparini and Margolies 1980), road systems (Hyslop 1984), and frontier fortresses and outposts[3]—and also in sacred places identified in the natural environment (e.g., Bauer 1998; Urton 1990; Zuidema 1986). Inka cognition of their landscape, space, and place was defined by state practices that integrated social, political, economic, religious, and historical management strategies (van de Guchte 1999: 151). The organization of Inka imperial space can be described as ideational or taxonomic—that is, derived from relational principles—but the ordering of their physical landscape was largely phenomenological, based on real, tangible entities.

Embodied Landscapes and Their Organization

Ethnohistorical and ethnographic sources reveal varied ways in which Andean peoples ordered their environment, many of which evidence principles common to early civilizations. For example, spatial organization was likely established by celestial activity, such as the daily and seasonal movements of the sun (Earls and Silverblatt 1978: 300) or perhaps the movement of the Milky Way (Urton 1981).

Another principle is anatomical: Andean peoples developed a complex system of metaphors and polysemy related to human and animal anatomy, the mountainous landscape, hydraulic systems of irrigation, and ayllus (Bastien 1978, 1985; Classen 1993). This cognitive organization is exemplified by the residents of the three ayllus occupying Mount Kaata, in western Bolivia northeast of Late Titicaca, who think of the features of their landscape as corresponding to features of the human body: head, eyes, arms, legs (Bastien 1978: 94, 97, 1985: 597). For these Qollahuayas (or Kallawayas), the mountain "is a triangular land mass, which signifies for all Kaatans ideas about their body, society, land, time, and history. Their rituals recall the similarities and relationships between the mountain and corporeal sickness,[4] lineage, marriage exchange, and ayllu solidarity" (Bastien 1978: 98). Garcilaso de la Vega, "El Inka" (1987b: 93), commented that "all Peru is long and narrow like a human body," and Cusco, laid out in the shape of a puma, was its navel. Jesuit father Bernabé Cobo (1983: 123) described the Inka ruler (*Sapa Inka*) Manco Capac as "the head and trunk" of both Cusco moieties. The mountain/body metaphor, by which mountains and river systems constitute heads and limbs, may have been the structuring principle of Andean landscape cognition (Bastien 1978: 99), with deep origins in earlier civilizations.

Administratively and conceptually, the capital of Cusco and the sacred valley landscape were divided in two at the "waist," that is, through the "navel"—Cusco's principal sun temple, the Qorikancha ("golden enclosure")—and the Río Huatanay into two parts or moieties: northern (upper, or *hanan*) and southern (lower, or *hurin*). These moieties were organized into ranked quadrants, or *suyus* (clockwise from north)—Chinchaysuyu, Antisuyu, Collasuyu, and Cuntisuyu or Contisuyu——hence the Quechua name of the empire: *tawa*, four; *ntin*, united; *suyu*, part (ibid.: 92). Suyus are commonly interpreted as spatial units, but in Cusco proper they originally may have been demographic or kin groups, each with a hierarchy of subdivisions and leaders (Ramírez 2005: 25). According to Tom Zuidema (1994: 156), each moiety was subdivided into five corporate groups called *panacas*, defined by ancestry and with an annual cycle of ritual duties. But quadripartition was the overarching mechanism.

By extension, all of imperial Tawantinsuyu was similarly organized and ranked: the hanan moiety consisted of Chinchaysuyu and Antisuyu, a tiny, rebellious area of the eastern Andean slopes; hurin encompassed Collasuyu, largest of the four quadrants, and Contisuyu (later hispanified to Condesuyos), a small wedge-shaped quadrant that included Moquegua. This meant that, in the north, Chinchaysuyu was hanan-hanan (the highest-ranked) and Antisuyu was hanan-hurin; in the south, Collasuyu was hurin-hanan and Contisuyu was hurin-hurin, the lowest ranked (see Bouysse-Cassagne 1986: 215–18; also Adorno 1986: 89).

To make matters still more complex, each of the four suyus had a similar *internal* division into upper and lower areas based on moiety organization (Urton 1990). Thus the Inkas cognized the spaces they occupied through a series of nested or "recursive hierarchies of identity" (Goldstein 2009: 279), from the ayllu to the empire.

Sacred Landscape Features

The Inkas ordered the Cusco valley and the vast space they later came to control through bipartition, tripartition, and quadripartition at various levels. In the Cusco valley, each suyu was divided conceptually into three parts by imaginary lines called *ceques*, conceptually radiating in groups from the Qorikancha (Bauer 1998; Zuidema 1964, 1986). Three of the suyus had nine ceques, but Contisuyu had fourteen or fifteen. The ceques are grouped into clusters of three, each line named and ranked: *collana* (highest), *payan*, and *cayao* (Bauer 1998: 35–38).[5] These lines extend over the landscape as much as 17 km from the city, following a series of cultural and natural shrines called *wakas* (*huacas*), the focus of group rituals and offerings (Bauer 1998).

Wakas were places that represented "anything in nature that was out of the ordinary," such as rock outcrops (carved or uncarved), desert springs, caves, and so on (ibid.: 2, quoting Garcilaso de la Vega). With more than 300 wakas in the system, these shrines constituted symbols and mnemonics as "instruments in the collective memory of origins and interrelationships with the supernatural, and as tools in the creation of their empire and the replication of icons of power in conquered territories" (van de Guchte 1999: 155). The existence of these wakas suggests that the Inkas perceived the sacred natural landscape of their heartland as animate and anthropomorphized, a "parallel physical world" in which "stones were put in the same mental categories that ruled the human world," such as kinship relations, physical movement, and receipt of tribute (ibid.: 162–63). The Inkas' geopolitical aesthetic was not one of portraying or imposing rigid imperial order over the natural and cultural environment but rather one of valuing "singularity" or alterity. Together, the ceque lines and wakas "demarcated the ritual topography of the valley of Cuzco" (ibid.: 161).

Boundaries

The 3,300-km (2,050-mi) north-south extent of the Inka empire held the potential for immense administrative challenges in maintaining allegiances, secure borders, and boundaries between kin groups. Indeed, the bounding of spaces and particularly the construction of high-walled compounds, residential and civic-ceremonial, was a fundamental element of pre-Inka Andean site organization, as evidenced at Wari and Tiwanaku in the south (Isbell and Vranich 2004) and at Chan Chan on the north coast of Peru (Moseley and Day 1982), but also back into the Preceramic period (see Moseley 1992).

Inka rulers placed boundary markers to mark the north, south, and eastern limits of their imperial explorations. Also, in an Aymara province of Umasuyu, the Inka ruler settled a dispute about grazing lands by establishing "landmarks, where he thought fit, so that each province should know its own land and not trespass on its rival's. These landmarks were, and still are today, preserved with great veneration, for they were the first to be set up in all Peru by order of the Inca" (Garcilaso de la Vega 1987b: 158–59).

Two royal specialists in measuring land and marking borders were called *sayua checta suyoyoc* in Quechua ("one who creates boundaries with stone piles and trenches") and *amojonadores* in Spanish. The keywords are sayua and *mojon*, both meaning "marker." These amojonadores were called Cona Raqui ("to divide") from Hanan Cusco and Una Caucho ("to put up signs") from Hurin Cusco (Guaman Poma de Ayala 1980: 353; Zuidema 1983: 68). According to Felipe Guaman Poma de Ayala (1980: 353), Topa (Thupa, Tupac) Inka Yupanki sent them to every province and every pueblo of every ayllu to measure and mark fields, pastures, and irrigation canals and thus maintain administrative order.

In noting that Guaman Poma's illustration of amojonadores shows "builders and engineers, not land surveyors," Ramírez (2005: 43–45) suggests that the setting of mojones might be a Spanish imposition rather than an Indigenous practice, given Spanish notions of private property and territorial politics. Also, some markers might have functioned for calendrical purposes. Guaman Poma's illustration, however, shows the construction of a more substantial boundary marker than a mere pile of stones; for example, a fortress.[6] In any case, it is unlikely that the two individuals from Cusco did all the survey work throughout the entire empire; local leaders such as kurakas or others were probably authorized to execute that responsibility within their ayllus. Regardless of who physically accomplished the demarcations, it is clear that physical markers existed throughout the vast Inka territory. Anyone tampering with the established boundaries faced severe penalties (Julien 1983: 28).

Physical boundaries carried important symbolic meanings. For example, both Inka and Tiwanaku architecture emphasized portals or gateways (including Tiwanaku's "Gateway God") for separating different kinds of ritual spaces and places. These features can be said to possess agency (sensu Latour 2005), as people passing through them may have experienced "important social and political transformations" (Morris and von Hagen 1993: 103). Inka doorways and interior niches were typically carefully constructed trapezoids, frequently with double jambs that accentuated their boundary-defining function. In addition, Pedro de Cieza de León (2005: 175) noted that at Cusco there were "gatekeepers, collectors of tolls, and guards, who were stationed to see who went in and out" of the city.[7]

Another architectural feature—the carefully fitted stone walls of Inka civic-ceremonial structures (Hyslop 1990), often "grafted" onto rock outcrops (Dean 2007)—can be considered in terms of boundary perspectives by focusing not on the stones but rather on the joins or borders between them. In some walls, in which the sizes and shapes of the "nibbled" (ibid.: 509–10) blocks are fitted and extremely uniform, the narrow, mortar-less joins between perfectly horizontal courses are virtually invisible, giving the appearance of a solid facade. In other structures, the stones have pillowed faces and irregular ("polygonal") shapes, accentuating—especially in raking sunlight—their unusually hewn individuality and the sinuous tracery of their precisely matched and sunken boundaries. The former is to Western eyes more "perfect" in its uniformity and appears to have been used for the most prestigious structures. Varied aesthetic, political, and economic considerations could account for the second, which may copy fieldstone architecture (ibid.: 517n43; Gasparini and Margolies 1980: 324–31).

As noted, ceques and wakas often served boundary functions, and ceremonial circuits or processions along them underscore performative celebrations of social and cosmic order. Gary Urton (1990: 120–23) links the dual (moiety), triple (ceque), and fourfold (suyu) partitioning of Cusco and central Tawantinsuyu to the Inka ancestors' mythical journey to the capital. He speaks of an Inka "preoccupation with boundary groups and other such social, temporal, and spatial 'border' categories in the organization of Cuzco and of the empire . . . The journey [of the ancestors] was a theoretical construction and a normative expression of the relationship between geopolitical boundaries and border categories [as intermediaries] in the overall organization of the empire" (ibid.: 123–24). Ancestor-based ritual performance highlights the role of these paths and monuments in an Inka landscape of memory and power: they declared rights to land and symbolized identities, exemplifying how movement over a landscape is fundamentally a "political act" (Snead, Erickson, and Darling 2009: 17).

IMPERIAL EXPANSION:
THE LAKE TITICACA BASIN AND THE AYMARA

Inka activity in the Osmore drainage was mediated by the peoples of the basin of Lake Titicaca, or "the Collao" as it was known, so it is appropriate to examine Inka expansion into this region. After the fall of Tiwanaku around AD 950, the Titicaca basin saw the same mobility, cultural regionalization, and decentralization apparent in other areas of the Andes. The region was wracked by political instability, as formerly suppressed inter-ethnic hostilities erupted, exacerbated by competition over resources (Kolata 1993: 299). By the late fourteenth century, some of these "micro-polities" (ibid.) had consolidated into variably sized señoríos in the Titicaca basin. One was Omasuyus to the east of the lake; another was Pacajes in the area of Tiwanaku in the south (Janusek 2004: 257–70). The largest and most powerful were those of Aymara-speakers on the northwestern shore.

Aymara Space

The Aymara-speaking Qolla and Lupaqa polities, on the northern and western edges of the lake, respectively, engaged in increasing hostilities throughout the LIP. This is indicated archaeologically by their distinctive hilltop fortifications (*pukaras*) and the differing distributions of their ceramics (Arkush 2008; Bouysse-Cassagne 1986: 205; Covey 2008: 301; Julien 1985: table 9.1; Van Buren 1996: 343). The Qollas' initial political and economic primacy in the northern Titicaca basin may be underscored by the toponym of the basin region as a whole: Collao = Qollao. However, after the Lupaqa reportedly defeated the Qolla, the former's political importance was enhanced through alliance with the Inkas (Hyslop 1979).

Aymara space has been described as "oriented around a northwest-southeast axis" based on the alignment of the Río Azángaro, Lake Titicaca, and the Río Desaguadero (Bouysse-Cassagne 1986: 216). In accordance with this axis, the Aymara ordered their landscape into two gendered divisions based on topographic elevation or vertical space—a de facto east-west geographic distinction—and on socioeconomic status. These two divisions were *urcosuyu* (Quechua; Aymara *alaasaa*) and *umasuyu* (*maasaa*). Urcosuyu/alaasaa was male, mountainous, and of high status; umasuyu/maasaa—the same name as the señorío east of the lake—was female, flatland (near water), and less valued (ibid.: 202; see also Rostworowski 1988).[8]

The coastal valleys, such as the Osmore, settled by Aymara colonists were classified as *alaa yungas*. Although topographically lower than urco, they were still considered high status (Bouysse-Cassagne 1986: 210). Moquegua, in the alaa yungas, was "low" not only in the sense of lower than urco in Aymara landscape ideology but also by existing in Contisuyu, the lower of the two hurinsaya moieties of Tawantinsuyu (ibid.: 215). The people who occupied the alaa yungas were "*koli*," characterized as "lively, intelligent," sociable, "urbane and civilized," and with "privileged links" to urcosuyu (ibid.: 210, 211, 212).

INKA ORIGINS

With respect to late pre-Inka times and the Inka conquest of the Lake Titicaca basin, modern understanding of the reality of events is complicated by differing Inka origin myths and mythic histories, including king lists (Covey 2006; Hiltunen and McEwan 2004). Because the Inkas were non-literate, the information we have today about pre-Hispanic life has been filtered and transmuted by both native informants and Spanish chroniclers (Hiltunen and McEwan 2004: 250–51; Julien 1985: 216–22). On the one hand, Spanish chroniclers' understanding of what they witnessed and were told was incomplete at best, and they possessed varying degrees of ability to work in native languages (Covey 2006). Some, like Sarmiento, endeavored to portray the Inkas as "cruel tyrants" and barbaric, while others, such as Garcilaso, painted a far more benign picture (Hiltunen and McEwan 2004: 253–54).

At the same time, the stories told to the Spaniards were also colored by the status, ethnicity, goals, and other interests of the Indigenous informants. These differences were in part a consequence of multiple Andean elites' maneuvering to reposition themselves during the social and economic turmoil of the post-conquest period. In relating their mythic histories to Spanish authorities, elites manipulated the details of their families and genealogies to their personal advantage. "Advantage" included increases in prestige, accumulation of land, economic exemptions from taxes, tribute, or labor (Urton 1990: 24, 124–28), an opportunity to redirect or mislead the interrogator (Murra 1968: 128), and protection of their current situation.

One set of myths proclaims Inka origins in Pacariqtambo, near the Cusco region, apparently a recent manipulation of political history in response to colonialism (McEwan 2006: 86; Urton 1990). An alternative history places their beginnings in Aymara territory on an island in southern Lake Titicaca (see Hiltunen and McEwan 2004: 238–40).[9] The Titicaca argument is given some support by the names of Inka kings, which are "predominantly Quechua, but a significant portion . . . are clearly Aymara and some Puquina" (ibid.: 246). Archaeological evidence suggests longstanding ties between Cusco and the

TABLE 3.1 Comparison of various Spanish accounts of Inka conquest of the Collao

Chronicler	Inka Ruler	Qollas	Lupaqas	Follow-up
Garcilaso[a]	Lloque Yupanki	Submitted to Inka	Submitted later	Qollas favored by Inka
Cobo[b]	Pachacuti	Defeated by Inka	Submitted to Inka	Lupaqa loyal, favored
Sarmiento[c]	Pachacuti	Defeated, rebelled	??	Inka conq'd Qolla three times
Cieza[d]	Viracocha	Attacked Lupaqa	Defeated Qolla at Paucarcolla	Lupaqas major power; Inka daughter to Qari; Inka-Lupaqa alliance
Tschopik[e]	Viracocha	Attacked Lupaqa	Allied w Inka, fought Qolla	
	Pachacuti	Defeated by Inka	Defeated by Inka	
	Topa Yupanki	Rebelled; sent to coast		Hatunqolla an Inka admin. center

Sources: [a]Garcilaso de la Vega (1987b); [b]Cobo (1983); [c]Sarmiento de Gamboa (2007); [d]Cieza de León (2001); [e]Tschopik (1946).

altiplano (McEwan 2006) while also supporting the autochthonous origins of the Inkas and their empire in the Cusco valley, as opposed to immigration from outside (Covey 2006: 172–73; McEwan 2006; Urton 1990). These two sets of Inka origin stories may relate to the two Cusco moieties, hanan as a conquering Aymara group with origins in the Titicaca basin shortly after the fall of Tiwanaku and hurin as the original residents of Cusco who migrated from Pacariqtambo (Hiltunen and McEwan 2004: 250–51). The Inka Pachacuti might have reinvented state history to resolve the competing myths and their factional proponents, "merging the stories into a hybrid tradition in which the creation occurred in Titicaca and the Inca emerged at Pacariqtambo" (ibid.: 250).

CONQUEST OF THE COLLAO

As part of these mythic histories, numerous—and wildly differing—versions of the conquest of the Collao exist, but only five are reviewed here (table 3.1): those of Garcilaso de la Vega (1987a, 1987b: 106–14), Bernabé Cobo (1983), Pedro de Sarmiento de Gamboa (2007), and Harry Tschopik's (1946) synthesis.

The most detailed account comes from Garcilaso. According to his report, the conquest was accomplished by the ruler Lloque Yupanki, third in the line of Inka kings (Garcilaso de la Vega 1987b: 106). The Sapa Inka and his army set out from Cusco toward the Collao, stopping in the "great province called Cana" where he "sent messengers to the natives requiring them to submit to and obey and serve the child of the Sun, abandoning their false and wicked sacrifices and beastly customs" (ibid.: 107–8).[10] The Canas supposedly agreed, but the Ayaviris nearby did not and were soundly defeated by the Inka force.

Some years thereafter, Lloque Yupanki and an army again marched southward, this time stopping in Pucará and sending messengers to two Qolla towns, Paucarcolla and Hatunqolla, with the same demand (ibid.: 109). The Qolla area was "a very extensive province embracing many peoples and tribes," and the Qolla leaders "told the Inca that they were content to be his vassals" (ibid.). Thereafter, Lloque Yupanki "and his descendants showed great favor and honor towards both towns, but especially Hatun Colla, for the service they had performed by receiving him with signs of love" (ibid.: 110). Still later, the Inka ruler and 10,000 warriors proceeded to "the borders of Chucuitu [Chucuito], a famous and populous province." In response to the Inka's demand for submission, the Lupaqa people of Chucuito responded "that they would obey him with love and goodwill" (ibid.: 111). Over the next few years the Inka ruler extended his domain farther south through the Collao by achieving the submission of other Lupaqa towns including Ilave, Juli, Pomata, and Zepita (ibid.: 112). Garcilaso's account, then, suggests that the Inka-Aymara alliance began with the Qolla and later incorporated the Lupaqa.

Cobo's account is considerably different and far briefer. According to him, the conquest of the Titicaca region was by the Inka Pachacuti, who "destroyed the town of Ayavire" and beheaded "all the people his men could lay hands on" (Cobo 1983: 140). The Qolla king fought the Inkas and lost. The Lupaqa cacique who lived in Chucuito, however, "took sounder advice, because he received the Inca in peace and turned over his state to him. Thus, the Inca honored him very much and in order to show him more favor, he stayed in Chucuito for a few days" (ibid.). Little else is said, except for mention that during a visit to Chucuito by Topa Inka Yupanki, Pachacuti's successor, the Lupaqa offered to serve in his army; the next Inka ruler, Wayna Qhapaq, "liked the Lupaca Indians . . . and since they were very loyal to the Incas, they deserved their unwavering favor" (ibid.: 144, 154).

Sarmiento de Gamboa (2007) agreed that the conquest of Collao was accomplished by the Inka Pachacuti. At the time, the Qolla kuraka Chuchi Ccapac (or Chuchi Colla) controlled a large area of what is now southwest Peru and northern Chile (ibid.: 114). When Pachacuti advanced toward the Titicaca basin, he and his army were met by Chuchi Ccapac, who awaited them at

Hatunqolla (ibid.: 111–13). Pachacuti demanded that the Qolla leader submit, but he refused; in the subsequent battle, the Qollas were defeated. Chuchi Ccapac was taken prisoner and brought to Cusco, where he was beheaded and the other Qolla prisoners were allegedly fed to wild animals. This reportedly brought about the unforced surrender of other kurakas in Contisuyu, who did not wish to suffer the same fate (ibid.). According to Sarmiento, the Qollas resisted Inka control—including staging a major rebellion while the Inka ruler was conquering Antisuyu, east of Cusco—and had to be defeated several times (ibid.: 124, 143–44).

Tschopik's (1946: 508–9) account is based on an unpublished paper by John Rowe that synthesizes various early ethnohistoric sources, including those of Sarmiento and Pedro de Cieza de León (2005). Tschopik traces the history to the eighth Sapa Inka, Viracocha, and his conquests beginning about 1430. According to legend, the caciques of both the Qolla and Lupaqa polities received word of the Inka's advances and sent emissaries to Viracocha "asking for his friendship" (Tschopik 1946: 508). The Inka ruler decided, apparently reluctantly, to ally with the Lupaqa, which prompted a Qolla attack. In response, Qari (Cari), cacique of the upper Lupaqa moiety, defeated the Qollas and sacked their capital, Hatunqolla. The next Inka, Pachacuti (1438–71), apparently distrusted alliances as a sound strategy for imperial administration and, on hearing of unrest in Collao, sent an expedition to conquer both the Qolla and Lupaqa polities. The conquest of Chucuito probably occurred around 1445 (Tschopik 1950: 198). Further disturbances erupted in Collao while Pachacuti was invading Antisuyu (also Cieza de León 2005: 169), and the revolt was quelled by his son, Topa Yupanki (1471–93). Topa also subdued and "garrisoned" the rest of the Aymara polities (Tschopik 1946: 508). As part of the imposed discipline, many Aymara were sent to coastal regions as agricultural colonists, and "Hatuncolla was made a center of Inka administration" (ibid.).

All of these accounts agree on the Inkas' desire to control the Collao because of the region's wealth. But they disagree on which Inka king accomplished the conquest: Viracocha? Lloque Yupanki? Pachacuti? They also disagree on which group was favored by the Inka, the Lupaqa (Cobo) or the Qolla (Garcilaso), and which led rebellions. Cieza de León (2005: 175) claims that after pacification following the last rebellion, the Inka declared that only 1,000 Qollas would be allowed in Cusco at any one time. Later, Aymara troops reportedly aided Manco Inca in the siege of Spanish-controlled Cusco, but the siege was lifted by Diego Almagro (Tschopik 1946: 509). After Manco's defeat, the Lupaqa attacked the Qolla, who sought help from the Spaniards, and Hernando Pizarro came in to defeat the Aymara (and presumably repress both Qollas and Lupaqas).

In reading and comparing these early accounts, however, it seems that distinctions between the Lupaqas and the Qollas were not always carefully made, and the two were often conflated or even confused. For example, Catherine Julien (1985: 219) noted that Cieza "never mentions Lupacas or Pacajes, and clearly for him, these people were Qollas." One intriguing question is why Garcilaso's version is so much more detailed than the others and why it portrays the Qollas in a much more favorable light.

Today, the general consensus among ethnohistorians and others is that Inka control of the northwestern Titicaca basin was achieved by the ruler Pachacuti, probably with military assistance directed by his son and successor, Topa Yupanki. This area appears to be the earliest imperial territory in what became Collasuyu, the large southern quadrant of Tawantinsuyu, so named because of the importance of the Qollas and Collao (Garcilaso de la Vega 1987b: 109). In light of post-conquest documentation, it seems clear that the Inkas favored the Lupaqas, as this wealthy polity and its capital, Chucuito, paid tribute directly to the crown rather than to individual Spaniards. As John Murra (1968: 120) comments, the wealth represented by camelid herds managed by the Lupaqa was "readily convertible in both the Andean and the European economies."

INKA RE-SPATIALIZATION

The Inkas were highly preoccupied with organizing their spaces into partitioned places, the landscape composed of nested systems of ayllu lands inscribed with the lines of ceques, roads, and irrigation canals and sprinkled with wakas and markers. The material of choice for accomplishing this partitioning was stone, which was cut, carved, and shaped for incorporation into civic-ceremonial statements of imperial power or venerated in a rough state, as outcrops or large boulders jutting out of the earth, massive reminders of chthonic power.

At least some of the Inkas' concepts about spatial order in their empire's heartland appear to have been imposed as they conquered outlying territories. If spatialization involves defining (or redefining), (re)bounding, (re)naming, and otherwise cognitively (re)structuring a space, how might these processes be identified in the southwestern Peru region? Beginning with their intrusion into the altiplano, the Inkas engaged in several re-spatialization activities that transformed the landscape of the Lake Titicaca basin. Physically, they changed the Aymara settlement system, moving populations from their easily defended fortified hills to accessible centers on the lakeshore, where they still exist today as Puno, Chucuito, Acora, Ilave, Juli, Pomata, Zepita, and Yunguyo

(Bouysse-Cassagne 1986: 209). Ethnohistorical sources say that Hatunqolla became an administrative center for the Inkas (Tschopik 1946: 508), which appears to be evident in the layout of the town as mapped by archaeologists. The location of the original Qolla town of Hatunqolla is unknown, however (Julien 1983: 107), but it was likely a typical LIP hilltop fortress.

As the Inka empire expanded to take over provinces increasingly distant from Cusco, new settlements were created and peoples from one area were resettled in far distant locations. The relocation strategy was implemented for numerous reasons, including facilitating the production and distribution of goods and improving security. Re-spatialization occurred in the altiplano and, as discussed in chapter 4, also in the Torata valley in Moquegua. The degree to which the Inkas disturbed existing land-use patterns in the middle Moquegua valley is unknown, but given the paucity of Inka remains, they appear to have administered with a light touch.

NOTES

1. Yanaconas are variously defined as groups not belonging to a larger ayllu, or home community, or, among the Spaniards, as indentured servants.

2. This up-valley movement seems to have been a common pattern in several parts of the Andes during the LIP, including northern Chile, and may relate to changes in availability of water (see Zori 2011: 192).

3. One wonders why the Inkas built fortresses if it were not for concerns about control over territory (contra Ramírez 2005). Investigations on the southeastern Inka frontier in Bolivia suggest a "soft" military perimeter of outposts sited by topography that functioned primarily as deterrents to movement but allowed interaction (Alconini 2004). By contrast, the northern frontiers in Ecuador can be considered a "hard" frontier, with dozens of defensive constructions including "concentric, walled and moated installations in elevated terrain . . . [and] walled terraces around hilltops" (ibid.: 394, 2005: 118). In northern Chile, Inka settlements along the highway as far as Copiapó were well defended and controlled access to water (Rivera 1991: 39).

4. The Kallawaya were widely known as herbalists and itinerant healers (Bastien 1978, 1985; Tschopik 1946: 569).

5. Colleen Zori (2011: 84), citing Heather Lechtman's (2007: 323) reference to an Inka creation myth in which gold is *collana*, silver is *payan*, and copper is *cayao*, says these clusters symbolize "hierarchical social and gender relationships that structured social organization in the Inka empire."

6. Ramírez (2005: 348) provides "tower" as one translation of *mojon*, and indeed a tower is shown in the background of Guaman Poma's drawing.

7. Gatekeepers and guards also existed elsewhere in the empire. A *relación* written in 1534 reports on the findings of two explorers Francisco Pizarro sent to explore gold mines in the altiplano. The Spaniards found guarded strongholds "so that no one can steal gold or leave without being seen," and miners returning home from the mines enter "through a gate where the managers responsible for the gold receive from each miner the gold that has been mined" (Petersen 2010: 41, citing Pedro Sancho de la Hoz).

8. See also parallel discussions for the Inkas by R. Tom Zuidema (1964) in which hurin/lower refers to existing residents and metaphorical feminine attributes and hanan/upper as conquering, masculine warriors (Hiltunen and McEwan 2004: 247–49).

9. The Inkas may also have expanded their origin stories to incorporate certain aspects of the origins of the people they conquered (Sallnow 1982: 732).

10. This sounds suspiciously like a performance similar to one of the Spanish procedures of conquest, which involved first reading to the natives a document called the *Requerimiento* (Seed 1992), demanding of them exactly the same acquiescence.

4

Inka Spaces and Places

The Inkas in Moquegua

> Land and people to work it on a reciprocal basis formed a single unity which one can separate for analytical purposes but which we have to put together again if we want to understand them in Andean terms.
> —John Murra (1968: 134)

Sometime in the late fifteenth century, the Inkas inserted themselves into the region that is now southwestern Peru. In contrast to the multiple accounts of real or legendary events of Inka imperial expansion, only one written account is known of the Inkas' intrusion from the Titicaca basin into the Osmore valley: the 1609 *Royal Commentaries of the Incas and General History of Peru* by Garcilaso de la Vega, "El Inka" (1987a, 1987b: 143–45). According to Garcilaso, the conquest of this area in the Contisuyu quarter of Tawantinsuyu took place under the Inka ruler Mayta Qhapaq (Capac), whose army set out from Hatunqolla toward Cuchuna (Cochuna), the name for the lower Torata valley in what is now Moquegua.

> From Hatuncolla [the Inka ruler] sent the army with its four commanders westwards with orders to cross the desert[1] called Hatunpuna, the edge of which had been won by the Inca Lloque Yupanqui, and to reduce to his service the tribes that might be found on the other side of [it], as far as the shores of the Southern Sea. Under no circumstances were they to offer battle to the enemy . . . With these instructions and a great store of supplies . . . the captains marched across the snow-capped range, with some difficulty since there was no road . . . They reached a province called Cuchuna, with a loosely scattered though considerable population.

DOI: 10.5876/9781607322764.c004

Hearing of the arrival of this army, the natives built a fort and shut themselves up with their wives and children. The Incas surrounded it, but out of respect for the orders of their king, were unwilling to attack it, though it was very weak . . .

[The army held the people at siege "for above fifty days" . . .] But the natives were sorely pressed by hunger . . . since the sudden arrival of the Incas had prevented them from laying in provisions; nor had they thought the Incas would persist in the siege . . . the children were unable to bear it and went out to find herbs in the fields. Many [children] went over to their enemies . . . The Incas received them and fed them and even gave them a little food to take back to their parents, sending the usual messages of peace and friendship. Seeing this, the natives, who no longer hoped for relief, decided to surrender unconditionally . . .

The Inca captains reported all that had happened in this conquest and asked for colonists to settle in two towns there, for the land seemed fertile and capable of supporting far more people than it held. It was proposed also to leave a garrison [*presidio*] there to assure the possession of what had been won, and for any emergencies that might occur. The Inca sent the required settlers with their wives and families, and the two towns were peopled. One was at the foot of the mountains where the natives had built their fort. It was called Cuchuna, the name of the mountains. The other was called Moquehua. The towns are five leagues apart. (Garcilaso de la Vega 1987b: 143–44)

INTERROGATING THE ACCOUNT

Because Garcilaso's is the only known report of the Inka conquest of the upper Osmore drainage, it is useful to examine (or "unpack") his account in greater detail to investigate underlying themes and processes it and its narrator contribute to a greater understanding of this moment in the region's history.

Who Was Garcilaso de la Vega, "El Inka"?

Born in 1539, Garcilaso was the illegitimate son of a Spanish father, Capt. Sebastián Garcilasso de la Vega Vargas, and an "Inka princess" (*ñusta, palla*) named Chimpu Ocllo (Livermore 1987: xx, xxii). Known by her baptismal name, Isabel Suárez Chimpu Ocllo, and also as Isabel Palla and Isabel Yupanqui, Chimpu Ocllo was a relative of the Inka ruler Wayna Qhapaq, generally thought to be his daughter (figure 4.1). However, sorting out the factual details and chronology of the Inka rulers—much less their offspring from multiple wives—is notoriously difficult (Covey 2006). Wayna Qhapaq was likely a son of the ruler Topa Yupanki, who in turn was the son and military commander of Pachacuti. All were

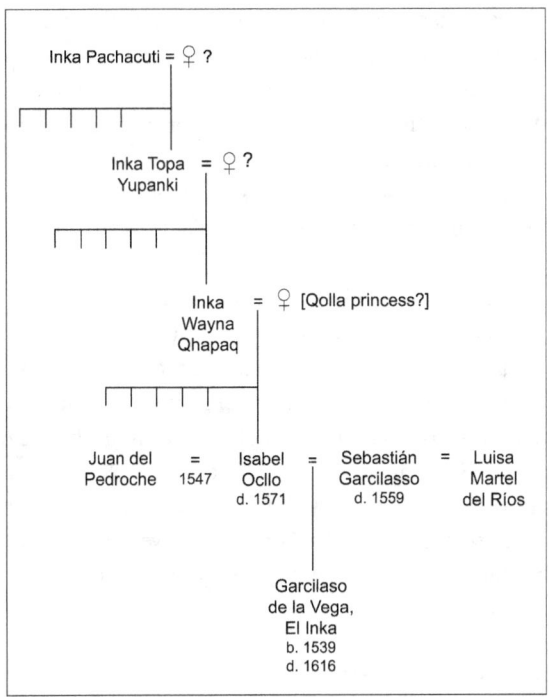

FIGURE 4.1 *The family tree of Garcilaso de la Vega, "El Inka."*

from hanan Cusco (associated with the Chinchaysuyu ceques; Bauer 1998: table 4.5), and the last two are generally considered responsible for the conquest of the Titicaca basin (D'Altroy and Schreiber 2004: table 13.1). If Isabel were Wayna Qhapaq's daughter, she would have been a granddaughter of Topa Yupanki. Other interpretations suggest Isabel might have been Wayna's sister or niece.

The Spanish crown, ever preoccupied with "*limpieza de sangre*" (purity of bloodlines), was increasingly concerned about informal unions between Spanish men and Indigenous women in the colonies and urged men to marry Spanish women. Thus in 1547 Sebastián may have felt obligated to separate himself from Isabel, marrying her off to Juan del Pedroche, an "obscure" Spaniard, perhaps a soldier or trader (Livermore 1987: xx; Marchena Fernández 1992: 396; http://histfam.familysearch.org/getperson.php?personID=I41&tree=Peru). Shortly thereafter, Sebastián married a Spanish woman, doña Luisa Martel de los Ríos, effectively alienating both Garcilaso and his mother, Isabel (Livermore 1987: xx). After his father died, Garcilaso left for Spain in 1560, where he lived the rest of his life. Isabel died in 1571 (ibid.: xxii).

Garcilaso is not regarded as the most reliable of chroniclers because he penned his account with the agenda of vindicating and celebrating the peaceful rule of his Andean mother's royal family, in contrast to the cruelty of the Spaniards. He also might have been reacting to the negative portrayal of the Inkas written by Pedro de Sarmiento de Gamboa (2007 [1572]) at the behest of Viceroy Toledo, to contrast that tale of violence with his own view of Inka beneficence. Or he might have been revealing his bitterness at his father's treatment of himself and his mother.

Regardless, considering the relatively small size and seeming unimportance of the Osmore drainage in general and of Cuchuna in particular, it is remarkable that this conquest event survived in any legend. We can only assume that Garcilaso's mention of it was transmitted to him in the stories his maternal relatives told, his mother apparently having held something like a European "salon" for Inka elites in early Colonial times (see Livermore 1987: xxi). Garcilaso's mention of Cuchuna raises the possibility that his mother's relatives (perhaps related to Qollas, given his favored treatment of them?) were not merely aware of the expedition to that region but were among the participants.

The Inka Ruler and Conquest

Garcilaso attributes the conquest of Cochuna to Mayta Qhapaq, fourth in the Inka king list. Mayta Qhapaq was the only son and heir of Inka Lloque Yupanki, both from lower, or hurin, Cusco, specifically the Collasuyu quarter (Bauer 1998: table 4.5; D'Altroy and Schreiber 2004: table 13.1). Mayta Qhapaq apparently did not have a reputation as a strong ruler, however. Pedro Cieza de León (2005: 106) reports that the "*Orejones*" (royal elites with large ear ornaments) of Cusco said only that he reigned for several years and died before getting to Condesuyos; Samuel Markham (quoted in ibid.: 106n1) critiques Garcilaso's glorified view of the king in attributing other conquests to him.

It is not clear when Mayta Qhapaq ruled: Moquegua's historian says 1114 to 1152 (Kuon Cabello 1981: 31), which appears too early for the archaeologically attested Qolla settlement in the upper valley and certainly for imperial Inka influence. According to conventional scholarship, the conquest of the Moquegua region more likely occurred during the reign of Pachacuti after his son, Topa Yupanki, took control of the military beginning in 1463 (D'Altroy and Schreiber 2004: 262).

There are hints of agreement in chroniclers' accounts of how the Titicaca basin was brought under Inka control: the procedure for the conquest of new polities was for the king, his captains, or other envoys to first demand submission before attacking or holding siege (Rowe 1946: 281–82). Garcilaso expresses this directly in his account of the conquests of the Collao and Cochuna. In expanding their empire, Garcilaso (1987b: 111) claims, the Inka rulers "always thought it better to advance gradually and impose order and reason, so that their subjects should appreciate the mildness of their rule ... rather than ... appear ambitious and covetous tyrants" ("like the Spaniards," one can imagine him thinking). Thus Mayta Qhapaq's instructions to his army were to achieve submission of the people of the lower sierras—settlers from the powerful and rebellious Qolla province in the Collao—and take control of the region without resort to warfare.

The chroniclers' occasional failure to distinguish between the Lupaqa and the Qolla is not clarified in Garcilaso's account. The Inka captains are said to have departed westward from Hatunqolla, the Qolla capital, which is reasonable given that both the chroniclers (e.g., Sarmiento de Gamboa 2007: 114) and archaeological evidence (Stanish 1991, 1992) agree that this part of the Titicaca basin had been under the control of the powerful Qolla since sometime in the thirteenth century. At least one account claims that Hatunqolla became "a center of Inka administration" (Tschopik 1946: 508), which is also verified archaeologically, as the town displays an Inka-based orthogonal grid plan defined by two main roads (Hyslop 1990: 195–96). The assertion that the administrative center at Hatunqolla was a new settlement is further supported by the lack of earlier remains recovered in excavations (Julien 1983: 107). Garcilaso (1987b: 110) claims that Inka rulers particularly favored Hatunqolla for their submission, but other sources suggest that the Qolla led multiple revolts against Inka control. If Garcilaso's account is correct, it appears that the Inka captains were sent to Cochuna from the new Hatunqolla capital (the pre-Inka Qolla center unidentified archaeologically) before the takeover of the Lupaqa.

Other reports suggest that the Inka rulers increasingly favored the Lupaqas for their loyalty (Cobo 1983: 144, 154) and also because the kuraka of the hanansaya moiety, Qari/Cari, had attacked and defeated the rebellious Qolla (Tschopik 1946: 508). When the Inka ruler allied with the Lupaqa, he gave Qari one of his daughters, presumably as consort (Hyslop 1979). This might have elevated Qari into an "Inka-by-privilege" (as opposed to Inka-by-royal-blood), a semi-noble provincial administrator in the empire (Conlee et al. 2004: 230; Urton 1990: 28; see Bauer 1992: 23–24, 27–29, 150n7).

Finally, an Inka intrusion into the Osmore drainage might have been promoted by the Lupaqa kurakas of Chucuito as a strategy of revenge against the Qolla. The Lupaqas not only claimed an earlier victory over the Qolla but were also allies of the powerful Inkas. A strong military alliance could have wrested control of the fertile Moquegua breadbasket from the Lupaqa's former Qolla enemies.

The Fort

The fort where the residents of Cuchuna took refuge is traditionally believed to be Cerro Baúl (Moseley, Feldman, and Pritzker 1982), the dramatically isolated, butte-like formation occupied by Wari settlers in the MH. But Cerro Baúl can hardly be described as "very weak" defensively. Its towering summit, rising 600 m (1,968 ft) above the surrounding terrain and visible for miles, was protected by natural and artificial fortifications—the most prominent being the adjacent Cerro Mejía, which controlled access from the north (Moseley 1990: 249–50). In addition, Cerro Baúl very likely would have been described by the Spaniards then, as it is today, in the singular, as a *cerro* (hill, mountain). In Garcilaso's (1987a: 144) original Spanish, however, the refuge is identified in the plural as a *sierra* (mountains, mountain range), and the location of the newly founded Cuchuna is "at the foot of these mountains where the natives had made their fort; they called it Cuchuna, which was the name of the mountains."[2] According to this account, then, Cuchuna is the name of a province and a mountain range or ridge and also of a new town founded at its base. Given Inka reverence for mountains (apu), it is peculiar that Garcilaso's account—possibly related by an elderly participant in the expedition?—makes no mention of Baúl's looming presence.

I propose that the refuge for the local people was more likely the fortified hilltop site (pukara) known as San Antonio (see figure 3.1). This site lies slightly less than the specified 5 leagues (about 20+ km or ~12 mi) from modern Moquegua; Cerro Baúl is significantly closer (ca. 12 km or 7.5 mi). Garcilaso suggests, rather improbably, that the residents found time to build this fortification after learning of the Inka army's approach but failed to take in adequate provisions to withstand a siege. His inference of recent construction might relate to the idea that the fortification was weak.

New Colonists in Moquegua

Garcilaso's (1987b: 143) informants led him to describe the Cochuna area as having "a loosely scattered though considerable population"; in addition, "the land seemed fertile and capable of supporting far more people than it held." Indeed, as noted in chapter 2, a section of the lower Río Torata's floodplain represents the third-largest area of cultivable land in Moquegua. The best soils—deep and moisture retentive—are found in the upper mid-valley immediately adjacent to the Tumilaca and Torata Rivers and their confluence.

After the fort surrendered, the Inka sent agricultural colonists (*mitimaes*) from the altiplano to establish settlements known as Cuchuna and Moquehua.

The captains who brought about the surrender of the Cuchuna valley also recommended that the Inka ruler leave a garrison there "to assure the possession of what had been won, and for any emergencies" (Garcilaso de la Vega 1987b: 144). If Tschopik's (1946: 508) synthesis is valid, this deployment can be seen on the one hand as part of Topa Yupanki's punishment of the Aymara for their rebellions against the Inkas. Some of the colonists might have been Qollas, who already occupied the area and San Antonio itself and were likely considered untrustworthy after their revolts. On the other hand, as indicated by archaeological investigations in the Torata area, most of the LH settlers were Lupaqas, the Qollas' southern neighbors and enemies and the Inkas' recent allies (Stanish 2003: 271). They likely came from Chucuito and other newly relocated Lupaqa towns along the lake edge, such as Acora and Ilave (Kuon Cabello 1981: 32). This would suggest the new settlements in Cochuna were established between 1471 and 1493. Other colonists in the Osmore tributaries were likely Pacajes from the southern Titicaca basin (Stanish 1992: 99).

Garcilaso adds a footnote to the conquest: while the Inka captains were busy establishing the new towns in Cochuna, they heard that the local people used a disfiguring poison against their enemies in some kind of sorcery or witchcraft: "It was a gentle poison which was only fatal to those of weak constitution. Those who were robust survived, though at the expense of losing the use of their senses and members and remaining half-witted and deformed in body and appearance. They were indeed repulsive, being covered with patches and blotches of black and white" (Garcilaso de la Vega 1987b: 144–45).

The Inka ordered that anyone guilty of the practice should be burned alive, which so greatly pleased the people in this province "that they themselves sought out the criminals and executed the sentence, burning the guilty alive with everything in their houses, which were pulled down and the site strewn with stones as accursed places. Their flocks were burnt, and their estates destroyed . . . and the land was left abandoned" (ibid.: 145). This poison might have been mercury, which can cause neurological impairment and skin disfigurement and was used medically by the Aymara in the twentieth century to treat syphilis (Tschopik 1946: 568).

INKA SITES IN THE OSMORE DRAINAGE

Several Late Horizon Inka-related sites lie in the upper tributaries of the Ríos Tambo and Osmore (see figure 3.1). These sites probably represent settlements of altiplano agricultural colonists, Qollas, Lupaqas, and perhaps also Pacajes. In the upper tributaries of the Osmore, the small site of Polvorín, with a possible Inka road nearby, lies in the valley of the Río Otora, which flows into the Huaracane (Stanish 1992: 152). But Garcilaso's account, combined with archaeological data (architecture and ceramics), suggests that the resettlement focus was the Torata valley: Cochuna and especially the archaeological sites known as Torata Alta, Sabaya, and Camata. In all, to judge from the varied types of pottery recovered at these sites, particularly at Torata Alta, it is clear that the region was populated by colonists from various Inka-allied señoríos in the Titicaca basin.

Cuchuna/Cochuna was established at the base of the hilltop fortification of San Antonio in the hill(s) and region/valley also called Cuchuna. It was earlier suggested that the site of Torata Alta was Cochuna (Stanish and Pritzker 1983: 10), but a more likely candidate for this settlement may be the site of Sabaya. Sabaya (Bürgi 1993: 176–271) occupies a low rise on the north side of the Río Torata, slightly north of the modern town of Torata. Covering an area of 5–6 ha (12.3–14.8 acres) (figure 4.2), the site has been heavily damaged, including the looting of four small LIP cemeteries. Nonetheless, Sabaya (17° 07'S, 70° 85'W) displays several features typical of Inka provincial administrative siting: proximity to springs (*puquios*), including an apparent "aqueduct" that channeled water downhill to holding tanks (ibid.: 199); several plazas; an enormous 55-m-long *kallanka* (multi-door great hall, which appeared to have been abandoned before 1600; ibid.: 213); and an *usnu* (stone altar platform)[3] (ibid.: 178–79). More than 100 structures and other features (terraces, cemeteries) are dispersed in seven small, separate clusters, some of which resemble Inka compounds (kanchas). Construction combined *pirca* stonework with adobes.

Surface materials at Sabaya included Chucuito, Saxamar, and provincial Inka pottery types, as well as *botijas* (amphora-like Spanish storage and transport jars). Str. 31, a large, well-constructed building in the north-central part of the site, was probably an elite residence. It yielded unusual quantities of pottery probably related to food production and feasting, including two large unslipped jars sunk into the floor; several other buried whole vessels, including an aryballus; and, in a stone-lined cist, a cache of five plates decorated in Inka style plus a "face jar" (ibid.: figures 71–84). A post-1600 burial of a very young child was intruded into the floor. Post-1600 construction and European artifacts, including glass beads, iron (n = 2), and botija fragments, were identified in subsurface contexts.

At least seven post-1600 burials were noted in excavations in the northeast corner of Str. 2A (ibid.: 202, 231–32), on the opposite side of the plaza from the kallanka. This 15 × 15 m structure may have been the atrium of a church to the east, now destroyed; commoners were frequently buried in atria. Individuals were interred in an extended position (N-S), wrapped in shrouds pinned with

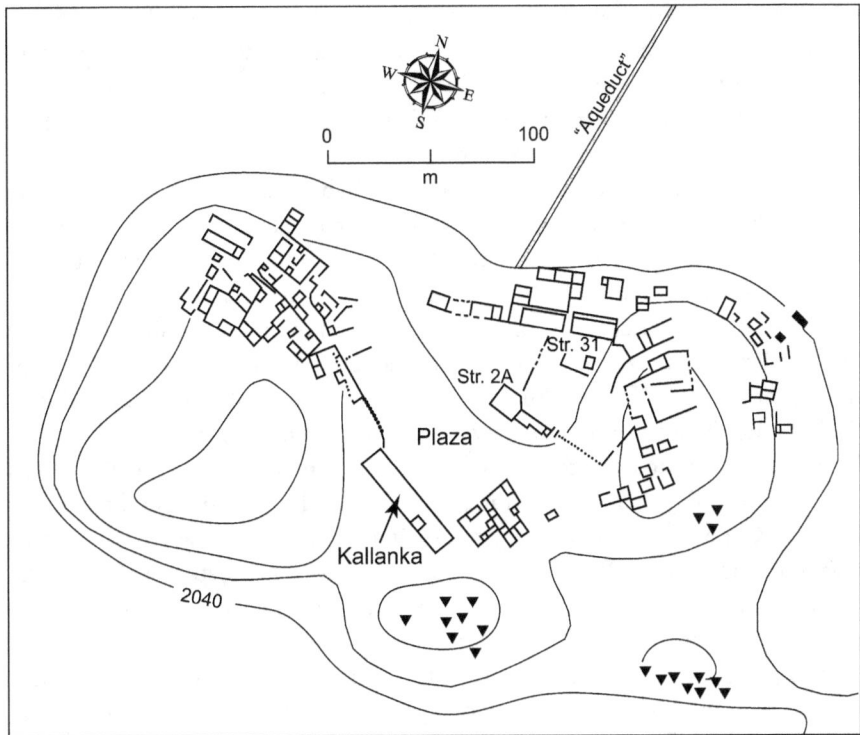

FIGURE 4.2 *Core area of the site of Sabaya, showing structures and features discussed in text. Clusters of inverted triangles are pre-Hispanic cemeteries. Contour interval 4 m. After Burgi 1993: figure 41.*

copper *tupus* (shawl pins with broad ends); one tupu had a cross inscribed on it. The post-1600 date was determined by the presence of volcanic ash in and around the burials. In addition, a possible Colonial-period homestead, identified by scatters of glazed pottery, was identified to the southeast of, and downslope from, the main part of the site. Clearly, Sabaya was occupied well into the Colonial period—apparently by Qollas, to judge from documentary evidence—when it was part of an encomienda. Residents of San Antonio and other nearby LIP Qolla-related hilltop sites had very likely been moved to this riverside location by the Inkas.

Torata Alta (chapter 8; Rice 2012) is likely the location of the garrison, or presidio, advocated by the Inka captains. The site perches on the same ridge top as San Antonio but at a slightly higher elevation and a few hundred meters to the northeast. Alternatively, the recovery of Inka remains in Str. 20 at San Antonio raises the possibility that this fortified site might have been briefly repurposed as the garrison Garcilaso mentioned or been occupied during the construction of Torata Alta. Torata Alta lacks evidence of LIP and earlier occupation and activity and exhibits a distinctive gridded layout similar to that found at other Inka (re)settlements in southern Peru.

The site of Camata, roughly 5 km north of Sabaya and Torata Alta, consists of two adjacent components at an elevation of approximately 2,800 m. One is the fortified LIP hilltop settlement, whereas the other is a later Inka tambo; the two may be at least partly contemporaneous (Mathews 1989: 430).[4] The tambo is a triangular complex of forty-three storehouses comprising three long rectangular structures around an open plaza approximately 130 m southeast of the earlier site (Stanish and Pritzker 1983: 11–12). With walls up to 2 m high, the facilities are thought to have had a capacity of around 700 m^3 (ibid.: 11). A pre-Hispanic road approaches the plaza from the east and heads into the mountains on the west, with other smaller storage facilities and residential buildings along it (ibid.). Camata also has a nearby reservoir and an immense system of terraces on the hillsides of the Río Torata valley, the largest such system known in the Osmore drainage (Mathews 1989: 427–28). Rare fragments of Colonial-period pottery (tin-enameled ware) were noted on the site surface.

"Moquehua," the second town founded by the Inkas, is believed to underlie the modern city of Moquegua, on the left (south) bank of the lower Río Tumilaca on the Pampa Chen Chen. If we accept this occupational continuity, then there is additional support for the likelihood that San Antonio, rather than Cerro Baúl, was the location of the Cochuna "fort," given the distances separating these sites. Situated at the confluence of the Osmore's three tributaries, Moquehua's location would have provided residents with the advantage of monitoring human travel along the Osmore, both heading down-valley through the tributaries and coming up from the coast. It also would have provided oversight of the greatest area of high-quality soils in the drainage. Given this advantageous siting, it would not be surprising if the town had been built over an earlier Qolla LIP settlement and that settlement over an even earlier Tiwanaku-related town, given the proximity of the MH Chen Chen mortuary site.

Some Inka materials were recovered at Cerro Baúl, but south of the tributaries' confluence, evidence of LH settlement is sparse and largely limited to scatters of provincial Inka polychrome ceramic fragments (R. Feldman, pers. comm. July 20, 1992):

- A badly disturbed small site on the road east-southeast of the modern pueblo of Estuquiña at Km 13, which yielded Inka and Estuquiña materials and also gold

- The area of the airport and tourist hotel on the left bank of the Río Tumilaca, across from modern Moquegua, in the settlement originally known as Escapagua
- Surface scatters on three terraces south of Omo
- At the winery site of Locumbilla (chapter 9), where forty-seven sherds of fine Sillustani (Qolla) provincial polychromes were mixed with European material in basal levels (secondary contexts) under the colonial pottery kiln.

As best can be judged, during the LH the middle valley was largely unsettled, instead devoted to irrigation farming by colonists who lived in the higher elevations. On the coast, the Inkas established an agricultural community at Quebrada (or Pueblo) Tacahuay, 27 km southeast of Ilo (Covey 2009).

INKA RE-SPATIALIZATION IN MOQUEGUA

Of the multiple reasons the Inkas relocated peoples in conjunction with imperial expansion (Julien 1983: 78–79), five appear to apply to the Late Horizon re-spatialization of the Osmore drainage:

- When a new territory was organized as a province, "for security reasons and to aid in the acculturation of the inhabitants to their role as subjects of the empire." This would explain Torata Alta, Sabaya, and Moquehua.
- "To frontier areas to serve as garrisons": Torata Alta.
- "As colonies in underpopulated regions to bring them into production": the Torata valley.
- To grow or collect "certain plants unavailable at home, like maize, coca and a variety of fruits": the Torata and Moquegua valleys and particularly the storage facilities at Camata Tambo.
- "From hilltop locations to more level ground": abandonment of San Antonio and removal to the new town of Cochuna (Sabaya?).

Inka-Lupaqa activities in the drainage exemplify one important imperial strategy the Inkas practiced throughout the Andes: modifying the landscape for economic purposes by mobilizing land and labor to support the state. Moquegua provides an example of appropriation of land and creation of enclaves for agricultural production in fertile valleys and for administration in strategic communication and transportation loci, staffed by *mitmaq* (non-local) labor (La Lone and La Lone 1987: 49; see also Acuto 2005: 220–25). Unlike the earlier Tiwanaku colonization of the Osmore, the Inkas seem to have had little interest in placing actual settlements in the agriculturally favored portion of the Moquegua valley. One wonders if this might reflect the need to capture for irrigation the low flow of the river resulting from the preceding centuries of drought in the southwest region (Kolata 1993: 297).

Part of Inka re-spatialization was incorporation (or reincorporation) into the pan-Andean system of nested dual political organization, reflected in sixteenth-century documents. In 1567 Moquegua and Torata were under the jurisdiction of don Martín Cusi, cacique principal of the lower (hurinsaya) moiety of Chucuito (Diez de San Miguel 1964: 27), with Moquegua the upper (hanan) parcialidad and Torata the hurin. In the late sixteenth century, each community also had internal upper and lower moiety divisions, as is clear in a later document (Guíbovich P. 1984: 296).

Inka landscape transformations are most evident in the Torata valley through settlement reorganization, and the Torata and Moquegua valleys can be viewed together as an Inka "production enclave" settled and worked by altiplano colonists (La Lone and La Lone 1987; Mathews 1989: 431). In line with this model, both Sabaya and Torata Alta appear to be Inka administrative centers established to oversee agricultural production and reorganization of its settlement and landholding systems. The two sites probably had different specific functions. Sabaya, with its Inka pottery and kallanka, might have been "Cuchuna" and occupied by elites. Torata Alta may have been the "garrison" the Inka army captains advocated. Camata was described in an early document as "*junto a otro pueblo* named Incuraque" (Barriga 1939: 47), which might reference the two neighboring archaeological sites now known as Camata and Camata Tambo. With its immense terrace system and storage facilities, Camata would have been a staging area for accumulating maize, coca, ají, textiles, and other locally produced goods for transport to the altiplano along the existing road (now the modern road to Puno). The Inkas also might have had some early dealings with the people of San Antonio, as small amounts of Late Horizon pottery were recovered there.

The Inka-Lupaqa also constructed (or rebuilt) roads, which represent politically powerful organizational infrastructure to facilitate information and material exchanges (Snead, Erickson, and Darling 2009; Trombold 1991). If we take Garcilaso (1987b: 143) at his word, there were no roads to or in the area at the time of the Inka siege: "the captains marched across the snowcapped range, with some difficulty since there was no road" from Hatunqolla in the altiplano into Cuchuna.[5] However, on the basis of admittedly scanty evidence, we might postulate the creation of a late pre-Hispanic "Cochuna road" (called "Collasuyo road" by Cavagnaro Orellana 1988: 101). The proposed Torata Alta garrison, for example, is likely to have had a trail coming to or near it, and early surveys of the Torata valley suggested the existence of a "major ancient road" adjacent to

Torata Alta that heads into the mountains (Stanish and Pritzker 1983: 10). At Camata, a road enters the plaza from the east, then heads up into the mountains, possibly joining the path evident at the small LH site of Polvorín in the upper Río Otora (Stanish 1992: 152). There is also the possibility of a "major transport route" between Moquegua and the altiplano, suggested by the discovery of three small Inka sites near Lake Suches at 4,300 m (14,100 ft) elevation (Stanish and Pritzker 1983: 12–13). These sierra road segments facilitated the movement of goods from the Osmore colonies to Chucuito, the Lupaqa capital, thereby provisioning this part of the expanding Inka state. Early Spanish travelers' accounts note a road passing from Arequipa through Moquegua and continuing southeast through the lower sierra into what is now Chile. This "coastal" road might have been joined by a spur extending southward through the Moquegua valley.

Does Moquegua exhibit the characteristics Félix Acuto (2005: 222) described for marginal, peripheral Inka settlements? Generally, yes. The Inkas sought indirect (through the Lupaqas) rather than "direct control over natural resources or human labor" in Moquegua. It also might be said that the Inkas (sort of) transformed the Osmore valley into a "new regional center of power" by the establishment of Moquegua, Torata Alta, Sabaya (with its large kallanka), and Camata Tambo. They moved some nodes of control from LIP hilltop forts (e.g., San Antonio) to lower elevations and thereby "changed local ideas of how power and social order were exhibited and materialized in the region" (ibid.). Torata Alta thus might be considered one of the Inkas' "secondary" or "New Cuzcos" (ibid.: 224), with its orthogonal layout, walled compounds, and possible kallanka. At the time of conquest the entire Moquegua region exhibited nested upper-lower moiety divisions.

One point of difference with this model concerns the statement that new Inka sites were "concentrated apart from local settlements" (ibid.: 223). In the Torata valley, the Inka tambo at Camata was situated adjacent to the existing LIP settlement, and Torata Alta was built only a few hundred meters away from the LIP "fort" of San Antonio, on the same ridge top. In addition, no ceques, huacas, large administrative centers, or fortress complexes have been identified in the Moquegua drainage as they have in other provinces of the Inka imperium (e.g., ibid.: 226; D'Altroy and Schreiber 2004: 269–70). Although distinctive local landscape features such as mountains (Cerro Baúl), which have been seen throughout the Andes as "constitutive aspects of social life" and ancestors (Acuto 2005: 227–28; Bastien 1978, 1985), were likely appropriated as major ritual centers or shrines, this is not clear from available archaeological evidence. All of this confirms Moquegua's continuing minor and peripheral role as hurin-hurin in the Late Horizon.

NOTES

1. Garcilaso identifies this high-altitude plain as *el despoblado* (lit. "depopulated"; uninhabited, wilderness), which Livermore misleadingly translates as "desert."

2. "al pie de la sierra donde los naturales habían hecho el fuerte; llamáronle Cuchuna, que era nombre de la misma sierra."

3. *Usnu* (or *ushnu*) platforms typically appear in plazas in conquered territories (Hyslop 1990: 70–71), where they may serve as thrones for a visiting Inka lord or have varied state functions.

4. The two Camatas, like the paired sites of San Antonio and Torata Alta, indicate continuity of settlement from LIP to LH times, similar to that in the Collagua province in the Colca valley (Wernke 2007a: 157).

5. It is possible that the Wari might have built a road in the region (see Schreiber 1991), considering their colony at Cerro Baúl, but that route did not pass through the northern Titicaca basin. Similarly, given Tiwanaku's investment in a major center at Omo and irrigation works in the middle valley, it would not be surprising if they created a mid-valley road.

5

Language and Toponyms

> Places come into being out of spaces
> by being named.
> —Charles O. Frake (1996: 235)

Moquegua's long history on the peripheries of empire meant that people with varied ethno-politico-linguistic identities colonized the region during the Middle Horizon (MH), Late Intermediate Period (LIP), Late Horizon (LH), and Colonial Period. Whether their presence in Moquegua was forced or voluntary, these colonists and migrants established settlements that came to be known in later written ethnohistories and through archaeological excavations. Although Indigenous voices were not registered directly in the earliest Spanish records of their encounters in the Andes (Ramírez 2005: 2), they are heard through toponyms. These toponyms provide twenty-first-century scholars with clues to the occupants of Moquegua's spaces and places.

TOPONYMY

A toponym is a proper noun—a name—that designates a unit of space as a place (see Martin and Ringham 2006: 203). The naming of places articulates humans' relations with their environment and brings order to undifferentiated space. More specifically, the fact that a given space has a name reveals that it possesses meaning within that order and that there is a need to distinguish it unambiguously in various kinds of discourse. If existing place names are unknown to a newcomer or different spaces become important, the newcomer gives them names, thus beginning an alternative spatial history (Carter 1987).

DOI: 10.5876/9781607322764.c005

Names can be drawn from numerous sources—for example, describing a key characteristic of a place, memorializing an event that occurred there, remembering a homeland, or honoring a person or religious figure. Not surprisingly, toponyms "encapsulate and unleash" memories and identities. Every place name "can and does peg some sort of story for someone, and a broad spectrum of possibilities surrounds the extent to which those stories are shared, significant, meaningful, or memorable through time for particular individuals or social groups" (Feld 1996: 111–13). Thus toponyms are part of an "emotional geography" (Kearney and Bradley 2009). Clearly, this was true in the Spanish naming of as-yet-unexplored territories in the Southern Hemisphere: the names were chosen from the most dramatic Christian *reconquista* successes in Muslim-controlled Iberia—(Nuevo) Toledo and (Nueva) Granada—plus the most Christian of all provinces, (Nueva) Castilla.

For Indigenous groups or natives of an area, whether ancient or modern, "place names are more than remnants of an earlier time; they deny any notion of an innocent or arbitrary history . . . Naming place is a declaration of ownership, it expresses the inalienable right to know and call into being the places" that define collective identity (Kearney and Bradley 2009: 81). For example, the renaming of streets in modern times has become a matter of politicization and resistance (Rose-Redwood, Alderman, and Azaryahu 2010). In situations of colonialism, the removal of Indigenous toponyms and imposition of new ones is a naked exercise of power. Such erasure is a silencing of voice, a denial of identity, an act of linguistic hegemony (Rose-Redwood and Alderman 2011), and a "neutralizing of otherness" (Carter 1987: 61). Similarly, the withholding of information about the origins and meanings of place names, as in Indigenous responses to Spanish questions in the late-sixteenth-century *Relaciones Geográficas*, can be an exercise of resistance (Scott 2009: 56–57). Place names and place naming, then, are critical to the social production of place and, as such, are often contested (Rose-Redwood, Alderman, and Azaryahu 2010).

At the same time, the creation of toponyms is an essential component of praxis, the processes of spatializing the physical world (Martin and Ringham 2006: 190, 203) and directing meaningful (and safe) movement through it (Whitridge 2004). Because of the recurrent flow of migrants into the Osmore drainage, the area can be thought of as having multiple re-spatializations. In addition to the Aymara-speaking Qolla and Lupaqa from the northern and western parts of the Lake Titicaca basin, respectively, residents included Pacajes (Pacaxes) from the southern basin (Stanish 1992: 99), Pukina/Puquina-speakers east of the lake (see Browman 1994), and probably some Quechua-speakers from the central highlands, plus Koli-speakers on the coast.

INDIGENOUS TOPONYMY IN MOQUEGUA: PRE-HISPANIC MULTIVOCALITY

In general, late pre-Hispanic colonists in the Osmore drainage appear to have been primarily Aymara-speakers from the northern Titicaca basin: Qollas in the LIP and Lupaqas in the LH (Conrad 1993; Stanish 1989). A section of the lower Río Torata, just above where it is joined by the Huaracane, is still known as Ocolla, perhaps linked to this Colla occupation. The domestic architecture of the LIP site of San Antonio, farther up the Río Torata, shares attributes of Qolla sites higher in the sierras (Conrad 1993).

Earlier, the MH occupants of the southern Lake Titicaca basin might have been Aymara or proto-Aymara speakers (Browman 1994), or they might have spoken Pukina (see Bouysse-Cassagne 1986: 208). This latter point is contentious,[1] and Charles Stanish (2003: 59) points to the few Pukina toponyms in the Tiwanaku valley as evidence that that city was not Pukina-speaking. The language is now extinct, but in the sixteenth century Pukina was spoken in the southern and eastern altiplano and adjacent areas (Julien 1983: 47–49) and was considered a language of "high prestige" (Campbell 2000: 189), perhaps explaining why some Inka kings' names are Pukina (Hiltunen and McEwan 2004: 246). The modern Kallawaya (Callahuaya) language, based primarily on lexical items from Pukina and morphology from Quechua, is used primarily by itinerant male curers from the Department of La Paz, Bolivia, who travel widely throughout this region of the Andes (Campbell 2000: 190). An Umasuyu polity of Kallawaya was apparently in existence in MH times (Janusek 2004: 49).

At the time of Spanish contact, the southwestern region is said to have included "*un notable sector de puquina-hablantes*" (Galdos Rodríguez 1996: 293). Pukina-speakers may have moved into the southwestern sierras, including the area of the tributaries of the Tambo and Osmore Rivers, during the LIP to join colonists who remained there following Tiwanaku's demise. A town named Puquina existed in a tributary of the Río Tambo, north of Arequipa, in the sixteenth century.

The possibility of Pukina-speakers in the Osmore drainage is suggested by abundant toponyms ending with -*huaya*, -*waya*, -*baya*, -*paya*, -*baha*, -*laque*, -*laca*, and -*coa*, which are said to be Pukina markers (Adelaar 1987: 373; Browman 1994: 246; Galdos Rodríguez 1984: 178, 1990: 206). These toponyms include Sabaya,[2] Chiribaya, Ilubaya, Tumilaca, Porobaya, Paralaque, and Tacahuay. Indeed, the toponym "Moquegua," sometimes spelled Moquiguaya or Moquingoa[3] in early Spanish writings, might have been drawn from an LIP Pukina settlement in the area, later appropriated by the Inkas. However, the common ending -*gua* or -*hua* in Moquegua and other toponyms could also be from Quechua—perhaps a "Quechuanization" of the Pukina *waya*—which would account for toponyms such as Moquegua, Samegua, Charsagua, and Escapagua. Moquegua is popularly translated through Quechua as "quiet place," although in Aymara it is *muki-wa* 'humid place.' Another translation would have it as *tierra templada productora de granos o semillas* 'temperate land of seed and grain production' (Anonymous 1998: 814), based on *muhu/moho*, meaning "seed, grain" in Quechua and "temperate zone" in Quichua.

It is generally agreed that coastal agricultural peoples spoke Koli (also Coli, Coles)[4], a term that is also an ascription of pleasant personality and character traits of coastal peoples (Cavagnaro Orellana 1986: 102; Julien 1979). Koli-speakers may have moved from the coast into the middle Moquegua valley, as suggested by features of the domestic architecture in the LIP sites of Estuquiña and Tumilaca (Conrad 1993: 65; Julien 1979). Koli, like Pukina, is extinct today, but references to a Koli language were noted as late as 1790 and even later in parts of Chile (Rostworowski 1988: 142, 144), and both Pukina and Koli were spoken as late as 1813 in Andagua, north of Arequipa (ibid.: 144). In addition to Qollas, Lupaqas, Pukinas, and Kolis, Pacajes colonists from the southern Titicaca basin might also have been in the southwestern region (Galdos Rodríguez 1985: 25; Rostworowski 1988: 144; Stanish 1992: 99).

Some of Moquegua's Indigenous toponyms are common elsewhere in the southern Peruvian Andes and altiplano, suggesting that peoples resettled in pre-Hispanic times carried the names of their former homes to the new colonies—as did the later Spaniards. Ancestral communities and possibly also ancestors of ayllus may have been resituated, a common practice among immigrants as they produce new places by reproducing old ones (see Amith 2005: 163). In addition to the archaeological site of Camata in the Torata valley, two communities named Camata exist around southern and eastern Lake Titicaca (see Bauer and Stanish 2001: 92; Hyslop 1984: 121, 123; Julien 1983: 50). Similarly, a Yunguyo exists in the southern Titicaca basin and in the Osmore drainage, and other Indigenous duplicates might be Chincha and Sabaya. Unfortunately, the idiosyncrasies of sixteenth- and seventeenth-century Spanish orthography often make it difficult to determine if a single place is being referred to or if there are two or more identically named locations, such as Torata/Tarata and Ilabaya/Ilubaya. The colonies' names might also reveal something of their administrative status. For example, the toponym Torata (also Tarata) may be traced etymologically to Quechua *thurita*, meaning "stand firm, seize without falling" (Kuon Cabello 1981: 470), which suggests obvious links to the legendary Inka seige of Cochuna. Camata is a common place name and may be derived from *kamach* 'to govern or order' (Stanish and Pritzker 1983: 11). The new places bear these toponyms permanently, such "tagging" coming to stand as testimony to the valley's history.

Collasuyu, Contisuyu/Condesuyos, Colesuyu

By the time of Spanish intrusion into the Andes, the Inkas had developed a geo-demographic administrative system for ordering their vast empire of Tawantinsuyu into four quarters, or suyus (see figure 3.2). The southern quarter was known as Collasuyu because it encompassed the Collao, or the Lake Titicaca basin, dominated by the Aymara-speaking Qolla peoples. As can be seen in figure 5.1, a large area of the upper tributaries of the rivers of the Pacific watershed in what is now southwestern Peru and northern Chile was occupied by Aymara-speakers and controlled by the Collao. This region may have constituted one of roughly eighty provinces organized by the Inka (D'Altroy and Schreiber 2004: 266; see also Wernke 2006).

Significantly, the early Spanish chroniclers Sarmiento and Cieza refer to the existence of a pre-Inka "polity larger than the [existing] Lupaca province . . . which controlled adjacent territories including a good portion of Arequipa, and which existed for two or more generations before" Inka annexation (Julien 1985: 216). This late LIP polity, which stretched south into what is now Chile, was at the time of Inka conquest the domain of the Qolla (ibid.: 217–20) and the southern extreme of what became the small western quarter of Cuntisuyu or Contisuyu (figure 5.2). Named for either West/sunset (Quechua *konti*) or after a town (Kunti) in the region, this quarter was later hispanified to "Condesuyos," perhaps related to the later corregimiento of Condesuyos north of Arequipa (ibid.: 217).

The core area of Contisuyu, the small vertex in the Cusco valley defined by its ceques, is fairly well-known thanks to Brian Bauer's (1998) fieldwork, but its precise boundaries are not. Tom Zuidema (1986: figure 11.2) suggested that in the Cusco region, Contisuyu's northern boundary with Chinchaysuyu extended directly west of the city to the Río Apurimac, and its southeastern boundary with Collasuyu extended about 13° east of South. However, it is not known if or how far these boundaries can be directly extended to the Pacific coast or some other terminus to define the actual imperial suyu. If Contisuyu's northern boundary continued directly west (cf. Moseley 1983: 187, figure 5.3, 1992: figure 10), it would intersect with the Pacific Ocean just north of the Río Pisco. This seems appropriate, considering the presence of an Inka road in the area linking the wealthy polity of Chincha (for which Chinchaysuyu is named) to Cuzco (Hyslop 1984: 100–102). The southern boundary of Contisuyu has been proposed

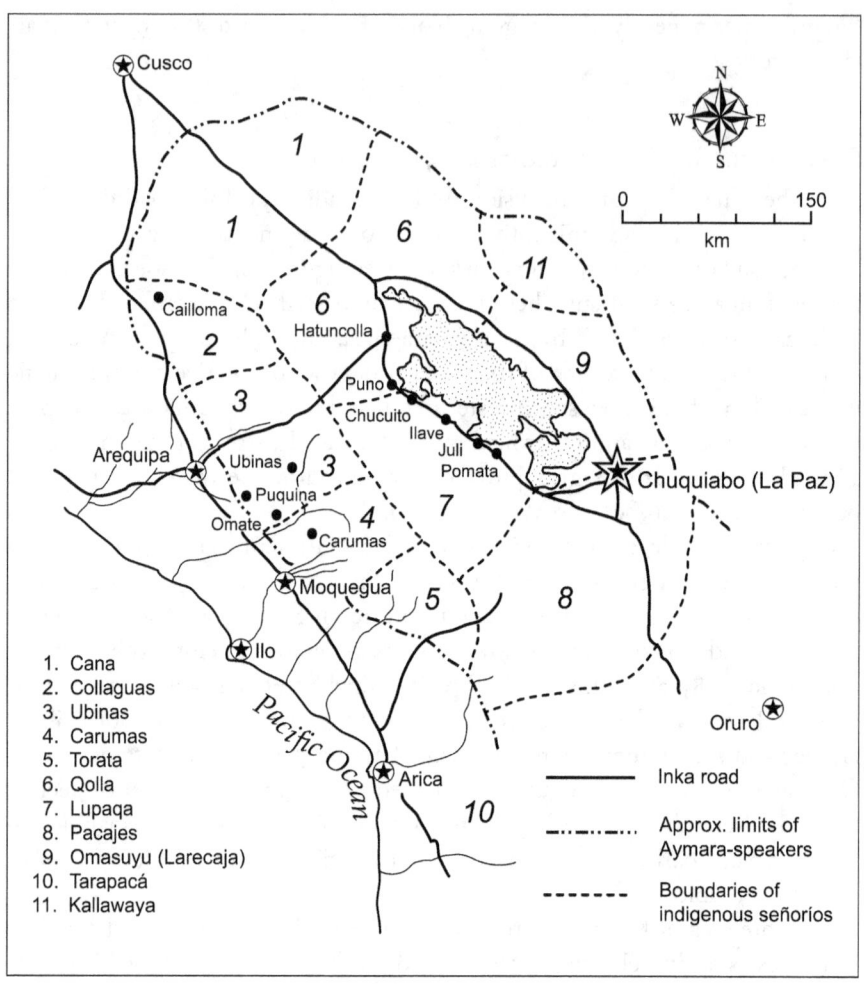

FIGURE 5.1 *Aymara señoríos in the upper sierras and altiplano (the Collao).*

to be the coastal portion of the Río Osmore (the "Río Ilo") (Moseley 1983: 187, 1992: figure 10). I suspect, on the basis of what is known about Inka expansion and later Spanish spatializations, however, that it extended into Chile, with its southern border near Tarapacá.

Colesuyu is a conundrum. María Rostworowski (1986: 127, 1988: 140) suggests that southwestern Peru and northern Chile may have had three divisions, or suyus—Omasuyu, Orcosuyu, and Colesuyu—which she considers pre-Inka distinctions (cf. Bouysse-Cassagne 1986). She considers Colesuyu (figure 5.3)

74 LANGUAGE AND TOPONYMS

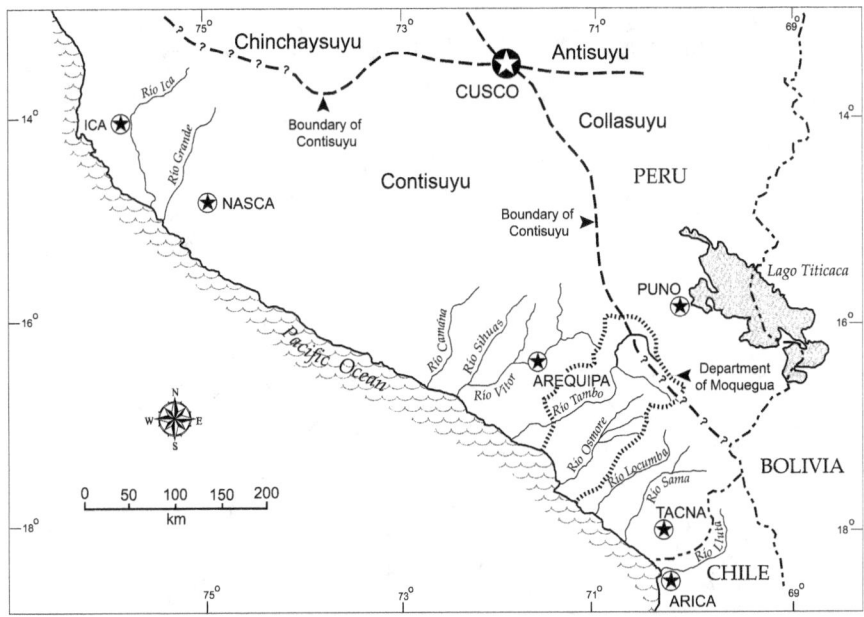

FIGURE 5.2 *The Contisuyu quarter of Tawantinsuyu, showing approximate boundaries.*

an Indigenous coastal territory that included the lower valleys of Río Majes southward through the Osmore and Sama valleys to the Río Lluta (Arica) and beyond, to Tarapacá in present-day Chile (Rostworowski 1988: 139). This possibility receives some corroboration from the extent of the early coastal award of tributary populations assigned to Lucas Martínez Vegaso. The toponym Colesuyu was likely derived from Koli, and the Inka coastal road between Arequipa and Tacna may have marked this division's upper boundary. Orcosuyu and Omasuyu would then be upper and lower sierra areas of agricultural colonization established during the LIP by the Qolla.

However, references to Colesuyu appear only in early colonial documents (Rostworowski 1986: 128), and the spatial boundaries of this province—particularly its extent inland from the coast into Contisuyu—are highly variable. In 1565 Colesuyu referred to the upper sierras of the Ríos Tambo and Osmore, rather than the coast (as Rostworowski would have it), because it included the tributary populations of Pocsi, Puquina, Umate, Quinistaca, the two Carumas, and the crown province of Ubinas (Galdos Rodríguez 1996: 293). Franklin Pease G. Y. (1984: 152–53) also refers to the upper Osmore region as the "Corregimiento of Colesuyo."

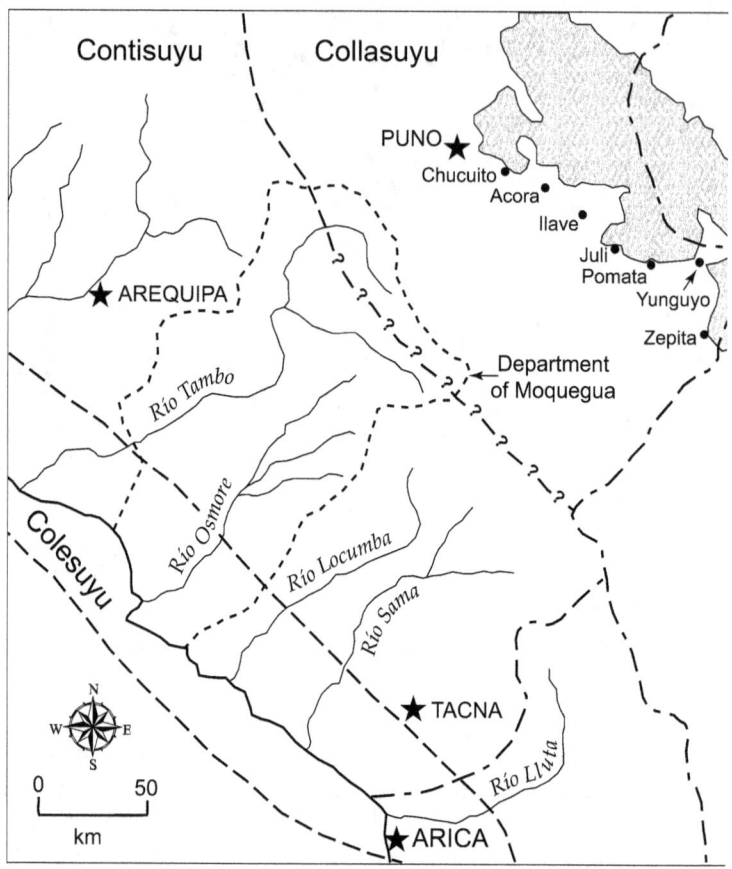

FIGURE 5.3 *Southern Contisuyu, showing proposed coastal area of Colesuyu.*

Cochuna

The Cochuna toponym (see Rice 2011a) is particularly problematic because it had multiple meanings in Indigenous and Spanish usage and because it long ago fell into disuse. In the sixteenth century, Cochuna/Cuchuna referred to a natural place (a valley and nearby mountains), to an Inka-established town, to an encomienda award that appears to incorporate both, and also to parts of the upper-middle Moquegua valley. As best I have been able to define it, the area the Spaniards in Moquegua referred to (inconsistently) as Cochuna or the Cochuna valley included the lower Río Torata extending south to the north bank of the Río Tumilaca. The northern and western extent of Cochuna as place is not clear, but it might incorporate the entire Río Osmore drainage as far north as the Río Tambo.

"Cochuna" appeared in Spanish encomienda records in 1540 as the name of a kuraka and his people. More information comes from a 1542 encomienda award document: the lower moiety of this parcialidad, "*valle* Cochuna," had 125 colonists from Hatuncolla under its kuraka principal Alique, 55 in "Suhuba," and 70 in "Capavaya" (Barriga 1955: 29).[5] As the Osmore valley began to be settled by Spaniards, "Cochunas" were said to live in Escapalac, across the Río Tumilaca from modern Samegua; Carumas lived in or around Samegua, Estuquiña, Huaracane, and Yaracachi in the upper mid-valley and at Calaluna and Coanto near Omo farther downstream (Galdos Rodríguez 1985: 31–33). Luis Cavagnaro Orellana (1988: 101) equates Cochuna with modern Torata and notes that this community, located on what he calls the "Collasuyu road" (my proposed "Cochuna road"), was the "port of entry, coming from the south, to the rich and populated zone of the Omates, the Carumas, the Puquinas, the Ubinas, and the Quinoestacas."[6]

By the beginning of archival record keeping in Moquegua in 1587, however, the term *Cochuna* had ceased to refer to an encomienda and had become a toponym: the spatio-geographical entity encompassing the lower valley of the Río Torata and the north (right) bank of the Río Tumilaca. Early documents often conjoin the two Indigenous places Cochuna and Moquegua, with activities identified as occurring in, or individuals being from, "the valley of Cochuna and Moquegua," which appears to specifically indicate the confluence region. This term seems also to acknowledge Indigenous dual political organization, in which Moquegua and Torata/Cochuna constituted the upper and lower moieties, respectively, of a parcialidad, with one ruler over both (Cañedo-Argüelles Fábrega 2005: xix). With the ascendancy of Moquegua (on the left bank of the Tumilaca) as the primary Spanish settlement in the valley, reference to Cochuna was dropped in the early seventeenth century, and the Cochuna toponym no longer exists.

It is not known what the Osmore river system, its streams and valley land, were called during the MH or the LIP. Throughout the sixteenth century, what is now known as the Río Osmore was simply referred to in documents as "the river that divides this valley," suggesting that it was otherwise unnamed. The Río Tumilaca, putative boundary of Cochuna, also was not identified by name. The lack of a name for these rivers, sources of the precious water that irrigated Indigenous and Spanish fields, is curious and may relate to questions of "ownership" of places. That is, because these streams were boundaries between districts, pre-Hispanic and Spanish, they had multiple nested meanings and perceptions, none of which permitted claims of "ownership" through the powerful act of naming (see Kearney and Bradley 2009: 81; Keith and Pile 1993a: 6).

TOPONYMY IN SPANISH-COLONIAL MOQUEGUA

Toponyms in twentieth-century Moquegua reveal how the Spaniards re-spatialized and re-politicized the Osmore drainage. The Spanish viceroys, for example, applied new religious and personal appellatives to the urban politico-religious centers they created—such as Villa San Francisco "de Esquilache" and Villa Santa Catalina "de Guadalcázar" in Moquegua—in keeping with the high valuation they placed on urban life, religion, and titles of nobility and power. Rural places, however, largely retained their Indigenous place names, even when prefixed by a saint's name as an official *doctrina* (parish), and this toponymy is a distinctive feature of the landscape of Moquegua today.

Bodgas

Rural bodega sites in the middle Moquegua valley are identified with a mixture of Indigenous and Spanish toponyms. Sixteenth-century documents record many Indigenous place names, including Chimba, Estopacaje, Samegua, Escapalac, Yaravico, Locumbilla, Omo, and Cupina, among others. These records helped the Moquegua Bodegas Project organize the valley's 130 wineries, or bodega sites, into fourteen "toponymic zones" in which most of the sites shared a common name. Six large zones comprised most of the middle and lower Moquegua valley in the late twentieth century. Initial large landholdings were subdivided beginning in the sixteenth century by sale or inheritance and perhaps most recently in the 1960s land reforms. Thus some winery sites came to be known by their owners' names as modifiers of the zones. Examples include bodegas known as Corpanto Ghersi and Corpanto Pomareda in the Corpanto zone and various sites named "Omo." Others bear only an owner's name, such as Montalvo and Gascon in the Locumbilla area. Only 11 of the 130 bodega sites (8.5 percent) identified during project surveys had religious or saints' names (see figure 1.2 and chapter 10).

Cerro Baúl

Throughout the Andes, the Tiwanaku and particularly the later Inka cultures venerated a multitude of significant places disposed over vast sacred landscapes. These places commemorated ancestral journeys, mythic histories, and feats of supernaturals and were memorialized by unusual landscape features, monuments, elaborate architectural portals, and other meaning-laden diacritics celebrated in ritual performances. Detailed lists of wakas and ceques in Cusco were recorded in the sixteenth century, and similar topographic information may have been maintained for every Inka-controlled town and valley, including the Titicaca basin (Arkush 2008; Bauer and Stanish 2001; Cobo 1890; van de Guchte 1999: 161). No such wakas are identified in the Moquegua region today, likely because Moquegua, on the periphery of the Inka empire, did not have a role or even participate in their imperial cult of ancestral gods, ritual, and mythological origins.

Still, it is curious that no Indigenous toponym has been retained for Cerro Baúl, a geophysical alterity and the most dramatic topographic feature of the Osmore drainage. The flat summit of this citadel-like butte, 600 m above the surrounding terrain, provides a spectacular vista of the lower valley to the southwest and the distant snow-covered volcanic peaks of the high sierras to the north and east (Chacaltana and Nash 2009: 161; Williams and Nash 2006). A local *curandero* (shaman) noted that Cerro Bául is a sacred mountain, or apu, one of a chain of such sites of pilgrimage in the circum-Titicaca area (ibid.: 462–64). Moquegua is thus part of a larger ritual landscape, probably created in the MH if not earlier, formed of chains of visible and invisible (because of distance) apu stretching from Cusco to La Paz. These ritual chains might be regional parallels to Cusco's ceques, perhaps "owned" by different ethnolinguistic or descent groups.

Cerro Baúl might have had some minor shrine functions after its MH Wari occupation, as small quantities of Late Horizon pottery were found on the summit, but remains did not include artifacts typical of Inka sacred shrines such as small animal figures of metal (Moseley and de France, pers. comm. November 5, 2010). A small offering, intrusive into wall collapse, consisted of human hair braided through copper bell-shaped ornaments; this might represent some sort of "witchcraft," given Inka symbolism associated with human hair (Chacaltana and Nash 2009: 173–74). At least four post-Wari *ofrendas* (cached offerings) were recovered in excavations, one just below the 1600 Huaynaputina ash, suggesting the butte's continued veneration (ibid.: 173–75). A modern shrine exists at the northeast corner of the summit of Cerro Baúl, where rituals are carried out today in late July or early August by local residents as well as pilgrims from Bolivia (ibid.: 161–64; Williams and Nash 2006). In general, apu are sites of annual feasts on varying dates in February and August (ibid.: 458), which might coincide with rituals celebrating second solar zenith and solar nadir, respectively. Modern offerings include llama fat, flowers, incense, coca leaves, wine, chicha, commercially produced beer, and other items.

In this context, it is striking that Cerro Baúl is known today by a Spanish toponym instead of retaining an Indigenous one. Such renaming might have been a conscious decision by the Spaniards: negate any ancient meanings and idolatrous associations with this distinctive feature by expunging its Indigenous name.[7] As noted in chapter 1, such toponym removal and replacement is an exercise of hegemonic power, silencing the voices and neutralizing the identities of Others (Carter 1987; Rose-Redwood and Alderman 2001).

Corregimiento in Moquegua

Examination of the colonial institution of *corregimiento* in the Moquegua region reveals how the Spaniards in some instances understood and reproduced boundaries between Indigenous ethno-political units while in others, as in the case of Colesuyu, they simply confused things (Rice 2011a). Some administrative actions were responses to pressure from Lupaqa kurakas in the crown repartimiento of Chucuito. Lupaqa leaders wanted their settlers in the sierra valleys to be returned to their jurisdiction rather than maintained in the hands of the encomenderos. For example, in 1557, in response to the petitions of Andean leaders, 144 Lupaqa mitimaes in two towns in the Lluta and Azapa valleys (part of Lucas Martínez Vegaso's encomienda), at that time under the jurisdiction of Arequipa, were returned to Chucuito (Trelles Aréstegui 1982: 169). In other cases, Spanish authorities took advantage of the deaths of some of the encomenderos to assign their encomiendas to Chucuito. After Francisco Noguerol de Ulloa was forced to return to Spain in 1556 for his bigamy trial (Trelles Aréstegui 1982), Viceroy Hurtado de Mendoza turned his Ubinas encomienda over to Chucuito in 1561 (Málaga Medina 1975: 74). All such reassignments served to strengthen the power of the Spanish kings vis-à-vis the encomenderos, maintain good relations between the crown and the Lupaqas (Julien 1985: 196; Kuon Cabello 1981: 48–49), and allow the new corregidores of Chucuito to exercise jurisdiction over these areas (Málaga Medina 1975: 74).

The situation with the middle Osmore valley—the "Moquegua valley"—is particularly difficult to deconstruct as formal administrative units were established all around it but the valley itself was little more than an add-on. For example, in 1561 the "*valle de* Moquegua" was added to the Corregimiento of Chucuito (Kuon Cabello 1981: 53). In 1565 the Corregimiento of Arica was established, with its northern boundary in the Moquegua valley registered by the mojon (marker) separating the "lands of the Carumas Indians and the [Spanish] jurisdictions of Moquegua and Arica" (ADM 10). This marker might have been one of many the Inkas established to differentiate the labor responsibilities of coastal and highland populations, especially in valley lands with mixed uses (Guaman Poma de Ayala 1980: 852–66; Ramírez 2005: 33–34, also 248n57). The Indigenous administrative separation between coastal Koli and sierra Carumas peoples might have been appropriated later by the Spaniards in establishing corregimiento jurisdictions. In simultaneously incorporating concepts of Indigenous and Spanish boundaries, this marker makes a telling statement about hybrid colonial spatializations.

The official formation of this corregimiento is also an indication of the importance of the coastal area—especially the port of Arica—in the new colonial economy. The jurisdiction encompassed a large area covered by encomiendas, including Ilo, Arica, Tarapacá, and Pica belonging to Martínez Vegaso; fishing communities in Tacna, Codpa, and La Quiaca of Pedro Pizarro; and Hilabaya, Cochuna, and "Cauaya" of Juan de Castro (Galdos Rodríguez 1996: 287). In fact, these last two communities in the Osmore drainage, Cochuna and Cauaya (Sabaya), were named as the corregimiento's (northwestern) boundary (Málaga Medina 1975: 54, 74). Not long thereafter, the coastal portions of Ilabaya, Locumba, and Sama were separated from Chucuito and included in the corregimiento. Much of the vast area of this corregimiento comprised Martínez Vegaso's original encomienda, and its loss may be related to Martínez's impresarial machinations: his vacillating support of the encomenderos versus the royalists during the mid-century civil wars, and his complex trading, bequests, and counter-petitioning of encomiendas, during which parts of the coastal area may have been lost.

Administrative districting of the coastal area of the southwestern region was thus settled relatively early in the Colonial period, but the sierras—with their declining Indigenous populations claimed by Chucuito—were another matter entirely. In early colonial times, the sierra region of what is now Moquegua was variously known as Colesuyu in 1560 (Galdos Rodríguez 1996: 293); Corregimiento of Colesuyu (Pease G. Y. 1984: 152–53); Corregimiento of Carumas and Ubinas (Julien 1985: tables 9.3 and 9.4); Province of Chucuito, Moquegua, and Sama in 1568 (Kuon Cabello 1981: 49); Corregimiento de Collesuyo, Corregimiento de Ubinas y Moquegua (Málaga Medina 1975: 74); and Corregimiento de los Ubinas y Valle de Moquegua in the early 1600s (Cavagnaro Orellana 1988: 109; Kuon Cabello 1981: 51).

The fact that the region slowly came to be known as Moquegua suggests that as the pueblo of Moquegua grew during the late sixteenth century, the province was increasingly identified in administrative contexts by the name of its principal Spanish town, and Indigenous toponyms such as Ubinas or Colesuyu were abandoned (Brown 1986: 14). But the fact that it took decades to straighten out the administrative name and status of the valley in the colonial organizational structure underscores Moquegua's peripherality (Rice 2011a, 2011b).

THE REGION AND THE LEGACY OF INDIGENOUS PROVINCES

As mentioned, early Spanish accounts of the Inka conquest of southwestern Peru note a large "pre-Inka" (i.e., LIP) polity that extended from Arequipa into Chile, settled by Qolla agricultural colonists whose administrative center was in the Collao, the northwestern basin of Lake Titicaca in the altiplano (Julien 1985: 216). This southwestern watershed polity can be said to constitute an Indigenous "region" in a political ecology sense. After the Collao was annexed by the Inkas, the basin became part of Collasuyu, the largest quarter of the empire of Tawantinsuyu. Its southwestern colonies, however, were part of the small quarter of Contisuyu, although it is not clear what this conceptual separation might have meant in political praxis beyond a continuation of tribute obligations. In the status- and power-related moiety organization of the Inka empire, the Contisuyu quarter was the lowest (hurin-hurin) of the four. If Contisuyu resembled other quarters, it was probably organized into numerous smaller provinces, or *wamanis*; these, in turn, would have been divided into smaller units called *warangas*, consisting of (ideally) 1,000 male tributaries. Warangas were divided into pachacas, consisting of 100 male taxpayers. All these units were part of and divided by the nested, ranked moieties the Spaniards called parcialidades.

Four sociopolitical units (warangas?) have long been identified ethnohistorically in the southwestern sierra region of Contisuyu (Rowe 1946: map 3): Collaguas north of Arequipa, Ubinas to its southeast, and Carumas and Tarata farther to the south. Collaguas was populated by Quechua-speaking Cabanas peoples and Aymara-speaking Collaguas/Qollas. Ubinas and Carumas were peopled by Aymara-speakers (both Qollas and Lupaqas). Not all of these provincial identifications have been grounded in the hierarchical and dualistic principles of Andean sociopolitical organization, however. For example, it is known that the Collaguas were divided into upper/hanan and lower/hurin moiety divisions, but such divisions are not clear for Moquegua. Some provinces and villages in the Inca empire, including Collaguas, had three subdivisions (ayllus) reminiscent of ceque structuring, irrespective of ethnicity and moiety structure (Wernke 2006: 202; Zuidema 1964: 221).

By the time of Spanish contact, this entire southwestern region might have encompassed a series of nested moieties or parcialidades (figure 5.4, table 5.1). They are speculatively identified here as Levels 1 through 5.

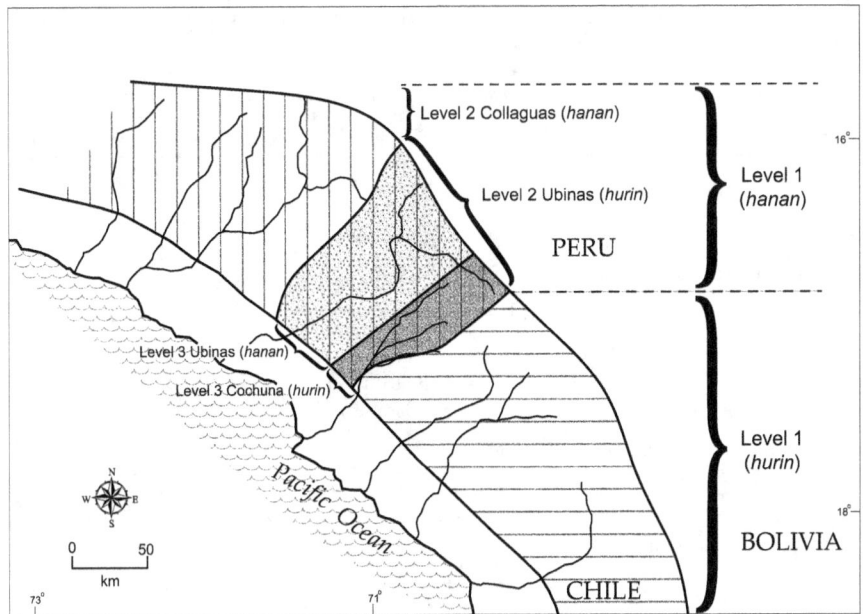

FIGURE 5.4 *Southwestern Peru, showing proposed nested moieties.*

- Level 1 would encompass the four Aymara-speaking sierra provinces just discussed as the hanan, or upper, division: Collaguas (around Arequipa), Ubinas (centered on the Río Tambo), Carumas (the Río Osmore), and Tarata (Ríos Locumba[8] and Sama). The area from Tacna south into Chile was the hurin, or lower.
- At Level 2, the upper division of the southwest would have been divided into Collaguas (Arequipa) and Ubinas as hanan, with Carumas and Tarata as hurin. This was the core of the area known as Condesuyos and formed a colonial corregimiento district. Ubinas was named after its largest population node, which lay on a pre-Hispanic road.
- In Level 3, the more southerly area that would become the Department of Moquegua comprised Ubinas (upper Río Tambo drainage) as hanan (the lower, or hurin, part) and "Carumas" (upper Osmore drainage) as hurin (but the hanan, or upper, part of it).
- In Level 4, Ubinas had two divisions or parcialidades, Ubinas (upper) and Omate (lower), while the divisions of "Carumas" were Carumas and Cochuna. Thus Ubinas was hanan-hanan, Omate was hanan-hurin, Carumas was hurin-hanan, and Cochuna was hurin-hurin.

LANGUAGE AND TOPONYMS   83

TABLE 5.1 Proposed moiety nesting and sixteenth-century tributary[a] populations of kurakazgos in the Osmore and Tambo drainages

Level	Upper (Hanansaya) Upper	Upper (Hanansaya) Lower	Lower (Hurinsaya) Upper	Lower (Hurinsaya) Lower	Population Early[b]	Population Late[c]
1: Lower Contisuyu	SW Peru		Tacna/ Tarata and N Chile			
2: Condesuyos	Collaguas	Ubinas	Carumas	Tarata		
3: River drainages	Ubinas	(R. Tambo)			> 1000	
			Carumas (R. Osmore)			
4: Parcialidades	Ubinas	Omate	Carumas			
				Cochuna	692	
5: Communities	Ubinas					532
	Pocsi					440
		Omate				128
		Quinistaca				206
		Puquina				125
			Carumas (U and L)		249	415
				Cochuna	125	73
				Sibaha	?	
				Camata	?	
				Moquegua	?	303
				Torata	?	117

a Males ages 18–50.
b At time of encomienda award; Julien 1985: tables 9.3 and 9.4.
c Galdos Rodríguez 1984: 180.

- Subdividing further (Level 5, communities), we know from late-sixteenth-century sources that early Cochuna had two sociopolitical divisions, Moquegua (hanan) and Torata (hurin), each of which was further divided into moieties. Carumas also had upper and lower divisions.

With more information, it might be possible to parse the sierra regional system differently, perhaps into a tripartite structure. The coastal area at lower

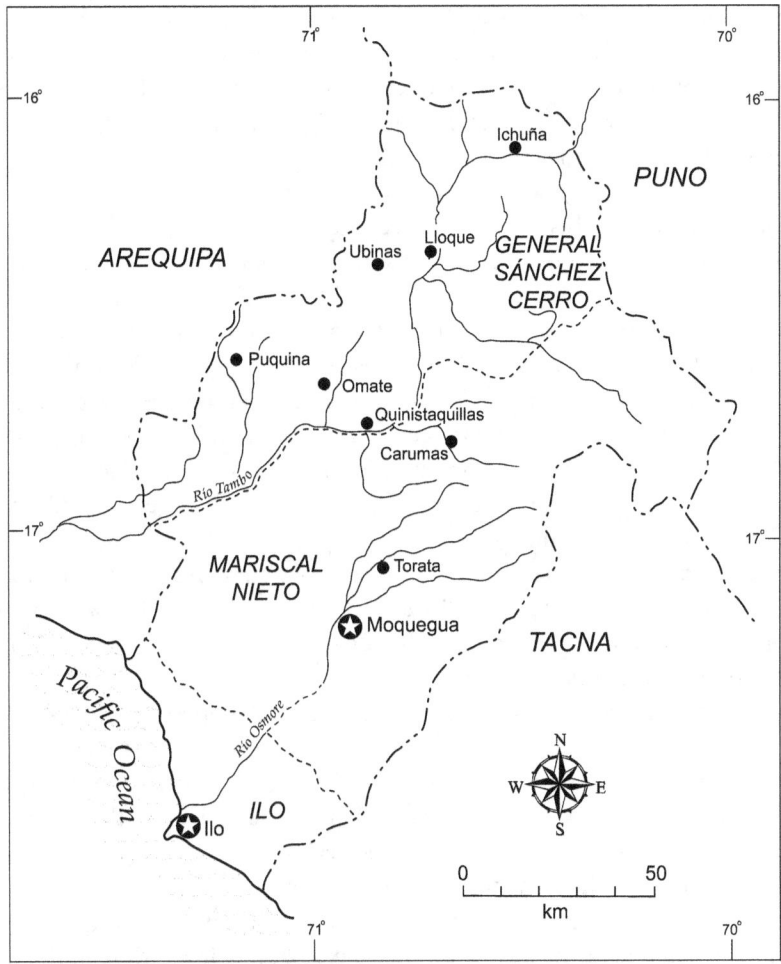

FIGURE 5.5 *The three administrative provinces of the modern Department of Moquegua.*

elevations, for example, seems to have been a separate province independent of this altiplano-focused organization, although it might have had its own moiety divisions.

These Indigenous divisions, based on pre-Hispanic Aymara agricultural colonization of river systems, were maintained not only in early Spanish spatializations but also in the administrative units of the modern Department of Moquegua. Two of its three *provincias*, created in 1936, maintain these divisions (figure 5.5). The northern province, General Sánchez Cerro, was named for Luis

Miguel Sánchez Cerro (1889–1933), an assassinated foreign ambassador. Briefly president of Peru, Sánchez appears to have had some connections to southern Peru and Arequipa but none to Moquegua specifically (http://es.wikipedia.org/wiki/Luis_Miguel_Sanchez_Cerro). Communities in this province, centered on the upper Río Tambo, include Coalaque, Matalaque, Puquina, and Yunga, which were part of the early-sixteenth-century provinces/encomiendas of Omate, Ovinas, Puquina, and Tassa Ovina, respectively.

The contemporary province of Mariscal Nieto is named for grand marshal don Domingo Nieto (1803–44), a local favorite son (Alayza y Paz Soldán 1987; Basadre 1987; Denegri Luna 1987; Minuto 1987; Rivero Velez 1987). Nieto was born in Moquegua (although it is not clear where; Alayza y Paz Soldán 1987: 97) and played a leading role in the fight for Peruvian independence through participation in the Battles of Moquegua and Torata (ibid.: 98). This province has six districts encompassing communities in the sierra tributaries of the Río Osmore, including modern Carumas, Cuchumbaya,[9] Samegua, San Cristobal de Calacoa, Moquegua, and Torata.

Moquegua's third modern province, Ilo, is coastal, representing what might have constituted a distinct sociopolitical unit, Colesuyu, in pre-Hispanic or contact-period times. It is not clear to what degree Koli-speaking coastal peoples in the southwest might have absorbed Aymara colonists (or vice versa) or were incorporated into the Inka imperial system or by the proposed moiety system.

Toponyms in use in twenty-first–century Moquegua and its environs represent a mix of those brought by waves of immigrant settlers. Speaking varied languages over a period of centuries before the arrival of the Spaniards, these settlers produced places out of the area's dry and craggy mountainous spaces. Colonial officials retained many Indigenous place names in denominating administrative districts, for example, Arica, Ubinas, and Moquegua. Ilo also continued as the name of the department's coastal province, while in the early twentieth century two other provinces were named for more recent military-political figures in Peruvian history, only one of whom had a connection to Moquegua. As with Cerro Baúl, the principle that place names should have meanings related to the people who produced them, and thereby embody collective or personal identity and social memory (Feld 1996: 111; Rodman 1992: 642–44), is easily subverted by those holding power.

NOTES

1. Even more contentious is the identity of a Pukina-speaking group in the basin called Uru. Did the term refer to an ethno-linguistic group (Kolata 1993: 241), a tax

category (Julien 1983: 52; Stanish 2003: 56), low social status (Rostworowski 1988: 143), or some combination? After Inka-Aymara expansion in the western Titicaca basin, Pukina-speakers were probably pushed eastward, and both Pukina- and Uru-speakers came to be viewed pejoratively (Bouysse-Cassagne 1986: 206, 208; see Wachtel 1986).

2. Sabaya is the name of a volcano in Oruro, subject of a legend and a cult (Bastien 1985: 608; Gisbert 1980: 22). The volcano may have erupted in 1600, coincidentally with Huaynaputina, destroying a nearby village.

3. Moquingoa is said to have been the pre-Hispanic name for the valley (Galdos Rodríguez 1984: 180n5).

4. Non-agricultural fisherfolk on the coast were called Camanchacas (Rostworowski 1988: 141–42).

5. Rostworowski (1988: 141), citing documents in Moquegua's archives, says that the people of Cochuna were known as Capangos. In the last years of the sixteenth century their kuraka principal was Pedro Onagua (Anagua) from Escapagua.

6. My translation: "ubicada en el camino de Collasuyo, era la puerta de entrada, viniendo del sur, a la rica y poblada zona de los Omates, los Carumas, los Puquinas, los Ubinas y los Quinoestacas."

7. A similar situation might obtain with respect to San Antonio, the legendary "fort" where (I believe) the Indigenous inhabitants resisted the Inka siege. This site is now known by a Spanish—and a saint's—name, but that name may be very recent. At the start of Programa Contisuyu the site might have been called "Torata Viejo."

8. It is interesting that the Río Locumba, south of the Osmore, is rarely mentioned in colonial documents, unlike the Río Sama, to the south of Locumba and north of the Río Caplina (Tacna). The difference is likely the greater amount of arable soil in the Sama valley, as compared with Locumba.

9. Cuchumbaya could easily be a garbled version of Cochuna. A new community by that name was established north of Carumas in 1944.

Part III
Spanish-Colonial Spaces and Places

Salient questions in situations of conquest and colonization concern power relations: How was knowledge of an unfamiliar space acquired, assimilated, and strategically applied in imposing new forms of administrative control and social order? In terms of Moquegua's experience, such questions can be rephrased in several ways: How were Indigenous spaces and places (re-)identified by the foreigners and incorporated into Spanish knowledge systems? How were these spaces and places "made, imagined, contested, and enforced" (Rockman 2003: 4)? How did the Spaniards learn about the southwestern Peru region, particularly the Río Osmore drainage? How did they accumulate locational, limitational (ibid.: 4–5), geographical, technical, and social (Hardesty 2003) knowledge about the region's routes, climatic regimes, and resources (Meltzer 2003)? How did Spanish interests come to supersede those of the area's multiethnic and multivocal Indigenous populace? How was the Moquegua region reconstructed, re-politicized, and re-spatialized with the entry of capitalist market forces? The burgeoning literature on landscape, space, and place emphasizes the interrelations of praxis and power in the creation of these entities and of their meanings to the peoples who populated them (e.g., Gupta and Ferguson 1997a, 1997b; Keith and Pile 1993a, 1993b; Lefebvre 1991; Rodman 1992; Smith 2003).

As reviewed elsewhere (Rice 2011a), Spanish efforts to control and establish order in their vast new empire were accomplished by adapting numerous administrative institutions from medieval Iberia to their new transatlantic circumstances. These institutions were social, political, economic, juridical, and religious; as discussed in the chapters in part III, they "worked" in different ways and to different degrees in different places.

Conquered spaces and places were immediately claimed for Spain through the traditional ceremony of "taking possession." This was followed by awards of encomienda to participants in the conquest: encomiendas were grants of Indigenous populations, not of land itself. Private ownership of land was imposed by various mechanisms, its availability increased by the drastic decline of Indigenous populations through disease and overwork and through the forced resettlement of those dwindling communities through the policy of reducción.

To construct a new Moquegua as a distinctly Spanish "place," crown officials imposed additional concepts and practices associated with urban and rural spaces brought from the Iberian homeland. These included units of political administration, such as *audiencia* and corregimiento, and units of religious jurisdiction, firmly anchored by cathedrals, convents, and chapels liberally spread throughout the cities and the countryside. These traditional Spanish concepts were frequently modified by the realities of life in this new world and even more by agrarian capitalism and monoculture, transforming the Moquegua valley into a uniquely viticultural landscape.

Spaniards' different approaches to defining, bounding, and using space and place are discussed in the five chapters in part III. Chapter 6 provides an introduction and overview of political and economic spatializations, beginning with general institutional and jurisdictional constructs and moving to the particulars of the built spaces of Moquegua's colonial wine agro-industry. Chapter 7 explores the role of encomiendas by focusing on two wealthy and powerful encomenderos, Hernán Bueno *y familia* and Lucas Martínez Vegaso, and their contrasting strategies for identifying and exploiting new spaces and resources in southwestern Peru. The site of Torata Alta is the focus of chapter 8, its brief administrative history having begun under the Inka imperium, usurped by the Spaniards as a reducción, and ended by volcanism. Chapter 9 discusses historical and material data pertaining to Locumbilla, the only bodega site in Moquegua with an archaeologically detected sixteenth-century occupation and use, and part of the extensive Bueno family landholdings. In chapter 10, Spanish religious considerations are reviewed along with the reorganizations of space in Moquegua that accompanied the introduction of Christianity into the valley.

6

Spanish Order and Re-spatializations

> Christianization had amounted to a reorganization of [Andean] space ... but the countryside remained pagan.
> —Sabine MacCormack
> (1985: 459, 465)

In Iberia, the centuries immediately preceding Spain's invasion of the Western Hemisphere were dominated by the events and myths surrounding *reconquista* (reconquest), the prolonged internal warfare and "wave of advance" colonization that characterized the Christian retaking of the peninsula after its fall to Islamic control in AD 711 (see, e.g., Glick 2005; Reilly 1993). Reconquest had begun almost immediately in the rugged Pyrenees Mountains in the north but required eight centuries of southward crawl for successful completion. Throughout the conflict, saints, the nobility, the Catholic Church, and Spanish identity were deeply entangled through militant, evangelical Christian colonialism and "ethnic chauvinism" manifest in the concept of *limpieza de sangre* (Weinstein and Bell 1982: 191): the ability to prove Christian purity of familial bloodlines, that is, a lack of Jewish or Muslim ancestry. Correctly or incorrectly, historians have often considered Spain's New World venture as an extension of the centuries-long process of reconquest; and it is evident that, at a minimum, many of the institutions and "spatializations" established in the transatlantic colonies were based on that experience.

Not surprisingly, given this protracted struggle, significant religious differences emerged between northern (Christian) and southern (Islamic) Spain (figure 6.1), their separation approximated by the Río Tajo/Tagus (Christian 1981). In the late twelfth century,

DOI: 10.5876/9781607322764:c06

FIGURE 6.1 *The Iberian Peninsula, showing modern political divisions, rivers, towns, and other places mentioned in the text.*

military-religious orders were established to secure the frontiers of the new Christian kingdoms, and, importantly, these orders gained papal recognition (Reilly 1993: 149). The best-known—Calatrava (established in 1158), Santiago (1170), and Alcántara (1176)—conferred elite status on the knights and their descendants, a status that continued to be recognized throughout the sixteenth-century overseas expeditions of conquest. The Order of Calatrava was housed in a fortress on the Río Guadiana in Castile/La Mancha, and the Order of Alcántara occupied a fort on the Río Tajo in Extremadura; both had oversight from the Cistercian (religious) Order. The home of the Order of Santiago, or the Military Order of Saint James of the Sword (*de la Espada*), is disputed, but it may have been in Uclés, in La Mancha. Established to protect Christian pilgrims from Muslim harassment on the road to and from the tomb of the apostle Saint James (Santiago) in Compostela, the order also founded hospitals and convents in Spain.

NEW WORLD CONQUEST AND AGENDAS

Europeans sailed to the "New World" and the land of "Birú" in pursuit of multiple agendas: those of the church, the Spanish kings, and the individual travelers. For the church, the ostensible justification for conquest of Indigenous peoples throughout the Western Hemisphere in the late fifteenth century was religious: a collaborative arrangement through which the Roman Catholic Church, not yet the powerful entity it would later become, allowed the Spanish crown to explore/exploit newly discovered lands on the condition that they bring the natives' idolatrous souls to salvation through Christianity. Similar permissions had earlier been granted to Portugal[1] for exploration and absolute rights to lands in Africa, for example, and such arrangements had begun in Spain during the final years of reconquest (Dussel 1981: 38–39).

For the adventurers who embarked upon these expeditions of discovery, the agenda was more straightforward: "to serve God and his Majesty, to give light to those in darkness and also to get rich," in Bernal Díaz's pithy summation (quoted in Hennessy 1978: 19). In reality, their emphasis was on the last of these goals: to acquire personal wealth represented by land and servants (or slaves). They brought the same norms and expectations for rewards as those that prevailed during the late reconquest: establishing themselves in towns and urban estates, with productive lands in the countryside where the conquered peasantry—farmers and artisans—were servants and manual laborers.

The agenda of Spain's "Catholic kings," the devout Isabel of Castile and Ferdinand of Aragón, was both economic and religious: a joint venture of colonizing, evangelizing, and exploiting under the banner of the Catholic Church. Much of the stimulus for exploration was trade: the famous spice trade associated with Columbus's sailing westward to the "Indies" but also a desire for new sources of gold ("capital") to rival the amounts acquired by the Genoese and Portuguese in Africa (see Banaji 2003). As in the peninsular reconquest, Spain's effort was a collaborative military-religious enterprise. In the crown's eyes, the New World spaces were to become exclusively Christian places, occupied only by Christians and using only goods produced in Christian Spain. Toward this end, restrictive policies were issued to award travel licenses only to "true" (or "old") Christians (as determined through limpieza) and prohibiting trade with other countries and even among the colonies.

The crown began the reorganization of alien Andean spaces by transferring many of the same practices, policies, and institutions that had been instrumental in reordering Muslim Iberia into Christian Spain (Rice 2011a). Not all of these policies were overtly spatial, but through their application—by the Spanish crown, which wanted Christian order, and by individuals who desired wealth—they came to carry a strong physical component. The emphasis quickly focused on "capital" more broadly defined: productive agricultural land and the human labor and mineral resources associated with it.

SPACE-RELATED SPANISH INSTITUTIONS

Spaniards' relations with land and landscapes were complex. They recognized a medieval tradition of communal usufruct (Gilmore 1977; Vassberg 1984: 5–16) in which, for example, residents along Christian-Muslim borders often made agreements to share pastureland (López de Coca Castañer 1989). But the Spaniards also brought to the New World many capitalist concepts relating to the generation of wealth and its legal underpinnings, particularly land as private property, to which one held title and which could be bought, sold, and rented. These activities and concepts not only implemented the re-spatialization and re-politicization of Andean South America into a Christian space but also paved the way for the viceroyalty's entry into the emerging world of commodity production and capitalism. In Moquegua, this new economic world was one of growing grapes and making wine and brandy (Rice 2011b).

CAPITULACIONES

The first glimmers of geographical knowledge about Andean South America were obtained by Francisco Pizarro and his men while sailing along parts of the northwest coast of the continent. Spanish learning of the continent's landscape began by what has been called a "point-and-arrow" model (Rockman 2003): explorers sailed southward, guided by the Pacific coastline and information from natives they captured, and they moved inland guided by Inka roads. Incomplete as this early learning was, it provided a basis for royal *capitulaciones* (contracts) the Spanish crown granted to the early adventurers, permitting them to mount expeditions of exploration and conquest.

Awarded under the crown's dual military-religious authorization, capitulaciones authorized the recipients to declare themselves governor and captain-general of the region in question. Four such contracts were issued for South America between 1529 and 1534 (figure 6.2): Pizarro received Nueva Castilla,

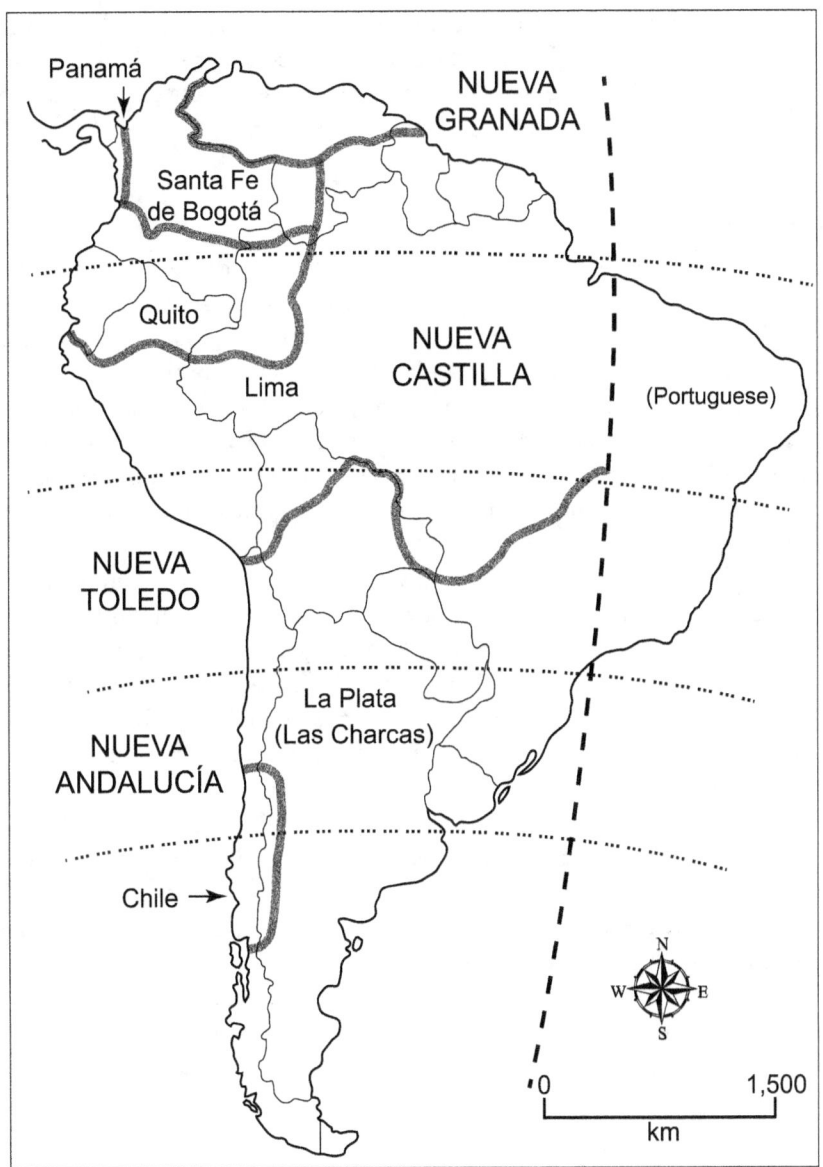

FIGURE 6.2 *Approximate boundaries of the early-sixteenth-century Spanish capitulaciones (dotted lines) and audiencias (shaded lines) in South America with those of modern nation-states. Boundaries of capitulations are approximate because of vague measurements of "leagues" and disagreements between Spain and Portugal about the longitude (heavy dashed line) specified in the Treaty of Tordesillas.*

extending 200 leagues south from Santiago (Ecuador), and Diego de Almagro was awarded Nuevo Toledo, extending 200 leagues farther south into what is now northern Chile. These were the first steps in the process of European re-spatialization and re-politicization of the Andean world.

Taking Possession

When the Spanish invaders encountered New World peoples, they first staged a performance in which they read the extraordinary document known as the *Requerimiento* ('requirement'). This document drew upon ancient Roman law to declare to Indigenous peoples that the Spanish rulers claimed dominion over the land and that they, the inhabitants, were to allow Spanish priests to preach to them (Seed 1992). Informed acquiescence by the uncomprehending, non–Spanish-speaking audience was unnecessary; the mere act of reading the *Requerimiento* was deemed sufficient legitimation. Indigenous resistance was met with violence.

Upon seizing land or founding a town, the Spaniards staged another performance: the formal ceremony of "taking possession." In founding Arequipa in southern Peru in 1540 (Barriga and Victor 1939: 79) and San Sebastián de Escapagua in the Moquegua valley in 1618 (Cúneo-Vidal 1978: 553–62), the ceremony involved asserting dominion over the natural space by cutting tree branches, pulling up grass, and tossing clods of dirt—and creating a cultural place by erecting a cross and a *picota* (pillory), among other symbolic acts. When the Jesuits of Cusco took formal possession of the Yaravico vineyard and estate in Moquegua in 1610, they were accompanied by a judge, the vicar of Moquegua, and others, all of whom participated in taking "actual and normal possession, opening manually the houses, bodega [wine cellar], [walled] vineyard and orchard; closing the doors, cutting branches from the vines; walking the property from one side to the other in quiet and patient signal of taking possession" (ADM 44). "Taking possession" of existing places, in other words, involved entering and (re)defining its spaces, including breaching boundaries such as doors and walls.

Encomienda

Encomiendas (from *encomendar* 'to commend, entrust') were not awards of land (these were called *mercedes de tierra*) but rather were grants of native peoples as tributary laborers. Largely ignoring the technicalities, however, encomenderos took a broad view, assuming that, along with the human populations, they were also entitled to the lands the natives worked, the goods they produced, and the resources—such as minerals—in the area.

The institution of encomienda had roots in medieval Spain, as Christian forces wresting the peninsula from Muslim control demanded tribute and labor from the inhabitants of newly conquered areas (see Keith 1971: 433–34; Reilly 1993: 144–47; Sánchez-Albornoz 1963; Vassberg 1984: 124–25). Similarly, as the Spanish conquerors moved across the Americas, they were rewarded with Indigenous populations to provide labor and tributary income, along with tracts of land in newly platted colonial towns. The grants were for two generations (*dos vidas*), those of the original encomendero and his immediate heir, after which the award reverted to the crown. The spatial extent of encomiendas in the Moquegua region is unclear, but these awards apparently excluded the fertile lands of the confluence of the Río Osmore's tributaries and the narrow valley below.

Reducción

Reducción was a cornerstone of Spanish administration of Indigenous populations throughout their colonies, including Andean South America. Etymologically, the word *reducción* comes from *reducir(se)*, which means roughly "(to be) convince(d) or persuade(d)," with the implication of doing things for the better (Hanks 2010: 2). Reducir can be traced to the Latin *reduco*, which means not a minimization of size or number but rather a "physical movement toward something" and "to bring to a certain state or condition" (Cummins 2002a: 203; also Gose 2008: 119). Reducción can be considered an idea, an ideal, and a social space of encounter for transforming identities and practice based on Christianity (*policía cristiana*) (Hanks 2010: xv–xvii, 2–3). These goals were accomplished by inculcating a new "habitus" in the recently conquered populations through imposed codes of conduct and organization of space and through formal interactions between Spaniards and natives that contributed to altered linguistic structures to explain both (ibid.; see also MacCormack 1985).

The desired psychological "state or condition" of faith and reason among the Indigenous populations was thought to be attained spatially, in part through a policy of physical concentration in reducciónes de indios or *congregaciones*. Congregación involved forcibly dislocating native peoples from their small, dispersed home communities and gathering them into new, larger towns or sometimes consolidating these groups in existing settlements (Lockhart and Schwartz 1983: 173). New reduction towns were created through formal building programs that were structured, like those of colonial cities inhabited primarily by Spaniards, according to specific standards: centered on a plaza with a grid of wide, straight streets dividing the community into residential blocks (Crouch 1991; Crouch, Garr, and Mundigo 1982; Cummins 2002a; Gade and Escobar 1982; Low 1995; Nuttall 1922; Stanislawski 1947; Zéndegui 1977). Public buildings—most important a church but also houses for Spanish officials and the Indigenous leader (kuraka, cacique)—were distributed around the plaza. Individual residences were to be occupied by nuclear families, with separate rooms for males and females and doors opening to the street rather than into shared courtyard spaces. The goal was to segregate the sexes, especially unmarried daughters, and thereby limit potential sexual contact among relatives (Cummins 2002a: 214, 217–18, 236–37n56). This proscription may relate to an old Spanish legend whereby non-Christian women were characterized as licentious and dangerous to the social, moral, and political order (Grieve 2009; for Spanish negative characterizations of women, see Boxer 1975; Silverblatt 1987).

In the new reduction communities, the "pagans" could be watched, taxed, and indoctrinated in the Christian faith as part of "persuading" them to live according to the ideals of *civitas*: a spatially ordered (urban), religiously ordered (Christian), and socially ordered, civilized life. There, the indigenes could be integrated into a "non-Andean structure of landholding and taxation" and separated from their ancestral wakas, some of which were viewed as places of origin: "Leaving one's home therefore brought with it not only material, but also spiritual, upheaval and confusion" (MacCormack 1985: 453).

The concepts, plans, and royal edicts promoting reduction in the Spanish colonies can be traced back to 1503, but for Peru the most significant was the 1549 *cédula* issued by Holy Roman Emperor Charles V (Cummins 2002a: 208; McAlister 1984: 172). Resettlements, which began in the 1570s, came on the heels of two critical circumstances for Christian administration: a decade of Indigenous rebellions, especially against Christianity, such as the Taki Onkoy movement to revitalize the cults of wakas and ancestors, and, even earlier, the broad Catholic religious reforms promulgated by the Council of Trent (1545–63) (Gose 2008: 120). Under the administrative reforms of Viceroy Francisco de Toledo (1569–81), more than 1,000 reductions were established, relocating perhaps 1 million–1.5 million native Andeans (Andrien 1991: 125; Gade and Escobar 1982: 430, 432).

Political Jurisdictions

Virtually all of Andean South America—plus unexplored tropical lowlands extending to the east—was included in a single viceroyalty, the Viceroyalty of

Peru, created in 1543. As elsewhere in the new and growing Spanish empire, the viceroyalty was subdivided into various audiencias (supreme court jurisdictions), with frequently shifting boundaries until two new viceroyalties were created under House of Bourbon rule in the eighteenth century.

In Moquegua, the Río Osmore and its tributary Río Tumilaca constituted the boundary between two *audiencias*, that of Lima (including Arequipa) to the north, created in 1542, and Charcas, or La Plata (Alto Peru, including wealthy Potosí), to the south, created in 1559. This demarcation meant Spanish citizens in the community of San Sebastián, on the north side of the river, had recourse to one set of colonial authorities, whereas those increasingly choosing to settle in Moquegua, on the opposite side of the Río Tumilaca, had to deal with another. Indigenous residents of the valley, regardless of which side of the river they occupied, were administered by the Lupaqa kurakas in Chucuito, a crown property since 1540.

Corregimientos, or provincial governorships, were smaller colonial administrative units subdivided into repartimientos. The Osmore valley was crosscut by two corregimientos: Arequipa (created in 1548), which included the upper mid-valley, and Arica (1565), which included the coastal area and lower mid-valley. The boundaries of these political units also changed frequently.

Religious Jurisdictions

Catholicism was brought to the Spanish colonies by the "secular" clergy, the hierarchy of officials in the Catholic Church, and the "regular" clergy, the missionary friars. The latter especially were from among the mendicant orders: Dominicans and Mercedarians arriving in the early 1530s, Franciscans in 1548, and Augustinians in 1552. Two Dominican friars accompanied Pizarro's expeditions in the Andes; one of them, Father Hernando Luque, became the first Peruvian bishop (of Tumbes) and protector of the Indians (Lockhart and Schwartz 1983: 107). The friars established missions, preached among the poor, and were exempt from diocesan jurisdiction.

Because the Catholic Church and the Spanish crown were so closely entangled politically and economically in the enterprise of colonization and evangelization, the crown was reluctant to allow persons born in the colonies—known as *criollos*—or non-*peninsulares* entry into the highest levels of the church hierarchy. Of the 535 bishops and archbishops in South America, only 64 (12 percent) were American-born (Greenleaf 1971: 6). In addition, with a few exceptions, the religious orders, including the Jesuits who arrived in 1568, did not accept native Andeans or persons of mixed race into their ranks until the mid-eighteenth century (Tibesar 1971b: 100–101). The consequences of these policies have been far-reaching: unlike the bishops, the lower levels of the clergy were largely anti-royalist (Greenleaf 1971: 7), a populist stance with echoes in today's liberation theology.

In carrying out the religio-military enterprise, the Spanish crown, led by the "Catholic kings" Ferdinand and Isabel, created and zealously protected a series of rights granted by the church. These royal patronage concessions—the *patronato real*—allowed Spanish kings tremendous independence in their New World enterprise, including the right to collect tithes, construct churches and monasteries, establish dioceses and their seats, pre-approve all church literature, and appoint bishops and require them to swear an oath of loyalty to the crown (Dussel 1981: 39; Greenleaf 1971: 2; McAlister 1984: 194–96; Scholes 1971: 21–22). Important for Peru, the patronato dictated that the crown would supply its colonies with sacramental wine and olive oil for the ritual needs of the church and its personnel.[2] Eventually, the crown was also able to interfere in matters of religious dogma, with little objection.

Spain quickly created a number of dioceses or bishoprics in Andean South America. Initially under the archdiocese of Sevilla, these entities were established in areas of anticipated population growth and frequently had to be revised (van Oss 1978). Ultimately, they corresponded fairly closely to actual patterns of urban growth and hierarchical political jurisdictions in the viceroyalty (table 6.1). The archdiocese of Lima was created in 1541, with four dioceses in its jurisdiction. One of these was the Cusco diocese, later divided into three bishoprics: Cusco, Huamanga, and Arequipa. The Osmore drainage was initially part of the diocese of Cusco from 1553 to 1612 (Kuon Cabello 1981: 50–51), after which it was placed into that of Arequipa. In 1619, as part of efforts to resolve the longstanding disputes between the Spanish communities of Escapagua and Moquegua, the valley of Moquegua and Torata, which had been combined into a single doctrina, or parish (center of religious instruction), was separated: one became the mostly Spanish doctrina of Moquegua, and the other included the largely Indigenous communities of Torata, Tumilaca, and Yacango. At the same time, Torata began building its church dedicated to the Virgen de la Candelaria.

SPANISH (RE-)SPATIALIZATION AND (RE-)POLITICIZATION IN MOQUEGUA: CONTESTATION

Spanish settlement in the Osmore region began in the area of the tributaries' confluence, specifically on the banks of the lower Río Tumilaca and Río Torata. It is not clear exactly when the first Spaniards entered the valley, but it was

Table 6.1 Archdioceses and dioceses in early Colonial South America

Archdiocese	Date	Diocese	Date	New Diocese	Date
Lima	1541	Cusco	1537–38		
				Arequipa	1577–1609
				Huamanga	1609
		Quito	1546	Trujillo	1577–1609
Santa Fe de Bogotá	1564				
Las Charcas/ Sucre	1608	Charcas	1552		
		La Paz	1605–8		
		Córdoba	1570		
		Santa Cruz	1605		
		Buenos Aires	1620		
Caracas	1638				

probably in the mid-1530s. Apportionment of the Indigenous populace of the drainage into encomiendas began shortly thereafter, as did the region's incorporation into other political and religious administrative divisions.

Attempts to inscribe new kinds of social and political spaces over Moquegua's landscape were highly contested by Spaniards and Indigenous people alike because they were disconformant with praxis: they did not "fit" either resident Spaniards' or Andeans' meanings or expectations for use. For example, as noted, the Río Tumilaca was part of the boundary between the Lima and Charcas audiencias and the royal jurisdiction of Chucuito, a circumstance that caused interminable conflicts between settlers on opposite sides of the river. These disagreements were resolved early in the seventeenth century, but that resolution was disputed. In 1618 the Peruvian viceroy renamed the San Sebastián settlement Villa San Francisco, promoting it from *pueblo* (village) to *villa* (town). He also ordered the Spanish citizens of Moquegua to move across the Río Tumilaca to the new town and prohibited Chucuito from interfering in Indigenous valley affairs (Cúneo-Vidal 1978: 558–62; Kuon Cabello 1981: 54–57). The citizens of Moquegua refused to comply with the directive, and for years the two towns traded heated accusations about general desirability of place, including health, safety, and religiosity. The conflict was not settled until 1625, when a new viceroy promoted Moquegua to Villa Santa Catalina and declared it the capital of a new province variously known as Colesuyos or Ubinas in the audiencia of Lima (Kuon Cabello 1981: 62).

Apart from the influx of new Spanish settlers, the major contributor to the re-spatialization of the Moquegua valley was the severe demographic decline of Indigenous populations as a result of disease, overwork in the mines, and other stresses. By the time of a 1572 *visita*[3] by fray Pedro Gutiérrez Flores (Cañedo-Argüelles Fábrega 2005), the native population of Torata and Moquegua had declined by 50 percent (Cañedo-Argüelles Fábrega 2004: 33). This population loss had unavoidable consequences for the (re)production and contesting of spaces by both Spaniards and Indigenous peoples.

One consequence was the forced removal of Andeans from their small, scattered communities in the sierras and resettlement in new locations. In Moquegua, one such congregación was the site of Torata Alta (chapter 8). A related problem was severe disruption of the Indigenous moiety-based system of social and political organization. This led to a long dispute among local kurakas about the legitimacy of Indigenous leaders in Torata and Moquegua and their successors. The leaders of Torata argued that there should be only one kuraka over the two communities rather than separate lords because historically there had been only one ruler over both: Tacasi in Torata, who had been named by the Inka Wayna Qhapaq (~1493–1526) in Cusco, along with his *accompañado*, or *segunda persona*, Inga Pari (table 6.2; Cañedo-Argüelles Fábrega 2005: xix). The Toratans claimed further that the current kuraka of Moquegua, Carlos Pacaxa, was not legitimate because his father, Visa, had been named in Chucuito instead of in Cusco.

No matter how the Spanish authorities attempted to resolve the dispute, neither side was satisfied. Inga Pari's son and then his grandson, don Pedro Conta, pressed these claims for twenty years. The Spaniards were generally sympathetic toward Torata's position, doubtless because they wanted to eliminate Indigenous claims to much-desired lands in the Moquegua valley (Cañedo-Argüelles Fábrega 1994: 18–19, 2004: 24). Teresa Cañedo-Argüelles Fábrega (1995: 129) asserts that in 1592, the Spaniards acknowledged don Martín Cutipa of Torata as the region's single legitimate kuraka, but a 1594 document in the Moquegua archives (ADM 7; Guíbovich P. 1984: 296–97) names don Pedro Conta as the kuraka of the hanansaya moiety and don Martín Cutipa as kuraka of the hurinsaya moiety.

Still another repercussion of the population loss and resettlement process was the sale of real estate in the final decades of the sixteenth century. For example, documents in the Moquegua archives reveal that in 1575, Juan de Castro, encomendero of Cochuna, purchased 80 *topos* (ca. 50 acres) of land from "*sus indios en el valle de Cochuna*" (Davies 1975: 32, 37). These "Indians" might already have been reduced to San Mateo de Zunilata. In the 1590s, land in various parts of

TABLE 6.2 Names of *kurakas* in Torata and Moquegua

Date	Torata Kuraka Principal	Acompañado	Moquegua Kuraka Principal
1493–1526?	Tacasi	Inga Pari	
?	Curata		Visa
1543	Carlos Layme		
1559	Gaspar Cutipa	Francisco Poma[a]	
1572			Carlos Pacaxa[c]
1573	Francisco Chimo		
1573	Martín Cutipa	Pedro Conta[b]	
1592	Martín Cutipa		

Source: Cañedo-Argüelles Fábrega 2004: *cuadro* 3.
a Son of Inga Pari.
b Son of Francisco Poma.
c Son of Visa.

the valley owned by Toratans, including Pedro Conta and his sons, was sold outright, and abandoned lands were put up for auction in Arica. In 1600 the reduced Capangos (Capantos?) sold lands in "Suañalay," a toponym lost by the twentieth century.[4]

ECONOMIC RE-SPATIALIZATION: MOQUEGUA'S WINE *HEREDADES*

Rural real estate in colonial southwestern Peru was known by the term used in Spain: *heredad*, which emphasizes possession through inheritance. The term was initially used in sixteenth-century Peru "in a broad sense to denote a person's possessions," but by the end of the century it referred to a rural estate (Davies 1984: 196n62). A better-known term for Spanish agricultural estates— but inappropriate in colonial Moquegua—is hacienda. Hacienda is a distinctive socioeconomic formation usually characterized by a powerful, paternalistic landowner (*hacendado*), a large, dependent labor force, and limited capital, which can affect the penetration of new technologies (Van Young 1983; Wolf and Mintz 1957: 380, 393–94).

Some of the earliest—and most heavily damaged—heredades (here called "bodegas") were noted in the confluence area, both on the high-quality soils of the flatlands and on hilltops (figure 6.3). As Spanish settlement grew and expanded south from the tributaries' confluence and the town of Moquegua,

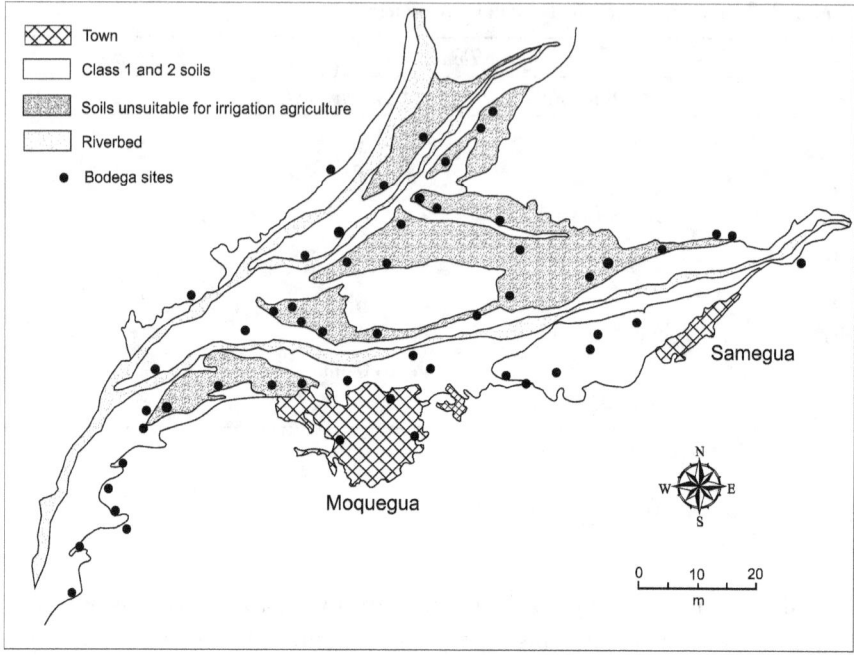

FIGURE 6.3 *The upper Moquegua valley (confluence area) showing locations of bodega sites relative to soil quality (see figure 2.2).*

winery structures were constructed along the valley margins. Vineyards were particularly important in the early colonial economy because Spain had proven incapable of supplying the viceroyalty with sufficient wine for ecclesiastical and domestic use. Indigenous groups also learned to make wine as an entry into the new economy, with Torata producing wine from its vineyard in Moquegua by the late 1560s (Diez de San Miguel 1964: 245; Guíbovich P. 1984: 222–23, 299; Pease G. Y. 1984: 164). This was the beginning of Moquegua's wine and pisco (grape brandy) agro-industry, which dominated the valley's colonial economic history through repeated boom-and-bust cycles over three-and-a-half centuries (Rice 2011b).

Over time, as Spanish population grew, Moquegua's rural estates were repeatedly subdivided by inheritance and sale. The small size of these properties stands in contrast to that in the neighboring Locumba valley to the south, which is broader than the Osmore valley, but Moquegua has better agricultural soils. Individual landholdings in Locumba appear to be much larger, but we were unable to directly investigate the valley by means of pedestrian surveys.[5]

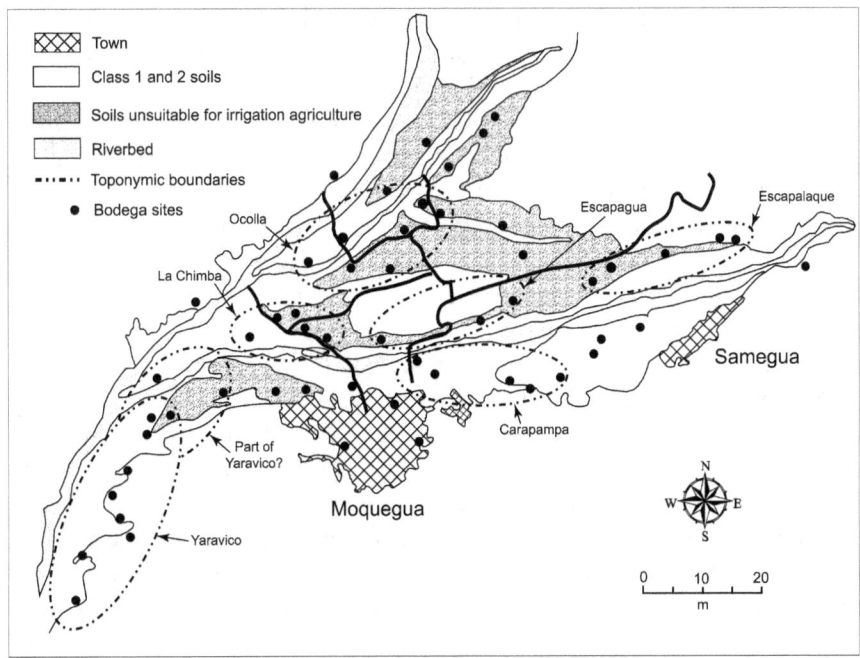

FIGURE 6.4 *Core areas of toponymic zones in the confluence area of the Río Osmore.*

TOPONYMIC ZONES

The process of land division in Moquegua is clearly demonstrated through what I have called "toponymic zones" in the valley. These are areas in which most of the identified bodega sites share a common toponym—frequently very old—plus a modifier reported by local residents (usually a recent owner's name) or assigned by the Bodegas Project. Many of these zones' toponyms are associated with multiple holdings of Indigenous residents of the valley in the late sixteenth century, particularly the Carumas, although it is not easy to determine which of the moieties.

Five toponymic zones can be identified in the upper mid-valley where the Osmore's three tributary streams flow together (figure 6.4). The Ocolla zone straddles the lower Río Torata valley (with a second possible zone, Estuquiña, including Yahuay bodega, just upstream). Much of this area is interrupted by fingers of desert hills probing westward, and irrigable agricultural lands lie almost entirely on the valley floors (see figure 2.2).

The lower Río Tumilaca valley has four toponymic zones, three of them on the north, or right, bank. Escapalac lies farthest to the east, with Escapagua just downstream, although whatever existed in early colonial Escapagua appears to have been destroyed. Several seemingly old adobe haciendas and structures were noted in the 1980s on the north bank (e.g., Buena Vista, Charsagua) but lacked evidence of wine making. Still farther downstream is the Chimba zone, where six bodega sites were identified just above the confluence of the Ríos Tumilaca and Torata. This zone appears to have been misidentified as "Chacba" through an error in some transcriptions of sixteenth-century documents.

The main zone of the southern, or left, bank of the Río Tumilaca is Carapampa, at least to judge from early documents, with Samegua to its east. Another possible zone is the area of the modern city of Moquegua, where only the Villegas bodega in the Huayco region was functioning in the 1980s.

Past the confluence of the tributaries, the valley turns south and is sharply confined between bordering hills. Zones in this middle valley area are easily defined (see Rice 2011b: figure 11.3). The Yaravico zone lies on the left/south bank of the Osmore, just below the confluence. In its settlement characteristics, this zone is in some ways transitional between the upper and middle portions of the mid-valley and may be grouped with either. In earlier descriptions I identified nine bodega sites in the Yaravico zone, including several early colonial heredades, but I now believe two others to the north, Estopacaje and Yaracachi, may belong as well. Locumbilla occupies the southern Yaravico zone.

Just below Yaravico is the small Calaluna zone, with nine bodega sites. These sites lie on both banks of the Río Osmore, as this is the only part of the middle valley where irrigable flatlands are found on the west side of the river course. Native Andeans of Torata claimed 6 fanegadas (1 fan. = 1.6 acres) of land in Calaluna, bordered on the north with vineyards in Locumbilla and on the south by lands in Omo worked by the Carumas (GGR1: f. 331).

The Omo zone lies south of Calaluna, and its bodega sites preserve the Indigenous name of Omo known from sixteenth-century documents. In this zone the river abuts the hills on the west bank, and virtually all arable land lies to the east. Here, the Carumas had 20 fanegadas (20 fan. = 32 acres, or 0.5 mi^2) in Omo in the *asiento* of Coanto. The northern boundary of Carumas land was a broad *quebrada* (gorge) (almost directly opposite Ventillata bodega) and a "*mojon de piedras y palos*" (marker of stones and wood). Fifteen bodegas and haciendas are tightly packed along this eastern edge of the valley, suggesting intense subdivision through inheritance or sale. One site (Ventillata) perches above a tiny pocket of cultivable land on the west side, and Omo Viejo lies on bottomland.

South of Omo is the Coanto, or, today, the Corpanto, zone. As in the Omo zone, the river flows against resistant rock at the western boundary of Corpanto. Here, too, sites are strung along the eastern valley margin, although with broader spacing than in Omo. In the southern part of Corpanto the riverbed shifts back to the middle of the valley floor.

In the lower mid-valley, bodegas can be found on both the right and left banks of the river. Most (perhaps all) of this area was known in colonial times as Cupina, and it appears to have been held originally by Carumas. The area can be divided into four zones: two on the left/east bank and two on the right/west bank. On the east side of the river, the northern portion is the Chamos zone, with tightly spaced (and heavily disturbed) bodegas along the valley margins; the Rinconada zone lies to the south. The western (or right) bank has the best-preserved bodegas in the valley (although they might simply have been more recently remodeled). In the northern Cupina zone, the names of bodegas—Cupina, Merced, and saints such as Santo Domingo and Santa Ana—echo the area's early colonial history, which was tied by bequest to the Convent of La Merced in Cusco. In the far south, the Sacata zone, difficult to access, is home to large standing structures today. The toponym Sacata was known in the seventeenth century as Sillacta.

Bodega Layouts

As described elsewhere (Rice 1996a, 1996b), the built environment and technology of the colonial and later wineries in Moquegua reveal continuities of "place making," with roots in Roman estates. Standing structural remains in the valley can be described in terms of two functional sectors, "industrial" (wine making; *pars rustica*) and residential (*pars urbana*). These sectors were arranged in four site plans: segregated, integrated-block, integrated-linear, and specialized. In the segregated plan, residential and industrial sectors were physically separated; in the integrated layouts, the two were connected in either a linear or a block-like arrangement. Specialized sites exhibited only wine- and brandy-making facilities, with no standing remains likely to have served a residential function. These facilities were probably constructed to augment the productivity of the more multifunctional hacienda-like complexes during the heady years of Moquegua's eighteenth-century "brandy boom."

There are virtually no comparable data on wine hacienda layouts from elsewhere in southern Peru. Earlier interest in the wine haciendas was directed primarily toward religious—especially Jesuit—estates (e.g., Cushner 1980; Davies 1984) in larger and wealthier valleys to the north on the south-central coast. It can be questioned, therefore, whether it is reasonable to expect architectural parallels between them and the smaller, generally secular heredades of the Moquegua valley. Nonetheless, the published plan of a Jesuit heredad in the Vitor valley of Arequipa dating to the 1650s (Cushner 1980: 61, plate 2) seems roughly comparable to the integrated-block layout in Moquegua, with three functionally distinct sectors arranged around a patio. On one side of the patio is the "industrial sector," consisting of lagars, bodegas, and pottery workshops; opposite this sector is a small building with three rooms or enclosures where the mayordomo resided. Between them, on the third side of the patio, is a structural block with cells for the priests, living room, chapel, and kitchen and a veranda in front facing the courtyard. A wall or fence links the rear portion of the "industrial" portion with the rear of the priests' quarters.

Bodega Components

The industrial sectors of Moquegua's bodegas have many components and arrangements that can be traced back to Roman times, as can the combined layouts of residences and wine-making facilities. As discussed elsewhere (Rice 1996b, 2011b: 277), the wine heredades produced a variety of other goods related to making and shipping wine, an ancient pattern variously known as estate production, secondary industrial production, or upstream ("backward") vertical integration.

One such facility is the *lagar*, a square or rectangular (circular only at Hacienda Grande and Testamento) stone tank, usually plastered on the interior, where harvested grapes were deposited to be crushed by foot or mechanically in a beam-and-screw press.[6] From the upper lagar(s) the juice flowed into one or more lower tanks (*puntaya*), where the sugars were measured and quantities checked. An opening at the base of the puntaya allowed the expressed liquid, or must (*mosto*), to drain from the lagar to the fermentation facilities. Lagars were typically (but not exclusively) located in pairs at a relatively elevated area of a bodega, to take advantage of gravity in moving the liquid through the entire process (see Rice 1996a). Ideally, lagars were enclosed to maintain cool temperatures and avoid insect-borne contamination, but such enclosures were likely of perishable materials and evidence of them was not common (they were present at nineteen sites) at the Moquegua heredades.

At some point in the seventeenth century, Moquegua's vintners began distilling wine into brandy, locally called pisco. The pot-still distillery, known as a *falca*, was typically located at a lower elevation in "front" of the fermentation structure. This is an area that at virtually all bodega sites was badly damaged by modern irrigation canal construction, and only fourteen distillery facilities were located in project surveys; another eleven were located by other means (e.g., air photographs, informants). At four bodegas, a large lagar-like tank sat in this area.

At the better-preserved sites in Moquegua, the fermentation bodegas held rows of large earthenware tinajas partially buried in the floors (Rice 1996a).[7] Tinajas were significant capital investments in the wine industry, as reflected in documentary sources as early as the Romans. In 1570, Hernán Bueno y García paid 2 pesos apiece for 54 tinajas (108 pesos), each holding 30–35 *arrobas* (2.6 gal. in a "wine arroba") of wine (Davies 1975: 39). In 1616, the Jesuit heirs to the Yaravico estate attempted to sell it, and former owner Alonso de Estrada's itemized property included "una vodega con cincuenta y una tinajas dentro della, que hazen dos mil y quienientas botijas de vino" along with another "siete tinajas para harina y vinagre" (ADM 48). The value of the vessels is not provided.

These large, heavy vessels could crack or break during fermentation, necessitating repair or replacement, but the frequency of such events is unknown. Wine makers in southern Spain reported that their much larger tinajas lasted sixty to seventy years. Patterns of dates on tinajas in Moquegua's fermentation bodegas clearly indicate that they were often replaced in batches. When the Moquegua tinajas cracked, they were repaired with some kind of sealant such as pitch or plaster, and tin suture-like strips were placed across the cracks.[8]

Available evidence does not permit a clear understanding of the decision-making sequence and socioeconomic organization involved in the production of these tinajas and the religious inscriptions on them. The inscriptions clearly were incised into the clay before the vessel was fired, presumably by the *tinajero*. But did a church, chapel, or cofradía that wanted a dedicated wine supply contract with a tinajero to make a jar? Or did religious organizations contract with a heredado to produce the wine, and then he (rarely she) contracted with the tinajero, specifying whether anything should be inscribed on the vessels, such as a date, a cross, or a religious figure or event? It is likely that tinajas were produced by itinerant potters, who placed their own marks on the jars.

At many of the bodega sites, circular updraft kilns were constructed at some distance from the industrial facility, and they were of two types (Rice 1994; Rice and Van Beck 1993). Large kilns were used to fire tinajas and botijas; smaller kilns were used for calcining lime, gypsum, or both.

FOUR EXCAVATED BODEGA SITES IN MOQUEGUA

Chincha

Chincha was, at the time of project surveys, a large, well-preserved bodega on the right (west) bank of the Río Osmore (17° 20'S; 71° 00'W), perched on a low hill overlooking the far southern extreme of the valley (figure 6.5). The standing walls and roof of the site have since disappeared, likely destroyed in recent

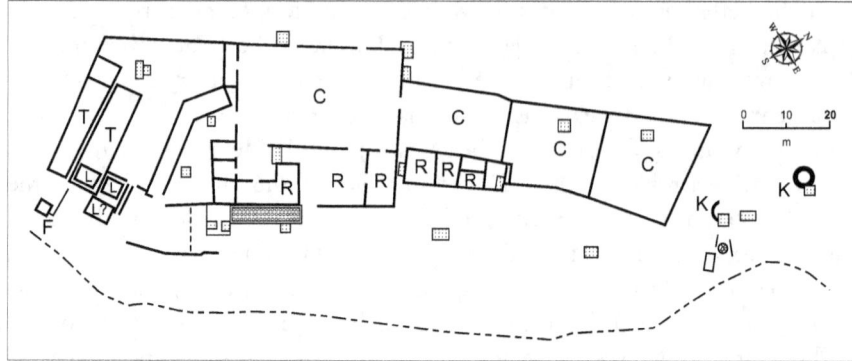

FIGURE 6.5 *Chincha bodega site plan, showing the location of excavation units (stippled squares). T = tinaja room; L = lagar; F = falca; R = residential; C = corral; K = kiln (note grinding platform, Feature 9, to the southeast; see figure 6.6a). Feature 4 (see figure 6.6b) was revealed in excavations in the large enclosed space to the southwest.*

earthquakes. The adobe structural ruins covered an area of approximately 200 m north-south by 50 m east-west, in an integrated-linear layout. Seventeen tinajas were noted but only two dates: 1796 and 1797. As described by Greg Smith (1991: 227), the site consisted of

> two industrial sectors, one at the north and one to the south, with an area of residential use located between the two on the highest part of the hill. The southern part of the bodega consists of two tinaja rooms, a large open room thought to have been used for tonel [large wooden container] storage, and a partially destroyed distillery apparatus, or falca. While not clearly apparent, the lagares for crushing grapes appear to have been located slightly northeast of the tinaja rooms.

Two kilns stood off the northeastern corner of the structural complex, along with a circular platform of cut limestone, apparently for grinding calcined gypsum (figure 6.6a). The residential area, consisting of several adobe rooms, was fronted (to the east) by an attractive stone mosaic patio, and four animal corrals lay behind the complex.

Chincha was sampled by 89 shovel tests, of which 24 were sterile, and by 20 larger excavation units (ibid.: 118, 227–39). Two fragments of pig bone were recovered below volcanic ash in one unit (deFrance 1993: 298). Two bricks recovered in surface collections bore the stamp of the Rufford Company of Stourbridge, England (Smith 1991: 227), a well-known nineteenth-century producer of firebrick. Excavation data suggested primarily eighteenth- and nineteenth-century occupations of Chincha by relatively wealthy residents (Rice 2011b: 255).

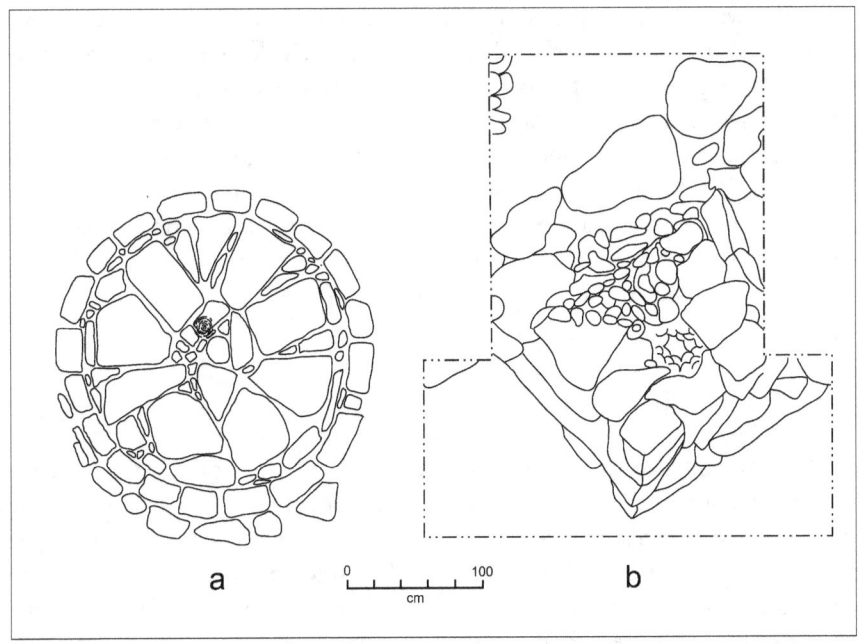

FIGURE 6.6 *Features at Chincha bodega: (a) Feature 9, a grinding platform for calcined lime; (b) Feature 4, an unknown stone construction (see text).*

Feature 4 (figure 6.6b) in the northernmost room of the industrial sector was an unusual construction, roughly 2.2 m square and 1.4 m tall, composed of "very large, crudely shaped blocks of *moro-moro* [local sandstone] set on top of large river cobbles and cemented with a mixture of clay and lime" (Smith 1991: 234–36). To the north of this pyramidal structure was a dense deposit, up to 55 cm thick, of cow and goat bone, which appeared to be refuse from butchering and leatherworking (deFrance 1996: 28). Analysis of features nearby and partial excavation of Feature 4 itself yielded few artifacts and no basis for inferring the function of the juxtaposition of the stone structure and bone deposit, but both are believed to be colonial in date.

Estopacaje

The documentary identification of an early bodega with the name Estopacaje[9] (López and Huertas 1990) prompted investigation of a valley location with that toponym. Located on the right (north) bank of the lower Río Tumilaca, just above its join with the Río Torata and opposite Yaravico, Estopacaje (17° 11'S;

70° 57'W) was settled in the sixteenth century by Pedro Guevara. The bodega site with this name was inhabited in the 1980s, and little open space was available for testing. A total of only twenty-one shovel tests, spaced at 5-m intervals, was placed in an area of 60 m north-south by 30 m east-west; six of these tests were sterile (Smith 1991: 190–91). Three excavation units were placed at the site. Neither shovel tests nor excavations encountered volcanic ash or sixteenth-century occupation traces. Instead, most of the artifacts recovered suggested occupation in the eighteenth and nineteenth centuries, including several coins dated to the 1870s (ibid.: 250–51). Dates on tinajas ranged from 1740 to 1832.

Locumbilla

The Locumbilla bodega site (17° 12'S; 50° 57'W), in the middle of the Yaravico toponymic zone in the northern part of the Locumbilla subdivision, was the most intensively investigated of the four bodega sites chosen for work by the Bodegas Project (chapter 9). The site was selected for excavation for several reasons, most importantly the documentary evidence that a winery by that name existed in the late sixteenth and early seventeenth centuries. Also, Locumbilla was unusually well preserved, perhaps because the Ministerio de Agricultura owned the property in the late 1980s, although we found it occupied by squatters who kept their goats penned in the enclosed spaces. Fieldwork began in 1987 with the excavation of 92 shovel tests, the largest number at any of the 28 tested sites. This program was followed by more extensive and intensive areal excavation of 16 units in 1987, 4 in 1988, and 12 in 1989.[10]

A related site, of particular interest given Bodegas Project interest in the Yaravico toponymic zone, was one we named Yaravico Viejo because it yielded the valley's oldest in situ tinaja, bearing a religious inscription and a date of 1590.[11] Yaravico Viejo (figure 6.7) sat at the base of a hill on the west side of the Panamerican Highway near the confluence of the Río Tumilaca with the Río Torata. The Mercedes Carbonara elementary school occupied the southeast corner of this wine heredad, and bulldozing associated with modern additions to the school, plus road widening and irrigation canal construction—all witnessed by the Bodegas Project in the late 1980s—have now completely obliterated the site. Nonetheless, we were able to identify walls of fermentation bodegas (the southern structural complex is more recent than the northern one) and crushing vats (one with part of a winepress), and eventually we noted traces of a possible kiln exposed on the hillside just below the "new wall." In 1987 the area deemed testable measured approximately 100 m north-south and 60 m east-west and was investigated

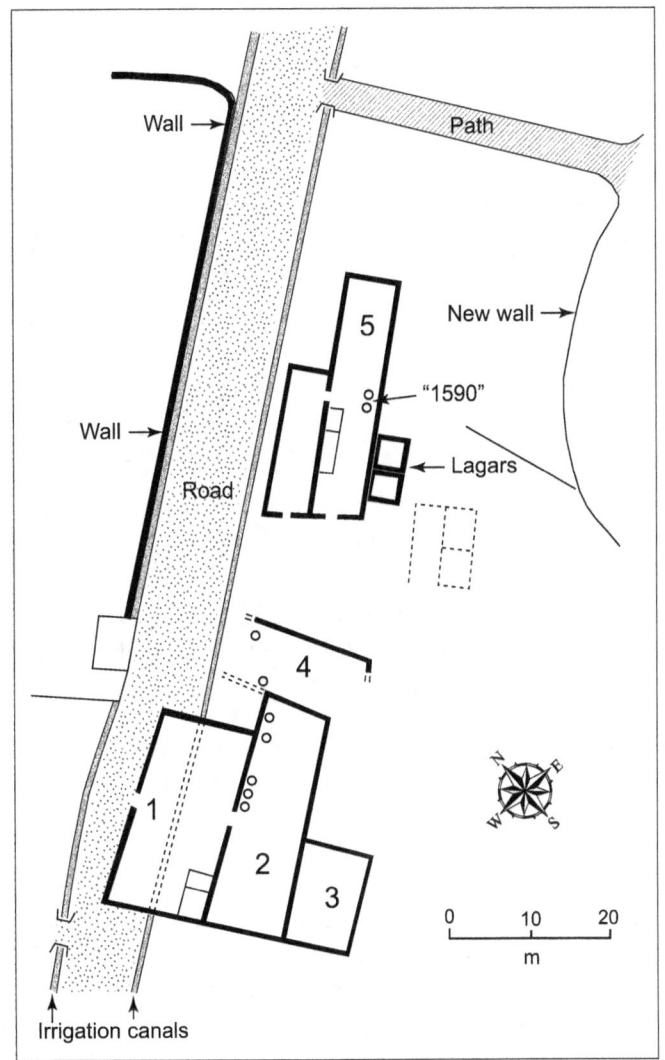

FIGURE 6.7 *Plan of now-destroyed Yaravico Viejo bodega site, drawn from 1970 air photographs and field observations. A former resident gave us the following information about use: (1) held wooden barrels of various sizes: 18–20* toneles *and 60* pipas; *(2) held 6 earthenware* tinajas *(5 remaining in situ) and 8* cubas; *had a* lagar *with a press in the corner; (3) held 36 clay* tinajas *and 3 tin* tinajas *(for brandy); (4) held 8* tinajas *to store grain; 2 remaining in situ; (5) property belonging to another landowner; note location of the in situ 1590* tinaja.

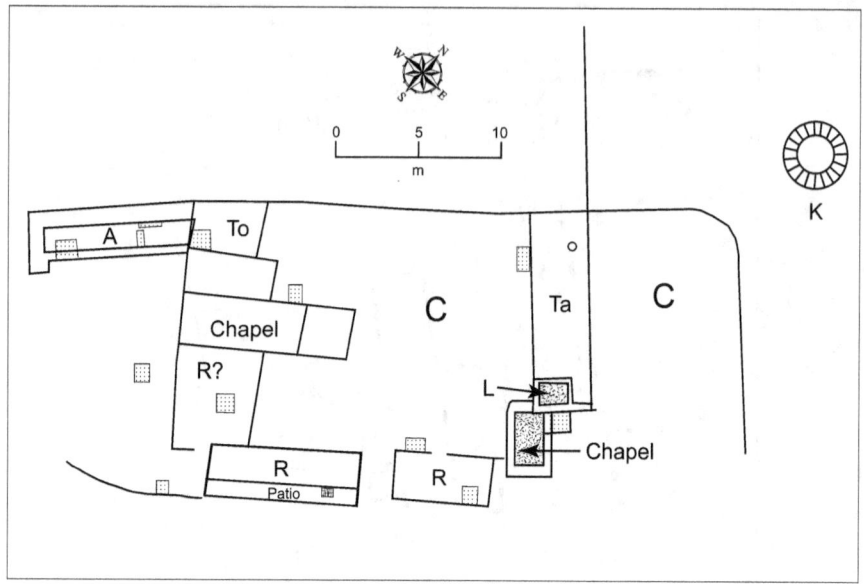

FIGURE 6.8 *Yahuay bodega site plan, showing location of excavation units (stippled squares). Ta = tinaja room; To = tonel room; L = lagar; R = residential; C = corral; K = kiln; A = "arch room," with multiple arches and niches.*

by twenty-six shovel tests, of which three were sterile (Smith 1991: 169). Because of the extensive damage, no excavations were undertaken at Yaravico Viejo.

Yahuay

Yahuay bodega (17° 09'S; 70° 56'W; figure 6.8) is a well-preserved site in the far northwestern valley on the west side of the Río Torata. Measuring roughly 40 m north-south by 100 m east-west, the bodega has an integrated-linear site plan and was investigated by thirty-eight shovel-test units and thirteen excavation units (ibid.: 185–88, 243–49). Yahuay is distinguished by two chapels, one on the south side of the site and the other, smaller chapel on the east. The latter had a niche with a statue of San Isidro Labrador, still venerated at the time of the Bodegas Project (see Rice 2011b: figure 11.6). Three tinajas, most likely fired in the large, heavily buttressed kiln off the northern corner of the structure, bore a date of 1744. Most excavations and excavated material suggest primarily an eighteenth-century and later date of occupation.

The Yahuay heredad was donated to the Dominican monastery in Moquegua as a source of income and supplies for the friars (ibid.: 125, 177, 203, 256).

Perhaps because—or in spite—of that heritage, a lot of local folklore focused on Yahuay. One tale was that a long, narrow room with arched cells along its walls, probably used to house novitiates, was used for keeping slaves (see ibid.: figure 11.7). In addition, Bodegas Project investigations revealed that Yahuay had been heavily disturbed by looters seeking the rumored buried treasure of long-ago wealthy bodega owners, and holes and tunnels had been dug in many rooms as well as outside them (Smith 1991: 244–48). Such treasure-hunting activities might also account for the local lore about tunnels, underground passages, and tombs at Yahuay.

Excavations in a room south of the large corral revealed a brick floor, below which was a wall running north-south that appeared to date to the Middle Colonial Period. Greg Smith (ibid.: 248) suggests that this wall may have been part of a kitchen structure because a variety of ceramics and organic material, including bone and shell, were recovered in the area. The excavation also yielded "several earthenware pipe fragments, a green glass bead, and a clear glass rosary bead with a wire attachment" (ibid.). The presence of *Ricinus, Datura*, and *Sapindus* among the botanical remains at Yahuay (Jones 1990: tables 7.1, 7.2) may indicate that, as at Locumbilla, the Dominican friars were producing medicines and soap.

NOTES

1. In 1481 the pope decreed that all land south of the Canary Islands belonged to Portugal, but with Christopher Columbus's voyages, the question arose about lands to the north. The 1494 Treaty of Tordesillas was intended to resolve disputes between Spain and Portugal and established that all lands west and south of a meridian 100 leagues west and south of the Azores would belong to Spain. Squabbles prompted by this division continued for more than 250 years.

2. This "right"—on which southwestern Peru's wine industry was partly founded—ultimately became a burdensome obligation in Spain's distant Pacific colonies because of problems of supply and spoilage during the ocean voyages. As a result, Peru and Chile were allowed to produce their own wine and oil but were forbidden to export them.

3. A *visita* is an official inspection tour of Indigenous communities in a region to carry out a census and determine tax assessments.

4. This is a confusing situation that may be a consequence of Spaniards mis-hearing and mis-transcribing early toponyms. Although Suañalay no longer exists as a place name, a small settlement called "Canilay" is located near Torata. "Suañalay" might have been garbled into both Canilay and Zunilata—a reducción community—by substitutions of S, C, and Z and the common "-ata" ending of local toponyms. Oddly, the

document identifying the communities reduced to Torata does not mention Suañalay (Cañedo-Argüelles Fábrega 1995: 130) or "Sualanay above [presumably north of] Yacango" (Pease G. Y. 1985: 155).

5. A drive-through visit in 1988 identified seven bodegas or probable bodegas, to judge from rows of sunken tinajas at three locations and toneles (large wooden container) (and one falca) at two others, all close to the town of Locumba. Grapes were grown in a very small area, with most of the valley planted in ají or pasture. See Davies 1984: 104–15 for discussion of land fragmentation in the Arequipa area.

6. The wooden screws of a beam-and-screw press were noted at only a few sites: La Banda, Yaravico Bajo, Yaravico Viejo, Calaluna 1, Garbanzal, Corpanto Ghersi, Testamento, and Santa Ana.

7. Fermentation bodegas at twenty-eight sites had "internal lagars" (called *preparadoras*) excavated into the floors, but I was unable to ascertain their specific function.

8. The Roman writer Cato's attention to viticultural practices included directions for pitching the interior and exterior of wine jars (*dolia*), cleaning their mouths to prevent contamination, and preparing a plaster of resin, wax, sulfur, and pulverized gypsum to repair cracks in the jars (see Younger 1966: 180).

9. This toponym is also seen as Estopacaja and Estopacaxes, perhaps reflecting a place once occupied by Pacajes from the southern Titicaca basin.

10. These totals exclude most of the units excavated in the kiln area, except for four in 1987, which have been reported elsewhere (Rice 1994).

11. A hacienda in the Vitor valley, just north of the city of Arequipa, has seventy-two tinajas with inscribed dates of 1590 (Quiroz Neyra 2006: 174).

7

Encomiendas in Moquegua

> What were granted in encomienda were not territories or even Indians in the strict sense, but kurakas.[1]
> —Efraín Trelles Aréstegui
> (1982: 158)

Spanish colonization of the Andean landscape was implemented through the institution of encomienda, grants of Indigenous populations awarded to individual conquerors. These awards began to be made as Francisco Pizarro and his men crossed the northern Peruvian desert and were later implemented with conquest of the south, quickly reaching the Arequipa/Moquegua area. Although the Indigenous town of Moquegua was known to early Spaniards such as Diego de Almagro, who followed an existing road through the southwestern region on his return to Cusco from Chile in 1537, this community and the middle Moquegua valley itself apparently never constituted a distinct, named encomienda.[2] This might be because it was part of Cochuna or, more likely, because its Lupaqa settlers were so closely identified with Chucuito.

ENCOMIENDAS IN PERU

In Peru, the earliest encomiendas were assigned by local governors, beginning with Pizarro, rather than by the Spanish crown because the expeditions of exploration and conquest were financed by private citizens. After 1543, however, with the first encomenderos having been killed in uprisings and Peru having become a viceroyalty, the viceroy, as crown agent, redistributed them. In awarding encomiendas, one goal of the Spanish monarchy was to provide inducements for

DOI: 10.5876/9781607322764.c07

Spaniards to colonize the new lands and make them productive for the homeland. A second crown (and papal) goal was evangelization. By accepting an encomienda, the grantee assumed extensive obligations, set out in the Laws of Burgos in 1512 (Bakewell 2011), for indoctrinating the natives in the Catholic faith. Duties included building a church, maintaining priests, and attending services with their tributaries. The priests fulfilled the encomenderos' responsibilities for confession, baptism, catechistic (e.g., the Ten Commandments, Seven Deadly Sins) and moral (wearing clothing; not having multiple wives) instruction, and testing the tributaries on their religious knowledge. Not all encomenderos complied with these responsibilities, particularly if their encomendees lived some distance from major Spanish towns. Besides, the goal of the encomenderos, like that of later settlers, was decidedly material rather than spiritual: to get rich.

Encomienda awards varied in size and value depending on the recipient's financial investment, length of service and loyalty to the crown, and bravery in the enterprise of exploration. As a result, they were simultaneously sources and reflections of social, economic, and political power among their holders. They were also sources of conflict, as encomenderos' power was viewed as a threat to the crown and resented by later settlers who lacked these tickets to wealth. In response, the "New Laws of the Indies" were promulgated in 1542 to reiterate the principles of Burgos, as well as to limit encomenderos' holdings to a single lifetime, forbid the creation of new encomiendas, and prohibit the slavery of Indigenous peoples. These stipulations precipitated an encomendero revolt in Peru, and the New Laws were never implemented.

As the epigraph suggests, the key figure in an encomienda was the kuraka(s), for these local leaders ultimately controlled production of goods and services, often by ayllu members who lived at some distance. For example, in 1572 the kuraka of hanansaya Chucuito, Martín Cari, claimed to have twenty-five retainers in Moquegua to plant maize (Julien 1985: 201). Although encomiendas were formally population units, for most purposes they were effectively spatial: roughly coterminous with the ill-defined spatial limits of a particular ayllu, its agricultural lands and other resources, and, ideally, Indigenous ethno-political districts. In the Inka heartland and perhaps elsewhere in the Andes, the earliest encomienda populations may have been delimited on the basis of official boundary markers, or mojones, drawn by the amojonadores (Julien 1983: 28; cf. Ramírez 2005: 36–37). If so, this Inka practice conferred upon these markers significant agency (sensu Latour 2005) in defining community politico-economic relations that lasted into the next imperial regime: that of the Spaniards.

Throughout the provinces, discontinuous settlement patterns and multi-ethnicity made it difficult for the Spaniards to avoid conflict among the encomenderos themselves as well as vis-à-vis their tributary populations. Nevertheless, despite—or perhaps because of—the imprecision of spatial boundaries, encomenderos also claimed whatever resources, agricultural or mineral, their populations exploited. In the mineral-rich southern Andes, these resources represented significant wealth. Gradually, as the Spanish population swelled through in-migration and the Indigenous population declined because of introduced diseases and abusive labor demands, a cash-based capitalist economy began to dominate Peru. Native lands were increasingly sold, usurped, or passed into the hands of the Spaniards through other means. Encomenderos and their descendants constituted the first hereditary elite class.

Unlike the heavily populated sierra and coast of northern and central Peru, the southwestern region lacked large, late, pre-Hispanic centers of population. Instead, the narrow valleys of the watershed were occupied by small groups of agricultural colonists from the larger, wealthy señoríos in the altiplano. The existence of only small, scattered Indigenous populations meant that encomiendas in this area were less attractive than they were elsewhere. Perhaps in acknowledgment, Francisco Pizarro recruited Spanish settlers for the southwestern region from among his "less distinguished" followers, expecting that "few very important people" would want to give up their lives in urban Cusco or Lima to live in this relatively empty frontier (Davies 1984: 14).

Juan Pizarro began to award encomiendas in the southwest in August 1535. It is not clear how the region's villages had come to be known, but such knowledge likely originated in census data provided to the Spaniards by the Inkas in Cusco through their provincial Aymara allies in Chucuito. In early 1534 Francisco Pizarro sent an expedition from Cusco to explore the Collao and adjacent regions for forty days (Petersen 2010: 41), a foray that seems to have reached Moquegua. In 1535 Diego de Almagro began an arduous trip south from Cusco to Nuevo Toledo (Chile), where he had been granted governorship. Foolishly taking the altiplano road southward, he returned in 1537 by the coastal route through the Atacama Desert, traveling through Turacapa (Tarapacá) and Tacana (Tacna) before continuing northward along the road toward Arequipa (Cavagnaro Orellana 1986: 119–20; Hyslop 1984: 153; Oviedo y Valdés 1959: V: 149). In his journey he passed through Moquegua, including "los pueblos de Moquiguaya y Araguaya e Quinoaestaca e Umati e Sana" (Oviedo y Valdés 1959: V: 150), confirming the existence of a known travelway in at least part of the valley.

The largest and broadest swaths of agricultural land in the southwestern region lie in Arequipa and Tacna, and Francisco Pizarro gave the Andeans in these valleys to his cousin Pedro in 1538. In 1540 he declared the wealthy Lupaqa kingdom of Chucuito, on the west side of Lake Titicaca, a crown *repartimiento*, or share (Julien 1983: 17). At the same time, Pizarro awarded between ten and sixteen encomiendas in the upper reaches of the Río Tambo and Osmore drainages to those who had served him in Cajamarca, Cusco, and in the early settlement at Camaná, near the mouth of the Río Majes. Those awardees also received plots of urban land to build residences in the newly founded town of Arequipa and cultivable terrain along the adjacent Río Chili.

The new encomenderos in the southwest directed their Andean laborers to plant Iberian crops, particularly grapevines, wheat, and stone fruits, alongside the traditional maize (corn), coca, and ají peppers. Spaniards in Moquegua appropriated the Indigenous irrigation canal system to water their fields and, to the dismay of the native inhabitants, violated the schedule of water rights said to have been established by the Inka (Diez de San Miguel 1964: 247).[3] The products of the encomiendas were typically tribute items. By 1548 the encomendees in Carumas, Ilo, Arica, and Tarapacá were paying taxes and tribute in a mix of Indigenous and introduced items: cotton and wool cloth and thread, coca, maize, wheat, beans, ají, birds (chickens), eggs, pigs, livestock, seal skins, jars (100 *cántaros* from Tarapacá), salt, salted fish, and sandals, as well as personal service such as watching cattle (Trelles Aréstegui 1978: 34).[4]

Of the thirty-four early encomenderos Pizarro named in the southwest, most died as a result of participation in the civil wars and other turmoil in the early viceroyalty. Only ten survived a decade, and only five of the holdings passed to a second generation (Davies 1984: 70). As a result, the region's encomiendas were frequently reassigned by the viceroys and then reassigned again on the basis of political loyalties and disputes about ownership. In Arequipa as in other early Spanish towns, encomenderos became *vecinos*—wealthy, propertied, and influential citizens who could vote and hold municipal office. Two such encomenderos were Hernán Bueno and Lucas Martínez Vegaso.

THE BUENOS AND CARUMAS

The Buenos in Moquegua

Captain Hernán (or Fernán) Bueno *el viejo* (elder, senior) was the patriarch of a petty dynasty in Moquegua (Boyd-Bowman 1968: 60, 62; Cúneo-Vidal 1978: 90, 183; Martínez 1936: 342–53; Miró Quesada Sosa 1982: 86–87; Rice 2011b: 101–5). Hernán was one of three Buenos in Peru in the 1530s; the other two were sailors Juan and Martín.[5] Juan operated between Panama and Peru and was living in Lima in 1537 (Boyd-Bowman 1968: 155). Hernán's brother Martín, from Peñafiel, Valladolid, was a ship master and one of the "Men of Cajamarca" (del Busto Duthurburu 1981: 259–64; Cúneo-Vidal 1978: 75, 88; Lockhart 1972: 99). He accompanied Pizarro from Cajamarca to Cusco and participated in the 1534 expedition from Cusco to the Lake Titicaca region. During his explorations, Martín Bueno discovered the area of Carumas, also known as the "valley of Catari" (its kuraka), in the sierras of what is now Moquegua. In 1535 or 1536 he may have returned to Spain a wealthy man from his share of the spoils of Atahualpa's ransom (del Busto Duthurburu 1981: 259–64; also Boyd-Bowman 1968: 155–56) and, one might speculate, an encomienda in Carumas. He apparently returned to Peru and died in 1538 in the Battle of Salinas, fighting on Pizarro's side against the almagrist rebellion (Cúneo-Vidal 1978: 88).

Hernán Bueno, like his brother, was a native of Peñafiel. He married Beatriz García—her surname is variously given as Zea y Pareja and Gascón—of Aranda de Duero, Burgos. Their son, Hernán (Fernán) Bueno y García (or Zea), known as *el mozo* (younger, junior), was born in Aranda, probably around 1525. It is not clear if Hernán viejo's wife and son traveled with him to Peru or if he sent for them after he was settled in Arequipa, although it is claimed that Bueno senior came to Peru "with his son, and he fought in the most bloody combats, and also took part in the principal revolts between the conquerors" (Alastaya n.d.: n.p.; cf. Cúneo-Vidal 1978: 90). The elder Bueno was one of the earliest settlers in Arequipa in 1539 (Fernández Dávila 1947: 121), where he owned a substantial residence in center city at the corner of Calle Mercaderes. In 1542 he was awarded an encomienda in Carumas by Governor Cristóbal Vaca de Castro. The late date of this award suggests that Bueno viejo arrived in Peru after the conquest was largely finished, perhaps accompanying his brother Martín on his return from Spain, and received what was once his Carumas encomienda. Hernán Bueno viejo was killed on October 20, 1547, in the Battle of Huarina, fighting on the royalist side in the violence accompanying the rebellions against Gonzalo Pizarro.

Like his father, Hernán Bueno y García (Bueno mozo) was allied with the royalists against Gonzalo Pizarro, who removed his encomiendas and persecuted the Buenos with "unspeakable rigor" (Cúneo-Vidal 1978: 89). In 1548, however, the year after Bueno viejo's death, Governor Pedro la Gasca awarded the Carumas encomienda to his son, the award confirmed in 1557 by Viceroy Hurtado de Mendoza. In Arequipa, Bueno mozo was recognized as a vecino and inherited the houses of his parents. In 1560 he married doña Jerónima Cárdenas y Carabantes y Arana, daughter of the conquistador don Fernándo Cárdenas y Zapata of Madrid and doña María Catalina de Carabantes y Arana of Soria (Cúneo-Vidal 1978: 89, 109–12; Martínez 1936: 344).[6]

Bueno mozo maintained property and a high social and political profile in Arequipa, serving as *alcalde* (mayor) in 1566, 1570, and 1576. In Moquegua he had an urban home ("*su propia casa habitual de vivienda*") and was identified as a *residente* of Escapalac. He was also a heredado with substantial landholdings in the valley (presumably the lands cultivated by his tributary Carumeños), including a country home ("*al lado del rio, era de campo*") in what appears to have been a vast estate of Yaravico in the confluence zone (Miró Quesada Sosa 1980: 16). Doña Jerónima died before 1588. Bueno mozo's will (GGR1) is dated May 9, 1596; he died three days later, on May 12, 1596, in Moquegua. According to his wishes, his remains were buried in the church of Santo Domingo in Arequipa, on the left side of the chapel that he, his wife, and his in-laws had built (Alastaya n.d.).

Bueno mozo and doña Jerónima had seven children born in Arequipa, three sons and four daughters. The oldest son, Hernán Bueno de Arana—the third-generation Hernán Bueno—was prominent in Moquegua's affairs. He married doña Mariana de Saavedra y Vasco, daughter of Juan Vasco and doña Beatríz de Saavedra.[7] The couple had nine children, three of whom married into the prominent Mazuelo and Montalvo families, surnames that continued to be associated with bodegas in the Moquegua valley in the late twentieth century. One daughter, doña Beatriz Bueno de Arana, married don Diego de Vizcarra y Estrada, "a knight who belonged to an ancient lineage of Vizcaya (Biscay)" and was corregidor (provincial governor) of Moquegua in 1582 (Alastaya n.d.: n.p.). They had two children, Alonso and Isabel, who were effectively orphaned at a young age when their father, Diego, died and their mother, Beatriz, joined a nunnery in Arequipa.

The orphans were raised by Beatriz's sister, doña Jerónima de Miranda Bueno de Arana, and her husband, Alonso de Estrada, who was Diego de Vizcarra's brother (i.e., the Vizcarra de Estrada brothers married Bueno sisters). When nephew Alonso de Vizcarra married in 1605, the Estradas gave him land known as Locumbilla. At that time, I surmise, Locumbilla comprised the southern part of the Yaravico toponymic zone. Their niece, doña Isabel de Vizcarra y Bueno de Arana, married don Diego Fernández Maldonado, offspring of a union between the Fernández and Maldonado families of Salamanca, who held a patent of nobility signed by Kings Ferdinand and Isabel in 1518. Fernández Maldonado moved to Moquegua in 1585. At the time doña Isabel married, her dowry included 500 pesos worth of land (Guíbovich P. 1984: 244–45), which documentary evidence suggests was just south of her brother's parcel in Locumbilla.

TABLE 7.1 Sixteenth-century population of Carumas

	Year	Kuraka	Tributaries	Total Pop.
Hanansaya?	1540	Catari	249	
	1571–73		415	
	????		199	975
Hurinsaya?		Diego Catari		
	????		216	1121

Source: Julien 1985: tables 9.3 and 9.4.

THE CARUMAS ENCOMIENDA

The modern town of Carumas lies 50 km (31 mi) north of the present city of Moquegua at an elevation of 2,985 m (9,793 ft) on the Río Carumas, a southern tributary of the Río Tambo. In the early sixteenth century, Carumas consisted of two Lupaqa communities, doubtless representing two moieties, both under Chucuito in the altiplano. One, headed by the kuraka Catari el viejo, was the upper, or hanansaya (*alaasaa*), moiety; the other, under Catari's son Diego, was the lower, or hurinsaya, moiety (table 7.1; Trelles Aréstegui 1982: 23, 141–42).

The Carumas moieties have a complex history in encomienda. In 1535 Juan Pizarro awarded both Carumas communities to Lucas Martínez Vegaso, a fellow native of Trujillo in Spain (Trelles Aréstegui 1982: 23, 141–42). This raises the possibility that Martínez accompanied Martín Bueno in his discovery of Carumas, and the encomienda was assigned to him with the knowledge that Bueno was returning to Spain. Later, the two Carumas encomiendas were removed from Martínez and given to Gómez de Tordoya Várgas, a native of Badajoz who had come to Peru with Pedro Alvarado and was a founding citizen of Cusco and Arequipa (Martínez 1936: 154–58). In 1542, however, following the deaths of both Pizarro and Tordoya in the Battle of Chupas, the encomienda was divided and awarded yet again: Governor Vaca de Castro gave the people of Catari el viejo to Hernándo de Silva and those of Diego Catari to Hernán Bueno viejo, rewarding both for their service to the crown (Trelles Aréstegui 1982: 164; also Barriga 1955: 28–30, 211; Julien 1985: table 9.1; Kuon Cabello 1981: 34, 46). Martínez disputed the assignment to Silva, however, and eventually the governor returned the Catari moiety to him.

At some point after the Carumas encomienda was awarded, Bueno viejo (likely accompanied by his son, Bueno mozo), Hernán Rodríguez de Huelva, Pedro Cansino, Juan de Castro, and other Arequipeños ventured into the Osmore drainage and established themselves on the high north (right) bank of the lower Río Tumilaca. They founded a community they called San Sebastián in an area known as Escapagua, believed to lie in the general vicinity of the modern airport and tourist hotel. At the time, the Moquegua valley was lightly occupied by Aymara-speaking agricultural colonists of several ethno-political affiliations from the Lake Titicaca basin high in the altiplano. The extended Bueno family's vast lands in the rich soils of the upper mid-valley, accessed by means of their Carumas encomienda, constituted a singular capital resource that catapulted them to wealth by the early seventeenth century.

The precise boundaries of the Carumas' lands in the Moquegua valley are not well-known, particularly as they relate to the moieties and encomiendas. Nonetheless, their toponyms continue to exist and, at least in the middle valley, are roughly coterminous with toponymic zones. Documentary references suggest the Carumas claimed large areas of the upper valley, including places still known as Samegua, Estuquiña, Huaracane, and Yaracachi (Galdos Rodríguez 1985: 31–33; Julien 1985: 198). Yaracachi lies just north of Yaravico.

The Carumas' extensive holdings in Omo were described as bordered on the south by lands belonging to the Carumas encomiendas of Hernán Bueno and María de Avalos (María Dávalos) (GGR1 f. 355). This suggests that these Carumas natives were of the lower moiety initially awarded to Bueno, whereas those of María Dávalos were part of the upper moiety encomienda retained by Lucas Martínez Vegaso, which became hers after their marriage and his death. The mojon (boundary marker) in Omo that established the northern boundary of Carumas lands and later separated those lands from "the [colonial] jurisdictions of Moquegua and Arica" (ADM 10) likely referred to these southern Carumas holdings.

LUCAS MARTÍNEZ VEGASO AND COCHUNA

Lucas Martínez Vegaso was a participant in the Peruvian conquest, and his encomienda awards plus astute business acumen made him an enormously wealthy and powerful vecino in colonial southwestern Peru in the sixteenth century. He is the subject of a biography by Efraín Trelles Aréstegui (1982; unless otherwise specified, the page citations in this section refer to this source).

Of legitimate birth in Trujillo around 1511, Martínez was fully literate, sailed to Panama in 1530, and was recruited the following year by Francisco Pizarro as a foot soldier in the Peru expedition (13–15). He was one of the men of Cajamarca (Lockhart 1972: 300–305) and used the 3,330 gold pesos that were his share of the reward to buy two horses (18). In 1533, after the fall of Cusco, Martínez was rewarded with another 2,000 gold pesos, 1,517 silver pesos, and textiles (23).

His literacy and wealth underwrote an early business career in trade, and he established a foundry for precious metals (24). Martínez left Cusco as part of Pizarro's plan to settle in Arequipa, lured by the promise of a large encomienda—a promise that was amply fulfilled with awards of several coastal communities. Martinez's encomiendas have complex histories of being withdrawn and bestowed upon other participants in the conquest and internal fighting and then returned to him after lengthy petitioning.

In 1535 Juan Pizarro gave Martínez a generous encomienda that included coastal groups plus the sierra communities of Carumas and Ubinas in the upper Río Tambo drainage (23, 141–42). Carumas and Ubinas were among the most valuable encomiendas in the far southwest because of their relatively large populations. The coastal encomienda, extending from the Río Osmore south to Tarapacá in Chile, might seem on first glance to have been undesirable, for although it included a large number of native tributaries, they were extremely scattered. But under Martínez's management the encomienda became hugely lucrative because of its mineral resources—the Huantajaya and Tarapacá silver mines (Zori and Tropper 2010)—and potential in various shipping enterprises: Martínez established the port of Arica and was instrumental in providing emergency supplies to Pedro de Valdivia's forces in the conquest of Chile (Cúneo-Vidal 1978: 277–78).

In 1540, as the southwestern region was beginning to be occupied by Spaniards, Francisco Pizarro granted numerous encomiendas in the upper tributaries of the Ríos Tambo and Osmore, centered on communities along the Inka road between Arequipa and Moquegua. As part of these assignments, Pizarro reaffirmed Martinez's coastal encomienda but removed Ubinas (30). At the time, Ubinas, also known by the variant spelling "Ovina," was a common term used by the Spaniards to refer to much of the upper Tambo and Osmore drainages. Ovina/Ubinas comprised twenty-one small, Indigenous communities with more than a thousand tributaries (Barriga 1955: 21–22; Julien 1985: table 9.1).

In reaffirming Martinez's coastal encomienda, Pizarro included ninety-four Andeans called "Cochumas" (Cavagnaro Orellana 1988: 101), who apparently were part of a large parcialidad (moiety) within Ovina/Ubinas under a "cacique Cochuna" (see table 5.1). This parcialidad held 692 tributaries in 13 pueblos (Cúneo-Vidal 1978: 25, cited in Cavagnaro Orellana 1988: 101), three of which were Sibaha, Camata, and Tarata (Barriga 1955: 21). These toponyms recall the archaeological sites known as Sabaya, Camata, and Torata (Alta) in the Torata valley, and this 1540 document—apparently awarding Cochuna in encomienda—seems to be the earliest Spanish mention of a settlement called Torata in the Osmore region.

In 1542, 125 of Martínez's Cochuna tributaries were given to Hernando de Silva by Peruvian governor Vaca de Castro, who also divided the Carumas encomienda in two (the lower moiety going to Hernán Bueno viejo). The Cochunas were said to be Qolla colonists (mitimaes) in two pueblos, Suhubaya (i.e., Sabaya)[8] and Capavaya (Capanto? Camata?) (ibid.: 29; Julien 1985: table 9.1; Málaga Medina 1975: 78; Martínez 1936: 145). The lack of mention of Torata in this award is of interest because its settlers—like those of "Moquehua"—were Lupaqas affiliated with Chucuito, which Pizarro had distinguished as a crown property. It thus appears that Torata (and Moquegua?) were no longer part of the Cochuna component of the Ubinas encomienda. In any case, Martínez claimed the Cochuna tributaries were his, and Vaca de Castro eventually returned them to him.

Martínez proceeded to pursue some shrewd trades, swapping encomiendas to consolidate his coastal holdings. For example, he made a deal with Silva to reacquire the latter's tributaries in Cochuna; in exchange, Silva was given Martínez's encomienda in Yuminas near Arequipa (166n27). Martínez then gave his newly acquired Cochunas as dowry to Isabel Palla/Yupanqui, said to be the sister of a kuraka Tix in Nasca, who gave her to Martínez (166–67; Altman 1989: 228). He supposedly raised her as a daughter, but it was widely assumed that she was Martínez's mistress. Described as the "*cacica de los indios Cochunas de Moquegua*" (Cúneo-Vidal 1978: 214), Isabel brought the Cochuna tributaries as part of her dowry in 1544, when she married the Spaniard Martín Pérez de Villabona, a residente in Moquegua-Cochuna (Cavagnaro Orellana 1988: 82). Martínez likely arranged and subsidized their union (Lockhart 1972: 302; Marchena Fernández 1992: 350), in much the same way Sebastián Garcilasso arranged a marriage for his Isabel Chimpu Ocllo in Cusco. A vecina of Arequipa, Isabel found that when her husband died he had somehow "neglected" to return this property to her in his will, and in 1551 she took legal recourse to demand restitution (167). At Isabel's death, Cochuna reverted once again to Martínez.[9]

In 1559 Martínez made another trade, this time with Juan de Castro. Castro was encomendero of Socobaya and Pica, the former near Arequipa and the latter on the Chilean coast. Martínez gave his Cochuna tributaries to Castro in exchange for Pica, thereby further enlarging his coastal holdings (170). And the Qollas in Moquegua came to be part of the encomienda of Juan de San Juan (Julien 1985: 224n14), which might explain the recovery of European artifacts at Sabaya.

Martínez died in Lima in 1567, shortly after having married doña María Dávalos de Ribera, daughter of Nicolás de Ribera, an immensely influential conquistador by virtue of being one of Pizarro's "Gallo Thirteen." María inherited all his property, including Carumas-worked landholdings in the Moquegua valley.

DISCUSSION

The stories of encomenderos Hernán Bueno viejo and Lucas Martínez Vegaso illustrate two very different paths to immigrant success in the early post-conquest frontier of southwestern Peru. They exemplify distinct, and distinctly capitalist, strategies of identifying and exploiting new spaces and places, along with the people occupying them.

Martínez, one of the original participants in the early stages of conquest, profited from his literacy and sharp business sense. For example, he invested his share of the liquid assets (gold and silver) from the conquest of Cajamarca and Cusco in capital resources for further success: first buying horses and establishing a foundry, and then shrewdly litigating and trading ("flipping," in modern parlance) his encomiendas in a strategy aimed at maximizing profit from coastal mineral and shipping enterprises. He had no legitimate children.

Bueno viejo, who was not among the initial conquistadors, and his son Bueno mozo pursued a different trajectory that was clearly agrarian-capitalist in its goals but rooted in traditional Iberian patterns of familial social advancement. Bueno viejo's initial good fortune was a consequence of well-placed relatives (brother Martín) and access to the Carumas encomienda, augmented by entrepreneurial talents and accumulating the knowledge necessary to profit from the kinds of opportunities and uncertainties frontier situations presented. The Bueno family's multi-pronged strategy included (1) expanding out from an urban base in Arequipa to accumulate substantial productive agricultural lands in the Osmore valley; (2) arranging strategic marriages, especially into immigrant families of higher status and political power, to create a small, locally powerful familial dynasty; (3) subdividing valley landholdings among heirs; and (4) building business opportunities through commodity (wine and sugar) production and trade.

The Bueno descendants benefited dramatically from the peculiar social and economic circumstances of the early southwestern region. The wealth accumulated from these first- and second-generation endeavors permitted their children's and grandchildren's strategic marriages into distinguished families of conquistadors or Spanish peninsulares immigrating to Peru—for example, the Fernandez de Córdoba family[10] (Rice 2011b: 288n7; Zavala Oyague 1946: 41–45), thereby further enhancing the family's regional status.

NOTES

1. My translation. The original reads: "lo que se encomendaba no eran territorios, ni siquiera indios en sentido estricto, sino curacas."

2. The question of an encomienda in Moquegua, like the related issue of an encomienda in Cochuna, is problematic because of imprecise Spanish toponymy and orthography and the complex relations of Lupaqa settlers in the Osmore drainage to the crown encomienda of Chucuito. A Diego García of Cáceres (1513–86), who participated in the conquest of Chile with Valdivia in 1540, is mentioned in one source as having an encomienda in Moquegua (Boyd-Bowman 1968: 79), but this is doubtful.

3. The longstanding Indigenous irrigation regime calls up the idea of "landesque capital," which refers to investments in "landscape infrastructure" that allow "labor to be environmentally banked" (Fisher and Feinman 2005: 64, citing Brookfield). These investments increase productivity and sustainability as long as labor inputs can be maintained—a problem in situations of demographic decline.

4. In the 1570s Viceroy Toledo introduced payment of silver pesos for tribute and lowered other requirements (Trelles Aréstegui 1978: 35).

5. Several "Martín Buenos" appear in conquest records.

6. Another story calls her the daughter of Hernán Velásquez (or Blazquez) Dávila, of Avila, and doña Catalina de Arana, born in Santo Domingo (Fernández Dávila 1947: 121).

7. Doña Beatríz may have been the daughter of Captain Juan de Saavedra (d. 1554), who accompanied Almagro on his journey through the southern Andes. In Spain from 1439 on, the Saavedra lineage had controlled a border patrol oversight office for ransoming Christian captives in Granada (López de Coca Castañer 1989: 140). Juan de Saavedra was taken prisoner in the war of Río Verde (1448), and his story is celebrated in a famous ballad (ibid.: 135n21, 137). In 1564 another Juan de Saavedra (a relative?) was briefly president of the Lima audiencia.

8. A tiny modern community of Sujabaya exists beside a small pocket of cultivable bottomland in the Tumilaca valley, east of Cerro Baúl, but it does not appear to be associated with an LIP or LH archaeological site.

9. Another version of the story holds that Isabel died a year after her marriage and Pérez held the encomienda for a few more years until, presumably at his death, it reverted once again to Martínez.

10. Diego Fernández de Córdova y Aguilar, who married Clara Bueno, was the scion of a prominent Andalucían family with ancestry traceable back to the thirteenth century (Zavala Oyague 1946: 41–45). He is said to have had an encomienda in "Cochuna" (ibid.: 41), likely in the Torata valley in the confluence zone.

8

Torata Alta

From Inka Administrative Center to Spanish Congregación

> To be able to live up to their hospitality and display obligations the [Andean] kings needed vast quantities of food, beer and wool . . . which they distributed to "their" cultivators, wives, soldiers and peers. The king would increase his power by extending his network of "mutual" obligations to new wives, new weavers, more herders.
> —John Murra (1968: 130)

By the early 1570s, the Indigenous communities of Torata and Moquegua were greatly diminished, while Spanish occupation of the confluence zone of the Osmore's tributaries was expanding. For the Spaniards, moving small groups of natives out of the Moquegua valley and sequestering them in a separate settlement was not only a convenience for administrative order but also an expedient mechanism to free up lands for increasing numbers of emigrants from Arequipa. Thus the Inka-Lupaqa community of Torata Alta became a Spanish resettlement of local Indigenous groups. Here I review archaeological and documentary data pertaining to the occupation of Torata Alta for less than two centuries as a Spanish-colonial administrative center (see Rice 2012).

REDUCCIÓN IN MOQUEGUA

The Spanish policy of reducción was implemented in southwestern Peru, as elsewhere in the colonies, by gathering the populations of small Indigenous communities into larger towns called *reducciónes de indios* or *congegaciónes*. These towns, either newly built or preexisting communities appropriated for the purpose, were not that

DOI: 10.5876/9781607322764.c08

different in some senses from the imperial resettlements of the Inkas, and they allowed the Spaniards to force the natives to adhere to Spanish ideas of civilized, Christian spatial order.

In Moquegua, reductions were structured by a 1567 visita (see chapter 6, note 3) in the Moquegua-Chucuito region undertaken by a Spanish official, Garci Diez de San Miguel. Diez (1964: 223) commented that 280 pueblos in three colonial provinces, including Moquegua, could be reduced to 58, although he did not name specific towns. In the early 1570s, 226 small communities in Moquegua and Arica were reduced to 22 (Cavagnaro Orellana 1988: 140; Vargas Ugarte 1949: 243). Eleven named sites are known in Arica (now northern Chile), including San Pedro de Tacna (Cavagnaro Orellana 1988: 140–44) and San Lorenzo de Tarapacá, the latter one of four in Martínez Vegaso's former encomienda (Zori 2011: 236). Archaeological investigations at the Tarapacá Viejo site did not reveal the presence of a church (Núñez Henríquez 1984), but perhaps it was dismantled (Zori 2011).

If these Indigenous settlements were actually reduced to 22, with 11 in Arica, the remaining 11 were likely in Moquegua. Unfortunately, few reductions are known there through documents: the populations of Carumas (presumably its two moieties) were reduced to the towns of San Cristóbal de Saro and San Felipe de Coata, and the community of Pocsi, closer to Arequipa, became San Francisco de Pocsi (Málaga Medina 1975: 76, 78). Some of the residents of Cochuna were resettled in the village of San Mateo de Zunilata (Tumilaca? Málaga Medina 1972: 398); those of Puquina were reduced to two towns, San Bernardo and San Salvador de Puquina; and Ubinas was reduced to San Felipe (Levillier 1929).

Recent archival studies, however, have clarified that a place called Torata in the Osmore drainage—more specifically in Cochuna—was a colonial administrative center of congregación (Cañedo-Argüelles Fábrega 1995: 130). According to documents, the reduced communities included "Yacango, Tumilaca, Pocata, Chuquisquea, Otora, Queli, and Iluvaia" (ibid.). Yacango is the current name of an archaeological site and a small community south of Torata on the river's east bank. Tumilaca, possibly a continued occupation of the Late Intermediate Period (LIP) site, and Pocata are located on the Río Capillune, just east of its join with the Río Coscori (both tributaries of the Tumilaca). Otora is an upper tributary of the Río Huaracane, where eight sites have evidence of Late Horizon occupation (Stanish 1992: 136–56). Chuquisquea is doubtless Chuqusquea, just below the site of Camata on the left bank of the Río Torata, and Queli (possibly Quellaveco) lies 14 km beyond. Chuqusquea and Queli, in the modern district of Torata, were associated with early-twentieth-century copper mining (Kuon Cabello 1981:

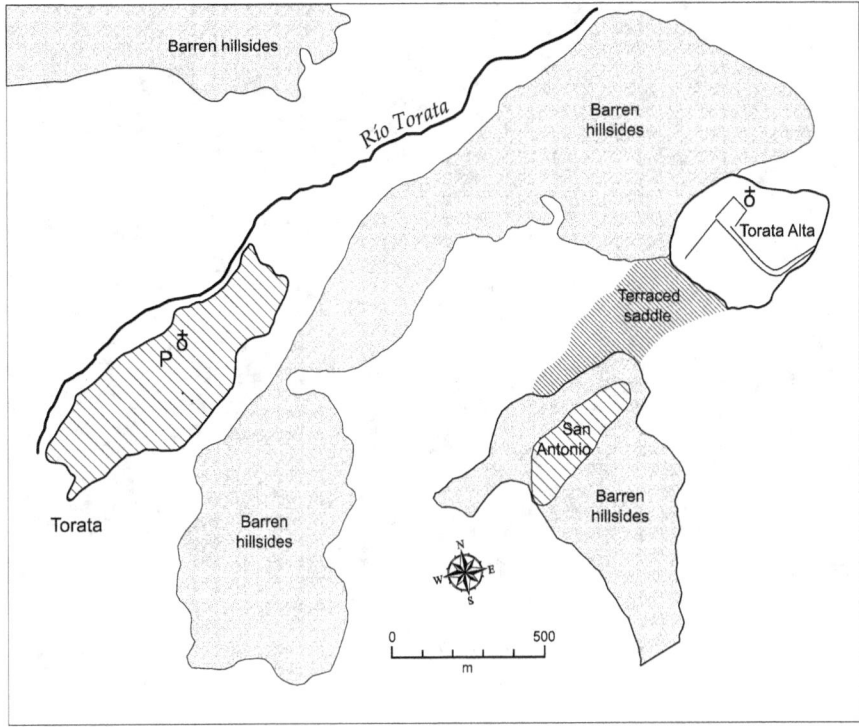

FIGURE 8.1 *Location of the ridge-top sites of San Antonio and Torata Alta and the modern community of Torata in river bottomland.*

396–400) and were joined by a "bad road with many dangers and cliffs" (Cañedo-Argüelles Fábrega 1995: 130). Ilubaya was a community across the Río Torata from Torata Alta, at the same elevation (Van Buren, Bürgi, and Rice 1993: 137).

TORATA ALTA: LAYOUT AND STRUCTURES

The history of Torata begins with Garcilaso de la Vega's account of Inka conquest in the Osmore drainage and the establishment of new settlements of Lupaqa agricultural colonists from the altiplano (chapter 4). Certain elements of that account are corroborated by evidence from the archaeological site of Torata Alta. Torata Alta (17° 4'S; 70° 49'W) occupies a hilltop, perhaps artificially leveled,[1] on the same ridge as the LIP fortified site of San Antonio (figures 8.1, 8.2) but about 400 m to the northeast and at a slightly higher elevation (2,600 m). Spatially ordered by an orthogonal grid of streets defining two

FIGURE 8.2 *The Torata valley, looking west-southwest: Torata Alta lies in the right-center and San Antonio in the left-center. Note heavily terraced modern fields in the foreground and barren mountains in the background. Photo by the author.*

dozen rectangular, walled room blocks or compounds (kanchas)[2], Torata Alta (figure 8.3) occupies approximately 7–8 ha. More structures likely existed on the northeast and east, but at the time of Bodegas Project fieldwork these areas were occupied by agricultural terraces and modern squatters, the latter vainly hoping to build new, permanent housing. The site has been badly damaged by recent activities, particularly the cutting of irrigation canals on the northeastern and southwestern margins.

Fieldwork

Bodegas Project fieldwork at Torata Alta was organized by kancha. Selection of kanchas, their subdivisions (quads), and individual structures for further investigation was purposive in some cases and randomized (by drawing numbers out of a hat) in others. Structures and quads were surface-collected in sixteen compounds; the others (Kanchas 4, 5, 6, 11, 14, 17, 18, 19, 24, 25) were not collected because of extensive disturbance or lack of time. Strs. 137, 138, 140, 156, 161, and 268 were purposively selected for excavation.

TABLE 8.1 Approximate chronology of Torata Alta[a]

Period	Dates
Inka-Lupaqa	~1450/1475–~1535
Contact	~1535–~72
Early Reducción	~1572–1600
Late Reducción	1600–~20

a The only absolutely certain date in this chronological approximation is that of the February 19, 1600, eruption of Huaynaputina volcano.

The stratigraphy at Torata Alta features four or five cultural strata overlying sterile or nearly sterile deposits of two kinds: reddish- to orangey-brown sandy-pebbly material representing exfoliating bedrock and dark brown clay resembling modern cultivated soil, apparently placed to level bedrock (e.g., in Strs. 62 and 64 in Kancha 8, Str. 120 in Kancha 13, and Str. 210 in Kancha 20). Indeed, some structures on the site peripheries may have been constructed over old agricultural fields (Van Buren 1993: 361).

Cultural/construction deposits are typically light grayish-brown clayey-silty strata, sometimes incorporating pebble- through cobble-sized rocks; they may evidence hard packing, trampling, or both. Prepared floors are finer-grade deposits of this material. Construction/occupation episodes were frequently interrupted by domestic hearths and burned areas, rodent nests, animal feces (guinea pig, llama), and constructional decomposition (wall collapse, "melted" mortar, decomposed adobes, organic roofing). The uppermost stratum is a thin aeolian deposit of gray-brown sand. The occupational history of Torata Alta (table 8.1) is anchored by tephrochronology, a layer of ash from the February 1600 eruption of Huaynaputina volcano. Some of Torata Alta's structures partially collapsed during the temblors, and the community was blanketed by a 10-to-12-cm-thick layer of white-to-gray volcanic ash, readily distinguishable in excavations. In some excavation units the ash graded from finer to coarser from top to bottom of the deposit, indicating an extended period of deposition.

SITE PLAN AND ARCHITECTURE

Torata Alta's gridded layout, oriented approximately 41° east of north (measured at its NW corner), is substantially different from that of earlier (LIP) San Antonio (Conrad 1993) but is not uncommon in Inka site planning. The kanchas enclose multiple structures, primarily rectangular in plan, that are usually attached to the compound walls, with their long axes extending into the

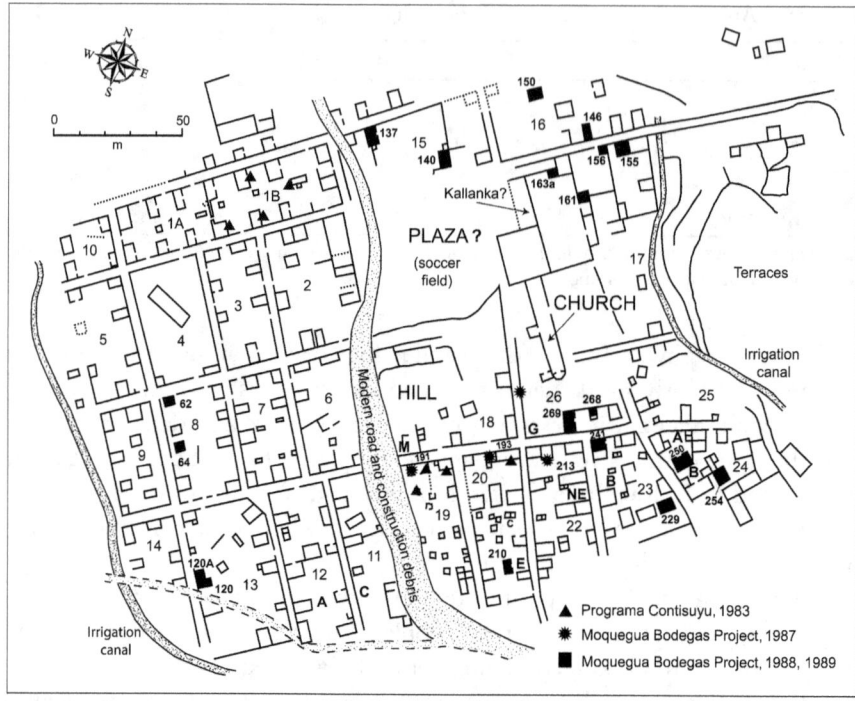

FIGURE 8.3 *The site of Torata Alta, showing numbered kanchas, the church and possible kallanka, and locations of excavated structures (numbered) and trenches (letters). Reprinted by permission from* Latin American Antiquity, *vol. 23, no. 1: figure 2, p. 7. © 2012 Society for American Archaeology.*

open courtyards and their entrances slightly off-center in one of the long walls. Other structures are free-standing. All are of pirca construction: uncut, largely uncoursed and unbonded fieldstone with mud mortar, typically but not invariably two courses wide.

A road bulldozed through the center of Torata Alta may trace an original Inka path (Stanish and Pritzker 1990: 169). An open area near the site center may have been a plaza, but it has been partially bulldozed into a modern soccer field. Plazas in Inka settlements sometimes lie on the peripheries of sites and often correspond to moiety divisions (Gade and Escobar 1982; Hyslop 1990: 201). Aerial photographs suggest the possibility of a smaller plaza at the southeast of Torata Alta, but it has been obliterated by modern settlers.

A possible kallanka, or great hall, sits on the eastern edge of this putative central plaza. Kallankas, which typically open onto plazas, are common at provincial

Inka administrative centers along roads and may have lodged mobile groups, as at tampu (tambos) (Hyslop 1984: 285–86). South of the plaza a bedrock outcrop vaguely recalls the Inka pattern of creating usnu platforms and integrating carved bedrock projections into site planning in or on the edges of conquered territories (Dean 2007: 514; Hyslop 1990: 70–71), but at Torata Alta the rock exhibits no sign of having been worked—perhaps such labor had been deferred. Large, sometimes immense (up to 2.5-m) boulders[3] are strewn throughout the site, in kanchas as well as in the streets, and were frequently incorporated into structure walls. This latter practice, "marrying" the built environment to living rock, is a visible expression of the union of the Inka with Mother Earth (Dean 2007).

Site Sectors

The modern road that crosses Torata Alta separates two architecturally distinct sectors of the site, here identified simply as western and eastern. In the western sector the architecture is relatively formal, with straight streets creating large, open rectangular blocks. Kanchas 1A and 1B are highly standardized, with large structures measuring 8 × 4 m in size and entries opening to the northeast. Four units Programa Contisuyo excavated in Kancha 1B revealed a lack of domestic debris; and doorways, some with jambs of large loaf-shaped stones set on end, were sealed before the 1600 ashfall. The structures in these compounds are believed to have been storage facilities. These two kanchas, plus eight others that are relatively undisturbed (Kanchas 2, 3, 5, 7, 8, 9, 12, 13), hold a total of 80 large buildings (ranging from n = 6–10; mean 8 per block), plus 4 attached and 13 unattached structures.

In the eastern half of Torata Alta the orderly rectangular layout was markedly disrupted. Some disturbance was from modern activity (e.g., a soccer field, irrigation canals, squatter settlement), but other interruptions of the grid are associated with the construction of the reduction church. The northeastern quadrant, east of the "plaza" and the church, lacks the orderly residential compounds and structures found in the west and also small, bin-like storage features. Instead, it is characterized by large buildings and open spaces.

The southeast, by contrast, is crowded with structures of varied sizes and orientations—some irregularly shaped—and heavy constructional debris, sometimes including dressed stones. Kanchas 19 through 24[4] comprise a total of 56 large, presumably residential buildings (range n = 7–14, mean 11.2), 16 small attached structures, and 26 small bins. Those originally mapped as circular *chullpas* were found to be highly variable in plan—some round, some square, some intermediate—and many were looted. The fill of these small buildings included decayed bone as well as potsherds and some shell. In Kancha 23 several structures were looted or almost destroyed, and some were possibly mis-mapped (e.g., Str. 237 might be round rather than square). Colonial materials recovered in surface collections included European majolica and a fragment of porcelain.

Mapping, surface collections, and excavations indicate that different parts of Torata Alta had different kinds of structures. Three categories of structure forms can be identified: large rectangular (sometimes squarish) buildings, some attached to kancha walls and others freestanding, presumed to be primarily residential; small attachments, possibly kitchens or storage bins; and small, unattached structures or bins, suggesting ties to local LIP patterns (e.g., at San Antonio). No round structures, characteristic of LIP settlement in the Titicaca basin, were definitely identified.[5] The internal spaces of nineteen excavated structures fell into four discrete dimensional categories (table 8.2), smaller than those of the Colca valley (Wernke 2006: 195), but they cannot be considered a truly representative sample of size variation at Torata Alta. In the eastern sector of the site, the ratio of small to large buildings is 0.75, meaning that for every four large structures there are three small ones; in the west the ratio is 0.21 (one small per five large). Also, small structures in the east are frequently paired: eight pairs in the five kanchas plus three others, compared with only one pair in the west (in Kancha 12).

These different distributions of structure sizes and shapes likely relate to different functions and relative dates of occupation/use not only of the structures themselves but also of the kanchas. The western and eastern sectors may correspond to occupation by different moieties or to pre- and post-reduction settlement. Or the uniformity of structures in the western sector, especially in Kanchas 1A and 1B, might indicate that they housed administrative activities for the Inka-Lupaqa agricultural colonies in Cochuna: if Torata Alta were the presidio advocated by the conquering Inka soldiers, the barracks-like structures of Kanchas 1A and 1B might have been where they were quartered.

It has long been assumed that at least part of western Torata Alta was abandoned before 1600; the doorways of a few structures in Kancha 1B were closed and sealed,[6] with the seals' bases stratigraphically below the base of the volcanic ash deposit. These structures were interpreted as Inka storerooms (Stanish and Pritzker 1983: 10), sealed around the time of Spanish intrusion. The recovery during surface collecting of rare tin-enameled pottery (e.g., a manganese purple-and-blue-on-white sherd, probably made in Panama), botija fragments, and a large *batan* (grinding stone) suggest the possibility of some continuing post-reduction or post-ashfall activity in this area. However, in general, surface collections and excavations revealed that "European artifacts are rare, middens

TABLE 8.2 Internal area of nineteen excavated structures at Torata Alta

	Kancha	Structure	Length (m)	Width (m)	Area (m^2)
Small (3.0–4.5 m^2)	13	120A	1.85	1.7	3.14
	15	138	2.0	2.0	4.0
	17	156	2.5	1.7	4.25
	26	268	2.0	2.0	4.0
Medium small (9.0–15.0 m^2)	8	62	3.7	2.6	9.6
	8	64	4.1	2.6	10.66
	13	120	5.5	2.7	14.85
	16	146	5.5	2.4	13.2
	16	150	5.0	2.5	12.5
	20	210	4.1	2.8	11.48
	23	241	3.4	3.2	10.88
	24	250	3.9	3.3	12.87
Medium large (20.0–24.0 m^2)	15	140	6.0	3.75	22.5
	15	137	7.0	3.0	21.0
	23	229	6.0	4.0	24.0
	26	269	6.5	3.5	22.75
Large (> 30.0 m^2)	17	155	7.0	5.5	38.5
	17	161	8.9	3.9	34.71
	24	254	7.5	4.0	30.0

Source: Reprinted by permission from *Latin American Antiquity*, vol. 23, no. 1: table 1, page 10. © 2012 Society for American Archaeology.

are absent, and deposits are shallow" in this part of the site (Van Buren 1993: 120).

The eastern sector of Torata Alta was clearly occupied after 1600, as excavations in five structures in Kanchas 23, 24, and 26 (Strs. 229, 241, 250, 254, 269) recovered Indigenous and European artifacts and domestic midden material above the ash deposit and wall-fall. At least three buildings in Kancha 23 (Strs. 231, 235, 241) had fragments of Indigenous pottery incorporated into wall mortar, suggesting relatively later (re)construction. Two radiocarbon dates were obtained from excavated charcoal samples in this sector (see table 1.2). One was from wall collapse of Str. 213 in Kancha 22, a structure that had been swept clear of volcanic ash in the interior but ash was found outside. The one-sigma

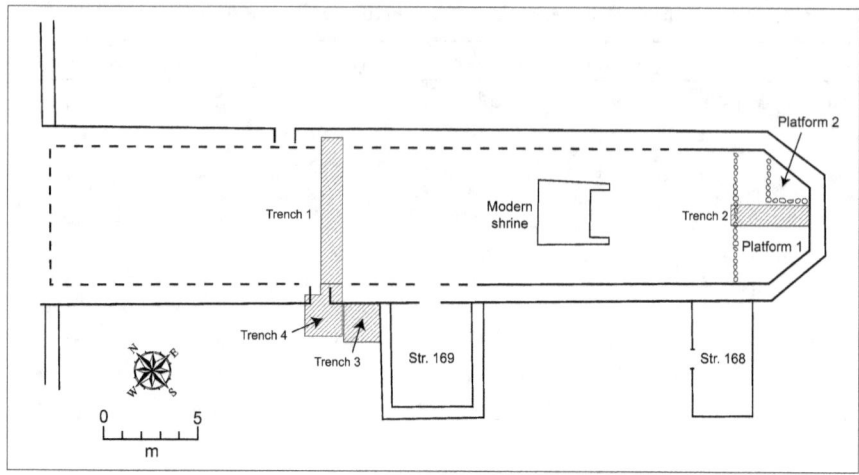

FIGURE 8.4 *Plan of the Torata Alta church, showing attached structures, modern shrine (see figure 8.9), and locations of excavations. Reprinted by permission from* Latin American Antiquity, *vol. 23, no. 1: figure 3, p. 11. © 2012 Society for American Archaeology.*

calibrated date range was AD 1431–1640 (Van Buren, Bürgi, and Rice 1993: 139; Rice and Smith 1990: 212). A second sample, from a hearth below a floor in Str. 193, Kancha 20, was calibrated from 1640 to the present (Rice and Smith 1990: 212).

The Church

A structure on the east side of the plaza conforms generally to the plan of sixteenth-century churches in many areas of the Spanish-colonial realm (figure 8.4; see, e.g., Graham 2011: 224–32): it is oriented southeast ("liturgical east") at 130° and has an unusually long, narrow nave, possibly incorporating a narthex, measuring approximately 38 × 7 m on the interior.[7] There was no sign of a bell tower in the late 1980s, although an earlier aerial photograph appears to show one to the left (east) of the door.[8] Two small auxiliary structures were attached to the southwestern wall. One, near the apse, had a door opening to the exterior and may have been the sacristy; another to the northwest, Str. 169, may have been a baptistery. Neither annex was excavated.

The main entry to the church was likely through a large atrium or open court between the church and the possible kallanka. As in later cathedrals, the atrium "provided a dramatic setting with the façade of the building as backdrop, for the various ceremonies and colorful processions" that were part of religious life (Kelemen 1971: 241). Two other entrances were found on opposite walls, slightly offset from each other. Excavations in the southwest wall uncovered two shaped stones—one L-shaped, suggesting a lintel—that may have been placed to mark doorways after the structure's collapse. A local informant reported that a font had been attached to the church wall near this entry.

An early church with a footprint strikingly similar to that of Torata Alta was excavated at Magdalena de Cao Viejo, on the north coast of Peru (Quilter n.d.). This building, with its apse to the southwest, was constructed of adobe and also appears to have been destroyed by an earthquake that toppled the walls. Ancillary structures were identified through excavations—including a sacristy off the southeast corner, a baptistery off the western wall, and nearby kitchen facilities, including a hearth, ovens, and a grinding station.

The Torata Alta structure was of pirca and adobe construction, likely roofed with *quincha* (cane and daub). Standing walls are 1.1 m wide and roughly 1.1 m high, but elderly informants reported that they used to be higher and plaster-covered. The relatively small amounts of stone debris suggest that the walls were not very high originally and their upper portions were of adobe, as these slabs were found among the stones in the wall collapse. The Inka used a similar construction technique in structures with stone foundations more than 1 meter in height (Hyslop 1990: 12). Graziano Gasparini and Luise Margolies (1980: 131) remarked that "important structures frequently combine [stone and adobe] in their walls, with stone to a height of two to four meters and adobe up to the top."

We placed four excavation units at the church, two inside (Trenches 1 and 2) and two outside (on the southwest wall), with four to five depositional strata identified. Inside the structure (figure 8.5) a level layer of brown silty sand topped the subsoil, whereas on the outside the subsoil was topped with ash. Wall-fall lay both above and below the ash, mixed in the interior with clayey soil from decomposed adobes. Recovered artifacts were primarily sherds of Indigenous Chucuito Polychrome (black-on-light red-to-orange) pottery.

Only in Trench 3, in the corner formed by the exterior southwest wall of the church and the exterior of Str. 169, could we identify a primary deposit of ash directly abutting the walls. Its absence elsewhere was a consequence of the complex mixture of wall-fall, ash filtering into spaces among the rocks, and disturbance by rodents and scrubby vegetation. In any case, these stratigraphic data support the interpretation of a sixteenth-century date of construction of the church and its collapse sometime during the ten-day Huaynaputina seismic event. It appears that the structure collapsed to the northeast, as rubble lies outside the northeast wall and inside the southwest wall.

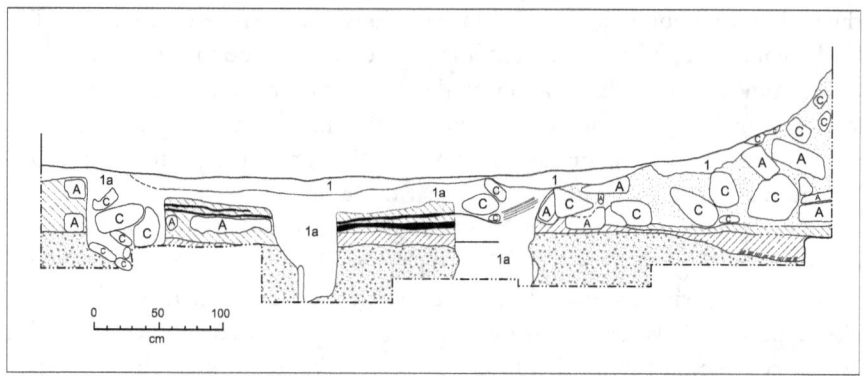

Figure 8.5 *Profile of the southeast wall of Trench 1, a transverse trench through the nave of the church. Note heavy zone of wall-fall on the interior west side; major construction stones (C) and adobes (A) are illustrated. Diagonal hachure indicates clayey-silty deposits, mostly of decomposed adobes. Zone 1 is aeolian sand; 1a is a mix of surface sand and underlying clayey adobe melt. Two pits cut through the deposits represent burials. Reprinted by permission from* Latin American Antiquity, *vol. 23, no. 1: figure 4, p. 12. © 2012 Society for American Archaeology.*

Adobes were used in various parts of the church interior. Trench 1 revealed that, in the central part of the nave, the floor or sub-floor was constructed of adobes laid perpendicular to the structural axis, on and into the brown sand. Adobes were also set in two tiers on the floor against the western wall in the nave (figure 8.6; see also figure 8.5) and might have constituted a bench for seating; a similar feature might also exist against the east wall. A line of tilted adobes, lying on edge, was also found near the wall, atop collapsed stones (Rice et al. 1989).

The church has a polygonal apse, in which fragments of red- and black-painted plaster or whitewash were recovered, although this coating was largely damaged by melt of the brown clay mortar used in construction. Excavations in the apse were carried out by means of Trench 2, a 4 × 1 m unit through its center, paralleling the church's longitudinal axis. This unit revealed that the foundations of the apse were large boulders set atop small rubble in a possible foundation trench[9] in the reddish, sandy, and nearly sterile subsoil (figure 8.7). After the church was abandoned, the apse was covered with a layer of fill material and in recent times two rubble platforms were constructed, their edges faced with rock. Platform 1 rose 55–60 cm above the ground surface and extended 4 m from the wall. Platform 2, 25–30 cm high, was constructed over Platform 1 in

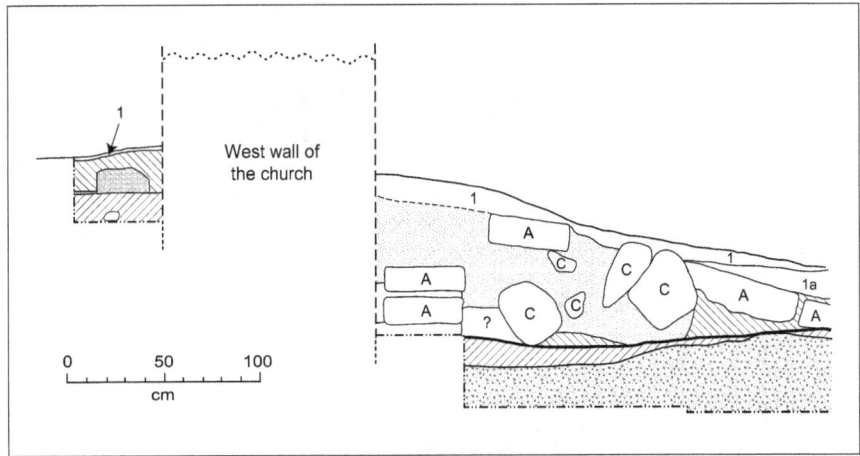

FIGURE 8.6 *Composite profile of the northwest wall of Trench 1 and part of Trench 4, showing deposits outside the wall (including volcanic ash), the west wall of the church, and the bench-like adobe structure against the interior wall. Exterior excavations stopped at sterile exfoliating bedrock. See figure 8.5 caption for key.*

the eastern corner of the apse (figure 8.8); on the west side a "stone bin" (dimensions unrecorded) was constructed atop Platform 1. Trench 2 bisected the area between these two features. It was expected that this trench would reveal an altar, but no Colonial-period or religious features were found.

Informants indicated that both platforms were refurbished within the last decade in connection with activities associated with a modern adobe shrine structure in the nave near the apse (figure 8.9; Rice et al. 1989; Van Buren, Bürgi, and Rice 1993). This shrine measures about 2.75 × 3 m and stands 3–4 m tall, with two steps. Low bench-like wings project from the structure's southeastern wall to enclose a small area bearing traces of fire. On the facade, a carved stone face of the Virgin rests in one of three small niches, along with candles and flowers, and atop the shrine stood two wooden crosses and an arch decorated with colorful paper flowers and streamers. In certain respects, this shrine resembles the "Mother Atoja" altar near Chucuito, in that it is a "U-shaped platform with parallel arms extending eastward" (Tschopik 1946: 561) and possible offerings on the sides. We were told that the shrine was used regularly by valley residents as a ritual locus and that it has a feast day (*tiene su dia*) in late May.

Excavations at the church revealed Christian-style extended burials both inside the nave (two adults) and apse and on the outside. Most of these were "recent" (early-twentieth-century?) interments of infants, occasionally with

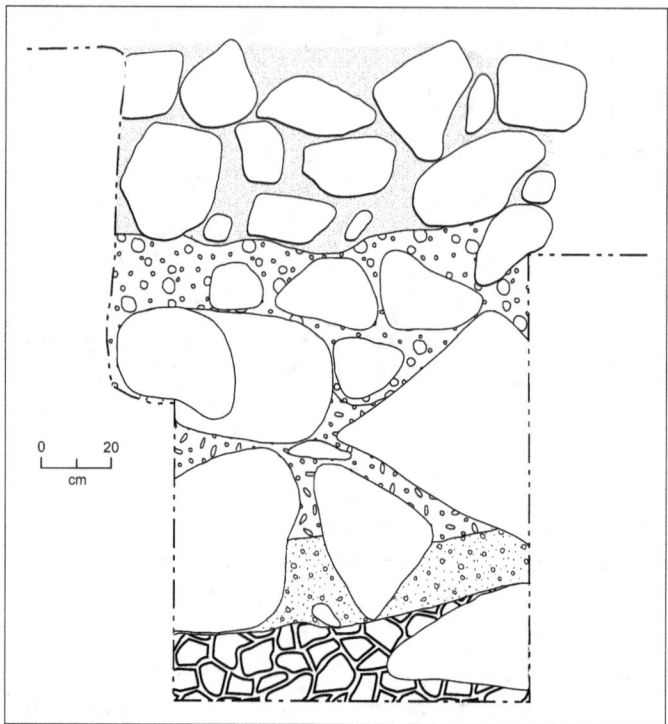

FIGURE 8.7 *Construction of the lower center wall of the apse, exposed in the southeastern end of Trench 2 (the wall continues upward beyond the stones illustrated). Loose fill lies at the base of the builder's trench. Note large size of basal construction stones.*

traces of textile wrappings, buried in oval pits. The remains were not removed. According to informants, these were probably children who were not baptized.[10] Informants also indicated that under the platforms in the apse there had been an earlier crypt (*bóveda*) for the poor, now closed and filled in. Sub-floor burials were also noted at the Magdalena de Cao Viejo church.

After damage by the 1600 earthquakes, the Torata Alta church appears to have been cleared of ash and its reconstruction planned, or perhaps this activity occurred after a second, even stronger earthquake in 1604. The angled adobe alignment suggests accumulation of construction materials, and some adobes were manufactured of a mixture of earth and volcanic ash.

There is a slight possibility of a second church at the site: a rectangular enclosure in Kancha 4, oriented 100° east of north and at an angle to the overall

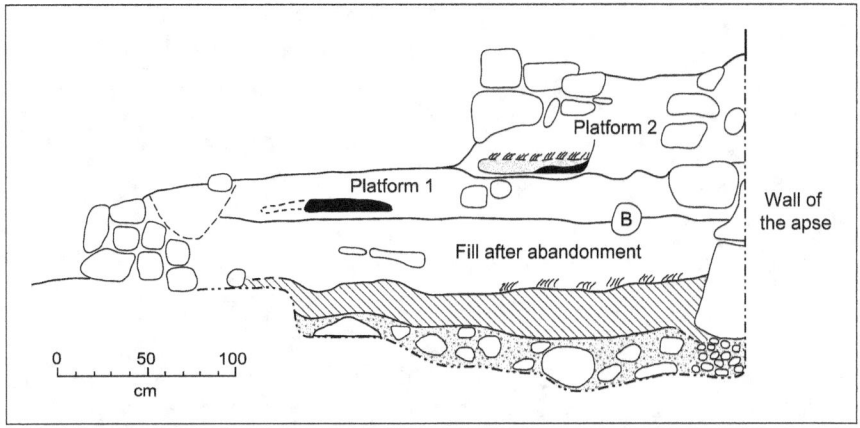

FIGURE 8.8 *Profile of the northeastern wall of Trench 2, through Platform 1 in the apse of the church. For illustrative purposes, Platform 2 is shown above Platform 1, but it was not excavated and is actually offset 25–30 cm east of the trench and this profile (see figure 8.4). Sterile exfoliating bedrock at the base of the excavation is topped by a possible floor (diagonal hachure). Small diagonal hachure represents area of flaked plaster. B marks burial.*

site grid (Rice et al. 1989). In plan and in the massiveness of the stone walls, this structure seems similar to the larger church near the plaza. Spanish-colonial settlements sometimes had a pair of churches—either separate churches for Spaniards and Indigenous peoples or one earlier and one later (e.g., at Lamanai, Belize; Graham 1998: 51). Unfortunately, this odd structure was never investigated further, and it is equally, if not more, likely that it is a modern construction.

Public Areas and Structures

If the Torata Alta congregación were architecturally and functionally similar to missions in other areas of the Spanish-colonial world, it is likely that the area near the church, including Kancha 17 to the east and northeast and the putative kallanka to the north, might have had public or ceremonial functions. In comparison with the rest of the site, Kancha 17 displays large open spaces, smaller walled courtyards, and few internal structures. Originally, some of the enclosed area in the kancha might have been crossed by multiple walls or even buildings, suggested by large boulders with adhering traces of mortar. Two buildings in Kancha 17, Strs. 161 and 156, were excavated.

FIGURE 8.9 *The modern adobe shrine in the nave of the Torata Alta church, as seen in the late 1980s. View to the northwest. Photo by the author.*

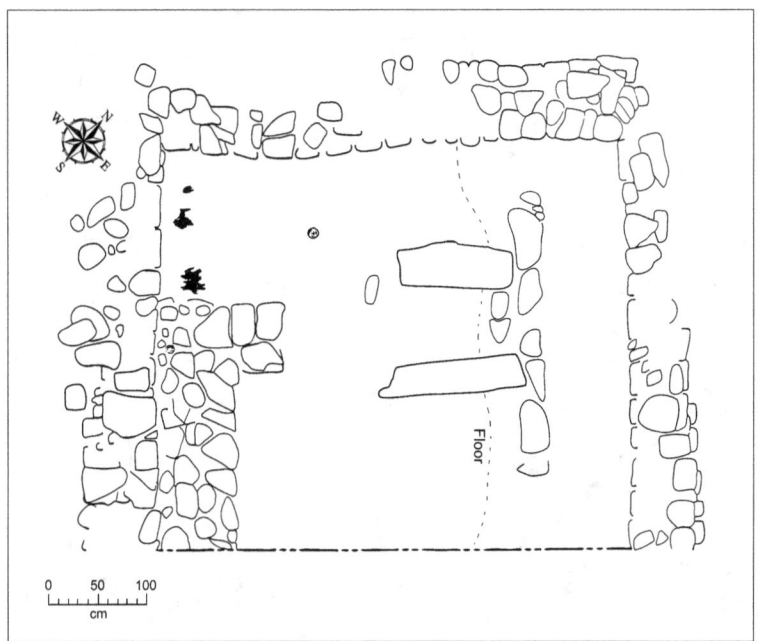

FIGURE 8.10 *The northwestern half of Str. 161 (Kancha 17). Note L-shaped platform against southwest wall and unusual box-like feature of bedrock and a crude wall in the center, apparently used to mix clay mortar. After Van Buren and Bürgi 1990: figure 4.10. Reprinted by permission from* Latin American Antiquity, *vol. 23, no. 1: 14. © 2012 Society for American Archaeology.*

Adjacent Strs. 161 and 162, opening to the west toward the church, might have been a *convento*, or friary, the residence of a friar either living on-site or visiting periodically. Str. 161 (figure 8.10) was excavated only in its northern half, north of its west-facing doorway. This carefully constructed building is large (measuring 8.9 × 3.9 m internally), with 80-cm-wide stone walls standing up to 2 m high. A crude bin-like rock feature lay on bedrock and was apparently used for mixing the mortar for the initial construction. The structure's prepared clay floor exhibited signs of having been whitewashed. A large, L-shaped stone bench, 50 cm high, was constructed against the western wall. Sometime later, Str. 161 was filled to the level of the bench, and then the whole area was covered with another clay floor, over which lay wall-fall. No volcanic ash was encountered, suggesting the structure's refurbishment and use occurred after 1600. The floor and walls may have been coated again with plaster or whitewash. Little domestic midden

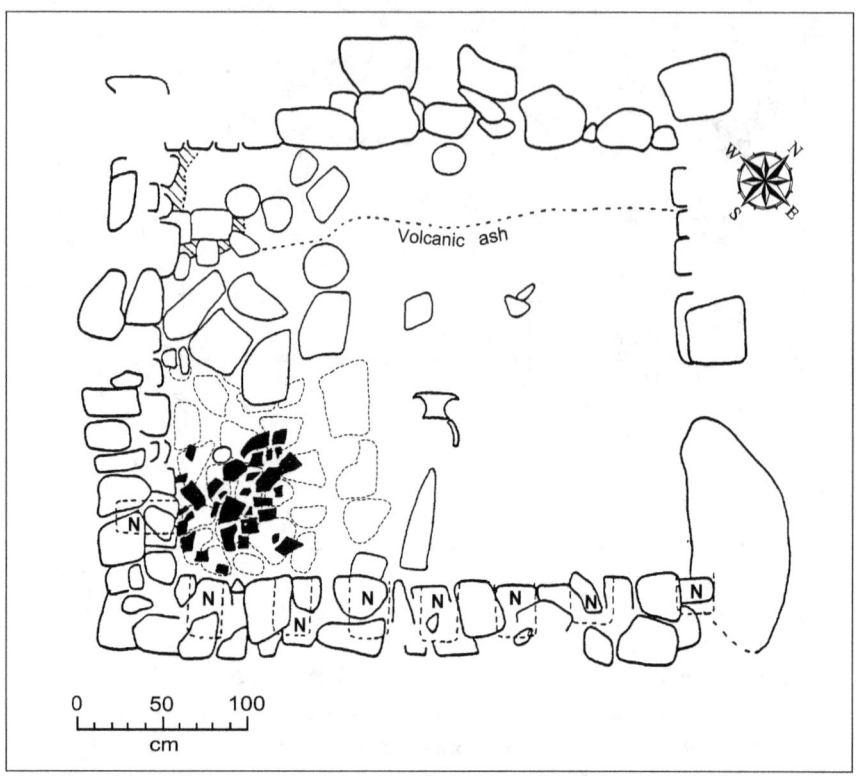

FIGURE 8.11 *Str. 156 (Kancha 17), Level 2 (surface of volcanic ash). Note niches (N) in the southeast wall, sherds in the south corner (overlying a stone platform), and fragment of aríbalo (urpu) in the center. After Van Buren and Bürgi 1990: figures 4.7 and 4.8. Reprinted by permission from* Latin American Antiquity, *vol. 23, no. 1: 14. © 2012 Society for American Archaeology.*

material was recovered in Str. 161; artifacts included Indigenous decorated pottery but little utilitarian ware (except in fill). Other artifacts included botijas, copper pins, iron, glass, and mineral pigment.

Str. 156 also opened into the patio from the north end of Kancha 17 (figure 8.11). Small (interior 2.5 × 1.7 m), with standing walls up to 1.2 m high, this structure was built over bedrock, with a possible prepared floor. Volcanic ash lay atop domestic ash, above which was wall-fall. Eight small closed niches, approximately 20–25 cm on a side and 30 cm deep, appear in the interior walls—seven in the southeast wall and one in the southwest, about 45 cm above the floor.[11] A stone spindle whorl was the only artifact recovered in the niches. In the southern

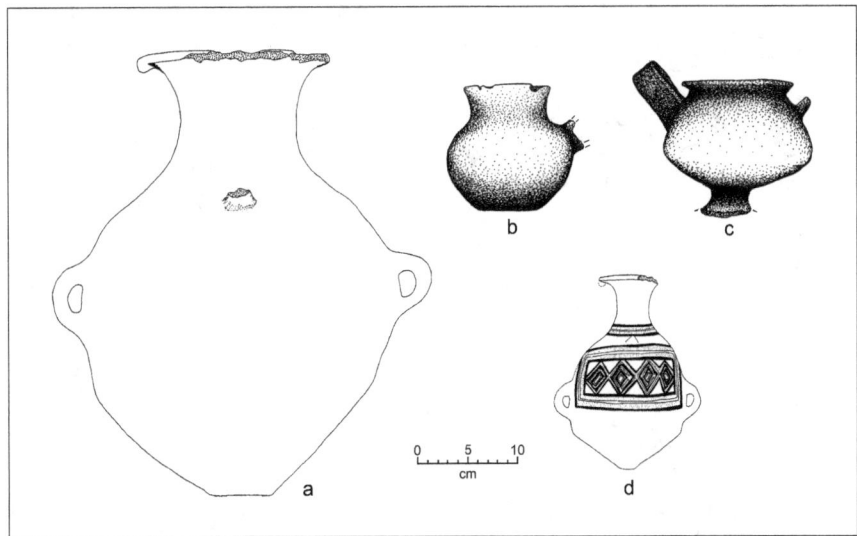

FIGURE 8.12 *Pottery recovered in excavations at Torata Alta: (a) reconstructed brownish-orange slipped, flared-rim jar from Str. 156 (Van Buren 1993: figure 44); (b, c) Inka-related vessels from Str. 156, both sooted (modified from ibid.: figure 43); b has a purplish-red slip; c is a double-handled "pedestal vessel"; (d) a small Chucuito-Inka aríbalo from Trench I in Kancha 26, possibly associated with a burial (ibid.: figure 27). Reprinted by permission from* Latin American Antiquity, *vol. 23, no. 1: figure 7, p. 15. © 2012 Society for American Archaeology.*

corner of the structure, a stone platform measuring 1.2 × 1.25 m had been constructed, on top of which was a large concentration of Indigenous pottery.

Str. 156 had a thin layer of domestic ash, probably from three hearth-like features in the northern corner, overlying the floor. The structure appears to have been abandoned hastily, perhaps after the Huaynaputina eruption, with de facto refuse including several nearly whole or reconstructible bowls and jars (figure 8.12a–c; Van Buren 1993: 296–303, table 13). Fragments of flared-rim utilitarian jars were especially abundant—fifty-five of them, nearly three times as many as in any other provenience—and a distinctive Inka cooking vessel was recovered: a footed or pedestal-based *olla* with an angled strap handle. Other artifacts included large batanes, part of a basket, spindle whorls, two nearly intact bowls, a string of gastropod shells, iron, and copper. Bone, pottery, a horseshoe, stone balls, and a copper tupu were found in the wall-fall, and varied artifacts were in the volcanic ash layer: bone, corncobs, shell, spindle whorls, copper tweezers,

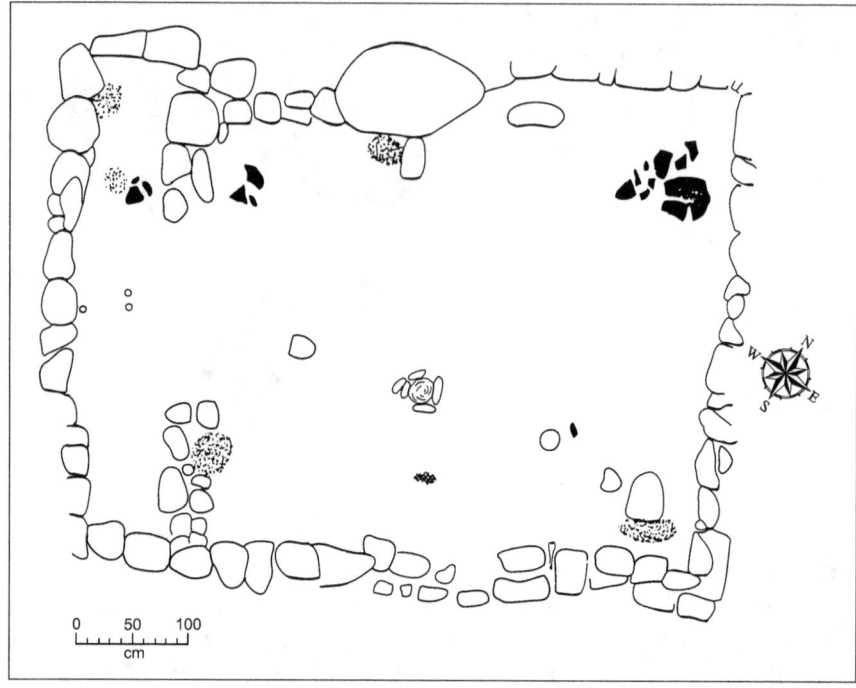

FIGURE 8.13 *Str. 229 (Kancha 23). Note stone partitions in the south and west corners, stone-rimmed postmold in the center, small hearth against a boulder in the northwest wall, and botija fragments in the north corner. Modified from Van Buren and Bürgi 1990: figure 4.12. Reprinted by permission from* Latin American Antiquity, *vol. 23, no. 1: figure 10, p. 17. © 2012 Society for American Archaeology.*

and a stone plaque engraved with a cross. This structure was likely used for food preparation (ibid.: 365–66), making Str. 156 at least superficially analogous to the kitchen area at the Magdalena church, although, as discussed later, its function seems to have been closely tied to brewing maize beer.

Domestic Structures

Two domestic structures at Torata Alta, Str. 229 and Str. 269, yielded both pre-1600 construction and post-1600 domestic refuse (including European earthenwares) above the ashfall, indicating continued occupation after that destructive event. Str. 229 (figure 8.13), approximately 6 × 4 m, sits in the southeast corner of Kancha 23, with entry from the southeast. Its walls, preserved to a height of

1.7 m, incorporate two massive boulders. Two "bins" with low stone walls were constructed in the south and west corners before the 1600 Huaynaputina event. They contained the only volcanic ash noted during excavation of the structure, the main living space having been swept clean. These bins were subsequently filled in over the ash, and a new floor was laid over them. Wall-fall overlay this flooring, suggesting that after the 1600 eruption the structure was refurbished and then damaged in the more severe 1604 earthquake.

Substantial quantities of Indigenous as well as colonial artifacts were recovered in pre-1600 fill and later refuse deposits at Str. 229. Indigenous decorated pottery included fragments of Chucuito (Lupaqa) and Sillustani (Qolla) bowls and especially Chucuito-Inka jars, along with utilitarian vessels. Other traditional Indigenous artifacts are associated with textile production: twelve spindle whorls, including eight of stone and one of wood, plus a *wichuña* (a weaving tool made from a camelid metapodial) and a cache of eight copper straight pins. Several grinding stones and a well-made batan measuring 60 × 40 cm were also found. Spanish artifacts include large quantities of botija fragments in the northeastern side of the structure above the floor, a small coin, thirty-five fragments of glass, six nails, a twisted Nueva Cádiz bead, three horseshoes or fragments, and 55 g of miscellaneous iron (Van Buren 1997: table 16.1). One sherd of porcelain was recovered. This rich artifact inventory, compared with that of other structures, suggests that Str. 229, although not unusually large, was the residence of elites.

A somewhat similar interpretation might be applied to Str. 269 in Kancha 26, immediately southeast of Torata Alta's church. Str. 269, measuring 6.5 × 3.5 m and with standing walls up to 1.4 m, had some unusual architectural features, including an ovoid floor-level niche in the southwest corner and an adobe platform measuring 1.5 × 1.2 m in the northwest corner, constructed before the 1600 eruption. The residents of Str. 269 appear to have been involved in textile production, as suggested by the recovery in excavations of six spindle whorls of a fine-grained green stone with incised decoration and others of pottery, plus copper scissors, a thimble, and straight pins. European-associated artifacts include a glass bead, a silver decorative pin, a nail, a brass bell, a small Spanish coin, a lead slug, a horseshoe, and 28 g of miscellaneous iron fragments (ibid.; Van Buren and Bürgi 1990: 78).

Str. 269 did not yield comparable quantities of non-Chucuito decorated Indigenous serving vessels, as were found in Str. 229. However, Trench G in the southern corner of Kancha 26, close to the Str. 269 compound, was excavated in an area that appeared to contain a midden associated with the structure. This 3 × 3 m excavation had two deposits of domestic refuse, a thin one above and a

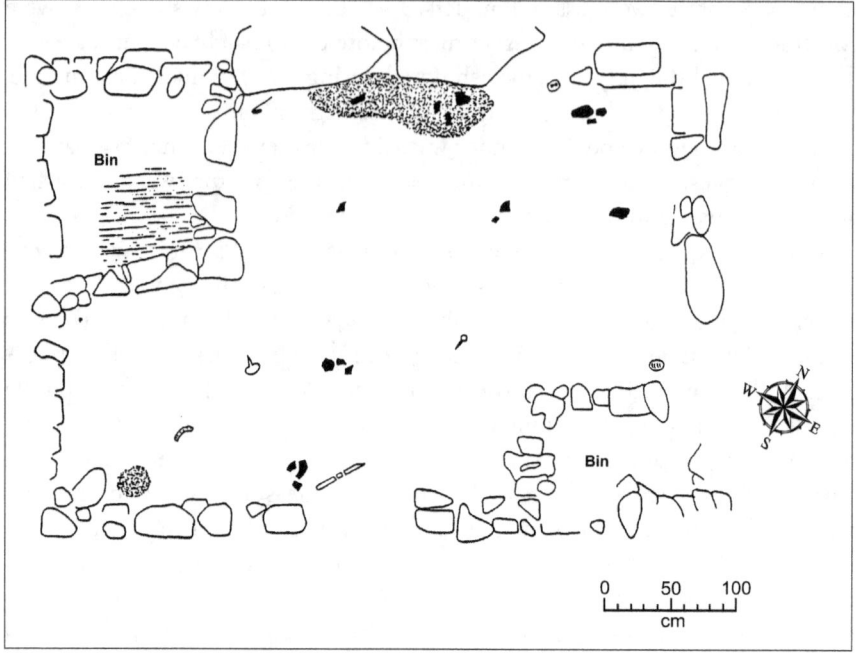

FIGURE 8.14 *Str. 150 (Kancha 16). Note stone "bins" in the east and west corners, large hearth at the base of two boulders in the northwest wall, and two tupus on the floor. After Van Buren and Bürgi 1990: figure 4.4.*

deeper one below a thick layer of volcanic ash; sterile subsoil was encountered 45 cm below surface. The midden below ash yielded large fragments of beautifully decorated Indigenous polychrome bowls and especially jars, undecorated utilitarian wares, and European earthenwares and a few majolica sherds (Van Buren 1993: tables 9, 12, 15, 18). Also present were quantities of bone, primarily camelids, and plant remains including maize, grapes, gourd, squash, and peppers (Van Buren and Bürgi 1990: 79–80).

Eight domestic structures had small interior platforms, usually in the corners. These were constructed of stone and clay mortar and measured about 1–1.5 m on a side and 20–25 cm high; the platforms in Strs. 150 (figure 8.14) and 229 are edged with low stone walls, making them bin-like. Platforms in four structures appear to have been constructed before the 1600 eruption (in Strs. 150, 156, 229, 269?), and the others (Strs. 210 [figure 8.15], 250 [figure 8.16], and 254) were likely constructed afterward. Associated artifacts suggest that the platforms may represent the equivalent of tables on which to keep objects elevated and away from

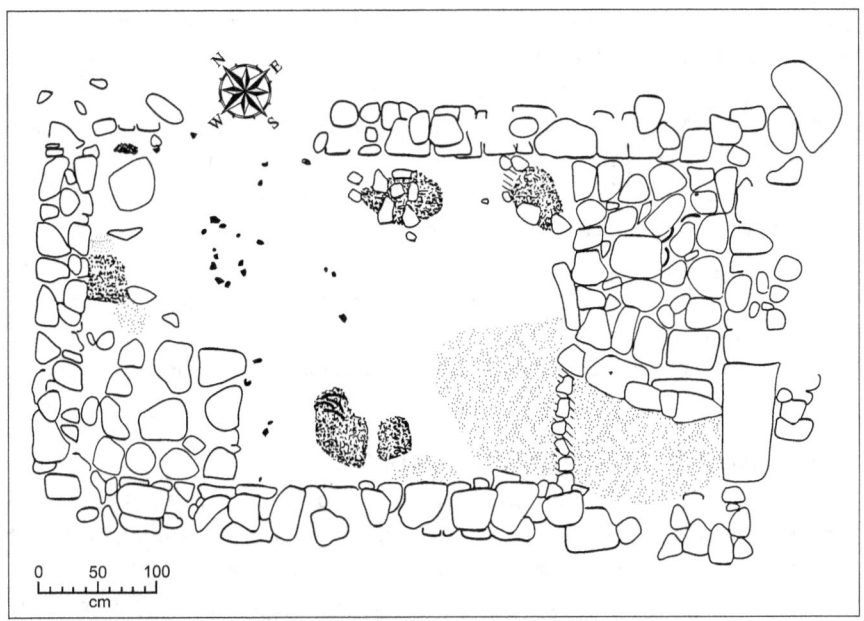

FIGURE 8.15 *Str. 210 (Kancha 20). Note the stone platforms in the east and west corners, five hearths, and volcanic ash (light stipple in south corner). After Van Buren and Bürgi 1990: figure 4.11. Reprinted by permission from* Latin American Antiquity, *vol. 23, no. 1: figure 8, p. 16. © 2012 Society for American Archaeology.*

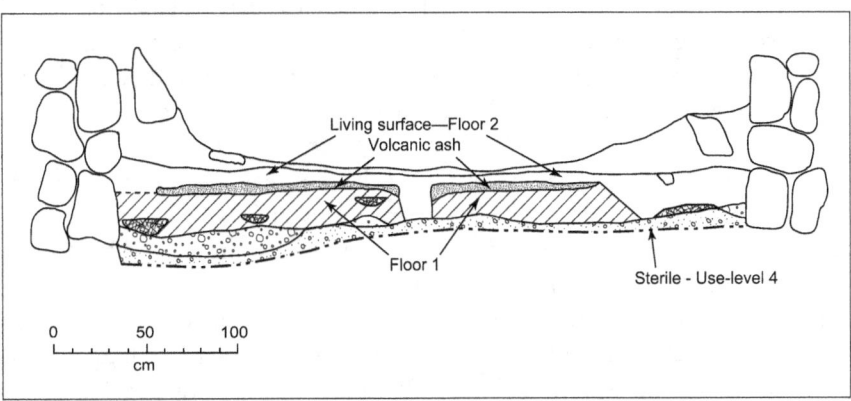

FIGURE 8.16 *West profile of Str. 250 (Kancha 24), showing two living surfaces/floors separated by volcanic ash (the ash and Floor 1 interrupted by a posthole). Modified from Van Buren and Bürgi 1990: figure 4.15. Reprinted by permission from* Latin American Antiquity, *vol. 23, no. 1: figure 9, p. 16. © 2012 Society for American Archaeology.*

damage from normal household activities. In particular, botija fragments were noted on and around these bins.

Alternatively, Thomas Cummins (2002a: 217–18), in discussing the Spanish concern with sexual segregation and moral order in the structure of reduction communities, suggests that archaeologists should consider how residential interiors were divided into discrete spaces, especially for sleeping. Spanish clerics were appalled by the Andean lack of appreciation for female chastity (Boxer 1975: 108), and the low platforms in the Torata Alta structures might represent efforts to comply with Spanish strictures. Otherwise, internal spatial partitioning was rare, either on structure surfaces or in excavations, although partitions might have been created by perishable materials such as quincha (cane) or cloth curtains.[12]

MATERIAL CULTURE AND ECONOMY

The most ubiquitous categories of artifacts at Torata Alta were pottery, weaving/sewing implements, and grinding tools. Chipped lithic artifacts were not systematically identified in surface collections because of the difficulty distinguishing intentionally flaked artifacts from flakes, spalls, and shatter of the native rock. An exception is Kancha 10, in the western extreme of the site, where numerous lithics such as scrapers and drills were identified, along with small flakes of exotic pinkish chert-like stone. Few lithic artifacts were recorded in excavations (Van Buren 1997: table 16.1).

Grinding implements, whole and fragmentary, were identified in surprising numbers, both inside structures and in open areas of the kanchas; fourteen were recovered in Kancha 23 alone. Batanes were apparently too heavy and low-valued to be transported when the hilltop community was abandoned. Smaller mortars were usually square and less common; handstones were comparatively rarely noticed.

Spinning thread, weaving, and textile production seem to have been important activities throughout Torata Alta, particularly at Strs. 229 and 269, given the recovery of spindle whorls, pins, and other related artifacts (table 8.3). A total of 54 spindle whorls was found at the site, manufactured of varied materials: ceramic (25), stone (19), sherds (8), and one each of bone and wood (Van Buren 1993: table 1). Many of these whorls were similar in shape, technology, and decoration to examples from Qolla and Pacajes sites in the altiplano. Unbroken whorls varied in weight from 2.1 g to 32 g, with weight generally thought to vary with type of use: lighter weights for spinning and for short (e.g., cotton) fibers; heavier weights for plying and long (e.g., wool) fibers (ibid.: 157–59, tables 19, 20). Twenty-eight of the 37 complete whorls (75.7 percent) were at the lighter

TABLE 8.3 Occurrence of textile-related implements from excavated contexts[a] at Torata Alta

	Structures						Trenches		
	120	156	229	250	254	269	G	M	Site Total
Spindle whorls	7	3	12	4	8	6	2	3	54
Wichuña	1		1	2	2				6
Copper scissors						1			1
Copper pins			8		8	X			?
Copper tweezers		1							2
Thimbles						1			2
Mandibles[b]			x	X			x	x	12

Sources: Van Buren 1997: table 16.1; deFrance 1993: 180.
a Combined pre- and post-1600 contexts.
b Camelid mandibles showing usewear, thought to be involved in processing hides.

end of the range, weighing between 2.1 and 9.9 g, suggesting use in spinning thread from the cotton grown in the Moquegua valley.

In addition to the wichuña in Str. 229, five more of these tools were recovered in excavations (Van Buren 1997: table 16.1), along with other artifacts formed of camelid bone. They include twelve mandibles (seven right side, four left, one unknown) showing nonabrasive wear, recovered from Str. 250, Str. 254, Trench G, and Trench M (deFrance 1993: table 4–48). Resembling similar tools from Tiwanaku and related sites, these worn mandibles may have been used in hide processing or textile production (ibid.: 180). The hides, thread, and textiles produced at Torata Alta were all likely for tribute payment.

Pottery recovered from excavations and surface collections (a total of 29,473 analyzed sherds; Van Buren 1993: 254n1)[13] was almost entirely characteristic of Indigenous Late Horizon/Inka-period wares. Jesuit friar Bernabé Cobo (1983: 169) commented on the abundance of pottery associated with making, storing, and drinking chicha (beer): the Andeans "have more tools and jars than for all their [other] foods. They use jars, the biggest of which hold from four to six arrobas [ca. 12–18 gal.], while others are smaller; large numbers of vases, large and small; and three or four kinds of cups and glasses." The pottery from Torata Alta appears to fit this pattern. The majority of serving and utilitarian wares were closely related in form and decorative style to pottery from the altiplano, and a small but distinctive component demonstrated ties to Inka vessel forms.

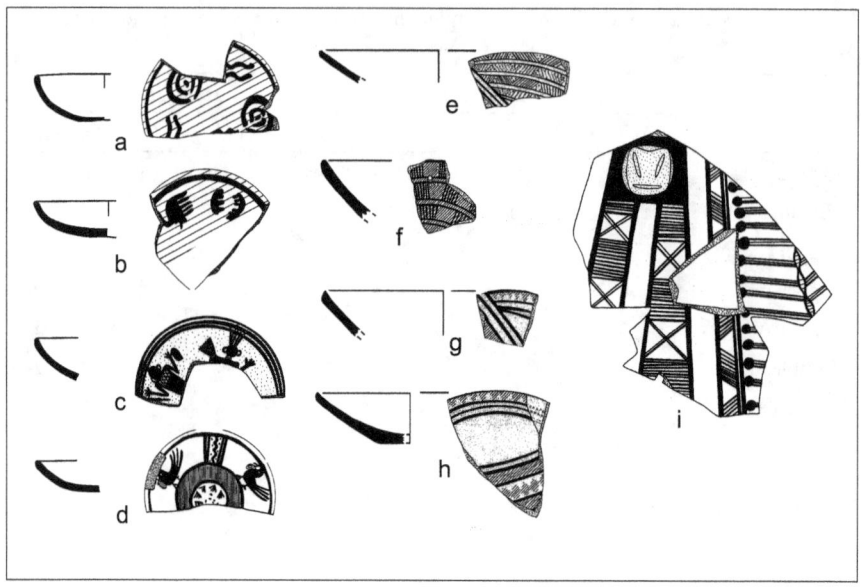

FIGURE 8.17 *Indigenous decorated pottery recovered at Torata Alta: (a–b) Chucuito Black-on-red; (c) unnamed black-and-red on white; (d) Chucuito Polychrome; (e–i) Inka-style decoration, (i) body sherd of a large aríbalo. After Van Buren 1993.*

Among the most common decorated vessels were small, shallow dishes (*chúas*) typically measuring 12–14 cm in diameter (range 10–19 cm; Van Buren 1993: 255). Decorated in the styles of their altiplano Lupaqa equivalents, these were probably individual eating utensils (figure 8.17a–h). Chucuito and Chucuito-Inka polychromes were found both below the 1600 ashfall and above it, suggesting continuing production of, and access to, these wares by the Lupaqa into the early seventeenth century (ibid.). Small amounts of other polychrome pottery types from the Titicaca basin were also found (ibid.: tables 7–9): Sillustani or possible Sillustani types, associated with the Qolla, were more common in post-1600 contexts than earlier, and rare sherds of Saxamar (Pacajes; characterized by painted *llamitas*) were noted (table 8.4).

Undecorated utilitarian wares also closely resemble those of the altiplano (ibid.: 152–53). The most common unslipped form is a globular cooking pot, or olla (*p'uk'u* in Aymara; Tschopik 1950: 206, figure 60i), with a short neck and small vertical strap handles. Mouth diameters most commonly measure 14–16 cm (range 10–30 cm; n = 43). Similar forms were used in the Estuquiña/Estuquiña-Inka period in the Osmore drainage and throughout the southern Peruvian Andes and altiplano

TABLE 8.4 Non-Chucuito-Inka decorated bowl sherds from Torata Alta.

	Kancha	Structure or Trench	Possible Sillustani	Sillustani Polychrome	Sillustani-Inka	Pacajes
West part of site						
	8	64	1	—	—	—
	15	140	3	—	—	—
	16	140	—	—	—	1
Church area						
	17	155	1	—	—	—
	17	156	2	—	—	1
	17	161	4	—	—	—
	17	163	—	—	—	1
East part of site						
	18	M	28	—	—	—
	20	C	5	—	—	—
	22	NE	12	—	1	1
	23	229	14	2	3	—
	24	254	35	1	2	2
	24	A	11	—	—	—
	24	B	2	—	—	—
	26	269	1	—	—	—
	26	G	72	2	3	2

Source: Van Buren 1993: tables 8 and 9. Reprinted by permission from *Latin American Antiquity*, vol. 23, no. 1: table 2, p. 19. © 2012 Society for American Archaeology.

in the Late Horizon, when they may have functioned in making chicha, among other uses. At Torata Alta these olla sherds represented 29 percent of all undecorated fragments that could be classified by vessel form (ibid.: 295).

Certain vessels at Torata Alta are part of the Inka "state" ceramic assemblage, of which two forms seem particularly common in the provinces (Bray 2000, 2003: figure 5). One is the pedestalled olla already mentioned; the other is the long-necked aríbalo jar (Quechua *urpu*), represented by 83 percent of all decorated jar sherds classifiable by vessel form (see figure 8.12d). Rim diameters of the urpus (n = 67) range from 6 cm to 32 cm, although 94 percent fall between 12 and 28 cm (Van Buren 1993: 266, figure 26). One large sherd from

Str. 156 exhibits the typical Cuzco Polychrome A decorative style featuring vertical bands with X-motifs flanked by "ferns" (Bray 2000: 172), and a miniature jar from Trench I bears another common style: a horizontal band with nested rhombs (ibid.: 173). Of particular interest are fragments of undecorated flared-rim jars, representing 20.4 percent of undecorated classified forms (Van Buren 1993: 301). With rim diameters varying from 10 cm to 44 cm (n = 51; ibid.: figure 46)—significantly larger than their decorated analogs—these vessels have been referred to as "fermenting jars," presumably for chicha.

Some pottery might have been produced on-site, as materials indicative of such activity—small lumps of red pigment, a grinding palette (Str. 146), polishing stones, sherd scrapers, and worn llama mandibles—were recovered (ibid.: 145). No LIP pottery, either decorated or of typical utilitarian forms, has been identified in excavations at Torata Alta,[14] despite its proximity to San Antonio; indeed, the two sites exhibit few continuities in material culture (Van Buren 1997). This supports the interpretation that Torata Alta's LH residents were largely non-local.

As for European manufactures, both surface collections and excavations yielded various kinds of goods. Fragments of botijas were recovered primarily in kanchas east and south of the church and were particularly common above the floor of Str. 193 in Kancha 20 and Str. 229 in Kancha 23. Str. 229 yielded roughly 420 fragments of non-Indigenous earthenwares (including botijas), nearly an order of magnitude more than in any other excavated context (Van Buren 1993: table 18). The presence of the botijas might be explained by the need for wine to accompany the holy sacrament. Some of the botijas were identifiable as Spanish-made, with green or yellow interior lead glazing, but most were produced in Peru, very likely in the kilns at the winery sites at lower elevations in the Moquegua valley (Rice 1994; Rice and Van Beck 1993).

Tin-enameled pottery—commonly called "majolica," or *loza* (see chapters 11–13)—was relatively uncommon at Torata Alta, with only twenty-two sherds recovered in excavations and only a few fragments stratigraphically below the 1600 volcanic ash layer. More sherds were recovered in surface collections, including fragments of Mas Alla Polychrome (Rice 1997), possibly manufactured in Cusco. Imports include Sevilla (or Ligurian) Blue-on-blue (five fragments of brimmed plates in Trench G), one sherd possibly of Sevilla Blue-on-white, a few sherds produced in Panama and Mexico, and six fragments of porcelain (Van Buren 1993: 309–16). The presence of porcelain and Spanish- or Panama-made majolica at this site in distant, rural, far southern Peru is likely a consequence of the presence of the reduction church and the use of these wares in religious service. Alternatively, these fragments might reflect ties of the

TABLE 8.5 Non-ceramic European objects recovered in excavations in residential structures at Torata Alta

	Structure Numbers										
	Abandoned pre-1600					Abandoned post-1600					
	62	120	140	146	155	229	241	250	254	269	T
Needle	—	—	1	—	—	—	—	—	—	—	1
Thimble	—	—	—	—	1	1	—	—	—	—	2
Straight pin	—	—	—	—	—	8	—	2	8	—	18
Glass bead	—	1	1	—	—	—	—	1	—	—	3
Metal orn.	—	—	—	—	—	5	4	2	1	4	16
Glass	—	1	—	—	—	35	1	1	5	—	43
Iron knife	—	1	—	—	—	—	—	—	—	—	1
Iron nail	1	—	—	1	1	6	1	3	2	1	16
Horseshoe	—	1	—	1	—	3	1	—	—	1	7
Brass bell	—	—	—	—	—	—	—	—	—	1	1
Lead slug	—	—	—	—	—	—	—	—	—	1	1
Coin	—	—	—	—	—	1	—	—	—	1	2
Total	1	4	2	2	2	59	7	9	16	9	111
Misc. iron (g)		3.0	19.7			55	11.8	11.5	196	28.2	

Sources: Van Buren and Bürgi 1990; Van Buren 1997: table 16.1. Reprinted by permission from *Latin American Antiquity*, vol. 23, no. 1: 158. © 2012 Society for American Archaeology.

Note: Structures 156, 161, and 168 were excluded because they were not residential. Data for Str. 120 include the kitchen, Str. 120a. No European artifacts found in Str. 64.

site's populace to Indigenous and Spanish settlement and churches in wealthy Chucuito, which had access to porcelain (Tschopik 1950: 204).

In addition to ceramics, the residents of Torata Alta had access to other kinds of Spanish goods both pre- and post-1600 (table 8.5). Among them are thirty-six glass beads, including chevron and especially Nueva Cadiz type (Van Buren 1993: 92). Metal items include tools, nails, and several small coins, one of which is a silver eight-*real* piece minted in Potosí no later than 1633 (Van Buren, Bürgi, and Rice 1993: 137). Only four introduced plant taxa were recovered: grape, castor bean, peach, and apricot (table 8.6). Of five excavations in patio areas and middens outside structures, four yielded European artifacts (and one—Trench G in Kancha 26—yielded grape seeds) from below undisturbed volcanic ash (ibid.: 139).

TABLE 8.6 Botanical remains from Torata Alta

Introduced Taxa	Native Taxa
Vitis vinifera (grape)	*Lagenaria siceraria* (gourd)
Ricinus communis (castor bean)	*Cucurbita moschata* (squash)
Prunus persica (peach)	*Capsicum annuum* (ají pepper)
Prunus armeniaca (apricot)	*Zea mays* (corn)
	Cyperus sp. (sedge)
	Schinus molle (peppertree)
	Armatocereus sp. (pitahaya)
	Salicaeae (willow family)
	Fabacaea (bean family)
	Dicotyledoneae (hardwoods)
	Gynerium sagitatum (cane)
	Cactaceae (cactus family)

Source: Jones 1990: tables 7.1, 7.2.

Very few religious items were found, most notably a medal bearing the image of Christ on the cross below volcanic ash in Str. 213 and a stone plaque engraved with a cross from under wall-fall in Str. 156. More religious items might have been recovered if additional excavations had been carried out near the church, especially in attached Strs. 168 and 169.

Faunal material from three excavation units—Trench M (Kancha 18), Str. 250 (Kancha 24), and Trench G (Kancha 26)—led to identification of a minimum number of individuals (MNI) of 183 in 47 taxa (see table 8.7; Trench G not included in table) and provided considerable information about economic activities (deFrance 1993, 1996). One unusual find was a mountain lion (*Felis concolor*) humerus with cut marks in pre-1600 levels of Trench G (deFrance 1993: 178, figure 4-9). Varied marine fish and shellfish were brought to Torata Alta from the coast as food resources, probably through continuation of pre-Hispanic exchange routes (deFrance 1993: 206–7, 1996: table 5). European dietary fauna includes chickens and pigs, both of which were rare at the wine haciendas in the valley. Laying hens were present in pre- and post-1600 contexts (deFrance 1993: 143), probably to produce eggs for tribute payments. Caprines (sheep/goats) and Old World rodents were found in pre-1600 deposits. Large European quadrupeds used for transport or agro-industry—cattle, horses, burros, mules—were not recovered at Torata Alta.

TABLE 8.7 MNI and edible meat weight (EMW) of fauna in pre-1600 levels from two contexts at Torata Alta

	Trench G[a]		Str. 250[b]	
	MNI	EMW (g)	MNI	EMW (g)
Guinea pig	1	54	—	—
Camelids	13	38,071.2	7	18,933.8
Caprines	2	541.9	1	270.8
Other (mammal)	—	53,067.1	—	13,267.6
Chicken	3	158.5	1	49.8
Osteichthyes	5	109.8	1	66.5
Total	24	92,002.5	10	32,588.5

a From deFrance 1993: table B-91. Eleven contexts from ¼-inch screening (table A-8) and 50 liters screened through 1/16-inch mesh (table A-9).
b From deFrance 1993: table B-94. Eleven contexts from ¼-inch screening (table A-8) and 61+ liters screened through 1/16-inch mesh (table A-9).

Age profiles of the camelid remains reveal the presence of all age classes, indicating that a breeding population was present at or near the community (ibid.: 184). In addition, variability in the size of camelid bones suggests that at least two species were present (ibid.: 154, 191), presumably llama and alpaca, both domesticated. Some bones show pathologies indicative of weight-bearing activities, such as wine transport (ibid.: 141, 191, 1996: 37). This is not unexpected, as documents indicate that the Torata kurakas organized llama caravans to transport wine to the altiplano (Guíbovich P. 1984: 337–38). Isotope analysis revealed that the beasts were probably pastured in the wet *puna* grassland regions of the Titicaca basin (Van Buren 1993: 242–44). Camelids were probably also butchered for meat (dried into *charqui*) and their wool, especially that of smaller alpacas, which was spun and woven into textiles. In general, the community seems to have maintained conservative and pre-colonial patterns of animal use with respect to both protein consumption and economic activity (deFrance 1993: 207, 1996: 44).

COLONIAL (RE-)SPATIALIZATION AND (RE-)POLITICIZATION

As discussed in chapter 3, the Torata valley—known as Cochuna in late pre-Hispanic times—experienced considerable settlement turnover, with population movements and colonization by external polities in response to drought and political unrest. Two archaeological sites can be identified as Inka administrative centers: Sabaya (possibly Cochuna?) and Torata Alta. Both presumably oversaw agricultural (especially maize) production for the state, as well as reorganization of its settlement and landholdings. Torata Alta might be the garrison or presidio recommended to the Inka, its early residents serving as agricultural overseers or soldiers, perhaps living in the barracks-like structures of Kancha 1A and 1B.

In the early 1570s, the Spaniards appropriated Torata (Alta) to resettle the residents of numerous small communities around the Río Osmore's tributaries. Interestingly, Sabaya and Camata are not mentioned among the reduced communities. This is probably because these two pueblos, known in early documents as Suhubaya (see chapter 7, note 8) and "Capavaya" (?), continued to be occupied by Qolla colonists—perhaps descendants of the earlier LIP/EI colonists in the valley, for example, at San Antonio.

Spaces and Places

The distinctive, albeit brief, historical trajectory of Torata Alta—as first a forced Inka resettlement and then, approximately a century later, a Spanish one—means that Torata Alta should, in theory, carry the imprint of culturally distinct concepts about the organization and use of space. The fact that the site does not, in large part, carry such an imprimatur, and neither do other Inka settlements appropriated as colonial reductions (see Hyslop 1990: 191–92), merits discussion.

Both Inka and Spanish resettlements were organized by some kind of orthogonal arrangement. In Inka examples, units of residential space (kanchas) created by the intersection of streets were irregular, sometimes rectangular but often polygonal (ibid.: 234–39). Orthogonality was the Spaniards' primary footprint, based on models drawn from Classical antiquity (see Rice 2011a): when the Spaniards established new towns, there was a concerted effort to make its internal spaces regular and equal in size. In co-opting Inka spaces for their own purposes, existing variability did not appear to require significant architectural adjustment. The orthogonal layout of Torata Alta, plus its relatively high-level Indigenous administrative structure associated with Chucuito, would have attracted Spanish authorities in Moquegua seeking a location to congregate native Andeans.

Nonetheless, places, as distinctive components of spaces holding particular meanings, were defined differently by the Inka and the Spaniards. For example, open plazas for public gatherings in Inka resettlements were frequently on the edges of the community (Gade and Escobar 1982; Hyslop 1990: 194–201), suggesting uses not for general community solidarity but rather places of restricted "ownership" by each moiety. In Spanish towns and reductions, by contrast, the plaza was central; it was the focus of civic order, with structures representing the institutions responsible for maintaining that order—the church, government, and elite residences—displayed around and bounding it. Similarly, the status of residents declined with distance from this central place.

At Torata Alta, modern disturbance makes it difficult to discern the original locations of any plaza or plazas. Nonetheless, one may have existed on the southeast side. The construction of the colonial church in the east-central part of the site appears to have occasioned major disruption of the Inka grid organization: destruction of kanchas, internal buildings (although foundation walls may remain), and streets. The modern soccer field may have simply involved widening a Spanish (or earlier Inka) plaza space. Spaces associated with gathering residents to the Torata Alta church were bounded but unroofed.

The orientations of Inka resettlements were variable. Torata Alta's primary orientation is southwest-northeast, as established by its longest and straightest streets, with shorter cross-streets irregularly spaced between them. The grid, measured from the site map at the intersection of Kanchas 10, 1A, 4, and 5, has the two streets oriented to azimuths 41° east and 137° south. This latter orientation is only a few degrees from the Inkas' "special interest in the southern circumpolar region from about 146 to 155 degrees" (Hyslop 1990: 224). Various constellations arose, and the Milky Way was centered, in this area of the sky (ibid.). Torata Alta's northeastern orientation is perpendicular to the preferred axis of Aymara space, said to run northwest-southeast, as established by the 320°–140° (i.e., ca. 50° west) alignments of Río Azángaro, Lake Titicaca, and Río Desaguadero (Bouysse-Cassagne 1986: 216).

Inter-cardinally oriented orthogonal grids occur in Inka site planning at Cusco and elsewhere, but they were not common (Hyslop 1990: 59–61, 192–202). Chucuito and Hatunqolla in the Titicaca basin and Tarapacá Viejo in northern Chile are, along with Torata Alta, among the southernmost examples of such site plans (see ibid.: 191–92; azimuths are not given). Torata Alta's kanchas differ from those at most Inka sites, however, where structures' long axes are parallel, rather than perpendicular, to the compound walls.

The plan of Tarapacá Viejo, in northern Chile, is remarkably similar in many ways to that of Torata Alta. Both sites have an orthogonal site plan, a southwest-northeast primary axis incorporating an Inka road, construction incorporating large boulders, variable use of double courses of stone, and internal structures oriented orthogonally to the kancha walls (Núñez Henríquez 1984: 55; Zori 2011: 486, 490–91, 493, 501, figures 3.14, 3.15). Nonetheless, they also differ in several respects: Tarapacá Viejo was built over an LIP settlement, it lacks a plaza, and walls were set into foundation trenches (e.g., ibid.: 486, 490, figures 6.35, 6.36, 6.76), which were not apparent at Torata Alta. Spanish artifacts were scarce at

Tarapacá Viejo, although fragments of liturgical music noted earlier (Núñez Henríquez 1984) suggest some Spanish presence there, perhaps while the reduction community of San Lorenzo was being constructed across from the site. The apparent absence of fragments of botijas associated with provisioning wine and olive oil to the settlement is unusual.

The similarities of site structure raise the possibility of some kind of suprasite planning after the Inka annexed the present-day southwestern Peru and northern Chile region into Contisuyu. Inka administration of this formerly Qolla-controlled area seems almost designed to replicate that unity, perhaps as an outgrowth of fairly rapid and peaceful conquest achieved by a single ruler (Pachacuti? Topa Yupanki?) and subsequent construction and resettlement overseen by a single official or team in charge of such affairs.

Spaces and Functions

Architectural and artifactual variability, as revealed in mapping, surface collections, and excavations, suggests that different parts of Torata Alta had different functions and relative dates of occupation/use. Compared to the western sector of the site, the southeast evidenced different structural characteristics and ordering of space: "a larger number of contiguous rooms, a higher frequency of European artifacts, and more domestic refuse. Walls are also wider and preserved to a greater height than those elsewhere . . . [The masonry] is usually double-coursed, and the construction stones tend to be roughly the same size" and sometimes dressed (Van Buren and Bürgi 1990: 52; also Van Buren, Bürgi, and Rice 1993: 143).

Many factors can account for these differences. One is time: the southeastern sector generally seems to have been occupied longer and later than the western side of Torata Alta. Another is function: at some Inka sites, such as Ollantaytambo, an orthogonal layout is evident in the residential area occupying one side, whereas the other half of the site, locus of ceremonial or military functions, lacks a strict grid arrangement (Hyslop 1990: 194).

Variations might also be a consequence of pre-Hispanic social and ethnic relations, the ethno-political affiliations of the occupants re-spatialized in the new reduction settlements (see, e.g., Gutiérrez 1993: 228). The Torata community, or parcialidad, had both hanan and hurin moieties (Guíbovich P. 1984: 296), and the more substantial construction in the southeast part of Torata Alta might indicate occupation by the higher-status moiety. Or perhaps Torata Alta itself was the hanan moiety settlement, and the hurin parcialidad was at a lower elevation, such as the valley-floor "Cochuna" settlement. Also, differences in structure sizes and ratios could represent a distinction between initial Inka-Lupaqa and larger, later reduction occupations. The presence of multiple small facilities, often paired, in the eastern kanchas might relate to the grouping of peoples of different ayllu, moiety, or ethnic backgrounds who wished to maintain separate domestic resources.

After the implementation of reduction, if not earlier, Torata Alta may have been a fairly diverse community occupied by people with varied altiplano ethno-political and possibly also ethno-linguistic connections. This is suggested by the several types of pottery recovered not only at Torata Alta but also at other sites in the Osmore drainage; the material is primarily Lupaqa (Chucuito), but small quantities of pottery from other Inka-allied señoríos in the Titicaca basin—Qollas (Sillustani) and Pacajes (Saxamar)—were also present.

Kurakas, Feasting, and Tribute

In the eastern part of Torata Alta, several structures—Strs. 156, 229, and 269—may have had special functions commonly associated with Inka state control of a province. Excavations in Str. 156, for example, yielded several nearly whole or reconstructible flared-rim jars and bowls, a pedestalled olla, large batanes, spindle whorls, and a tupu. These artifacts suggest that this structure was a small-scale brewery.[15] The batanes would have been used in milling dried, malted corn for chicha de jora; the undecorated flared-rim jars were for storage (or possibly fermentation); the hearths and ash were residues of cooking the mash; and the tupu supports the role of elite women in brewing beer. The finished beer would have been sieved and decanted into the slightly smaller *aryballoid* jars with Inka-type decoration, from which the chicha would have been poured into wooden or ceramic beaker-like *keros* for drinking. Decorated jars, small, decorated eating bowls, and special drinking vessels were scarce in Str. 156 (only nineteen bowl fragments), suggesting that these activities preparatory to serving took place elsewhere.

The estimated volume of a reconstructible flared-rim jar found in Str. 156 is 37 liters, just under the "large" size capacity in ethnographic household assemblages for brewing chicha for weekly household consumption or for contributions to community labor feasts (Jennings and Chatfield 2009: 214–15, 217). This jar had a rim diameter of approximately 20 cm, in the lower half of the range measured at Torata Alta. If rim diameters are roughly proportional to capacity in this form category (admittedly a dubious proposition), the three largest rims of 36, 38, and 44 cm may represent jars with enormous capacities of more than 150 liters. These, together with the two fragments of large double-handled ollas with rim diameters of 28 and 30 cm, suggest production of beer or other foods at Torata Alta in amounts well above simple household consumption.

Much of the chicha produced at this proposed brewery might have been consumed in Strs. 229 and 269. The rich artifact inventory of Str. 229, particularly decorated serving wares—jars and bowls—compared with that of other structures, suggests that it might have been the residence of elites with access to valued Indigenous goods as well as imported items. In particular, the substantial quantities of serving wares and botijas might reflect household production for work-party feasts kurakas provided as generous reciprocity for community labor (see Dillehay 2003; Gose 2000: 86). The other residents of Kancha 23 appear to have supported such endeavors, as fourteen batanes or fragments were noted in the compound.[16]

Numerous fragments of botijas littered the open area around Str. 156 and were found inside Str. 229. Given the apparent association of these two structures with grinding and brewing activities (presumably of maize), the botijas could have been used to store or carry dried corn and ground cornmeal. Alternatively, considering that the Toratans had a vineyard in Moquegua and were producing wine by the late 1560s (Diez de San Miguel 1964: 245; Guíbovich P. 1984: 222–23, 299; Pease G. Y. 1984: 164), the botijas at Str. 229 might have held wine consumed in religious celebrations and feasts, or they might have been repurposed to hold chicha.

Str. 269, as noted, did not have the quantities of Inka-related serving vessels as were recovered in Str. 229, but the midden in nearby Trench G included bowls and jars decorated in altiplano styles, plus European materials and plant and animal remains. The material in this deposit also suggests the kinds of feasting activities and consumption of chicha as those in Str. 229, although neither yielded keros. Both the proposed chicha production at Str. 156 and the feasting at Str. 269 pre-date the 1600 ashfall, although this dating is less clear in Str. 229.

Who were the residents of Str. 229 in Kancha 23 and Str. 269 in Kancha 26? Most likely they were Indigenous elites, likely families of the kuraka principal don Martín Cutipa or his persistent rival, don Pedro Conta (Rice 2011b: 130–31). If the structures were occupied by kurakas, the proposed feasting events reflect the large-scale festivities these leaders sponsored in return for labor, as Murra noted in this chapter's epigraph. Str. 229 lies near the possible peripheral plaza in the southeast of the site. State-sponsored reciprocal hospitality (*mink'a*) is based on "Inka tributary principles in specifying that labor should be received and food reallocated" (Gose 2000: 86). The food and drink for these feasts were typically prepared by *aqllas* ("chosen women"), beautiful young women who lived apart from society in their own dedicated compound (*aqllawasi*) and who could be found "in virtually all settlements" (ibid.: 86–87). In addition to brewing beer, aqllas were also skilled weavers. Kancha 23 was possibly an aqllawasi.

The residents of Torata Alta paid tribute directly to Chucuito and the Spanish crown; because they were not required to provide labor service at the mines, they may have been required to provide substitutes. It is not unlikely that the solutions Cutipa and Conta chose involved collaborating with their new Spanish overlords in the region's emerging wine-based, capitalist economic system. By growing grapes, making wine, and organizing llama caravans for transport of goods through the sierras, they enriched themselves and attempted to solidify their authority over their subjects.

ABANDONMENT

The apparent pre-1600 (perhaps even pre-1567) abandonment of Kanchas 1A and 1B could relate to population decimation or to changes in labor patterns, either seasonally or because of demographic decline. In response to questions during the 1567 visita, don Martín Qari, kuraka principal of the upper moiety of Chucuito, indicated that colonists under his jurisdiction included both temporary and permanent residents, some of whom worked the maize fields and others of whom transported lowland goods to the altiplano (Van Buren, Bürgi, and Rice 1993: 142).

The recovery of artifacts atop the volcanic ash layer, the sweeping of domestic floors to remove the ash, and the thin, trampled lenses of ash near walls reveal that the settlement continued to be occupied after the devastating 1600 eruption and earthquakes toppled the church and other structures. Efforts were made to rebuild the church with adobes before or after another severe earthquake in 1604, which doubtless hastened the community's departure. As Mary Van Buren (1993: 355) commented, most of the artifacts recovered from occupational surfaces at Torata Alta were "broken objects that were no longer useful" or small personal items that were probably lost: "This suggests that either site abandonment occurred slowly, and/or with considerable foreknowledge, or that useful items were scavenged after abandonment took place."

It is not known exactly when the Torata congregación was abandoned. Antonio Vásquez de Espinosa (1948 [ca. 1629]: 463) passed through the region in 1618 and gave the population of Torata as 546 people—117 tributaries, 29 old men, 129 boys, and 271 women and girls—but it is not clear from which census he drew these findings. Nor is it clear if this population refers to the archaeological/reduction site, the riverside community, or the general valley area. At some point Torata Alta's residents moved downhill to the river valley, presumably to the location of the modern town of Torata. In 1619, when San Agustín de Torata was established as a doctrina (rural parish) separate from Moquegua, construction began on a new church, which was built over a period of twenty-three years (Kuon Cabello 1981: 472). Remains of this old church can be seen under Torata's police station.

NOTES

1. Both the Inka and the Spaniards leveled and graded ground surfaces of areas chosen for construction before beginning to build (Zori 2011: 380). This was likely a matter of concern for structural stability, given the region's frequent earthquakes.

2. The plan for Inka kanchas might have been derived from the north coast (Chimú; Gasparini and Margolies 1980: 181) or the site of Pikillakta, a Middle Horizon Wari center north of Cusco (McEwan 2006: 98).

3. At Tarapacá, similar boulders frequently bore petroglyphs (Zori 2011: 232, for example), but such carvings were not noted at Torata Alta.

4. There is no kancha numbered 21 on the current map. A Kancha 21 was originally proposed as a southeastward extension of Kancha 20, but subsequent pedestrian surveys and mapping determined that such a designation was not justified because of disturbance.

5. Circular and square structures occur at the site of Malata, in the Colca valley, however, identified as a very early or "pre-reducción" settlement (Wernke 2006).

6. Some closures, however, might be low-threshold entries, as seen in Inka *qollqas* (storage structures).

7. Given this size and shape, it is possible that the church structure originally could have been a kallanka.

8. This blurry, undated air photo also shows possible structural features inside the church, within the atrium, and in the large open area east of the church. Similar features seem to have existed in the plaza before the bulldozing obliterated them.

9. Unlike the reduction settlement of Tarapacá Viejo in Arica (see Zori 2011), which has a similar history, and also the large Str. 1 at Sabaya in the Torata valley (Bürgi 1993: 216), structure walls at Torata Alta were generally not set into foundation trenches.

10. Our Andean workers were disturbed by these burials, so we ceased excavation upon their exposure. As a consequence, few excavation units inside the church reached bedrock. We covered the remains with plastic before backfilling. Because of limited excavations in and around the church, it is not known if the Colonial-period residents might have exhumed bodies buried in the church and reburied them in ancestral burial grounds, as occurred as part of Andean resistance in other parts of Peru (MacCormack 1985: 459).

11. In a structure at the small LH site of Polvorín in the Otora valley, three wall niches measuring about 20 × 25 cm were placed about 1 m above the ground surface in two walls. One niche was open through the wall, and the other two were closed (Stanish 1992: 152).

12. Excavation of Strs. 5 and 6 at Sabaya revealed multiple postmolds that might reflect such partitioning; Str. 6 also had a large corner platform (Bürgi 1993: figs. 65, 66).

13. Van Buren's analyses of excavated materials were restricted to her own excavations in 1989 and excluded the church units and Strs. 137, 150, and 210 (see Van Buren 1993: 122).

14. Typical features of San Antonio pottery, including "exterior striations, bright orange slip, and bowls with steeply incurved rims," were not part of the Torata Alta assemblage (Van Buren, Bürgi, and Rice 1993: 144).

15. Chicha production in the Andes seems to have followed three models (Marcus 2009: 316; Moore 1989: 688–89): two were large-scale production for state or elites, as at Cerro Baúl (Moseley et al. 2005); the third was small-scale household production. In the Aymara area, two vessel forms were used in making chicha in Chucuito in the mid-twentieth century—a wide-mouthed fermentation jar and a tall, restricted-neck jar for storage, both with paired vertical handles on the lower sides (Tschopik 1950: 206).

16. These batanes include one incorporated into a wall, six north of Str. 228, two south of Str. 238, two overturned south of Str. 240, and three rectangular slabs (locations unrecorded).

9

Locumbilla

A Colonial Wine Heredad

> Wine is bottled poetry.
> —Robert Louis Stevenson

Evidence of early Spanish transformations of the Moquegua landscape is evident in the Yaravico toponymic zone in the upper mid-valley. The Yaravico toponymic zone is a large area of high-quality agricultural land on the east side of the upper Moquegua valley, on the south (left) bank of the Río Tumilaca and immediately below its join with the Río Torata (figure 9.1). Historical data suggest that in the sixteenth century, much of this land came to be held by Hernán Bueno viejo and his descendants, and, beginning in the very early seventeenth century if not before, the southern portion of this zone was differentiated as Locumbilla. Nine bodega sites were identified in project surveys in this zone, representing the long process of successively dividing this huge property through inheritance and sale. These bodega sites, from north to south, are Yaravico 1, Yaravico 2, Yaravico Viejo, La Banda, Yaravico Bajo, Locumbilla, Gastón, Belén de Locumbilla, and Montalvo (table 9.1). Other sites that were initially part of the extended Bueno family holdings include Chimba (with five bodega ruin sites), on the north side of the Tumilaca, and possibly two sites in the intervening area: Yaracachi and Estopacaje. Hernán Bueno y García (Bueno *mozo*) and his son, Hernán Bueno de Arana, also had land in Escapalac (Escapalaque), on the far eastern end of the north bank of the Tumilaca valley.

DOI: 10.5876/9781607322764:c09

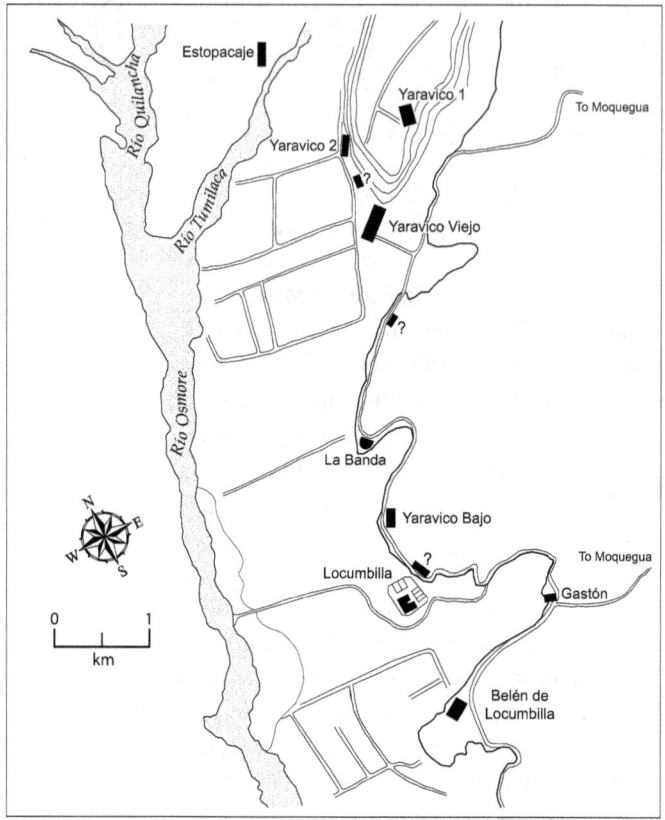

FIGURE 9.1 *The Yaravico toponymic zone, showing the location of bodega sites and old roads.*

YARAVICO AND LOCUMBILLA: THE BUENOS AND ESTRADAS

In the sixteenth century, lands known as Yaravico became the property of Hernán Bueno and his extended family. It is not presently known how he came to hold this land, although it was presumably by appropriating the fields cultivated by the people of his Carumas encomienda. Available documentary data begin in 1577, when Bueno's granddaughter, doña Jerónima de Miranda, daughter of Hernán Bueno mozo, married Captain Alonso de Estrada y Vizcarra, bringing a handsome dowry that included land in Yaravico (Miró Quesada Sosa 1982: 86). The Yaravico Viejo bodega site, with its in situ tinaja inscribed with religious symbols and the early date of 1590, was of particular interest, but unfortunately, it could not be associated with any specific members of the Bueno family.

TABLE 9.1 Bodegas in the Yaravico zone and their industrial facilities

	Plan[a]	Bodega	Lagar	Press	Kiln	Falca	Tinaja	Dates
Yaravico 1	spec.	1	?	?	?	?	5	1761, 1787
Yaravico 2	spec. (nearly destroyed)							
Yaravico Viejo	segr.	4	4	1	1	?	36	1590, 1751, 1771
La Banda	I-Bl.	1	3	1	—	—	8	1699, 1790
Yaravico Bajo	spec.	2?	2	1	?	—	12	1757
Locumbilla	I-Bl.	3	3	—	1	1	18	1771, 1790, 1803
Gastón	spec.	—	2	1	—	1	—	1769 (3), 1782 (2), 1789, 1808 (2)
Belen de Locumbilla	destr.	—	4	—	—	—	2	1791 (2)
Montalvo	?	?	3	—	—	—	10	1793, 1976, 1811

a Plans or layouts are specialized ("spec."), segregated ("segr."), and integrated-block ("I-Bl.").

Estrada and doña Jerónima were wealthy and lavishly generous with their relatives. In 1593, for example, they donated a vineyard and land on the north side of the lower Río Tumilaca, north of Yaravico, to the sons of doña Jerónima's illegitimate brother, Hernán García Bueno (Guíbovich P. 1984: 277). This heredad is variously identified as "Chacha" or Chacba, but both are probably mis-transcriptions referring to the area known as Chimba. The location of the notary's record is given as Yaravico, suggesting that this Chacha/Chimba was originally part of the Buenos' landholdings. Also in 1593, Estrada claimed to have in his possession an act of sale of lands in Yaravico, sold either to him or to his father-in-law by a native woman, Ana Poma (ADM 5).

The Estradas had no children of their own but were guardians of their orphaned niece and nephew, whose parents were Alonso Estrada's brother,

Diego Vizcarra, and Jerónima's sister. When nephew Alonso de Vizcarra married in 1605, the Estradas gave him land known as Locumbilla. "Locumbilla" probably then referred to the southern part of the Yaravico zone, where four bodega sites have been identified: Locumbilla, Gastón, Belén de Locumbilla, and Montalvo. The name Gastón is unusual and may be a variant of Gascón or Chacón: Mariana Chacón/Gascón was married to Cristóbal Bueno de Arana, doña Jerónima's brother. Montalvo may have retained the matronym of the husband of doña Jerónima's niece through her youngest sister, doña Inés de Villamisar Bueno Cárdenas y Arana. Doña Inés married Captain Gonzalo de Mazuelo, and their daughter, Aldonsa Mazuelos Villamisar, married Captain Juan de Mesa Montalvo.

When doña Jerónima Miranda de Estrada passed away in February 1606, Alonso Estrada was left with considerable property: Yaravico and its vineyard, orchard, bodega, earthenware vessels, mill, houses, slaves, animals, clothes, and household goods. She also willed property to the native peoples of Torata and Carumas (Kuon Cabello 1981: 360).[1] Alonso Estrada died on May 11, 1610. In his will, dated a month earlier on April 11, he left all his property to the Jesuit school in Arequipa. He also founded a cofradía, or religious brotherhood, at Moquegua's Iglesia Matriz (ADM 49, 50). In addition to the rural heredad in Yaravico, Estrada left one or more houses in Moquegua, which had been sold at public auction at unjustifiably low prices, and the Jesuits repossessed them (ADM 44). He also left a ranch in Ilo on the coast, 19 slaves (one of whom he freed), 7 mules, 9 burros, and 250 goats (Miró Quesada Sosa 1982: 93–107).

The Jesuits formally took possession of the Yaravico heredad and on November 12 sold it to Bachiller Juan Guerrero de Vargas, vicar of Moquegua. In the sale document, the boundaries of Estrada's Yaravico lands are stated as "above [north] with the Torata Indians' lands, on one side [west] with the river of this valley [the Osmore], on the other side [east] with the camino real ... to the valley and town of Locumba ... [and] down below [south] with the alfalfa field of Diego Fernández Maldonado" (ADM 44). The camino real likely refers to the old road on the eastern edge of the hills bordering the valley rather than the track of the present Panamerican Highway through the middle Moquegua valley. Fernández Maldonado was married to Estrada's niece, Isabel Vizcarra, sister of Alonso. The fact that the south boundary of the Yaravico estate "belongs to" Fernández may reflect the fact that Isabel's dowry included 500 pesos worth of land (Guíbovich P. 1984: 244–45), likely somewhere in the Yaravico toponymic zone. The 1610 sale document also reveals a complex pattern of ownership within the Yaravico estate, Estrada having given or sold parts of it to several others: the southern area of Locumbilla to Alonso de Vizcarra, as noted, plus parts to Cristóval Pérez (possibly one of the sons of doña Jerónima's illegitimate brother) and, on the north, to Felipe de Estrada (an illegitimate son of Alonso Estrada).

At the time of sale to Guerrero, Estrada's Yaravico estate included the following (ADM 44): a vineyard with 38,000 vines and an orchard with Spanish and native fruit trees, both enclosed by walls with doors and keys; a bodega with 25 large and 15 small tinajas; 2 lagars and their "appurtenances"; a "*contrabodega*" (storage cellar) with 6 good medium-sized tinajas, quantities of wine in tinajas and botijas, and equipment; a *botijería* (potter's workshop) with wheel, door, and key, and a botija kiln that held 420 vessels, with basins to levigate the clay (the document also mentions a piece of land "*al principio de la quebrada donde se saca el barro para botijas*" [f. 139r]); a room for the majordomo and another room between the botijería and the bodega, with doors and keys; a grain mill; a workshop with a forge and tools; copper utensils; a chapel with door, key, ecclesiastical vestments, chalice, altar, missal, Host container, and decanters; an alfalfa field; 8 slaves; several mules, 7 donkeys, 7 yokes and harnesses for oxen (presumably for grinding sugarcane), and 250 goats; and all the household goods, including bedsteads, cabinets, chairs, and tools. At the time, Estrada's estate, or some portion thereof, was occupied by Bartolomé Conde, a salaried employee and probably the site manager, or majordomo. Vicar Guerrero was also obliged to pay Estrada's substantial debts of 30,459 pesos and 2 *tomines*.

In 1614 Vicar Guerrero, the purchaser of Yaravico, formed a four-year *compañía* (business partnership) with Gerónimo de Cárdenas of Chucuito to transport the estate's various products to Torata, Candabaya, and Cochabamba (Rice 2011b: 178–79; ADM 46). These products included wine and also sugar and syrup made at a new mill (*trapiche*) he was planning to construct there. Sugarcane seems to have become an important crop in the valley after the 1600 Huaynaputina eruption and the end of the sixteenth-century wine boom (Rice 2009: 389).

But Guerrero soon began trying to sell the heredad, first to Dr. Alberto de Acuna, an *oidor* (judge) in the Audiencia of Lima, on June 25, 1616 (ADM 48). At that time, the northern and southern borders of the property were identified slightly differently than in the earlier sale: north with the Torata Indians' land and also that of Felipe de Estrada and south with the lands of Isabel Vizcarra, part of her original dowry that came back to her when her husband, Fernández Maldonado, died in 1613. Isabel also held land bought from her brother Alonso de Vizcarra (ibid.), presumably in Locumbilla, which included the heredad of Francisco Rodríguez Bayon.

The listed property at the Yaravico estate is largely the same in 1616 as it was in 1610. No new vines were planted, but the itemization included 3,400 botijas of wine from the current year's harvest; 51 tinajas, with a capacity of 2,500 botijas (suggesting a capacity of ca. 50 botijas per tinaja); 23 slaves; dwellings; a trapiche and equipment; a canefield; the botijería, with 3 *"cuerpos"* (work stations?); copper implements (including a large basin near the bodega proper to make *"arrope"* [boiled wine syrup] to add as a sweetener); a new alfalfa field; a long list of agricultural implements and tools, including those of the estate's blacksmith; 2 granaries for wheat and corn; 200 cows; a stable and 3 corrals; 6 pulling horses; 8 donkeys; and a chicken coop.

That sale apparently fell through, as two months later there is yet another document of sale of the estate or more likely only part of it, this time to Francisco López de Cáceres, dated August 24, 1616. The much abbreviated list of rooms, fields, household goods, and so on also mentions three training horses. The price was reduced by one-third (from 60,000 pesos to 40,430 pesos; ADM 49), slightly below the 1610 sale price. Apparently, a visiting church attorney from Cusco, soon to be Bishop of La Plata, had "demanded" that Vicar Guerrero sell the property within a year.

On January 24, 1618, the Yaravico heredad was sold yet again (ADM 50). López de Cáceres sold it to Juan Rodríguez de Ves, husband of Juana de Arana, daughter of Hernán Bueno de Arana. The purchase price of 45,430 pesos included wine made from the entire incoming harvest and delivered to Arica in January 1619. The document specified that the botijas have the standard capacity used in Arequipa—16 *cuartillos* (ca. 2 gal.; a cuartillo is approximately 1 pint)—sold for 2 pesos 6 reales per botija of fermented wine or 1 peso 6 reales if sold as *"caldo"* (fermented but unaged wine). The description of the property refers to a vineyard of Ana Rodríguez Corte Real, apparently inherited or bought from Francisco Rodríguez Bayon.

It is difficult to understand why the Yaravico property was so difficult to sell in the early seventeenth century. Keith Davies (1984: 102) claims the land Estrada and his heirs were trying to sell was barren. This is unlikely, unless the reference is specifically to the northern part of the Yaravico zone. The ruined heredades we named Yaravico 1, Yaravico 2, and Yaravico Viejo are arrayed around the western point of an area of unproductive land, although they are immediately adjacent to a swath of Class 1 soils and a narrow strip of Class 2 soils (see figure 6.3). It is equally likely that the Jesuits preferred cash to this distant rural property. Or the vicar may have had insufficient funds to maintain the estate; perhaps similar financial difficulties plagued subsequent purchasers. In any case, Rodríguez de Ves held on to the property for some time, thus keeping it in the extended Bueno family.

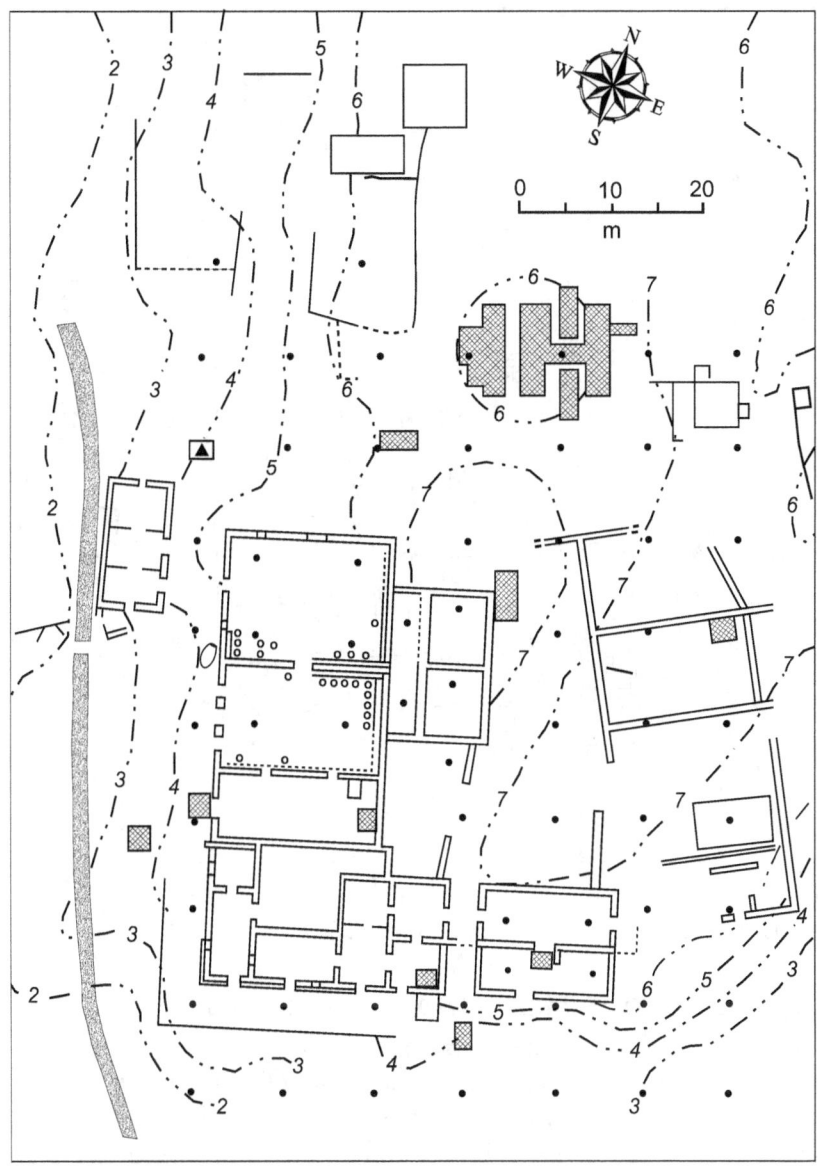

FIGURE 9.2 *Locumbilla site plan. Boxed triangle = datum; contour lines show relative elevations in meters. Double lines indicate walls of standing structures; single lines mark destroyed walls. Hollow circles = tinajas. Solid circles = shovel tests. Crosshatched areas = excavation units (southeastern corner omitted; see figure 9.8). Note irrigation canal west of the structural complex.*

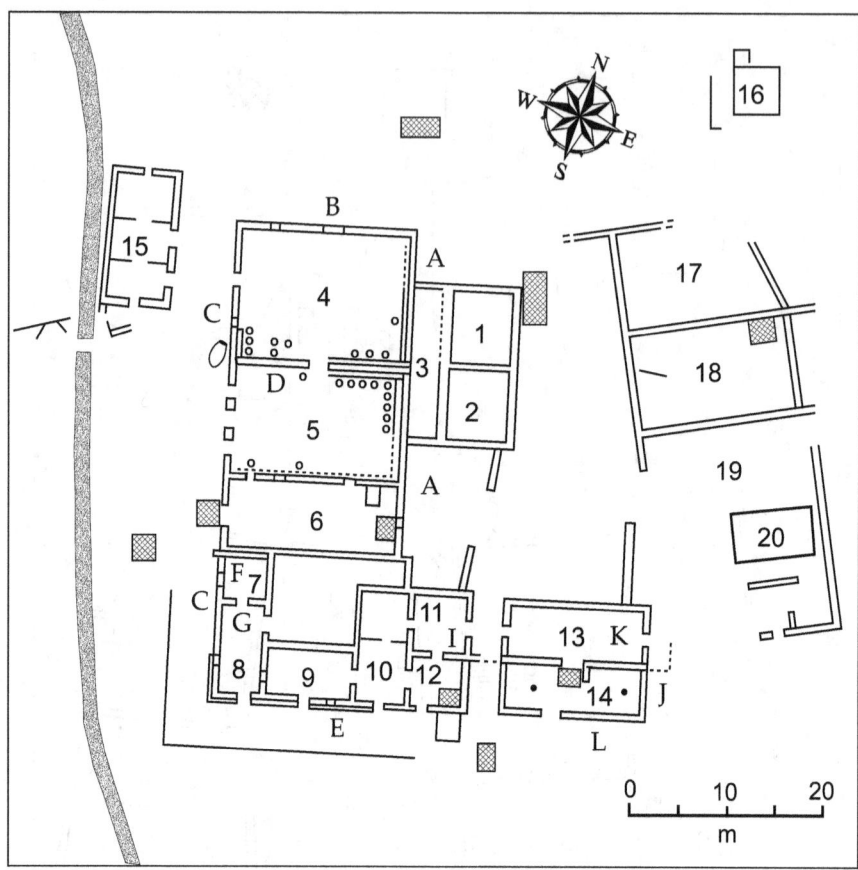

FIGURE 9.3 *Standing remains at Locumbilla. Structures, rooms, and enclosures are numbered for discussion in text; walls are labeled with letters.*

LOCUMBILLA BODEGA: THE INDUSTRIAL SECTOR

The Locumbilla bodega site (figures 9.2, 9.3, 9.4) lies in the southern part of the Yaravico toponymic zone, on the left (east) bank of the Osmore. Considering current toponymy, it is apparent that this property was the southern part of Estrada's wife's Yaravico estate, given to nephew Alonso de Vizcarra at his marriage in 1605. Standing structures oriented slightly east of north perch on a low rise at the base of a broad projecting desert hill. This hill forms part of the undulating eastern edge of the Osmore floodplain, just north of a pocket of flat land that pokes eastward into the mountains. Another, probably older, arrangement of low adobe walls was visible on a low rise north of the complex in 1970s

FIGURE 9.4 *The Locumbilla site, viewed from behind and looking to the southwest. Lagars 1 and 2, with adobe roof supports, are in the center; fermentation bodega Str. 4 is to their right, and open corral 17 is partially visible in left-center. Roofs cover (left to right) Strs. 11/12, Strs. 8–10, and Str. 6. Author photo, 1988.*

aerial photographs, but by the time of Bodegas Project fieldwork, only faint traces of the foundations of some of these structures were visible. Most had been destroyed by modern activities or covered by scrubby vegetation, and they were not explored.

Locumbilla has an integrated-block site plan, with its industrial and residential sectors adjoining, the former north of the latter. Excavations were placed purposively to examine correlations between these assumed functions and the kinds of artifactual and other material recovered therein, as well as times of construction and occupation (see discussion in Smith 1991: 198–226). Visible structures were primarily late in date, but, as discussed later, earlier remains were identified through excavations in the southeastern part of the site. For purposes of description, individual spaces—industrial and residential—and their walls are discussed here using the alphanumeric identifiers on figure 9.3. Because of the good preservation of the Locumbilla site, a variety of standing features of the industrial sector of the bodega could be investigated.

Lagars

Locumbilla had three visible crushing facilities, or lagars. Two small lagars (1 and 2) drained through small, arched adobe apertures in their western walls. Their liquid spilled into a slightly lower and larger tank (3), situated "behind" (i.e., east of and slightly above) the fermentation bodegas. The exterior walls of Lagars 1 and 2 are thick, composed of one header and one stretcher, the arrangement of headers and stretchers alternating in eight successive courses. The south wall of Lagar 2 measured 1.4 m high. Lagar 3's walls appear to be late additions, their construction incorporating brick and cobbles. The dressed stones or plaster commonly used to line the interiors of lagars were missing.

Eight pillars, up to 1.9 m high and with thirteen courses of adobes, were constructed on the basal walls of Lagars 1 and 2. These pillars featured notches or holes to support horizontal beams, suggesting that the lagar complex probably had "walls" of perishable quincha and perhaps also a cane roof.[2] An excavation unit at the northeast exterior corner of Lagar 1 (Rice 1996a: 193) revealed that the base of the 1.4-m-high foundations was composed of large river cobbles up to 75 cm in maximum dimension, set into a foundation or builder's trench (figure 9.5). This trench, extending 55 cm from the edge of the cobbles and 68 cm deep, intruded into lenses of guano, lime, and ash. A fragment of British Pearlware pottery in the fill indicates construction after 1778, the beginning of comercio libre in Spain's colonies.

Fermentation Structures

Locumbilla's three large, adjoining rectangular rooms—"bodegas proper"—for fermenting and storing wine (table 9.2) have complex construction histories.[3] Only Rooms 4 and 6 were roofed. Rooms 4 and 5 held tinajas in situ. Room 4 appears to have been a later addition to Room 5 or a division of it: the east side walls (Wall A; only one header wide) of the two rooms do not meet precisely. The adobes of Room 4 (see table 9.3 for measurements) were laid on two courses of cobbles, and the north wall (B) has a blocked doorway. Room 6 probably originally held tinajas but was apparently converted into a "tonel room" that held a variety of large wooden containers for wine in the late eighteenth century, when wooden receptacles began to be used (Kuon Cabello 1981: 366). A low stone platform was noted near the northeast corner, probably to support such a barrel. One doorway was originally wider but had been partially filled to create a narrower entry, and another doorway in the east wall (A) was blocked.

Wall C, the long western facade of this complex that constitutes the "front" of these three rooms, appeared to have been built as a single construction

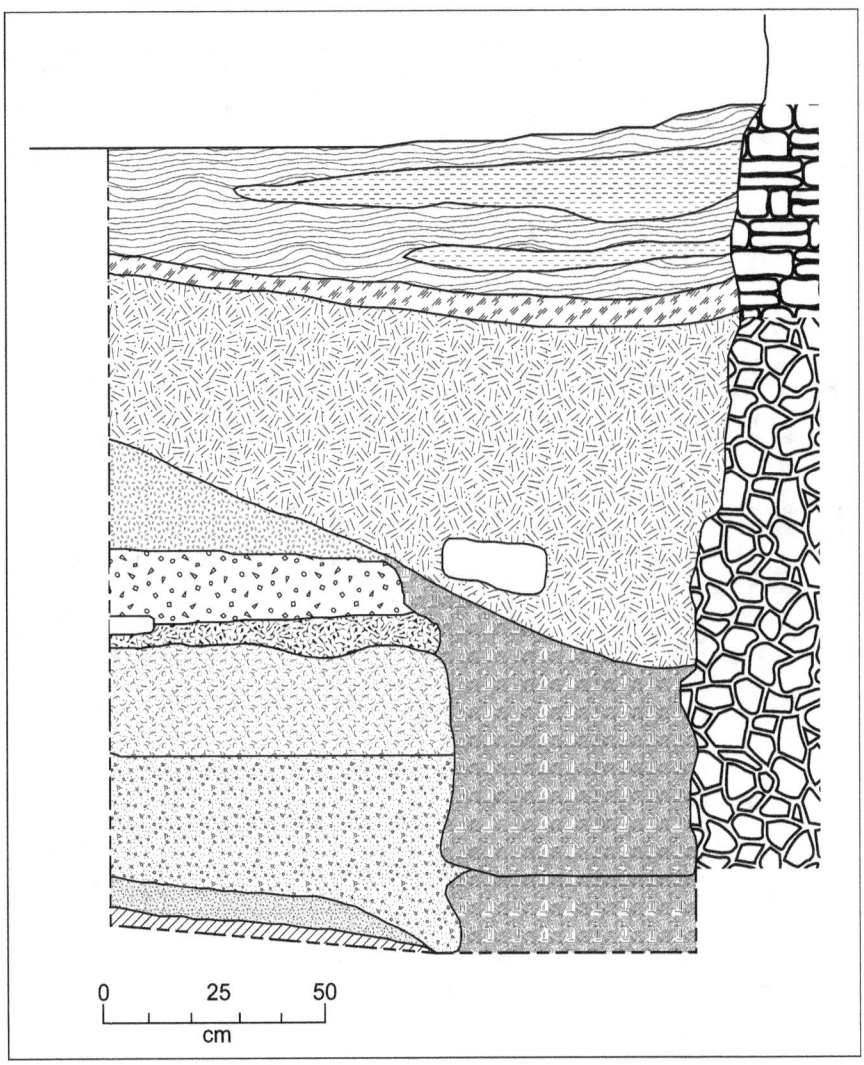

FIGURE 9.5 *South profile of the foundation trench excavated at the northeast corner of Lagar 1, showing builders trench.*

episode. It was built after the east-west room-divider walls: the adobes of Wall D between Rooms 4 and 5 were not bonded into it, although those of the wall between Rooms 5 and 6 are so bonded. The mortar of Wall C incorporates tinaja and botija fragments. Nonetheless, the variable height of Wall C and that of the roofs, plus the differential arrangement and alignment of windows

TABLE 9.2 Dimensions (m) of fermentation bodegas in the Yaravico zone

Site	Str. #	Length	Width	Area (m²)
Locumbilla	4	18	14	252
	5	18	11.5	207
	6	18	8	144
Yaravico Viejo	1	30	6.5	195
	2	29	10	290
Yaravico Bajo	1	35	15	525
Gaston	1	35	4	140
Moquegua valley mean		29.3	8.16	234.3
Total N measurements		45	40	39

TABLE 9.3 Dimensions (in cm) of adobes used in constructions

Location	Length	Width	Thick	Mortar	Comment
Locumbilla					
Str. 2, S wall	65–66	28–30	12	Little	Very stony
Str. 4	64	30	13–15	8–9	2–4-cm stones
Str. 15	64	28–29	11–12	4–5	Modern
Huaracane					
Older str.	61.5	29	13.5	4–7	
Newer str.	—	27–28	—	6–8	Pebbly mortar
Yahuay resid.	57	30	13.5	—	Fibrous material

and doors, suggests a lack of architectural planning for an integrated, unitary facade.

The must flowed from Lagar 3 into these fermentation rooms by way of drains cut through the walls, which fed into narrow stone or plaster channels (*canaletas*) that run around the interior perimeter. In Room 4, for example, the canaleta is about waist-high, supported by a one-course widening of the lower interior walls on the eastern, southern, and southwestern sides; there is no channel on the northern wall (B). In Room 6 the lower walls were poorly preserved, probably as a consequence of damage to (or removal of) the channel-supporting adobes. The fact that a canaleta had originally been present is evidenced by two drains in the wall with Room 5: one in the middle of the wall (blocked on the

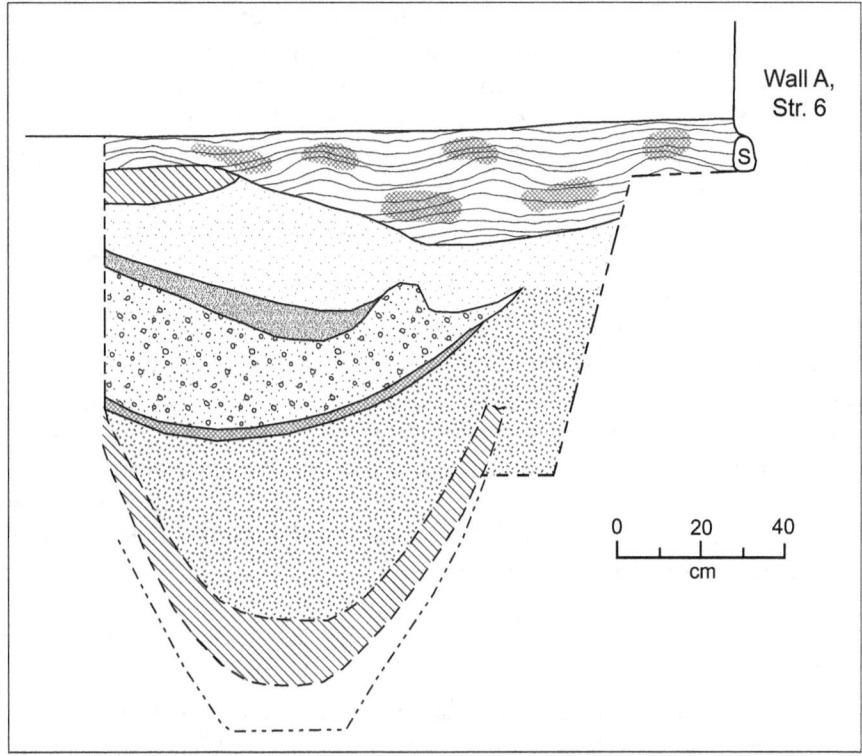

FIGURE 9.6 *North profile of the excavation unit in Structure 6 against the east wall, showing (as cutaway) the lower broken section of a tinaja exposed by the excavation. Sandy soil, organic matter, and a thick layer of grape seeds filled the depression.*

Room 5 side) and the other just inside the western facade wall (C). An excavation unit in the interior of Str. 6, at the base of the blocked doorway on the east side (Wall A), revealed the broken lower halves of two tinajas under a layer of grape seeds (figure 9.6).

Tinajas

Only seventeen tinajas were noted in situ in Rooms 4 and 5; another had been removed and lay outside. Seven vessels were dated to the years 1790 (n = 3), 1791, and 1803 (n = 3) by the inscriptions on their shoulders. The large tinaja lying outside Wall C had an unusually long and narrow shape compared with earlier vessels, such as the Yaravico Viejo 1590 tinaja, which were egg-shaped with high shoulders. Measuring 2.7 m long with a 23-cm-diameter base and an interior mouth diameter of 48 cm, its inscription is "Año de 1803." On two tinajas the dates were part of larger inscriptions: "16 de Maio Año de 1791†^{YB}" and "No. 18 Año De 1790^{YB}." The late dates—and lack of religious references—on these vessels probably reflect the late constructional modifications of the fermentation bodegas (indicated by the Pearlware sherd) and the eighteenth-century commercial focus on brandy (pisco) making.

The YB (sometimes YB^{co} or B^{co}) inscribed on these jars is of some interest. It is tempting to relate this notation to the toponymic zone name Yaravico, often spelled Yarabico. In addition to Locumbilla, it is found on two other sites in the Yaravico/Locumbilla zone and at seven sites in the Calaluna, Omo, and Corpanto zones in mid-valley (table 9.4). Associated dates begin in 1768 and extend to 1797, but most (n = 18 of 22; 82 percent) fall between 1783 and 1793. YB and its variants are likely maker's marks of some sort, signifying the potter(s) who made the tinajas. This tinajero might have been an itinerant potter—perhaps one of several—and possibly attached to one of the heredades in the Yaravico zones, who formed and fired tinajas up and down the valley, "signing" his manufactures for recordkeeping purposes.

Falca

At Locumbilla, the distillation facility was located in front (west) of, and at a lower elevation than, the tinaja rooms (Rooms 4 and 5; Wall C), just to the west of the modern irrigation canal and southwest of Str. 15. It sat near a low platform of old adobes incorporated into a more recent wall, all of which might have been part of a receptacle for holding the liquid. A brick channel 3.5 m long ran from this wall/platform to a shallow circular depression (2.4 m diameter; figure 9.7), which would have held the flat-bottomed copper basin used in distillation. The interior of this depression, lined with stones and tinaja fragments, had a floor of fired brick.

A tiny filled-in arch at the base of Wall C in Room 4 appears to be the opening through which the fermented wine could flow (by way of piping or a plaster channel) toward this putative now-destroyed tank or some other container prior to distillation in the falca. This ground-level opening in Room 4 is reasonably well aligned with the falca traces.

Kiln

The botija kiln at Locumbilla and its large excavation units have been amply described elsewhere (Rice 1994: 331–37; Rice and Van Beck 1993: 74–75), and

TABLE 9.4 Occurrence of "YB" and variant inscriptions on tinajas at bodega sites by toponymic zone

Zone	Inscr.	Date	Site	N	Other Inscription
Locumbilla	YB	1790	Locumbilla		No 18
	YB	1791	Locumbilla		16 maio
	YB	1791	Belén de Loc.	3	11 maio, 14 maio, 16 maio
	Bco	1793	Montalvo		San Angel de la Guarda
Calaluna	YB	788	San Antonio	2	
	YBco	1779	Calaluna		
	YBco	1791	Calaluna		
	Bco	1791	Calaluna		
	Bco	179	Calaluna	5	
	RBco	1797	La Cuevita		
	Ysco	797	Sorsano		
	Y	1768	Sorsano		Gran Poder de Dios las Bale
Omo	YBco	788	Omo Chico	3	9 octubre, 3 noviembre
	Bco	178	Omo Garibaldi		
	Bco		Omo Garibaldi		Las Bendites Animas
Corpanto	YB	788	Corp. Viejo South		S de octubre 20
	Bco	1783	Corp. Viejo South		San Roque Avogado
	Bco	1783	Corp. Viejo South		Sto. Domingo de Gusman
	EBco	1783	Corp. Viejo South		Nra Sra Aransasurano [?]
	BcoCro	1783	Corp. Viejo South		San Cristobal

details are only summarized here. This round updraft kiln was constructed in a large, sloping pit, about 6 m north-south and 3 m deep, that expanded a natural depression in rocky sterile subsoil. Built of adobes, the kiln had a 2.2-m-high firebox and a ware chamber approximately 4.6 m in diameter, with standing walls 90–95 cm high. Its mouth opened by way of a tunnel sloping down from the east; the upper surface of this tunnel was first detected in a 1987 excavation unit. The kiln collapsed from overheating during firing. After it cooled, workers emptied the ware chamber of its load of botijas, which were badly warped or broken. More than 900 kg of these ceramics were recovered in a 40–50-cm-thick stratum excavated in a 3.0 × 1.5 m unit on the east side. The dump of botija wasters from the failed firing also included small quantities of pottery not recovered at other sites, including "setters" or "stacking rings" and

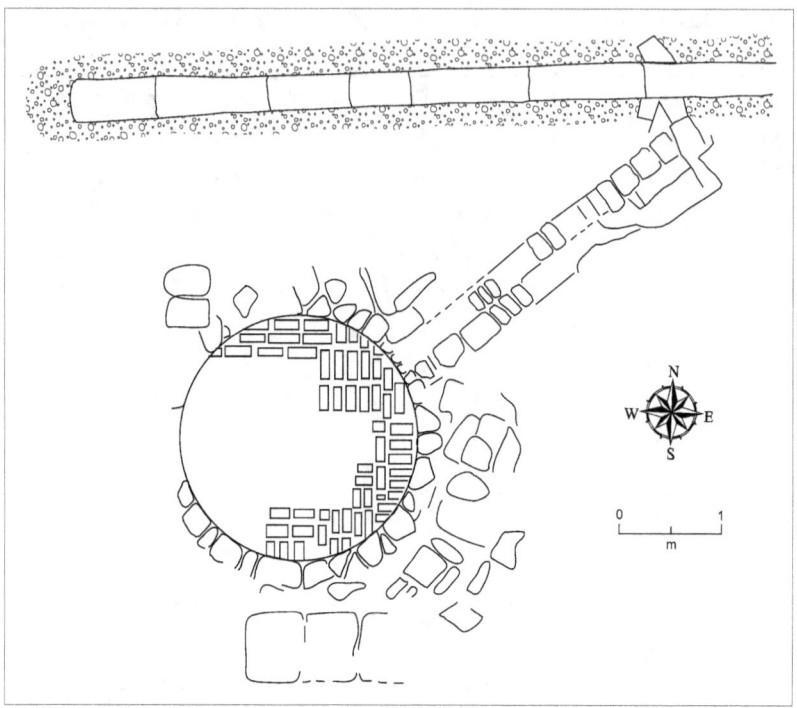

FIGURE 9.7 *Falca complex at Locumbilla (southwest of Str. 15 on figures 9.2 and 9.3), showing the adobe wall, a stone-lined drain, and the patterned brick-lined base for the copper basin of the pot-still.*

Mechero Plain jars (Smith 1991: 341d). A radiocarbon date (Beta–33725) on charcoal from the floor of the firebox yielded a 1-sigma calibrated range of AD 1586–1726 (see table 1.2).

After its collapse, the kiln was abandoned and the depression filled with trash. Post-collapse stratigraphy is complex, with lenses of ash, sand, clay, and lime below and above large boulders up to 80 cm in diameter. Possibly, the kiln depression was used as a basin for levigating clay for later pottery manufacture, which would explain the contoured laminar deposits and the peculiar moisture retention noted in deposits in the firebox and elsewhere around the kiln.[4]

NORTH SIDE

As noted, unexplored platforms, lines of stone, and wall foundations lie on the slope northwest of the buried kiln. One low, square platform of cobbles had a smaller, rectangular adobe platform off its southwestern corner. Because these walls and platforms were not investigated, it is difficult to know what they might represent.

Similarly, no function is known for a small, approximately 50-cm-high adobe platform (Str. 16) in the northeast corner of Locumbilla, north of the possibly modern corrals. This low platform is topped by flues or channels constructed of tinaja fragments, and tinaja and botija fragments were scattered around it, along with slag-like vitrified material, suggesting some activity involving high-temperature fires and air circulation. Two units excavated at the platform's northwest corner (not shown on figure 9.2) revealed an east-west rock-and-mortar wall running from the base in the general direction of the kiln, and a line of adobes lay immediately below the surface, along with lime and limestone. Perhaps this low structure was part of the long-sought pottery workshop or was an area for heating and applying pine pitch after collapse of the kiln. Alternatively, it might have been involved in cooking the liquid from crushed sugarcane to make sugar.

Str. 15, off the northwest corner of Room 4 at the "front" of the bodega, appeared to be another fairly recent building. The northern part of its western wall was heavily damaged by canal construction, which exposed a thick layer of guano underlain by deposits of grape seeds from emptying a lagar. Str. 15 was built of adobes set over seven courses of cobbles; the corners combined headers and stretchers, and the walls were almost entirely headers. Two doorways penetrated the east wall, and the interior of the structure was divided into three spaces by partitions of quincha.

East Side

Three large, corral-like enclosures (Strs. 17, 18, and 19) stood on the east side of Locumbilla and appeared to be relatively recent (particularly 18, constructed of *adobónes* [tamped earth blocks]). They opened to the west, into a central courtyard area, but we could not determine whether access to these spaces was intentionally left open or if original gates or walls had been scavenged. A smaller, roughly rectangular adobe enclosure (20) was constructed in Enclosure 19, its interior lined with quincha.

Three excavation units (see Smith 1991: 224–26) in Enclosures 18 and 19 were excavated in hopes of encountering walls of a botijería to accompany the excavated kiln. Deposits of micaceous clay, similar to that used for Mechero Plain pottery, were noted in the units, but volcanic ash was not identified. In one unit in Enclosure 18, a low, east-west adobe wall, interrupted by a jog or zigzag, was composed of two courses of adobes over a foundation of large stones, with prepared flooring on either side. This wall was built over the micaceous clay, which in turn overlay a stratum of gray clay and botija fragments, resting on sterile subsoil. No analyses were carried out to explore mineral or petrographic comparisons between the micaceous clay deposits in this area and Mechero Plain ware.

In another unit, in the northern part of Enclosure 19, we encountered a wooden post and posthole that appeared to be associated with tethering animals rather than construction. Two small pit features were identified nearly a meter below surface, underlying a thin layer of calcareous material: one held a concentration of corncobs; the other, larger and deeper, contained burned mammal bone. A radiocarbon sample from the latter yielded a 1-sigma calibrated range of 1570–1690 (Beta–22433; table 1.2). A Peruvian colleague commented that similar deposits in northern Peru were thought to be refuse left by workers involved in construction activity.

Southeast Corner

After initial shovel testing suggested the possibility of pre-1600 material in the southeastern portion of the Locumbilla site, we carried out intensive excavations over three seasons that opened more than 60 m² of the total area of 330 m² (figure 9.8; see Smith 1991: 205–19 for detailed discussion). These excavations revealed the builder's trench for Str. 13, abundant deposits of grape seeds and botija fragments, and thin (up to 15 cm) deposits of volcanic ash in association with at least two Early and one Middle Colonial–period structures. These constructions, here labeled Strs. X, Y, and Z,[5] had stone and clay foundations and frequently included posts, postholes, and burned straw (especially Str. Y), suggesting that they were roofed or enclosed. This was the only location at any of the bodega sites where we were able to recover sixteenth-century materials from stratigraphically controlled excavations.

Structure X: Str. X, measuring approximately 10 m southwest-northeast, was represented by three wall segments about 65–70 cm thick and 50 cm high. Constructed of medium to large rocks in clay mortar, this wall was dated to the sixteenth century on the basis of the volcanic ash layer abutting it above its base. The discontinuous distribution of ash inside and outside Str. X (its north wall) appears to correspond to the robbing of construction stones. Ash from the 1600 Huaynaputina eruption was sealed in the small doorway in the central standing section, which was mortared closed after the event. Some botija fragments were recovered under the floor of Str. X.

Structure Z: A small corner wall of another southwest-northeast–oriented structure, parallel to Str. X, was encountered approximately 4 m to the north.

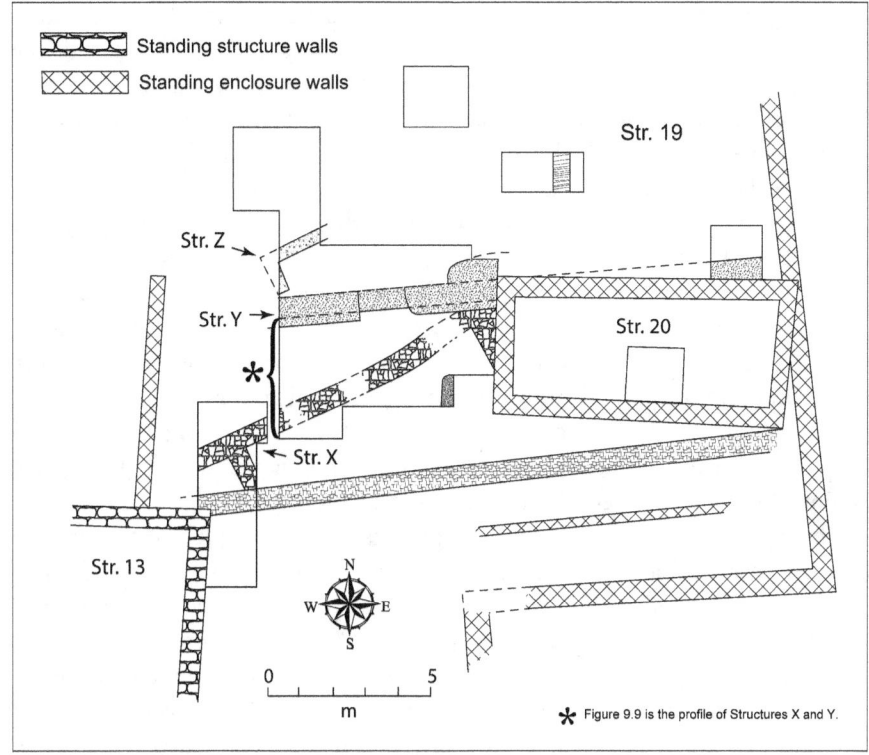

FIGURE 9.8 *The southeastern corner of the Locumbilla site, showing excavation units and numbered structures and enclosures. Walls of individual structures uncovered in excavations are indicated by various patterns of hachure and stipple. Asterisk indicates the location of figure 9.9.*

Because these walls were only about 40–45 cm thick, we designated it a separate building, Str. Z, rather than a northernmost wall of Str. X. The volcanic ash layer butted up to the north side of its wall, indicating that it, too, was an early structure and likely functioned with Str. X. This Str. X-Z complex appears to have been a sixteenth-century lagar arrangement destroyed by the Huaynaputina event.

Structure Y: Str. Y, interpreted as an early-seventeenth-century lagar, consists of two substantial walls, north and east, built directly above volcanic ash in two stages: gray clay and rock in the lower, wider portion and pinkish clay and rock above. These walls, standing approximately 1 m high and up to roughly 90 cm thick, were constructed with large stone foundations, many scavenged from Str. X. This suggests an effort to build a sounder and more stable lagar structure here, compared with its predecessor. (Similar construction was also noted in an east-west wall exposed at the corner of Str. 13.) A sealed doorway was identified in the northern wall of Str. Y; the lack of European artifacts in the fill of the doorway suggests it was blocked before 1780. Outside the doorway was a dense zone of botijas, lime, undecorated pottery, and small rocks. Deposits of grape seeds, 10–50 cm thick, were noted inside Str. Y as well as under and abutting its walls.

Inside the northwest corner of Str. Y, excavations revealed a prepared clay surfacing, 13–20 cm thick and mixed with rock, directly above volcanic ash, with a 20-cm-high riser against the north wall. A 20-cm-thick stratum of grape seeds lay upon this surfacing (figure 9.9), and grape seed deposits of variable thickness were also noted under and abutting the structure's walls. Similar interior floor surfacing was not evident in the northeast corner, where several posts and a thin layer of burned straw suggested a perishable roof or enclosure wall. The Str. Y interior also held other deposits of wall-fall capped by a thick layer of grape seeds mixed with earth, pitch-lined botija fragments, and small particles of lime, similar to the deposit outside this structure.

The lagar foundations and botija fragments below the volcanic ash layer in the southeastern part of Locumbilla probably represent the earliest locus of wine production on the heredad. This area was part of Yaravico between 1577, when it was given to doña Jerónima upon her marriage to Alonso Estrada, and the 1600 Huaynaputina eruption. The Str. Y lagar surfacing extended southward 1.4 m, at which point it was damaged by wall-fall from Str. X, which suggests that Str. Y was built between the 1600 eruption and the devastating 1604 earthquake. This early-seventeenth-century rebuilding thus seems to have preceded the gift of this land—as Locumbilla—to their nephew Alonso de Vizcarra in 1605. These southeastern facilities were abandoned at some unknown later time, with wine making moved to the northwest where the standing structures date to the late eighteenth century.

Other Excavations: Several other units were excavated in the southeast sector of Locumbilla. One, inside and against the southern wall of Str. 20, uncovered a thick layer of grape seeds above volcanic ash. Pottery from the lowest levels was plain and unglazed, and a few provincial Inka polychrome sherds were noted. A unit outside the northeast corner of Str. 20 revealed a small charcoal-filled pit below a clay floor, covered by volcanic ash; fragments of botijas and Mechero Plain lay below the ash. A wall displaying the same two-tier construction as that of Str. Y and deposits of grape seeds were also revealed in the excavation.

In another unit, excavations below the ash yielded a fragment of Panamanian tin-enameled pottery, Mechero Plain ware, peach pits, and tinaja sherds. Finally, a unit in the extreme southeastern corner of the site was excavated in hopes of locating a pre-1600 workshop or kiln because large quantities of botija wasters

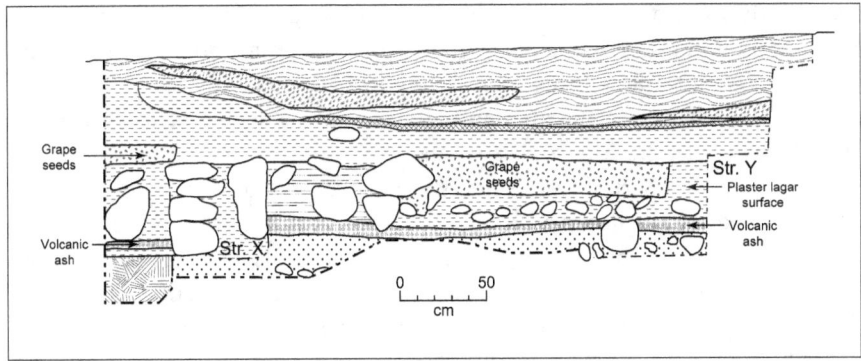

FIGURE 9.9 *Western profile of the excavation of the lagar of Structure Y, showing the clay-plaster surfacing covered with grape seeds. See figure 9.8 for location of profiled excavation wall.*

(and also bone) were noted in the area in shovel testing. Unfortunately, nothing indicative of the sixteenth century could be identified.

RESIDENTIAL SECTOR

Locumbilla's residential spaces lie south of Room 6, with eight rooms (7 through 14) and an open patio. Room 9 was occupied by squatters in the late 1980s. A stone mosaic patio wraps around the southwestern corner of the complex, extending about 5 m from the adobe structure walls. The exterior base of the corner of Room 8 and the southern wall (Wall E) of Rooms 9 and part of 10 were set off by a low ledge atop this patio.

The front, or west, wall (Wall C) of Rooms 7 and 8, in the southwest corner of the complex, exhibits signs of complex remodeling of these rooms. For example, the north (F) and south (G) walls of Room 7 may originally have extended farther to the west, but at some point they were cut flush with the western facade Wall C (of Rooms 4, 5, and 6). Part of the west wall (C) of Room 7 was missing and the opening closed with cane, set above a low adobe wall segment (Wall H, unlabeled on figure 9.3), with dressed, stepped masonry *calicanto* capping it. The cut south wall (G) separating Rooms 7 and 8, perforated by a door between the two rooms, also appears to be set atop this low Wall H segment. Wall H continues southward across the lower western side of Room 8, with new adobes used in a wall atop a central section.

Room 8 is entered from the south through a doorway with stone jambs. The room has traces of blue and red paint on its plastered interior, as well as red paint on the exterior south wall (Wall E), and yielded a fragment of stucco with gold leaf on it. It also boasts a herringbone-patterned brick floor extending into the patio. We interpreted this room as a possible chapel (Rice and Watanabe 1990: 260), perhaps a reconstruction built on remains of the sixteenth-century chapel constructed by Alonso de Estrada.

The east-central part of the residential sector consists of Rooms 10, 11, and 12. Room 10 had a well-preserved roof and a wooden plank floor in the southern half or two-thirds of the interior, with a large square hole in its center. The room seems to have served at least in part as a kitchen for the current squatter residents. A large flat slab of rock in the southeastern corner may be a batan, and a small beehive-shaped oven was constructed in the northeast corner, the wall behind it markedly fire-blackened.

Rooms 11 and 12 are separated by Wall I. The north wall of Room 11 was built of adobes that were darker brown (more organics?) than the mortar, which undercut their edges. Numerous fragments of botijas and tinajas were incorporated into the mortar between the adobes (also noted in the western facade Wall C), which were primarily headers. Room 12 appears to have been added on to 11 because the adobe courses do not match and the floor is lower. The northeast corner of the floor was paved with dressed stones to raise it. The interior walls were plastered, and the doorway in the east wall was blocked. An excavation into the southeast corner of Structure 12 revealed a low stone banquette or bench along the east wall constructed upon the lowest of three floors, this one of paving brick and small cobbles set into mortar. A small adobe platform had been constructed outside Room 12 at its southeastern corner.

At one time, Rooms 11 and 12 might have been attached to Str. 13/14, just to the east. This two-room structure appears to be a fairly recent construction, however, perhaps built upon earlier foundations. The rooms have plastered interiors and a floor of brick pavers in a herringbone pattern; walls were built on cobbles. Room 13 had a doorway and window in the eastern wall (J) and a window in the gable of the western wall. Room 14 had traces of a north-south dividing wall just east of the doorway in the wall (K) between the two rooms. The south wall (L) of Room 14 appeared to have been built or rebuilt at some time over a broader base of cobbles, with calicanto quoins inserted into the lower SE and SW corners. The adobe courses of Wall L did not match those of the earlier Wall J.

The east-west Wall K separating Rooms 13 and 14 appears to be an eastward extension of Wall I separating Rooms 11 and 12, as they are almost perfectly aligned, although the intermediate section of the putative wall was missing in the 1980s. The two paired structures are now separated by a narrow passageway.

The same transverse Wall K may have extended farther east beyond Rooms 13 and 14, as indicated by a small, low area of cobbles and mortar on the exterior. The east wall (J) is all headers, except in the area of the dividing Wall K, which appears to have been removed and then rebuilt with stretchers.

SPECIALIZED ANALYSES

Ceramics

More than 6,500 sherds of domestic ceramics were recovered out of a total of 9,100 artifacts in excavations at Locumbilla. Half (49.4 percent) were fragments of various undecorated "white wares," primarily European, including cream wares, transfer-printed (26.2 percent), and ironstone (17.6 percent) produced in the late eighteenth century and later.

In the early sixteenth century, prior to the arrival of the Spaniards, the site that would become the Locumbilla winery was likely occupied by Aymara-speaking colonists from the Lake Titicaca basin, as were the lower reaches of the Osmore's tributary streams. Excavations into basal levels of the small quebrada where the kiln was constructed yielded forty-seven sherds of provincial Inka (Sillustani) polychrome mixed with European material. This was not a primary context, and Inka sites in general are rare in the Moquegua valley. Alternatively, the colonial-period owner, Estrada, might have had access to finely decorated Indigenous tablewares through various contacts with native Andeans, including the relatives of doña Jerónima's illegitimate brother. The deposit might reflect an instance of "eating like an Indian": negotiating social and power relations between Spaniards and Indigenous elites through shared meals (Rodríguez-Alegria 2005).

The imported tin-enameled pottery, or loza, recovered in Moquegua differs from the better-known loza of North America and the Caribbean in displaying primarily green and black-brown (rather than blue) painted decoration over a brick-red paste (see chapters 11–13). Two sherds of Peruvian-made loza, Mas Alla Polychrome and Corregidor Polychrome types, were recovered in excavation below the 1600 Huaynaputina ashfall in the southeastern corner of Locumbilla (cf. Smith 1991: table 7.2), supporting a late-sixteenth-century date of production.

Other Artifacts

In addition to pottery, numerous other categories of artifacts were recovered at Locumbilla, especially various kinds of personal objects (see Rice 2011b:

239–44). These items attest to the likelihood of winery workers and their families living in scattered perishable huts around the site:

- Personal items (clay pipestem, 5 coins, comb, key, Swedish matchbox, part of a watch, carved handle, leather knife sheath, cross)
- Toys, entertainment (3 parts of dolls, 2 pottery gaming disks)
- Sewing implements (clay spindle whorl, 2 brass spools, 3 brass pins, 2 brass thimbles, 2 iron scissors fragments; miscellaneous pieces of fabric and cordage, including a small Inka textile of cotton [William Conklin, pers. comm. May 7, 1991])
- Jewelry (3 beads, 2 pieces of jewelry)
- Clothing (13 buttons, 2 pieces of shoe leather, hook-and-eye)
- Metal: horse hardware, and
- Miscellaneous (fragment of an oil painting on canvas).

Archaeofauna

Large quantities of faunal material were recovered in the three seasons of excavations at Locumbilla and were analyzed by Susan deFrance (1993: 98–109, 1996: table 5). Only 15 taxa were recovered from Early contexts, but Middle contexts exhibited considerable diversity, with 31 taxa, and 23 taxa were identified in Late contexts (deFrance 1993: table 4-7). Mammals were the most common in terms of numbers of taxa, minimum numbers of individuals (MNI), and edible meat weight (EMW).

In Early contexts (the southeastern corner of the site), mammals represented 99.6 percent of the remains; these were dominated by camelids (llamas), with 13 MNI (31.7 percent of mammals) and 28.45 percent of the EMW (ibid.: table 4-6). The next-most-common mammals in terms of EMW were cattle and caprines (sheep and goats) in MNI. Chicken was present in small amounts.

Middle and Late contexts were also dominated by camelids, caprines, and cattle, but remains of "pigs, horse, either burros or mules, guinea pigs, other rodents, cats, and dogs" were also present (ibid.: 98). Bird remains include chickens, muscovy ducks, and doves; coastal resources are represented by fish (corvina, mackerel, mullet, anchovies) plus a variety of snails, mussels and other bivalves, and crab and urchin (ibid.: 109).

In general, the diet of Moquegua's winery residents emphasized introduced species (cattle and caprines) and deemphasized indigenous fauna such as camelids (which declined to 14–15 percent of EMW in Middle and Late contexts at Locumbilla), guinea pigs, and marine resources.

TABLE 9.5 Botanical remains at Locumbilla bodega

Introduced Taxa	Native Taxa
Vitis vinifera (grape)	*Lagenaria siceraria* (gourd)
Ricinus communis (castor bean)	*Cucurbita maxima* (squash)
Citrullus vulgaris (watermelon)	*Cucurbita moschata* (squash)
Prunus persica (peach)	*Capsicum bacatum* (rocoto chili)
Olea europaea (olive)	*Capsicum annuum* (ají pepper)
Medicago sativa (alfalfa)	*Zea mays* (corn)
Ficus carica (fig)	*Phragmites communis* (cane)
Triticum sp. (wheat)	*Phaseolus vulgaris* (bean)
Opuntia ficus-indica (cactus)	*Solanum tuberosum* (potato)
Bactris gasipaes (coco chileno)	*Anona cherimolia* (cherimoya)
Gymnospermae (softwoods)	*Acacia* sp. (acacia)
	Cyperus sp. (sedge)
	Neoraimondia macrostibas (cactus)
	Arachis hypogaea (peanut)
	Sapindus saponaria (soapberry)
	Inga feuillei (pacae)
	Schinus molle (peppertree)
	Typha angustifolia (cattail)
	Panicum sp. (grass)
	Datura sp. (datura)
	Salicacaeae (willow family)
	Fabacaea (bean family)
	Poaceae (grass family)
	Dicotyledoneae (hardwoods)

Source: Jones 1990: tables 7.1, 7.2.

Botanical Remains

Archaeobotanist John Jones (1990) analyzed the plant remains recovered in excavations at Locumbilla (table 9.5). Eleven introduced plant taxa were identified, six of which were Old World comestibles: grape, olive, wheat, peach, fig, and watermelon. Non-food introductions included alfalfa and castor beans. Locumbilla's botanical suite was dominated by native taxa, categorized as items of food, construction or fuel, and "other." Consumable plants and seeds included corn, beans, squashes, potatoes, peppers, avocado, cherimoya, and coca. Construction materials and fuel included various grasses (cane, sedge, catttails, some of which might have been used to make mats, baskets, room dividers, and roofs) and trees (mesquite, acacia, pacae, molle, willow, and hardwoods).

The interiors of sherds of Mechero Plain jars commonly displayed a black encrustation, sometimes as much as 10 cm thick at the base, believed to be pine pitch. Analysis of a sample of this material (Jones 1993) yielded pollen from nine taxa, primarily wind-pollinated species including abundant *Pinus* (84 percent) and also Poaceae, ragweed-type plants, cheno-ams, *Quercus* (oak), and Malvaceae. Phytoliths in the sample were dominated by panicoid grasses (such as sugarcane), *Cyperus*, two types of palms, and abundant *Heliconia*. Other materials in the residue included charred grass and plant remains and marine and freshwater diatoms. Most of the taxa represented by the pollen and phytoliths in the Mechero sample were not identified among the macrobotanicals from Locumbilla. Jones speculated, but drew no conclusions, about the origin of this tarry material in his report. We believe it represents pine pitch obtained from Pacific coastal Mexico, Honduras, or Ecuador. It is known from the 1593 will of Alonso de Adrada that Moquegua residents obtained pitch from Huatulco, Mexico (Guíbovich P. 1984: 373, 375). The presence of these large Mechero Plain jars among the botija wasters surrounding the kiln suggests that they were placed at the kiln to heat and liquefy the pitch prior to application as a sealant on the interior of the botijas.

Two introduced plants are of particular interest and perhaps similar uses: castor bean (*Ricinus comunis*) and soapberry (*Sapindus saponaria*). Castor bean seeds were found in pre-1600 contexts at Locumbilla and in such quantities elsewhere around the site that Jones (1990: 98) suggested that their abundance "cannot be accounted for by any but an industrial usage."[6] *Ricinus* seeds are widely crushed to extract the oil, which has medicinal uses, for example, as a purgative and to aid various digestive problems and skin disorders (Scarpa and Guerci 1982). Castor oil has varied industrial uses, including lubrication of machinery, such as trapiches (sugarcane mills) (Gade 1975: 183) and ships' gear (Gil 1975: 66n25), in a blue dye for fabric (Zori 2011: 475), and in making soap. Castor oil was probably a cheaper alternative to olive oil, a key ingredient in Castile soap. Similarly, the seeds of *Sapindus*, when crushed, produce a lather and have a long pre-industrial history of being used as soap, as suggested by its common name. Soapberry has also been administered medicinally as an emetic, among other uses.

A possible explanation for the abundance of *Ricinus* and *Sapindus* at Locumbilla comes from early-eighteenth-century documents. In 1725 Locumbilla's owner, don Antonio Isidro Fernández Maldonado y de la Raya of the Sacred Bethlemite Hospitaler Order, donated property to the order to establish a hospital in his home. According to traditional history in Moquegua, this hospital—the Convento Hospital Beletmítico de San Antonio de Padua (or San Antonio Abad [Anonymous 1998: 816], one of the oldest hospitals in the country)—was constructed the following year to care for native Andeans throughout the valley who became sick while working in the vineyards. Fernández treated them and gave them "medicines" (Montenegro y Ubalde 1987a: 165), which undoubtedly included castor oil. It is not clear whether the bodega site identified as Locumbilla or the now-destroyed site to the south that retains the name Belén de Locumbilla (Rice and Watanabe 1990) is the location of this eighteenth-century hospital.

Two native plants with medicinal uses were recovered at Locumbilla and Yahuay bodegas (Jones 1990: table 7.2). One, *Datura* sp., can be useful as a painkiller as well as for other ailments, although it can be toxic in large doses. Similarly, the leaves and berries of the *molle* (*Schinus molle*) tree have various uses in herbal medicine, including topical application as an antiseptic to heal wounds and skin disorders and, taken internally, for respiratory, urinary, and menstrual disorders and as a digestive stimulant (Bras et al. 2011).

One of the products of the bodegas, brandy, was also probably useful for medical purposes. The distillation process is said to have been "discovered" by a medieval Italian doctor; and brandy, or *aqua vitae*, was initially produced by doctors, apothecaries, and monks for medicinal use, administered "particularly against plague, gout and loss of voice" (Braudel 1981: 242; also Read 1986: 196; Seward 1979: 16; Singer, Holmyard, and Hall 1955: 142; Unwin 1991: 236).

LATER HISTORY OF YARAVICO AND LOCUMBILLA

Information about early activity at Locumbilla (and Yaravico more broadly), although scanty and perplexing to integrate, nonetheless provides some tantalizing glimpses into the foundations of the centuries-long history of wine and brandy production in the middle Osmore valley. The Yaravico area enjoyed considerable importance in the history of the valley, probably as a consequence of multiple factors: associations with the wealthy and influential Bueno family, proximity to the town of Moquegua, and relatively large expanses of good-quality agricultural soils. Despite Locumbilla's association with the Buenos, the artifact assemblage recovered in excavations suggests a middle- to lower-class occupation (Rice 2011b: 255–56). This may be historically "real"—the rural bodegas were generally occupied primarily by staff and workers rather than by their

TABLE 9.6 Owners of the Yaravico/Locumbilla estate in the sixteenth through eighteenth centuries

Name	Owner	Dates of Ownership
Yaravico	Hernán Bueno	??
Yaravico	Jerónima de Miranda and Alonso de Estrada	1577–1610
Locumbilla	Alonso de Vizcarra	1605
Yaravico	Jesuits in Arequipa	1610
Yaravico	Vicar bach. Juan Guerrero de Vargas	1610–16
Yaravico	Francisco López de Cáceres	1616–18
Yaravico	Juan Rodríguez de Ves	1618–??
Yaravico	José Hurtado Zapata y Echagoyen	??–1708
Yaravico	Jesuits	1708–67
Locumbilla	Antonio Isidro Fernández Maldonado y de la Raya	1725–1767??
Yaravico	José Fernández Cornejo	

owners—and also a consequence of Bodegas Project excavations focusing on industrial rather than residential sectors of the sites.

The Locumbilla winery/bodega/heredad is an example of estate production or upstream vertical integration, engaging in multiple "industrial" activities: wine and pisco making and probably also vinegar, to be sure, but also producing botijas and possibly soap and medicines in the eighteenth century for an on-site or nearby hospital facility. One wonders if the peculiar firing facility in the northeast corner of the Locumbilla grounds might have been involved in this latter activity rather than in pottery or sugar production.

The Yaravico estate was left to the Jesuits in the early seventeenth century, but they immediately sold all or part of it into private ownership. In 1708 (table 9.6), Yaravico's then owner, Captain don José Hurtado Zapata y Echagoyen, left his vineyard, bodega, and heredad to the Jesuits to establish a school for young men (Brown 1986: 141–42). They opened the Colegio de San Josef? in 1713, and in 1735 the hacienda Santo Domingo in the "*pago* of Cupina" was donated to its support. In 1763 they constructed a new bodega at Yaravico (ibid.: 142; Cúneo-Vidal 1978: 231–32). After the Jesuits were expelled from Peru in 1767, Yaravico was purchased by José Fernández Cornejo (Brown 1986: 157). In the late twentieth century Locumbilla was owned by the state as an agricultural research station.

NOTES

1. This may be an example of the payments of restitution church fathers urged wealthy Spaniards, especially conquistadors and encomenderos, to make to native Andeans to counter the rapacity of conquest.

2. The southernmost bodega in the Yaravico zone, Montalvo, boasted four wooden, bell tower–like features at the corner of the roof over a large lagar. One tower actually did have a bell at some time in the past, and two were topped by weather vane–like ornaments.

3. The present text describes the condition of Locumbilla and other sites as they were at the time of Bodegas Project fieldwork. On Saturday, August 8, 1987, a 5.5-magnitude earthquake centered in Arequipa lasted nearly a minute. Part of the upper south wall of Room 13 and the dormer window collapsed and fell into the room. Since then, it is evident from Google Earth™ that the roofing on all but one structure (Room 9) and numerous walls (especially Wall C, the front wall of Rooms 4, 5, and 8) have disappeared, probably in the magnitude 8.4 earthquake in 2001 or a slightly less severe temblor in April 2006.

4. The moisture retentiveness of the clay adobes and mortar in this area made it nearly impossible to distinguish individual adobe bricks in excavations until after they had dried for some time—typically as much as two to three weeks. Consequently, we found ourselves in the awkward situation of understanding little about what we were digging through until well after we had dug it.

5. These structures were identified as Strs. 1, 2, and 3 in previous reports (e.g., Smith 1991) but are re-labeled here to avoid confusion with the numbering of standing structures.

6. Castor beans were also present at Chincha and Yahuay bodegas and at Torata Alta (Jones 1990: table 7.1), but not in such great quantities. *Sapindus* was also noted at Yahuay. By contrast, a single *Ricinus* seed was found at Tarapacá Viejo (Zori 2011: 475). Although castor oil is widely used medically, *Ricinus* plants, especially the seeds, are extremely toxic (because of the presence of ricin) if ingested.

7. Saint Joseph is a protector of young children and is associated with orphanages (Flynn 1985: 343).

10

Religion . . . and Resistance?

> Religious customs may be similar or different . . . [but] they all have one thing in common: they are tied to a specific place and a historical constituency. All practice takes place somewhere.
> —William A. Christian Jr. (1981: 178)

Christian practice in medieval Europe can be differentiated spatially and temporally, a key variable being the role of popular, local cults versus that of the papacy and institutions of the Roman Catholic Church (Weinstein and Bell 1982: 182–91). Catholicism operated on two levels. One was "the Church Universal, based on the sacraments, the Roman liturgy, and the Roman calendar," whereas the other was local and particularistic, operating in a sacred landscape created from locally venerated "places, images, and relics, locally chosen patron saints, idiosyncratic ceremonies, and a unique calendar built up from the settlement's own sacred history" (Christian 1981: 3). "Local Catholicism" is a place-based set of beliefs, devotions, festivals, relics, and shrines devoted to a religious patron, either a saint or the Virgin Mary, believed to intercede against natural disasters (Christian 1981).

Spain's unique experience of reconquest, coupled with broader religious transformations in Europe, "led to a kind of Christianization of the landscape in the form of shrines and chapels,"[1] followed by "a shift away from holy sites in the countryside" to more centralized, urban devotional activity (ibid.: 91, 199). As discussed in chapter 6, Spanish conquest of the "New World" was a collaborative military-religious enterprise between the kings of Spain and the Roman Catholic

DOI: 10.5876/9781607322764.c10

Church, based on an agreement that the latter would allow Spain to exploit the foreign land's riches in exchange for converting its heathen residents to Christianity. These circumstances led to a distinctive Spanish Catholicism that was carried to the Americas.

LOCAL CATHOLICISM IN PRE-MODERN SPAIN

Early Christianity had long been dominated by the proliferation of local cults and shrines based on relics of saints, preferably brought from the Holy Land but also relics of local martyrs, hermits, or bishops miraculously "discovered" as signs of divine intervention (Brown 1981: 188–94; Christian 1981: 21). Northern European saints tended to be associated with furthering establishment (elite, monarchical) interests, whereas those venerated in Iberia and Italy were more likely to have come from the lower classes, been involved in "intense family conflict," and lived lives working miracles for ordinary petitioners (Weinstein and Bell 1982: 182–83). In early modern Spain, the landscape was peopled not only by human inhabitants but also "by other beings . . . the remembered dead . . . fairies . . . giants . . . and the pantheon of supernatural figures associated with Catholicism" (Christian 2010: 75). By the thirteenth century, however, these cults of local saints were replaced by devotions to the Blessed Virgin Mary, whose popularity had swept across Christian Europe (Christian 1981: 123–24).[2]

Marianism

During the eleventh and twelfth centuries, the Virgin Mary gained a marked following in Spain (Hall 2004: 19),[3] as she already had in the Mediterranean area. Her heightened importance is at least in part a consequence of the introduction of religious imagery, as opposed to relics, as a focus of devotions: because of the belief in Mary's heavenly assumption at death, there could be no remains of her body to be kept as relics (Christian 1981: 21). In addition, the Muslim takeover of the Iberian Peninsula, beginning in the south, meant local Christian shrines and relics of early martyrs were often destroyed or taken northward by those fleeing the Muslim advance (ibid.: 141).

Attitudes toward the Virgin Mary were modified by churchmen during a time when women in general suffered an ambiguous, dichotomized status in Iberia. They were feared and despised and therefore had to be controlled because of the power of their sexuality (Boxer 1975; Grieve 2009). Chastity was prized above all other female virtues and was indexed to social, political, and moral order. Women were symbols of nations and the salvation of men's souls;

virginity was equated with nation building and unchaste women with national downfall, evidenced in a legend about a beautiful Muslim girl seducing an early Christian ruler and precipitating the Muslim takeover (Grieve 2009: 114–15). Thus Marianism was particularly notable on the frontiers of reconquista in the southern peninsula: "Typically, the major church in a reconquered town would be named for Mary ... It was usually located on the site of the chief mosque" (Hall 2004: 27).

Mary has been described as a "divine non-specialist," or generalist, in terms of her devotions, as opposed to "specialist" saints appealed to under specific circumstances, such as illness, insect pests, hail, and so on (Christian 1981). The growing supplications to Mary as a positive, compassionate mediator between the heavenly and the earthly were accompanied by a movement away from viewing natural disasters as punishment of an angry god. Instead of assuming a community's collective responsibility for both bringing ill fortune and deflecting it, medieval Christian religion and worldview became more individualistic, with Mary advocated to ward off individual misfortune (ibid.: 206–8). Mary was viewed as an intercessor with her son, Jesus Christ, in petitions for divine assistance.

Cofradías

A singularly important expression of local or popular Catholicism is the institution of cofradía, also known as confraternity, lay brotherhood, *hermandad*, or *mayordomía*. Originating in medieval Europe, these organizations elected members (*cofrades*), often from the same trade or profession or the same neighborhood and typically from generations of the same families, who shared a desire to pay homage to a particular saint (Foster 1953). Confraternities performed various social, religious, and charitable services for their members and society.

Socially, these organizations were particularly important in urban contexts, where they created a type of fictive kinship (Lynch 2003), much like modern sororities, fraternities, and trade brotherhoods. They gave loans and credit, helped members who were sick and gave them funerals, and aided travelers who had no relatives in a particular city. They also provided "a kind of group insurance" for the afterlife (Christian 1981: 143).

Religious functions included veneration of a particular saint or holy event, activities pursued most vigorously during Holy Week and on the saint's feast day, with a special mass, processions, and fiestas. Dedication to a particular saint was often community-wide for protection against epidemics, insects, or natural disasters, meaning confraternities played an important role in local identity formation (ibid.: 50–52).

Charitable activities were developed in line with Catholic teachings that the path to salvation was to imitate Christ through acts of mercy: "feeding the hungry, giving drink to the thirsty, clothing the naked, visiting the sick, ransoming captives, lodging the homeless, and burying the dead," following Matthew 25 (Flynn 1985: 336). Some confraternities aimed to satisfy these needs for paupers, thereby "creating a welfare program for society" (ibid.: 338). Others directed their works toward building hospitals, roads, and bridges; caring for pilgrims; hearing masses said for all manner of souls; protecting orphans, including giving dowries to orphan girls; freeing prisoners from local jails (ibid.: 339–43); and redeeming captives in foreign lands (Brodman 1986).

Efforts to institutionalize such welfare programs in the hands of governments, as in northern Europe, were soundly rejected in Spain, where cofradías were especially popular: "Charitable ritual had defined relations between rich and poor in Spain, placing paupers in privileged spiritual positions with the power to help transport their benefactors to salvation through prayers of gratitude for charity ... Spaniards preferred this spiritually fulfilling, personal contact with the poor, and rejected ... attempts to replace ritual with bureaucratic organization of poor relief" (Flynn 1985: 348).

Sixteenth-Century Spain

By the sixteenth century, the papacy had developed multiple concerns: Marian devotions were too popular, confraternities were too independent, feasts and festivals were too secularized, and expenses for charity would be better centralized (Flynn 1985, 1989). To address these issues, the church held a series of meetings known as the Council of Trent, which promulgated changes known as the Catholic, or Counter, Reformation.

One 1564 decree from the council articulated the value of sacred images in painting or sculpture for didactic purposes in inspiring devotional emotion, especially among the illiterate and uneducated. Images could be used provided they were not treated as "idols" and were presented with "decorum," that is, "neither indecent nor profane in either dress or ornamentation" (Rodríguez G. de Ceballos 2010: 20). Particularly encouraged were images that referred to events and symbols of Christ's Passion, especially the cross. This Tridentine position promoted the creation of cult, devotional, and processional images in religious art, along with a "multiplication of altars, altarpieces, shrines, and oratories where they were exhibited" (ibid.: 29).

The overall impact of Trent was the imposition of "a more strict devotional and doctrinal program to conform with the church's new and more narrow definition of orthodoxy" (Flynn 1989: 5). This program included reassertion of the doctrine of transubstantiation in the Eucharist, resituating Mary beneath Christ as a mature mother sorrowing for her adult son (rather than a young mother holding the infant), and promoting new confraternities and other rituals devoted to the sacraments and the Passion (Flynn 1985: 342, 1989: 122–23, 125). Beginning with the Council of Trent and the Counter Reformation, significant religious transformations swept over Europe and incorporated Enlightenment notions, especially individual responsibility for good and ill, modernity, and the rise of capitalism.

Political consolidation of the Iberian kingdoms that had begun under Isabel and Ferdinand was accompanied by religious consolidation, including strengthening of formal Catholicism vis-à-vis lay practices (Christian 1981: 158–61). New cofradías were dedicated to the Holy Sacrament (Santísimo Sacramento; established in 1542), the True Cross (Vera Cruz), the Souls in Purgatory (Las Ánimas de Purgatorio, who "continued to demand aid from the living"), and the Holy Name of Jesus (Flynn 1989: 122–23). The "motif of the Mother of God contemplating the Passion was the most highly developed" in Spain; and confraternities were dedicated to Our Lady of Sorrows (Nuestra Señora de Dolores), Solitude (de la Soledad), the Rosary (del Rosario), the Immaculate Conception (de la Concepción Inmaculada), and so on (Christian 1981: 181–90; Flynn 1989: 126). Cults of individual saints never disappeared, although those that survived the Counter Reformation were primarily "health-bearing patrons" such as San Roque, San Antonio, and San Blas (Flynn 1989: 124).

CATHOLICISM IN EARLY PERU: FORMAL AND LOCAL

Christianity was brought to the Andes with the first expeditions of exploration and, following conquest, by a full complement of secular clergy (Catholic Church officials) and regular clergy (the religious orders). The early decades of introduction of Christian religious institutions in the Andes have been variously periodized, depending on whether the focus was on regular or secular clergy (Cavagnaro Orellana 1988: 89; Dussel 1981: 49–61; Kubler 1946: 341–54; Tibesar 1971a: 54–55; van Oss 1978: 30–31). I propose these overlapping periods for sixteenth-century southwestern Peru:

1. 1529–40: initial missionization with the entry of regular clergy (Dominicans and Mercedarians) accompanying the conquistadors and explorers.

2. 1537–69: the unsettled period of warring Spanish factions and native uprisings, which saw the founding of the first dioceses (see table 6.1); incorporation of regulars as doctrineros in encomiendas (1540–53); arrival of Franciscans (1548); First (1551) and Second (1567–68) Provincial Councils of Lima; establishment of formal, permanent doctrinas (missionary parishes) for instruction of natives (1557); and founding of monasteries.
3. 1570–75: establishment of reducciones de indios; establishment of the Inquisition in Lima (1570).
4. After 1575: partitioning of existing dioceses and establishment of new ones (including Arequipa and La Paz); Third Council of Lima (1582–83), which provided for teaching the catechism in Quechua and Aymara (Dussel 1981: 57; see also MacCormack 1985: 448–50).

Religious Orders and Saints

The Dominican Order became especially important in the Lake Titicaca basin, where the crown repartimiento of Chucuito was assigned to them. Fray Tomás de San Martín arrived there in 1539 to begin building churches and monasteries (Tschopik 1946: 509); Chucuito's Iglesia Santo Domingo, one of as many as fifteen sixteenth-century churches, may be the earliest surviving church in South America (Fraser 1990: 11).[4] Although Franciscan influence was felt most strongly in the northern Andes, the Recollect Franciscans had a monastery in Arequipa, the Convento de San Francisco, founded in 1552 on land donated by Lucas Martínez Vegaso (Málaga Medina 1975: 58, 1990: 289, 292). The Augustinians established a church in Arequipa in 1574 (Málaga Medina 1975: 58, 1990: 290). The Mercedarians (Orden de la Merced) were a non-mendicant order that supported Gonzalo Pizarro. They became prominent in northern Chile—four friars accompanied Almagro on his journey and seven went with Valdivia (Cavagnaro Orellana 1988: 20, 26, 89–90)—and established the Iglesia de Nuestra Señora de la Merced in Arica. They held a large property in the lower middle Moquegua valley.

The wealthy Jesuits, the Compañía or Society of Jesus, arrived in South America in 1568, well after the Dominicans and Franciscans. They built numerous schools throughout the viceroyalty, including a college in Juli in 1576, and in 1621 they established the Royal School of San Francisco de Borja in Cusco, which taught the sons of many kurakas in southern Peru (Stern 1982: 167). Their beautiful monastery in Arequipa was built in the late sixteenth century, and they owned significant property in Moquegua (below), where they established a school in 1711[1713?]. The Jesuits, who believed their authority was derived from the papacy rather than from kings (Dussel 1981: 58), were expelled from Peru in 1767 by order of King Charles III, their vast landholdings confiscated by the crown and sold in public auction.

Three Peruvians were elevated to sainthood (Dobyns and Doughty 1976: 105–7), primarily for their work with native Andeans and the poor: San Martín de Porua, San Toribio Mogrovejo, and Santa Rosa. San Martín de Porua or Porres (1579–1639), patron of the sick, poor, enslaved, and orphaned, was beatified in 1837; his feast day is November 3. Martín was the child of a Spaniard from (perhaps a knight of?) Alcantara, Juan de Porras, and Ana Velásquez, a free black woman from Panamá. Rejected by his father for his African features and socially marginalized, Martín became a Dominican tertiary (a lay practitioner under the Third Order of Saint Dominic) and was known for his work with the sick and care of animals.

San Toribio Mogrovejo (1538–1606) is patron of Latin American bishops; his feast day is March 23. San Toribio, a former Grand Inquisitor of Granada and archbishop of Lima, organized the Third Council of Lima to improve the ministry to Indigenous peoples, especially in northern Peru. He is said to have personally baptized hundreds of thousands of native Andeans in Peru and initiated numerous reforms.

Santa Rosa (1586–1617) is patroness of Lima, of Peru, and of all of Spain's lands in the Americas, the Indies, and the Philippines. Beatified in 1668 and canonized in 1671, Santa Rosa's feast day is August 23. Rosa was born Isabel de Flores in Lima, to Gaspar de Flores (from Puerto Rico) and María de Oliva. She modeled her life after Saint Catherine of Siena and became a Dominican tertiary. According to legend, she attempted martyrdom in association with the repulsion of Dutch (Protestant) pirate invaders of Lima's port of Callao in 1615. The cult of Santa Rosa de Lima was "hotly contested" in power struggles between Spaniards and native Andeans (Morgan 2002: 67–97; Palmer and Pierce 1992: 41; see also Hampe Martínez 1997).

Ecclesiastical Architecture

Crown efforts to establish a framework of Christian order in the colonies were marked by the creation of large cathedrals in the colonial cities and small chapels in rural areas. Both kinds of churches represent dramatic instances of exercising power to redefine space and register distinct syncretism, or transculturation, because they were frequently constructed atop Indigenous religious structures. Although the preferred building materials were fine masonry, stone, tile, and brick, the earliest structures often had to be built of the materials available, often simply adobe walls with thatch or cane roofs (van Oss

1978: 40–45; Wethey 1949). Nonetheless, the urgent need for a church structure—any structure—dictated rapid construction, with the rude early buildings replaced as soon as possible by more imposing edifices. The builders of these edifices were thoroughly aware of the weighty impression the exteriors made on the natives—"the ornament and splendor of church is essential to lift up their spirits and move them to the things of God" (Hanks 2010: 65)—as well as the subtler impressions of the rituals carried out in the interiors: "oral performances . . . coordination of body postures . . . music . . . interior acoustics, light, mass, volume, and density of signs, would greatly amplify the sense of collective copresence with the 'mystery of God'" (ibid.: 64).

It is unfortunate that virtually nothing remains of the early colonial churches in Moquegua because southern Peru exhibits a mix of traditions of ecclesiastical architecture. These hybrid styles have been given various labels, including *mestizo* (Wethey 1949), Andean Hybrid Baroque (Bailey 2010), and numerous versions of *criollo* (creole) and "*ibero-indigena*"—its very naming a controversial and politically loaded, often racially charged issue similar to that of toponymy (see Dean and Leibsohn 2003). This style, described as "the most original contribution of the Hispanic colonial period" in Peru (Wethey 1949: 20), is typified by florid ornamentation that draws on Spanish Catholic roots and pre-Columbian Andean traditions. Motifs include rosettes, grapes and vines, papayas, bananas, apples, pomegranates, the Andean *ccantu* lily, corn plants, fronds, shells, mermaids, monkeys, birds, and pumas. The ornate *portada* (facade) of the Iglesia de Santo Tomás in Chumbivilcas, for example, is decorated with a sun and moon, birds, fish, monkeys, chinchillas, serpents, and flowers (Gisbert 1980: 61). Much of the iconographic vocabulary in this regional style is tropical, perhaps relating to an Indigenous artistic tradition of complex wood carving in the tropical forests on the eastern flanks of the Andes.[5]

"Mestizo"-style designs appear to have been composed and executed either by Indigenous artisans or criollos who had minimal contact with European canons (Cummins 1988: 121; Wethey 1949: 20). The style is primarily found outside the main colonial centers, for example, in Arequipa (Quiroz Paz Soldán 1991a) and the Titicaca basin, and it contrasts with churches in Lima, which more closely resembled Sevillian architecture (Wethey 1949: 1–12, 71–72, 261). This hybrid architecture reflects the greater freedom permitted in peripheral or frontier contexts for combining artistic elements in asserting identities (see Harth-Terré 1965).

A second architectural tradition is *mudéjar*, named for Muslim artisan producers (see chapter 11), and it is characterized by a mixture of Muslim and Christian motifs, materials, and techniques. In the viceroyalty of Peru, *mudejarismos* in carpentry were seen in marquetry-like ceilings of churches (Bernales

Ballesteros 1986; Gutiérrez 2002: 47–67; San Cristobal 1995) and the enclosed wooden balconies of elite residences in Spanish cities, including Moquegua.

LOCAL CATHOLICISM

Local Catholicism in Peru is a combination of beliefs and practices colonists brought as part of the local culture of their home communities, plus divine intercessors and advocates, to accommodate the new circumstances of their lives. These local belief systems provide a unique window into the interactions between Spanish authorities and the colonists and between Spaniards and Indigenous peoples.

Cofradías were established as part of popular religious practice, but those in the colonies differed from confraternities in the homeland—particularly in rural areas—by virtue of their role in spreading the Catholic faith to the natives. These brotherhoods were actively encouraged by the clergy, and in Peru, particularly southern Peru, they reflected the changes imposed by Trentine reforms. As a consequence of Spanish ethno-racial exclusionism, cofradías in the Andes were primarily "Spanish" in membership, with native Andeans, mestizos, and blacks forming their own organizations (Foster 1953: 22; García-Bryce 2004: 30–33).[6] Study of these brotherhoods has revealed variations and changes in their activities. In Lima, as in other cities and in the Spanish homeland as well, many artisan groups—tailors, shoemakers, silversmiths—formed their own confraternities as well as occupational guilds (*gremios*) and participated in civic and religious celebrations (García-Bryce 2004).

Another aspect of local Catholicism is the establishment of shrines, many of which were placed over former Inka wakas (Sallnow 1982). A prime example—also illustrating the continuing role of Marianism in frontiers (Hall 2004: 27)—is the Inkas' sacred Island of the Sun/Copacabana in Lake Titicaca, which became a Marian shrine (and also a cofradía) dedicated to Nuestra Señora de Copacabana. The Virgin Mary was conflated with Pachamama (earth mother) in early paintings showing Mary's triangular-shaped spreading cloak sheltering or embodying Cerro Potosí (Gisbert 1980: 17–22, figures 2–5).

RELIGION IN EARLY MOQUEGUA
FORMAL CATHOLICISM: URBAN CHURCHES, CHAPELS, SCHOOLS, AND SHRINES

In the early Spanish settlement that became today's Moquegua, churches, chapels, and religious schools and hospitals were built by secular and regular clergy (see Gutiérrez and Viñuales 1977; Rice 1995: 376–79), largely financed through donations and bequests of wealthy heredados. Religious schools were established in Moquegua by the Dominicans in 1652 and by the Jesuits in 1711[1713?] (Kuon Cabello 1981: 189). Most of them were rebuilt and enlarged repeatedly after collapsing in the region's earthquakes. Several were dedicated to protection of vineyards, the foundation of Moquegua's colonial-period prosperity.

The earliest Christian establishment in the Osmore valley was the Iglesia San Sebastián in Escapagua (ibid.: 189–91). According to local tradition, Escapagua was the first Spanish settlement in the valley, founded on January 20, 1541, the day of Saint Sebastián, although the town's formal founding (as Villa San Francisco de Esquilache) was in 1618 (see Cúneo-Vidal 1978: 553–62 for the *Acta de la Fundación*). The precise location of this church is unknown, as is the date of construction, thought to be in the 1560s. Dismissed as "only a chapel" in the early discord between Escapagua and Moquegua, the structure was unused by the Spaniards after 1624, when the focus of colonial life in the valley shifted to the opposite side of the river. Saint Sebastian, an early Christian and martyr of Narvona (Kuon Cabello 1981: 59), is a protector against the plague and, among viticulturists, against diseases of the vine (Weinhold 1978: 101).

Across the Río Tumilaca, the main church in the town of Moquegua was the Iglesia Santa Catalina de Alejandría, known as La Matriz ("mother church"). Santa Catalina, virgin and martyr, was an early Christian saint and patron of preachers; her feast day is November 25. Built on land purchased from Capt. Alonso de Estrada on the north side of today's Plaza de Armas, the church's history began with a series of chapels (Gutiérrez and Viñuales 1977: 83–86; Kuon Cabello 1981: 191–94; Watanabe 1984). The first was the Chapel of San Pedro, built at a cost of 3,000 pesos by the first *teniente corregidor* in Moquegua, don Pedro León de Guevara Sisa (mozo), son of the conquistador of the same name and doña Catalina Sisa, both of Cusco. After this chapel was destroyed by the 1604 earthquake, Estrada began construction of what was to become the Iglesia Matriz in the same location, with two chapels: San Juan and San Antonio de Padua. The latter held images of San Antonio, Nuestra Señora de la Candelaria, and Nuestra Señora de la Purísima Concepción that Estrada ordered made in Juli (Miró Quesada Sosa 1982: 95). Some years later don Cristóbal Pérez Cugate, from Valencia, added the chapel of Nuestra Señora del Rosario. A still later chapel was dedicated to the Peruvian Santa Rosa.

During the early-seventeenth-century quarrels between settlers on opposite sides of the Tumilaca, Moqueguanos were able to proudly tout their Iglesia Santa Catalina, with its "baptistery, choir, towers, and bells" (Kuon Cabello 1981: 190). However, the church and its chapels suffered heavy damage from earthquakes and experienced at least five major rebuilding episodes through the generosity of benefactors (Gutiérrez and Viñuales 1977). By the late eighteenth century, La Matriz had a 60-m-long sanctuary, walls of stone, a vaulted roof, eight (possibly fourteen) chapels, and five high altars with *retablos* (carved wood panels). The church was abandoned after the 1868 temblor because, given the economic situation of the valley and its vineyards in the late nineteenth century, money for repairs could not be raised.

A shrine to San Bernabé (feast day June 11) was established in 1596 by the *ermitaño* priest Gaspar Fernández de Lugo Cabeza de Vaca, on a hill at the northeast corner of the town of Moquegua (Miró Quesada Sosa 1980: 14). San Bernabé was declared patron of the vineyards in the valley of Moquegua and second patron of Moquegua itself (Gutiérrez and Viñuales 1977: 83; Kuon Cabello 1981: 194–95). For many years Moquegua held an annual festival dedicated to San Bernabé, in which each hacienda took turns contributing a measure of wine from the recent vintage to defray its costs. This festival ceased to be observed in 1807.

In 1604, Fernández de Lugo also left property in Moquegua to the Cofradía del Santísimo Sacramento for the Recollect Franciscans to establish a religious house (Gutiérrez and Viñuales 1977: 86–90; Kuon Cabello 1981: 202–7; Montenegro y Ubalde 1987b). Eventually built primarily of adobe and cane by the Jesuits, the Iglesia San Francisco was occupied briefly by the Observant Franciscans after the Jesuits were forced out of Peru in 1767, then by the Franciscans de Propaganda Fide from Bolivia after 1776. The church's wooden retablo, which served as an altar, held *bultos* (polychrome wooden images) of San Francisco de Borja (patron against earthquakes), San José, San Ignacio, and San Francisco Xavier; there was also a *nicho* for Nuestra Señora de Loreto, invoked as a patron of Moquegua after an earthquake in 1713 (Kuon Cabello 1981: 193).

In the early seventeenth century a chapel known as San Juan in the "El Huayco" region on the east end of town was demolished, and its place was taken by the Iglesia Belén, constructed in 1613 by the Orden Hospitalaria Beletmítica (Gutiérrez and Viñuales 1977: 90; Kuon Cabello 1981: 207–16). This order, whose patroness was Nuestra Señora de Belén, also had charge of the Convento Hospital Beletmítico de San Antonio de Padua, built in 1726 at the Locumbilla or Belén de Locumbilla wine heredad (Montenegro y Ubalde 1987a). First built of adobe, then of stone in 1830, the church was damaged by the region's earthquakes but was repaired and kept functioning. The patron of the hospital and the church, San Juan de Dios, is celebrated each year on the Sunday after his day (March 8). The church also celebrates the Peruvian San Martín de Porres on November 3 (Kuon Cabello 1981: 210).

The Iglesia and Convento Santo Domingo, at the southeast corner of the Plaza de Armas, became the principal church of the Moquegua parish after the destruction of La Matriz. The church was originally constructed of cane and adobe in 1652 as a monastery and then became a school of the Hospederian Dominicans of the Sacred Order of Predicadores (preachers) of Arequipa (see Gutiérrez and Viñuales 1977: 86; Kuon Cabello 1981: 197–202; Montenegro y Ubalde 1987a). It was known as the "Hospedería de Nuestra Señora del Rosario" of that order. Shortly after its construction, the Yahuay heredad was donated in 1655 to support the Dominicans. Destroyed by an earthquake in 1784 and rebuilt of stone and plaster, the Iglesia Santo Domingo has been called "the richest establishment outside the city of Arequipa," excluding the Jesuit properties (Brown 1986: 142).

Like the Iglesia Santo Domingo, the San Francisco complex was completely rebuilt with stone and masonry roof vaults after the strong 1784 earthquake. In 1793–96 the remains of Santa Fortunata were recovered in Rome and given to Father Tadeo Ocampo, head of the Moquegua Franciscans de Propaganda Fide (Kuon Cabello 1987; Miranda Nieto 1987). Brought from the Mediterranean Sea through various countries to the port of Ilo (Anonymous 1998: 832), these relics finally arrived in Moquegua, where they rest in the Iglesia San Francisco. The saint is celebrated every October 14 (http://www.turismomoquegua.com.pe/sf.html). The oldest part of the church was destroyed in the 1868 earthquake.

Local Catholicism: The Rural Moquegua Valley

Moquegua's "local Catholicism" is given unique expression through its wine industry, as seen in the names, chapels, and tinaja inscriptions at the many wine heredades strung along the valley. Eleven (8.5 percent) of the 130 identified bodega sites bore overt religious names—Belén de Locumbilla, San Antonio, Santa Ana, San Bernabé, Santo Domingo, San Francisco, San José, San Julian, San Luis, San Pedro, and Santa Rosa—and other sites' names may have religious significance: María (Cupina), La Merced, and Soledad. Sacatita and Sacatilla, both with chapels, might earlier have been part of the sixteenth-century Mercedarian property. It is unclear if any significance can be attached to the location of most of the religious toponyms in the far south of the valley, other than that a large property (Cupina) was given to the Order of Merced. Only three wine heredades with religious names are in the upper valley (San Bernabé, San Francisco, Santa Rosa), and two are in the middle valley (Belén, San Antonio).

In addition to the churches and chapels in the town of Moquegua, many rural heredades also boasted religious facilities. In the early nineteenth century the inhabitants of the valley could practice their faith in at least thirty-six churches, chapels, and *"oratorios,* richly adorned and furnished" (Pereyra y Ruiz 1987: 44). This was apparently a common practice within Spanish popular Catholicism. In Cusco, for example, wealthy hacendados with chapels on their rural properties effectively established their own religious jurisdictions by sponsoring saints' festivals, thereby co-opting religious activities in Indigenous communities and parishes and coming into conflict with official religious activities (Urton 1990: 99–100).

Chapels were identified at ten bodega sites on the basis of surveys and documentary sources. Some are clearly associated with ownership of the property by religious houses. Yahuay, for example, which was donated to the Dominican Order, had two chapels; one exhibited modern veneration of an image of San Isidro Labrador. The two María Cupina heredades, Alta and Baja, were donated to the Mercedarian order, and each had a chapel (ADM 58, 59). Chapels were also identified at Sacatita and Sacatilla, the latter by arched niches to hold saints' images. Other chapels were noted at Totoral, Conde 1, and San Pedro; documents report chapels at Yaravico and Locumbilla.

INSCRIPTIONS ON *TINAJAS*

Additional information about local-level religious activity in the valley comes from inscriptions on the shoulders of the large earthenware jars (tinajas) used to ferment and store wine (Rice 1995). A total of 1,424 tinajas was inventoried in Bodegas Project surveys, of which 191 (13.4 percent) carried religious notations and 379 (26.6 percent) bore dates. Unfortunately, these data, along with other information on the jars, represent only a small sample of what might originally have been recorded. For example, of the 379 inscribed dates, only 5 (1.3 percent) fell in the sixteenth and seventeenth centuries. This means that the first century and a half of Moquegua's wine industry is essentially unrepresented in the tinaja inventory. Also, the sample of 1,424 jars itself represents only a small fraction of these fermentation and storage containers in use at the valley's 130 wine haciendas during the four centuries of its vinicultural enterprise, given that jars frequently broke and had to be replaced and that the vessels were commonly extracted from the bodegas in modern times for use as yard ornaments.

Despite these caveats, the saints and others to whom the valley's churches and chapels were dedicated and who were invoked on the tinajas reveal considerable information about early colonial Moquegua (table 10.1). They constitute a kind of toponymy, a sample of the unique set of patrons and protectors chosen by Moquegua's wine hacendados and others charged with responsibility for the valley's economic well-being and for its citizens' spiritual lives while here on earth and for their souls after death. More specifically, the tinajas' naming of saints and cofradías and events in the annual cycle of religious celebrations might indicate to whom or what the wine was destined: which chapel, which cofradía, which religious procession or feast. Because the tinajas' use-lives could last decades (or centuries), such a dedication suggests long-term contractual arrangements.

Saints

Saints in rural Latin America have "assumed an importance among the folk far beyond that specified by official orthodoxy" (Gudeman 1976: 709). They symbolize family and community and constitute a focus of ritual and pleas for divine intercession; but also, in a broader sense, they symbolize social order, and "to order is to give meaning" (ibid.: 709, 726). Veneration of saints establishes a community's ritual calendar. The private devotions to particular saints, the sacred places and landscapes where public celebrations occur, and their annual rhythms during the liturgical year all contribute to the unique flavors and meanings of local Catholicism. The system of saint veneration is "at the edge of 'structure'" in two senses: it is "a juncture between public symbols and private meanings," and it also establishes a balance "between the past, remembered and recreated as a series of meaningful events, and the future" (ibid.: 727).

Ninety-six (6.7 percent) inscriptions on the Moquegua tinajas mentioned saints: 82 referenced 36 male saints and 14 mentioned 9 women. Fifteen references can be described as "livelihood-related": patrons and protectors of the valley's agricultural enterprise. Of these, 10 saints or titles of the Virgin Mary[7] are related to viticulture: 3 appear to be general patrons of vineyards (against diseases) and vintners, plus San Bernabé, who is more of a generalist related to harvests but was appropriated for Moquegua's vineyards. The other 6 were "wine saints" in Europe, associated with particular days of harvesting and wine making, two specifically in Jerez.[8] But because of the inversion of the growing and harvesting seasons in the Southern Hemisphere, the saints' days that governed these activities in Europe were no longer properly timed in the Andes. Their invocation in Moquegua suggests that they were mentioned because of traditional associations, or they may have had other realms of protection.

Two other saints were generalists for farmers and harvests, and three were patrons of livestock. Two apostles named on the tinajas—San Pedro (n = 4) and San Andrés (n = 3)—were patrons of fishermen, raising the possibility that the wine they contained was intended to be consumed in coastal communities. Four

TABLE 10.1 Saints and religious themes referenced in Moquegua

Area of patronage	Saint/Theme	Feast day	Specific patronage
Wine-related	San Sebastián	January 20	Against diseases of the vine
	San Vicente de Zaragoza[a]	January 22	Vintners
	San Bernabé	June 11	Moquegua's vineyards
	San Roque	August 17	Against vine pests and diseases
Wine in Europe	San Gines (Agnes) de la Jara	January 21	Jerez vintners
	San Lorenzo[a]	August 10	Ripening of grapes
	NS de la Asunción	August 15	Beginning of vintage
	NS de Natividad	September 8	First day of vintage in Jerez
	San Andrés	November 30	Must is fermented into wine
	San Juan Evangelista	December 27	First tasting of new wine
Farmers	San Isidro Labrador[a]	May 15	Farmers
	San Bernabé	June 11	Harvests
	San Antonio de Padua	June 13	Harvests
Livestock	San Marcos	April 25	Fertility of cattle
	San Pascual[a]	May 17	Sheep and sheep raisers
	San Juan Bautista[b]	June 24	Sheep and sheep raisers
Fishermen	San Pedro[b]	June 29	
	San Andrés[b]	November 30	
Earthquakes	NS de Loreto	August 15	
	San Francisco de Borja[a]	October 10	
	Santa Catalina de Alejandria	November 25	
Construction	San Vincent Ferrer[a]	April 5	Builders
	San Antonio de Padua	June 13	Masons and bricklayers
	Santo Tomás[b]	July 3	Architects and builders
	San Lucas Evangelista[b]	October 18	Painters and glass workers
	San Josef	March 19	Carpenters
Founders	San Pedro, San Pablo, San Agustín, San Jerónimo		Of the Christian Church

continued on next page

TABLE 10.1—*continued*

Area of patronage	Saint/Theme	Feast day	Specific patronage
	San Ignacio de Loyola[a]		Of Jesuits, 1540
	San Francisco de Asis		Of Franciscans
	San Pedro Nolasco[a]		Of Mercedarians
	Santo Domingo[a]		Of Dominican Order of Preachers
	Santa Clara		Of Franciscan nuns (Poor Clares)
	San Bernardo		Of Cistercians
Others	San Antonio de Padua	June 13	Chapel in La Matriz, built by Alonso de Estrada
	Santa Catalina de Alejandría	November 25	La Matriz church in Moquegua
	San Diego		Chapel in La Matriz, early seventeenth c.
	San Josef	March 19	Father of Jesus; protector of young children and patron of orphanages
	San Francisco de Borja	October 10	Image in the Jesuit Colegio San José, Yaravico; head of Jesuits in 1565; viceroy of Catalonia
	San Francisco Xavier		Image in the Jesuit Colegio San José, Yaravico
	San José		Image in the Jesuit Colegio San José, Yaravico
	San Ignacio	July 31	Image in the Jesuit Colegio San José, Yaravico
	San Juan de Dios	March 8	Patron of Iglesia Belén (constr. 1613) and hospital (constr. 1726 at Locumbilla)
	San Martín de Porres		b. 1579 in Lima; animals?
	San Ildefonso	August 23	Seventh-c. archbishop of Toledo
	San Pedro		First chapel/church in Moquegua; destr. 1604

continued on next page

TABLE 10.1—*continued*

Area of patronage	Saint/Theme	Feast day	Specific patronage
	San Vicente Ferrer	April 5	b. 1350, Valencia, noble; Dominican
	Santo Domingo		
Virgin Mary	Nuestra Senora del Rosario		Chapel in La Matriz, early seventeenth c.
	Nuestra Senora de Belén		Bethlemite Order and hospital
	Nuestra Señora de Loreto		Image in the Jesuit Colegio San José, Yaravico

a Basque, or born in Spain.
b Apostle.

saints/apostles were patrons of construction activities. Perhaps related to this, three others were invoked for protection against earthquakes; Nuestra Señora de Loreto became a patron of Moquegua after an earthquake in 1713 (Gutiérrez and Viñuales 1977: 88). Founders of the Christian Church and of six regular orders were named on the jars, suggesting the provision of wine for the friars and rituals of those houses.

In terms of the origins of the saints, the individuals named were almost exclusively Iberian/Spanish, Italian, or from the Holy Land. Those from the Spanish homeland include San Vicente de Zaragoza, San Vicente Ferrer, San Lorenzo, San Isidro Labrador, San Ildefonso, San Francisco de Borja, and three founders of the religious orders: San Ignacio de Loyola, San Pedro Nolasco, and Santo Domingo.

Religious references were more common at sites in the upper valley, suggesting that the wine was produced for activities taking place in the town. The Iglesia Santa Catalina (La Matriz) in particular played a central role in the religious life of not only the Osmore valley but the entire parish of Moquegua. Both La Matriz and the Jesuit college at Yaravico had chapels and altars dedicated to various saints and Marian advocations, and it is not unreasonable to suggest that much of the wine was produced for Catholic ritual in that church. The annual consumption of wine by individual churches is unknown, but in a small, under-populated area like Moquegua, it was surely orders of magnitude less than that at the cathedral at Sevilla. There, 24 altars celebrated 400 masses a day, using 10,750 liters (roughly 2,840 US gal.) of wine annually (Francis 1972: 165).

Importantly, however, consumption of Moquegua's wines took place largely outside Moquegua. Some of the wine was likely headed to Ilo, and six tinajas mention Torata or its patron saint. Much of the wine was shipped to Chucuito and its numerous churches on the edge of Lake Titicaca, which might account for many of the inscriptions, particularly those with Dominican references. Despite the multiple reasons for interest in the religious notations on the wine tinajas throughout the valley, it is important to reiterate that the large majority of jars lacked such mention. This is easily explained by the fact that vast quantities—literally millions of liters (Rice 1996c, 2011b)—of wine and brandy, especially in the eighteenth and nineteenth centuries, were transported to the highly secular mining regions of Potosí, Bolivia. Even there, at least some of the shipments must have been for religious service.

Cofradías and Holy Days

Some of the tinajas' inscriptions refer to known cofradías. Because the confraternities in Moquegua would have been established after the Trentine reforms, it is not surprising that three of them, in existence by 1590, were the Santísimo Sacramento, Las Ánimas de Purgatorio (ADM 19), and Nuestra Señora de la Concepción (Gutiérrez and Viñuales 1977). In his 1610 will, Alonso de Estrada bequeathed twenty pesos to each for masses to be said upon his death (Miró Quesada Sosa 1982: 95). By the mid-eighteenth century the cofradías of San Francisco de Paula and Nuestra Señora de Dolores also existed in the Iglesia Matriz.

Recalling the Trentine influence on orthodoxy concerning confraternities, sacraments, saints, and their advocations, there were twenty-three mentions of biblical subjects or holy days on the tinajas: Gran Poder de Dios, Jesus, Feast of Kings, La Santísima Cruz, La Santísima Trinidad, and La Sagrada Familia and the cofradía of Las Bendites Ánimas (en Purgatorio). Another seven referred to angels (including San Gabriel and San Miguel), and fourteen mentioned six apostles. Nonetheless, invocations of Mary continued to be very popular, as fifty-one inscriptions referenced thirteen titles of the Blessed Virgin. These, plus the abundant inscriptions invoking male saints, suggest significant retentions of pre-Trentine practices of local Catholicism. It would not be surprising if many of them were also cofradías.

Other Inscriptions

The Yaravico Viejo bodega was of particular interest, its name coming from discovery of an in situ tinaja with religious inscriptions, a cross, and the early date of 1590—which ties the bodega to the time of ownership by the Buenos and Estradas. One religious inscription consists of the letters AM: Ave María or 'Hail Mary,' the beginning of the Rosary prayer. The other is the letters IHS, generally thought to invoke the phrase Jesus Hominum Salvator 'Jesus Savior of Mankind,' although it may also refer to the first three letters of the name of Jesus in Greek (IHSUS) (Weinhold 1978: 270). IHS is also a symbol of the Jesuits.

Sixty-two of the Moquegua tinajas had crosses inscribed on their shoulders, some of them elaborated to the point that they resembled stylized chapels. The tips of the arms of the crosses on the tinajas, as well as on churches, were frequently embellished with the three circles or curves ("budded" crosses) said to represent the trinity. The cross is a potent symbol of Christianity, a symbol of military reconquest of the Iberian Peninsula and crusades in other lands against the infidels. In addition, in "late medieval theology, the cross was a sign of great power to turn back the devil" and a weapon to ward off other evils and enemies, whether human (religious, disease) or natural (hail, drought, insects) (Christian 1981: 184).

Avians were also frequently incised on the jars. They are largely unidentifiable as to species (even genus), but one might be a rooster, associated with the Passion; another could be a dove. Other nonreligious inscriptions include the names of individuals and initials and other signs (e.g., YB^{co}) that might be marks of the tinajeros who produced the vessels.

REDUCCIÓN AND RESISTANCE AT TORATA ALTA?

Indigenous resistance to Spanish culture and Christianity has not been examined as closely in the Moquegua area as elsewhere in the southern highland, but two possibilities merit greater attention. One concerns legends relating to Huaynaputina's eruption; the other is prompted by artifacts at the congregación site of Torata Alta.

With respect to Huaynaputina, local lore holds that the *hechiceros* (shamans) had been told of the impending eruption by the water serpent Pichinique. He and the evil deity Supay announced that the destruction was punishment because the people had accepted Christianity and baptism and ceased sacrificing ten or twelve maidens by hurling them into the mouth of the volcano (Cañedo-Argüelles Fábrega 2004: 41). Another story (MacCormack 1985: 460) concerns a dispute between two volcanoes in the Arequipa region, Omate (Huaynaputina) and Arequipa (probably Misti).[9] Omate wanted Arequipa to join him in an eruption to destroy the Spaniards in the region, but Arequipa refused, claiming he was now a Christian. So Omate erupted alone in 1600—and laid waste to the town of Arequipa.

Torata Alta is of interest in the context of early-seventeenth-century campaigns to extirpate idolatry. One common problem for the Christian missionaries was Andeans removing the bodies of their dead from Christian cemeteries and reburying them in their own traditional burial sites (MacCormack 1985: 459). Old waka cults had been suppressed, but some had "quickly reemerged in a new guise, typically as devotions focused on shrines commemorating apparitions of Christian personages at or near the pre-Hispanic sacred sites" (Sallnow 1982: 733). Examples include the Virgin Mary at Copacabana in 1583 and Pachacamac in 1601. It was not until about 1660 that the Spanish priests' campaign against idolatry drew to a close, accompanied by "the crystallization of a new, syncretic Andean religion" and establishment of "the Iberian complex of village patron saints and fiesta sponsorship . . . partly displacing the cults of the local tutelary spirits" (ibid.).

As noted (chapter 8), few Christian religious items were recovered in excavations at Torata Alta: only a medal bearing the image of Christ and a stone plaque engraved with a cross. Other artifacts and features suggest practices Christian priests would frown upon—possibly subtle forms of idolatry or "resistance"?—in the community. For example, Str. 241 (Kancha 23) yielded a small ritual feature or offering of uncertain date: a shallow pit dug into the floor in the southwest corner containing a deliberately folded tupu and a small piece of sheet copper in dark earth (Van Buren and Bürgi 1990: 71). Str. 269, in Kancha 26—an elite residence, perhaps a kuraka's—yielded a fragment of a "Tiwanaku-type puma censer" and a guinea pig burial (ibid.: 78). None of these items can be precisely dated, but the fact that they occur in the southeastern part of the site, where post-Inka occupation is most obvious, seems telling.

The walls of Torata's domestic structures frequently incorporated large boulders, recalling the well-known Inka veneration of rocks and stone outcrops, many of them large and elaborately carved (Dean 2007; Hyslop 1990: 102–28). In six residences at the site, hearths—often multiple—were positioned at the base of these boulders (or against bedrock) (see, e.g., figures 8.13, 8.14, 8.15). This recalls longstanding Indigenous practices of burning offerings to stones, use of fire in divination (Rowe 1946: 303), and Aymara belief in "house spirits" (Tschopik 1946: 559). Only one such hearth is in the western part of the site; the other five are in the later-occupied east, and three are in Kanchas 16 and 17 near the church.[10]

Most perplexing is a seeming fetishization of horseshoes at Torata Alta. Ten horseshoes or horseshoe fragments were recovered in domestic structures

TABLE 10.2 Co-occurrence of hearths and horseshoe recovery at Torata Alta

Kancha	Structure	Hearths[a]	Horseshoes
13	120	1	1
15	137	?	1
16	146	1	1
	150		1
17	156	—	1
23	229	1	3
24	1	1	1
24	254	1	—
26	269	—	1

Source: Reprinted by permission from *Latin American Antiquity*, vol. 23, no. 1: table 4, p. 23. © 2012 Society for American Archaeology.

a Hearths built against boulders or bedrock inside structures.

(Van Buren 1997: table 16.1). In addition, a small horse's head with reins, modeled of clay, was found in Str. 140; and a flat horseshoe-shaped chipped lithic object, 10 cm long, was found in surface collections in Str. 146. Seven of the horseshoes were found in five structures with hearths against boulders, and all but one were in the eastern half of the site (table 10.2). In four structures where secure contexts of recovery can be determined, all suggest a pre-1600 date: in Str. 120, below the ash; in Str. 137, above a floor and below the ash; in Str. 150, under a floor above sub-floor fill and leveling; and in wall-fall in Str. 156 (Van Buren and Bürgi 1990).

The recovery of these horseshoes at the Torata Alta congregación is unusual for several reasons. Down-valley at Moquegua's wine estates, horse hardware (and bones of equids) were uncommon.[11] Horseshoes are not mentioned among items of material culture typically recovered in Mesoamerican or North American missions, particularly in Indigenous contexts (Graham 1998; B. McEwan, pers. comm. September 22, 2011). However, four horseshoes were recovered at the site of Cchaucha del Kjula Marca, an early colonial-period Indigenous village in the Lake Titicaca basin in Bolivia (Rydén 1947: 304, cited in Chatfield 2007: 140). In addition, eleven horseshoes were found in excavations inside Indigenous structures at Spanish-colonial Ocelocalco (Pacific coastal Chiapas, Mexico; Gasco 1987: 340).

Horses were singularities, relatively rare and extremely expensive in Peru, especially immediately after conquest. They were also ambiguous creatures, although the apparent fusion of human and beast was quickly deconstructed. On the one hand, horses were feared: Garcilaso de la Vega (1987b: 580–81) claimed that horses terrified native Andeans to such an extent that they refused to learn blacksmithing—despite the long Indigenous history of Andean metalwork—and how to shoe the animals. On the other hand, horses were desired, given that they were diacritical symbols of Spanish status and wealth. Spaniards noted that many kurakas became "horsemen and good hunters, and have fine horses and harquebuses in their houses," worrying that these military skills could threaten Spanish interests (Spalding 1984: 213). In the context of mid-sixteenth-century native uprisings, it was proposed that kurakas be forbidden to own horses (Gade 1992: 467; Spalding 1984: 213). But at the time of Diez's 1567 visita in the southwest, he noted that many natives who were not caciques had horses and mules and demanded that their communities supply food for them (Diez de San Miguel 1964: 252).

Perhaps not surprisingly, horses were part of the post-conquest merging of Andean deities with Christian saints. Santiago/St. James the Greater, longstanding patron of Iberian reconquest and symbol of warrior success and military power, melded with Andean mountain gods and related deities. In particular, Santiago on his white horse with loud, death-dealing firearms was identified with the Andean supernatural Illapa, associated with thunder and lightning. The result was a hybrid complex of "andeanized santiagos" and "Hispanified mountain gods" (Silverblatt 1988).

It is not known what horseshoes might have symbolized for early contact-period Andeans, and the scant available evidence is equivocal.[12] Early in the conquest, Andeans believed horses' feet were of silver (Kubler 1946: 380). In central Mexico, after the Tlaxcalans killed one of Cortés's horses, they took the shoes to offer to their "idols" (Díaz del Castillo 1998: 109). The horseshoes (and figurine and lithic) at Torata Alta recall the colonial Quechua appropriation of European artifacts as *conopas* (household gods or amulets; Kubler 1946: 397; Tschopik 1946: 563). In a broader context of conquest and resistance, the horseshoes can be related to the wider practice of conquered peoples appropriating power-laden foreign objects—here, symbols of the fearsome horses and the technology of crafting the shoes—to derive symbolic power from them (see, e.g., Helms 1993; Silliman 2005: 66–68). The possession of horseshoes might be considered "positive contagion" of power from the foreign source, as "certain goods reserved for elite performances may act as metonyms 'of a whole system of power, prosperity, and status'" (Pugh 2009: 374, quoting Appadurai 1986: 52). Another analogy might be to the "spirit bundles" of African slaves in Annapolis (Leone 2005; Orser 2010: 123).

A final operative consideration might not relate to horses at all but rather to the fact that the shoes were made of iron, a highly valued and previously unknown metal with foreign production practices. Iron artifacts were significant valuables, with both practical and symbolic functions, in many settings of European colonialism. In addition to the horseshoes, other iron recovered in eleven of the excavated structures at Torata Alta included one knife, sixteen nails, and 316.2 g of miscellaneous iron; 196 g (62 percent) of the last came from Str. 254 (Van Buren 1997: table 16.1).

All these features at Torata Alta might have totally innocent explanations, except when considered in light of Pedro Conta and his struggle to become cacique principal over Torata and Moquegua. Spanish authorities repeatedly accused and punished Conta for various offenses, including idolatry and witchcraft; he was described as a *"notorio"* and *"famoso hechicero"* (Cañedo-Argüelles Fábrega 1994: 22, 2005: li–lii). Spaniards described hechiceros as sorcerers who heard Indigenous versions of "confession" and supervised cults dedicated to various wakas (MacCormack 1985: 452). Torata Alta's hearths and horseshoes may be material vestiges of community-wide clandestine practices led by Conta and others who manipulated symbols of agency and power to negotiate their ambiguous existence between two colliding worlds. On the one hand, the kurakas privately exercised and protected idolatry and sorcery or witchcraft (*hechicería*) as a "prop" to uphold their traditional authority and control recognized by their subjects (Millones 1979). At the same time, however, they were forced to publicly profess rejection of such practices to maintain their positions in the new colonial/Christian authority structure.

NOTES

1. It is not too farfetched to see similarities in the establishment of a sacred Christian landscape by means of shrines housing saints' relics with that of the Inkas and their shrines to ancestors, gods, and mythical events (see chapter 3).

2. Two centuries later in northern Europe, Protestants increasingly scorned or abolished popular saints' cults as idol worship, laying the groundwork for the Protestant Reformation (Weinstein and Bell 1982: 184–91).

3. In southern Spain a cathedral dedicated to Santa Maria had been built in Toledo in the late sixth century (Hall 2004: 19–20). San Ildefonso, the seventh-century archbishop of Toledo, was especially devoted to Mary.

4. A 1590 document in the Moquegua archives, prepared in Juli, records that Juan Gómez, master carpenter, requested that documents pertaining to the finished

carpentry and masonry of ten to sixteen churches in the Chucuito area be given to the viceroy so the costs could be paid (Guíbovich P. 1984: 202–3).

5. Cummins (1988: 121, 377), commenting on woodworkers who supplied the Inkas with their carved and painted wooden keros, notes ethnohistorical data on native groups called "Queros" and Chunchos who lived on the mountain slopes east of Cusco.

6. It is not known if there were Indigenous cofradías in rural colonial Moquegua as there were in central Peru. There, Indigenous cofradías were wealthy and economically stratified on the basis of owning cattle, land, and other resources. As such, a cofradía functioned not only as a religious institution but also economically "as a kind of control and mediation between the hacienda and the community" (Celestino 1983: 149).

7. The Virgin Mary had been a traditional patroness of viticulture and wine making throughout post-Roman Europe: "Mary in early Christian tradition was seen as the vine upon which the grape of Jesus grew . . . the grape of life . . . the grape Madonna" (Weinhold 1978: 103). Particular titles of Mary were associated with European vintages: Our Lady of the Assumption (August 15) is associated with the beginning of the vintage (ibid.), and Our Lady of the Nativity (September 8) is the first day for starting the vintage in Jerez, Spain (Jeffs 1982: 25).

8. European wine saints include Saints Vitus, Davinius, Urban, Morandus, Medardus, Sixtus, Donatus, Cyriacus, and Bartholomew (Weinhold 1978: 101–3). Saints Gregory and Pantaleón conferred protection for grapevines and other crops against insects.

9. Tradition holds that Misti volcano had erupted earlier and violently in the mid-fifteenth century (Kuon Cabello 1981: 134).

10. Two similar features were found in the kallanka structure at Sabaya (Bürgi 1993: 209, figure 54, 213): small areas of fire ash and burned material (sherds, bone, and earth) with encircling stone walls. One in the corner had a small outcrop of bedrock.

11. Of the twenty-eight sites shovel tested, only eleven yielded horse-related artifacts (n = 13). In surface collections, an iron horse bit was recovered from Sacatita and shoe fragments from Corpanto Viejo and Chimba Alta 2 (Smith 1991: 129, 145, 172). At Yahuay, two horseshoes were from Middle contexts; at Locumbilla and Chincha, all horse hardware came from Late contexts.

12. In some areas of the Andes, the dark spots visible in the full moon are seen as a woman riding a horse (Urton 1981: 81).

Part IV

Decorative Spaces and Decorating Places: Andean "Majolica" Pottery

As explained in the preface, the chapters in this volume explore spatialization—the production and meanings of spaces and places—in colonial encounters. The emphasis is primarily on spaces and places in a physical landscape, both natural (a region) and built, and also on political ecology in terms of the power relations expressed in the use of resources and in commodity production. In part IV, I pursue this latter theme with reference to a particular kind of commodity: tin-enameled (or "majolica") ceramic wares.

Ceramics with a glossy, opaque, pale coating, commonly known as *majolica*, constitute an important item of material culture in medieval Iberia and imperial Spain and an important artifact category at Spanish-colonial archaeological sites. The antecedents of this pottery bespeak a journey in time, space, and ideology, as they were produced in ninth-century Persia and were inspired by even more distant wares made in China. Tin-enameled pottery began to be produced in early Muslim Spain and featured green and brown-black (verde y morado) decoration, later elaborated through Italian influences to include blue, yellow, and orange. The three original colors—green, black, and white—are symbolic for Muslims. Although interpretations differ, in general green is associated with paradise, life, and luxuriant vegetation and is an indicator of descent from the Prophet; black is associated with the Abbasid dynasty (Bloom and Blair 2011: 14–15, 31; Casanovas 2003: 51; Fierro 2011: 82; Mahmoud 2011: 112; Rosselló Bordoy 1992: 98). White is a symbol of purity, the color of creation, and is associated with the Umayyid dynasty. A white undercoat, whether architectural stucco or plaster on wood surfaces—or enamel on pottery—contributed to the important aesthetic of luminosity of color in the Islamic world (Bush 2011: 73). As the Iberian Peninsula was slowly transformed into a Christian land during centuries of reconquista (reconquest), new Christian elites continued to depend on Muslims or *moriscos* (Muslims newly converted to Christianity) or mudéjars (producers of Islamic-style arts in Christian kingdoms) for artisanal and craft production—including pottery making (Gavin et al. 2003; Pleguezuelo 2003a). Much of the majolica was produced by Muslim artisans in southern and eastern Spain.

Pottery of this tradition, both imported from Spain and locally produced, is widely recovered in Ibero-America. Until relatively recently, historical archaeological research and historical archaeologists' studies of these beautiful, multicolored wares have been focused on artifacts from the northern regions of Spain's colonial empire: Mexico, the Caribbean, "La Florida" (the southeastern United States), and the southwestern United States. The decorative palette of the earliest and most widely studied examples of this tin-lead-"glazed" (or "enameled") earthenware pottery, whether imported from Spain or produced in the colonies, is primarily blue-based: blue-on-white or polychromes with blue as the predominant color, accented by green, black, yellow, or orange, over the white ground. In Mexico, green-on-white and green-and-black-on-white decorated pottery was a common-grade ware; in Panama, small quantities of green-and-black/brown decoration were subsumed typologically within the variability of polychromy.

In South America, historical archaeology as a discipline has developed more slowly than in the north (Funari 1996, 1997; Jamieson 2005; Politis 1995, 2003; Van Buren 2010; Williams and Fournier-García 1996; Zarankin and Salerno 2008). Although John Goggin's pioneering study of majolica in the New World makes brief reference to such wares in Venezuela, Colombia, and Ecuador, the only mention of Peru is in connection with a theory that Panama Polychrome type was produced there (Goggin 1968: 42–48). Only recently has Andean tin-enameled pottery begun to be seriously studied by archaeologists (Chatfield 2007; Jamieson 2001; Jamieson and Hancock 2004; Rice 1997, 2013), but little documentary information is available on sources of imported majolica or the beginnings of local production: no kiln sites are published, evidence is often anecdotal, and little archaeological work has been carried out that would shed light on these issues. As the pottery of the Andes is becoming better known, however, it is evident that the medieval tradition of verde y morado decoration is a common decorative combination and that blue is relatively lesser known.

The chapters in part IV address the likelihood that Andean tin-enameled wares, or loza (tableware), were produced by artisans representing one particular Muslim-related tradition of Spanish production. My interests are in how this ware transcended boundaries between various kinds of spaces, physical and social, and also created new spaces; in how different kinds of resources, human and mineral, interacted in these spaces; and in how resources were ordered in the spaces on the pottery itself. Specifically, I focus on Muslim-influenced, green-and-black-decorated, tin-enameled pottery and argue that inattention to, or devaluation of, this material—and of Muslim influence in the early colonies in general—has silenced one of the voices in the dialogue of Spanish colonization.

The possibility of morisco manufacture of Andean loza prompts questions about the background and traditions of potters in Spain's colonies because, according to official policy, only "old" Christians were permitted to travel to the New World. The social and economic roles morisco potters possibly occupied in Ibero-America have received little attention from historians and archaeologists. This is surprising, especially given archaeologists' interest in material culture and identities and the fact that moriscos were widely recognized as skilled artisans and craftsmen. Most of the attention to possible mudéjar influence in the colonies has come from art and architectural historians, with a focus on architecture (e.g., Gutiérrez 2002: 47–67; López Guzmán 1993; Ortíz Crespo 1993). Mudéjar/morisco influence on pottery has been acknowledged but little explored (cf. Lister and Lister 1982: 80–90; Natt 1997; Rice 2013).

The three chapters in part IV adopt a political ecology approach to tin-enameled wares in discussing three kinds of space and places: cultural/ideological, technological, and decorative. Chapter 11 reviews the historical development of these wares—literally encircling the globe, from China to Persia to Spain to the New World, and then adding Chinese influence again—within the context of early imperial Spain's anti-capitalist political and economic policies underlying their production and exchange in the emerging world economy. Chapter 12 examines the manufacturing technology of these wares and particularly the sources of, and access to, resources necessary for their manufacture. Of particular interest are two decorative "series," blue-based and green-based, of loza in Spain's transatlantic colonies. Distinguished largely by the presence and absence, respectively, of cobalt for blue pigment, these geographic spheres were constructed by unique historical contingencies and structure two landscapes of not only style but also commerce. Chapter 13 discusses decorative space with respect to a comparative hierarchical design structure analysis of painted loza from several areas of the Spanish-colonial empire. The focus is on Andean South America, specifically pottery recovered in the Moquegua valley of southern Peru. The purpose is not a 1970s-style interpretation of learning, information exchange, or other intimate interactions among producers and users. Rather, the concern is to examine this pottery in terms of the generative relations of decorative styles widely separated in space.

11

Transcending Worlds

> A good part of Spanish historiography has been systematically dedicated to underestimating the influence of Islam in Christian Spain, closing the eyes to the overwhelming evidence of the monumental Islamic footprint.[1]
>
> —Gonzalo Borrás Gualis
> (1993: 15)

Majolica is the Anglicized term for a western European fine earthenware ceramic known in Spanish as *mayólica* and in Italian as *maiólica*. Other terms include *faience* and *faenza* (French and Italian, respectively) and delft in the Netherlands and England. The term *majolica/maiólica* may have originated with fourteenth- or fifteenth-century Italians who obtained this pottery in trade with the island of Majorca (Mallorca), in the Spanish kingdom of Aragón, and erroneously believed it was produced there (Lister and Lister 1982: vii). Alternatively, the term may arise from a specific ware produced in Málaga[2] in southeastern Spain (Casanovas 1983: 24; Gavin 2003: 2; Glick 2005: 240–41). Whatever the etymology, majolica ceramics are characterized by a light-colored, opaque, tin-lead–based coating and multicolored painted designs. They are more generally referred to in functional terms in Spanish as a high grade of *loza* (tableware, "china"), sometimes distinguished as *loza fina*, *loza blanca*, or *loza tradicional* (in contrast to *loza común* or *basta*, often only lead glazed).

HISTORICAL BACKGROUND

The tin-enameled ware encountered at the Moquegua bodegas has a long history that can be distantly traced

DOI: 10.5876/9781607322764:c11

to the Neo-Assyrian empire of Mesopotamia in the first half of the first millennium BC. Palaces in the cities of the time, such as Nimrud (northern Iraq), were decorated with wall panels composed of glazed bricks or plaques: terracotta blocks with glaze-painted decoration. Ninth-century plaques from three sites revealed that the clay was a calcareous sediment, tempered with "stalk-like vegetal matter," and painted with glazes colored black, opaque white, green, and yellow (Freestone 1991); elsewhere blue was also used. This glaze-painting practice was later lost or abandoned for more than a millennium.

The origins of today's majolica and related tin-enameled wares are more directly discerned in complex intercultural exchanges between the Abbasid caliphate (AD 750–1258) of Persia (modern Iran and Iraq) and T'ang-dynasty China (618–907) by way of the fabled Silk Road. Islamic "merchant capitalist" traders developed vast sea and overland caravan routes extending as far as China (Banaji 2003; Labib 1969), which was a source of highly desired silk and other valued goods, including pottery (Carswell 1999; Rouguelle 1996). These traders also established colonies along the routes to facilitate commerce, including one at Canton (now Guangzhou), a major southern port city on the maritime trade route of the Silk Road between China and the Arabian Sea.[3]

The role of ceramics in this trade is evidenced by the discovery of Chinese pottery in the ninth-century Muslim center of Samarra on the Euphrates River (Wykes-Joyce 1958: 51) and examples in museums in Baghdad. Even more striking is the recent discovery of *Batu Hitam*, a ninth-century "Arab" (Arabia or Persia) or Indian trading vessel, shipwrecked off-course near Beitung Island between Sumatra and Borneo (see Flecker 2000, 2001). The ship's cargo was entirely Chinese, including around 55,000 items of pottery produced primarily at the Changsha (or Tongguan) kilns in Hunan province in south-central China (ibid.; Chiew 2005). Most of this pottery displays an unusual technique developed by potters at the Changsha kilns: under-glaze painting, featuring brown and green (also rarely blue) decorative motifs, many of which are Muslim (Chiew 2005). Abbasid potters also appear to have been influenced by other T'ang glazed wares, particularly *sancai* ("three colors") decoration in green, brown, and yellow.

The practice of adding tin as an opacifier to glass and lead glazes began in the Near East (see chapter 12) using tin imported from southern Burma and Malaysia (Molera, Vendrell-Saz, and Pérez-Arantegui 2001: 332). Knowledge of producing opaque, whitish, tin-lead glazes or enamels began spreading throughout the Islamic world of the Near East and the Mediterranean (e.g., Waage 1934). However, the technique's adoption was slow, especially in Christian Europe: "so long as Christians could import the wares, they did not produce them at home" (Glick 2005: 241). The later explosion of tin-enameled ware production is thought to have been an effort to imitate the background color of true porcelains, which were developed in China in the fourteenth century (Gavin 2003: 2; Pleguezuelo 2003b: 110; Tite 1988).

Islamic arts and technologies were introduced to Christian Iberia after the peninsula was forcibly incorporated into the Muslim world following an invasion by Berber Arabs from North Africa in AD 711. Islamic forces surged northward, quickly seizing control over nominally Christian Visigothic territory. Shortly thereafter, Christian kings in the Pyrenees Mountains began the slow and uneven process of recapturing the peninsula, ultimately an eight centuries–long series of south-moving battlefronts known as reconquista (reconquest) (see Harvey 1990; Reilly 1993). Throughout this long period, Muslim rule—along with technological superiority in construction, agriculture, and artisanry (Glick 2005: 217–47)—was most firmly entrenched in the cities of al-Andalus, the southern and eastern regions of what is now Spain.

By the tenth century, tin-enameled pottery with green and manganese-based purplish-black/brown (verde y morado) painted decoration was produced near the Umayyad caliphate's capital of Córdoba (Fierro 2011: 82) (table 11.1). From there it spread among potters farther south, then east and northeastward (Molera, Vendrell-Saz, and Pérez-Arantegui 2001: 332; Pinedo and Vizcaino 1979: 2; Pleguezuelo 2003a: 26; Zozaya 1981: 42–45). This spread was accompanied by an "early proliferation of schools of design," some relatively austere but others more extravagant, with floral motifs (Rosselló Bordoy 1992: 98). In the early eleventh century, the Umayyad caliphate suffered an internal revolt and collapsed into numerous *tā'ifas* (petty kingdoms or emirates), which weakened Islamic control and permitted the Christians of Old Castile–León to push deeper southward (Reilly 1993: 96–100). Following this collapse, many of Córdoba's potters migrated to other areas, introducing the techniques of tin enameling throughout the new Christian kingdoms (Glick 2005: 241). Green-and-manganese-decorated pottery was more widely produced, including in the tā'ifas of Toledo in central Spain (recaptured by Christians in the late eleventh century); Málaga, Granada, and Sevilla in the far south; and Zaragoza to the northeast in Aragón (Pinedo and Vizcaino 1979: 26; Pleguezuelo 2003a: 26). By the end of the century, Muslim rule was pushed to the southern half of the peninsula, roughly south of the Río Tajo and extending northeast across the Ebro beyond Tarragona. As Muslims retreated, Jews enjoyed a "golden age" in twelfth-century Spain.

Several important innovations in eastern Iberia's medieval pottery manufacture occurred in the twelfth century. The 1171 fall of the wealthy and powerful

TABLE 11.1 Muslim dynasties in Spain and their capitals

Berber/Umayyad	Córdoba	756–1010
Almohad	Sevilla	1010–1248
Nasrid	Granada	1248–1492

Source: Crow 1985: 54–75.

Fatimid dynasty in Egypt coincided with the appearance of innovations in designs and techniques in the pottery of the southeastern coastal port cities of Iberia and Italy (Pleguezuelo 2003a: 27; Whitehouse 1980). One of these introductions in Spain was "luster ware," distinctively decorated with metallic oxides and possibly copied from Egyptian glass (Barber 1915a; Canby 1997: 112; Gavin 2003: 5; Lister and Lister 1987: 87–89; Van de Put 1911: 2). For Islamic elites, luster-painted pottery was an acceptable substitute for one forbidden category of luxury good—eating utensils of silver and gold—allowing Muslims to circumvent the Prophet's injunction against using them until the afterlife. Málaga, in the Nasrid tā'ifa of Granada, became the most important Iberian center of luster ware production in the thirteenth century (see note 2; Pleguezuelo 2003a: 27), augmented by Persian potters fleeing the Mongols (Glick 2005: 240). In subsequent centuries the luster technique spread through the peninsula, passing northward into Valencia and west to Sevilla (Gavin 2003: 5).

MUDÉJAR STYLE

By the early thirteenth century, as the Christian reconquest proceeded southward, Muslims were increasingly confronted with a difficult decision: convert to Christianity or hope to continue practicing their faith in areas newly conquered by Christians. Those who chose the former and converted came to be identified as moriscos; those who opted for the latter were known as mudéjars.[4] With the Christian conquest of Sevilla in 1248, tens, perhaps hundreds, of thousands of Muslims, including potters, were given "three days to pack or sell their possessions and to leave Sevilla and environs. The king generously provided a fleet of fourteen ships to transport evacuees" to Morocco, while others moved to Jerez and Granada (Lister and Lister 1987: 66–67).

Moriscos and mudéjars were highly skilled artisans, craftsmen, and laborers who worked for Christian overlords. Their distinctive artistic and architectural creations are known collectively as the mudéjar style, characterized by a mixture of Muslim and Christian motifs, materials, and techniques. Both

Christian and morisco artisans worked in this style, meaning that mudéjar art and ethno-religious mudéjar identities are not isomorphic (Borrás Gualis 1993: 15–16). Decorative motifs in the mudéjar style were derived from the Near East and Egypt. In architecture, these motifs included calligraphy, geometric patterns (including interlaced bands), stylized flora (*ataurique*; twining foliage), and fauna (Jeffery 2003). Similar decoration appeared on mudéjar-style pottery, which combined green, purplish-brown, luster, and newly important blue[5] pigments on a light-colored tin-enameled ground. Motifs included animals (especially birds and deer), plants, human figures,[6] and geometric designs (see chapter 13; Barber 1915a: 33–35; Gavin 2003: 5; Lister and Lister 1987: 42–54). Forms reflect a similar hybridity: for example, large covered basins with green and manganese mudéjar decoration were produced for Christian rites of baptism (see Pleguezuelo 2003a: figure 1.4). However, in 1671 the Bishop of Málaga prohibited the production of ceramic baptismal fonts (figure 11.1) by mudéjar potters and ordered that henceforth they be made of stone, as they had been much earlier (Sánchez-Pacheco 1981b: 97; see also Lister and Lister 1987: 78).

The kingdom of Aragón in eastern Spain (figure 11.2) was an important center of mudéjar artisanry, and as much as half of the population of Aragón might have been mudéjars (Harvey 1990: 3, 6–7). Comprising the coastal states of Catalonia (Catalunya in Catalán) and Valencia, along with interior Aragón, the kingdom had longstanding ties to Naples and Sicily, the latter having come under short-lived Islamic control shortly after Iberia and produced similar pottery (Lister and Lister 1982: 69). Aragón struggled with France for control of these kingdoms, solidifying its dominant role in 1373 and by the early fifteenth century controlling an immense territory from southeastern Spain through France and into southern Italy. This gave Aragón a key role in Mediterranean trade, and potters in the eastern peninsula continually experienced new influences from the circum-Mediterranean region.

In Catalonia, Barcelona's potters produced wares similar to those of Valencia, but with closer stylistic ties to Italy and France, doubtless at least in part a consequence of geographic proximity (Pleguezuelo 2003a: 28; see also Casanovas 2003: 50; Sánchez-Pacheco 1986). Potters in Barcelona were Christians (Casanovas 2003: 50) and, like all of that city's artisans, organized into powerful guilds (see Corteguera 2002). Those who produced painted loza fina were known as *escudellers* (Ainaud de Lasarte 1981: 132), their barrio still identifiable by a street of the same name near Barcelona's port.

The mudéjar architectural style was particularly associated with the city of Teruel in southern Aragón, but mudéjar pottery (figure 11.3) is best known from the neighboring towns of Paterna and Manises, just outside the modern city

FIGURE 11.1 *A verde y morado baptismal font; Teruel, fifteenth century. Green and morado painted decoration varies from weak/pale to medium-strong colors. Note variable line widths of the morado. Computer rendering of color photograph (Sánchez-Pacheco 1986: 25) into black-and-white drawing by Don S. Rice.*

of Valencia (Alvaro Zamora 1981: 113–16; Pinedo and Vizcaino 1979).[7] Valencia was brought under Christian rule in 1238, when the king of Aragón defeated the Muslims. By then, the area's pottery was well known; and King Jaime I ordered the protection of the morisco potters, their wares (for his use), and their kilns (Pinedo and Vizcaino 1979: 23–24). The towns produced two types of decorated pottery known as Hispano-Moresque ware: traditional medieval Ibero-Islamic verde y morado and luster painted with or without cobalt blue. Sometimes blue and manganese were used together to paint Muslim motifs (ibid.: 40–41).

By the end of the fourteenth century, the traditional Iberian style was dubbed "vulgar" by a chronicler of the time, and Paterna's green-and-manganese pottery was eclipsed by the blue and gold[8] painted pottery of Manises (ibid.: 33). Manises luster pottery was coveted throughout "Christendom," including by the pope and cardinals, who may have obtained it *"per special gracia"* (ibid.: 67).

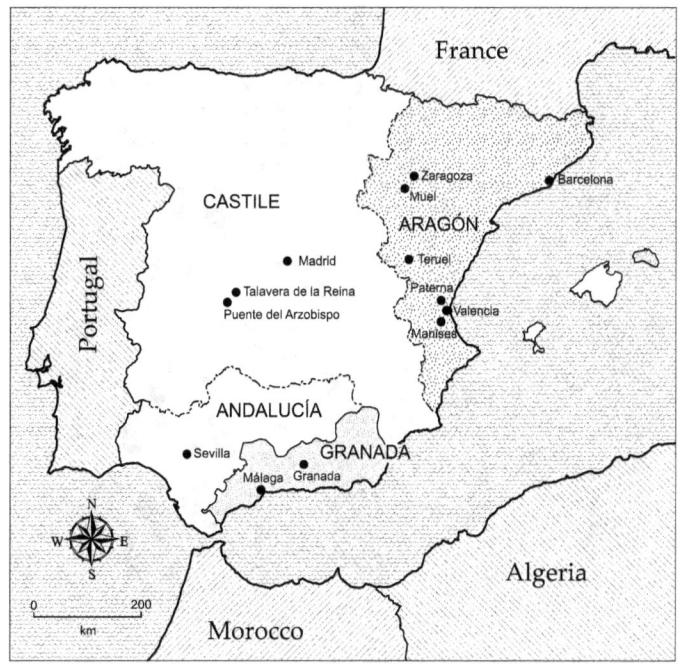

FIGURE 11.2 *The Iberian Peninsula in the late sixteenth century, showing major pottery centers and other places mentioned in the text.*

The secrets of luster ware production were allegedly introduced to that city by an influential lord of Valencia, don Pedro Buyl (or Boil) (Lister and Lister 1987: 92; Van de Put 1911: 13). In 1454 and 1455, Mary of Castile, consort of Alfonso V of Aragón, requested of Buyl two orders of the blue and gold ware—misnamed "Obra de Malaga"—including plates, cups, pitchers, and porringers (Van de Put 1911: ix, 11–12). Contracts for these wares record payment "in-kind," including valuable potters' resources such as cobalt, lead, and tin, but also "in grain and other articles of diet; in horses and mules; in textile fabrics and garments. A pair of silk gloves and a sword" (ibid.: 14). Manises's luster ware retained its high status through the sixteenth century before declining in the seventeenth, in part as a consequence of the broader circumstances—severe economic depression[9]—gripping Spain at the time (Pinedo and Vizcaino 1979: 83).

Alongside the Hispano-Moresque tradition in the east, a second tradition developed, known as Italianate or Renaissance (Thornton 1997). The style's origins are associated with three major production centers—Montelupo, Liguria (Genoa), and Faenza—that arose in the late fifteenth century in north-central

FIGURE 11.3 *A modern (ca. 1980s) green-and-manganese-over-cream footed plate painted by Domingo Punter of Teruel, Aragón, Spain. Punter, along with his father, began reproducing medieval styles of Teruel verde y morado pottery in the 1950s, using vessels in regional museum collections as models (Llorens Artigas and Corredor-Matheos 1979: 39). The green is a bright grassy green; the manganese varies from strong black to brown-black. Compare the black flower motifs on the brim with the motifs on the walls of the bowl of the baptismal font in figure 11.1. Diam. 25 cm. Collection of the author. Computer rendering by Don S. Rice.*

Italy, and it came into vogue in Sevillian pottery with the arrival from Pisa of the Genoese potter Francisco Nicoluso (a.k.a. Nicoluso Pisano) in 1498 (Lister and Lister 1982: 69–78, 140–41). Nicoluso's famed delicate painting style and colorful palette of blue, green, orange, yellow, and manganese began with making large tile pictures for walls and quickly spread to tableware (Lister and Lister 1987: 119, 137–40; Sánchez-Pacheco 1981b: 95). These Italianate-style wares are especially renowned as products of kilns in Sevilla and in Talavera de la Reina (Castilla). To encourage further Italian contributions to various kinds of artisanry, in 1484

Spain's rulers began offering ten-year grants of tax exemptions to induce both Italian and Flemish artisans to relocate there (Lister and Lister 1982: 13, 75).

By the late fifteenth century, Spanish and especially Italianate-style tin-enameled wares were imported into northern Europe, "a market virtually devoid of decorated ceramic" (Gaimster 1999b: 1; see also Hurst 1977). These majolicas were wildly popular, especially the plain white-enameled Faenza White type popular in the last half of the sixteenth century, heralded for its "clean white surfaces" appropriate for painting religious iconography such as Marian devotional scenes and the sacred trigram IHS (Gaimster 1999b: 1–2, also 1999a; Lister and Lister 1982: 76–78, 92; Pleguezuelo 2003b: 111–12). Not surprisingly, the desirability of both plain and decorated majolicas led to widespread imitations, including faience in France and delftware in the Low Countries.

In Sevilla, artisans were from varied religious backgrounds: Christian, Muslim, and Jewish. Settlement and production were spatially isolated into various districts, often walled, that reinforced social distinctions either between Christians and non-Christians or between select craft workers and others. The potters' districts housed hundreds of clay workers and painters and scores of kilns. The most famous barrio is Triana; others include Adarvejo de los Moros and the Genoese quarter of Puerta Real (Sánchez-Pacheco 1981b: 95). The Adarvejo was a walled quarter of Muslim settlement established after the Christians retook Sevilla in 1248, when King Ferdinand III of Castile ordered craftsmen to settle together in specific barrios (Pike 1972: 135, 154).

Sevilla became a center of mudéjar architecture relatively late, with roughly 200 mudéjar masons, carpenters, potters, and tile and glass makers in 1420 (Fernández 1993), although potters had long produced traditional Iberian styles of pottery and other goods. In the sixteenth century, much of the production was luxury goods; and artisan producers may have been primarily *conversos* (baptized former Jews) rather than moriscos, impoverished "social outcasts" unassimilated (and deemed unassimilable) in Christian society (Pike 1972: 130–70). The population of Muslims and moriscos steadily increased, however, and after the unsuccessful Alpujarras rebellion of Muslims in Granada in 1568, moriscos from that region poured into the city (ibid.: 154–55).

In the mid-sixteenth century, pottery making—which included production of a variety of shipping containers as well as tablewares—"was ranked eighth in importance" in a list of 53 occupations within the city, with 50 pottery workshops (Lister and Lister 1987: 45, 131, 160). By the boom years of the export trade with the Americas, however, Sevilla housed 5,000 potters, painters, and other workers in five barrios; and potters were the third-largest group of artisans in the city (ibid.: 124, 160). Even in 1721, well after the Sevillan ceramic industry's decline, there were "only" 82 glazed-ware kilns used by "only" 346 workers (Sánchez-Pacheco 1981b: 99).

Importantly, the urban- and region-based ceramic traditions of southern and eastern Spain were neither unique to nor bounded by those cities and regions. Potters frequently moved, particularly as a consequence of political and economic upheavals during the final stages of the Christian reconquest and later in response to the economic boom surrounding the supply of goods for Spain's overseas colonies. In addition, considerable counterfeiting was practiced, attributing the wares of one place to another production center viewed as having higher status. For example, loza produced in interior cities, such as Talavera, was more expensive for shippers because of the added costs of transport to coastal ports, so it was only

> logical for the ceramists of the port city [Seville] . . . to imitate these products and sell them at a more competitive price. This is what happened with Talveran loza shipped from Sevilla. It was soon supplanted by imitations made by potters in Triana, who came to be called "painters of Talavera mayólica" in the same way that years before they had called themselves "painters of Pisa and Venice mayólica" when those were the best-selling products. With equal audacity, in the 1600s they called themselves "painters of Chinese mayólica," and in the 1700s "Dutch-style painters." (Pleguezuelo 2003b: 114)

Changes in majolica production in medieval Iberia—including centers of manufacture, religious identities of producers, and decorative colors and motifs—resulted from the impacts of complex political, ideological, economic, and technological currents, both internal and external, sweeping the peninsula. These changes reflect not only the affairs of political leaders and economic elites but also humbler vicissitudes of daily life. In the late twelfth and early thirteenth centuries, greater decorative variability was accompanied by an increase in the number of named shapes of vessels, as gleaned from glossaries and cookbooks (Rosselló Bordoy 1992: 100). This likely reflects an increase in specialized uses of the ceramics. For example, one thirteenth-century innovation in Sevilla was a plate form for individual servings, which had not been produced previously and might distinguish Christian versus Muslim dietary patterns (Lister and Lister 1987: 75). Related to this, the loss of status of traditional verde y morado wares in fourteenth-century Paterna has been linked to ordinary folk using pottery eating vessels instead of traditional wooden ones (Pinedo and Vizcaino 1979: 24, 36). The popularity of imported Spanish and Italian majolica wares in northern Europe was in part "a response to changes in contemporary dining practices which had developed into a more ritualistic activity designed to demonstrate status ... [enabling] middle class consumers to imitate the dining habits of the elite ... The development of maiolica production illustrates how changing customs and social attitudes, rather than simple economics, form the motivation for technological innovation" (Gaimster 1999b: 2).

CHRISTIAN PERSECUTIONS AND RESTRICTIONS ON TRADE

The so-called *convivencia* in which Christians, Muslims, and Jews supposedly lived harmoniously in Iberia (see note 1)—living together but separately in walled barrios—ended in the late fifteenth century, after Isabel of Castile married Ferdinand of Aragón in 1469. When the two assumed the thrones of their respective kingdoms, Isabel in 1474 and Ferdinand in 1479, they achieved political unification of northern and central Spain. In 1492 they wrested Granada from Nasrid Islamic rule and united Spain under God and a fervent Christianity.

Shortly thereafter, and with the assistance of the Inquisition (see Kamen 1997), these "Catholic kings" began a program of ethnic cleansing to purge Spain of non- and doubtful Christians, the latter believed to be practicing their former religion secretly (as "crypto-Jews"). The principal targets were "New Christians," first the conversos, soon followed by persecution of moriscos. The litany of harsh decrees and edicts (table 11.2) demanded that moriscos/Muslims in various key cities and regions be converted and baptized or punished by expulsion from Spain. In the first decades of the sixteenth century, Islam was tolerated only in Aragón, largely because of the willingness of lower-class Muslims to engage in manual labor, including various kinds of skilled craftwork. Nonetheless, forcible baptisms of moriscos began in Valencia in 1520, immediately following an epidemic of plague, prompting four years of rebellions initiated by the beleaguered artisan guilds. In 1526 all Muslims in Aragón were ordered to convert or be exiled (ibid.: 215–17). In 1568 moriscos in Alpujarras (Granada) revolted against the Christians but, after being subjugated, were forced to resettle in Castile or were sold into slavery (ibid.: 224); some were resettled in the Triana potters' quarter of Sevilla (Lister and Lister 1987: 127, 272). Following heightened conflict and repression,[10] the crown issued new decrees of expulsion in 1609 and 1610. About 300,000 moriscos were forced into exile, beginning in Valencia in 1609 (Kamen 1997: 227), with 7,500 moriscos expelled from Sevilla the next year (Lister and Lister 1974: 45, 1987: 272). The Spanish crown also forbade transatlantic travel of moriscos/Muslims to the colonies, a violation punishable by death. Many of the moriscos moved south to Morocco, where Fez and other cities had long been welcoming destinations for persecuted Spanish Muslims (Lister and Lister 1987: 125, 175–88).

TABLE 11.2 Spanish decrees related to Muslims

1501	decree: Muslims in al-Andalus must accept Christian baptism
1502	decree: Muslims in Castile must be baptized or expelled
1520	decree: forcible baptisms of moriscos in Valencia
1526	decree: all Muslims ordered to convert
1543	decree: forbade travel of non-Christians to colonies
1557	decree: expulsion of non-Christians from colonies
1568	Alpujarras revolt of moriscos in Granada
1574	decree: limitations on non-Christians' artistic freedoms
1607	decree: death penalty imposed on unlicensed travelers to colonies
1609	decree: expulsion of moriscos from Spain, beginning in Valencia
1610	decree: expulsion of moriscos from Sevilla

Sources: Fernández 1993; Jeffery 2003: 293; Kamen 1997: 215–17, 227; Lister and Lister 1974: 45. See also Qamber 2006: 29–31.

The impact of the expulsions is difficult to measure. The literature on pottery production in Spain suggests that, over time—that is, with reconquest, forced conversions, and expulsions—the proportions of Muslim and Christian potters changed, but by the end of the fifteenth century the craft had become largely Christian and it became even more so after the influx of Italian and Flemish artisans (Lister and Lister 1987: 272). In Aragón, however, the pottery-producing towns of Teruel, Muel, and Villafeliche were left almost completely depopulated, and the area's new Christian overlord had to issue contracts to repopulate the towns (Alvaro Zamora 1978: 13–16). Many of the new potters were Christian *escudilleros* from Catalonia (e.g., Reus, Barcelona) or Castile, including Talavera (ibid.: 18–19).[11] In Manises the changes can be tracked incrementally. In 1610 there were 150 houses of "Old Christians" and only 45 of moriscos, of which 28 were those of potters (Pinedo and Vizcaino 1979: 94). In 1614 enough Christian luster ware potters were present to create the statutes of a guild of "Mestres de la Obra de Terra" dedicated to Saint Hippolytus, signed with the approval of "don Felip Boyl señor de Manises" (Van de Put 1911: 17, 65). In 1617 the "lord" of the city (presumably the same Philip Buyl) issued an order prohibiting any potter other than a "master of firing lusterware" from making that pottery (Pinedo and Vizcaino 1979: 94). This edict was reiterated a century later, which suggests considerable imitation of these highly desired wares. In some cases, for example, yellow paint was used in place of the metallic gold (ibid.).

FROM THE OLD WORLD TO THE NEW

As Spain established colonial settlements of various kinds (mission, military, mining, agricultural) in what is now the Caribbean, southeastern United States, and Mexico, the crown developed stringent mechanisms and policies to supply the colonies with necessary goods from the homeland. One such policy was that trade should be conducted only in Castilian goods, carried only by "properly licensed Castilian merchants" in "Castilian bottoms" (ships) (McAlister 1984: 243). Fleets of these transport vessels—the *carrera de Indias*—sailed under armed escort from Sevilla (later Cádiz) in late spring or summer. After re-provisioning in the Canary Islands, some ships headed for ports in Havana and New Spain (Mexico) or, if supplying South America, to Cartagena (Veracruz) and Nombre de Diós.

The port of Nombre de Diós (called Portobelo after 1597), on the Caribbean coast of Panama (see Ward 1993), was the official supplier of goods to Andean South America—the viceroyalty of Peru. Across the isthmus on the Pacific coast, Panamá La Vieja, founded in 1519, was the strategic commercial hub for moving Spanish goods south to Peru's port of Callao near Lima. In contrast to the comparatively rapid subjugation of Aztec Mexico by 1521, the conquest, pacification, and colonial settlement of Peru required the better part of three decades to achieve, as a consequence of feuding factions of conquerors and Indigenous uprisings (see Lockhart 1968). Thus it was not until the 1550s and later that colonists began moving to Peru in large numbers and began to need comparable quantities of tablewares.

Despite the persecution of morisco artisans in Spain and restrictions on their travel, striking *mudejarismos* are evident in Spain's transatlantic colonies. Mudéjar influence in Ibero-American architecture, for example, was not merely tolerated but encouraged (Henares Cuéllar and López Guzmán 1993; Jeffery 2003; Kaufmann 2003; Toussaint 1946), even in those most Christian of all edifices: the new churches and monasteries intended to symbolize Catholic dominion over the colonial landscapes. Mudéjar artisans were called upon to build the new structures—as they had built churches and other prominent structures in the newly Christianized Spanish homeland—because they were knowledgeable, experienced, and inexpensive workers (Fernández 1993; Jeffery 2003; Lister and Lister 1987: 119, 271).

Moreover, the earliest regular clergy in the New World, the Franciscans and other missionaries, were from Andalucía and other areas of Spain where they were accustomed to living among moriscos/mudéjars and their architectural products of stone, wood, and tile. They thus shared a collective memory, vocabulary, and expectations about what the new churches should look like. In addition, perhaps the appropriation and extension of mudéjar architectural traditions to the New World constituted an effort by civic and ecclesiastical leaders to express their authority in terms the immigrant populations were familiar with, that were meaningful, and that they could understand (Fernández 1993). It is of no little interest that, during the early years in the colonies, loza production was chiefly supported by the religious orders, both for hollow ware (used at table or in religious services, as baptismal and holy water fonts) and architectural tiles. Thus when "the extension of the Church in Mexico was checked and its influence began to decline," so did the tile industry (Barber 1915b: 17).

Mudéjar/morisco design contributions to architecture are seen in brickwork and carpentry, such as the elegant marquetry-like *artesonado* ceilings of colonial churches in many parts of Latin America, including Peru (e.g., Bernales Ballesteros 1986; Gutiérrez 2002: 47–67; López Guzmán 1993; Ortíz Crespo 1993; San Cristobal 1995). In Lima, Cusco, Moquegua, and other Andean cities, one of the primary architectural features attributed to Islamic influence is the beautiful overhanging, enclosed wooden "box" balconies (*ajimeces*) that adorn the palatial residences of the cities' elites, as well as public buildings around the main plazas (Kaufmann 2003: 48).[12] In Moquegua, perhaps the most famous of these is the mahogany balcony of the eighteenth-century home of don Diego Fernández de Córdova, on the south side of the Main Plaza.

Mudéjar-style pottery also reached the colonies, where it is known by archaeologists as "Morisco ware" (Goggin's [1968: 207–8] "Medieval Tradition"; see Deagan 1987: 55–61; Lister and Lister 1982: 45–65, 83–90, 1987: 113). Morisco ware had its beginnings in early-fifteenth-century Spain, with the growing market created by commoners' access to pottery tableware, and Muslim and Christian potters in the Triana district of Sevilla began to mass-produce common-grade tableware for largely poor city dwellers. Made using the light-colored clay from the bank of the Guadalquivir River near Sevilla (Lister and Lister 1987), Morisco ware consisted of simple, thick-walled, Muslim-style bowl and plate forms lacking foot-rings. Vessels had a heavily flawed, off-white surface, occasionally painted with simple lines or stylized Kufic inscriptions (*alafias*). This pottery was shipped to the colonies until about 1550 and has been given type names by archaeologists: Columbia Plain (plain white glazed), Isabela Polychrome (blue and purple or morado), Yayal Blue-on-white, and Santo Domingo Blue-on-white (see http://www.flmnh.ufl.edu/histarch/gallery_types/type_list.asp). In 1508 a load of 240 cartons of Columbia Plain carinated bowls was shipped across the Atlantic to Santo Domingo by a merchant in Sevilla (Lister and Lister 1974: 20, 1987: 202). In 1509 three men—including Diego Fernández de Morón of Sevilla,[13] identified as an *ollero* (potter; lit. maker of ollas [pots])—traveled to

Santo Domingo accompanied by enormous quantities of diverse ceramic goods, including nine boxes of loza from Valencia (presumably luster ware)[14] and wall tiles, all assumed to be for retail sale (Gavin 2003: 8; Lister and Lister 1982: 69, 1987: 202, 204, 311).[15]

Potters in Spain (also Portugal and Italy) produced not only vast quantities of majolica tablewares but also architectural tiles (*azulejos*; Arabic *az-zulaij* 'ornamental tile') painted in the Italianate style, particularly at the famous centers of Talavera de la Reina and nearby Puente del Arzobispo, southwest of Madrid in Castile (Seseña 1981). In addition to use in the homeland—for example, at King Philip's court—these goods were shipped to the transatlantic colonies and other European and Mediterranean[16] consumers (Gavin et al. 2003; Goggin 1968; Lister and Lister 1987; Sánchez-Pacheco et al. 1981). Talavera and Puente ceramics of the sixteenth through eighteenth centuries were decorated in blue, yellow, orange, and manganese and strongly influenced the styles of colonial loza manufactured in the Caribbean and New Spain.

Imported majolica was used in the colonies in dining, religious, and medical service: goods included not just tableware (for serving and eating) but also pharmaceutical jars (*albarelos*) and items for personal hygiene (urinals, or *bacines*; spittoons, or *escupideras*) and ornamental or other use (vases, candleholders, inkwells, and so on) (Fournier-García 1997: 53; Lister and Lister 1987: 128). But ceramics are bulky and fragile cargo for transatlantic ocean voyages and expensive for consumers once they arrive at their destination, so it is not surprising that centers of loza production were established in the colonies.

The whos, hows, and whens of this process are not at all clear, particularly in the early years. Under Spanish direction, a variety of composite or hybrid wares, also called colono-wares (Wheaton 2002) or transculturational ceramics, were produced that fused European and Indigenous technologies, styles, and forms. In what is now the Dominican Republic, for example, Indigenous potters used both traditional hand-building and wheel-based techniques to produce Spanish forms with traditional Arawak designs (Ortega and Fondeur 1978). In Mexico after the 1521 conquest, Spanish-introduced lead glazes and new forms (candle holders, chamber pots) were combined with native methods (molds), shapes (tripod bowls), and red-firing paste to create loza *amarilla* ("yellow"; Blackman, Fournier, and Bishop 2006; Fournier and Blackman 2008: 7).

Later, in 1537 and 1538, two Spanish potters (olleros) were given lots in the newly platted town that is now Mexico City, and they were followed by others in the early 1540s—bringing both morisco/mudéjar and Italianate traditions of forming, decorating, and firing loza from Andalucía (Lister and Lister 1982: 13, 88, 89; 1987: 202, 221). Around 1550 Diego Vargas Pina, a Spanish potter, moved to Mexico City but left after five years because he was unable to find the proper raw materials, particularly siliceous sand (Gómez, Pasinski, and Fournier 2001: 36, 45). In 1555 another potter, Juan de la Talavera, from Alcalá de Guadaira near Sevilla, traveled to New Spain but it is not known where he settled (ibid.: 54); the substantial sum he paid to make the journey might indicate that he was a morisco. Two years later, in 1557, Bartolomé Carretero, a potter from Talavera, petitioned to emigrate to Mexico, claiming to be one of only four old-Christian potters in all of Spain (ibid.: 35). He noted that the residents of the new viceregal capital desired fine ceramics but most potters were morisco or mudéjar and thus prevented from traveling.

MYTHS AND VOICES

Green-and-brown/black–decorated majolica has a long history in medieval Iberia, but this color combination and its underlying Islamic heritage have been little studied in loza manufactured in the Christian New World. Bold verde y morado decoration contrasts sharply with the delicate, blue-based Italianate polychromy common in Spanish-colonial North America and Panama. So, who were the immigrant potters/painters who produced the New World material? This question needs to be investigated in a larger context of rethinking the standard history of the Spanish conquest and colonization of the Americas. Matthew Restall began this process with a book titled *Seven Myths of the Spanish Conquest* (2003).[17] I suggest two additional "myths" that should be critically evaluated.

The first concerns migration. In theory, only "Old Christians" could obtain the necessary royal licenses from the Consejo de Indias to emigrate from Spain to its colonies. To obtain the license, those who wished to emigrate were required to produce three unrelated witnesses who would testify to their "old-Christian" status (Gómez, Pasinski, and Fournier 2001: 45). Essentially, in the Spanish crown's view of Christian order, certain privileged spaces and places could only be occupied by certain kinds of people; Others (Jews, Muslims) could live there but only "not there": that is, walled off from Christians. It was the Spaniards' sacred duty to cleanse their new lands of the heathens and infidels who already occupied them and refuse entry to others.

But this policy, like so many, was unreasonable and counterproductive. If it were actually true, as Bartolomé Carretero claimed, that he was one of only four old Christian potters in all of Spain in 1557, then who—other than potters of the religious orders, such as the Dominicans—established the new majolica industries throughout the American colonies? As noted elsewhere (Rice 2013), it seems telling that locerías in major early colonial capitals or commercial centers (e.g., Puebla and Oaxaca in Mexico; Antigua, Guatemala; Panamá La Vieja; Lima and Cusco in Peru) were established around 1580, give or take a decade, shortly after the morisco expulsion from Alpujarras. Another flurry of new pottery centers can be seen in the second quarter of the seventeenth century, perhaps a consequence of the morisco purges of 1609–1610.

Crown migration policies were ineffectually implemented and regularly ignored by anyone—Christian, Muslim, or Jew[18]—with enough money and cleverness to either bribe officials or avoid the procedures entirely. Prohibited individuals might not have been named on passenger lists[19] or might have disguised their occupation if it could be linked to something as clearly Muslim-related as pottery making or other artisanry. Moriscos were permitted to accompany legal migrants if they were claimed as slaves or servants who had practiced Christianity since age 10–12 (Qamber 2006: 22–23). In addition, morisco artisans frequently changed their names to disguise their identities, sometimes taking on the names of Christian potters who were colleagues or godparents; this, however, "did not erase the blood line; it merely confused accounting" (see Lister and Lister 1987: 270–71). Perhaps they left Spain for some other country and then sailed across the Atlantic from there or from the Canary Islands.

Peter Boyd-Bowman's (1968, 1973, 1976) studies of patterns of emigration from Spain to the Americas between 1493 and 1600, in which both origin and destination are known from official documents, are of interest. First, his maps (Boyd-Bowman 1976: maps 2, 4, 5) showing Spanish provinces of origin, coded by numbers of emigrants (from 200 to more than 10,000), reveal that most migrants to Mexico and Peru came from southern and central Spain. Significantly, provinces along Spain's eastern and southeastern coast—centers of mudéjar art and majolica production, such as Barcelona, Teruel, Valencia, Málaga, and Granada—contributed conspicuously few emigrants to Peru, despite the rampant persecution in these provinces. It is very likely that people from these areas made the journey but did not disclose their origins. Second, Boyd-Bowman (1973: 53) identified 114 non-Spaniards (3.5 percent) among 3,248 emigrants (of identified origin) to Peru between 1540 and 1559; more than half were Portuguese but there were also Italians, Flemish, Greeks, French, and Hungarians. This figure dropped to 1 percent between 1560 and 1579 (ibid.: 83).

Travelers' stories about the wealth and opportunities in the New World colonies, contrasting sharply with the poverty and growing oppression in the peninsula, would have contributed strongly to both "pull" and "push" stimuli for morisco potters and other artisans to make the transatlantic journey. However the non-Christians and others circumvented the rules, it is evident from all that is known of the early history of the Spanish colonies that "non-Spaniards, especially Portuguese and Italians, could be found everywhere" (Kamen 2003: 134). The Spanish chronicler Oviedo commented that by 1535 in the new Spanish city of Santo Domingo (Hispañola), "every language can be heard . . . from Italy, Germany, Scotland, and England, with Frenchmen, Hungarians, Poles, Greeks, Portuguese, and all the other nations of Asia and Africa and Europe" (quoted in ibid.). There is little reason to assume that morisco artisans could not have been among these peoples. Although Oviedo's statement might be a bit hyperbolic, the frequent reiteration of official decrees restricting migration reveals the futility of efforts to prohibit the travels of "undesirables." And, of course, the rules could be ignored when expedient: for example, the mother of Viceroy Antonio de Mendoza of New Spain (1535–50) was said to be part Jewish and part Muslim (Lister and Lister 1982: 89).

A second, and not unrelated, "myth of the Spanish conquest" concerns trade. In principle, again, Ferdinand and Isabel's monopolistic and mercantilist policies regulating trade with the colonies permitted the importation of only Castilian goods by only Castilian ships sailing only from Sevilla/Cádiz and into only a few American ports. But closer analysis reveals that this rigid anti-capitalist policy was as ineffective—and as frequently countermanded—as the policies concerning migration. In 1529, for example, the monarchs' grandson, Charles V, opened the movement of goods and settlers to ships sailing from ports in Biscay, Barcelona, and Málaga (Haring 1963: 303). This policy was reversed by Philip II in 1573.

Further evidence of gaps in Spain's protectionist net is evident with respect to the Canary Islands, a Spanish crown possession that was a provisioning station for duly licensed ships of the Spanish trade flotillas. In 1534 the citizens of the islands were permitted to participate in transatlantic commerce, and by mid-century the islands were opened up to French, British, Flemish, and Scottish merchants (ibid.). It is therefore not surprising that compositional analysis of twenty-two pottery fragments from the Canary Islands revealed that they were produced not only in Sevilla but also in Manises, Barcelona, the Netherlands, Italy, Portugal, and unknown areas (Iñañez et al. 2009). Through these mechanisms, pottery from many non-Castilian/non-Sevillan (i.e., mudéjar) Spanish and non-Spanish production areas could easily have been transported from the Canaries to the American colonies, whether legally or illegally. In all, as much as five-sixths of the cargo shipped to the Americas might have been supplied by countries other than Spain (Lister and Lister 1987: 210).

Despite Spanish functionaries' propensity to classify people into racial and religious categories, there has been little attention to identifying the presence of

Muslims and moriscos in Spain's American colonies and their role in bringing the colonies into the global capitalist network of production.[20] Officials could not expect to formally identify non-Christians in censuses, of course, because they were not supposed to be there in the first place. James Lockhart (1968: 196–98), in discussing the presence of moriscos in Peru between 1532 and 1560, considered them to be primarily black slaves (although he noted that the Spaniards "frequently . . . called moriscos white" Spaniards). Women outnumbered men and were thought to be primarily concubines; the "few male morisco slaves who can be identified were highly valuable artisans or trusted bodyguards" (ibid.), but no artisanal specialties are mentioned. According to surviving Inquisitorial records, only seven moriscos were tried in Peru between 1560 and 1700 (Qamber 2006: 41).

It seems clear from architectural studies that substantial numbers of architects and craftsmen skilled in the mudéjar style traveled to the Americas. These generally anonymous artisans were essential, given that discussions of pre-imperial Spanish society emphasize the growing elite depreciation of manual labor, which was, in turn, part of a status system created to highlight the differential identities and power of the victorious Christian overlords vis-à-vis their Muslim subjects and vassals. This status-based labor avoidance was likely transferred to the colonies, meaning that Muslim artisans, craftsmen, and laborers were essential components of the economy—particularly for production of elite goods[21]—but simultaneously discriminated against. Confirmation of the presence of morisco artisans comes from restrictions against the "Moorish rise in the craft guilds" in Mexico, such as prohibitions against non-Christians attaining the rank of *maestro*, or master potter (Lister and Lister 1982: 89, 1987: 273).

NOTES

1. My translation. The original reads "Una buena parte de la historiografía Española se ha dedicado sistemáticamente a minusvalorar el influjo del Islam en la España Cristiana, cerrando los ojos a la evidencia arrolladora de la huella monumental islámica." The relative influence of, and tolerance among, the various cultures in Iberia has been a longstanding preoccupation among Spanish historians: "The principal adversaries in the contest, Américo Castro and Claudio Sánchez-Albornoz . . . have debated the proposition that Spanish culture is the result of centuries of intimate contact between Christians, Muslims, and Jews. Castro, who supports this position, has been attacked as un-Christian; Sánchez-Albornoz, who opposes it, has been denounced as a racist" (Glick and Pi-Sunyer 1969: 138).

2. In the fifteenth century, Málaga in Granada was a well-known center of production of the popular and elegant luster ware, as was Manises in Valencia (Pinedo and Vizcaino 1979: 64–67; Van de Put 1911: 11–26). With the conquest of Málaga (Malíca, Malequa, Melicha) by the Christians in 1487, production ceased. Apparently the term *obra de Malíca* (or de Melicha) came to be used not only for Spanish luster ware of Manises (see ibid.: 3–5, 11–26) but also for luster ware in general, and in the variable orthography of the time *malíca* may have evolved into *maiolica* (Thornton 1997: 116).

3. This sea route may have been disrupted in 878, when Guangzhou was sacked and foreign merchants were murdered; according to a contemporary account, around "120,000 Muslims, Jews, Christians and Parsees" were killed (Flecker 2001: 350). The consequence for Arab merchants was loss of direct trade and increased reliance on Chinese middlemen (ibid.: 353).

4. The term *mudéjar* comes from Arabic *al-mudajjanun* or *al-muta'akhkhirun*, meaning "those permitted to remain, those who stayed behind" after subjugation (Fernández 1993; Jeffery 2003: 289). In fifteenth-century Valencia, contract documents frequently refer to potters as "Saracens" (Van de Put 1911: 13).

5. Blue decoration on Chinese ceramics—the blue imported from the Near East—became common during the Yuan dynasty (AD 1279–1368), but Spanish majolica is more closely related to the porcelains of the succeeding Ming (1368–1644, especially the Wan Li period, 1590–1620) and Qing (1644–1912) dynasties. Much of this is known as "Kraak porcelain" after the Portuguese ships, or *carracks*, that carried large cargoes of the ware (Kuwayama 1997: 17, 26n35).

6. There is some confusion regarding the portrayal of human figures in Islamic art. Although it is often said that such representations are prohibited, the Qur'an only prohibits the worship of idols (Bloom and Blair 2009). Attitudes toward depictions of humans varied among Muslims through time and space.

7. Other centers of mudéjar pottery production were Teruel, Muel, and Villafeliche in Aragón and Barcelona, Lleida, Villafranca del Penedès, and Reus in Catalunya (Iñañez et al. 2009).

8. Gold and blue are paired on some very prominent Islamic works, including the seventh-century Dome of the Rock in Jerusalem, several mosques in Spain, and the "Blue Koran," and they may be related to Roman art (Nees 2011: 160). Blue is the primary decoration in the much-esteemed Chinese porcelains and is also associated with the Virgin Mary and Christians more generally, especially in western Europe (Bloom and Blair 2011: 37; Fierro 2011: 96n5, 97n24). Tile work in two shades of blue, turquoise (copper-based) and dark blue (cobalt-based), was common in the Islamic Near East through the thirteenth century (O'Kane 2011).

9. In the seventeenth century Spain suffered from declining imports of gold and silver bullion from its colonies, plummeting tax revenues, and resultant bankruptcies.

The nation was mired in costly wars, experienced an epidemic early in the century, and suffered a series of natural disasters in the south (droughts, torrential rains, floods, an earthquake, harvest failures, and famine); farmers were reducing grain production in favor of wine grapes (Lynch 1981: 283–85; Vassberg 1984: 198–99). This, plus the nation's protectionist economic policies, resulted in "Castile's total administrative and economic collapse" (Elliott 1964: 360).

10. For example, moriscos were forbidden to bear arms, enter taverns, or live more than two to a house; they were forced to pay special taxes but were allowed to wear traditional clothes (Lister and Lister 1987: 272; Qamber 2006: 31–33).

11. The Catalan term *escudellers* (Sp. *escudilleros*) ceased to be used by the end of the seventeenth century, and potters producing tin-enameled wares were referred to as *vaxillero* (*baxillero, vagillero*), from *vajilla* 'ware' (Alvaro Zamora 1978: 20–21).

12. See also http://www.go2peru.com/webapp/ilatintravel/articulo.jsp?cod=200002218; http://www.go2peru.com/webapp/ilatintravel/articulo.jsp?cod=1998840).

13. Fernández de Morón is also identified as one of the guarantors of the venture (Lister and Lister 1987: 311), suggesting some wealth for this potter.

14. Luster ware is rare in the American colonies, found primarily in the Caribbean, although some was recovered in the Mexico City cathedral excavations (Lister and Lister 1982: 63, 68–69, table 2.2). See also (http://www.flmnh.ufl.edu/histarch/gallery_types/type_index_display.asp?type_name=LUSTERWARE).

15. Enormous quantities of basic construction materials, such as bricks and roof tiles, were also shipped in these and other vessels, prompting the question why no ceramic manufacturing industry had begun in the Caribbean settlements (Lister and Lister 1987: 203–4). The answer may relate to both the Spaniards' dislike of the manual labor involved in producing such goods (and the loss of native laborers to do so) and the fact that such heavy materials were useful as ballast for the ships and salable at their destination. The ninth-century Indo-Arab shipwreck *Batu Hitam*, with its cargo of pottery, was also found to be carrying 10 tons of lead ingots as salable ballast (Flecker 2000: 209–10).

16. The famous Italian painter Francisco Nicoluso worked out of Triana, and his decorated *cuenca* tiles were shipped back to Italy for use in the chapel of Leo X in the Castel Sant' Angelo in Rome, as determined by instrumental neutron activation analysis (INAA) (Hughes 1991: 55–56).

17. Restall's (2003) seven myths include conquest by a small king's army of exceptional white men and extended concepts relating to imperial completion, miscommunication, native desolation, and Spanish superiority.

18. Confirmation that Conversos, or "Crypto-Jews," migrated to South America despite the early prohibitions comes from genetic analyses of people from southern Ecuador (Velez et al. 2012). Specific genes can be traced to Sephardic Jewish ancestry in the Iberian Peninsula.

19. For example, the claim that "no Spanish potters came to the Americas in the first hundred years following contact (1492–1592)," based on the lack of mention of potters in passenger lists (Duncan 1998: 20), is obviously incorrect.

20. Reportedly, roughly "200 *morisco* soldiers were in the army that aided the conquest of Peru" (Lister and Lister 1987: 349n26, citing Ávilez Moreno 1980: 656).

21. For example, Lister and Lister (1982: 89, 1987: 273) refer to a proposal to send a group of moriscos to New Spain to aid in cultivation of silk worms.

12

Technological Spaces and Transfers

> Such choice loza and good glazed ware is made that Talavera ware is not missed, because a few years ago they began to make counterfeit Chinese ceramics that were very similar, particularly that made in Puebla de los Angeles in Mexico and in this city of Lima, which is very good and with fine glaze and colors.
>
> —Fr. Bernabé Cobo
> (1890 [1653]: 243)[1]

Spanish majolica has a centuries-long multicultural history that spans all of the Old World and combines the refined technological know-how of glass working and metalworking with the ancient craft of making earthenware pottery.[2] Majolica's foundations lie in glass making in the Near East where, by the fourth century AD, Persian glass makers had learned that tin oxide (SnO_2) was an opacifier: tiny (200–900 nanometers) crystals of the tin ore-mineral cassiterite in the glaze scatter light and thus create an opaque appearance (Molera, Vendrell-Saz, and Pérez-Arantegui 2001: 334; Vendrell, Molera, and Tite 2000).[3] By the ninth century, tin, in amounts of 5–8 percent or more, had gradually replaced other traditional agents (quartz, feldspar, calcium, air bubbles) as the sole opacifier of Near Eastern lead-based glazes (Mason and Tite 1997).[4]

In decoration, potters in the Near East were influenced by imported Chinese T'ang-dynasty ceramics of the eighth through tenth centuries, which included tri-color decoration featuring copper green, iron-based brown, and yellow pigments. Interestingly, this is also the color scheme of the Neo-Assyrian glazed bricks, although some of the colorants differed: black-brown was produced from manganese, opaque white

DOI: 10.5876/9781607322764:c12

from a calcium-antimonate pigment, green from copper, and yellow from lead-antimonate (Freestone 1991). Potters also might have been influenced by the rare, early, blue-on-white decoration on Chinese pottery using cobalt imported from Persia.

The technology of covering pottery surfaces with an opaque, light-colored tin enamel spread throughout the Mediterranean, perhaps earliest in Egypt, and was brought to the Iberian Peninsula in the tenth century, shortly after lead glazing was introduced (Lister and Lister 1987: 39–40). Chinese-inspired decoration on these wares gave rise in Andalucía to the long-lived medieval tradition of decorating tin-enameled pottery with copper (CuO) green and purplish-black/brown from manganese (MnO_2) instead of iron (see ibid. for a detailed history of Andalucían ceramics). Known as verde y morado, this Ibero-Islamic style featured motifs painted on a white or cream-colored ground that sometimes had a light bluish or greenish tint, depending on chemical impurities in the lead or tin oxides.

In the twelfth century the technique of producing luster ware (also known as *reflejo metálico*; *dorado*) was introduced to southeastern Spain, probably from Fatimid Egypt. This ware, especially famed in Málaga (Granada) and later Manises (Valencia), was fired twice (bisque and glost), then overglaze painted with gold or pinkish-gold decoration having a metallic luster, fired a third time at low temperature in a reducing atmosphere, and cooled under reduction (Canby 1997: 112; Gavin 2003: 5; Rhodes and Hopper 2000: 308–9; Thornton 1997: 119). These colors and luster are created by pigments made with metal salts (oxides): silver nitrate, copper sulfate or carbonate, or gold chloride. The ingredients and processes of luster-paint manufacture in Muel (Aragón) are described in 1585 and 1785 (Barber 1915a: 17–21). In 1585 the pigment was a mixture of powdered silver, "vermilion" (or cinnabar, which is mercury-based and toxic), red ochre, and "a little wire" (?), combined with strong vinegar and applied to the fired glazed ware with a feather. In 1785, 3 ounces of copper, a 1-*peseta* silver coin, and 3 ounces sulfur were combined, heated, and pounded into a powder. Then 12 ounces of red ochre and 3 pounds of earth or "scoriae" (metal slag?) were added; and the mix was powdered, mixed with water, and heated in a kiln for six hours. Finally, this mixture was powdered yet again, mixed with a quart of vinegar, and applied to the glazed vessels, which were fired using only dried rosemary as fuel. In addition to being technically complex, labor- and fuel-intensive, and thus expensive, luster wares had an extremely high failure rate; one observer estimated only 6 in 100 pieces were successful (Thornton 1997: 119).

In Manises, luster ware production appears to have been controlled by the Buyl family, prominent in Valencia since the thirteenth century, with don Pedro

Buyl (Peter Boil) described in the fifteenth century as the "lord of the castle and town of Manises" (see Van de Put 1911: v, 11–26). It is said that Pedro Buyl (likely an ancestor with the same name), an entrepreneur and Valencian diplomat to the Muslim court in Granada, discovered the secrets of luster ware production in Málaga and shared them with his Manises potters (Lister and Lister 1987: 92).

Together, these decorative treatments featuring green and black-brown, metallic luster, and cobalt blue pigments became known as mudéjar style or Hispano-Moresque ware.

SPANISH MAJOLICA: RESOURCES AND PRODUCTION TECHNOLOGIES

The production technology of tin-enameled pottery has long been studied through historical records (e.g., Picolpasso 1980), and some of the findings have been synthesized by Florence and Robert Lister (1982: 81–90, 1987). More recently, the technology of Spanish majolicas has been investigated through physicochemical analyses of the paste, glaze, and pigments—including instrumental neutron activation analysis (INAA), X-ray fluorescence spectrometry (XRF), petrography, electron microprobe, lead isotope, and laser ablation–inductively coupled plasma–mass spectrometric (LA-ICP-MS) analysis. One of the earliest of these investigations, which analyzed the paste of 178 fragments from Spain and New World sites, found clear distinctions in chemical composition between these two general proveniences (Olin, Harbottle, and Sayre 1978). It also identified differences within the New World sample, which included three sherds from Panamá La Vieja and three from Andean South America (from Quito, Ecuador, and Cusco, Peru), indicating multiple locations of Ibero-American production.

Clay Bodies

Another key finding of this analysis was that some of the Spanish earthenware bodies had a high calcium content, which later studies revealed to be the result of mixing two clays: one white-firing and calcareous (a.k.a. marly, calcitic, chalky) combined with a red-firing and non-calcareous clay (Lister and Lister 1987: 256–57; Magetti, Westley, and Olin 1984). Calcareous pastes are typical of Italian majolicas and earlier Islamic luster wares, with the clay having as much as 15–25 percent lime (Thornton 1997: 117).

Calcium-bearing clay bodies have numerous aesthetic and technical advantages and disadvantages. One advantage is lightening the fired color, perhaps in an effort to mimic the body color of early Chinese wares. With this mixture, any iron (Fe) in the non-calcareous clay is incorporated into the structure of calcium silicates and thus not fully oxidized to red.[5] This means the amount of expensive imported tin needed to create the opaque white glaze coating can be reduced (Magetti, Westley, and Olin 1984: 169). More important, the thermal expansion of high-lime pastes is similar to that of lead glazes, meaning that their high shrinkage puts the glaze under compression and overcomes the tendency of low-temperature glazes to be flawed by crazing (ibid.; Molera, Vendrell-Saz, and Pérez-Arantegui 2001: 339).

One disadvantage of calcareous clays in arid environments is a possible need for slightly greater amounts of water to make them plastic. Another potential disadvantage is the damage caused by the dissociation of calcium-carbonate ($CaCO_3$) particles at firing temperatures above roughly 700°C. To avoid this problem, these clays were likely carefully pre-processed (by levigation, sieving, or fine-screening) to remove large inclusions. Florence and Robert Lister (1982: 87) cite a 1301 treatise claiming that the ingredients were sifted through silk. This problem of "lime popping" can also be avoided by firing at temperatures above about 850°C, because calcareous clays develop a "very stable microstructure when fired in the range 850–1050°C (Freestone 1991: 55).

The technique of mixing calcareous and non-calcareous clays was used in various Spanish majolica production centers, including Talavera and also Paterna and Manises in Valencia (Caiger-Smith 1973: 200; Jornet, Blackman, and Olin 1985; Molera et al. 1996). Calcium (Ca) and sodium (Na) are negatively correlated in Valencian as compared with Málaga pottery (Hughes 1991: figure 4), suggesting a possible way to distinguish those centers' wares by chemical analysis. High calcium (ca. 18 percent) was found in majolica produced in Murcia, but it is not clear if this resulted from a mixture of two clays (Molera, Vendrell-Saz, and Pérez-Arantegui 2001: 336).

Few studies (cf. Joel et al. 1988; Lister and Lister 1982: 85–88; see also Rice 2013) have pursued the geological sources of the resources (lead, tin, copper, manganese) used in the production of this pottery, although raw materials found in archaeological excavations of a fourteenth-century workshop in Paterna have been analyzed (Molera et al. 1996). In Sevilla, potters used the light-colored calcareous clay found on the west bank of the Guadalquivir River across from the city (Lister and Lister 1987: 41, 49, 73, 75, 102–3). Their pastes contained inclusions of very fine quartz (maximum diameter 0.03 mm; silt-size), and sea-urchin spicules were occasionally visible (Magetti, Westley, and Olin 1984: 159, figure 3), suggesting the calcareous clay was a marine deposit.

Glazes

The mountainous Iberian Peninsula is rich in minerals, and lead—usually mined as galena or lead sulfide (PbS)—and manganese were relatively abundant. However, other ingredients were often imported, and different cities had different sources. Until the fourteenth century, glaze ingredients were prepared as frits, that is, combined and heated to a melt, with the resultant glass cooled and ground into a powder (Molera, Vendrell-Saz, and Pérez-Arantegui 2001: 339). It is not clear if Spanish potters followed the practice in Iran of first calcining tin with lead and then combining this mixture with quartz and soda, heating and cooling it, and crushing it (see Mason and Tite 1997: 57). Tin, the essential opacifying ingredient, was imported from Cornwall, England, after the thirteenth century (Lister and Lister 1982: 85), although Talavera imported tin from Portugal until the mid-seventeenth century (Pleguezuelo 2003b: 109). Analyses of the glazes on tin-enameled pottery produced in various workshops in eastern Spain indicate that the amount of tin ranged from 5 percent to 10 percent; less than 5 percent would not provide the desired opacity (Iñañez et al. 2009; Molera, Vendrell-Saz, and Pérez-Arantegui 2001).

An important ingredient to enhance fluxing ("melting") of the glaze during firing was an alkali of some sort. In Italian pottery, the white ground (*bianco*) was created with an alkali silicate frit (*mazzacotto*, masicote) made of wine lees, which contributed potassium (Kingery and Aronson 1990: 230; Thornton 1997: 117). In Islamic areas, where wine and alcohol were proscribed, the alkali was sodium. In Sevilla, for example, sodium or soda ash was obtained from burned marsh grasses (*barilla*), a legacy of earlier Muslim practice despite the large numbers of Christian potters and the abundance of Andalucían vineyards in later centuries. The prepared enamel was applied over a bisque-fired earthenware body, decoration was painted on the surface, and then the vessels were given a second (*glost*) firing (see Thornton 1997: 119). Italian wares frequently had a clear glaze *coperta*, or covering, over the painting.

Tin-enameled pottery was glazed on both surfaces, interior and exterior. At Zaragoza, Aragón, the white opaque enamel was used on the visible surface, such as the exterior of jars or the upper surface (obverse) of plates, whereas the other side (interiors or undersides/reverse) might be covered with a yellow or "honey"-colored (*melado*) lead glaze[6] (see Molera et al. 1997) or an opaque white coating. In the case of white secondary glaze-enamels, their compositions differed from that of the primary glaze (table 12.1), and small amounts of calcareous clay were sometimes added. Both primary and secondary enamels at Zaragoza included smaller amounts of lead (PbO) compared with other glazes analyzed. These differences indicate distinct recipes for primary versus

TABLE 12.1 Variable composition of white tin glazes in Zaragoza, Spain

Ingredient	Primary Glaze (wt. %)	Secondary Glaze (wt. %)
Tin oxide (SnO_2)	9–14	5–7
Silicon (SiO_2)	44–48	39–41

Source: Molera, Vendrell-Saz, and Pérez-Arantegui 2001: 337, table 2, figure 3.

secondary glazes, with smaller amounts, impure sources, or careless processing of expensive ingredients marking the latter.

Pigments

Many pigments for the painted decoration of tin-enameled wares were obtained as by-products of other industries, some of which were local; copper was obtained from cauldron makers and iron from blacksmiths (Pleguezuelo 2003b: 109). Yellow pigments were produced from a mixture of antimony and iron oxide, with Italian painters said to prefer the rust from ships' anchors (Lister and Lister 1982: 25).

Blue pigment was produced from expensive imported cobalt ore or oxide (CoO). Cobalt occurs widely but in generally low concentrations in the Earth's crust (element ranked number 33, at 0.002 percent), and it is generally mined today as a by-product of nickel, copper, silver, or arsenic operations (CDI 2011: 53–54). The cobalt for Spain's majolica pottery was from an arsenical deposit in Persia (Iran/Iraq) or the closer Levant and imported by Genoese merchants (Pleguezuelo 2003b: 109). It was "ground with potash and borax, moistened with grape syrup, and rolled into cakes, which were stored until needed. When used the cakes were crushed with fine sand and the mixture was then applied to a vessel wall with a gum substance or a bit of the glaze solution" (Lister and Lister 1987: 88). Morocco was another possible early source of cobalt (ibid.: 74–75, 223, 325–26n177).

The "Persian" source of cobalt was also that used for underglaze decoration on Chinese ceramics beginning in the Yuan dynasty, AD 1279–1368 (examples exist in the National Museum of Iran (http://www.cultural-china.com/chinaWH/html/en/Arts1741bye3395.html). Because the local cobalt in China was contaminated with manganese and fired to a lighter color, potters imported the arsenical cobalt pigment—which they called Mohammedan blue or sacrificial blue—for underglaze decoration (Hamer and Hamer 2012: 233; Wykes-Joyce 1958: 57; Zhang Fukang 1985: 173).

By 1470 Spain's cobalt source may have been Saxony, Germany—first Schneeburg, then later the Erzgebirge Mountains—where a silver-mining boom had begun in the twelfth century (CDI 2011: 3; Zucchiatti et al. 2006: 132–33). These changes in cobalt sources were revealed in chemical analyses of blue pigments on Valencian pottery, but they also occurred more widely among majolica/faience producers in Italy and France as a general "European technological event" around 1515–20 (Pérez-Arantegui et al. 2008: 1279; Zucchiatti et al. 2006). Cobalt had become "a real industrial product" rather than a mere by-product, with the ore roasted to a compound known as *zaffre* in newly developed reverberatory furnaces (Zucchiatti et al. 2006: 150–51).

MAJOLICA AND LOZA IN THE AMERICAS

Spanish-made pottery, the potters and painters who made the wares, and the knowledge of the resources and techniques for their production all traveled to Spain's New World colonies beginning in the early sixteenth century as part of the initiation of massive early capitalist technology transfer (Rice 2013, n.d.). Tin-enameled wares produced in the Spanish colonies are referred to here as loza to distinguish them from the Euro-specific cultural term *majolica*.

Although art historians have been interested in colonial Spanish American loza since the early twentieth century (e.g., Barber 1915b), archaeologists' attention began with John Goggin's (1968) typology of sherds recovered from sites primarily in the southeastern United States and the Caribbean. American-produced loza is generally easily distinguished from its imported majolica counterparts by paste color: Spanish- (and Italian-) made majolicas typically have light-colored (cream to yellowish to tan) pastes resulting from the use of calcareous clays or the addition of lime (Molera et al. 1996). New World loza pastes vary from pinkish (some Mexican products, which also incorporated calcareous clays) to orange to brick red; among the last, separate producing sources are often difficult to differentiate visually. In addition, inclusions were frequently volcanic or granitic, materials absent from Spanish majolicas (Magetti, Westley, and Olin 1984: 159–60, figure 8).

Efforts to trace the history of development of colonial workshops for making Spanish- and Italian-style tin-enameled pottery in Mexico and Central America (e.g., Jamieson 2001; Lister and Lister 1974, 1982: 5–12, 1984, 1987) suggested that production began in Mexico City in the late 1530s and in Puebla de los Angeles, to the southeast, perhaps by 1550. In present-day Guatemala, majolica manufacture probably began in the capital city of Santiago de los Caballeros (modern Antigua) around 1580, spreading into other cities (e.g., Totonicapán) during the seventeenth century and to Honduras in the eighteenth century (Luján Muñoz 1975: 22–24; see also Rodríguez Girón 2008).

Technology of Mexican Loza Production

Studies of pottery recovered in excavations into sixteenth-century contexts around the Metropolitan Cathedral in Mexico City led to its classification into three wares on the basis of technological variables: Mexico City ware (in fine and common grades), Valle ware, and Indigena ware (Lister and Lister 1982). Considerable information is available about the manufacture of these and similar ceramics, thanks to work by Florence and Robert Lister. Their investigations, since supplemented by compositional analyses, have revealed production practices closely modeled on those of Sevilla, presumably the home of immigrant "Old Christian" potters (ibid.: 13). The origins of the beautiful polychrome wares of Puebla, known as Talavera Poblana, are unclear, although it is claimed the craft was introduced by potters from the Dominican Order in Talavera, who instructed native potters (Tschopik 1950: 201n42; see also Barber 1915b; cf. Lister and Lister 1982: 69, 1987: 233).

Substantial quantities of calcium in the paste of Mexico City ware (Olin, Harbottle, and Sayre 1978) resulted from production technology copying that of Spanish products: mixing a calcareous clay with a non-calcareous one (Joel et al. 1988: 188). Indeed, ordinances dictated by potters' guilds, which were not established in Mexico City until 1677, specified three grades of pottery, *común*, *entrefina*, and *fina*, and the amounts or ratios of ingredients for paste and glaze for each (Gómez, Pasinski, and Fournier 2001: 53). For fine-grade ware, a mixture of ten basketloads of white (calcareous) clay to twelve of gray clay was required (Lister and Lister 1982: 14). This indicates that a widespread technological practice in Spain was transferred to Mexico. Producers of lower-quality Valle ware and of loza elsewhere in the Americas, for example, in Panama and Andean South America, did not adhere to this practice of mixing, as evident by the brick-red paste of the pottery.[7] It is not known, however, if this alternative practice was a consequence of a lack of locally available calcareous clays or of a different technological heritage among the potters.

Compositional analysis of the Mexican sherds revealed that the pastes used by Mexico City and Puebla potters could be distinguished chemically (Joel et al. 1988). These studies also indicated that, when the data were statistically manipulated to eliminate the calcium carbonate, the composition frequently matched that of Indigenous Aztec wares and the volcanic ash present in some of the pottery was characteristic of certain local clay sources (ibid.: 188). These data not only reveal continuity of resource use from pre-Hispanic through Colonial times but also suggest that these clays and the new paste formulations were able to withstand the higher temperatures of Spanish kiln-firing technology (see Chatfield 2010: 727).

Locating appropriate resources for the glazes and pigments of majolica manufacture was an early barrier to development. A source for the sand that Diego Vargas Pina had fruitlessly sought was located 260 kilometers away in what is now Veracruz (Blackman, Fournier, and Bishop 2006: 209). Tin (cassiterite), however, was a problem. Sources were known near Taxco and the mineral was mined in Guerrero as early as 1524, although not heavily until the late eighteenth century (Foshag and Fries 1942: 103; Gómez, Pasinski, and Fournier 2001: 47; see also Lister and Lister 1982: 85, 87, 1987: 222). Instead, tin might have been imported into the viceroyalty from the same sources in England, Flanders, and Portugal that were used by Spanish potters (Gómez, Pasinski, and Fournier 2001: 47). Except for prohibitions against intercolony trade (frequently circumvented), tin might also have come from Peru. A 1654 contract for the purchase of Puebla-manufactured tin-enameled ware to be shipped to Peru specified that partial payment for the wares was to be made with 900 pounds of tin (Goggin 1968: 216).

Different patterns of raw material usage can also be identified in the enamel of various grades of wares in Mexican pottery. As with pastes, these are typically spelled out in guild ordinances: for example, the lead-to-tin ratio (in pounds, based on an *arroba* of 25 pounds) in the enamel for common-grade ware was 25:2; for middle-grade it was 25:4; and 25:6 for fine (Gómez, Pasinski, and Fournier 2001: 53; Lister and Lister 1982: 14, 25). Potters appear to have used lead from galena sources in the western and southwestern parts of central Mexico, which is isotopically distinct from the lead in Spanish majolicas (Joel et al. 1988: 189). The alkali used in glazes in Mexico City was a rocklike edible salt called *tequesquite*, obtained from the saline lake beds of northern Lake Texcoco and elsewhere (Lister and Lister 1974: 25, 1982: 87; Parsons 1994).

Blue pigment was produced from cobalt on fine-grade wares, but with a mix of copper and zinc on those of lower quality (Lister and Lister 1982: 25, 27). Guild ordinances prohibited the use of green decoration on fine wares, and it only appeared on loza común (ibid.: 14). It was suggested that the brown-black was produced by an iron oxide (ibid.: 25), but chemical analysis suggested a mixture of iron and manganese oxides (Padilla et al. 2005: 204).

Panamá La Vieja: Trade and Loza Production

Spain's protectionist, mercantilist trade policies posed immense logistical difficulties for supplying goods to Andean South America. In late summer the nominally annual (but increasingly unpredictable) supply fleet from Sevilla arrived in Panama at the official Atlantic port of Nombre de Diós (later Portobelo). There, merchants from Lima purchased goods and loaded them onto mule trains for the overland journey to Panamá La Vieja, where everything was reloaded onto vessels of Spain's Pacific merchant fleet for transport to Lima's port of Callao.

Supply-side realities in the wealthy Peruvian viceroyalty and elsewhere on the Pacific coast forced acknowledgment of, and creative solutions to, the problem that colonists' demand for homeland tablewares (and other goods, such as wine) could not be met by this cumbersome and unreliable fleet supply system. Sometime in the late sixteenth century, one or more entrepreneurial potters established kilns at Panamá La Vieja and began producing tin-enameled loza and other wares to supply the Pacific colonies (Goggin 1968; Long 1967; Rovira 2001; Rovira et al. 2006). Archaeologists have classified the products into "types" (table 12.2) with sequential but overlapping histories: Panama Plain (1575?–1650), Panama Blue-on-white (1620–71), and Panama Polychrome (1631–71) (Jamieson 2001: 48–49).

Blue-on-white decoration was produced, here as elsewhere, in imitation of Chinese porcelains, and polychromes mimicked Spanish and Italian decoration. The Listers (1974: 44, 45, 1987: 340n82) suggested that Panama loza is stylistically related more to eastern Spain than to southern wares, although they also proposed that the potters of Panamá La Vieja might have come from Granada after the Alpujarras rebellion, bringing firing methods and technology typical of Sevillian/Genoese potters. Production at the Panamá kilns ceased in 1671, when the English buccaneer Henry Morgan sacked and burned the city.

Loza in the Viceroyalty of Peru

Continuing unrest in the Peruvian viceroyalty until the 1560s meant the colony remained small and primarily male; there was perhaps one European woman for every seven or eight males (Lockhart 1968: 152). Most of the imported goods and newly established artisanry were associated with military affairs and building infrastructure (especially churches), not in provisioning domestic households. A study of artisans named by profession between 1532 and 1560 identified 824: tailors, shoemakers, smiths, farriers, carpenters, masons, silversmiths, muleteers, barber-surgeons, pharmacists, bakers, musicians and instrument makers, artillerymen and powder manufacturers, carters, gardeners, and candlemakers (Harth-Terré 1945; Lockhart 1968: table 5). Nowhere are potters mentioned, although they might have been included among the 44

TABLE 12.2 Tin-enameled loza types produced at Panamá La Vieja

Panama Plain		Some forms like morisco Columbia Plain; others like Italian
Panama Blue-on-white		Chinese motifs
Panama Polychrome		Blue, manganese, green, black; rarely yellow
	Var. A	Blue, manganese, green, black; rarely yellow
	Var. B	Blue "lacy" decoration[a] (Deagan 1987: 91)
	Panama Vieja Polychrome	Green, blue, and black on white (Long 1967; cf. Baker 1968)
	Unnamed	Green-and-manganese decoration (Long 1967: 16)
Panama Blue-on-blue		Like Seville/Ligurian (Genoa) Blue-on-blue
Panama Blue		Blue exterior, white interior
Caparra Blue		Blue exterior and interior

Sources: Deagan 1987; Goggin 1968; Rovira 2001.
aSimilar to products of Puebla and Talavera.

"miscellaneous" artisans. In any case, artisans and craftsmen were of low status in colonial Peru, their relative rankings based "primarily on the value of the raw materials worked" (Lockhart 1968: 29). Thus silversmiths were of higher status than potters, who worked with clay. Potters were primarily native Andeans or slaves: "all the clay pots that the Spaniards use in this kingdom ... are made by Indians" (*todas las ollas de barro que usan los españoles en este reino ... son hechas por indios;* Cobo 1891 [1653]: 241).

Four types of glazed wares were made in colonial Peru: lead-glazed (total or partial coverage), architectural tiles, tin-enameled ("majolica"), and *falsa mayólica* (Acevedo 1986: 22). As can be seen in table 12.3, wares given a green or melado lead glaze were widely produced, including figurines, cooking and tablewares, and large jars associated with the wine and olive oil agro-industries. Architectural tiles were apparently manufactured only in Lima, although information about the colors of decoration is not available. Tin-enameled ware production is associated with Lima and the southern highlands, particularly Cusco

TABLE 12.3 Production of glazed wares in Colonial-period and later Peru

	Century			Colors of Glaze/Decoration				
	Sixteenth	Seventeenth	Eighteenth	Green	Marrón[a]	Melado[a]	Yellow	Blue
Glazed ware								
Arequipa[b]	X	X		X	X			
Cusco	X	X	X	X			X	
Huancavelíca			X					
Ica[b]	?	X	X	X				
Lima	X	X	X	X				
North Coast	X[c]			X		X		
Puno[b]			X	X	?			
Tiles								
Lima	X	X			?	?		?
Tin-enameled[d]								
Cajamarca					?			?
Cusco	(X)	X	X	X	X		X[e]	X[f]
Lima	(X)	X	X	X	X			X
Falsa mayólica								
Cusco region?								
Puno			X	X	X	X	X[g]	

Sources: Acevedo 1986: 20–26; Stastny 1981.

a The term *marrón* means dark brown (sometimes purplish or black), roughly equivalent to *morado*. Melado is a clear, honey-colored glaze.
b Glazing appeared on botijas associated with the wine and olive oil industries.
c The earliest of these were whistles and Inka forms in the Chimu area.
d Except where indicated, the background enamel of these wares was white, cream, or creamy white. The background color in Cusco and Puno often varied toward yellowish or greenish.
e Used in the eighteenth century and later. Yellow was also used as a background color.
f Used in the eighteenth century and later.
g Used as a background color in the nineteenth century.

and the area around Puno in the northern altiplano, which could have supplied the Titicaca basin and the wealthy and heavily populated mining regions of Alto Peru (modern Bolivia). Painted decoration was in green and manganese brown-black (*morado*; *marrón*); the use of blue is rare and late.

It appears that production of loza in Andean South America, as in Guatemala and Panama, began in the late sixteenth century. In what is now Ecuador, for example, loza with a "*blanco verdoso*" (greenish-white) background color has been found in association with a sixteenth-century coin and Indigenous (Inka) pottery near Quito (Fournier-García 1989: 63). The earliest known loza workshop, however, is one Jesuits established in Quito by 1635 (Buys 1992: 32). The most common loza recovered archaeologically in and around Quito features green or green-and-manganese painting on a cream to pale-greenish enamel ground (Jamieson 2000: 190; see also Goggin 1968: 9, citing Lozoya 1945: 623; Holm 1971: 268; Jamieson and Hancock 2004). Pottery produced in Cuenca includes a ware with green, brown, or both decoration on a yellow to "mustard" background color (Jamieson 2000: 193). Loza might also have been a later colonial product farther to the north in Popoyán, in southwestern Colombia (Londoño 2001).

Lima Area: In what is now Peru, the beginnings of the colonial ceramic industry are hazy, and little physically remains of it (Stastny 1986b: 1). At one time it was thought that loza was not made there until the first half of the seventeenth century, with the documented presence of *ollerías* (pottery workshops) and *pintores de azulejos* (tile painters) in 1639 (Harth-Terré 1945: 168). But by 1619 a Sevillian tile maker, Juan Martín Garrido, was in Lima producing azulejos (Connors McQuade 2003: 207). As noted in the epigraph, locally made loza was appreciated, although Father Cobo (1890 [1653]: 243; see note 1) commented less favorably on local tiles, calling them "very interesting" but adding that, in comparison with Spain's, they "do not have such fine colors."

It now seems that tin-enameled wares were made in Peru earlier than originally thought. Documents reveal that potters' guilds (gremios) existed in Lima by 1577, for example (Frothingham 1969: 78), probably for tile makers. However, loza workshops have not been located in the city; nor have Lima-produced ceramics been definitively identified. Cajamarca appears to have been a late viceregal production center in the north, known for blue-and-white and blue-and-black-on-white decorated loza (Stastny 1981: 99, figures 45, 89), but it is not clear when this center was established or how long it produced the ware.

Early studies of loza recovered in excavations are of little help in determining location of manufacture. Description of 105 decorated plate and bowl fragments of loza from Huaca Palomino, on a colonial ranch between Lima and Callao, indicated the use of blue (ranging from dark to light), brown/black, green, and yellow pigments, of which green-and-brown (n = 34) and blue-on-white (n = 24) were most common (Cárdenas Martin 1971). Pastes were fine-textured, lacking visible inclusions (although the color was not described), but the cream to light greenish enamel quality is poor and carelessly prepared and fired (Cárdenas Martin 1973). The illustrated decorations suggest that the vessels could have come from Mexico or Panamá. Fifteen sherds of porcelain were also recovered (Cárdenas Martin 1971: 66).

Materials from the Casa Osambela (or Oquendo) in Lima—once part of a Dominican monastery—included loza, porcelain, and architectural tiles and were divided into four chronological intervals: pre-Hispanic, Early Colonial (to ca. 1550), Colonial I (ca. 1550–1746), and Colonial II (1746–1806) (Flores Espinoza 1981). Six unnamed "types" of loza were distinguished. Two (designated L-1 and L-2) from the Early Colonial period are probably equivalent to what is now called Morisco ware (plain, with a greenish enamel) (ibid.: 40–41, 50). Blue-on-white (L-3) and polychrome-on-green (L-5) types are thought to be of Peruvian manufacture in the long and, unfortunately, undifferentiated Colonial I period, as are some red-paste azulejos (ibid.: 41–42, 44–45, 51). The L-4 and L-5 loza types are more likely Panama Polychrome, believed at the time to have been Peruvian products (ibid.: 42, 51–52). A residuum included varied wares from Spain, Mexico, France, and England.

Lima continued to import loza in the seventeenth century, at least some of which was likely contraband. Sara Acevedo (1986: 19) cites a 1630 *Memorial* by fray Buenaventura de Salinas y Córdova, who noted that in Lima there were baskets and *bateas* (hampers) of loza, some locally made but also wares from Panama, China, Portugal, and Venice. Lima also received a shipment of the highly esteemed loza produced in Puebla, Mexico (Lister and Lister 1974: 37). At the same time, thousands of tiles were shipped from Sevilla to decorate the monasteries of Santo Domingo and San Francisco (Connors McQuade 2003: 207), prominent locations where illicitly obtained materials would have been inappropriate. Goggin (1968: 8–9, 41–49, 163–65) believed the majolica he recovered in small quantities at widely scattered sites in South America might have been manufactured in Lima, not an unreasonable proposal. However, compositional analysis has shown that some of his material was produced by the Panamá La Vieja kilns (Rice and Blackman n.d.), which were not known at the time of his study.

Southern Peru: In the south-central highlands, a four-year contract was drawn up in Cusco in 1588 to establish a workshop for making loza (Acevedo 1986: 21, citing Cornejo Buroncle 1960: 337), and a colonial kiln is said to have been found on the edge of the city (I. Oberti Rodríguez, pers. comm. 1989). Cusco would have been a pragmatic early location for tin-enameled ware production, given that it was the former Inka capital and the Inkas had controlled exploitation of the tin ore (cassiterite) deposits in Bolivia and northwestern Argentina (Zori 2011: 167). Moreover, a number of pre-Hispanic potting communities were outside the city, including Sanyo (San Sebastián) and Racchi (Stastny 1986b: 9).

A study of pottery recovered in excavations in four structures in historic Cusco provides some temporal information about tin-enameled ware availability from the sixteenth through nineteenth centuries. The earliest pottery was decorated with green and brown-black, blue paint was used later, and the combination of green and blue was rare (Oberti Rodríguez 1999: 141; see also Benavente 1982: 176). Tri-color decoration—blue, green, and morado—was most common in the eighteenth century (Oberti Rodríguez 1999: 141). Although it is a convenient assumption, it is not necessarily the case that all of the recovered pottery in these structures was manufactured in Cusco.

Loza recovered at the wine haciendas of the Moquegua valley, in far southern Peru (Rice 1997, 2011b; Smith 1991), included earthenware with a reddish-brown paste covered with a thin, cream to pale greenish tin-enamel coating and decorated in green and manganese; it was given the type name Mas Alla Polychrome (figure 12.1). Other fragments featured green-and-manganese decoration over a bright yellow background (probably eighteenth or nineteenth century?), and still other pieces were characterized by the presence of a green or brown lead glaze in addition to the verde y morado enamel decoration (Rice 1997).[8]

INAA of samples of the green-and-manganese-decorated pottery from Moquegua indicated that it was not made in any known location in Mexico, Spain, or Panama (Rice and Blackman n.d.). Instead, it was most likely produced in southern highland Peru, probably in Cusco. Two sherds of this enameled ware were recovered at the Locumbilla bodega site in a context sealed below volcanic ash from the February 1600 Huaynaputina eruption, thus confirming a late-sixteenth-century date of the start of manufacture. In addition, pottery with decoration virtually identical to that of Mas Alla was recovered in stratigraphic excavations at the Inka site of Aqnapampa, 80 km southeast of Cusco (Chatfield 2007: figure 8.9).

Farther south, in the altiplano region of Lake Titicaca, loza with green, dark brown, and yellow lead glaze was manufactured in two neighboring communities roughly 60 km north of the lake—Santiago de Pupuja and Pucará—and perhaps also in Chucuito near the lake's western shore (Murra 1978; Paredes Eyzaguirre 1989; Stastny 1981: 101; Tschopik 1950: 202, 204; see also Hyslop 1979:

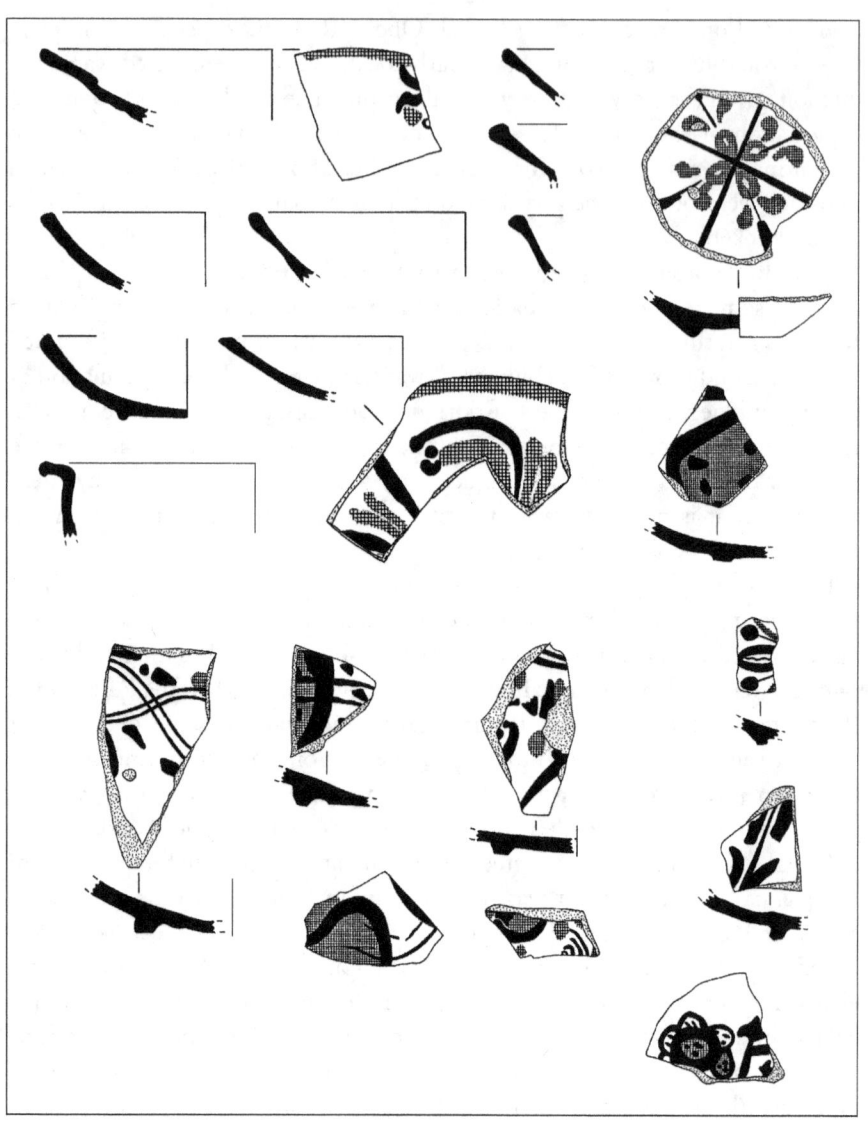

FIGURE 12.1 *Fragments of Mas Alla Polychrome recovered at the wine heredades in the Moquegua valley. Green indicated by crosshatching, manganese by black lines of varying thickness.*

FIGURE 12.2 *A carelessly painted twentieth-century green-and-manganese shallow bowl (chúa, food dish) produced in the northwestern Lake Titicaca basin. The central motif is a catfish, or* suchi *(compare with figure 11.3), also a popular motif on late pre-Hispanic Aymara pottery in the region (Tschopik 1950: 197). Below the catfish is a plant, probably maize, also common on Indigenous pottery executed in Inka style. The manganese black is thin and carelessly applied. Computer rendering of color photograph (Stastny 1981: figure 90) into black-and-white drawing by Don S. Rice.*

65–68). It is not known when this industry began, although glazed wares in general in this area date to the seventeenth century and later (Acevedo 1986: 24, 26), and the industries flourished in the eighteenth and nineteenth centuries. Decoration consists of "bold, cursive, floral patterns" (Tschopik 1950: 204), as well as fish (figure 12.2) and bulls,[9] also seen in the Cusco area (figure 12.3). Some of these materials have a clear glaze over a white slip rather than a true tin-enamel and are called "false majolica" (Acevedo 1986: 23; for a similar product in Guatemala, see Luján Muñoz 1975: 24).

FIGURE 12.3 *A footed dish, probably Late Colonial or early Republican in date, purchased in a Cusco (Peru) shop in the 1980s. The central decoration of this dish or shallow bowl features a bull standing on vegetation, the motifs outlined in black with green used as dots or filler, plus a wide rim band. The interior enamel is grayish-beige; the underside lacks any glaze or enamel. Diam. 19.8 cm. Collection of the author. Computer rendering by Don S. Rice.*

A publication on the "popular arts" in Peru includes illustrations of tin-enameled pottery, mostly from the eighteenth century. Much of this represents a revival of traditional Inka styles, particularly motifs drawn from keros, associated with the Tupac Amaru II uprising in late 1780 (Stastny 1981, 1986a). These styles frequently appeared on vessel forms associated with the earlier Inka imperium, such as urpus (long-necked aríbalos or aryballus jars); decorative themes include making offerings to the Sapa Inka and the Inka wars against the people of Antisuyu (Stastny 1986a: 11–17). One vessel from Cusco is decorated in green, yellow, blue, and black on a white ground (Stastny 1981: figure

54). Another from the "southern sierra" is a deep bowl (*lebrillo*) painted in green, blue, and black on yellow in a fine-line Italianate-type decoration, with leafy vegetation (*frondosidad*) and in the center a deer pursued by a dog (ibid.: figure 91). An Inka aryballus had the neck and shoulder covered with white enamel; its decoration in green, blue, and black featured a face on the neck and the double-headed Hapsburg eagle on the shoulder (ibid.: figure 93).[10] However, this vessel likely dates to the late sixteenth or seventeenth centuries, before the end of the Spanish Hapsburg ruling line. Another glazed and painted aryballus shows Spaniards or mestizos and blacks and is presumed to date to the first half of the seventeenth century (Tschopik 1950: 204n68).

TWO IBERO-AMERICAN LOZA SPHERES

As more is learned about loza in the early viceroyalty of Peru, it becomes evident that two "cluster regions" (Rice 2013), spheres, or commercial networks of ceramic production and exchange existed in the early Spanish-colonial world, a possibility suggested some time ago by the Listers (1974: 45–49; also Rice 1997; Rovira 2001).[11] One sphere is northern (figure 12.4), centered on the circum-Caribbean basin and extending through La Florida, New Spain, and the southwestern United States; the other is southern and western, centered on the east-central Pacific basin and the Andean highlands. The most obvious difference between the two spheres appears to be access to resources, with rare and expensive cobalt the critical variable.

The blue pigment used on the New World imitations of Spain's majolica was primarily produced from cobalt oxide (CoO). In the absence of other information, it can only be assumed that cobalt from the same source (or sources) used by Spanish painters was exported to the colonies to support the fledgling ceramic-ware industry. However, the extra distance traveled, and perhaps policies controlling its export, likely made the material even rarer and more expensive, and thus in Mexico it was only used in fine-grade wares. The range in tones of the blue-painted decoration on loza, from clean and bright to light blue or grayish, has several possible explanations, including different amounts of cobalt in the prepared pigments, different levels of refinement of the ore, and different ore sources. If poorly refined, the cobalt fired not to a clean, bright blue but rather to a "dirty greyed or slate tone" that was typical in the sixteenth century. In the absence of cobalt, a "dull, washed-out" blue could also be created by a cheaper mixture of copper dioxide (CuO_2) and zinc, which was used on common-grade wares in Mexico (Lister and Lister 1982: 25, 27).[12]

FIGURE 12.4 *The two spheres of tin-enameled ware circulation in the Spanish-colonial New World (using modern political boundaries and names), showing places mentioned in text. Stars indicate known loza production centers; dots indicate cities and archaeological sites of recovery of analyzed loza. Curving lines indicate approximate boundaries of the "northern" and "southern" spheres of production and exchange discussed in the text.*

A recent chemical analysis suggests that the cobalt used for blue paints on loza produced in Puebla, Mexico, may have been from a different source than that used in Spain. Spanish and Italian samples had higher amounts of calcium (Ca) mixed with the cobalt, whereas the Puebla pigment had more iron and potassium (Padilla et al. 2005). Furthermore, in the seventeenth century, Puebla's potters had access to a new source of cobalt pigment that yielded a "clear, intense color" in low relief and was packaged distinctively "in boxes in dry powder form" (Lister and Lister 1987: 239–40, see also 345n124). Still another cobalt source may have been used by late-sixteenth-century producers in Panamá La Vieja, where the blue lacks the relief and density of Puebla decoration (Lister and Lister 1974: 45).

It is not known if these painters in New Spain were using one or more different Old World sources or if a source(s) had been found in the Americas. Small veins of cobalt are now known in Mexico (Lister and Lister 1982: 88), and significant quantities of cobalt are mined today in eastern Cuba (http://havanajournal.com/business/entry/update-on-cuba-nickel-and-cobalt-production/), but it is unknown if either of these sources had been identified by early prospecting Spaniards. One wonders if, after the 1565 beginnings of commerce with the East Indies, administered through the Viceroyalty of New Spain, traders on the Manila galleons might have had access to internal (rather than imported) cobalt sources used by Chinese porcelain painters (see Nilsson 1998–2010) and other resources used by producers elsewhere in southwest Asia (e.g., cobalt was produced in Burma by 1651 [CDI 2006: 3]). This material could have been shipped to Pacific ports, such as Acapulco, and from there to Panamá La Vieja or Lima.

The existence of these two spheres of loza decorative production is simultaneously revealing and obscuring. The regionalization may reveal something of the backgrounds and preferences or aesthetic tastes of both pottery producers and consumers in the two areas, but at the same time it points to broader issues of political ecology (Rice 2013, n.d.) in terms of policies surrounding commerce and access to resources. All of these issues have implications for understanding the cultural and ethno-religious identities of the painters of the pottery and the economic integration of Spanish-colonial society.

For example, the prominence of blue-decorated loza in the northern Ibero-American colonial sphere could be a consequence of varied factors, singly or in combination:

- On the producers', or supply, side:
  - The earliest pottery painters to arrive from Spain exercised agency and chose to decorate with blue out of custom and because they
    - Were "old" Christians from Sevilla, trained in the blue/Italianate tradition for upper-class consumers (à la Lister and Lister 1982: 13); or
    - Were from communities or regions producing in the blue/Italianate tradition (especially Sevilla but also Talavera);
  - Pottery workshops in Mexico had ready access to cobalt (or its suppliers) for pigment;

- Copper (for green) was less available or abundant and therefore undesired/rejected; or
- For whatever of these (or other) reasons (color impermanence), potters' guilds in Mexico stipulated that green decoration could not appear on fine-grade ware.
- On the consumers', or demand, side, buyers in the northern sphere may have preferred blue-painted (Renaissance-style) pottery because:
    - It was most popular in Christian Spain;
    - It was most popular in their home region;
    - It was an upper-class ware;
    - It resembled Chinese porcelains;
    - It possessed as-yet unknown technical or performance characteristics; or
    - Green or green-and-manganese decoration was actively rejected.

Tin-enameled pottery produced in the Pacific/southern sphere, on the other hand, prominently features green-and-manganese, Hispano-Moresque–like decoration, and blue-on-white pottery is relatively uncommon or late (insofar as presently known from excavations). Green-and-manganese decoration had enduring symbolic and economic associations with Muslims since medieval times, not only in Iberia but throughout the Near East. The emphasis on green, as opposed to blue, colors in the southern colonial sphere could be a consequence of several factors:

- On the producers'/supply side:
    - The earliest pottery painters to arrive in this region exercised agency and chose to decorate with green and manganese because they
        - Were moriscos from Spain trained in this mudéjar tradition;
        - Were from communities or areas producing in the green-manganese tradition (whether in Spain or lower-grade wares elsewhere in the New World);
        - Lacked the specialized knowledge to prepare cobalt pigments; or
        - Lacked ties to cobalt suppliers;
    - Pottery workshops in this region had easy access to copper and manganese for pigments; or
    - Cobalt for blue was excessively costly or unavailable.
- On the demand side, consumers preferred green-and-manganese-decorated pottery:
    - For aesthetic/cultural reasons (e.g., use in their home regions of Spain);
    - Because these vessels were cheaper and more readily obtained;

- Because of as-yet unknown technical or performance characteristics; or
- Consumers lacked preference or were unable to exercise choice for any alternative.

Issues of access versus preferences (exercise of choice and decision-making) on both producers' and consumers' sides are difficult to tease apart on the basis of available information. Document-based histories would suggest that the politico-economic circumstances of colonial life in Peru outside Lima meant little access to upper-class blue-on-white pottery, whether Spanish- or American-made or Chinese porcelain. Yet excavations at an early colonial site in wealthy Chucuito, in the Titicaca basin, yielded no blue-and-white loza but "surprising" numbers of porcelain fragments (Tschopik 1950: 204), again raising the issue of contraband. In addition, it is of no little interest that the Panamá La Vieja kilns produced both "blue series" and "green series" decorated wares.

In early archaeological studies of the Panama kilns' products, pottery decorated with blue painting on a white ground was separated typologically from Panama Polychrome type (with blue, green, and black), presumably because it was seen to have cultural significance as an imitation of Chinese porcelains. Unfortunately, 178 sherds with green-and-manganese decoration (Long 1967: 16) were apparently presumed to lack comparable cultural significance and were incorporated into the polychrome type in subsequent studies (Baker 1968: 56–59).[13] Panama Polychrome may have been produced relatively late, from 1630 to 1671 (Jamieson 2001), but incorporating two-color (verde y morado) decoration into the type precludes consideration of the possibility that, as in Cusco, this latter was an early (late-sixteenth-century) product.

INAA studies of pottery recovered from various sites in the southern sphere, including Cuenca and Quito in Ecuador, identified some green-and-manganese-decorated ware produced at the Panamá La Vieja kilns, as well as some locally made (Jamieson and Hancock 2004; Rovira et al. 2006). Another INAA study of tin-enameled wares in archaeological collections from Peru, including Moquegua, and Panama[14] (Rice and Blackman n.d.) revealed that 7 of 44 sherds recovered from and geochemically sourced to Panamá La Vieja had green-and-manganese decoration, and another from Huaca Palomino in Peru was this same Panama green-and-manganese. A sherd of an unidentified type with a green background and black and blue paint from the Convento de la Concepción in Panama was geochemically identified as having been manufactured at the Panama kilns.

Moreover, pottery produced at the Panamá La Vieja kilns was widely traded "along the Pacific watershed (from Guatemala to Chile)" (Rovira 2001: 291). At Ocelocalco in Soconusco, south-coastal Mexico, 6 sherds from Panamá La

Vieja—1 blue-on-white and 5 polychrome—were recovered (Rovira 2001: 299), and 268 sherds of an unnamed green- or green-and-brown-on-cream ware were recovered there (Gasco 1987: 307–8). Compositional analysis of a sample of the latter did not match with a known source, however (Gasco et al. 2006). Beatriz Rovira (2001: 301) notes the perplexing fact that pottery from the La Vieja kilns was not recovered in Portobelo or elsewhere on the Atlantic coast and links this observation to social preferences: European majolica was desirable everywhere as a high-status good, but the "local" Panamanian products were not desired in Portobelo. Such preferences in Portobelo, which had direct access to Spanish goods, might also relate to the general value-added aspect of foreign versus local goods.

However, these explanations for preferences do not speak to the issues of interest here: the cultural and economic implications of the green-and-manganese-decorated pottery in the larger Spanish-colonial world and the apparently restricted or delayed availability of cobalt in Peru. Panama is physically located between the two cluster regions, northern/Atlantic/blue and southern/Pacific/green, and participated in both. Panama had access to at least one source of blue pigment, whether cobalt or not. Why, then, didn't potters in the wealthy Viceroyalty of Peru have similar access?

MORISCO WARES AND INFLUENCES IN SPANISH AMERICAN POTTERY

Morisco influences on the pottery assemblages of Spain's American colonies are evidenced by actual vessel imports as well as mimesis: decorative techniques, motifs, and color combinations, as well as forms. With respect to importation, pre-1550 contexts in Mexico and the Caribbean yielded plates and bowls of Sevilla-produced "Morisco wares" (Lister and Lister 1982: 45–57; Myers et al. 1992), either with a plain cream enamel or painted with simple blue or blue-and-purple decoration.

Muslim-influenced *sgraffito* ("scratched") ware, known as Romita Sgraffito or "Indigena ware" in Mexico, was initially thought to have been made by Indigenous (Nahua/Aztec) potters in central Mexico (Lister and Lister 1982: 34–40, 1987: 228–29). It is now known from compositional as well as motif analyses that it was more probably produced in Europe (Rodríguez-Alegría et al. 2003). Like green-and-manganese-decorated wares, sgraffito decoration had been produced in the Middle East and eastern Mediterranean regions since medieval times, replacing *cuerda seca* (glazed areas separated or outlined by an unglazed line) decoration (Rosselló Bordoy 1992: 100). It featured lightly applied green, brown, or yellow pigment over a white slip (not a tin enamel) and was covered with a lead glaze, the same technique of the "false" majolicas produced in Guatemala and the Lake Titicaca region (and also at the ninth-century Changsha kilns). By the sixteenth century, however, graffito decoration had ceased to be a Muslim product.

Feldspar-inlaid ware is also Muslim-related, a translation into ceramics of a traditional mudéjar ornamentation technique using patterns of precious woods or ivory inlaid into furniture and doors in both domestic and religious settings. Feldspar-inlaid wares were produced in Mexico (Rodríguez-Alegría et al. 2003), and a fragment of this ware from the Florida Museum of Natural History collections was sourced to the Panamá La Vieja kilns (Rice and Blackman n.d.; see Fairbanks 1966).

As for motifs, the "lacy" decoration of Panama Polychrome Variety B (Deagan 1987: 91), similar to Talavera wares and to blue-and-black-decorated Puebla Polychrome type from Mexico, has been attributed to morisco influence (Lister and Lister 1987: 238–39; Seifert 1977: 22). Goggin (1968: 181) called attention to similarities with green-and-manganese wares from Paterna in Spain.

Relative to blue-series fine wares, little attention has been devoted to the production or significance of green- or green-and-manganese-decorated loza in the New World. Loza decorated with green paint was among the earliest products made in New Spain: the type called Mexico City Green-on-cream began to be produced there in 1540 and may have continued to be produced through the seventeenth century (Lister and Lister 1982: 28; see http://www.flmnh.ufl.edu/histarch/gallery_types/type_list.asp). This early appearance might be a consequence of the first potters being morisco or of early lack of access to cobalt. By the seventeenth century, however, potters' guild regulations appear to have directly acknowledged changed consumer tastes (and, more indirectly, class formation) by forbidding the use of green on fine-grade wares.

Building on previous work by Goggin (1968) and his students, the Listers gave relatively short shrift to green-decorated pottery. They suggested a possible "Spanish prejudice against green" because of its Muslim significance, proposing that the potters who came to New Spain "were more firmly tied to the ceramic traditions of Andalucía or northwestern Castile" (i.e., Talavera) and Italian/Renaissance blue decoration (Lister and Lister 1982: 14; see also 1974: 33, 48). They also commented that the earliest majolicas were used in Mexican households "presided over most often by Indian ladies," who probably lacked the Spanish bias against Muslims (Lister and Lister 1982: 89). Thus green-decorated pottery was for the lower classes, and green was devalued compared to blue: "This lower regard for green decoration is understandable inasmuch

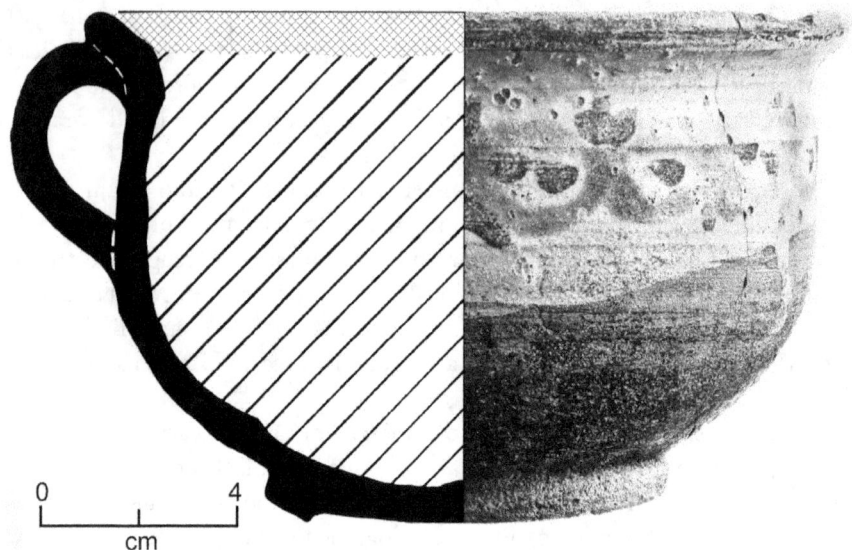

FIGURE 12.5 *One-handled chamber pot–like footed vessel, probably Late Colonial or early Republican in date, purchased in a Cusco (Peru) shop in the 1980s. This pot has carelessly painted apple green–and-manganese embellished chain decoration over a greenish-cream opaque enamel on the upper exterior surface; the interior has a green lip stripe and is glazed over the entire surface. The glaze is thin and appears tan in color because of the strong red-brown of the paste showing through. The lower exterior is unglazed and has faint facets and concentric marks, suggesting it was finished by scraping. Height 9 cm. Collection of the author. Computer rendering by Don S. Rice.*

as green lead glaze, *verde claro*, had been old hat since the Romans, and green and brown decoration had been in use in Spain since the Cordovan Caliphate. Blue, on the other hand, was associated with all that was new and rich in both Oriental and European courts" (Lister and Lister 1974: 33). For colonial producers and consumers alike in New Spain, it seems that the color green was imbued with negative connotations and symbolism carried neither by forms nor by stylistic motifs or modes (feldspar inlay, sgraffito) otherwise associated with Muslim manufacture. Alternatively, the explanation could be less ethnocentric: according to Mexico City guild regulations, green decoration was prohibited on fine wares because it was not permanent ("*por no ser de permanencia*") (Gómez, Pasinski, and Fournier 2001: 53).

In the Viceroyalty of Peru, however, green-and-manganese-decorated loza appears to have played a much more central role than in other areas of the

FIGURE 12.6 *A pitcher, probably Late Colonial or early Republican in date, purchased in a Cusco (Peru) shop in the 1980s. It has a thin, opaque, "cream" (very pale yellowish-green) enamel on the upper exterior surface and handle. Decoration consists of a band of simple, swooping frondosidad: four triangular flowers topped with "buds," outlined in black-brown with their centers painted apple green. The band is bordered top and bottom by single black-brown lines. The handle has alternating black and green horizontal stripes. The lower exterior is unglazed and poorly finished, with scraping marks and other blemishes also evident under the enamel. Height 21.2 cm. Collection of the author. Computer rendering by Don S. Rice.*

colonial empire (figures 12.5, 12.6; Stastny 1981: 101). Documentary and archaeological evidence suggests that pottery with this decoration began to be manufactured in Peru in the late sixteenth century, with a workshop established in Cusco in 1588. Bernabé Cobo's seventeenth-century observation—that the loza and tiles produced in Peru "do not have such fine colors" as those of Spain and Mexico—may be a reflection of this traditional mudéjar palette. The possibility of an "Andean complex" of early tin-enameled wares was based on only a few sherds from the Lima area, but the Listers (1974: 49) were prompted to suggest that "the motifs . . . the habit of only partial glazing, the restricted use of green and brown with only a bit of yellow and virtually no blue . . . makes one suspect that the potters who got to the southern viceroyalty or their descendants had roots in the Spanish Levante [eastern Spain] or southeastern Castile."

TRAVEL, TRADE, AND TECHNOLOGY

It is tempting to try to link the manufacture of morisco/mudéjar styles of pottery in the Americas to the many royal decrees forcing moriscos to choose between baptism or expulsion from Spain (see table 11.2; also Qamber 2006: 29–31). In particular, the flowering of new loza production centers in the late sixteenth century—from Guatemala through Honduras, Panama, Ecuador, and Peru after 1575 or so—may be a consequence of the 1568 Alpujarras revolt of moriscos against Christians in Granada, which resulted in the former's forced resettlement or enslavement. Morisco potters from Valencia and Sevilla who immigrated to the American colonies after additional expulsions beginning in 1609 might have joined these new centers and could have been responsible for establishing new types of green-and-manganese-decorated pottery. For example, San Luis Polychrome, described as a second-grade ware probably produced in Mexico City between 1650 and 1750, is common at rural sites in the Teotihuacan valley to the northeast (http://www.flmnh.ufl.edu/histarch/gallery_types/type_list.asp; Goggin 1968: 166–68; Lister and Lister 1976: 125; Magetti, Westley, and Olin 1984: 181; Seifert 1977: 67).

Answers to many questions are elusive. Were the immigrant potters and painters Christians who painted in mudéjar style? Were the loza painters in Peru late migrants as a consequence of increasingly harsh edicts banishing moriscos from Spain or demanding their conversion? Did more morisco artisans migrate to the Viceroyalty of Peru than to other colonies? Did the decoration, blue versus green, on the loza on colonial consumers' dinner tables not constitute statements of Hispano-Christian social identity or class (in contrast to common archaeological assumptions)? Did green-and-black decoration retain its pejorative Muslim and lower-class associations in the early Caribbean and Mexico settlements but lose them in the distant colonies in the Andes, where settlement according to Spanish ideas of civic order was established later? Was there a greater tolerance for morisco or crypto-morisco people and styles in the politically and socially disordered circumstances of the early southern viceroyalty?

Answers to these questions can be sought in closer examination of the "political ecology" of Andean loza from the viewpoint of both producers and consumers. With respect to the former (Rice 2013), it is clear that loza production exemplifies the contingent circumstances and contested politics of commodity production in a region, particularly conflicts over resources (Neumann 2010: 371). From the viewpoint of consumers, the relations between loza (both fine and common) and class need to be examined in the context of emerging distinctions and power relations in the early viceroyalty and their complex social, political, and economic circumstances vis-à-vis Spain (see, e.g., Fournier-García 1997).

In the northern sphere of loza production and exchange, archaeologists typically consider fine tablewares, whether imported from Spain or locally produced, to be items of status display (Deagan 1983: 262, 1985: 23–28; Lister and Lister 1982: 94; McEwan 1992: 104). They were expensive: Spanish *mayólica* cost 400–800 percent more in Mexico than in Spain (Gómez, Pasinksi, and Fournier 2001: 50). But displays of status—or, better, class—in early colonial Peru may have been escalated far above that of mere loza, however. Earthenware table service was for commoners: cabildo records from Lima in 1570–74 deal with the regulation of prices of loza because "in this city there are many poor people . . . who eat from loza . . . and they cannot pay" for it (Acevedo 1986: 21).[15] Stated more bluntly, in wealthy viceregal Peru, "silver tablewares were privileged and the use of earthenware was a sign of poverty" (Stastny 1986b: 1).[16] More significant, silver tableware might have been specifically a marker of Christian elites because in Islam it was forbidden to eat or drink from vessels of silver or gold. This practice was not too different from late pre-Hispanic times in Peru, when the Sapa Inka and kurakas ate and drank from dishes of silver and gold rather than clay (see Cummins 2002b: 30–32).

NOTES

1. My translation. The original reads: "Lábrase tan escogida loza y tan bien vedriada, que no hace falta la de Talavera, porque de pocos años á esta parte han dado en contrahacer la de China, y sale muy parecida á ella, particularmente la que se hace en Puebla de los Angeles en la Nueva España y en esta ciudad de Lima, que es muy buena y

de lindo vedrio y colores; y así mismo se hacen muy curiosos azulejos, que antes se solían traer de España; si bien es verdad que no salen los de acá de tan finos colores."

2. Various categories of ceramics, such as earthenware and porcelain, are distinguished by composition and firing temperature. Earthenware is relatively coarse, low-fired (up to ca. 900–1000°C), porous, and typically red or brown (from iron) in color; it may or may not be glazed. Porcelain is fine, high-fired (~1300–1450°C), vitrified (glassy), and typically white in color, made from a kaolin clay-based formula.

3. An alternative interpretation sees the opacification of Islamic glazes as coming from Byzantine glass makers (Tite, Pradell, and Shortland 2008: 81–82). In some glazes, opacity may be a consequence of the presence of quartz or feldspar inclusions (Mason and Tite 1997) or small amounts of clay (Molera, Vendrell-Saz, and Pérez-Arantegui 2001: 337–38). For discussion of the earlier history of opacifying agents, see Tite, Pradell, and Shortland (2008).

4. By the sixteenth century, amounts well in excess of this percentage (up to 37 percent by weight) were used (Kingery and Aronson 1990: 231).

5. Many—perhaps most—of the descriptions I have read of the paste of Iberian verde y morado pottery suggest that it was reddish-brown. Contemporaneous ware from Paterna/Manises still is.

6. Lead glazes fire to a honey color in a reducing atmosphere and to green in an oxidizing atmosphere.

7. Compositional analysis of tin-enameled ware pottery from the site of Aqnapampa, southeast of Cusco, revealed one with a CaO content of 12.7 weight percent (Chatfield 2007: table 8.15), raising the possibility of mixing red and calcareous clays.

8. This dual finishing calls to mind the practice in Zaragoza, in which obverse/visible surfaces were decorated with tin enamel and the reverse (interiors or undersides) were given a yellow or brown lead glaze or a secondary white coating (Molera, Vendrell-Saz, and Pérez-Arantegui 2001: 337).

9. Modeled figurines of bulls, or *toros*, produced in Pupuja range in size from several inches to a foot or more in length. They may be completely covered with a green glaze or a white slip; with the latter they are decorated with red paint and green glaze. The bulls are colonial modifications of Inka carved stone figures (*conopas*) of legless, reclining camelids, with a small hole in the back to hold offerings. During the late eighteenth century conopas began to be made of glazed ceramic, in the early nineteenth century reclining bulls rather than native camelids were formed, and sometime later standing bulls with short legs began to be made (Stastny 1981: 60, 104–7). The bull replaced the llama as a beast of burden and became an important symbol of fertility in southern Peru, associated with various feasts and rituals. In one, the skin of the bull's neck is pierced to draw sacrificial blood, chicha is rubbed on the nostrils, and chilies are tied under the tail, causing the animal to lick its nostrils and raise its tail—precisely the characteristics of

the pottery toros. Pairs of bull figurines, placed on either side of a cross, often decorate the roof ridges of houses as symbols of luck and fertility.

10. A Hapsburg eagle was also painted on a polychrome plate produced in Guatemala (Lister and Lister 1974: 40).

11. The existence of different Mexican and Peruvian commercial "orbits," in a broader politico-economic sense, has long been recognized by historians (e.g., Lockhart and Schwartz 1983: 86–92).

12. They suggest, without explanation, that the copper in the Cu-Zn mixture for creating a blue pigment might have been "derived from scrap or coins rather than raw ore" (Lister and Lister 1982: 25).

13. It is possible, of course, that these fragments represent vessels that also bore blue paint but broke in such a way that only green-and-black decoration appears. Nonetheless, in future classifications of Panama wares, it would be useful to return to a "splitting" rather than "lumping" strategy and count these sherds as a possible distinct type, to determine if there are distinct patterns of circulation of these wares. They can always be included with a larger group later.

14. The analyzed sherds from Panama were from the collections of the Florida Museum of Natural History, sampled with the kind permission of Dr. Kathleen Deagan.

15. My translation. The original reads: "porque enesta cibdad ay gran suma de gente pobre . . . que comen en loca . . . y no pueden pagar."

16. My translation. The original reads: "una nacion donde primaban las vajillas de plata y el uso de loza era signo de pobreza." Presumably this refers to loza común, although there might have been a hierarchy of value of loza fina based on price, and this in turn was based in part on the cost of cobalt and on transport costs—including bribes for contraband.

13

Ceramic Spatialization

Southern Styles

Prudence M. Rice and
Wendy L. Natt

> In the semiotic analysis of art, the interest of the objects represented lies not only in their mimetic value as copies of objects in the real world, but also in the symbolic value of the place that they occupy on the pictorial field and the relationships that they may have to the objects surrounding them ... The center is the position of preferred value.
>
> —Rolena Adorno (1986: 89)

Tin-enameled earthenwares, commonly known as majolica or loza, have long been of interest to historical archaeologists working at Spanish-colonial sites. Existing studies are primarily descriptive and classificatory, often for purposes of deriving chronology (Deagan 1987; Goggin 1968; Lister and Lister 1974, 1982; Rice 1997). Increasingly, analyses have focused on chemical composition to identify location of manufacture, but few attempts have been made to either contextualize these compositional analyses within the social and economic background of production in Spain and Italy or to move decorative "styles" beyond art-historical, descriptive characterization. Anthropologically informed stylistic analyses have rarely been undertaken, regardless of where the pottery was produced or recovered.

MOQUEGUA'S BODEGAS AND LOZA

Of the 753 fragments of decorated tin-enameled and enameled-and-glazed wares recovered at the bodegas in the rural Moquegua valley, only 12 percent were imports from regions outside presumed centers of manufacture in southern Peru (Rice 1997: 72). Less

DOI: 10.5876/9781607322764:c13

than 3 percent was from Europe,[1] and a similar amount was visually identified as products of Panamá La Vieja, a provenience subsequently confirmed by instrumental neutron activation analysis (INAA) (Rice and Blackman n.d.). Primarily displaying the copper green-and-manganese purplish-brown-black (verde y morado) decoration associated with traditional, medieval Ibero-Islamic or Hispano-Moresque wares in Spain, these Moquegua materials were likely produced in the southern Andes, probably in Cusco and the Lake Titicaca basin, although not in Moquegua itself. Similar decoration is noted in Ecuador (Buys 1992; Goggin 1968: 9, citing Lozoya 1945: 623; Holm 1971: 268; Jamieson 2000: 190, 193; Jamieson and Hancock 2004).

The color palette used on the Moquegua pottery supports the existence of two distinct spheres of colonial Ibero-American loza production and exchange, northern and southern (chapter 12; Lister and Lister 1974: 45–46; Rice 1997: 174). The northern sphere (see figure 12.4) is characterized by the use of blue pigment and Italianate polychrome decoration, the wares referred to here as blue series. The southern sphere of Andean South America (Peru and Ecuador) features green and "black" decoration and is referred to as green series. Pottery produced in Panamá La Vieja participates in both series or traditions, blue and green.

The green-series loza recovered in Moquegua was classified into two wares and five types using the principles of the type-variety system (Rice 1997). The most common ware was named Contisuyu Tin-Enameled ware, with two types, Mas Alla Polychrome and Escapalaque Yellow Polychrome. Mas Alla Polychrome features green-and-purplish brown/black (presumably manganese) decoration over a tin enamel that is of generally poor quality: pale greenish rather than cream-colored (likely from copper impurities in the raw materials), thinly applied, and with numerous defects. Escapalaque Yellow Polychrome displays green-and-black decoration over opaque yellow enamel.[2]

The traditional green-and-manganese decorative palette of Iberian pottery is most distinctively associated with mudéjar/morisco potters in eastern Spain, particularly Teruel and Muel in Aragón and Paterna in Valencia (chapter 11). This shared color scheme contributes to striking visual similarities between southern Andean (and some Panama) loza and eastern Spanish Hispano-Moresque ware, but a salient question concerns whether subtler comparisons might be made: Do verde/morado, or green-series, wares exhibit a distinctive design style compared with the blue series? Can a specifically Muslim/morisco/mudéjar influence be identified in the southern Andean loza industry that is not evident in other areas of colonial production? These questions can be explored through a hierarchical design-structure stylistic analysis of a sample of New World lozas and Spanish majolicas.

SPACE AND STYLE: HIERARCHICAL DESIGN-STRUCTURE ANALYSIS

Hierarchical design-structure analysis (HDSA) is an investigation of the choices and decisions a pottery decorator, usually a painter, makes (or made) at each step of the decoration process (Friedrich 1970: 337–39). It begins with the potter's "decoding strategy," which is essentially a process of spatialization: creating a decorative landscape by ordering the various parts of a vessel's surface into design spaces to be combined into a perceptually unified pattern. The "structure" of the design comprises the rules for—or the logic behind—the spatial arrangement, organization, and combinations of its visible components in the formation of larger units and entire decorative schemes. HDSA of already-painted objects follows the stepwise processes of making these decisions—the painter's choices about where to place decoration and what kind of decoration to put there—in which earlier decisions affect later ones (Plog 1978: 161). By focusing on sequences of decisions and actions, HDSA shares the general perspectives of technological choice models (Lemonnier 1986, 1993) and agency theory (Giddens 1982) and is a useful approach to the structure-agency dilemmas inherent in implementing agency approaches (see Joyce and Lopiparo 2005; also Dornan 2002; Hegmon and Kulow 2005).

Wendy Natt (1997) applied a hierarchical model of ceramic design structure to the Moquegua and other loza following methods outlined by Margaret Hardin Friedrich (1970) in her ethnographic analysis of pottery design in the village of San José, Michoacán, western Mexico. Natt considered eighteen attributes of design structure, ten of which were taken from Friedrich's study. Attributes of particular interest here are the spatial layouts, the motifs and configurations placed in those defined spaces, and the combination and placement of the design elements that created those motifs and configurations.

- *Spatial division/layout* refers to the subdivision of the overall space to be decorated (e.g., the exterior of a jar; the upper surface of a plate) into distinct "design fields." This is "usually through the application of boundary markers ... [which] determine the shape, size, and location of multiple design fields" (Natt 1997: 108).
- *Configuration*s are complex, patterned "arrangements of design elements that are of sufficient complexity to fill a spatial division" (Friedrich 1970: 335). Among the painters Friedrich studied, the design configuration was the "basic concern in vessel decoding" (ibid.: 337).
- *Motifs*: Friedrich does not use the term *motif* in her 1970 study, but here a motif is distinguished as a "theme," typically but not necessarily consisting of

TABLE 13.1 Loza analyzed in Natt's HDSA

Type	N
Mas Alla Polychrome	70
Escapalaque Yellow Polychrome	26[a]
Panama Polychrome[b]	8
Panama Blue-on-white[b]	23
Total	127

a This sample includes one tile fragment.
b The samples from Panamá La Vieja were a sample of ca. 350 sherds from the collections at the Florida Museum of Natural History, on loan to Rice at SIUC.

recurrent components of a design. Motifs can be discussed in terms of both configurations and elements.

- A design *element* is "the smallest self-contained unit" of a design. Elements are "manipulated as a single unit although they may be constructed of one or more brush strokes" (Friedrich 1970: 335 (quote); Hardin 1983: 17). They may be distinguished as primary or secondary, depending on their use and placement.

Other aspects of loza decoration assessed in Natt's study included use of color and quality of execution of the painted decoration. Symmetry patterns were not investigated.

The samples Natt analyzed were primarily fragments of decorated hollow wares (plate and bowl forms) brought to Carbondale from archaeological sites in Moquegua and from the Panamá La Vieja collections at the Florida Museum of Natural History in Gainesville (table 13.1). In addition to these 127 sherds, she studied photographic slides of 183 rim and body sherds (or refits) from Moquegua.

Comparative data on decorative styles were gathered from illustrations and published photographs of several other kinds or sources of hollow ware pottery; some of these were published after Natt's original study and are discussed here. These data included loza from the southern Peruvian Andes believed to have been manufactured in Cusco in the south-central highlands and Puno farther south in the Lake Titicaca basin, as well as published material from Ecuador. Analyses also included photographs and illustrations of loza from Mexico City and Puebla and majolica from certain areas of Spain, but because of the longevity and vibrancy of production in that country, the focus was primarily on early (sixteenth- and early-seventeenth-centuries) wares. Moreover, because the interest lies particularly in comparisons between Andean material and Spanish verde y morado/Hispano-Moresque ware, comparisons focused on the pottery of Aragón, chiefly that of Teruel (González Martí 1944; Lister and Lister 1974: 48–49; Sánchez-Pacheco 1981a: 57; Stastny 1981: 101).

Finally, late pre-Hispanic and Colonial-period Indigenous earthenwares—slipped and painted but unglazed—from southern Peru were also examined. These include Chucuito and Sillustani Polychromes produced in the Titicaca basin and Chucuito-Inka Polychromes probably made in the same area but with Inka-like designs ("state" and "provincial" Inka types; Morris 1995: 426). The rationale for this comparison is the seventeenth-century observation by fray Bernabé Cobo that the earthenware vessels used by the Spaniards were made by native Andean potters (Cobo 1891 [1653]: 241; Lister and Lister 1974: 48).

The obvious limitations of the analyzed sample necessitate some caveats. One problem was working with fragments rather than whole vessels; this limited the ability to identify complete design layouts, led to an emphasis on rims and brims rather than overall interior decoration, and resulted in incomplete identification of motifs and configurations and their arrangements. Another problem was working from published photographs, especially black and white, which made color determination difficult if not clearly described in the captions. Some features—such as scrolls, arcs, hachure—were difficult to classify: are they elements or motifs? Despite the fragmentary state of the pottery, some motif classes were found to have "varietal" designations as simple versus complex or abstract versus naturalistic. All in all, data were not optimally comparable among culture areas; thus the findings are neither definitive nor conclusive but rather suggestive and warranting further investigation.

VESSEL FORMS

A key aspect of the decoration of tin-enameled pottery, particularly determinant of its placement (layout), is vessel form. Although Spain experienced little change in food preparation techniques between medieval and early modern times—the main meal was a liquid stew—serving wares changed from large common forms to individual dishes or plates (Lister and Lister 1987: 75; McEwan 1992: 97, 99). Unlike the North American colonial region, where "there were no aboriginal counterparts to the glazed, individualized dishes" for Spanish food service (ibid.: 104), small serving plates (chúas), bowls, and drinking beakers (keros) were common Indigenous decorated forms in the southern Andes.

Hollow ware bowl and plate forms can be distinguished as brimmed or unbrimmed (figure 13.1). The "brim" (also known as the marley) refers to a broad

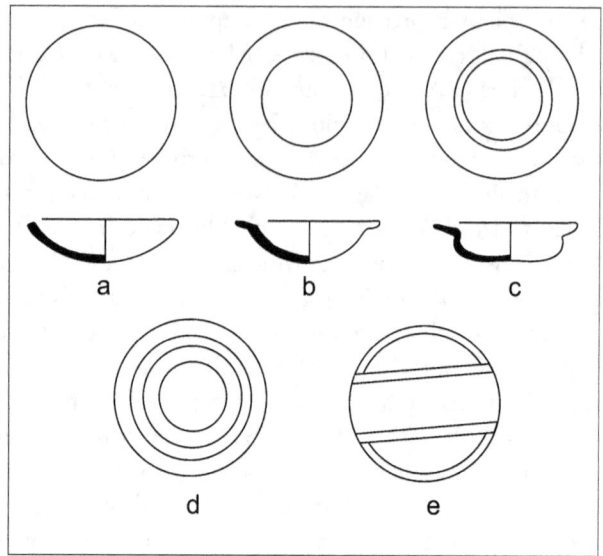

FIGURE 13.1 *Schematic diagram of the hollow ware forms and design layouts on the loza analyzed in this study: (a) open, (b) brim-center, (c) brim-cavetto-center, (d) concentric-banded, (e) horizontal- or transverse-banded. After Natt 1997: figure 5.1.*

rim angled from the hollow bowl of the interior (figure 13.1b). Brimmed bowls and plates may or may not have a "cavetto," the out-curved area between the base of plates or bowls and the brim (figure 13.1c). Tin-enameled Andean bowls and plates lacked cavettos, thus differing distinctively from Spanish, Panama, and Mexican forms. The cavetto on dishes from Teruel and Muel is often indicated more by decorative field than actual physical shape, the decoration overlapping onto part of the base or brim (Natt 1997: 214).

The ceramic assemblage recovered in rural Moquegua lacked several standard Spanish vessel forms, glazed and unglazed, variably found elsewhere in the colonial world, such as cooking braziers (*anafes*), mortars (*morteros*), deep bowls or basins (lebrillos), chamber pots (bacines), and so on (Deagan 1987: 47–53; Lister and Lister 1976; McEwan 1992: 104; Smith 1991: 92, 256). This could, of course, represent a biased sample reflecting Moquegua's relative remoteness from production centers, occupation of the bodega sites by lower-class laborers rather than wealthy owners, or other factors. Alternatively, the absence of these forms might indicate that the activities/functions associated with these Spanish vessels were not part of life at the Moquegua bodegas, or their functions were adequately met by other forms or media. For example, throughout the Andes, mortars were of readily available stone; and common Indigenous cooking ollas (p'uk'u) in the south since late pre-Hispanic times were nearly identical morphologically to Spanish *pucheros*. Copies of Chinese forms, such as the "ginger jars" made in Puebla and used for food storage, were not noted.[3]

COLOR USE AND APPLICATION

Variables relating to the use and application of color were evaluated subjectively and qualitatively (Natt 1997: 117. Note: except where specified, all page numbers below refer to that source.) Colors discussed here are almost exclusively green and purplish-black-brown pigments, with blue mentioned only by way of comparison or contrast. "Color use" was assessed in terms of design function (as filler, outliner, or in particular elements or forms) and relative frequency of use. Quality of painted design execution was assessed by four criteria: sharpness of edges, evenness of application, element reduplication, and relative placement of elements.

Moquegua and Southern Peru: In Mas Alla Polychrome, green and brown-black pigments exhibit varied hues and often seem to be used interchangeably. In execution, decoration was judged good to poor in all four criteria (150–51). In both Mas Alla and Escapalaque Polychromes, all fine-line work was done only in black or black-brown. Several types of loza found in small quantities at the Moquegua winery sites had lead glazing rather than tin-enamel on lower or exterior surfaces (Rice 1997).

Manganese purplish-black-brown, or morado, is generally more prominent than green and used mainly for outlining and primary design elements that structure a configuration or motif (figure 13.2; 147–48; discussed later). Painting is typically executed in a bold hand; most elements range from medium to medium-wide in width (2–7 mm). Dividing lines, as in quadripartite designs, are typically of medium width, ranging from 3 to 5 mm. The color ranges around 10R 4/2–3 and 10R 3/2; copper-based green varies from bright grassy green to light bluish-green (148, 150). It is used for relatively wide lip bands (see examples in figure 12.1, also 12.3 and 12.5) and as filler, as well as other elements composed of boldly (up to 11 mm wide) depicted lines.

The yellow enamel ground of Escapalaque Yellow Polychrome had Munsell color measurements of 5Y 7/4–6, 8/8, and 8/4. Compared to Mas Alla, the black decoration on Escapalaque (156–58) has sharper edges and is usually an opaque true black instead of purple-brown, which probably indicates a non-manganese pigment (iron?). There may be a slightly greater emphasis on green

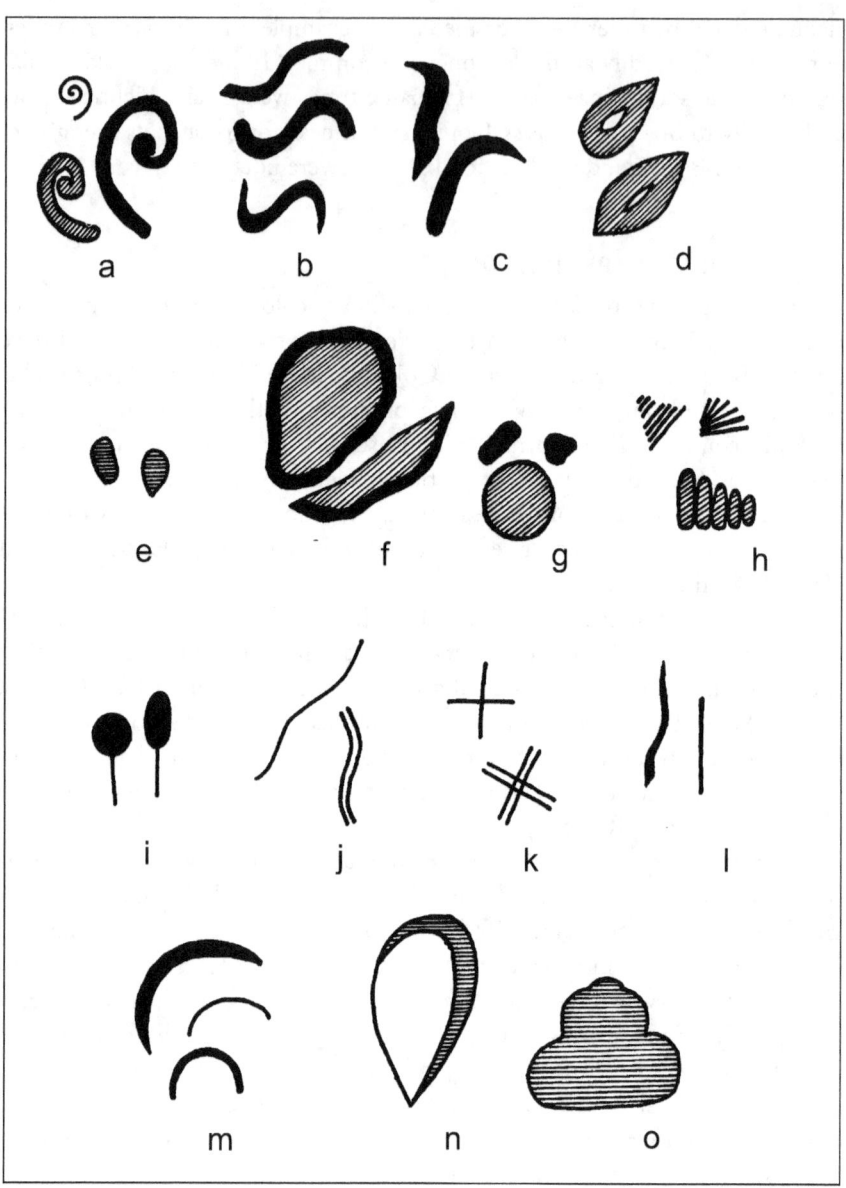

FIGURE 13.2 *Elements and motifs on green (diagonal hatching)-and-manganese loza recovered in Moquegua: (a) scroll; (b) S-scroll; (c) curled leaf; (d) ovoid leaf/petal; (e) tick-leaf; (f) large, leafy form; (g) dot/dash/splotch; (h) stacked, graduated lines; (i) "lollipop"; (j) meandering lines (single/double); (k) cruciform lines (single/double); (l) stem; (m) arc; (n) large petal-loop; (o) "cloverleaf." After Natt 1997: figure 5.2.*

as well as a different technique: pendant green fronds are painted first, with black outlines over the green. In general, the colors are darker and brighter as a result of use of more opaque, pigment-rich paints, and they do not show the range of color depth noted in Mas Alla.

In execution, designs on Escapalaque Yellow Polychrome appeared more consistent from vessel to vessel, although because these fragments were few and small, it was impossible to make reliable, systematic comparisons. The sharpness of painted edges was good, exhibiting less blurring and running compared to Mas Alla, as were evenness of paint application and relative placement of elements. Design element reduplication, best noted on brims, was judged fair to excellent.

Because the Moquegua loza—at least Mas Alla Polychrome type—is believed to have been produced in Cusco, the preceding characterizations of color use and application are pertinent to southern Andean Peru more generally. It is possible, of course, that the material recovered in distant, rural Moquegua was a poorer grade of loza than that available to the residents of Cusco (or elsewhere), but that possibility cannot be evaluated until more material is excavated from the city. Loza in Cusco antiquities shops, probably produced in the late eighteenth century and later, frequently lacked glaze on the lower and reverse surfaces (see figures 12.5, 12.6).

In Ecuador, loza recovered archaeologically commonly displays green, manganese brown, or green-and-brown decoration on a cream-to–pale greenish or yellow to mustard enamel ground.

Spain: In their analyses of Spanish majolica, the Listers clearly privileged the delicate Italianate "blue-series" styles of Sevilla and Talavera and gave little attention to the Aragonese materials. The bold decoration on Spanish imitations was deemed inferior: "Whether the Spanish decorator did not appreciate the precision of Italian line work or whether he lacked the control to achieve it, his interpretations tended to be bolder, improvised, suggestive rather than explicit, greatly restricted in theme and color, and imperfect" (Lister and Lister 1982: 76). Green was acceptable in Italian painting, but only as a minor color (ibid.: 14).

The background enamel of Aragonese wares rarely exhibits the pale greenish tone noted in Panama and Andean examples, which was probably a question of purity of the lead source used in the enamel. Pottery produced in Teruel and Muel included a blue series and a green (verde y morado) series; Muel also produced a blue, green, and manganese polychrome (213, 221–23), a palette shared with Panama Polychrome. Throughout the sixteenth century the pottery painters of Teruel used manganese for fine-line work and outlining,

TABLE 13.2 Decorated wares at Baños de la Reina Mora, Sevilla

Color of Decoration	N	%
Green, Green-on-white	217	7.0
Blue	1,150	37.1
Polychrome	45	1.4
Other (or undecorated)	1,690	54.5
Total	3,102	100.0

Source: McEwan 1992.

and green was equally prominent as filler or as dots and fronds. Green lip stripes were fairly common, sometimes with a thin, black bordering line on the interior.

Analysis of pottery recovered at the site of Baños de la Reina Mora in Sevilla, location of a sixteenth-century Augustinian convent dedicated to "repentant prostitutes," shows an apparent preference for blue over green (table 13.2; McEwan 1992). Of 3,102 sherds analyzed in eight form categories, 217 (7 percent) exhibited green or green-on-white decoration (excluding green lead-glazed), and only 45 were polychromes. Of the blue-decorated and polychrome wares, 305 (nearly 10 percent) were Morisco ware: 270 Yayal Blue-on-white, 23 Santo Domingo Blue-on-white, and 12 Isabela Polychrome.

Mexico: Loza produced in Mexico City and Puebla (and also that in colonial Guatemala) used a variety of colors and combinations involving multiple shades of blue, black-brown, green, yellow, and orange. Combinations of only blue, green, and black are rare (205). The Listers recognized only two grades of loza: fina, decorated primarily with blue and other colors, and común in two color series, blue and green. Blue in common-grade ware was produced not by cobalt but rather by a mix of copper and zinc, which often produces a dull color (Lister and Lister 1982: 25, 27). Green was "very dark and blurred at the edges . . . [and] was used for an exceedingly casual, rapidly applied, closely spaced decoration on plate or bowl obverses; it was limited on rims to hatchure [sic], fronds, and dots, and in centerpieces to a few brush swipes" (ibid.: 28). As noted, guilds banned green decoration on fine wares because it was not thought to be permanent (Gómez, Pasinski, and Fournier 2001: 53).

Panama: Panama's kilns produced undecorated tin-enameled pottery with a plain, white-to-cream-colored (rarely pale greenish) coating (Panama Plain) and also a blue enamel (sometimes combined with white on the reverse). The best-known product is Panama Blue-on-white, with a white-to-cream background decorated with blue (Chinese motifs). Panama Polychrome features a combination of blue, manganese purplish- or brownish-black, and green, rarely including yellow; sherds with green-and-manganese decoration are included in this type. Some pottery mimics Ligurian (Genoa) Blue-on-blue, with blue decoration painted over a lighter blue ground.

In Panama Polychrome (161–62, 187, 211), blue is used more frequently than green, and the green tends to be more "dull" (bluish) than the brighter green of the Peruvian decoration. Both blue and green may fill in bold forms; outlines and wide-line elements may be rendered in blue or black; fine-line elements are, with one identified exception, painted in black. Design edges are typically fuzzy, blurry, runny, or "watery"-looking; the blurry designs may be later than the finer-edged examples (Goggin 1968: 165).

Panama Blue-on-white sherds recovered in Moquegua displayed considerable variability in the color of blue pigment—bright, dark (navy), light, grayish—and in its application (line width, thickness, blurring). Similar kinds of variability were not evident in the collection of blue-on-white pottery from Panama itself. Perhaps the small amount of Panama pottery at Moquegua represents the work of a particular painter or kiln load or seconds. Sharpness of edges and evenness of application were judged fair and fair-to-poor, respectively (171).

Indigenous: Serving-ware pottery produced in the southern Andes at the time of contact and during the early colonial period was slipped and painted but unglazed. Polychrome decoration was primarily black and various tones of red (light, medium, transparent, purplish, orangey), with white sometimes applied as an accent color. Orange paint may be a new addition in the Cusco area (Tschopik 1950: 205, citing personal communication from John Rowe). Designs were usually framed by black lines. Background slips were generally light red/orange but sometimes brownish or white.[4]

LEVELS OF DESIGN STRUCTURE

The HDSA focused on three structural levels. In keeping with the spatial focus of the chapters in this volume, the first level is what might be called "ceramic spatialization": the design layout or placement of decoration on the vessel. Layout has been called the solution to the "decorative problem": what areas of the vessel surface are to be decorated, and how (Hardin 1983: 9)? Solutions to this problem—pottery painters' choices about how to decorate these areas—involve complex and difficult-to-isolate combinations of elements, motifs, and configurations in the majolica style traditions. They are surveyed in two somewhat overlapping levels: elements/motifs, combined into motifs and configurations.

Layouts and Boundary Markers

Three layouts can be identified in tin-enameled wares: open, brim-center, and brim-cavetto-center (figure 13.1a–c; Natt 1997: figure 5.1, table 5.7). They are often formalized by the placement of boundary lines to create discrete decorative zones, such as bands, panels, and central medallions.

The use of medallions and panels is both old and new in tin-enameled ware decoration. The painting of central medallions, especially floral, as the "solution to the design problem" has been considered to represent a "Muslim approach to composition" (Lister and Lister 1987: 240). However, medallions can also be related to several centuries of Chinese wares, bespeaking an interchange of ideas with Yuan dynasty blue-on-white porcelains exported to the Near East in the fourteenth century (Kuwayama 1997: 17–18). Similarly, "a central motif surrounded by evenly placed designs in panels or ogival reserve has wide precedent in the Islamic tradition" beginning in the Near East in the ninth century (ibid.). In an instance of convergent evolution, these configurations came to characterize both Hispano-Moresque wares and, centuries later, Portuguese-traded "Kraak porcelains" produced by the imperial kilns of Jingdezhen. Central medallions illustrate Adorno's observation about the "preferred value" of central space, noted in the epigraph.

Moquegua and Southern Peru: Brimmed plates of Mas Alla Polychrome recovered in Moquegua displayed a brim-center layout: brims and centers are separate design fields, each decorated with a single motif or configuration, although the fields are not separated by painted boundary markers. Bowls more commonly lack brims (see figure 12.1, upper left) and have an "open" layout: the entire interior is a single design field with no framed divisions (136). The only boundary marker on brimmed and non-brimmed bowls is a green lip stripe on the outer edge, often overlapping into the interior, thus demarcating the outermost edge of the design field. The decorative layouts on Escapalaque Yellow Polychrome appeared to follow those of Mas Alla (152–53).

Additional Peruvian loza was analyzed through illustrations of colonial vessels from Cusco and Puno[5] (Acevedo 1986; Stastny 1981). Materials from both centers show a brim-center (e.g., figure 12.2) or an open layout (e.g., figure 12.3). Lip stripes in both areas may be green or manganese brown-black; Puno wares may have a broad green band covering the brim and encircling a central design. Medallions were used in some eighteenth-century green-and-black revival wares (Stastny 1981: figure 91).

Spain: A full stylistic analysis of the products of Spain's many pottery centers was beyond the scope of Natt's study, which primarily considered the products of Aragón (214, 217, 223). Design layouts on Hispano-Moresque pottery produced in Teruel and Muel were commonly brim-center (see figure 11.3) and open (on unbrimmed bowls) with central medallions. Unlike Andean pottery but similar to that of Mexico and Panama, Aragonese majolica usually had painted boundary markers to demarcate spatial divisions; lip stripes were common, and those of Teruel were frequently green. Blank cavettos appear on vessels of the seventeenth century and may relate to copying of Chinese porcelains (Lister and Lister 1976: 33, 44).

Mexico: Decoration on loza fina produced in Mexico City and Puebla exhibited complex arrangements. Like those of Panama, Mexican wares had banded layouts, with decorated, bounded brims, a blank cavetto, and frequently a central bounded medallion (197–98). Boundary lines may number from one to three and were usually painted in blue or black. Common-grade wares from Mexico City and certain Puebla types typically lacked the formal boundary markers.

Panama: Vessels produced at Panamá La Vieja exhibit brim-center and brim-cavetto-center layouts. Brim decorations are typically bands marked by boundary lines: a lip stripe or a narrow encircling stripe (or both) at the top of the band, with one or more narrow stripes at the base of the band/brim (figure 13.3c, e). Placement of motifs in the brim sometimes creates an informal quadripartite division of that design space. In brim-cavetto-center layouts, the cavetto is typically left blank, set off from the brim by its lower boundary line (185; Rovira 2001: figure 3).

Indigenous: Indigenous-made earthenware bowls and plates in late pre-Hispanic southern Peru display regional and Inka-influenced styles, the latter especially evident on decorated forms common to Inka "state" assemblages in the provinces. Bowls lack brims and layouts are often open (see figure 8.17a–h), although two distinctive banded patterns are part of state designs (Bray 2000): "concentric-banded" and "horizontal-banded" (see figure 13.1d, e). Concentric-banded designs (see figure 8.17e, f), sometimes paneled, make use of one or two boundary lines (usually black) and lip stripes (occasionally red). Horizontal-banded—better described as transverse-banded—designs are distinguished by one or more bounded decorative bands across the interior maximum diameter of the chúas and similar forms (225). Jars, particularly urpus, tend to have vertical, multi-paneled, bounded decoration featuring rhombs and ferns (see figures 8.12d, 8.17i).

Elements and Motifs

Because of the complexity of the designs and the fragmentary nature of the pottery sample analyzed, it was often extremely difficult to consistently

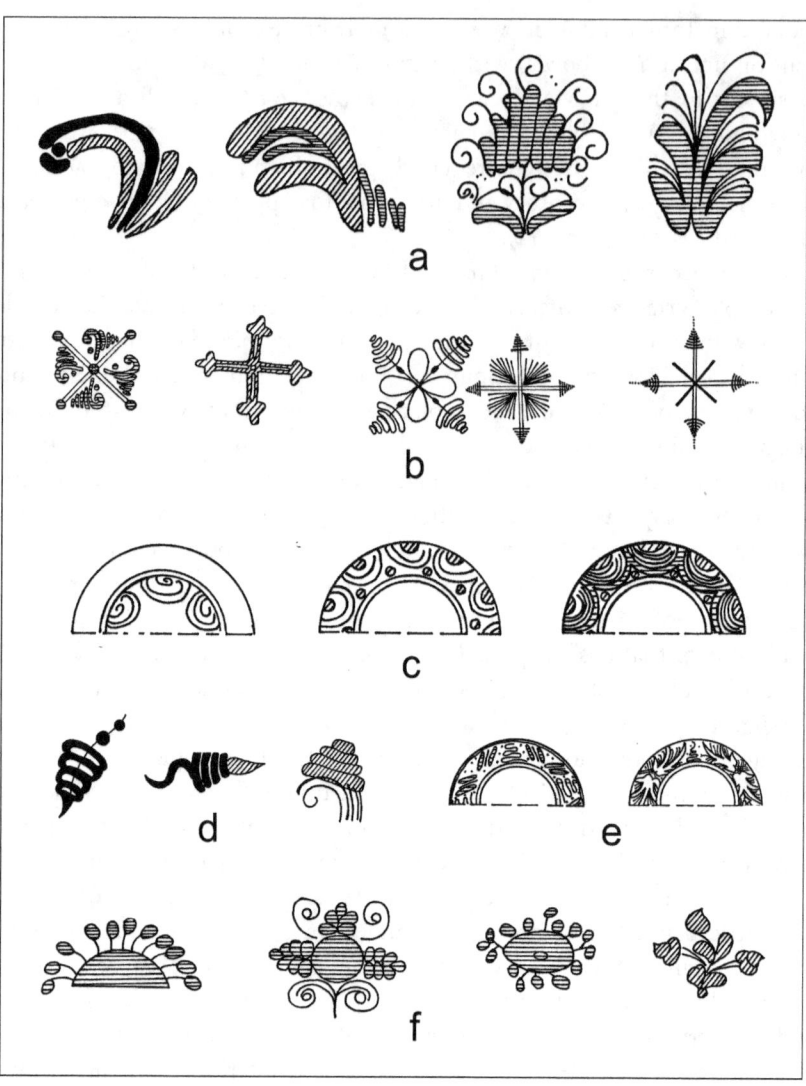

FIGURE 13.3 *Intra- and inter-regional loza design comparisons (types and locations left to right): (a) Mas Alla Polychrome, Pamama Polychrome, Panama Blue-on-white, Muel blue-on-white; (b) Cajamarca (?) blue-on-white, Ecuador green-on-white, Muel polychrome, Inka black-on-red; (c) Panama Polychrome, Panama Polychrome, Muel and Teruel polychrome; (d) Teruel verde y morado, Teruel verde y morado, Cusco green-and-black; (e) Panama Polychrome, Muel polychrome; (f), San Luis Blue-on-white (Mexico), Ichtucknee Blue-on-white (Sevilla), Panama Blue-on-white, Cusco green-and-black. After Natt 1997: figure 5.6.*

distinguish primary and secondary design elements. In addition, all loza studied—Mexican, Aragonese, and South American—displayed the same basic inventory of secondary elements and similar patterns of use (220). Dots or beads are particularly common as secondary elements of designs.

Moquegua and Southern Peru: Numerous primary design elements were identified in Mas Alla Polychrome; most also appear in Escapalaque Yellow Polychrome (Natt 1997: table 5.1). These elements include (table 13.3; figures 13.2, 13.3a, left) scrolls and S-scrolls, leaves (three kinds) and stems, petals and blossoms, dots, "lollipops," and linear elements. The linear elements may be stacked and graduated, single and double wavy lines or meanders, and single and double cruciforms. Some—such as arcs and nested arcs, cornucopias, dotted or wavy lines, and vegetal elements (flowers, leaves, fronds, plumes)—can be considered motifs on the basis of their repetition. In addition to lip stripes, green was used for large dots in black arcs, the tops of cornucopia motifs, scrolls, leaves, and other elements. Meandering lines (single and double parallel), floral elements, arcs, S-scrolls, and lollipops were generally painted in manganese (147–48). Some elements/motifs may be painted green *or* black; these include dividing lines, frond sprays, scrolls, small dots, and stacked lines.

Secondary design elements occur as embellishments of, or fillers in, primary elements. They include dots and splotches and also short lines/ticks, arcs, and scrolls. Only dots and ticks could be identified as secondary elements on Escapalaque pottery because of small sample size.

This inventory of primary and secondary elements was shared among other New World wares, along with similar patterns of use. Some secondary elements on other loza were not observed in the Moquegua material, such as hachure and fine-line lacy decoration. Crosshatching was uncommon in New World loza in general and rare in the Peruvian material as currently known (219–20).

Spain: Elements in brim bands in Italianate majolica produced in Sevilla and later in Castile included "encircling wavy lines associated with dot flowers, fronds, two-toned leaves, and lollipop dots terminating splayed lines" (Lister and Lister 1982: 75). Crosshatching was common, particularly in rendering palmette flowers in some Aragonese designs.

Mexico: Majolica decoration in Mexico City was not as delicately painted as Spanish Italianate styles, which, in turn, were simplified from the Italian originals. The Listers (ibid.: 76) describe the Mexican decorative repertoire negatively as a "partially digested diet of Italianisms that diffused via Sevilla across the Atlantic."[6] Elements include wavy rays, lollipops, leaves, undulating vines, palmettes, tendrils, dots (fillers), and flowers. Common motifs are "arc-dots; thin nested arcs; large-petaled flowers; frond sprays ... [and] palmettes" (199). This observed complexity

TABLE 13.3 Comparative occurrence of primary design configurations, motifs, and elements

		Andes[a]	Panama	Mexico	Aragón[b]
Brim configurations					
	S-scroll chain	X	X	(rare)	X
	Arc-dot chain	X	X	X	X
	Repeated fronds	X	X	X	X
Center configurations					
	Quadripartite-floral	X		(rare)	X
	Flower	X	X	X	X
	Human/animal	X[c]		X	X
	Bird	X	X	X	X
	Fish	X			X
	Human	(rare)		X	X
	"Spontaneous"	X			
Primary design elements					
	"Meanders"	X			X

Source: Natt 1997: table 5.7 and p. 254.
a Includes the Moquegua samples, as well as published photographs of pottery from Cuenca (Ecuador), Cusco, and Puno.
b Natt 1997: 218–20. Natt's analysis included pottery from Sevilla, Talavera, and Barcelona (ibid.: table 5.8), which are omitted here and Paterna is added (see text).
c Human and animal motifs were not noted on the Moquegua loza, although birds were often incised on the large earthenware tinajas used for fermenting and storing wine.

contrasts with seventeenth-century guild regulations, which specified not only the colors but also the decorative motifs on each of the three grades of ware, *común*, *entrefina*, and *fina* (Gómez, Pasinski, and Fournier 2001: 53): a small *berenjena* (eggplant) or blue motifs in the center of common ware; loops, dots, and branches on *entrefina*; and blue and black decoration, plus the master's mark, on fine ware. Decoration on Puebla pottery includes "fine-line cross-hatching, concentric arcs," fine-line lacework, and branches with leaf-like ticks (Lister and Lister 1982: 202).

Panama: Elements and motifs in the decoration on Panamanian tin-enameled wares included S-scrolls; nested arcs; arcs and lines of dots; stacked lines, often embellished with dots; cornucopias; and lollipops (Natt 1997: table 5.7). Others included some of the leaf forms (including clover-leaves), plumes, stems, and the meandering and cruciform line arrangements found in Moquegua. In general, all levels of the Panama loza design structure closely paralleled those of Mexico (201–5). One variety of Panama Polychrome features the lacy decoration also seen in Talavera and Paterna in Spain and Puebla (Mexico). Five possibly Chinese design elements and also maize plants appear on Panama Blue-and-white (Rovira 2001: 297).[7]

Indigenous: Decorative elements shared with Moquegua and other loza include dots (226) and wavy or meandering lines (Van Buren 1997: figures 21b, 24d, 31a, 32a, 32b, 35b). The interiors of two Chucuito Polychrome bowls were divided by cruciform lines, each quarter filled by an element such as a bird or a leaf, and a Chucuito-Inka vessel displayed an interior cruciform with embellishments on the ends and centers, much like Christian crosses incised on wine tinajas. Similar quadripartitioning is found on twentieth-century Aymara pottery (Tschopik 1950: figure 61a, b).

Motifs and Configurations

Design elements were combined into numerous motifs and configurations, some of which were widely shared and others that were unique to individual production regions. As noted, because this analysis was carried out primarily on pottery fragments, it was often difficult to identify these larger components of design structure. In addition, considerable variation existed in how elements were combined and where they were placed.[8]

The most common and widespread of the shared configurations/motifs in New World pottery, as in Spain, are broadly characterized as frondosidad: vegetal elements such as leaves, stems, tendrils, plumes or sprays of palm-like fronds, and flowers or blossoms combining boldly painted with fine-line (e.g., tendrils) work. Also common are medallions centered in the interior base of a dish, typically bounded by one or more circumferential lines. New World lozas generally emphasize vegetal, naturalistic, informal decorations rather than the intricate geometric designs (e.g., eight-pointed stars) seen in some late medieval Islamic wares in Spain, such as cuerda seca architectural tiles.

Moquegua and Southern Peru: In Moquegua, the brim configurations on Mas Alla Polychrome vessels usually consist of simple bands of interlocking or chained S-scrolls, double-concentric arcs, or widely spaced floral motifs, often embellished with dots or other secondary elements. Escapalaque Yellow Polychrome displayed two brim motifs not found on Mas Alla: diagonal hachure and repeated pendant frond sprays (154). Four Mas Alla dishes displayed a distinctive quadripartite or cruciform division of the design space, each quarter filled with a single motif (136; see figure 12.1, upper right). Central motifs on southern Peruvian loza may be floral (arrangements of flowers, fronds, leaves, meandering lines, cornucopias) or representational, featuring bulls, fish, and birds (144, 209), but they are not rendered as encircled medallions. Some of these motifs, such as flowers, vines, fronds, and birds, also occur in the early colonial mestizo architecture of southern Peru.

Spain: Frondosidad was common throughout Spain, although rendered in different ways in different regions. Decorative motifs on Castilian wares (Talavera and Arzobispo) included ferns (*helechos*), palmettes, and other plumy vegetation and also "butterflies" (*mariposas*).

The centers of hollow wares featured a multitude of motifs, with or without bounding into medallions (Lister and Lister 1982: 76; Seseña 1981: 84). In Castile and other Christian areas these motifs included elements such as signs for Ave Maria and Jesus (IHS), angels "framed by rayed lines," and Italianate motifs such as human busts in profile (see Lister and Lister 1982: 75). Other central representational figures included animals (mammal, bird), complex scenes, or other motifs. Many motifs—flowers (e.g., lotus) and trees, birds, fish, and other animals—recall the mix of Buddhist and Islamic influences on Changsha pottery from ninth-century China (Chiew 2005).

As noted earlier, the use of central medallions was a longstanding Hispano-Moresque tradition. Valencian majolica, for example, especially luster ware, was commonly decorated with centered heraldic emblems because of the patronage of local nobility, particularly the house of Buyl (Van de Put 1911: 19). The rest of the design space was typically filled with random dots or "horror vacui"-like patterns of tiny flowers, berries, or leaves (for Muslim/Moresque decoration in general, see Barber 1915a: 33–35; Lister and Lister 1987: 42–54, 234, 240–41).

Mexico: Mexican loza is said to have had "four distinct sources of inspiration": Muslim/Moresque, Italianate/Christian, Aztec, and Chinese (Barber 1915b: 13–15). Configurations include the various combinations of vegetation elements of frondosidad. Central medallions, often featuring palmettes, animals, and humans (especially in Puebla), were typically encircled by two or more boundary lines. Animal representations include birds (often perched on leafy vegetation), rabbits, horses, and deer, but fish are rare (208, 261).

Panama: Brim configurations on Panama Blue-on-white may include paneled floral motifs; arcs may be interchanged with vertical lines, and fourfold arrangements of fan-shaped wavy rays (sometimes embellished with dots) may establish the division of design space (203; Rovira 2001: figure 3d). Other configurations include frondosidad, central medallions, and cruciforms. In Panama Polychrome and Panama Blue-on-white, the medallion typically features floral or vegetal motifs, especially an arrangement of "thin, nested, curled leaves and wider leafy forms that usually radiate outward from a single stem" (204). The medallion is bounded with thin, encircling lines and set off from the brim by a blank cavetto (186, 203–4; Rovira 2001: figure 3).

Indigenous: Painted Indigenous designs in the southern Peruvian Andes are both linear and naturalistic (especially in the Chucuito tradition). Pre-conquest Inka-style polychromes were decorated with four types of motifs: geometric, phytomorphic (ferns, corn, peppers), zoomorphic (fish, llamas), and anthropomorphic (Fernández Baca 1971). They are distinct from all pottery described here—lozas and non-Inka Indigenous wares—in that they tend to emphasize geometric and linear motifs, such as diamonds, triangles, and Xs (see figure 8.17g–i), rather than curvilinear designs. This is true even in depictions of vegetation such as ferns, which on Inka pottery are stylized, linear, and abstract (see figure 8.17i, right side). Crude human figures are sometimes shown. Geometric motifs/elements on Inka pottery resemble *tocapus*—square, glyph-like elements with simple to complex designs, frequently quadripartite—that can be traced back to Wari iconography and appear in bands embroidered on Inka tunics and painted on keros (Eekhout and Danis 2004; Murra 1962; Zuidema 1994).[9] Later, in early Colonial-period Cusco, the K'uychipunku style featured "insects, flowers, plants, etc., mingled with geometric motives, instead of the almost purely geometric style of the Imperial period" (Tschopik 1950: 205, quoting John Rowe, pers. comm.).

In the Lake Titicaca region, centered representations include catfish (suches), which are particularly common on Chucuito Polychrome pottery, and painted birds (see figure 8.17b, d), which often appear to be native flamingoes; wings and bird footprints are also known (see figure 8.17d). One clearly post-conquest Chucuito Polychrome vessel depicted a rooster (Tschopik 1950: 205). Stylized llamitas appear in several different pottery types from the Titicaca basin (especially Saxamar/Pacajes) and also on Inka pottery (Van Buren 1993: 263, 289–90, 292, 294).[10]

SUMMARY OF COMPARISONS: TIN-ENAMELED WARE IN COLONIAL PERU AND ARAGÓN

Design schemes on verde y morado loza recovered archaeologically in the southern Peruvian Andes (Moquegua and Cusco; also the Lake Titicaca region), although currently incompletely known, differ in several respects from those of "northern" Spanish-colonial sites in the Caribbean, southeastern United States, and Mexico, as well as from producing centers in Spain itself. Study of forms and painting execution, plus comparative HDSA of Spanish majolica and colonial Ibero-American loza, indicates that the tin-enameled wares from Moquegua (Mas Alla Polychrome and Escapalaque Yellow Polychrome) and the southern Andean region more generally might be characterized as follows (189–96):

- Forms: generally simplified, lacking cavettos and frequently also brims.
- Layout: open and brim-center. Because hollow ware dishes and plates recovered in Moquegua lack cavettos, vessels lack the brim-cavetto-center layouts found elsewhere in the New World and Spain.
- Boundary markers: lip stripe only.
- Painting style: broad and bold, with quick or careless brushstrokes, shared with eastern Spanish majolica. This differs from the delicate fine-line work of the Italianate style of Sevilla and Talavera, its "degraded" version in fine-grade ("blue-series") Mexico City ware, and Mexico's even further "debased" common-grade wares (Lister and Lister 1982: 76).
- Elements and motifs: Moquegua's loza shares with all compared tin-enameled wares a wide repertoire of primary and secondary design elements and motifs, most commonly the leafy, plumy, viny, flowery elements of frondosidad but also dots and lines. Most of these elements were common in both Italianate and mudéjar decorative styles in Spain and thus seem to constitute a widely shared basic vocabulary for decoration of Spanish majolicas and their Ibero-American derivatives.
- Configurations: On brims, Moquegua's loosely interlocking S-scrolls, arc-dots, and fronds are broadly shared with Ibero-American loza and Spanish majolica. In southern Andean wares more generally, birds, fish, quadripartite/cruciforms, and unpatterned "spontaneous" decoration occur in interior centers of hollow wares. Humans are rare, and bordered medallions are generally not used.

Table 13.3 presents a tabulation of the Moquegua motifs shared with Spanish types/centers that produced the green-series/verde y morado/Hispano-Moresque wares (Teruel and Muel). Although not a quantitatively elegant illustration of the HDSA findings, this table shows that two levels of structure—configurations and elements—are broadly shared among the pottery recovered in Moquegua and that of the various Spanish centers/styles. The number of shared motifs and configurations differs sharply in comparing eastern versus southern/central Spain, however, regardless of blue- or green-series contexts.

Similarities between southern Peruvian loza and the mudéjar majolica of Aragón (especially Teruel and Muel) and Valencia (Paterna) exist at all levels of design and design structure. The most obvious point of comparison is color: the primary decorative palette is copper-based green and manganese-based brown-black pigments. In Teruel through the sixteenth century, manganese pigment was used for fine-line work and outlines, and green was prominent as dots, fronds, and fillers (222). In the early seventeenth century and later, green was also used for selected wide-line elements (arcs, fronds, birds) in the absence of manganese outlining. A green lip stripe was fairly common, and some early designs also featured a "thin black outline on the interior brim just below the lip stripe" (223). Designs are exuberant and painted with broad strokes. Some of the Moquegua material was similar to that of Zaragoza in having secondary or reverse surfaces covered with a lead glaze (Molera, Vendrell-Saz, and Pérez-Arantegui 2001: 337).

Among the shared elements, dots are used in the same way in the two regions—for example, to accent the edges of leafy elements, form "beading" on lines, and fill spaces between parallel lines, scrolls, or arc chains (219–20, 254).[11] Dots or beads can be traced back to ninth-century Changsha pottery, where they were "applied at random" or "arranged in circles, squares and lozenges" that resembled motifs on Near Eastern carpets (Chiew 2005), and they often call to mind the diacritics used in Arabic script. Wavy lines are a "signature feature of a particularly long-held decorative scheme at Teruel" (219; Ainaud de Lasarte 1952: figures 487–97; González Martí 1944: figures 672–702).

Representational images include birds (peacocks?) commonly perched amid frond-like motifs, as well as fish. A motif on the brim of some Teruel and Muel plates consists of "a series of thin, brown, double- or triple-concentric arcs framing large, green dots," which are "identical in color and composition" to those of Panama Polychrome and similar to Mas Alla Polychrome" (218). Quadripartite/cruciform arrangements were rare in Spanish majolica, except in eastern Spain. Two Muel plates exhibit a quadripartite configuration similar to that of Mas Alla Polychrome, although they incorporate blue painting.

Similarities also exist between Moquegua/southern Peruvian loza and Indigenous southern Andean slipped and (non-geometric) decorated wares, which were made before, during, and after the period of Spanish domination. These similarities include:

- Forms: small unbrimmed bowls and dishes for individual food service
- Decorative elements and motifs: especially linear elements, dots, and representations of birds and fish
- Cruciform configurations.

An interesting point of difference among Aragonese majolica, Indigenous Inka/Andean pottery, and southern Peruvian tin-enameled ware can be noted with respect to the occurrence of two features: boundary markers and central medallions. Aragonese pottery has both, Inka pottery uses boundaries but not medallions, and the local loza displays neither. The sharing of elements and motifs between Indigenous wares and southern Peruvian tin-enameled ware suggests that Spanish designs and technology were readily incorporated into new colonial pottery production systems. As mentioned, however, southern Andean loza did not incorporate two banded layouts of Indigenous dishes.

INTERPRETATIONS

This analysis explored two related, decades-old observations concerning the tin-enameled pottery produced in the Viceroyalty of Peru: these poorly known wares (1) resemble majolica of eastern Spain/Aragón, particularly Teruel, and (2) circulated in a southern commercial sphere distinct from that in the north (Lister and Lister 1974: 48; Rice 1997; Rovira 2001; Stastny 1981: 101). The data reported here (from Natt 1997) represent an early effort to apply formal HDSA to Spanish-colonial hollow ware pottery and Spain's majolicas and to investigate the decorative inspiration—along with the geo-spatial origins and identities— of potters in colonial or culture contact situations. The question underlying the HDSA was not so much "were Andean potters from Teruel/Aragón"— although an answer to that query is certainly highly desirable—but rather a more preliminary "given general similarities between Aragonese majolica and colonial Andean loza, what *kinds* of similarities do and do not exist, and why?"

Tin-enameled loza at New World Spanish-colonial sites has not been subject to rigorous stylistic analysis of the various sorts popular in late-twentieth-century American pre-Columbian archaeology and ethnoarchaeology. The reasons for this are unclear, but they may relate to the formidable complexity of this ware's florid decoration, which does not lend itself to disciplined analyses based on geometric motifs or symmetry principles. There might also be some underlying sense that the information gathered from stylistic analysis is pertinent to prehistoric materials but not to pottery from historically documented capitalist-market contexts.

Hierarchical Design-Structure Analysis

HDSA was developed and elaborated by Americanist ethnoarchaeologists in the 1970s and early 1980s to explore how the content and techniques of pottery decoration are transmitted and learned within communities and what the decoration communicated among the pottery's producers and consumers. Different levels of design structure were interpreted as reflecting different intensities of interactions among potters. Here, however, "interactions" represented by these levels are more loosely interpreted in terms of the generative relations among styles separated spatially by oceans and temporally by decades and centuries.

The interpretations of the HDSA of this loza can be considered in terms of a recent analysis of Mimbres (southwestern United States) pottery design. That study's basic premise is that "the act of painting a design on a vessel is a form of agency, and the overall style of that design in part can be conceptualized as a kind of structure" (Hegmon and Kulow 2005: 314). The Mimbres analysis was specifically oriented toward identifying decorative innovations, in which pottery painters (actors, agents) intentionally or unintentionally introduced something novel and thereby changed the structure of the design in terms of what was painted, where it was painted, or both. Much of the variability described here in terms of layouts, elements, motifs, and configurations of loza decoration from different production centers in Spanish-colonial America represents analogous processes of agency. But the Moquegua study is more normative in that it is difficult to identify what was innovative without first determining what was typical and what it was typical *of*.

Striking general resemblances exist among and between virtually all styles of New World loza and their Spanish majolica (Italianate and Hispano-Moresque) forebears. Similarities are evident in overall "style" and elements/motifs: for example, painters' decisions to produce luxuriant vegetation rather than the geometric forms/motifs common on tiles. In most general terms, HDSA revealed similarities in decoration of Andean and Aragonese (Teruel/Muel) wares at all levels of design structure: open layout, elements, motifs, and configurations, with the exception of medallions and boundary markers. Citizens of Aragón were among the early migrants to Peru before 1560, but only in small numbers—perhaps 2 percent of all known Spaniards—and few of them seem to have been artisans (Boyd-Bowman 1976; Lockhart 1968: 111, tables 1, 2). Given that loza was probably not produced in the viceroyalty until the late sixteenth century, the early Aragonese settlers might not have been potters themselves; but they could have established a small "founding colony" in Peru from which they built a "pipeline," encouraging relatives and neighbors to emigrate and join them.[12] To probe more deeply into the kinds of similarities and the reasons for them, it was necessary to explore the two New World spheres in which these wares were produced and exchanged: northern/blue/Italianate-influenced and southern/green/Hispano-Moresque.

Loza Decorative Spheres

The existence of two decorative spheres of Ibero-American loza is most apparent through the dominant painting colors used and their spatial distributions: cobalt blue in the north and copper green in the south. However, differences extend beyond color to include certain aspects of vessel form (e.g., presence/absence of a cavetto) that establish initial structural levels and layouts, such as definition of design spaces and their delineation by boundary markers. Other differences are seen in skill of execution: decoration on loza produced in the southern Andes was markedly simplified (the Listers would say "debased") compared with the Italianate-style fine wares of the northern sphere.

The development and maintenance of these spheres—indeed, of the New World loza industry as a whole—was a consequence of individual potters' and painters' agency, which began with decisions to migrate from Spain to the colonies. These decisions, in turn, were contingent on Spain's politico-economic and politico-religious circumstances between the late fifteenth and early seventeenth centuries. Potters/painters were mobile in Spain, particularly in Andalucía, with production of wares intended for the new colonies. In the south and east, especially in Aragón, Granada, and Valencia, however, mobility was a consequence of oppression of Muslim/morisco artisans.

It would be convenient to assume that the morisco response to centuries of persecution was for potters and other artisans to flee to the Americas. However, ascertaining the ethno-religious background and occupation of migrants to the New World is a difficult proposition (Qamber 2006; Velez et al. 2012). Further, Spanish potters were not solely moriscos and "new" Christians (Lister and Lister 1984: 88–89); many were Christians of long standing and some were from monasteries (Tschopik 1950: 201n42). Once safely across the Atlantic, morisco artisans were probably equally mobile as they searched out places with a sufficient consumer base to practice their craft in the growing colonies. Although potters are notoriously secretive about their techniques (see, e.g., Picolpasso 1980: 6), this human movement, along with the flow of commodities in legal and illegal trade within and among the colonies, would in principle have contributed to a vibrant interchange of ideas and stylistic elements and motifs.

A key issue here concerns not only why these distinct ceramic stylistic spheres emerged but why they overlapped, stylistically and commercially, in Panama. A resource (cobalt)-centered perspective was suggested in chapter 12. What more, if anything, can HDSA contribute to the disentangling of these complex social and economic relations of colonial ceramic production and exchange? For example, who founded the Panamá La Vieja loza industry? Did potters come to Panama directly from Spain, or might artisans have moved out of Mexico in search of new opportunities?

According to the Listers (1974: 44–45, 1987: 340n82), loza decoration suggests that potters (or painters) may have come to Panama from southeastern Spain, particularly Granada after the Alpujarras rebellion, bringing the firing methods and technology typical of Sevillian/Genoese potters. HDSA supports this idea, indicating that Panama's loza shares features—of layout, configuration form and placement, and patterns of color use—with mudéjar-style majolica produced in eastern Spain. Furthermore, the use of blue, green, and manganese decoration (Panama Polychrome), which is uncommon in Mexican pottery to the north, is also found in Muel. Moreover, Panama and Muel shared distinctive brim and basal configurations (248). Panama loza belongs primarily in the southern/Pacific design sphere along with Andean wares and exhibits fewer similarities with Mexico (247, 271–72).

Design-structure analysis highlighted multiple sources of influence on the "style" of southern Peruvian and Moquegua loza: Spain (Christian, Muslim, Italian), Panamanian, and Indigenous Andean. Were the Andean verde y morado loza production clusters founded by immigrants directly from Spain or by potters and painters moving out of Panama or even Mexico? The strong similarities between Panamanian and Andean ware, such that the two are part of the same green/southern sphere, suggest that potting centers in both areas might have been begun by immigrants coming directly from eastern Spain. Or, potters might have left Panama to establish workshops in the Andes. Alternatively, Andean loza painters, including those of Ecuador, might have simply borrowed "relatively complex design units from the Panamanian decorative repertoire," but their renderings were simplified (i.e., lacking secondary design elements) and less skillfully executed (244).

Because Italianate elements in Andean loza were combined into an overall design structure that was more morisco, "this would seem to indicate that Italian decorative influence entered into the South American decorative program via some route other than Andalusia" (258). In the southern Andes, the mudéjar design style seems to have easily incorporated aspects of Indigenous Inka decoration, likely through the incorporation of native potters/painters into the workshops.

The spatialization of decoration through layouts and the use of boundary markers and central medallions (table 13.4) might be considered core tactics in larger strategies of "us versus them" identifications of colonized and colonizer (and not so much between upper and lower classes), subtly encoding power

TABLE 13.4 Comparative occurrence of boundary markers and central medallions

Producer	Boundary Markers[a]	Central Medallion
Spain[b]	X	X
Mexico	X	X
Panama	X	X
Inka/Indigenous	X	No
S. Andes loza[c]	No	No

a Other than lip stripes.
b Both Italianate and Hispano-Moresque styles.
c As currently known.

relations through a relatively mundane technology. However, neither Spanish nor Andean potters or painters were familiar with the physical properties of the locally available raw materials needed for loza glazes and paints (copper, lead, tin), as evidenced by persistent flaws in application, and this inexperience might have been partially responsible for the structurally simple design repertoire (277).

Given strong anti-Muslim prejudices in tenuously Christian sixteenth-century Spain, it must be asked again why traditionally Ibero-Islamic– or Hispano-Moresque–style verde y morado loza was made and used in the southern Andes. In Mexico, green-series wares were common-grade wares, used by the poor and in rural areas. The Listers (Lister and Lister 1982: 14) suggest a possible prejudice against green among sixteenth-century Spaniards because of its association with Islam. (Blue, in contrast, is said to have been a "lucky color" for Muslims [ibid.: 88].) Was Andean green-series loza similarly viewed pejoratively? Did consumers in the Viceroyalty of Peru have to "settle" for green-series ware because more desirable Italianate (or Chinese) styles painted with blue were unavailable? Was the early predominance of green-and-manganese decoration a deliberate choice made by loza painters, or was it thrust upon them by a lack of reliable access to sources of blue pigment?

This last conjecture is unlikely for several reasons (see chapter 12). Cobalt was expensive, but blue could also be produced by combining copper with zinc, a mixture used on common-grade blue wares in Mexico (ibid.: 25). Blue decoration was used on Panama loza (and blue-on-white decoration seems to have been produced in Cajamarca, northern Peru, although perhaps later), raising the possibility that Panama potters were able to exert some influence on suppliers/traders to embargo its shipment farther south. Finally, if loza painters in southern Peru were accustomed to painting blue decoration but did not do so simply because the pigment was unavailable, the HDSA would have revealed greater stylistic similarities to Italianate blue-series wares of Mexico and Sevilla/Talavera (whether produced by moriscos or Christians).

Instead, the stylistic structure of Andean loza exhibits strong ties to the centuries-old verde y morado decoration of eastern Spain, suggesting painters' intentional decisions to maintain traditional styles. The HDSA reveals a remarkable decorative conservatism in all levels of green-and-manganese-decorated wares on both sides of the Atlantic. In colonial Peru, tin-enameled wares lacked the pervasive color and class associations seen in Mexico. Instead, wealth and class were proclaimed by silver.

NOTES

1. A few sherds of Ligurian Blue-on-blue type were recovered at Torata Alta.

2. The inspiration for this yellow background is unknown, although some late Spanish majolicas have a yellow ground, as do some Chinese porcelains. Lister and Lister (1974: 28, 35) mention yellow ground in Spain and Mexico and suggest English Canary Ware (1780–1835) as an inspiration. Yellow ground was seen in some nineteenth-century ware believed to have been produced in Puebla (Natt 1997: 212). Sherds with yellow tin-enamel backgrounds have also been noted in Honduras (Goggin 1968: 9), Brazil (Orser 1994: 12–13), and possibly Chucuito (Tschopik 1950: 204). Escapalaque Yellow Polychrome might have begun to be produced later than Mas Alla, perhaps as late as the nineteenth century.

3. Used to store valuable spices and other foods, such as ginger, vanilla, and chocolate, the Puebla jars often lost their lids to breakage and were fitted with replacement covers of iron or other metal, complete with lock and key (Barber 1915b: 12–13). In southern Peru in the eighteenth century, gourds (*mates*; *Lagenaria* sp.) were intricately carved and similarly fitted with metal—often silver—hinges and locks (Stastny 1981: 133–41).

4. Additional complex uses and meanings of colors may have pertained to Inka ceques and suyus in the Colonial period, with red and black associated with the first and second ranked and the lower ranks associated with blue and green (Zuidema 2007: 96n9). Alternatively, the unranked color associations might be black, white, red, and a tawny or "dark yellowish" (*leonada*) color, perhaps corresponding to the orange newly seen on pottery (ibid.).

5. Material manufactured in the Puno region has been called false majolica because it features decoration on a white slip under a clear lead glaze instead of painting over tin enamel.

6. A backhandedly positive assessment comes from Barber (1915b: 6, 15), whose wine-snob–like evaluation would be amusing were it not for its colonialist bias: Mexican

decoration and motifs are "childlike in their simplicity," executed with "a charmingly naïve crudeness of technique" and displaying a "manly vigor not found in the more effeminate products of Spain or Italy."

7. Stylized corn tassels, or *espigas de maiz*, appear in brim panels on two Sevillian copies of Chinese porcelain (Lister and Lister 1987: figure 106).

8. This sometimes led to identification of "classes" and "subclasses" of motifs and configurations in Natt's original analysis, but they are not discussed further here (see Natt 1997: 143–47).

9. The right to wear tocapus was granted to certain high-status Inka males by royal privileges (Murra 1962: 720; Zuidema 1994: 152). Tocapus may have been titles of rank; different tocapus in different arrangements were characteristic of males and females (ibid.: 152–53); they may have been heraldic emblems specific to individual Inka rulers (Eekhout and Danis 2004: 319); and they may have carried other meanings, including toponymy, social or military rank, calendrical intervals, or religious cults (ibid.; Zuidema 1994: 198). They are commonly thought to be a representational system, analogous to writing, that has not yet been decoded. The earliest Spanish chroniclers made no mention of tocapus individually, although they identified certain patterns of their integration and placement on tunics (Zuidema 1994).

10. A broad range of motifs is found in modern Chucuito pottery, including zigzags, crosshatching, rosettes or other flower, bird (dove, chicken, gallinule?), viscacha, catfish, star, and occasionally a human (Tschopik 1950: 213).

11. Wares recovered in Moquegua do not display the horror vacui style of some Hispano-Moresque wares in which random dots of paint or tiny clover-like vegetation are used as filler in large open areas or between motifs.

12. Spaniards displayed a great deal of loyalty to their home regions, encouraging relatives, friends, and neighbors to join them in the colonies. This is evidenced by many studies of patterns of migration to the New World (see, e.g., Altman 1989; Boyd-Bowman 1976; Lockhart 1968).

Part V
Conclusions

The preceding chapters considered the "espacio" Moqueguano, a small politically and ecologically distinct internal region within the greater Spanish-colonial espacio Peruano (Sempat Assadourian 1972: 11), from varying perspectives. These perspectives—temporally pre- and post-conquest, culturally those of colonized and colonizer, theoretically those of political ecology—reveal that today's Moquegua consists of many espacios that preserve the unique and complex historical contingencies underlying humans' relationships with their environments in this part of the Andean watershed. The palimpsested landscapes, spaces, and places of Moquegua were successively (re)negotiated, (re)constructed, and (re)produced during centuries of colonization and exploitation of its rich agricultural and mineral resources. This volume, then, is a contribution to a comparative, longitudinal, ethno-geography or political-economic history of Moquegua, the comparators subsuming four cultural periods and roughly six centuries of the late history of the area, beginning with the Middle Horizon (MH) colonies and their collapse. Throughout most of these centuries, the landscape of Moquegua was cognitively ordered by peripherality—as a frontier—by multiple societies (Rice 2011b).

14

Moquegua's Landscapes, Spaces, and Places through Time

> Landscapes are always in process, potentially conflicted, untidy and uneasy.
> —BARBARA BENDER (1993: 3)

The late prehistory of Moquegua illustrates Henri Lefebvre's point, in *The Production of Space* (1991), that space produces and is produced by power: Moquegua was for centuries a sociopolitically peripheral space of colonialism produced and reproduced by a series of powerful centers located outside the boundaries of the Osmore drainage. No large political centers comparable to Wari, Tiwanaku, or Cusco were ever established in Moquegua in pre-Hispanic times, although the MH Omo colony of Tiwanaku was certainly a substantial presence in the valley. Following the collapse of Tiwanaku and Wari, the middle valley was only sparsely occupied; the demographic weight moved upstream into the lower tributaries, which were settled by agricultural colonists from altiplano polities. Conquest by the Inkas in the late fifteenth century brought about Moquegua's incorporation into Tawantinsuyu, their socially, politically, and geographically quartered and nested universe. This kind of nested organization exemplifies the idea that multiple spaces are simultaneously present in any landscape (Keith and Pile 1993a: 6), all of which are differentially perceived, experienced, and "owned." The Moquegua region was part of the lower division of Contisuyu, the lowest of the four quarters of the empire.

The Inka presence in the Río Osmore drainage is barely visible archaeologically, doubtless because the Spaniards, who arrived soon after Inka conquest, arrogated many components of their significant imprint (landesque capital) on the landscape. For example, the

DOI: 10.5876/9781607322764.c14

Inkas established a system for allocating irrigation water among the various colonists' fields in the middle valley, a system the Spanish interlopers appropriated to their own ends. The Inkas also established the settlement underlying modern Moquegua, although it is more likely that they took over and enlarged an earlier community in this highly desirable location at the confluence of the Osmore's tributaries. In addition, they established the short-lived administrative center now known as Torata Alta, which the Spaniards preempted as a congregación: a forced resettlement of scattered Indigenous villagers. Even though Torata Alta was a quintessential node of oppressive colonial administration, epitomized by the emplacement of a church, it was not a Spanish community but rather an Indigenous one: its Lupaqa residents remained under the watchful gaze of Chucuito, a former Inka province in the Lake Titicaca basin that became a crown encomienda.

It is perhaps because of the area's marginality that Indigenous Moquegua residents' resistance in the face of these repeated usurpations seems to have been almost nonexistent. Cerro Baúl was burned at the end of its MH occupation, but that destruction was apparently intentional termination (Moseley et al. 2005). After the fall of Tiwanaku, populations from Omo and related settlements apparently moved up-valley, where they were joined by Qolla colonists from the altiplano. The Qolla established themselves on fortified hilltops, but it is unclear if this was because they were the familiar settlement choices of the homeland or if these colonists faced actual hostilities. Similarly, nothing suggests that Indigenous occupants of the Moquegua valley pursued any strong or active opposition to the Spaniards' intrusion, such as participating in widespread rebellions like Taki Onkoy. The Lupaqas were under the jurisdiction of Chucuito, essentially a crown agent. Thus the most overt instances of resistance were accommodated through colonial administrative channels—for example, the 1557 order by Chucuito's kurakas that all encomenderos in the southwest give up any Lupaqa tributaries, their repeated interventions in Lupaqa-Spanish relations in the valley, and testimonies given to *visitadores* by unfairly treated individuals (Diez de San Miguel 1964). The Torata Alta reducción might have been a center of Indigenous resistance in the form of apostasy, as the community's cacique was punished on numerous occasions for idolatry and witchcraft (Cañedo-Argüelles Fábrega 1994: 22, 2005: li–lii), which may be reflected in archaeological data.

The earliest stages of landscape construction in Moquegua are evident in Indigenous toponyms, which provide unique insights into the history of space, place, and landscape. Some toponyms have been retained for centuries and suggest the origins, languages, and social identities of late pre-Hispanic colonists.

Among the Aymara, the cultural affiliation of the Lupaqa/Qolla colonists, Indigenous landscape classifications identified the coastal valleys as low in elevation but high in status. Other toponyms bespeak the sacred landscapes created in rural Moquegua over the centuries. The fact that one singularly significant Indigenous place in Moquegua, the apu Cerro Baúl, conspicuously lacks an Andean toponym doubtless reflects Spanish eradication of associated idolatry.

Lefebvre (1991) describes space as an economic good, a commodity with use-value and exchange-value that, in Marxian dialectical fashion, both produces and is produced by power. The earliest Spanish settlers in the Moquegua valley provide an illustration of this process as part of their taking ownership and many approaches to re-spatialization. One approach was through religion: catholicizing the landscape by populating the surface with saints. For the early Spanish settlers, saints and other holy figures not only structured time through the Catholic ritual calendar but also ordered space. The many chapels and appellations of heredades throughout the valley established a network of places invoking protection against natural disasters and other calamities while also providing an overlying grid of Christian order, meaning, and identity.

Another path of re-spatialization was economic: reordering the Osmore's valuable but restricted productive space—irrigable valley flatland—making it Spanish not only by the power of forcing it to yield new products (peaches, grapes, wheat, sugar) but also through the alienation and private ownership inherent in capitalism. As Andean populations dwindled and communities were increasingly unable to pay the taxes their new overlords demanded, the Spaniards were able to acquire land as private property through legitimate sale, auction, or appropriation (Pease G. Y. 1985: 153–56). In so doing, the identity of Moquegua's agro-pastoral landscape was commodified in the transition from Andean to Spanish.

Moquegua was also re-spatialized politically, although the region's political-economic peripherality changed only slowly with the arrival of the Spaniards. For much of the first century of early Spanish occupation, colonial authorities regarded the area not as a meaningful place but rather as interstitial—essentially negative or empty—space between more important places. The Osmore drainage was re-politicized and partitioned, Theissen polygon-like, through lengthy and highly contested processes of drawing and redrawing various boundaries to define the jurisdictions of surrounding power centers rather than to accommodate the interests of the residents of the valley itself (Rice 2011a). These boundaries might be seen in terms of Lefebvre's (1991) "representations of space." However, they were fundamentally inadequate representations because of the complexity of Peru's spaces, not only those of the natural environment but especially as they were defined ethno-politically by ayllus and moieties at different levels. The shifting boundaries of audiencias and dioceses (and other units of spatial ordering—corregimientos, partidos, provincias, and so on) in the early Viceroyalty of Peru can be seen as an indication of the Spaniards' difficulties in learning this area and its socio-spatial organization, from the lowest levels up to the Inka empire and its provinces.

It was only through the region's identity negotiations and participation in larger church versus state debates in the late sixteenth and early seventeenth centuries—articulated by the strident voices of the citizens of San Sebastián/San Francisco on one side of the river and residents of Moquegua/Santa Catalina on the other, along with the muted whispers of Lupaqas, Qollas, and other native peoples in Torata Alta and elsewhere—that the spaces of Moquegua were "emplaced," that is, created and named and empowered. This history calls to mind Margaret Rodman's (1992: 642, quoting Berdoulay 1989: 135) observation that "a place comes explicitly into being in the discourse of its inhabitants, and particularly in the rhetoric it promotes." The conflicts also exemplify the ways in which "marginalized communities [are] able to inscribe themselves into new geographies" by taking advantage of "gaps, contradictions, folds and tears" in existing spatial representations (Keith and Pile 1993b: 36). It is of no little interest that Moquegua's current *"zonificación política-administrativa"* (Sempat Assadourian 1972: 12), although bearing toponyms of modern Peruvian politics, reproduces Indigenous administrative separations dating back to the fifteenth century or earlier.

Concepts of space and place in colonial settings can also be explored through pottery, domestic and imported, and its uses in varied spatial and functional contexts. Here, space can be considered on both macro and micro scales. The macro level is important in terms of both the places (countries, regions, towns) where a ware was produced and exchanged and the creation of new spaces in which pottery was assigned meanings for social production and reproduction. In the case of decorated vessels, space is also of interest in micro terms: the areas on the vessel surface that were identified as places to be decorated, and what kind of decoration was put in what place. In Spain and the Andes, specific associations between the macro and the micro permit insights into paths of movement of ideas about decorative spatializations and, tentatively, the ethno-religious identities of the makers.

In the Andes, considerations of decorative space can be explored with respect to various kinds of Inka pottery. A particularly interesting aspect of Inka pottery decoration is the use of boundary markers. This may relate to a longstanding Andean concern with bounding spaces (see Urton 1990: 120–23), particularly architectural spaces (e.g., Tiwanaku dates; Inka doorways), and controlling peoples' movements across these boundaries as key components of maintaining imperial order. Such movements "may have marked important social and political transformations" (La Lone 2000: 85, quoting Morris and von Hagen 1993: 103) or, in the case of pottery, statuses of participants in the public feasting that accompanied such ceremony and ceremonial vessels.

The relative absence of boundary markers on colonial Andean loza may be a consequence of the very different social and political contexts in which this pottery was used or, as in traditional interpretations of stylistic analyses, of different approaches to group identities (and so order) in pre-Hispanic versus colonial times. Boundary lines may also have different meanings. In the Ecuadorian Amazon, certain boundary placements on beer-drinking bowls correlate positively with political affiliation rather than ethnicity, as do the colors of primary design elements and the use of dots (Bowser 2000: 233, 235, 239–41). Andean vessels that might have such parallels are beaker-like keros, usually made of wood (see Cummins 1988, 2002b), used to drink chicha in ritual contexts. Among the Inkas, a distinctive pottery form associated with state-sponsored ritual feasting, particularly at provincial sites, is the slipped and painted arībalo, or urpu, used for storing and transporting the chicha. Interestingly, the upper decorated surfaces of at least two urpus that have survived to modern times were covered with tin enamel, thus neutralizing a widespread symbol of Indigenous power by smothering it with a new technology.

Moving outward to consider Spanish and Spanish-influenced tin-enameled pottery, two initial conclusions can be drawn from the comparative contextual study of loza in the Viceroyalty of Peru, including Moquegua. First, other than architectural tiles in the early Colonial period, little loza was imported from Spain into the Andean region. This created a need for local, that is, Pacific/Andean, production. Second, local production of loza began at the end of the sixteenth century, with wares painted primarily in copper green and manganese brown-black. This Andean decorative palette contrasted with that of wares produced in the Viceroyalty of New Spain, which prominently featured cobalt blue pigment, sometimes as the background color but primarily as decoration and often combined with black, green, yellow, and other colors. Green decoration was for lower-grade ware. In the imperial Spanish homeland, polychrome decoration featuring expensive, imported cobalt blue was particularly associated with the relatively new (fifteenth-century) Italianate- or Renaissance-style wares produced in Sevilla (near Spain's Atlantic export center) and Talavera. By the sixteenth century, Italianate majolica was identified with consumption by the highest statuses, including the Christian royal court. Green and brown, however, were part of a centuries-old verde y morado tradition that began shortly after the Islamic conquest of the Iberian Peninsula. These Ibero-Islamic wares were produced by Muslim potters and painters or those with such a heritage (morisco; mudéjar), primarily in eastern Spain.

Morisco/mudéjar contributions to the commodity supply of the Ibero-American colonies have generally been underemphasized and under-theorized in historical archaeological studies. This circumstance relates to the myths of glorifying the Christian Spanish conquest, of the sort highlighted in the "Columbian consequences" literature of the late twentieth century and, even earlier, the nineteenth-century romantic, Orientalist essentializing of the "Moor" as the "Other" (Dodds and Walker 1992). Conquest history is typically winner's history, which in the case of the Spanish-colonial world more narrowly constitutes crown/Roman Catholic history. The Spanish monarchs, beginning with Ferdinand and Isabel, and their officials were rabidly and mono-maniacally Christian, pathologically xenophobic, and afraid of anything and anyone they did not understand and could not control—not just people of other faiths but also "New" Christians: newly converted former Muslims and Jews.[1]

As Matthew Restall (2003: 12–14) has noted, most of the history of the Spanish conquest, and the basis for the "conquest mythology" that has been the received wisdom from historians for centuries, has come from letters, accounts, and reports written by the conquerors and missionaries.[2] These accounts employ a justificatory "ideology of imperialism that represented the Conquest as a dual mission, bringing both civilization and Christianity to the Americas" (ibid.: 14). This ideology was partly generated and certainly reinforced by late-fifteenth- and early-sixteenth-century Papal bulls. The great narratives compiled by Spanish chroniclers portray the conquest as a plan created by divine Providence "to bring the true faith to the whole world," with the Spanish conquerors acting as "God's principal agents" in implementing that plan for Christian order (ibid.; see also Cummins 2002a). As the story of conquest has traditionally been told through official Christian Spanish voices, the Muslims were infidels and heretics, the enemies of newly unified Spain, of Christianity, and of God's order. Related constructs and tropes about Spanish-colonial history, such as those concerning restricted migration and trade between Spain and the colonies, need to be reexamined.

The prominence of green-and-manganese, or verde y morado, colors on Andean tin-enameled ware prompts three reflections not only on the "meaning" of this traditional Muslim-associated decoration but also on the tangled relationship between style and identity and on the broader multicultural, multivocal contexts in these new spaces of colonial life. First, these wares made by potters and painters working in the mudéjar decorative tradition were variably acceptable in the New World colonies in the sixteenth century and later. It is possible that, by the late sixteenth century in the Americas, the original Islamic ethno-religious associations and meanings of these mudéjar contributions to ecclesiastical art and architecture style were lost (Fernández 1993), and the same is likely true with respect to any "messages" of identity and power sent by tableware bearing green-and-manganese decoration.

Second, potters and painters producing in this tradition might have been Christian, or they might have been Muslims/moriscos who traveled to the colonies despite a spate of royal decrees attempting to restrict such travel. In the reality of colonial life among settlers on the frontiers of colonial expansion in Ibero-America, the rigid dichotomization of us versus them and good versus evil might have been relaxed in a more pragmatic and tolerant atmosphere (at least aside from Inquisitorial investigations into active non-Christian practices). This may have been particularly true in the southern part of what is now Peru, where there was, at the time of conquest, a "cultural elasticity" and tolerance for peoples of varied ethno-linguistic backgrounds resulting from the long heritage of colonization, transhumance, and Inka resettlement (Galdos Rodríguez 1984: 183). It may also translate into acceptance as well as production of morisco styles of European pottery in the south.

Finally, two commercial clusters or spheres of production and circulation of tin-enameled wares emerged: northern/Atlantic and southern/Pacific. Although they seem to be part of larger viceregal commercial spheres (Lockhart and Schwartz 1983: 86–92), with respect to loza the most obvious difference is the presence/absence of blue/cobalt decoration. Explaining the reasons for this difference—resource availability? producers' preferences? consumer preferences?—is more complex and points to the difficulties in, for example, distinguishing among "intentions, consequences, meanings, and motives" in applying agency theory within real-world contexts of institutional/structural constraints (see Dornan 2002).

My goal in compiling the chapters of *Space-Time Perspectives* was to view Moquegua and its landscape at the time of Spanish contact and early colonialism through the analytical prism of spatialization and examine how, as with a beam of light, that prism separated the area's spectrum of spatialities that structured, and were structured by, power relations through time. I was interested in what Moquegua's experience might contribute to a broader understanding of spatialization in colonial encounters, as well as how spatializations in colonial encounters might illuminate Moquegua's experience. Because my intent was not to draw conclusions about the processes but rather to explore perspectives for investigating them, in Moquegua and elsewhere, what kinds of refracted perspectives—other than time and history—emerged from the prism?

One viewing perspective that can be highlighted is multi-valency: as with any landscape, that of Moquegua is today a mosaic of multiple spaces, old and new, differently perceived and experienced, abandoned and under construction—simultaneously present as a living, changing, unfinished production based on human interactions with the natural environment. Moquegua's spatializations were shaped, over more than a millennium, by size and natural resources: rich agricultural soils and valuable minerals but occurring in small, localized pockets. Over the centuries, many groups wanted to exploit Moquegua's spaces, but the spaces would only accommodate a small number of places—not mega-cities, either pre- or post-Hispanic—under existing technological regimes. From the view of natural spaces, then, Moquegua seemed destined to be peripheral.

A second perspective is that of globalization: the stages in the growth of capitalism, from the long era of merchant trade through recent global-industrial capitalism, have their own types or logics of space (Jameson 1991: 410–13). Early market capitalism is also associated with the initiation of the process of "desacralization of the world, the decoding and secularization of the older forms of the sacred . . . [and] the slow colonization of use value by exchange value" (ibid.: 410). These processes are clearly evident in early Spanish-colonial Latin America in general and in Peru and Moquegua in particular: land and labor were literally and figuratively colonized by secularization and commoditization.

In the late eighteenth century, Moquegua emerged as a small regional ("semi-peripheral") Spanish center in southwestern Peru. The reasons for the valley's evolution into a higher-order sociopolitical unit are economic: Moquegua became an important producer of wine and pisco (grape brandy) and the chief supplier of these beverages to the altiplano, especially to the wealthy silver-mining region of Alto Peru (modern Bolivia). The impetus behind these developments was, of course, emergent capitalism: as Spaniards acquired more and more land in the valley, they devoted increasing portions of it to vineyards, to the point of near monocropping. Even Indigenous groups learned to make wine as an entry into the new economy, with Torata producing wine from its vineyard in the middle valley by the late 1560s (Diez de San Miguel 1964: 245; Guíbovich P. 1984: 222–23, 299; Pease G. Y. 1984: 164). Moquegua was part of what is known in late-twentieth-century business argot as a cluster region—the southwest Peruvian wine and brandy agro-industry—seen today as representing "a new way of thinking about location" and economic resilience (Porter 1998: 78; also Rice 2013).

A third perspective is multivocality: this long-occupied landscape speaks with thousands of voices, relating anecdotes in the accretionary history of

Moquegua's socially embedded and meaningful places. Many of these voices are heard through the eyes: in documents (by Christian Spaniards and early educated Andeans and scores of modern scholars), in capitalism's blare, in pilgrims' offerings, volcanoes erupting, rivers flooding, and distributions of buildings and churches and wineries and artifacts. With respect to the last of these, I have devoted considerable attention to the history of tin-enameled pottery in Spain and its movement to the American colonies.

Historical archaeologists' and art historians' focus on blue-series wares in the Spanish colonies, along with obligatory references to emulation of porcelains and seeming disinterest in lower-grade green-series wares, has subtly perpetuated and valorized the reconquest ideology/mythology proclaimed by the crown, conquistadors, missionaries, and minor functionaries. But in ignoring the history and role of Muslim-influenced loza in the Americas, as well as the more general role of mudéjar/morisco potters, artisans, and styles in transatlantic societal production and reproduction, scholars have been privileging an elite Christian imperialist ideology of colonialism at the expense of creating a multilayered and multivocal narrative of transculturation and hybridization. The inattention to Muslim-influenced green-and-black-decorated loza has inadvertently silenced one of the voices in the dialogue of colonization. In the Andes, this voice spoke in colors.

NOTES

1. The monarchs were also deeply distrustful of the new elites in the colonies, insisting that crown officials in Peru at least be Spanish-born peninsulares. The most intractable problem, from the crown's perspective, would have been the presence of ethno-politically dangerous non-Christians in those difficult-to-control distant colonies. Consequently, the crown issued harsh but futile laws and punishments, including the Inquisition, to maintain the purity—or at least an illusion of purity—of Christian sanctity over the enterprise of conquest and colonization. The very fact that the institution of Inquisition needed to be established in the colonies—in both Mexico City and Peru in the early 1570s—signals the crown's perception of a problem (see Qamber 2006).

2. Many of these documents are in the form of *probanzas* (lit. 'proofs'), which were written to inform the crown—desperately trying to create an absolute, Christian-ordered, world monarchy—about "events and newly acquired lands, especially if those lands contained . . . settled native populations, and precious metals" (Restall 2003: 12). At the same time, these documents glorified and justified the writers' actions to underscore their merit for royal rewards of titles, land, and money.

Glossary

Ay, Aymara; Sp, Spanish; Q, Quechua

adobón (Sp) Large rectangular block of tamped earth, formed in a mold, for construction of buildings and walls (sometimes called *tapia*)

apu (Q) Mountain, particularly a sacred mountain

aqlla (Q) Chosen woman

aqllawasi (Q) Dedicated residential compound for *aqllas*

aríbalo (Sp) Decorated Inka jar with a tall, flaring neck; *aryballus*, *urpu*

arroba (Sp) Twenty-five pounds dry weight; 2.6 gallons of wine

audiencia (Sp) Supreme court jurisdiction in the Spanish colonies

ayllu (Q) Kin-based residential and landholding collective

azulejo (Sp) Glazed decorative architectural tile

batan (Q) Large grinding stone with a smooth, often dished upper surface

bodega (Sp) Winery; site where wine is fermented and stored; a room of *tinajas* for such storage

botija (Sp) Wheel-made, amphora-like jar, sometimes glazed, used for storage and transport

botijería (Sp) Workshop where *botijas* and other earthenware pottery were made

calicanto (Sp) Masonry, usually denoting dressed construction stone

cántaro (Sp) Water jar, usually with a flaring neck

cavetto (Sp) Out-curved area between the base and rim of a plate or bowl

cédula (Sp) Official order, edict, decree

ceque (Q) Imaginary lines for ritual processions over the landscape of the Cusco valley.

chicha Andean beer, usually made from maize (corn) or *molle* berries

chúa (Ay) Small, individual pottery serving dish

chullpa (Q) Stone burial towers; aboveground tombs

cofradía (Sp) Religious brotherhood, confraternity

compañía (Sp) Business partnership

congregación (Sp) Site of forced resettlement of Indigenous populations

conopa (Q) Small carved stone figures of animals used in Inka offerings; amulet

corregimiento (Sp) Provincial administrative district in the colonies

criollo (Sp) Born or originating in the colonies; creole

cuartillo (Sp) Liquid measure of approximately one pint

cuerda seca (Sp) Lit. "dry cord"; a type of decoration on tiles or pottery featuring glazed areas outlined or separated by unglazed lines created by painting with grease or wax, which melts during firing

encomendero (Sp) Owner of an *encomienda*

encomienda (Sp) Grant of native laborers to early Spanish conquerors

falca (Sp) Pot-still

frondosidad (Sp) Painted vegetal decoration on tin-enameled ware, featuring fronds, leaves, flowers, and tendrils

gremio (Sp) Guild

hanan (Q) Upper or higher ranked, as in moiety organization

hechicería (Sp) Sorcery; witchcraft

heredad (Sp) Small, rural hacienda-like estate

Hispano-Moresque Pertaining to Ibero-Islamic origins, especially pottery wares, types, and decoration

hurin (Q) Lower ranked, as in moiety organization

INAA Instrumental neutron activation analysis

kallanka (Q) Multi-door great hall

kancha (Q) Walled residential compound at Inka sites

kero (Q) Andean beaker-like drinking vessel of wood, pottery, or metal

khipu (Q) Knotted cords used to record economic and other information; *quipu*

koli Lively, sociable personality; language spoken in southwestern coastal Peru (capped)

kuraka (Q) Non-Inka Indigenous leader; *cacique*

lagar (Sp) Tank-like facility for crushing grapes to yield juice

limpieza de sangre (Sp) "Purity of blood"; absence of Muslim or Jewish biological heritage

loza (Sp) Pottery for table service, of various grades (e.g., *fina, común*)

majolica (Sp), **maiólica** (It) Tin-enameled fine earthenware pottery produced in the Iberian Peninsula and Italy

melado (Sp) Honey-colored glaze on pottery

mitmaq (Q) Worker moved from home community under Inka rule

moiety One of two ranked divisions of a community based on descent

mojon (Sp) Boundary marker

molle (Sp) Andean tree with peppery red berries (*Schinus molle*; peppertree)

morado (Sp) Manganese-based purplish-brownish-black pigment used in tin-enameled pottery decoration; see *verde y morado*

morisco (Sp) Muslim newly converted to Christianity

mosto (Sp) Must; unfermented grape juice; *caldo*

mozo (Sp) Junior, the younger

mudéjar (Sp) Islamic-style art and artisan in Christian kingdoms

olla (Sp) Ceramic cooking pot

parcialidad (Sp) Moiety

patronato real (Sp) Royal patronage; rights and obligations granted by the Catholic Church to the Spanish crown to carry out many religious duties

peninsular (Sp) Person in the colonies who was born in Spain

picota (Sp) Pillory

pirca (Sp) Construction of fieldstone

pisco (Sp) Grape brandy

pukara (Q) Hilltop fortification

qollqa (Q) Aboveground storage structures, primarily constructed of stone

quebrada (Sp) Lit. "broken"; a mountain gorge or valley

quincha (Q) Cane, or cane and clay, used in construction

Reconquista (Sp) "Reconquest"; the Christian campaign, 718–1492, to take back the Iberian Peninsula from Muslim rule

reducción (Sp) Colonial policy forcing resettlement of Indigenous populations (*congregación*)

Requerimento (Sp) "Requirement"; a legal document, written in Spanish, read to newly conquered peoples demanding their submission

retablo (Sp) Large, elaborately carved, painted, and gilded wooden structure behind the main altar of a church, displaying devotional images of saints and other holy figures or scenes

señorío (Sp) Petty kingdom, territory of a lord

suyu (Q) Quadrant

tambo (Sp), **tampu** (Q) Storage facility and way-station, usually on Inka roads

tinaja (Sp) Large earthenware jars used for storage, particularly of wine

tonel (Sp) Large, wooden, barrel-like container for fermenting and storing wine

trapiche (Sp) Mill for crushing sugarcane

tupu (Q) Large metal shawl pin with a broad, usually rounded, end

urpu (Q) *Aríbalo, aryballus*; decorated jar with a tall, flaring neck

usnu (Q) Carved stone altar platform, often an outcrop, in conquered territories

vecino (Sp) Wealthy, property-owning citizen

verde y morado (Sp) Green and brown-black; traditional Ibero-Islamic pottery decoration painted on tin-enameled ware since medieval times

waka (Q) Natural and cultural shrines; *huaca*

wichuña (Q) Weaving tool made from a camelid metapodial

References

ARCHIVAL SOURCES
(NUMBERING FROM *VINTAGE MOQUEGUA* [RICE 2011B: 293–96])

AAA1 Villa de Moquegua. Diezmos. Archivo Arzobispal de Arequipa. July 15, 1768.

GGR1 Apuntes referentes a documentos moqueguanos, cortesía de Guillermo Galdos Rodríguez, director del Archivo Departamental de Arequipa. Notes given to Lorenzo Huertas, 1988.

ARCHIVO DEPARTAMENTAL DE MOQUEGUA (ADM)
Documents by Escribano Diego Dávila, 1587–95, 1596–1600, 1610–14, 1616–19

ADM 5 Asiento of Yaravico in the valle de Moquegua, November 17, 1593. Donation of land. Fol. 281r–282v.

ADM 7 Pueblo de Moquegua, April 13, 1594. Power of attorney, kurakas of Torata. Fol. 326r–327v.

ADM 10 Asiento de Escapalaque, valle de Moquegua, November 27, 1594. Power of attorney. Fol. 373r–365v.

ADM 19 Valle de Moquegua, October 24, 1599. Codicil to will. Fol. 335r–335v.

ADM 44 November 12, 1610. Sale of Estrada estate in Yaravico. Fol. 136r–142v.

ADM 46 Pueblo y valle de Moquegua, March 29, 1615. Company to ship Yaravico wine, sugar, and syrup. Fol. 586r–587v.

ADM 48 Valle de Moquegua, June 25, 1616. Sale of Yaravico. Fol. 78r–81v.

ADM 49 Valle y pueblo de Moquegua, August 24, 1616. Sale of Yaravico. Fol. 110r–113v.

ADM 50 Valle de Moquegua, January 24, 1618. Sale of Yaravico. Fol. 334v–338v.

Other Documents

ADM 58 Villa de Santa Catalina de Guadalcázar, valle de Moquegua, April 28, 1694. Testimony about conditions at Cupina Baja hacienda. Escr. Thomás de Valcárcel, 1693–94, fol. 280v–282r.

ADM 59 Villa de Moquegua, June 22, 1694. Testimony about conditions at Cupina Alta. Escr. Thomás de Valcárcel, 1693–94, fol. 309r–310r.

PRINTED AND INTERNET SOURCES

Acevedo, Sara. 1986. "Trayectoría de la cerámica vidriada en el Perú." In *Vidriados y mayólica del Perú*, by Francisco Stastny and Sara Acevedo, 19–31. Lima: Museo de Arte y de Historia, Universidad Nacional Mayor de San Marcos.

Acuto, Félix A. 2005. "The Materiality of Inka Domination: Landscape, Spectacle, Memory, and Ancestors." In *Global Archaeological Theory: Contextual Voices and Contemporary Thoughts*, ed. Pedro Paulo Funari, Andrés Zarankin, and Emily Stovel, 211–35. New York: Springer. http://dx.doi.org/10.1007/0-306-48652-0_14.

Adelaar, W. 1987. "Commentary on Torero." *Revista Andina* 10: 373–75.

Adorno, Rolena. 1986. *Guaman Poma: Writing and Resistance in Colonial Peru*. Austin: University of Texas Press.

Ainaud de Lasarte, Joan. 1952. "Cerámica y vidrio." *Ars Hispaniae* 10. Editorial Plus Ultra, Madrid.

Ainaud de Lasarte, Joan. 1981. "Cataluña." In *Cerámica esmaltada española*, by Trinidad Sánchez-Pacheco, Maria Dolors Giral, Juan Zozaya, Natacha Seseña, Isabel Alvaro Zamora, Joan Ainaud de Lasarte, María Antonia Casanovas, and Balbina Martínez Caviró, 129–48. Barcelona: Editorial Labor.

Alastaya, Counts of. N.d. http://alastaya.com/history.htm (retrieved 8/12/10).

Alayza y Paz Soldán, Luis. 1987. "El mariscal Domingo Nieto, figura epónima de Moquegua." In *Pequeña antología de Moquegua*, ed. Ismael Pinto Vargas, 97–100. Lima: Ediciones El Virrey.

Alconini, Sonia. 2004. "The Southeastern Inka Frontier against the Chiriguanos: Structure and Dynamics of the Inka Imperial Borderlands." *Latin American Antiquity* 15 (4): 389–418. http://dx.doi.org/10.2307/4141585.

Alconini, Sonia. 2005. "The Dynamics of Military and Cultural Frontiers on the Southeastern Edge of the Inka Empire." In *Untaming the Frontier in Anthropology*,

Archaeology, and History, ed. Bradley J. Parker and Lars Rodseth, 115–46. Tucson: University of Arizona Press.

Aldenderfer, Mark S., ed. 1993. *Domestic Architecture, Ethnicity, and Complementarity in the South-Central Andes*. Iowa City: University of Iowa Press.

Altman, Ida. 1989. *Emigrants and Society. Extremadura and America in the Sixteenth Century*. Berkeley: University of California Press.

Alvaro Zamora, María Isabel. 1978. *Cerámica aragonesa decorada, desde la expulsión de los moriscos a la extinción de los alfares (siglos SVII–fines XIX/comienzos II)*. Zaragoza: Libros Pórtico.

Alvaro Zamora, María Isabel. 1981. "Aragón." In *Cerámica esmaltada española*, by Trinidad Sánchez-Pacheco, Maria Dolors Giral, Juan Zozaya, Natacha Seseña, Isabel Alvaro Zamora, Joan Ainaud de Lasarte, María Antonia Casanovas, and Balbina Martínez Caviró, 111–26. Barcelona: Editorial Labor.

Amerine, M. A., H. W. Berg, and W. V. Cruess. 1972. *The Technology of Wine Making*. 2nd ed. Westport, CT: AVI.

Amith, Jonathan D. 2005. "Place Making and Place Breaking: Migration and the Development Cycle of Community in Colonial Mexico." *American Ethnologist* 32 (1): 159–79. http://dx.doi.org/10.1525/ae.2005.32.1.159.

Andrien, Kenneth J. 1991. "Spaniards, Andeans, and the Early Colonial State in Peru." In *Transatlantic Encounters: Europeans and Andeans in the Sixteenth Century*, ed. Kenneth J. Andrien and Rolena Adorno, 121–48. Berkeley: University of California Press.

Anonymous. 1998. "Moquegua." In *Gran Enciclopedia del Perú, 807–43*. Lima: Lexus Editores.

Appadurai, Arjun. 1986. "Introduction: Commodities and the Politics of Value." In *The Social Life of Things: Commodities in Cultural Perspective*, ed. Arjun Appadurai, 3–63. Cambridge: Cambridge University Press.

Aragó, Buenaventura. 1878. *Tratado práctico-teórico sobre la fabricación, mejoramiento y conservación de los vinos españolas*. Madrid: Librería de Anlló y Rodríguez.

Arkush, Elizabeth. 2008. "War, Chronology, and Causality in the Titicaca Basin." *Latin American Antiquity* 19 (4): 339–73.

Ávilez Moreno, Guadalupe. 1980. "El arte mudéjar en Nueva España en el siglo XVI." *Anuario de Estudios Americanos* 37: 649–63.

Bailey, Gauvin Alexander. 2010. *The Andean Hybrid Baroque: Convergent Cultures in the Churches of Colonial Peru*. Notre Dame, IN: Notre Dame University Press.

Baker, Henry A. 1968. "Archaeological Excavations at Panama La Vieja, 1968." MA thesis, Department of Anthropology, University of Florida, Gainesville.

Bakewell, Peter. 2011. "1512–1513. The Laws of Burgos." http://faculty.smu.edu/bakewell/BAKEWELL/texts/burgoslaws.html (retrieved 2/25/11).

Banaji, Jairus. 2003. "Islam, the Mediterranean and the Rise of Capitalism." Paper presented at the Conference on Theory as History: Ernest Mandel's Historical Analysis of World Capitalism, Amsterdam, November 10–11. http://sacw.net/left/Amsterdam JB.pdf (retrieved 7/15/12). Revised and published in *Historical Materialism* 15 (1) (2007): 47–74.

Barber, Edwin Atlee. 1915a. *Hispano-Moresque Pottery in the Collection of the Hispanic Society of America*. New York: Hispanic Society of America.

Barber, Edwin Atlee. 1915b. *Mexican Maiolica in the Collection of the Hispanic Society of America*. New York: Hispanic Society of America.

Barriga R., Victor M. 1939. *Documentos para la historia de Arequipa, 1534–1558. Tomo I. Documentos inéditos de los archivos de Arequipa*. Arequipa, Peru: Editorial La Colmena.

Barriga R., Victor M. 1955. *Documentos para la historia de Arequipa, 1535–1580. Tomo III. Documentos inéditos del Archivo General de Indias*. Arequipa, Peru: Editorial La Colmena.

Barua, R. Victor. 1961. "Reconocimiento geológico—zona de Tacna y Moquegua." *Segundo Congreso Nacional de Geología, Anales*, part I, vol. 26, 35–59. Sociedad Geológica del Peru, Lima.

Basadre, Jorge. 1987. "Semblanza de Nieto." In *Pequeña antología de Moquegua*, ed. Ismael Pinto Vargas, 109–11. Lima: Ediciones El Virrey.

Bastien, Joseph W. 1978. "Mountain/Body Metaphor in the Andes." *Bulletin of the French Institute for Andean Studies* 7 (1–2): 87–103.

Bastien, Joseph W. 1985. "Qollahuaya-Andean Body Concepts: A Topographical-Hydraulic Model of Physiology." *American Anthropologist* 87 (3): 595–611. http://dx.doi.org/10.1525/aa.1985.87.3.02a00050.

Bauer, Brian S. 1992. *The Development of the Inca State*. Austin: University of Texas Press.

Bauer, Brian S. 1998. *The Sacred Landscape of the Inca: The Cusco Ceque System*. Austin: University of Texas Press.

Bauer, Brian S., and Charles Stanish. 2001. *Ritual and Pilgrimage in the Ancient Andes: The Islands of the Sun and the Moon*. Austin: University of Texas Press.

Bawden, Garth. 1993. "An Archaeological Study of Social Structure and Ethnic Replacement in Residential Architecture of the Tumilaca Valley." In *Domestic Architecture, Ethnicity, and Complementarity in the South-Central Andes*, ed. Mark S. Aldenderfer, 42–54. Iowa City: University of Iowa Press.

Bellido Bravo, Eleodoro. 1979. "Geología del cuadrángulo de Moquegua." *Boletín no. 15, serie A: Carta geológica nacional*: 35-u. Instituto Geológico, Minero y Metalúrgico, Lima.

Benavente, T. 1982. "La cerámica en el Cuzco." In *Arqueología de Cuzco*, ed. Italo Oberti Rodríguez, 169–76. Cusco, Peru: Ediciones Instituto Nacional de Cultura Región Cusco.

Bender, Barbara. 1993. "Introduction." In *Landscape: Politics and Perspectives*, ed. Barbara Bender, 1–18. Oxford: Berg.

Berdoulay, Vincent. 1989. "Place, Meaning, and Discourse in French Language Geography." In *The Power of Place*, ed. John A. Agnew and James S. Duncan, 124–39. London: Unwin Hyman.

Bernales Ballesteros, J. 1986. "Evolución estilística de Lima: Del mudéjar al neoclásico." In *Lima a los 450 años*, ed. Antonio Ortíz de Zevallos, 105–28. Lima: Universidad del Pacífico.

Blackman, M. James, Patricia Fournier, and Ronald L. Bishop. 2006. "Complejidad e interacción social en el México colonial: Identidad, producción, intercambio y consumo de lozas de tradición ibérica, con base en análisis de activación neutrónica." *Cuicuilco* 13(36): 203–22.

Bloom, J. M., and S. S. Blair. 2009. "A Global Guide to Islamic Art." *Saudi Aramco World* 60 (1): 32–43. http://www.saudiaramcoworld.com/issue/200901/a.global.guide.to.islamic.art.htm (retrieved 6/20/13).

Bloom, Jonathan, and Sheila Blair. 2011. "Introduction." In *And Diverse Are Their Hues. Color in Islamic Art and Culture*, ed. Jonathan Bloom and Sheila Blair, 1–51. New Haven, CT: Yale University Press.

Borrás Gualis, Gonzalo. 1993. "El arte mudéjar: Estado actual de la cuestión." In *Mudéjar iberoamericano: Una expresión de dos mundos*, ed. Ignacio Henares Cuéllar and R. López Guzmán, 9–19. Granada, Spain: Monográfica Arte y Arqueología, Universidad de Granada.

Borstel, Christopher L., Geoffrey W. Conrad, and Keith P. Jacobi. 1989. "Analysis of Exposed Architecture at San Antonio: Foundation for an Excavation Strategy." In *Ecology, Settlement and History in the Osmore Drainage, Peru*, ed. Don S. Rice, Charles Stanish, and Phillip R. Scarr, 371–94. Oxford: BAR International Series 545 (ii).

Bouysse-Cassagne, Thérèse. 1986. "Urco and Uma: Aymara Concepts of Space." In *Anthropological History of Andean Polities*, ed. John V. Murra, Nathan Wachtel, and Jacques Revel, 201–27. Cambridge: Cambridge University Press. http://dx.doi.org/10.1017/CBO9780511753091.018.

Bowser, Brenda. 2000. "From Pottery to Politics: An Ethnoarchaeological Study of Political Factionalism, Ethnicity, and Domestic Pottery Style in the Ecuadorian Amazon." *Journal of Archaeological Method and Theory* 7 (3): 219–48. http://dx.doi.org/10.1023/A:1026510620824.

Boxer, C. R. 1975. "The Cult of Mary and the Practice of Misogyny." In *Mary and Misogyny: Women in Iberian Expansion Overseas, 1415–1815, Some Facts, Fancies, and Possibilities*, by C. R. Boxer, 97–114. London: Duckworth.

Boyd-Bowman, Peter. 1968. *Indice geobiográfico de cuarenta mil pobladores españoles de América en el siglo XVI*, vol. 2: *1520–1539*. Mexico City: Editorial Jus.

Boyd-Bowman, Peter. 1973. "Patterns of Spanish Emigration to the New World (1493–1580)." Ms. in the file of the author.

Boyd-Bowman, Peter. 1976. "Patterns of Spanish Emigration to the Indies until 1600." *Hispanic American Historical Review* (HAHR) 56 (4): 580–604.

Bras, Cristina, Fernanda Gumilar, Norberto Gandini, Alejandra Minetti, and Adriana Ferrero. 2011. "Evaluation of the Acute Dermal Exposure of the Ethanolic and Hexanic Extracts from Leaves of *Schinus molle* var. *areira* L. in Rats." *Journal of Ethnopharmacology* 137 (3): 1450–56. http://dx.doi.org/10.1016/j.jep.2011.08.036.

Braudel, Fernand. 1981. *The Structures of Everyday Life: Civilization and Capitalism, Fifteenth–Eighteenth Century*, vol. 1. New York: Harper and Row.

Bray, Tamara L. 2000. "Inca Iconography: The Art of Empire in the Andes." *RES* 38: 168–84.

Bray, Tamara L. 2003. "Inka Pottery as Culinary Equipment: Food, Feasting, and Gender in Imperial State Design." *Latin American Antiquity* 14 (1): 3–28. http://dx.doi.org/10.2307/972232.

Brodman, James William. 1986. *Ransoming Captives in Crusader Spain: The Order of Merced on the Christian-Islamic Frontier*. Philadelphia: University of Pennsylvania Press.

Browman, David L. 1994. "Titicaca Basin Archaeolinguistics: Uru, Pukina and Aymara A.D. 750–1450." *World Archaeology* 26 (2): 235–51. http://dx.doi.org/10.1080/00438243.1994.9980274.

Brown, Kendall W. 1986. *Bourbons and Brandy: Imperial Reform in Eighteenth-Century Arequipa*. Albuquerque: University of New Mexico Press.

Brown, Peter. 1981. *The Cult of the Saints: Its Rise and Function in Latin Christianity*. Chicago: University of Chicago Press.

Bürgi, Peter T. 1993. "The Inka Empire's Expansion into the Coastal Sierra Region West of Lake Titicaca." PhD dissertation, Department of Anthropology, University of Chicago, Chicago.

Bush, Olga. 2011. "'Designs Always Polychromed or Gilded': The Aesthetics of Color in the Alhambra." In *And Diverse Are Their Hues. Color in Islamic Art and Culture*, ed. Jonathan Bloom and Sheila Blair, 53–75. New Haven, CT: Yale University Press.

Buys, Jozef. 1992. "La cerámica colonial." Paper presented at the 1992 Conference on Historical and Underwater Archaeology, Kingston, Jamaica.

Caiger-Smith, Alan. 1973. *Tin-Glaze Pottery in Europe and the Islamic World: The Tradition of 1,000 Years in Maiolica, Faience and Delftware.* London: Faber.
Campbell, Leon G. 1986. "The Historical Reconquest of 'Peruvian Space.'" *Latin American Research Review* 21(3): 192–205.
Campbell, Lyle. 2000. *American Indian Languages: The Historical Linguistics of Native America.* New York: Oxford University Press.
Canby, Sheila R. 1997. "Islamic Lusterware." In *Pottery in the Making: Ceramic Traditions*, ed. Ian Freestone and David Gaimster, 110–15. Washington, DC: Smithsonian Institution Press.
Cañedo-Argüelles Fábrega, Teresa. 1994. "Cacicazgo y poder en el valle de Moquegua (siglos XVII y XVIII)." *Revista Archivo Arzobispal de Arequipa* 1: 17–30.
Cañedo-Argüelles Fábrega, Teresa. 1995. "Las reducciones indígenas en el sur andino: Estrategias de producción y sus efectos en el medio ambiente." *Revista Complutense de Historia de América* 21: 123–40.
Cañedo-Argüelles Fábrega, Teresa, ed. 2004. *Al sur del márgen: Avatares y límites de una región postergada Moquegua (Perú).* Madrid: Instituto de Estudios Peruanos.
Cañedo-Argüelles Fábrega, Teresa. 2005. *La visita de Juan Gutiérrez Flores al Colesuyo y pleitos por los cacicazgos de Torata y Moquegua.* Lima: Fondo Editorial del Pontificia Universidad Católica del Perú.
Cárdenas Martin, Mercedes. 1971. "Huaca Palomino (Valle del Rímac): Fragmenteria vidriada fina con decoración en colores." *Boletín del Seminario de Arqueología* 10: 61–76. Instituto Riva-Agüero, Pontificia Universidad Católica del Perú, Lima.
Cárdenas Martin, Mercedes. 1973. "Cerámica de transición: Huaca Palomino (Valle del Rímac)." *Boletín del Seminario de Arqueología* 14: 30–34. Lima: Instituto Riva-Agüero, Pontificia Universidad Católica del Perú.
Carswell, J. 1999. "China and the Middle East." *Oriental Art Magazine* 45 (1): 2–14.
Carter, Paul. 1987. *The Road to Botany Bay. An Exploration of Landscape and History.* Minneapolis: University of Minnesota Press.
Casanovas, María Antonia. 1983. *La ceràmica catalana.* Barcelona: Coneguem Catalunya.
Casanovas, María Antonia. 2003. "Ceramics in Domestic Life in Spain." In *Cerámica y Cultura: The Story of Spanish and Mexican Mayólica*, ed. Robin Farwell Gavin, Donna Pierce, and Alfonso Pleguezuelo, 49–75. Santa Fe, NM: Museum of International Folk Art.
Cavagnaro Orellana, Luis. 1986. *Materiales para la historia de Tacna*, vol. 1: *Cultura autóctona.* Tacna, Peru: Cooperativa San Pedro de Tacna.
Cavagnaro Orellana, Luis. 1988. *Materiales para la historia de Tacna*, vol. 2: *Dominación hispánica (s. XIV).* Tacna, Peru: Cooperativa San Pedro de Tacna.
CDI (Cobalt Development Institute). 2006. "Cobalt Facts: History." http://www.thecdi .com/cdi/images/documents/facts/COBALT_FACTS-History.pdf (retrieved 6/17/12).

CDI (Cobalt Development Institute). 2011. "Cobalt Facts." http://www.thecdi.com/cobaltfacts.php (retrieved 6/17/12).

Celestino, Olinda. 1983. "Cofradía: Continuidad y transformación de la sociedad andina." *Allpanchis* 18: 147–66.

Chabert, F., and L. Dubosc. 1905. "Estudio sobre el viñedo de Moquegua y su reconstitución." *Boletín del Ministerio de Fomento* 8: 10–83.

Chacaltana, Sofía, and Donna Nash. 2009. "Análisis de las ofrendas en los Andes sur centrales. Las ofrendas como tradición de orígen prehispánico: El caso de Cerro Baúl, valle alto de Moquegua." In *Andes 7, Arqueología del Área Centro Sur Andina*, ed. Mariusz S. Ziółkowski, Justin Jennings, Franco Luis Augusto Belan, and Andrea Drusini, 155–79. Warsaw: Warsaw University Press.

Chapman, John. 2008. "Object Fragmentation and Past Landscapes." In *Handbook of Landscape Archaeology*, ed. Bruno David and Julian Thomas, 187–201. Walnut Creek, CA: Left Coast Press.

Chatfield, Melissa. 2007. "From Inca to Spanish Colonial: Transitions in Ceramic Technology." PhD dissertation, Department of Anthropology, University of California, Santa Barbara.

Chatfield, Melissa. 2010. "Tracing Firing Technology through Clay Properties in Cuzco, Peru." *Journal of Archaeological Science* 37 (4): 727–36. http://dx.doi.org/10.1016/j.jas.2009.11.003.

Chiew, Lim Yah. 2005. "Beitung Shipwreck–Revisit: Changsha Blue and Copper Red Wares and the Religious Motifs." http://www.koh-antique.com/lyc/belitung_shipwreck.htm (retrieved 6/17/12).

Christian, William A., Jr. 1981. *Local Religion in Sixteenth-Century Spain*. Princeton, NJ: Princeton University Press.

Christian, William A., Jr. 2010. "Images as Beings in Early Modern Spain." In *Sacred Spain. Art and Belief in the Spanish World*, ed. Ronda Kasl, 75–99. New Haven, CT: Indianapolis Museum of Art and Yale University Press.

Cieza de León, Pedro de. 1967 [1553]. *El señorío de los Incas* (second part of the *Crónica del Perú*). Lima: Fuentes e Investigaciones para la Historia del Perú, Instituto de Estudios Peruanos.

Cieza de León, Pedro de. 2001. *The Travels of Pedro de Cieza de Léon, A.D. 1532–50, Contained in the First Part of His Chronicle of Peru*. Trans. and ed. Clements R. Markham. London: Hakluyt Society.

Cieza de León, Pedro de. 2005. *Crónica del Perú, el señorío de los Incas*. Ed. Franklin Pease G.Y. Caracas: Fundación Biblioteca Ayacucho.

Classen, Constance. 1993. *Inca Cosmology and the Human Body*. Salt Lake City: University of Utah Press.

Clement, Christopher O., and Michael E. Moseley. 1989. "Agricultural Dynamics in the Andes." In *Ecology, Settlement and History in the Osmore Drainage, Peru*, Part 2, ed. Don S. Rice, Charles Stanish, and Phillip R. Scarr, 435–55. Oxford: BAR International Series 545, British Archaeological Reports.

Cobo, Fr. Bernabé. 1890 [1653]. *Historia del nuevo mundo*, tomo I. Sevilla: Sociedad de Bibliófilos Andaluces.

Cobo, Fr. Bernabé. 1891 [1653]. *Historia del nuevo mundo*, tomo II. Sevilla: Sociedad de Bibliófilos Andaluces.

Cobo, Fr. Bernabé. 1983 [1653]. *History of the Inca Empire*. Trans. and ed. Roland Hamilton. Austin: University of Texas Press.

Conlee, Christina A., Jalh Dulanto, Carol J. Mackey, and Charles Stanish. 2004. "Late Prehispanic Sociopolitical Complexity." In *Andean Archaeology*, ed. Helaine Silverman, 209–36. Malden, MA: Blackwell.

Connors McQuade, Margaret E. 2003. "The Emergence of a Mexican Tile Tradition." In *Cerámica y Cultura: The Story of Spanish and Mexican Mayólica*, ed. Robin Farwell Gavin, Donna Pierce, and Alfonso Pleguezuelo, 204–25. Santa Fe, NM: Museum of International Folk Art.

Conrad, Geoffrey W. 1993. "Domestic Architecture of the Estuquiña Phase: Estuquiña and San Antonio." In *Domestic Architecture, Ethnicity, and Complementarity in the South-Central Andes*, ed. Mark S. Aldenderfer, 55–65. Iowa City: University of Iowa Press.

Conrad, Geoffrey W., and Ann D. Webster. 1989. "Household Unit Patterning at San Antonio." In *Ecology, Settlement and History in the Osmore Drainage, Peru*, ed. Don S. Rice, Charles Stanish, and Phillip R. Scarr, 395–414. Oxford: BAR International Series 545 (ii).

Cornejo Buroncle, Jorge. 1960. *Derroteros de arte cuzqueño*. Cusco: n.p.

Corteguera, L. R. 2002. *For the Common Good: Popular Politics in Barcelona, 1580–1640*. Ithaca, NY: Cornell University Press.

Covey, R. Alan. 2006. "Chronology, Succession, and Sovereignty: The Politics of Inka Historiography and Its Modern Interpretation." *Comparative Studies in Society and History* 48 (1): 169–99. http://dx.doi.org/10.1017/S0010417506000077.

Covey, R. Alan. 2008. "Multiregional Perspectives on the Archaeology of the Andes during the Late Intermediate Period (c. A.D. 1000–1400)." *Journal of Archaeological Research* 16 (3): 287–338. http://dx.doi.org/10.1007/s10814-008-9021-7.

Covey, R. Alan. 2009. "Inka Agricultural Intensification in the Imperial Heartland and Provinces." In *Andean Civilization: A Tribute to Michael E. Moseley*, ed. Joyce Marcus and Patrick Ryan Williams, 365–77. Monograph 63. Los Angeles: Cotsen Institute of Archaeology, University of California.

Crosby, Alfred. 1972. *The Columbian Exchange: Biological and Cultural Consequences of 1492*. New York: Praeger.

Crouch, Dora P. 1991. "Roman Models for Spanish Colonization." In *The Spanish Borderlands in Pan-American Perspective. Columbian Consequences*, vol. 3, ed. David Hurst Thomas, 21–35. Washington, DC: Smithsonian Institution Press.

Crouch, Dora P., Daniel J. Garr, and Axel Mundigo. 1982. *Spanish City Planning in North America*. Cambridge: MIT Press.

Crow, John A. 1985. *Spain: The Root and the Flower; An Interpretation of Spain and the Spanish People*. 3d ed. Berkeley: University of California Press.

Cummins, Thomas B.F. 1988. "Abstraction to Narration: Kero Imagery of Peru and the Colonial Alteration of Native Identity." PhD dissertation, Department of Art History, University of California, Los Angeles.

Cummins, Thomas B.F. 2002a. "Forms of Andean Colonial Towns, Free Will, and Marriage." In *The Archaeology of Colonialism*, ed. Claire L. Lyons and John K. Papadopoulos, 199–240. Los Angeles: Getty Research Institute.

Cummins, Thomas B.F. 2002b. *Toasts with the Inca: Andean Abstraction and Colonial Images on Quero Vessels*. Ann Arbor: University of Michigan Press.

Cúneo-Vidal, Rómulo. 1978. *Diccionario histórico-biográfico del sur del Perú, vol. XI*. Lima: Gráfica Morsom, S.A.

Cushner, Nicholas P. 1980. *Lords of the Land: Sugar, Wine and Jesuit Estates of Coastal Peru, 1600–1767*. Albany: State University of New York Press.

D'Altroy, Terence N., and Katharina Schreiber. 2004. "Andean Empires." In *Andean Archaeology*, ed. Helaine Silverman, 255–79. Malden, MA: Blackwell.

David, Bruno, and Julian Thomas, eds. 2008. *Handbook of Landscape Archaeology*. Walnut Creek, CA: Left Coast Press.

Davies, Keith A. 1975. "La tenencia de la tierra en Arequipa colonial, 1540–1560." *Historia* 1: 29–46.

Davies, Keith A. 1984. *Landowners in Colonial Peru*. Austin: University of Texas Press.

Deagan, Kathleen A. 1981. "Downtown Survey: The Discovery of Sixteenth-Century St. Augustine in an Urban Area." *American Antiquity* 46: 626–34.

Deagan, Kathleen. 1983. *Spanish St. Augustine: The Archaeology of a Colonial Creole Community*. New York: Academic Press.

Deagan, Kathleen. 1985. "The Archaeology of Sixteenth Century St. Augustine." *Florida Anthropologist* 38 (1–2): 6–33.

Deagan, Kathleen A. 1987. *Artifacts of the Spanish Colonies of Florida and the Caribbean, 1500–1800, vol. 1: Ceramics, Glassware, and Beads*. Washington, DC: Smithsonian Institution Press.

Dean, Carolyn. 2007. "The Inka Married the Earth: Integrated Outcrops and the Making of Place." *Art Bulletin* 89 (3): 502–18.

Dean, Carolyn, and Dana Leibsohn. 2003. "Hybridity and Its Discontents: Considering Visual Culture in Colonial Spanish America." *Colonial Latin American Review* 12 (1): 5–35. http://dx.doi.org/10.1080/10609160302341.

deFrance, Susan Daggett. 1993. "Ecological Imperialism in the South-Central Andes: Faunal Data from Spanish Colonial Settlements in the Moquegua and Torata Valleys." PhD dissertation, Department of Anthropology, University of Florida, Gainesville. University Microfilms International, Ann Arbor, MI.

deFrance, Susan Daggett. 1996. "Iberian Foodways in the Moquegua and Torata Valleys of Southern Peru." *Historical Archaeology* 30 (3): 20–48.

del Busto Duthurburu, José Antonio. 1981. *La hueste perulera (selección)*. Lima: Pontificia Universidad Católica del Perú.

Denegri Luna, Félix. 1987. "La valentia de Nieto." In *Pequeña antología de Moquegua*, ed. Ismael Pinto Vargas, 100–109. Lima: Ediciones El Virrey.

de Silva, Shanaka I., and Gregory A. Zielinski. 1998. "Global Influence of the A.D. 1600 Eruption of Huaynaputina, Peru." *Nature* 393 (June 4): 455–58.

Díaz del Castillo, Bernal. 1998. *Historia verdadera de la conquista de la Nueva España*. Mexico City: Editorial Porrúa.

Diez de San Miguel, Garci. 1964. *Visita hecha a la provincia de Chucuito por Garci Diez de San Miguel en el año 1567*. Documentos Regionales para la Etnología y Etnohistoria Andina, vol.1. Lima: Ediciones de la Casa de la Cultura del Perú.

Dillehay, Tom E. 2003. "El colonialismo Inka, el consumo de chicha y los festines desde una perspectiva de banquetes políticos." *Boletín de Arqueología PUCP* 7: 355–63.

Dobyns, Henry F., and Paul L. Doughty. 1976. *Peru: A Cultural History*. New York: Oxford University Press.

Dodds, Jerilyn D., and Daniel Walker. 1992. "Introduction." In *Al-Andalus: The Art of Islamic Spain*, ed. Jerilyn D. Dodds, xix–xxiii. New York: Metropolitan Museum of Art.

Dornan, Jennifer L. 2002. "Agency and Archaeology: Past, Present, and Future Directions." *Journal of Archaeological Method and Theory* 9 (4): 303–29. http://dx.doi.org/10.1023/A:1021318432161.

Dregne, Harold E. 1968. "Appraisal of Research on Surface Materials of Desert Environments." In *Deserts of the World: An Appraisal of Research into Their Physical and Biological Environments*, ed. William G. McGinnies, Bram J. Goldman, and Patricia Paylore, 287–377. Tucson: University of Arizona Press.

Duncan, R. J. 1998. *The Ceramics of Ráquira, Colombia: Gender, Work, and Economic Change*. Gainesville: University Press of Florida.

Dunning, Nicholas P., Vernon Scarborough, Fred Valdez, Sheryl Luzzadder-Beach, Timothy Beach, and John G. Jones. 1999. "Temple Mountains, Sacred Lakes, Fertile Fields: Ancient Maya Landscapes in Northwestern Belize." *Antiquity* 73 (3): 650–60.

Dussel, Enrique. 1981. *A History of the Church in Latin America: Colonialism to Liberation (1492–1979)*. Trans. Alan Neely. Grand Rapids, MI: William B. Eerdmans.

Earls, J., and Irene Silverblatt. 1978. "La realidad física y social en la cosmología andina." *Proceedings of the 42nd International Congress of Americanists* 4: 299–325.

Eekhout, Peter, and Nathalie Danis. 2004. "Los tocapus reales en Guamán Poma: ¿Una heráldica Incaica?" *Boletín de Arqueología PUCP* 8 (3): 305–23.

Elliott, John H. 1964. *Imperial Spain, 1469–1716*. New York: St. Martin's.

Fairbanks, Charles H. 1966. "A Feldspar-Inlaid Ceramic Type from Spanish Colonial Sites." *American Antiquity* 31 (3): 430–32. http://dx.doi.org/10.2307/2694749.

Feld, Steven. 1996. "Waterfalls of Song: An Acoustemology of Place Resounding in Bosavi, Papua New Guinea." In *Senses of Place*, ed. Steven Feld and Keith H. Basso, 91–135. Santa Fe, NM: School of American Research Press.

Fernández, María Luisa. 1993. "Second Flowering: Art of the Mudejars." *Saudi Aramco World* 44 (1): 36–41. http://www.saudiaramcoworld.com/issue/199301/second.flowering-art.of.the.mudejars.htm (retrieved 6/19/13).

Fernández Baca, Jenaro. 1971. *Motivos de ornamentación de la cerámica inca Cuzco*. Lima: Libreria Studium.

Fernández Dávila, Guillermo. 1947. "Origen y genealogía de cuatro familias principales de Moquegua: Fernández Maldonado, Fernández Dávila, Alcazar y Vizcarra." *Revista del Instituto Peruano de Investigaciones Genealógicas* 2: 119–66.

Fierro, Maribel. 2011. "Red and Yellow: Colors and the Quest for Political Legitimacy in the Islamic West." In *And Diverse Are Their Hues. Color in Islamic Art and Culture*, ed. Jonathan Bloom and Sheila Blair, 77–97. New Haven, CT: Yale University Press.

Fisher, Christopher T., and Gary M. Feinman. 2005. "Introduction to 'Landscapes over Time.'" *American Anthropologist* 107 (1): 62–69. http://dx.doi.org/10.1525/aa.2005.107.1.062.

Flecker, Michael. 2000. "A 9th-Century Arab or Indian Shipwreck in Indonesian Waters." *International Journal of Nautical Archaeology* 29 (2): 199–217.

Flecker, Michael. 2001. "A Ninth-Century AD Arab or Indian Shipwreck in Indonesia: First Evidence for Direct Trade with China." *World Archaeology* 32 (3): 335–54. http://dx.doi.org/10.1080/00438240120048662.

Flores Espinoza, Isabel. 1981. "La cerámica." In *Investigación arqueológica-historica de la Casa Osambela (o de Oquendo)–Lima*, by Isabel Flores Espinoza, Rubén García Soto, and Lorenzo Huertas V., 34–59. Lima: Instituto Nacional de Cultura.

Flynn, Maureen M. 1985. "Charitable Ritual in Late Medieval and Early Modern Spain." *Sixteenth Century Journal* 16 (3): 335–48. http://dx.doi.org/10.2307/2540221.

Flynn, Maureen M. 1989. *Sacred Charity. Confraternities and Social Welfare in Spain, 1400–1700*. Ithaca, NY: Cornell University Press.

Foshag, William F., and Carl Fries Jr. 1942. "Tin Deposits of the Republic of Mexico." *Geologic Investigations in the American Republics, 1941–42, Bulletin 953-C*, 99–176. Washington, DC: United States Government Printing Office.

Foster, George M. 1953. "Cofradía and Compadrazgo in Spain and Spanish America." *Southwestern Journal of Anthropology* 9 (1): 1–28.

Fournier, Patricia, and M. James Blackman. 2008. "Production, Exchange and Consumption of Glazed Wares in New Spain: Formation of a Database of Elemental Composition through INAA." Report to FAMSI. http://www.famsi.org/reports/06014/06014Fournier.pdf.

Fournier-García, Patricia. 1989. "20 tiestos de mayólica procedentes de Ecuador." In *Tres estudios sobre cerámica histórica*, ed. Patricia Fournier-García, M. de L. Fournier, and E. Silva, 62–66. Mexico City: Instituto Nacional de Antropología e Historia.

Fournier-García, Patricia. 1997. "Tendencias de consumo en México durante los períodos colonial e independiente." In *Approaches to the Historical Archaeology of Mexico, Central and South America*, ed. Janine Gasco, Greg Charles Smith, and Patricia Fournier-García, 49–58. Institute of Archaeology Monograph 38. Los Angeles: University of California.

Fowles, Severin. 2010. "The Southwest School of Landscape Archaeology." *Annual Review of Anthropology* 39 (1): 453–68. http://dx.doi.org/10.1146/annurev.anthro.012809.105107.

Frake, Charles O. 1996. "Pleasant Places, Past Times, and Sheltered Identity in Rural East Anglia." In *Senses of Place*, ed. Steven Feld and Keith H. Basso, 229–57. Santa Fe, NM: School of Advanced Research Press.

Francis, Alan David. 1972. *The Wine Trade*. London: Adam and Charles Black.

Fraser, Valerie. 1990. *The Architecture of Conquest: Building in the Viceroyalty of Peru, 1535–1635*. Cambridge: Cambridge University Press.

Freestone, Ian. 1991. "Technical Examination of Neo-Assyrian Glazed Wall Plaques." *Iraq* 53: 55–58.

Friedrich, Margaret Hardin. 1970. "Design Structure and Social Interaction: Archaeological Implications of an Ethnographic Analysis." *American Antiquity* 35 (3): 332–43. http://dx.doi.org/10.2307/278343.

Frothingham, A. W. 1969. *Tile Panels of Spain, 1500–1650*. New York: Hispanic Society of America.

Funari, Pedro Paulo A. 1996. "Historical Archaeology in Brazil, Uruguay, and Argentina." *World Archaeological Bulletin* 7: 51–62.

Funari, Pedro Paulo A. 1997. "Archaeology, History, and Historical Archaeology in South America." *International Journal of Historical Archaeology* 1 (3): 189–206. http://dx.doi.org/10.1023/A:1027396931403.

Gade, Daniel W. 1975. *Plants, Man and the Land in the Vilcanota Valley of Peru*. The Hague: Dr. W. Junk B. V. Publishers.

Gade, Daniel W. 1992. "Landscape, System, and Identity in the Post-Conquest Andes." *Annals of the Association of American Geographers* 82 (3): 460–77. http://dx.doi.org/10.1111/j.1467-8306.1992.tb01970.x.

Gade, Daniel W., and Mario Escobar. 1982. "Village Settlement and the Colonial Legacy in Southern Peru." *Geographical Review* 72 (4): 430–49. http://dx.doi.org/10.2307/214595.

Gaimster, David, ed. 1999a. *Maiolica in the North: The Archaeology of Tin-Glazed Earthenware in North-West Europe c. 1500–1600*. British Museum Occasional Paper 122. London: British Museum Press.

Gaimster, David. 1999b. "Maiolica in the North: The Shock of the New." In *Maiolica in the North: The Archaeology of Tin-Glazed Earthenware in North-West Europe c. 1500–1600*, ed. David Gaimster, 1–3. British Museum Occasional Paper 122. London: British Museum Press.

Galdos Rodríguez, Guillermo. 1984. "Cuando el Kollisuyu incaico devino en Colesuyu colonial." *Revista del Archivo General de la Nación* 7: 177–84.

Galdos Rodríguez, Guillermo. 1985. *Kuntisuyu, lo que encontraron los españoles*. Lima: Fundación M. J. Bustamante de la Fuente.

Galdos Rodríguez, Guillermo. 1990. "Naciones ancestrales y la conquista incaica." In *Historia General de Arequipa*, ed. Máximo Neira Avendaño, Guillermo Galdos Rodríguez, Alejandro Málaga Medina, Eusebio Quiroz Paz Soldán, and Jorge G. Carpio Muñoz, 185–214. Lima: Fundación M. J. Bustamante de la Fuente.

Galdos Rodríguez, Guillermo. 1996. *Una ciudad para la historia, una historia para la ciudad: Arequipa en el siglo XX*. Arequipa, Peru: Ediciones de la Universidad Nacional de San Agustín.

García-Bryce, Iñigo L. 2004. *Crafting the Republic: Lima's Artisans and Nation Building in Peru, 1821–1879*. Albuquerque: University of New Mexico Press.

Garcilaso de la Vega, "El Inca." 1987a. "Reducense tres provincias, conquistanse otras llevan colonias; castigan a los que usan veneno." In *Pequeña antología de Moquegua*, ed. Ismael Pinto Vargas, 9–12. Lima: Ediciones El Virrey.

Garcilaso de la Vega, "El Inca." 1987b [1609]. *Royal Commentaries of the Incas and General History of Peru*, part 1. Trans. Harold V. Livermore. Austin: University of Texas Press.

Gasco, Janine L. 1987. "Cacao and the Economic Integration of Native Society in Colonial Soconusco, New Spain." PhD dissertation, Department of Anthropology, University of California, Santa Barbara.

Gasco, Janine, Hector Neff, and G. Evins. 2006. "Postclassic and Colonial Ceramics in the Soconusco: Patterns of Production and Exchange." Paper presented at the 71st Annual Meeting of the Society for American Archaeology, San Juan, Puerto Rico, April 27–30.

Gasparini, Graziano, and Luise Margolies. 1980. *Inca Architecture*. Trans. Patricia J. Lyon. Bloomington: Indiana University Press.

Gavin, Robin Farwell. 2003. "Introduction." In *Cerámica y Cultura: The Story of Spanish and Mexican Mayólica*, ed. Robin Farwell Gavin, Donna Pierce, and Alfonso Pleguezuelo, 1–23. Santa Fe, NM: Museum of International Folk Art.

Gavin, Robin Farwell, Donna Pierce, and Alfonso Pleguezuelo, eds. 2003. *Cerámica y Cultura: The Story of Spanish and Mexican Mayólica*. Santa Fe, NM: Museum of International Folk Art.

Giddens, Anthony. 1982. *A Contemporary Critique of Historical Materialism*. Berkeley: University of California Press.

Gil, Moshe. 1975. "Supplies of Oil in Medieval Egypt: A Geniza Study." *Journal of Near Eastern Studies* 34 (1): 63–73. http://dx.doi.org/10.1086/372396.

Gilmore, David. 1977. "The Class Consciousness of the Andalusian Rural Proletarians in Historical Perspective." *Ethnohistory* 24 (2): 149–61. http://dx.doi.org/10.2307/481740.

Gisbert, Teresa. 1980. *Iconografía y mitos indígenas en el arte*. La Paz: Editorial Gisbert y Cia.

Glave, Luis Miguel. 1986. "Agricultura y capitalismo en la sierra sur del Perú (fines del siglo XIX y comienzos del XX)." In *Estados y naciones en los Andes: Hacía una historia comparativa Bolivia–Colombia–Ecuador–Perú*, vol. 1, ed. J. P. Deler and Y. Sain-Geours, 213–43. Lima: Instituto de Estudios Peruanos and Instituto Francés de Estudios Andinos.

Glick, Thomas F. 2005. *Islamic and Christian Spain in the Early Middle Ages*. 2nd ed. Leiden: Brill.

Glick, Thomas F., and Oriol Pi-Sunyer. 1969. "Acculturation as an Explanatory Concept in Spanish History." *Comparative Studies in Society and History* 11 (2): 136–54. http://dx.doi.org/10.1017/S0010417500005247.

Goggin, John M. 1968. *Spanish Majolica in the New World: Types of the Sixteenth to Eighteenth Centuries*. Publications in Anthropology 72. New Haven, CT: Yale University.

Goldstein, David, and Robin Christine Coleman. 2004. "*Schinus molle* L. (Anacardiaceae) Chicha Production in the Central Andes." *Economic Botany* 58 (4): 523–29. http://dx.doi.org/10.1663/0013-0001(2004)058[0523:SMLACP]2.0.CO;2.

Goldstein, David J., Robin C. Coleman Goldstein, and Patrick Ryan Williams. 2009. "You Are What You Drink: A Sociocultural Reconstruction of Pre-Hispanic Fermented Beverage Use at Cerro Baúl, Moquegua, Peru." In *Drink, Power, and*

Society in the Andes, ed. Justin Jennings and Brenda J. Bowser, 134–66. Gainesville: University Presses of Florida.

Goldstein, Paul. 1993a. "House, Community, and State in the Earliest Tiwanaku Colony: Domestic Patterns and State Integration at Omo M12, Moquegua." In *Domestic Architecture, Ethnicity, and Complementarity in the South-Central Andes*, ed. Mark S. Aldenderfer, 25–41. Iowa City: University of Iowa Press.

Goldstein, Paul. 1993b. "Tiwanaku Temples and State Expansion: A Tiwanaku Sunken-Court Temple in Moquegua, Peru." *Latin American Antiquity* 4 (1): 22–47. http://dx.doi.org/10.2307/972135.

Goldstein, Paul. 2003. "From Stew-Eaters to Maize-Drinkers: The *Chicha* Economy and the Tiwanaku Expansion." In *The Archaeology and Politics of Food and Feasting in Early States and Empires*, ed. Tamara Bray, 143–72. New York: Springer. http://dx.doi.org/10.1007/978-0-306-48246-5_6.

Goldstein, Paul. 2009. "Diasporas within the Ancient State: Tiwanaku as Ayllus in Motion." In *Andean Civilization: A Tribute to Michael E. Moseley*, ed. Joyce Marcus and Patrick Ryan Williams, 277–301. Monograph 63. Los Angeles: Cotsen Institute of Archaeology Press, University of California.

Gómez, P., T. Pasinski, and Patricia Fournier. 2001. "Transferencia tecnológica y filiación étnica: El caso de los loceros novohispanos del siglo XVI." *Amerística* 4(7): 33–66. http://www.academia.edu/947016.

González Martí, M. 1944. *Cerámica del Levante español: Siglos medievales*. 3 vols. Barcelona: Editorial Labor.

Gose, Peter. 2000. "The State as a Chosen Woman: Brideservice and the Feeding of Tributaries in the Inka Empire." *American Anthropologist* 102 (1): 84–97. http://dx.doi.org/10.1525/aa.2000.102.1.84.

Gose, Peter. 2008. *Invaders as Ancestors: On the Intercultural Making and Unmaking of Spanish Colonialism in the Andes*. Toronto: University of Toronto Press.

Graham, Elizabeth. 1998. "Mission Archaeology." *Annual Review of Anthropology* 27 (1): 25–62. http://dx.doi.org/10.1146/annurev.anthro.27.1.25.

Graham, Elizabeth. 2011. *Maya Christians and Their Churches in Sixteenth-Century Belize*. Gainesville: University Press of Florida.

Greenleaf, Richard E. 1971. "Introduction." In *The Roman Catholic Church in Colonial Latin America*, ed. Richard E. Greenleaf, 1–15. New York: Alfred A. Knopf.

Grieve, Patricia E. 2009. *The Eve of Spain: Myths of Origins in the History of Christian, Muslim, and Jewish Conflict*. Baltimore, MD: Johns Hopkins University Press.

Guaman Poma de Ayala, Felipe. 1980 [1615]. *El primer nueva corónica y buen gobierno*. Critical ed. John V. Murra and Rolena Adorno; trans. Jorge L. Urioste. 3 vols. Mexico City: Siglo Veintiuno.

Gudeman, Stephen. 1976. "Saints, Symbols, and Ceremonies." *American Ethnologist* 3 (4): 709–29. http://dx.doi.org/10.1525/ae.1976.3.4.02a00090.

Guíbovich P., Pedro Manuel. 1984. "Indice del protocolo del escribano Diego Dávila (siglo XVI)." In *Contribuciones a los estudios de los Andes centrales*, ed. Shozo Masuda, 174–405. Tokyo: University of Tokyo.

Gupta, Akhil, and James Ferguson. 1997a. "Beyond 'Culture': Space, Identity, and the Politics of Difference." In *Culture, Power, Place: Explorations in Critical Anthropology*, ed. Akhil Gupta and James Ferguson, 33–51. Durham, NC: Duke University Press.

Gupta, Akhil, and James Ferguson. 1997b. "Culture, Power, Place: Ethnography at the End of an Era." In *Culture, Power, Place: Explorations in Critical Anthropology*, ed. Akhil Gupta and James Ferguson, 1–29. Durham, NC: Duke University Press.

Gutiérrez, Ramón. 1993. "Parroquias de indios y reorganización urbana en la evangelización americana." In *Mudíjar iberoamericano: Una expresión de dos mundos*, ed. Ignacio Henares Cuéllar and R. López Guzmán, 213–32. Granada, Spain: Monográfica Arte y Arqueología, Universidad de Granada.

Gutiérrez, Ramón. 2002. *Arquitectura y urbanismo en Iberoamérica: Manuales arte cátedra*. 4th ed. Madrid: Grupo Anaya.

Gutiérrez, Ramón, and Graciela Viñuales. 1977. "Arquitectura en Moquegua." *Documentos de Arquitectura Nacional y Americana* 4: 82–95.

Hall, Linda B. 2004. *Mary, Mother and Warrior: The Virgin in Spain and the Americas*. Austin: University of Texas Press.

Hamer, Frank, and Janet Hamer. 2012. *The Potter's Dictionary of Materials and Techniques*. 5th ed. London: A. C. Black.

Hampe Martínez, Teodoro. 1997. "Los testigos de Santa Rosa (una aproximación social a la identidad criolla en el Perú colonial)." *Revista Complutense de Historia de America* 23: 113–36.

Hanks, William F. 2010. *Converting Words: Maya in the Age of the Cross*. Berkeley: University of California Press. http://dx.doi.org/10.1525/california/9780520257702.001.0001.

Hardesty, Donald L. 2003. "Mining Rushes and Landscape Learning in the Modern World." In *Colonization of Unfamiliar Landscapes: The Archaeology of Adaptation*, ed. Marcy Rockman and James Steele, 81–96. London: Routledge.

Hardin, Margaret A. 1983. "The Structure of Tarascan Pottery Painting." In *Structure and Cognition in Art*, ed. Dorothy K. Washburn, 8–24. Cambridge: Cambridge University Press.

Haring, Clarence Henry. 1963. *The Spanish Empire in America*. New York: Harcourt, Brace, and World.

Harth-Terré, Emilio. 1945. *Artífices en el virreinato del Perú (historia del arte peruano)*. Lima: Torres Aguirre.

Harth-Terré, Emilio. 1965. "La arquitectura mestiza del sur peruano." *Revista Histórica* 28: 285–93.

Harvey, L. P. 1990. *Islamic Spain, 1250–1500*. Chicago: University of Chicago Press.

Hegmon, Michelle, and Stephanie Kulow. 2005. "Painting as Agency, Style as Structure: Innovations in Mimbres Pottery Designs from Southwest New Mexico." *Journal of Archaeological Method and Theory* 12 (4): 313–34. http://dx.doi.org/10.1007/s10816-005-8451-5.

Helms, Mary W. 1993. *Craft and the Kingly Ideal: Art, Trade, and Power*. Austin: University of Texas Press.

Henares Cuéllar, Ignacio, and R. López Guzmán, eds. 1993. *Mudéjar iberoamericano: Una expresión cultural de dos mundos*. Granada, Spain: Monográfica Arte y Arqueología, Universidad de Granada.

Hennessy, Alistair. 1978. *The Frontier in Latin American History*. London: Edward Arnold.

Hillier, Bill. 2008. "Space and Spatiality: What the Built Environment Needs from Social Theory." *Building Research and Information* 36 (3): 216–30. http://dx.doi.org/10.1080/09613210801928073.

Hillier, Bill, and Julienne Hanson. 1984. *The Social Logic of Space*. Cambridge: Cambridge University Press. http://dx.doi.org/10.1017/CBO9780511597237.

Hiltunen, Juha, and Gordon F. McEwan. 2004. "Knowing the Inca Past." In *Andean Archaeology*, ed. Helaine Silverman, 237–54. London: Blackwell.

Holm, Olaf. 1971. "La cerámica colonial del Ecuador (un ensayo preliminar)." Separata no. 116 del *Boletín de la Academia Nacional de Historia* (Julio–Diciembre): 265–78. Quito.

Hughes, M. J. 1991. "Provenance Studies of Spanish Medieval Tin-Glazed Pottery by Neutron Activation Analysis." In *Archaeological Sciences 1989: Proceedings of a Conference on the Application of Scientific Techniques to Archaeology, Bradford, September 1989*, ed. P. Budd, B. Chapman, C. Jackson, R. Janaway, and B. Ottaway, 54–68. Oxbow Monograph 9. Oxford: Oxbow.

Hurst, John G. 1977. "Spanish Pottery Imported into Medieval Britain." *Medieval Archaeology* 21: 68–105.

Hyslop, John. 1979. "El área lupaca bajo el dominio incaico: Un reconocimiento arqueológico." *Histórica* 3 (1): 53–79.

Hyslop, John. 1984. *The Inka Road System*. Orlando: Academic Press.

Hyslop, John. 1990. *Inka Settlement Planning*. Austin: University of Texas Press.

Iñañez, Javier G., Ronald J. Speakman, J. Buxeda i Garrigós, and Michael D. Glascock. 2009. "Chemical Characterization of Tin-Lead Glazed Pottery from the Iberian Peninsula and the Canary Islands: Initial Steps toward a Better Understanding of Spanish Colonial Pottery in the Americas." *Archaeometry* 51 (4): 546–67. http://dx.doi.org/10.1111/j.1475-4754.2008.00431.x.

Ingold, Tim. 1993. "The Temporality of the Landscape." *World Archaeology* 25 (2): 152–74. http://dx.doi.org/10.1080/00438243.1993.9980235.

Isbell, William H., and Alexei Vranich. 2004. "Experiencing the Cities of Wari and Tiwanaku." In *Andean Archaeology*, ed. Helaine Silverman, 167–82. Malden, MA: Blackwell.

Jameson, Frederic. 1991. *Postmodernism, or the Cultural Logic of Late Capitalism*. Durham, NC: Duke University Press.

Jamieson, Ross W. 2000. *Domestic Architecture and Power: The Historical Archaeology of Colonial Ecuador*. Contributions to Global Historical Archaeology. New York: Kluwer/Plenum.

Jamieson, Ross W. 2001. "Majolica in the Early Colonial Andes: The Role of Panamanian Wares." *Latin American Antiquity* 12 (1): 45–58. http://dx.doi.org/10.2307/971756.

Jamieson, Ross W. 2005. "Colonialism, Social Archaeology and *lo Andino*: Historical Archaeology in the Andes." *World Archaeology* 37 (3): 352–72. http://dx.doi.org/10.1080/00438240500168384.

Jamieson, Ross W., and R.G.V. Hancock. 2004. "Neutron Activation Analysis of Colonial Ceramics from Southern Highland Ecuador." *Archaeometry* 46 (4): 569–83. http://dx.doi.org/10.1111/j.1475-4754.2004.00174.x.

Janusek, John Wayne. 2004. *Identity and Power in the Ancient Andes: Tiwanaku Cities through Time*. New York: Routledge. http://dx.doi.org/10.4324/9780203324615.

Jeffery, R. B. 2003. "From Azulejos to Zaguanes: The Islamic Legacy in the Built Environment of Hispano-America." *Journal of the Southwest* 45 (1): 289–327.

Jeffs, Julian. 1982. *Sherry*. London: Faber and Faber.

Jennings, Justin, and Melissa Chatfield. 2009. "Pots, Brewers, and Hosts: Women's Power and the Limits of Central Andean Feasting." In *Drink, Power, and Society in the Andes*, ed. Justin Jennings and Brenda Bowser, 200–231. Gainesville: University Press of Florida. http://dx.doi.org/10.5744/florida/9780813033068.003.0008.

Joel, Emile C., Jacqueline S. Olin, James M. Blackman, and I. L. Barnes. 1988. "Lead Isotope Studies of Spanish, Spanish-Colonial, and Mexican Majolica." In *Proceedings of the 26th International Archaeometry Symposium*, ed. R. M. Farquhar, R.G.V. Hancock, and L. A. Pavlish, 188–95. Toronto: Archaeometry Laboratory, Department of Physics, University of Toronto.

Jones, John G. 1990. "Archaeobotanical Analyses." In Interim Report, Moquegua Bodegas Project, Fifth Season, 1989, ed. Prudence M. Rice, 95–98. Project files.

Jones, John G. 1993. "Analysis of Pollen and Phytoliths in Residue from a Colonial Period Ceramic Vessel." In *Current Research in Phytolith Analysis: Applications in Archaeology and Paleoecology*, ed. Deborah Pearsall and Dolores Piperno, 31–35. Philadelphia: MASCA Research Papers in Science and Archaeology 10.

Jones, Reece. 2010. "The Spatiality of Boundaries." *Progress in Human Geography* 34 (2): 263–67. http://dx.doi.org/10.1177/0309132509340610.

Jornet, A., James M. Blackman, and Jacqueline S. Olin. 1985. "13th to 18th Century Ceramics from the Paterna-Manises Area (Spain)." In *Ancient Technology to Modern Science*, vol. 1, ed. W. David Kingery, 235–55. Columbus, OH: American Ceramic Society.

Joyce, Rosemary A., and Jeanne Lopiparo. 2005. "PostScript: Doing Agency in Archaeology." *Journal of Archaeological Method and Theory* 12 (4): 365–74. http://dx.doi.org/10.1007/s10816-005-8461-3.

Julien, Catherine J. 1979. "Investigaciones recientes en la capital de los Qolla, Hatunqolla, Puno." *Arqueología Peruana*: 199–213. Lima.

Julien, Catherine J. 1983. *Hatunqolla: A View of Inca Rule from the Lake Titicaca Region*. Anthropology, vol. 15. Berkeley: University of California Press.

Julien, Catherine J. 1985. "Guano and Resource Control in Sixteenth-Century Arequipa." In *Andean Ecology and Civilization: An Interdisciplinary Perspective on Andean Ecological Complementarity*, ed. Shozo Masuda, Izumi Shimada, and Craig Morris, 185–231. Tokyo: University of Tokyo Press.

Julien, Catherine J. 1988. "How Inca Decimal Administration Worked." *Ethnohistory* 35 (3): 257–79. http://dx.doi.org/10.2307/481802.

Kamen, Henry. 1997. *The Spanish Inquisition: A Historical Revision*. New Haven, CT: Yale University Press.

Kamen, Henry. 2003. *Empire: How Spain Became a World Power, 1493–1763*. New York: HarperCollins.

Kaufmann, T. D. 2003. "Islam, Art, and Architecture in the Americas." *RES* 43: 43–50.

Kaulicke, Peter, Ryujiro Kondo, Tetsuya Kusuda, and Julinho Zapata. 2003. "Agua, ancestros y arqueología del paisaje." *Boletín de Arqueología PUCP* 7 (2): 27–56.

Kearney, Amanda, and John J. Bradley. 2009. "'Too Strong to Ever Not Be There': Place Names and Emotional Geographies." *Social and Cultural Geography* 10 (1): 77–94. http://dx.doi.org/10.1080/14649360802553210.

Keith, Michael, and Steve Pile. 1993a. "Introduction Part 1: The Politics of Place." In *Place and the Politics of Identity*, ed. Michael Keith and Steve Pile, 1–21. London: Routledge.

Keith, Michael, and Steve Pile. 1993b. "Introduction Part 2: The Place of Politics." In *Place and the Politics of Identity*, ed. Michael Keith and Steve Pile, 22–40. London: Routledge.

Keith, Robert G. 1971. "Encomienda, Hacienda, and Corregimiento in Spanish America: A Structural Analysis." *Hispanic American Historical Review* 51 (3): 431–46. http://dx.doi.org/10.2307/2512690.

Kelemen, Pál. 1971 [1967]. "Colonial Religious Architecture." Reprinted in *The Roman Catholic Church in Colonial Latin America*, ed. Richard E. Greenleaf, 237–50. New York: Alfred A. Knopf.

Kingery, W. David, and M. Aronson. 1990. "On the Technology of Renaissance Maiolica Glazes." *Faenza* 76 (5): 226–35.

Kolata, Alan L. 1982. "Chronology and Settlement Growth at Chan Chan." In *Chan Chan: Andean Desert City*, ed. Michael E. Moseley and Kent C. Day, 67–86. Albuquerque: University of New Mexico Press and School of American Research.

Kolata, Alan L. 1993. *The Tiwanaku: Portrait of an Andean Civilization*. Cambridge, MA: Blackwell.

Kubler, George. 1946. "The Quechua in the Colonial World." In *Handbook of South American Indians*, vol. 2: *The Andean Civilizations*, ed. Julian H. Steward, 331–410. Bureau of American Ethnology Bulletin 143. Washington, DC: Smithsonian Institution.

Kubler, George. 1948. "Towards Absolute Time: Guano Archaeology." *A Reappraisal of Peruvian Archaeology: Memoirs of the Society for American Archaeology* 4: 29–50.

Kuon Cabello, Luis E. 1981. *Retazos de la historia de Moquegua*. Lima: Editorial Abril.

Kuon Cabello, Luis E. 1987. "Santa Fortunata." In *Pequeña antología de Moquegua*, ed. Ismael Pinto Vargas, 139–42. Lima: Ediciones El Virrey.

Kuwayama, George. 1997. *Chinese Ceramics in Colonial Mexico*. Los Angeles: Los Angeles County Museum of Art.

Kuznar, Lawrence A. 1999. "The Inca Empire: Detailing the Complexities of Core/Periphery Interactions." In *World-Systems Theory in Practice: Leadership, Production, and Exchange*, ed. P. Nick Kardulias, 223–40. Lanham, MD: Rowman and Littlefield.

Labib, S. Y. 1969. "Capitalism in Medieval Islam." *Journal of Economic History* 29: 79–96.

La Lone, Darrell E. 1994. "An Andean World-System: Production Transformations under the Inca Empire." In *The Economic Anthropology of the State*, ed. Elizabeth M. Brumfiel, 17–42. Lanham, MD: University Press of America.

La Lone, Darrell E. 2000. "Rise, Fall, and Semiperipheral Development in the Andean World-System." *Journal of World-Systems Research* 6 (1): 68–99.

La Lone, Mary B., and Darrell E. La Lone. 1987. "The Inka State in the Southern Highlands: State Administrative and Production Enclaves." *Ethnohistory* 34 (1): 47–62. http://dx.doi.org/10.2307/482265.

Lamont, Michèle, and Virág Molnár. 2002. "The Study of Boundaries in the Social Sciences." *Annual Review of Sociology* 28 (1): 167–95. http://dx.doi.org/10.1146/annurev.soc.28.110601.141107.

Latour, Bruno. 2005. *Reassembling the Social: An Introduction to Actor-Network-Theory*. Oxford: Oxford University Press.

Lechtman, Heather. 2007. "The Inka and Andean Metallurgical Tradition." In *Variations in the Expression of Inka Power*, ed. Richard Burger, Craig Morris, and Ramiro Matos Mendieta, 313–55. Washington, DC: Dumbarton Oaks.

Lefebvre, Henri. 1991. *The Production of Space*. Trans. Donald Nicholson-Smith. Oxford: Blackwell.

Lemonnier, Pierre. 1986. "The Study of Material Culture Today: Toward an Anthropology of Technical Systems." *Journal of Anthropological Archaeology* 5 (2): 147–86. http://dx.doi.org/10.1016/0278-4165(86)90012-7.

Lemonnier, Pierre. 1993. "Introduction." In *Technological Choices: Transformations in Material Cultures since the Neolithic*, ed. Pierre Lemonnier, 1–35. London: Routledge.

Leone, Mark P. 2005. *The Archaeology of Liberty in an American Capital: Excavations in Annapolis*. Berkeley: University of California Press. http://dx.doi.org/10.1525/california/9780520244504.001.0001.

Levillier, Robert. 1929. *Ordenanzas de Francisco de Toledo, virrey del Perú, 1579–1581*. Madrid: Juan Pueyo.

Lister, Florence C., and Robert H. Lister. 1974. "Maiolica in Colonial Spanish America." *Historical Archaeology* 8: 17–51.

Lister, Florence C., and Robert H. Lister. 1976. *A Descriptive Dictionary for 500 Years of Spanish-Tradition Ceramics (13th through 18th Centuries)*. Special Publication Series 1. Columbia, SC: Society for Historical Archaeology.

Lister, Florence C., and Robert H. Lister. 1982. *Sixteenth Century Maiolica Pottery in the Valley of Mexico*. Anthropological Papers 39. Tucson: University of Arizona.

Lister, Florence C., and Robert H. Lister. 1984. "The Potter's Quarter of Colonial Puebla, Mexico." *Historical Archaeology* 18: 87–102.

Lister, Florence C., and Robert H. Lister. 1987. *Andalusian Ceramics in Spain and New Spain: A Cultural Register from the Third Century B.C. to 1700*. Tucson: University of Arizona Press.

Livermore, Harold V. 1987. "Introduction." In *Royal Commentaries of the Incas and General History of Peru, by Garcilaso de la Vega, El Inca*, xvi–xxxi. Trans. Harold V. Livermore. Austin: University of Texas Press.

Llorens Artigas, J., and J. Corredor-Matheos. 1979. *Cerámica popular española*. Barcelona: Editorial Blume.

Lockhart, James B. 1968. *Spanish Peru, 1532–1560: A Colonial Society*. Madison: University of Wisconsin Press.

Lockhart, James B. 1972. *The Men of Cajamarca: A Social and Biographical Study of the First Conquerors of Peru*. Austin: University of Texas Press.

Lockhart, James B., and Stuart B. Schwartz. 1983. *Early Latin America: A History of Colonial Spanish America and Brazil*. Cambridge, UK: Cambridge University Press.

Londoño, Wilhelm. 2001. "Hacia una interpretación antropológica de la cerámica vidriada de Popoyán." *Revista de Antropología y Arqueología* 13: 49–60.

Long, George A. 1967. "Archaeological Investigations at Panama Vieja." MA thesis, Department of Anthropology, University of Florida, Gainesville.

López, Leonor, and Lorenzo Huertas. 1990. "Relación de viñas y bodegas de Moquegua, siglos XVI y XVII." In *Trabajos arqueológicos en Moquegua, Peru*, vol. 3, comp. Luis K. Watanabe, Michael E. Moseley, and Fernando Cabieses, 255–58. Lima: Programa Contisuyo del Museo Peruano de Ciencias de la Salud and Southern Peru Copper Corporation.

López de Coca Castañer, José Enrique. 1989. "Institutions on the Castilian-Granadan Frontier 1369–1482." In *Medieval Frontier Societies*, ed. R. Bartlett and Angus MacKay, 127–50. Oxford: Clarendon.

López Guzmán, R. 1993. "Lo mudéjar en la arquitectura mexicana." In *Mudéjar iberoamericano: Una expresión de dos mundos*, ed. Ignacio Henares Cuéllar and R. López Guzmán, 189–212. Granada, Spain: Monográfica Arte y Arqueología, Universidad de Granada.

Low, Setha M. 1995. "Indigenous Architecture and the Spanish American Plaza in Mesoamerica and the Caribbean." *American Anthropologist* 97 (4): 748–62. http://dx.doi.org/10.1525/aa.1995.97.4.02a00160.

Lozoya, Juan de Contreras, Marqués de. 1945. *Historia del arte hispánico*, vol. 4. Barcelona: Salvat.

Luján Muñoz, Luis. 1975. *Historia de la mayólica en Guatemala*. Guatemala City: Serviprensa.

Lynch, John. 1981. *Spain under the Habsburgs*. 2nd ed., 2 vols. Oxford: Basil Blackwell.

Lynch, Katherine A. 2003. *Individuals, Families, and Communities in Europe, 1200–1800: The Urban Foundations of Western Society*. Cambridge: Cambridge University Press.

MacCormack, Sabine. 1985. "'The Heart Has Its Reasons': Predicaments of Missionary Christianity in Early Colonial Peru." *Hispanic American Historical Review (HAHR)* 65 (3): 443–66.

Magetti, M., H. Westley, and S. Jacqueline Olin. 1984. "Provenance and Technical Studies of Mexican Majolica Using Elemental and Phase Analysis." In *Archaeological Chemistry III*, ed. James B. Lambert, 151–91. Washington, DC: Advances in Chemistry Series, American Chemical Society.

Magilligan, Francis J., and Paul S. Goldstein. 2001. "El Niño Floods and Culture Change: A Late Holocene Flood History for the Rio Moquegua, Southern Peru." *Geology* 29 (5): 431–34. http://dx.doi.org/10.1130/0091-7613(2001)029<0431:ENOFAC>2.0.CO;2.

Mahmoud, Samir. 2011. "Color and the Mystics: Light, Beauty, and the Spiritual Quest." In *And Diverse Are Their Hues. Color in Islamic Art and Culture*, ed. Jonathan Bloom and Sheila Blair, 99–119. New Haven, CT: Yale University Press.

Málaga Medina, Alejandro. 1972. "Toledo y las reducciones de indios en Arequipa: Aspecto demográfico." *Historiografía y Bibliografía Americanistas* 16: 389–400. Publicaciones de la Escuela de Estudios de Sevilla, Spain.

Málaga Medina, Alejandro. 1975. "Los corregimientos de Arequipa, siglo XVI." *Historia* 1: 47–85.

Málaga Medina, Alejandro. 1990. "Organización eclesiástica de Arequipa." In *Historia General de Arequipa*, ed. Máximo Neira Avendaño, Guillermo Galdos Rodríguez, Alejandro Málaga Medina, Eusebio Quiroz Paz Soldán, and Jorge G. Carpio Muñoz, 275–308. Arequipa, Peru: Fundación M. J. Bustamante de la Fuente.

Manners, R. B., Francis J. Magilligan, and Paul S. Goldstein. 2007. "Floodplain Development, El Niño, and Cultural Consequences in a Hyperarid Andean Environment." *Annals of the Association of American Geographers* 97 (2): 229–49. http://dx.doi.org/10.1111/j.1467-8306.2007.00533.x.

Marchena Fernández, Juan. 1992. "Los hijos de la guerra: Modelo para armar." In *Congreso de Historia del Descubrimiento (1492–1556): Actas*, vol. 3, ed. Real Academia de la Historia, 311–420. Madrid: Confederación Española de Ahorros.

Marcus, Joyce. 2009. "A World Tour of Breweries." In *Andean Civilization: A Tribute to Michael E. Moseley*, ed. Joyce Marcus and Patrick Ryan Williams, 303–24. Monograph 63. Los Angeles: Cotsen Institute of Archaeology Press, University of California.

Marcus, Joyce, and Patrick Ryan Williams, eds. 2009. *Andean Civilization: A Tribute to Michael E. Moseley*. Monograph 63. Los Angeles: Cotsen Institute of Archaeology Press, University of California.

Martin, Bronwen, and Felizitas Ringham. 2006. *Key Terms in Semiotics*. London: Continuum.

Martínez, Santiago. 1936. *Fundadores de Arequipa*. Arequipa, Peru: Tipografía La Luz.

Mason, R. B., and S. Michael Tite. 1997. "The Beginnings of Tin-Opacification of Pottery Glazes." *Archaeometry* 39 (1): 41–58. http://dx.doi.org/10.1111/j.1475-4754.1997.tb00789.x.

Mathews, James E. 1989. "Dual Systems of Inka Agricultural Production: Evidence from the Osmore Drainage, Southern Peru." In *Ecology, Settlement and History in the Osmore Drainage, Peru*, vol. 2, ed. Don S. Rice, Charles Stanish, and Phillip R. Scarr, 415–33. Oxford: BAR International Series 545.

McAlister, Lyle N. 1984. *Spain and Portugal in the New World, 1492–1700. Europe and the World in the Age of Expansion*, vol. 3. Minneapolis: University of Minnesota Press.

McEwan, Bonnie G. 1992. "The Role of Ceramics in Spain and Spanish America during the 16th Century." *Historical Archaeology* 26 (1): 92–108.

McEwan, Gordon F. 2006. "Inca State Origins: Collapse and Regeneration in the Southern Peruvian Andes." In *After Collapse: The Regeneration of Complex Societies*, ed. Glenn M. Schwartz and John J. Nichols, 85–98. Tucson: University of Arizona Press.

Meltzer, David J. 2003. "Lessons in Landscape Learning." In *Colonization of Unfamiliar Landscapes: The Archaeology of Adaptation*, ed. Marcy Rockman and James Steele, 222–41. London: Routledge.

Millones, Luis, and William W. Stein. 1979. "Religion and Power in the Andes: Idolatrous Curacas of the Central Sierra." *Ethnohistory* 26 (3): 243–63. http://dx.doi.org/10.2307/481561.

Minuto, Attilio R. 1987. "Homenaje al maestro." In *Pequeña antología de Moquegua*, ed. Ismael Pinto Vargas, 111–15. Lima: Ediciones El Virrey.

Miranda Nieto, Froilan. 1987. "Santa Fortunata." In *Pequeña antología de Moquegua*, ed. Ismael Pinto Vargas, 192–94. Lima: Ediciones El Virrey.

Miró Quesada Sosa, Aurelio. 1980. "Apuntes para la historia: Santa Catalina de Moquegua." *Mensajes* 23. Southern Peru Copper Corporation, Lima.

Miró Quesada Sosa, Aurelio. 1982. "Nuevos datos sobre Alonso de Estrada." In *Nuevos temas peruanos*, by Aurelio Miró Quesada Sosa, 79–107. Lima: n.p.

Molera, Judit, M. García-Valles, T. Pradell, and Mario Vendrell-Saz. 1996. "Hispano-Moresque Pottery Production of the Fourteenth-Century Workshop of Testar del Molí (Paterna, Spain)." *Archaeometry* 38 (1): 67–80. http://dx.doi.org/10.1111/j.1475-4754.1996.tb00761.x.

Molera, Judit, Mario Vendrell-Saz, M. García-Valles, and T. Pradell. 1997. "Technology and Colour Development of Hispano-Moresque Lead-Glazed Pottery." *Archaeometry* 39 (1): 23–39. http://dx.doi.org/10.1111/j.1475-4754.1997.tb00788.x.

Molera, Judit, Mario Vendrell-Saz, and Josefina Pérez-Arantegui. 2001. "Chemical and Textural Characterization of Tin Glazes in Islamic Ceramics from Eastern Spain." *Journal of Archaeological Science* 28 (3): 331–40. http://dx.doi.org/10.1006/jasc.2000.0606.

Montenegro y Ubalde, Juan Antonio. 1987a. "Convento hospitalario de la sagrada religión de los RR. Beletmitas." In *Pequeña antología de Moquegua*, ed. Ismael Pinto Vargas, 164–66. Lima: Ediciones El Virrey.

Montenegro y Ubalde, Juan Antonio. 1987b. "Convento de Santo Domingo." In *Pequeña antología de Moquegua*, ed. Ismael Pinto Vargas, 161–62. Lima: Ediciones El Virrey.

Moore, Jerry D. 1989. "Pre-Hispanic Beer in Coastal Peru: Technology and Social Context of Prehistoric Production." *American Anthropologist* 91 (3): 682–95. http://dx.doi.org/10.1525/aa.1989.91.3.02a00090.

Moore, Jerry D. 1991. "Cultural Responses to Environmental Catastrophes: Post El Niño Subsistence on the Prehistoric North Coast of Peru." *Latin American Antiquity* 2 (1): 27–47. http://dx.doi.org/10.2307/971894.

Moore, Jerry D. 2004. "The Social Basis of Sacred Spaces in the Prehispanic Andes: Ritual Landscapes of the Dean in Chimu and Inka Societies." *Journal of Archaeological Method and Theory* 11 (1): 83–124. http://dx.doi.org/10.1023/B:JARM.0000014348.86882.50.

Moore, Jerry D. 2005. *Cultural Landscapes in the Ancient Andes: Archaeologies of Place*. Gainesville: University Press of Florida.

Morgan, Ronald J. 2002. *Spanish American Saints and the Rhetoric of Identity, 1600–1810*. Tucson: University of Arizona Press.

Morris, Craig. 1995. "Symbols to Power: Styles and Media in the Inka State." In *Style, Society, and Person: Archaeological and Ethnological Perspectives*, ed. Christopher Carr and Jill E. Neitzel, 419–33. New York: Plenum.

Morris, Craig, and Adriana von Hagen. 1993. *The Inka Empire and Its Andean Origins*. New York: Abbeville.

Moseley, Michael E. 1983. "Central Andean Civilization." In *Ancient South Americans*, ed. Jesse D. Jennings, 179–239. San Francisco: W. H. Freeman.

Moseley, Michael E. 1987. "Punctuated Equilibrium: Searching the Ancient Record for El Niño." *Quarterly Review of Archaeology* 8: 7–10.

Moseley, Michael E. 1990. "Fortificaciones prehispánicas y la evolución de tácticas militares en el valle de Moquegua." In *Trabajos arqueológicos en Moquegua, Peru*, vol. 1, comp. Luis K. Watanabe, Michael E. Moseley, and Fernando Cabieses, 237–52. Lima: Programa Contisuyo del Museo Peruano de Ciencias de la Salud and Southern Peru Copper Corporation.

Moseley, Michael E. 1992. *The Incas and Their Ancestors: The Archaeology of Peru*. London: Thames and Hudson.

Moseley, Michael E., and Kent C. Day, eds. 1982. *Chan Chan: Andean Desert City*. Santa Fe and Albuquerque: School of American Research and University of New Mexico Press.

Moseley, Michael E., Robert A. Feldman, Paul S. Goldstein, and Luis Watanabe. 1991. "Colonies and Conquest: Tiahuanaco and Huari in Moquegua." In *Huari Administrative Structure: Prehistoric Monumental Architecture and State Government*, ed. William H. Isbell and Gordon McEwan, 121–40. Washington, DC: Dumbarton Oaks.

Moseley, Michael E., Robert A. Feldman, and Irene Pritzker. 1982. "New Light on Peru's Past." *Field Museum of Natural History Bulletin* 53 (1): 3–11.

Moseley, Michael E., Donna Nash, Patrick Ryan Williams, Susan D. deFrance, Ana Miranda, and Mario Ruales. 2005. "Burning Down the Brewery: Establishing and

Evacuating an Ancient Imperial Colony at Cerro Baúl, Peru." *Proceedings of the National Academy of Sciences of the United States of America* 102 (48): 17264–71. http://dx.doi.org/10.1073/pnas.0508673102.

Murra, John V. 1962. "Cloth and Its Functions in the Inca State." *American Anthropologist* 64 (4): 710–28. http://dx.doi.org/10.1525/aa.1962.64.4.02a00020.

Murra, John V. 1968. "An Aymara Kingdom." *Ethnohistory* 15 (2): 115–51. http://dx.doi.org/10.2307/480555.

Murra, John V. 1972. "El 'control vertical' de un máximo de pisos ecológicos en la economía de las sociedades andinas." In *Visita de la provincia de León de Huánuco en 1562: Iñigo Ortiz de Zúñiga, visitador*, vol. 2, ed. John V. Murra, 429–76. Huánuco, Peru: Universidad Nacional Hermilio Valdizán.

Murra, John V. 1978. "Los olleros del Inka: Hacia una historia y arqueología del Qollasuyu." In *Historia problema y promesa*, ed. F. Miró Quesada C., Franklin Pease G. Y., and D. Sobrevilla, 415–23. Lima: Pontificia Universidad Católica del Peru.

Myers, J. Emlen, Fernando de Amores Carredano, Jacqueline S. Olin, and Alfonso Pleguezuelo Hernández. 1992. "Compositional Identification of Seville Majolica at Overseas Sites." *Historical Archaeology* 26 (1): 131–47.

Nash, Donna J., and Patrick Ryan Williams. 2009. "Wari Political Organization: The Southern Periphery." In *Andean Civilization: A Tribute to Michael E. Moseley*, ed. Joyce Marcus and Patrick Ryan Williams, 257–76. Monograph 63. Los Angeles: Cotsen Institute of Archaeology Press, University of California.

Natt, Wendy L. 1997. "A Structural Design Analysis of Tin-Enameled Pottery from Colonial Pacific South America." MA thesis, Department of Anthropology, Southern Illinois University, Carbondale.

Naveh, Zev, and Arthur Lieberman. 1993. *Landscape Ecology: Theory and Application*. 2nd ed. New York: Springer-Verlag.

Nees, L. 2011. "Blue behind Gold: The Inscription of the Dome of the Rock and Its Relatives." In *And Diverse Are Their Hues: Color in Islamic Art and Culture*, ed. Jonathan Bloom and Sheila Blair, 153–73. New Haven, CT: Yale University Press.

Neumann, Roderick P. 2010. "Political Ecology II: Theorizing Region." *Progress in Human Geography* 34 (3): 368–74. http://dx.doi.org/10.1177/0309132509343045.

Nilsson, J.-E. 1998–2010. "Cobalt on Chinese Pottery and Porcelain." http://www.gotheborg.com/glossary/?http://gotheborg.com/glossary/cobalt.shtml (retrieved 6/20/12).

Núñez Henríquez, Patricio. 1984. "La antigua aldea de San Lorenzo de Tarapacá, norte de Chile." *Revista Chungará* 13: 53–65.

Nuttall, Zelia. 1922. "Royal Ordinances Concerning the Laying Out of New Towns." *Hispanic American Historical Review* 5 (2): 249–54. http://dx.doi.org/10.2307/2506027.

Oberti Rodríguez, Italo. 1999. "Cerámica colonial cuzqueña." *Revista Universitaria* 138: 139–52.

O'Kane, Bernard. 2011. "Tiles of Many Hues: The Development of Iranian Cuerda Seca Tiles and the Transfer of Tilework Technology." In *And Diverse Are Their Hues: Color in Islamic Art and Culture*, ed. Jonathan Bloom and Sheila Blair, 175–203. New Haven, CT: Yale University Press.

Olin, Jacqueline, Garman Harbottle, and Edward V. Sayre. 1978. "Elemental Compositions of Spanish and Spanish-Colonial Majolica Ceramics in the Identification of Provenience." In *Archaeological Chemistry II*, ed. G. F. Carter, 200–229. Advances in Chemistry Series 171. Washington, DC: American Chemical Society. http://dx.doi.org/10.1021/ba-1978-0171.ch013.

ONERN (Oficina Nacional de Evaluación de Recursos Naturales). 1976. *Inventario, evaluación y uso de los recursos naturales de la costa: Cuencas de los ríos Moquegua, Locumba, Sama y Caplina. Oficina Nacional de Evaluación de Recursos Naturales*. Lima: ONERN.

Orser, Charles E., Jr. 1994. "Toward a Global Historical Archaeology: An Example from Brazil." *Historical Archaeology* 28 (1): 5–22.

Orser, Charles E., Jr. 2010. "Twenty-First-Century Historical Archaeology." *Journal of Archaeological Research* 18 (2): 111–50. http://dx.doi.org/10.1007/s10814-009-9035-9.

Ortega, Elpidio, and Carmen Fondeur. 1978. *Estudio de la cerámica del período Indo-Hispano de la Antigua Concepción de la Vega*. Serie Científica 1. Santo Domingo: Fundación Ortega Alvarez.

Ortíz Crespo, A. 1993. "Techumbres y cubiertas mudéjares en el Ecuador." In *Mudéjar iberoamericano: Una expresión de dos mundos*, ed. Ignacio Henares Cuéllar and R. López Guzmán, 265–86. Granada, Spain: Monográfica Arte y Arqueología, Universidad de Granada.

Oviedo y Valdés, Gonzalo Fernández de. 1959. *Historia general y natural de las Indias*, vol. 5. Madrid: Ediciones Atlas.

Owen, Bruce. 2005. "Distant Colonies and Explosive Collapse: The Two Stages of the Tiwanaku Diaspora in the Osmore Drainage." *Latin American Antiquity* 16 (1): 45–80. http://dx.doi.org/10.2307/30042486.

Padilla, R., O. Schalm, K. Janssens, R. Arrazcaeta, and P. Van Espen. 2005. "Microanalytical Characterization of Surface Decoration in Majolica Pottery." *Analytica Chimica Acta* 535 (1-2): 201–11. http://dx.doi.org/10.1016/j.aca.2004.11.082.

Palmer, Gabrielle, and Donna Pierce. 1992. *Cambios: The Spirit of Transformation in Spanish Colonial Art*. Albuquerque: Santa Barbara Museum of Art and University of New Mexico Press.

Paredes Eyzaguirre, Rolando. 1989. "La cerámica vidriada de Pucará, Puno." *Boletín de Lima* 61: 35–37.

Parsons, Jeffrey R. 1994. "Late Postclassic Salt Production and Consumption in the Valley of Mexico: Some Insights from Nexquipayac." In *Economies and Polities in the Aztec Realm*, ed. Mary G. Hodge and Michael E. Smith, 257–90. Albany, NY: Institute for Mesoamerican Studies.

Pease G. Y., Franklin. 1984. "Indices notariales de Moquegua, siglo XVI: Una introducción." In *Contribuciones a los estudios de los Andes centrales*, ed. Shozo Masuda, 151–73. Tokyo: University of Tokyo.

Pease G. Y., Franklin. 1985. "Cases and Variations of Verticality in the Southern Andes." In *Andean Ecology and Civilization: An Interdisciplinary Perspective on Andean Ecological Complementarity*, ed. Shozo Masuda, Izumi Shimada, and Craig Morris, 141–60. Tokyo: University of Tokyo.

Pereyra y Ruiz, Antonio. 1987. "Moquegua en el siglo XIX." In *Pequeña antología de Moquegua*, ed. Ismael Pinto Vargas, 42–47. Lima: Ediciones El Virrey.

Pérez-Arantegui, J., M. Resano, E. García-Ruiz, F. Vanhaecke, C. Roldán, J. Ferrero, and J. Coll. 2008. "Characterization of Cobalt Pigments Found in Traditional Valencian Ceramics by Means of Laser Ablation–Inductively Coupled Plasma Mass Spectrometry and Portable X-ray Fluorescence Spectrometry." *Talanta* 74: 1271–80.

Petersen, G. Georg. 2010. *Mining and Metallurgy in Ancient Perú*. Trans. William E. Brooks. Special Paper 467. Boulder: Geological Society of America.

Picolpasso, Cipriano. 1980. *The Three Books of the Potter's Art*. Trans. R. Lightbown and A. Caiger-Smith. London: Scholar.

Pike, Ruth. 1972. *Aristocrats and Traders: Sevillian Society in the Sixteenth Century*. Ithaca, NY: Cornell University Press. [For chapter 4, see http://libro.uca.edu/aristocrats/aristocrats4-1.htm].

Pinedo, C., and E. Vizcaino. 1979. *La cerámica de Manises en la historia*. Madrid: Editorial Everest.

Pleguezuelo, Alfonso. 2003a. "Centers of Traditional Spanish Mayólica." In *Cerámica y Cultura: The Story of Spanish and Mexican Mayólica*, ed. Robin Farwell Gavin, Donna Pierce, and Alfonso Pleguezuelo, 25–47. Santa Fe, NM: Museum of International Folk Art.

Pleguezuelo, Alfonso. 2003b. "Ceramics, Business, and Economy." In *Cerámica y Cultura: The Story of Spanish and Mexican Mayólica*, ed. Robin Farwell Gavin, Donna Pierce, and Alfonso Pleguezuelo, 102–21. Santa Fe, NM: Museum of International Folk Art.

Plog, Stephen. 1978. "Social Interaction and Stylistic Similarity: A Reanalysis." In *Advances in Archaeological Method and Theory*, vol. 1, ed. Michael B. Schiffer, 143–82. New York: Academic Press.

Politis, Gustavo G. 1995. "The Socio-Politics of the Development of Archaeology in Hispanic South America." In *Theory in Archaeology: A World Perspective*, ed. Peter J. Ucko, 197–235. London: Routledge.

Politis, Gustavo G. 2003. "The Theoretical Landscape and the Methodological Development of Archaeology in Latin America." *American Antiquity* 68 (2): 245–72. http://dx.doi.org/10.2307/3557079.

Porter, Michael E. 1998. "Clusters and the New Economics of Competition." *Harvard Business Review* 76 (6): 77–90.

Pugh, Timothy W. 2009. "Contagion and Alterity: Kowoj Maya Appropriations of European Objects." *American Anthropologist* 111 (3): 373–86. http://dx.doi.org/10.1111/j.1548-1433.2009.01139.x.

Qamber, Rukhsana. 2006. "Inquisition Proceedings against Muslims in 16th Century Latin America." *Islamic Studies* 45 (1): 21–57.

Quilter, Jeffrey. n.d. http://peabody2.ad.fas.harvard.edu/mcv (retrieved 7/20/13).

Quinn, W. H., V. T. Neal, and S. E. Antuñez de Mayolo. 1987. "El Niño Occurrences over the Past Four and a Half Centuries." *Journal of Geophysical Research* 92 (C13): 14,449–461.

Quiroz Neyra, Rosemary. 2006. "La agricultura en el valle de Vítor: retornando al vino y al pisco," 165–75. Arequipa, Peru: Universidad Nacional San Agustín. http://www.bvirtual-unsa.edu.pe/edicion8/13-historia-8-quirozneyra.pdf (retrieved 6/15/13).

Quiroz Paz Soldán, Eusebio. 1991a. "La arquitectura mestiza de Arequipa." In *Visión histórica de Arequipa, 1540–1990*, by Eusebio Quiroz Paz Soldán, 79–97. Arequipa, Peru: Universidad Nacional de San Agustín.

Quiroz Paz Soldán, Eusebio. 1991b. "Historia económica de la región sur del Perú." In *Visión histórica de Arequipa, 1540–1990*, by Eusebio Quiroz Paz Soldán, 271–99. Arequipa, Peru: Universidad Nacional de San Agustín.

Ramírez, Susan Elizabeth. 2005. *To Feed and Be Fed: The Cosmological Bases of Authority and Identity in the Andes*. Stanford, CA: Stanford University Press.

Read, Jan. 1986. *The Wines of Spain*. Rev. ed. London: Faber and Faber.

Reilly, Bernard F. 1993. *The Medieval Spains*. Cambridge, UK: Cambridge University Press. http://dx.doi.org/10.1017/CBO9780511818523.

Restall, Matthew. 2003. *Seven Myths of the Spanish Conquest*. New York: Oxford University Press.

Reycraft, Richard Martin. 2000. "Long-Term Human Response to El Niño in South Coastal Peru, circa A.D. 1400." In *Environmental Disaster and the Archaeology of Human Response*, ed. Garth Bawden and Richard Martin Reycraft, 99–118. Anthropological Papers 7. Albuquerque: Maxwell Museum of Anthropology, University of New Mexico.

Rhodes, Daniel, and Robin Hopper. 2000. *Clay and Glazes for the Potter*. 3rd ed. Iola, WI: Krause.

Rice, Don S. 1989. "Osmore Drainage, Peru: The Ecological Setting." In *Ecology, Settlement and History in the Osmore Drainage, Peru*, ed. Don S. Rice, Charles Stanish, and Phillip R. Scarr, 17–34. Oxford: BAR International Series 545 (i).

Rice, Don S., Charles Stanish, and Phillip R. Scarr, eds. 1989. *Ecology, Settlement and History in the Osmore Drainage, Peru*. Oxford: BAR International Series 545.

Rice, Prudence M. 1987. "The Moquegua Bodegas Survey." *National Geographic Research* 3 (2): 136–38.

Rice, Prudence M. 1994. "The Kilns of Moquegua, Peru: Technology, Excavations, and Functions." *Journal of Field Archaeology* 21 (3): 325–44.

Rice, Prudence M. 1995. "Wine and 'Local Catholicism' in Colonial Moquegua, Peru." *Colonial Latin American Historical Review* 4 (4): 369–404.

Rice, Prudence M. 1996a. "The Archaeology of Wine: The Wine and Brandy Haciendas of Moquegua, Peru." *Journal of Field Archaeology* 23 (2): 187–204.

Rice, Prudence M. 1996b. "Peru's Colonial Wine Industry and Its European Background." *Antiquity* 70: 785–800.

Rice, Prudence M. 1996c. "Wine and Brandy Production in Colonial Peru: A Historical and Archaeological Investigation." *Journal of Interdisciplinary History* 27 (3): 455–79.

Rice, Prudence M. 1997. "Tin-Enameled Ceramics of Moquegua, Peru." In *Approaches to the Historical Archaeology of Mexico, Central and South America*, ed. Janine Gasco, Greg Smith, and Patricia Fournier-García, 167–75. Monograph 38. Los Angeles: Institute of Archaeology, University of California.

Rice, Prudence M. 2009. "Volcanoes, Earthquakes, and the Spanish Colonial Wine Industry of Moquegua, Peru." In *Andean Civilization: A Tribute to Michael E. Moseley*, ed. Joyce Marcus and Patrick Ryan Williams, 379–92. Monograph 63. Los Angeles: Cotsen Institute of Archaeology Press, University of California.

Rice, Prudence M. 2011a. "Order (and Disorder) in Early Colonial Moquegua, Peru." *International Journal of Historical Archaeology* 15 (3): 481–508. http://dx.doi.org/10.1007/s10761-011-0151-0.

Rice, Prudence M. 2011b. *Vintage Moquegua: History, Wine, and Archaeology on a Colonial Peruvian Periphery*. Austin: University of Texas Press.

Rice, Prudence M. 2012. "Torata Alta: An Inka Administrative Center and Spanish Colonial *Reducción* in Moquegua, Peru." *Latin American Antiquity* 23 (1): 3–26. http://dx.doi.org/10.7183/1045-6635.23.1.3.

Rice, Prudence M. 2013. "Political-Ecology Perspectives in New World *Loza* (Majolica)." *International Journal of Historical Archaeology* 23 (1): 651–683. http://dx.doi.org/10.1007/s10761-013-0238-x.

Rice, Prudence M. n.d. "Algunas perspectivas política-ecológicas sobre la loza andina." In *Definiendo el derrotero: Posibilidades y perspectivas para una arqueología histórica en el Perú*, ed. T. A. Traslaviña, A. Chase, P. VanValkenburgh, and J. M. B. Weaver. Lima: Fondo Editorial PUCP. In press.

Rice, Prudence M., and James Blackman. n.d. "Colonial Andean Tin-Enameled Ceramics: New INAA Data from Peru." Ms. in prep.

Rice, Prudence M., Peter T. Bürgi, Mary Van Buren, and Geoffrey Conrad. 1989. "Torata Alta, an Inka-Spanish Settlement." Paper presented at the 54th Annual Meeting of the Society for American Archaeology, Atlanta.

Rice, Prudence M., and Donna L. Ruhl. 1989. "Archaeological Survey of the Moquegua Bodegas." In *Ecology, Settlement and History in the Osmore Drainage, Peru*, ed. Don S. Rice, Charles Stanish, and Phillip R. Scarr, 479–502. Oxford: BAR International Series 545 (ii).

Rice, Prudence M., and Greg C. Smith. 1989. "The Spanish Colonial Wine Industry of Moquegua, Peru." *Historical Archaeology* 27 (4): 65–81.

Rice, Prudence M., and Greg C. Smith. 1990. "Bodegas de vid de Moquegua: Tercera temporada, 1987." In *Trabajos arqueológicos en Moquegua, Peru*, vol. 3, comp. Luis K. Watanabe, Michael E. Moseley, and Fernando Cabieses, 207–30. Lima: Programa Contisuyo del Museo Peruano de Ciencias de la Salud and Southern Peru Copper Corporation.

Rice, Prudence M., Greg C. Smith, Susan M. deFrance, Sara Van Beck, Peter Bürgi, and Mary Van Buren. 1990. "Bodegas de vid de Moquegua: Quinta temporada, 1989." In *Trabajos arqueológicos en Moquegua, Peru*, vol. 3, comp. Luis K. Watanabe, Michael E. Moseley, and Fernando Cabieses, 241–53. Lima: Programa Contisuyo del Museo Peruano de Ciencias de la Salud and Southern Peru Copper Corporation.

Rice, Prudence M., and Sara L. Van Beck. 1993. "The Spanish Colonial Kiln Tradition of Moquegua, Peru." *Historical Archaeology* 27 (4): 65–81.

Rice, Prudence M., and Luis K. Watanabe. 1990. "Locumbilla o Belén de Locumbilla: Una bodega de vid de Moquegua, un Monumento Histórico, patrimonio del Perú." In *Trabajos arqueológicos en Moquegua, Perú*, vol. 3, comp. Luis K. Watanabe, Michael E. Moseley, and Fernando Cabieses, 259–63. Lima: Programa Contisuyo del Museo Peruano de Ciencias de la Salud and Southern Peru Copper Corporation.

Rivera, Mario A. 1991. "The Prehistory of Northern Chile: A Synthesis." *Journal of World Prehistory* 5 (1): 1–47. http://dx.doi.org/10.1007/BF00974731.

Rivero Velez, Enrique. 1987. "Nieto." In *Pequeña antología de Moquegua*, ed. Ismael Pinto Vargas, 116–23. Lima: Ediciones El Virrey.

Robbins, P. 2004. *Political Ecology: A Critical Introduction.* New York: Blackwell.

Rockman, Marcy. 2003. "Knowledge and Learning in the Archaeology of Colonization." In *Colonization of Unfamiliar Landscapes: The Archaeology of Adaptation,* ed. Marcy Rockman and James Steele, 3–24. London: Routledge. http://dx.doi.org/10.4324/9780203422908.

Rockman, Marcy, and James Steele, eds. 2003. *Colonization of Unfamiliar Landscapes: The Archaeology of Adaptation.* London: Routledge. http://dx.doi.org/10.4324/9780203422908.

Rodman, Margaret C. 1992. "Empowering Place: Multilocality and Multivocality." *American Anthropologist* 94 (3): 640–56. http://dx.doi.org/10.1525/aa.1992.94.3.02a00060.

Rodríguez-Alegría, Enrique. 2005. "Eating Like an Indian: Negotiating Social Relations in the Spanish Colonies." *Current Anthropology* 46 (4): 551–73. http://dx.doi.org/10.1086/431526.

Rodríguez-Alegría, Enrique, Hector Neff, and Michael D. Glascock. 2003. "Indigenous Ware or Spanish Import? The Case of Indígena Ware and Approaches to Power in Colonial Mexico." *Latin American Antiquity* 14 (1): 67–81. http://dx.doi.org/10.2307/972235.

Rodríguez G. de Ceballos, Alfonso. 2010. "Image and Counter-Reformation in Spain and Spanish America." In *Sacred Spain: Art and Belief in the Spanish World,* ed. Ronda Kasl, 15–35. New Haven, CT: Indianapolis Museum of Art and Yale University Press.

Rodríguez Girón, Zoila. 2008. "Investigaciones arqueológicas en el Convento de Santo Domingo, Antigua Guatemala, parte II: los materiales arqueológicos." *Utz'ib* 1 (8). Asociación Tikal, Guatemala City, Guatemala.

Rose-Redwood, Reuben, and Derek Alderman. 2011. "Critical Interventions in Political Toponymy." *ACME: An International E-Journal for Critical Geographies* 10 (1): 1–6. http://www.acme-journal.org/vol10/RoseRedwoodAlderman2011.pdf (retrieved 8/13/12).

Rose-Redwood, Reuben, Derek Alderman, and Maoz Azaryahu. 2010. "Geographies of Toponymic Inscription: New Directions in Critical Place-Name Studies." *Progress in Human Geography* 34 (4): 453–70. http://dx.doi.org/10.1177/0309132509351042.

Rosselló Bordoy, Guillermo. 1992. "The Ceramics of al-Andalus." In *Al-Andalus: The Art of Islamic Spain,* ed. J. D. Dodds, 97–103. New York: Metropolitan Museum.

Rostworowski, María. 1986. "La región del Colesuyu." *Revista Chungará* 16–17: 127–35.

Rostworowski, María. 1988. "La antigua región del Colesuyu." In *Sociedad andina: Pasado y presente. Contribuciones en homenaje a la memoria de César Fonseca Martel,* comp. Ramiro Matos Mendieta, 137–50. Lima: Fomciencias.

Rouguelle, A. 1996. "Medieval Trade Networks in the Western Indian Ocean (8–14th Centuries): Some Reflections from the Distribution Pattern of Chinese Imports in the Islamic World." In *Tradition and Archaeology: Early Maritime Contacts in the Indian Ocean*, ed. Himanshu Prabha Ray and Jean-François Salles, 109–14. New Delhi: State Publishers.

Rovira, Beatriz E. 2001. "Presencia de mayólicas panameñas en el mundo colonial: Algunas consideraciones acerca de su distribución y cronología." *Latin American Antiquity* 12 (3): 291–303. http://dx.doi.org/10.2307/971634.

Rovira, Beatriz E., James Blackman, Lambertus van Zelst, Ronald Bishop, C. C. Rodríguez, and D. Sánchez. 2006. "Caracterización química de cerámicas coloniales del sitio de Panamá Viejo." *Canto Rodado* 1: 101–31.

Rowe, John Howland. 1946. "Inca Culture at the Time of the Spanish Conquest." In *Handbook of South American Indians*, vol. 2: *The Andean Civilizations*, ed. Julian H. Steward, 183–330. Bureau of American Ethnology Bulletin 143. Washington, DC: Smithsonian Institution.

Rydén, Stig. 1947. *Archaeological Researches in the Highlands of Bolivia*. Goteborg: Elanders Boktryckeri Aktiebolag.

Sallnow, M. J. 1982. "A Trinity of Christs: Cultic Processes in Andean Catholicism." *American Ethnologist* 9 (4): 730–49. http://dx.doi.org/10.1525/ae.1982.9.4.02a00070.

Sánchez-Albornoz, Claudio. 1963. "The Frontier and Castilian Liberties." In *The New World Looks at Its History*, ed. A. R. Lewis and T. F. McGann, 27–46. Austin: University of Texas Press.

Sánchez-Pacheco, Trinidad. 1981a. "Paterna y Manises." In *Cerámica esmaltada española*, by Trinidad Sánchez-Pacheco, Maria Dolores Giral, Juan Zozaya, Natacha Seseña, Isabel Alvaro Zamora, Juan Ainaud de Lasarte, María Antonia Casanovas, and Balbina Martínez Caviró, 53–72. Barcelona: Editorial Labor.

Sánchez-Pacheco, Trinidad. 1981b. "Seville." In *Cerámica esmaltada española*, by Trinidad Sánchez-Pacheco, Maria Dolores Giral, Juan Zozaya, Natacha Seseña, Isabel Alvaro Zamora, Juan Ainaud de Lasarte, María Antonia Casanovas, and Balbina Martínez Caviró, 95–108. Barcelona: Editorial Labor.

Sánchez-Pacheco, Trinidad. 1986. *Guia del Museu de Ceràmica*. Guies breus de Museus 1. Barcelona: Ajuntament de Barcelona.

Sánchez-Pacheco, Trinidad, Maria Dolores Giral, Juan Zozaya, Natacha Seseña, Isabel Alvaro Zamora, Juan Ainaud de Lasarte, María Antonia Casanovas, and Balbina Martínez Caviró. 1981. *Cerámica esmaltada española*. Barcelona: Editorial Labor.

San Cristobal, A. 1995. "El carpintero mudéjar Bartolomé Calderón." *Revista del Archivo de la Nación* 12: 99–112.

Sandweiss, Daniel H., James B. Richardson III, Elizabeth J. Reitz, Jeffrey T. Hsu, and Robert A. Feldman. 1989. "Early Maritime Adaptations in the Andes: Preliminary Studies at the Ring Site, Peru." In *Ecology, Settlement and History in the Osmore Drainage, Peru*, ed. Don S. Rice, Charles Stanish, and Phillip R. Scarr, 35–84. Oxford: BAR International Series 545 (i).

Sarmiento de Gamboa, Pedro de. 2007. *The History of the Incas* (the 1572 *Historia de los Incas*, trans. and ed. Brian S. Bauer and Vania Smith, with an introduction by Brian S. Bauer and Jean Jacque Decoster). Austin: University of Texas Press.

Satterlee, Dennis R., Michael E. Moseley, David M. Keefer, and Jorge E. A. Tapia. 2000. "The Miraflores El Niño Disaster: Convergent Catastrophes and Prehistoric Agrarian Change in Southern Peru." *Andean Past* 6: 95–116.

Scarpa, Antonio, and Antonio Guerci. 1982. "Various Uses of the Castor Oil Plant (*Ricinus communis* L.): A Review." *Journal of Ethnopharmacology* 5 (2): 117–37. http://dx.doi.org/10.1016/0378-8741(82)90038-1.

Scholes, France V. 1971 [1936]. "An Overview of the Colonial Church." Reprinted in *The Roman Catholic Church in Colonial Latin America*, ed. Richard E. Greenleaf, 19–29. New York: Alfred A. Knopf.

Schreiber, Katharina J. 1991. "The Association between Roads and Polities: Evidence for Wari Roads in Peru." In *Ancient Road Networks and Settlement Hierarchies in the New World*, ed. Charles D. Trombold, 243–52. Cambridge: Cambridge University Press.

Scott, Heidi. 2009. *Contested Territory: Mapping Peru in the Sixteenth and Seventeenth Centuries*. Notre Dame, IN: University of Notre Dame Press.

Seed, Patricia. 1992. "Taking Possession and Reading Texts: Establishing the Authority of Overseas Empires." *William and Mary Quarterly* 49 (2): 183–209. http://dx.doi.org/10.2307/2947269.

Seifert, Donna J. 1977. "Archaeological Majolicas of the Rural Teotihuacan Valley, Mexico." PhD dissertation, Department of Anthropology, University of Iowa, Iowa City.

Sempat Assadourian, Carlos. 1972. "Integración y desintegración regional en el espacio colonial: Un enfoque histórico." *Revista Eure* 2 (4): 11–24.

Seseña, N. 1981. "Talavera y Puente del Arzobispo." In *Cerámica esmaltada española*, by Trinidad Sánchez-Pacheco, Maria Dolores Giral, Juan Zozaya, Natacha Seseña, Isabel Alvaro Zamora, Juan Ainaud de Lasarte, María Antonia Casanovas, and Balbina Martínez Caviró, 75–92. Barcelona: Editorial Labor.

Seward, Desmond. 1979. *Monks and Wine*. New York: Crown.

Shockey, Bruce J., Rodolfo Salas Gismondi, Phillip Gans, Annie Jeong, and John J. Flynn. 2009. "Paleontology and Geochronology of the Deseadan (Late Oligocene) of Moquegua, Peru." *American Museum Novitates* 3668: 1–24. http://dx.doi.org/10.1206/662.1.

Silliman, Stephen W. 2005. "Culture Contact or Colonialism? Challenges in the Archaeology of Native North America." *American Antiquity* 70 (1): 55–74.

Silverblatt, Irene. 1987. *Moon, Sun, and Witches: Gender Ideologies and Class in Inca and Colonial Peru*. Princeton, NJ: Princeton University Press.

Silverblatt, Irene. 1988. "Political Memories and Colonizing Symbols: Santiago and the Mountain Gods of Colonial Peru." In *Rethinking History and Myth: Indigenous South American Perspectives on the Past*, ed. Jonathan D. Hill, 174–94. Urbana: University of Illinois Press.

Silverman, Helaine. 2004. "Introduction: Space and Time in the Central Andes." In *Andean Archaeology*, ed. Helaine Silverman, 1–15. Malden, MA: Blackwell.

Sims, Kenny. 2006. "After State Collapse: How Tumilaca Communities Developed in the Upper Moquegua Valley, Peru." In *After Collapse: The Regeneration of Complex Societies*, ed. Glenn M. Schwartz and John J. Nichols, 114–36. Tucson: University of Arizona Press.

Singer, C., E. J. Holmyard, and A. R. Hall, eds. 1955. *A History of Technology*. Oxford: Oxford University Press.

Smith, Greg Charles. 1991. "Heard It through the Grapevine: Andean and European Contributions to Spanish Colonial Culture and Viticulture in Moquegua, Peru." PhD dissertation, Department of Anthropology, University of Florida, Gainesville. http://www.archive.org/stream/hearditthroughgroosmit/hearditthroughgroosmit_djvu.txt.

Smith, Monica L., ed. 2003. *The Social Construction of Ancient Cities*. Washington, DC: Smithsonian Institution.

Snead, James E., Clark L. Erickson, and J. Andrew Darling. 2009. "Making Human Space: The Archaeology of Trails, Paths, and Roads." In *Landscapes of Movement: Trails, Paths, and Roads in Anthropological Perspective*, ed. James E. Snead, Clark L. Erickson, and J. Andrew Darling, 1–19. Philadelphia: University of Pennsylvania Museum of Archaeology and Anthropology.

Spalding, Karen. 1984. *Huarochirí: An Andean Society under Inca and Spanish Rule*. Stanford, CA: Stanford University Press.

Stanish, Charles. 1989. "An Archaeological Evaluation of an Ethnohistorical Model in Moquegua." In *Ecology, Settlement and History in the Osmore Drainage, Peru*, ed. Don S. Rice, Charles Stanish, and Phillip R. Scarr, 303–20. Oxford: BAR International Series 545.

Stanish, Charles. 1991. "A Late Pre-Hispanic Ceramic Chronology for the Upper Moquegua Valley, Peru." *Fieldiana Anthropology* (n.s.) 16. Field Museum of Natural History, Chicago.

Stanish, Charles. 1992. *Ancient Andean Political Economy*. Austin: University of Texas Press.

Stanish, Charles. 2001. "Regional Research on the Inca." *Journal of Archaeological Research* 9 (3): 213–41. http://dx.doi.org/10.1023/A:1016698925820.

Stanish, Charles. 2003. *Ancient Titicaca: The Evolution of Complex Society in Southern Peru and Northern Bolivia*. Los Angeles: University of California Press. http://dx.doi.org/10.1525/california/9780520232457.001.0001.

Stanish, Charles, and Irene Pritzker. 1983. "Archaeological Reconnaissance in Southern Peru." *Bulletin of the Field Museum of Natural History* 54 (6): 6–17.

Stanish, Charles, and Irene Pritzker. 1990. "Reconocimiento arqueológico en el sur del Perú." In *Trabajos arqueológicos en Moquegua, Peru*, vol. 3, comp. Luis K. Watanabe, Michael E. Moseley, and Fernando Cabieses, 167–76. Lima: Programa Contisuyo del Museo Peruano de Ciencias de la Salud and Southern Peru Copper Corporation.

Stanislawski, Dan. 1947. "Early Spanish Town Planning in the New World." *Geographical Review* 37 (1): 94–105. http://dx.doi.org/10.2307/211364.

Stastny, Francisco. 1981. *Las artes populares del Peru*. Madrid: Ediciones Edubanco.

Stastny, Francisco. 1986a. "Iconografía Inca en mayólicas coloniales." In *Vidriados y mayólica del Perú*, by Francisco Stastny and Sara Acevedo, 7–18. Lima: Museo de Arte y de Historia, Universidad Nacional Mayor de San Marcos.

Stastny, Francisco. 1986b. "Introducción." In *Vidriados y mayólica del Perú*, by Francisco Stastny and Sara Acevedo, 5–6. Lima: Museo de Arte y de Historia, Universidad Nacional Mayor de San Marcos.

Stern, Steven J. 1982. *Peru's Indian Peoples and the Challenge of Spanish Conquest: Huamanga to 1640*. Madison: University of Wisconsin Press.

Thompson, Lonnie G., E. Mosley-Thompson, W. Dansgaard, and P. M. Grootes. 1986. "The Little Ice Age as Recorded in the Stratigraphy of the Tropical Quelccaya Ice Cap." *Science* 234 (4774): 361–64. http://dx.doi.org/10.1126/science.234.4774.361.

Thornton, Dora. 1997. "Maiolica Production in Renaissance Italy." In *Pottery in the Making: Ceramic Traditions*, ed. Ian Freestone and David Gaimster, 116–21. Washington, DC: Smithsonian Institution Press.

Tibesar, Antonine, O.F.M. 1971a [1953]. "The Early Peruvian Missionary Effort." Reprinted in *The Roman Catholic Church in Colonial Latin America*, ed. Richard E. Greenleaf, 53–62. New York: Alfred A. Knopf.

Tibesar, Antonine, O.F.M. 1971b [1955]. "Social Tensions among the Friars." Reprinted in *The Roman Catholic Church in Colonial Latin America*, ed. Richard E. Greenleaf, 98–107. New York: Alfred A. Knopf.

Tite, Michael S. 1988. "Inter-relationship between Chinese and Islamic Ceramics from the Ninth to Sixteenth Century A.D." In *Proceedings of the 26th International*

Archaeometry Symposium: Toronto 1988, ed. R. M. Farquhar, R.G.V. Hancock, and L. A. Pavlish, 30–34. Toronto: Archaeometry Laboratory, University of Toronto, Canada.

Tite, Michael S., T. Pradell, and A. Shortland. 2008. "Discovery, Production and Use of Tin-Based Opacifiers in Glasses, Enamels and Glazes from the Late Iron Age Onwards: A Reassessment." *Archaeometry* 50 (1): 67–84.

Toussaint, Manuel. 1946. *Arte mudéjar en América*. Mexico City: Porrúa.

Trelles Aréstegui, Efraín. 1978. "Cambios en la tributación en una encomienda del sur Peruano: Comparación de las tasas de La Gasca y Toledo." In *Etnohistoria y antropología andina*, ed. Marcia Koth de Paredes and Amalia Castelli, 33–39. Lima: Museo Nacional de Historia.

Trelles Aréstegui, Efraín. 1982. *Lucas Martínez Vegazo: Funcionamiento de una encomienda peruana inicial*. Lima: Pontificia Universidad Católica del Perú.

Trombold, Charles D., ed. 1991. *Ancient Road Networks and Settlement Hierarchies in the New World*. Cambridge: Cambridge University Press.

Tschopik, Harry, Jr. 1946. "The Aymara." In *Handbook of South American Indians*, vol. 2: *The Andean Civilizations*, ed. Julian H. Steward, 501–73. Bureau of American Ethnology Bulletin 143. Washington, DC: Smithsonian Institution.

Tschopik, Harry, Jr. 1950. "An Andean Ceramic Tradition in Historical Perspective." *American Antiquity* 15 (3): 196–218. http://dx.doi.org/10.2307/276763.

Unwin, Tim. 1991. *Wine and the Vine: An Historical Geography of Viticulture and the Wine Trade*. London: Routledge.

Upton, Dell. 1991. "Architectural History or Landscape History?" *JAE: Journal of Architectural Education* 44 (4): 195–99. http://dx.doi.org/10.2307/1425140.

Urton, Gary. 1981. *At the Crossroads of the Earth and the Sky: An Andean Cosmology*. Austin: University of Texas Press.

Urton, Gary. 1990. *The History of a Myth: Pacariqtambo and the Origin of the Inkas*. Austin: University of Texas Press.

Urton, Gary. 2005. "Khipu Archives: Duplicate Accounts and Identity Labels in the Inka Knotted String Records." *Latin American Antiquity* 16 (2): 147–67. http://dx.doi.org/10.2307/30042809.

Van Buren, Mary. 1993. "Community and Empire in Southern Peru: The Site of Torata Alta under Spanish Rule." PhD dissertation, Department of Anthropology, University of Arizona, Tucson.

Van Buren, Mary. 1996. "Rethinking the Vertical Archipelago: Ethnicity, Exchange, and History in the South Central Andes." *American Anthropologist* 98 (2): 338–51. http://dx.doi.org/10.1525/aa.1996.98.2.02a00100.

Van Buren, Mary. 1997. "Continuity or Change? Vertical Archipelagos in Southern Peru during the Early Colonial Period." In *Approaches to the Historical Archaeology of Mexico, Central and South America*, ed. Janine Gasco, Greg Charles Smith, and Patricia Fournier-García, 155–64. Institute of Archaeology Monograph 38. Los Angeles: University of California.

Van Buren, Mary. 2010. "The Archaeological Study of Spanish Colonialism in the Americas." *Journal of Archaeological Research* 18 (2): 151–201. http://dx.doi.org/10.1007/s10814-009-9036-8.

Van Buren, Mary, and Peter T. Bürgi. 1990. "Torata Alta Excavations." In Interim Report, Moquegua Bodegas Project, Fifth Season, 1989, comp. Prudence M. Rice, 51–82. Project files.

Van Buren, Mary, Peter T. Bürgi, and Prudence M. Rice. 1993. "Torata Alta: A Late Highland Settlement in the Osmore Drainage." In *Domestic Architecture, Ethnicity, and Complementarity in the South-Central Andes*, ed. Mark S. Aldenderfer, 136–52. Iowa City: University of Iowa Press.

van de Guchte, Maarten. 1999. "The Inca Cognition of Landscape: Archaeology, Ethnohistory, and the Aesthetic of Alterity." In *Archaeologies of Landscape: Contemporary Perspectives*, ed. Wendy Ashmore and A. Bernard Knapp, 149–68. London: Blackwell.

Van de Put, Albert. 1911. "Hispano-Moresque Ware of the XV Century: Supplementary Studies and Some Later Examples." *Art Workers' Quarterly*. Republished by General Books, London.

Van Dyke, Ruth M. 2008. "Memory, Place, and the Memorialization of Landscape." In *Handbook of Landscape Archaeology*, ed. Bruno David and Julian Thomas, 277–84. Walnut Creek, CA: Left Coast Press.

van Oss, A. C. 1978. "Comparing Colonial Bishoprics in Spanish South America." *Boletín de Estudios Latinoamericanos y del Caribe* 24: 27–66.

Van Young, Eric. 1983. "Mexican Rural History since Chevalier: The Historiography of the Colonial Hacienda." *Latin American Research Review* 18 (3): 7–61.

Vargas Ugarte, Rubén, S. J. 1949. *Historia del Perú: Virreinato (1551–1600)*. Lima: Empresa Periodística "La Prensa."

Vásquez de Espinosa, Antonio. 1948 [ca. 1629]. *Compendio y descripción de las indias occidentales*. Trans. Charles Upson Clark. Miscellaneous Collections, vol. 108, pub. 3898. Washington, DC: Smithsonian Institution Press.

Vassberg, David E. 1984. *Land and Society in Golden Age Castile*. Cambridge: Cambridge University Press.

Velez, C., P. F. Palamara, J. Guevara-Aguirre, L. Hao, T. Karafet, M. Guevara-Aguirre, A. Pearlman, C. Oddoux, M. Hammer, E. Burns, I. Pe'er, G. Atzmon, and H. Ostrer. 2012. "The Impact of Converso Jews on the Genomes of Modern Latin Americans." *Human Genetics* 131: 251–63.

Vendrell, M., J. Molera, and Michael S. Tite. 2000. "Optical Properties of Tin Opacified Glazes." *Archaeometry* 42 (2): 325–40. http://dx.doi.org/10.1111/j.1475-4754.2000.tb00885.x.

Waage, Frederick O. 1934. "Preliminary Report on the Medieval Pottery from Corinth: I. The Prototype of the Archaic Italian Majolica." *Hesperia* 3 (2): 129–39. http://dx.doi.org/10.2307/146525.

Wachtel, Nathan. 1986. "Men of the Water: The Uru Problem (Sixteenth and Seventeenth Centuries)." In *Anthropological History of Andean Polities*, ed. John V. Murra, Nathan Wachtel, and Jacques Revel, 283–310. Cambridge: Cambridge University Press. http://dx.doi.org/10.1017/CBO9780511753091.022.

Ward, Christopher. 1993. *Imperial Panama: Commerce and Conflict in Isthmian America, 1550–1800*. Albuquerque: University of New Mexico Press.

Watanabe, Luis. 1984. "Aspecto histórico y preservativo de la Iglesia Matriz de Moquegua." In *Iglesia Matriz de Moquegua*, by Luis Watanabe M. and Omar Benites D. Lima: Instituto Nacional de Cultura, Programa Contisuyo, Peru.

Weinhold, Rudolf. 1978. *Vivat Bacchus: A History of the Vine and Its Wine*. Trans. Neil Jones. Hertfordshire, England: Argus.

Weinstein, Donald, and Rudolph M. Bell. 1982. *Saints and Society: The Two Worlds of Western Christendom, 1000–1700*. Chicago: University of Chicago Press.

Wernke, Steven A. 2006. "The Politics of Community and Inka Statecraft in the Colca Valley, Peru." *Latin American Antiquity* 17 (2): 177–208. http://dx.doi.org/10.2307/25063046.

Wernke, Steven A. 2007a. "Analogy or Erasure? Dialectics of Religious Transformation in the Early Doctrinas of the Colca Valley, Peru." *International Journal of Historical Archaeology* 11 (2): 152–82. http://dx.doi.org/10.1007/s10761-007-0027-5.

Wernke, Steven A. 2007b. "Negotiating Community and Landscape in the Peruvian Andes: A Trans-Conquest View." *American Anthropologist* 109 (1): 130–52. http://dx.doi.org/10.1525/aa.2007.109.1.130.

Wethey, Harold E. 1949. *Colonial Architecture and Sculpture in Peru*. Cambridge, MA: Harvard University Press.

Wheaton, Timothy R. 2002. "Colonoware Pottery." In *Encyclopedia of Historical Archaeology*, ed. C. E. Orser Jr., 116–18. London: Routledge.

Whitehouse, D. 1980. "Protomajolica." *Faenza* 66: 77–89.

Whitford, J., and C. Potter. 2007. "The State of the Art: Regional Economies, Open Networks and the Spatial Fragmentation of Production." *Socio-Economic Review* 2007: 1–30.

Whitridge, Peter. 2004. "Landscapes, Houses, Bodies, Things: 'Place' and the Archaeology of Inuit Imaginaries." *Journal of Archaeological Method and Theory* 11 (2): 213–50. http://

dx.doi.org/10.1023/B:JARM.0000038067.06670.34.

Williams, Jack S., and Patricia Fournier-García. 1996. "Beyond National Boundaries and Regional Perspectives: Contrasting Approaches to Spanish Colonial Archaeology in the Americas." *World Archaeological Bulletin* 7: 63–86.

Williams, Patrick Ryan. 2001. "Cerro Baúl: A Wari Center on the Tiwanaku Frontier." *Latin American Antiquity* 12 (1): 67–83. http://dx.doi.org/10.2307/971758.

Williams, Patrick Ryan. 2002. "Rethinking Disaster-Induced Collapse in the Demise of the Andean Highland States: Wari and Tiwanaku." *World Archaeology* 33 (2): 321–74.

Williams, Patrick Ryan, and Donna Nash. 2002. "Imperial Interaction in the Andes: Huari and Tiwanaku at Cerro Baúl." In *Andean Archaeology: Variations in Sociopolitical Organization*, vol. 1, ed. William H. Isbell and Helaine Silverman, 243–65. New York: Kluwer Academic/Plenum.

Williams, Patrick Ryan, and Donna Nash. 2006. "Sighting the *Apu*: A GIS Analysis of Wari Imperialism and the Worship of Mountain Peaks." *World Archaeology* 38 (3): 455–68. http://dx.doi.org/10.1080/00438240600813491.

Wolf, Eric R., and Sidney W. Mintz. 1957. "Haciendas and Plantations in Middle America and the Antilles." In *Social and Economic Studies*, vol. 6, ed. H. D. Huggins: 380–412. Mona, Jamaica: University College of the West Indies.

Wykes-Joyce, M. 1958. *Seven Thousand Years of Pottery and Porcelain*. New York: Philosophical Library.

Younger, William. 1966. *Gods, Men, and Wine*. New York: World.

Zarankin, Andrés, and Melissa A. Salerno. 2008. "'Looking South': Historical Archaeology in South America." *Historical Archaeology* 42 (4): 38–58.

Zaro, Gregory, Kenneth C. Nystrom, Alfredo Bar, Adán Umire Alvarez, and Ana Miranda. 2010. "Tierras Olvidadas: Chiribaya Landscape Engineering and Marginality in Southern Peru." *Latin American Antiquity* 21 (4): 355–74. http://dx.doi.org/10.7183/1045-6635.21.4.355.

Zavala Oyague, Carlos. 1946. "Ascendencia de los Fernández de Córdova radicados en el sur del Perú." *Revista del Instituto Peruano de Investigaciones Genealógicas* 1: 41–87. Lima.

Zéndegui, G. de. 1977. "City Planning in the Spanish Colonies." *Americas* (supplement): s1–s12. Organization of American States, Washington, DC.

Zhang Fukang. 1985. "The Origin and Development of Traditional Chinese Glazes and Decorative Ceramic Colors." In *Ancient Technology to Modern Science,* ed. W. D. Kingery, pp. 163–80. Ceramics and Civilization, vol. 1. Columbus, OH: American Ceramic Society.

Zori, Colleen M. 2011. "Metals for the Inka: Late Prehispanic Transformations in

Social Organization and Metal Production in the Quebrada Tarapacá, Northern Chile." PhD dissertation, Department of Anthropology, University of California, Los Angeles.

Zori, Colleen M., and Peter Tropper. 2010. "Late Pre-Hispanic and Early Colonial Silver Production in the Quebrada de Tarapacá, Northern Chile." *Boletín del Museo Chileno de Arte Precolombino* 15 (2): 65–87. http://dx.doi.org/10.4067/S0718-68942010000200005.

Zozaya, Juan. 1981. "Cerámica andalusí." In *Cerámica esmaltada española*, by Trinidad Sánchez-Pacheco, Maria Dolores Giral, Juan Zozaya, Natacha Seseña, Isabel Alvaro Zamora, Juan Ainaud de Lasarte, María Antonia Casanovas, and Balbina Martínez Caviró, 37–50. Barcelona: Editorial Labor.

Zucchiatti, A., A. Bouquillon, I. Katona, and A. D'Alessandro. 2006. "The 'Della Robbia Blue': A Case Study for the Use of Cobalt Pigments in Ceramics during the Italian Renaissance." *Archaeometry* 48: 131–52.

Zuidema, R. Tom. 1964. *The Ceque System of Cuzco: The Social Organization of the Capital of the Incas*. Leiden, the Netherlands: E. J. Brill.

Zuidema, R. Tom. 1983. "Hierarchy and Space in Incaic Social Organization." *Ethnohistory* 30 (2): 49–75.

Zuidema, R. Tom. 1986. "Inka Dynasty and Irrigation: Another Look at Andean Concepts of History." In *Anthropological History of Andean Polities*, ed. John V. Murra, Nathan Wachtel, and Jacques Revel, 177–200. Cambridge, UK: Cambridge University Press. http://dx.doi.org/10.1017/CBO9780511753091.017.

Zuidema, R. Tom. 1994. "Guaman Poma and the Art of Empire: Toward an Iconography of Inca Royal Dress." In *Transatlantic Encounters: Europeans and Andeans in the Sixteenth Century*, ed. Kenneth J. Andrien and Rolena Adorno, 151–202. Berkeley: University of California Press.

Zuidema, R. Tom. 2007. "The Inca Calendar, the Ceque System, and Their Representation in *Exsul Immeritus*." In *Per Bocca d'altri: Indios, gesuiti e spagnoli in due documenti segreti sul Perù del XVII secolo*, by Laura Laurencich Minelli, Davide Domenici, Cesare Poppi, Paulina Numhauser, R. Tom Zuidema, and Vito Bongiorno, 75–104. Bologna, Italia: La Casa Editrice CLUEB (Cooperativa Libreria Universitaria Editrice Bologna). AMSACTA, Alma Mater Digital Library, University of Bologna, Italy. http://www.scribd.com/doc/74657543/The-Inca-Calendar (retrieved 7/25/12).

Index

Abbasid dynasty, 223, 228
Acevedo, Sara, 262
Acuto, Félix, 67
Adobe: and dating, 14, 17n4
Adrada, Alonso, 194
Aguardiente, 15
Alcántara, Order of, 92
Almagro, Diego: and Chile travel, 117, 119, 128n7, 204; and Nuevo Toledo, 95, 96; and rebellion, 121; and siege of Cusco, 51
Alpujarras rebellion, 235, 237, 243, 258, 276, 305
Altiplano, 31. *See also* Collao; Lake Titicaca; Lupaqas; Qollas
Alvarado, Pedro de, 123
Amojonadores, 45, 118
Antisuyu, 43, 44, 51, 266
Apu, 35, 60. *See also* Cerro Baúl
Aragón: majolica production in, 229, 231, 237, 238, 282; comparisons with Andean loza, 299–303
Arequipa: and Buenos, 121, 122, 172; churches in, 204; corregimiento of, 99; diocese of, 100, *101*, 204; encomiendas in, 119–120; and Huaynaputina eruption, 14, 217 (*see also* Huaynaputina); mining in, 21–22; and Moquegua settlement, 15, 123; and road to Moquegua, 67, 75, 125
Aríbalo. *See* Aryballus
Arica, 86; corregimiento of, 80, 99; port of, 81, 125; reduction in, 130. *See also* Martínez Vegaso, Lucas
Aryballus, 62, 155, 163; tin-enameled, 266, 267, 315
Atacama Desert, 20, 27
Audiencia: of Charcas (La Plata), 99, 101; of Lima, 99, 101, 173
Augustinian order, 99, 204
Ayllu, 27; and ancestors, 72; and boundaries, 45; definition of, 7–8, 17n2; and encomienda, 118; and landscape, 43
Aymara, 31, 33, 39, 82; and Inka origins, 48, 49; Inka resettlement of, 52–53; señoríos in Titicaca basin, *74*; and space, 47–48, 161. *See also* Collao; Collasuyu; Lupaqas; Qollas

Bauer, Brian, 73
Belén (de Locumbilla), 169, 171, 172, 195, 209
Bethlemite Order, 195, 209
Blue: in Islamic world, 246n8, 306; -painted loza decoration, 224, 225 (*see also* Majolica, Italianate style); resources for, 257, 306–307. *See also* Cobalt; Loza, New World production spheres of
Bodega(s), 9, *10*, 11, 103; functional sectors of, 107; locations relative to soils, *104*; names of, 78; plans of, 107–108; subdivision by sale, 104, 106. *See also* Moquegua Bodegas Project
Botanical remains: at Locumbilla, *193*–195; at Torata Alta, 157, *158*. *See also* Datura sp.; Molle; *Ricinus comunis*; *Sapindus saponaria*

Botija: capacity of, 173; at Locumbilla, 183; at Sabaya, 62; at Torata Alta, 12, 146, 149, 152, 156, 164
Boundary (~ies): and Inka site organization, 45, 46; meanings of, 315; natural, 5; physical, 5, 46, 314–315; of quarters of Tawantinsuyu, 73; and Spanish administration, 313–314 (*see also* Corregimiento). *See also* HDSA, and boundary markers; Mojon; Río Tumilaca; Taking possession
Boyd-Bowman, Peter, 243
Brandy. *See* Pisco
Bueno, Capt. Hernán (viejo), 120, 121; and Carumas encomienda, 123, 124, 126, 170; socioeconomic successes of, 127. *See also* Yaravico heredad
Bueno, Juan, 120
Bueno, Martín, 120–121, 123, 127, 128n5
Bueno de Arana, Cristóbal, 172
Bueno de Arana, doña Jerónima de Miranda, 122, 170; and family, 171–172; and Locumbilla, 188; will of, 172. *See also* Estrada y Vizcarra, Capt. Alonso de
Bueno de Arana, Hernán, 122, 169
Bueno y García, Hernán (mozo), 121–122, 169, 170; in Arequipa, 122, 127; and tinaja prices, 109
Built environment, 6
Buyl, 298; don Pedro, 233, 251; Philip, 238

Cacique, 8; cacique principal, 66. *See also* Kuraka
Cajamarca: loza production in, 261, 306; Men of, 121, 124; Spaniards' service to Pizarro in, 120
Calaluna, 77; toponymic zone, 106, 182; Toratan lands in, 106
Calatrava, Order of, 92
Callao, 239
Camaná, 120
Camata, 38, 62, 66, 68n4, 160; in Cochuna, 125; etymology of, 72; and LIP, 64; road at, 64, 67; Tambo, 64, 65, 67; and Titicaca basin, 72
Camelid, 52. *See also* Faunal remains
Canary Islands, 243; and colonial shipping, 239, 244
Cañedo-Argüelles Fábrega, Teresa, 102
Cansino, Pedro, 123
Capangos, 87n5, 103

Capavaya, 77, 126, 160. *See also* Sabaya
Capitulación, 94–95
Carapampa toponymic zone, *105*, 106
Cárdenas y Carabantes y Arana, doña Jerónima, 121–122
Carí. *See* Qari
Carumas, 22, 75, 82; encomienda of, 121, 122, 124; lands in Moquegua valley, 77, 80, 105, 106, 107, 124; moieties of, 122; in nested regional model, 83, 84; population of, 123; renamed reductions of, 130. *See also* Bueno, Capt. Hernán (viejo)
Castor bean. *See Ricinus comunis*
Castro, Juan de, 123; encomienda of, 81, 102, 126
Catari: Diego, 123; viejo, 121, 123
Catholicism, local, 199; in Moquegua, 210–211; in Peru, 207; in Spain, 200–203; and wakas, 207
Cauaya. *See* Sabaya
Cavagnaro Orellana, Luis, 77
Ceque, 44, 307n4; absence in Moquegua, 67; as boundary, 46. *See also* Cusco
Cerro Baúl, 35, 67, 312; as Cochuna fort, 60; Inka artifacts at, 64, 79; no Indigenous toponym for, 79–80, 86, 313; rituals at, 79; and sacred landscape, 79
Chamos toponymic zone, 107
Charles V, Holy Roman Emperor, 98, 244
Chen Chen, 37, 64
Chicha, 29, 36, 153, 163–164, 167n15, 315
Chile: conquest of, 125, 128n2; geology of, 21, 37; Peru war with, 16 (*see also* Pacific War)
Chimba toponymic zone, *105*, 106, 169, 171
China, early trade with Persia, 228
Chincha bodega, 11, 17n3, 109–111; site plan, *110*
Chinchaysuyu, 43, 44, 57, 73
Chronology 7, 13–15, 39, 133; of introduction of Christianity, 203–204. *See also* Huaynaputina
Chucuito, 50, 51, 117, 312; churches in, 204; as corregimiento, 80; as crown repartimiento, 52, 80, 99, 101, 120, 126; hanansaya, 118; hurinsaya, 66; as Lupaqa capital, 52, 59; and Moquegua, 61, 67, 216; plan of, *161*; province of, 50, 51. *See also* Lupaqas
Chucuito Polychrome, 139, 149, *154*, 285, 297, 299
Chupas, Battle of, 123

Church, Roman Catholic: in early Andes, 203–204; dioceses of, 100, *101*, 204; and formal Catholicism, 199, 203; and Spanish exploration, 93, 199–200. *See also* Catholicism, local
Church structures: architecture of, 205–207; mestizo style, 206; in Moquegua, 208–210 (*see also* La Matriz); mudéjar style, 206–207, 239–240; at Sabaya, 62; at Torata, 100, 166; at Torata Alta, 138–143, 165
Cieza de León, Pedro de, 46, 58; on Inka conquest of Collao, 49, 51, 52; on LIP polity in southwest Peru, 73
Coanto, 77, 106
Cobalt: colors produced, 267; sources of, 254–255, 269. *See also* Blue; Loza, New World production spheres of; Majolica, Italianate style
Cobo, fr. Bernabé, 43; on chicha production, 153; on colonial ceramics, 261, 276, 285; on Inka conquest of Collao, 49, 50
Cochuna (kuraka), 77, 125
Cochuna (settlement), 56, 60, 65, 76; as encomienda, 76, 77, 102 (*see also* Castro, Juan de); location of, 62, 66
Cochuna (valley): boundaries of, 76–77; and encomienda, 81, 125, 128n10; Inka settlement in, 62–64; Inka siege of, 55–56, 58, 59; as mountains, 60, 76; in nested regional model, 83, 84; Qolla colonists of, 126; as region, 60, 61, 77, 125. *See also* Torata valley
Cofradía, 172; in Andes, 207; Concepción Inmaculada, 203, 216; Las Animas de Purgatorio, 203, 216; in Moquegua, 216, 222n6; Nuestra Señora de Dolores, 203; Nuestra Señora de la Soledad, 203; Rosario, 203; Sagrado Nombre de Jesus, 203; Santísimo Sacramento, 203, 209, 216; in Spain, 201–202, 203; and Trentine reforms, 203, 207, 216; Vera Cruz, 203
Coins, 112, 149, 157, 192
Colca valley, 38, 68, 166n5
Colesuyu, 74–75, 76, 81; as modern Ilo province, 86; as Spanish province, 101. *See also* Koli
Coli. *See* Koli
Collaguas, 82; in nested regional model, 83
Collao, the, 47, 82; Inka conquest of, 49–52; as Inka province, 73. *See also* Aymara; Collasuyu; Lake Titicaca (basin); Lupaqa; Qolla
Collasuyu, 44, 52, 73. 82; in Cusco, 43, 58. *See also* Collao; Lake Titicaca (basin); Qollas
Colonialism, 4
Colono-ware, 241
Columbia Plain, 240
Comercio libre, 14
Compañía/Society de Jesus. *See* Jesuits
Compostela, 92
Condesuyos, 44, 58, 73; corregimiento of, 73; in nested regional model, 83. *See also* Contisuyu
Congregación, 97, 102. *See also* Reducción
Conta, don Pedro: as acompañado, *103*; as kuraka, 102, 164, 165; and lands in Moquegua valley, 103; and witchcraft, 221
Contisuyu, 43, 51, 55; boundaries of, 73–74, 75; and ceques in Cusco, 44; etymology of, 73; as hurin-hurin, 44, 48, 67, 83, 311; in nested regional model, 83–84
Contisuyu Tin-enameled ware, 282. *See also* Escapalaque Yellow Polychrome; Mas Alla Polychrome
Converso, 235, 237, 247n18
Copper, 53; ores in Peru, 21
Corpanto toponymic zone, 106–107, 182
Corregimiento, 80–81, 99
Counter Reformation, 202, 203
Cuchuna. *See* Cochuna
Cummins, Thomas, 152
Cuntisuyu. *See* Contisuyu
Cupina toponymic zone, 107, 196, 211
Cusco: and conquest of the Collao, 50, 51; diocese of, 100; hanan, 43, 57; hurin, 43, 58; and Inka origins, 48, 49; and La Merced convent, 107; moieties in, 43, 49. *See also* Ceque
Cusi, don Martin, 66
Cutipa, don Martín, 102, *103*, 164, 165

Datura sp., 195
Dávalos de Ribera, doña María, 124, 126
Davies, Keith, 174
Deagan, Kathleen, 11
deFrance, Susan, 192
Design analysis. *See* HDSA (Hierarchical Design Structure Analysis)
Díaz, Bernal, 93

Diet. *See* Botanical Remains; Faunal Remains
Diez de San Miguel, Garci, 130, 220
Doctrina, 78; of Moquegua, 100; of Torata, 100, 166
Dominican order, 99, 203, 205; in Lake Titicaca basin, 204; in Moquegua, 114, 208, 210, 211 (*see also* Yahuay); and pottery production, 256
Dual organization, 7–8, 46, 66, 82. *See also* Moiety

Earthquake, 14, 20; damage at Locumbilla, 197n3; damage in Moquegua, 197n3, 208, 209, 210; damage at Torata Alta, 142, 149; patron saints against, 209. *See also* Huaynaputina, eruption of
Ecological complementarity model, 12
El Niño. *See* ENSO events
Encomienda, 96–97, 117–120. *See also individual communities and regions*
ENSO events, 28–29, 37, 40
Escapagua, 65, 87n5, 124, 208; and dispute with Moquegua, 100, 101, 208, 314; toponymic zone, *105*–106. *See also* San Sebastián; Villa San Francisco de Esquilache
Escapalac (Escapalaque), 77; and Buenos, 122, 169; toponymic zone, *105*
Escapalaque Yellow Polychrome, 282, 307; and HDSA, 287, 289, 292, 295, 297
Estopacaje, 116n9; bodega, 11, 106, 111–112, 169
Estrada, Felipe, 173
Estrada y Vizcarra, Capt. Alonso de, 109, 122, 170; and family, 171–172, 173; and La Matriz, 172, 208; and Locumbilla, 190; will of, 172, 216. *See also* Bueno de Arana, doña Jerónima de Miranda; Vizcarra y Estrada, don Diego de

Falca, 108
False majolica, 265, 273, 307n5
Faunal remains: at Locumbilla, 192; at Torata Alta, 158–159
Feldspar-inlaid ware, 273
Ferdinand and Isabela, 93, 100, 122; and Muslim persecutions, 237; and trade policy, 244
Fernández de Córdova y Aguilar, Diego, 127, 128n10, 240
Fernández de Lugo Cabeza de Vaca, fr. Gaspar, 209

Fernández Maldonado, don Diego, 122, and lands bounding Yaravico, 172. *See also* Vizcarra y Bueno de Arana, doña Isabel de
Fernández Maldonado y de la Raya, don Antonio Isidro, 195
Franciscan order, 99, 204; in Moquegua, 209, 210
Frontier: Inka, 53; and Marianism, 207; Moquegua as, 7, 15, 309

García, Diego, 128n2
García Bueno, Hernán, 171
Garcilaso de la Vega, "El Inka": as chronicler, 58; family of, 56–57; on horses, 220; on Inka conquest of Collao, 48, 49–50, 52, 58–59; on Inkas in Moquegua, 55–56, 58, 60, 61, 62; and landscape, 43
Garrison, 56, 63, 66. *See also* Torata Alta site, as presidio
Gastón bodega, 170, 171, 172
Glass beads, 62, 115; Nueva Cadiz, 149, 157
Goggin, John, 224, 255, 262, 273
Granada: and luster ware, 230; and majolica, 229
Green: and loza decoration, 224; in Mexico, 224, 273–274, 306; Muslim symbolism of, 223. *See also* HDSA; Loza, New World production spheres of; Verde y morado in New World; Verde y morado in Spain
Green-and-manganese. *See* Verde y morado in New World; Verde y morado in Spain
Guaman Poma de Ayala, Felipe, 45, 53n6
Guerrero de Vargas, Bach. Juan (vicar), 172, 173–174
Guevara, Pedro, 112
Guilds: in Catalonia, 231; in Lima, 207, 261
Gutiérrez Flores, fr. Pedro, 102
Gypsum, 22, 30

Hacienda, 103
Hanan (-saya, -suyu), 8, 54n8; in Chucuito, 118; in Cusco, 43; and Moquegua, 66; in Tawantinsuyu, 43–44; in Torata, 162
Hardin Friedrich, Margaret, 283
Hatunqolla: and colonists in Cochuna, 77; and conquest of the Collao, 49, 50 (*see also* Collao); as Inka administrative center, 51, 53, 55, 59; as LIP fortress, 53; as Qolla capital, 59 (*see also* Qolla); site plan of, 161

HDSA (Hierarchical design structure analysis), 283–284, 285, 302; and boundary markers, 292–293, 295, 300, 302, 305, *306*, 314; and color use, 287–291, 301; comparisons of, 300–302, 303, 305–307; and configurations, *296*, 297, 300; and elements, 284, 295, 297, 300, 301; and Escapalaque Yellow Polychrome, 287, 289, 292, 295, 297; and forms, 285–287, 300; and frondosidad, 297–299, 300; and Inka decoration, 293, 305, 314; and Italianate elements, 305; and layout, 283, 285, *286*, 291–293, 300, 302; and Mas Alla Polychrome, 287, 289, 292, 295, 297, 298, 301; and medallions, 292, 298, 299, 302, 305, *306*; and Mexico, 293, 295–296, 298; and motifs, 283–284, *286*, *294*, 298, 300; and Muel/Teruel, 286, 289, 300, 301; and Panama La Vieja, 290–291, 293, 296–297; and quadripartition, 297, 298, 301
Hispano-Moresque ware. *See* Majolica, Hispano-Moresque ware
Horses, 219–220
Horseshoes, 147, 218–221, 222n11
Huaca. *See* Waka
Huantajaya silver mine, 125
Huaracane, 77, 124
Huari. *See* Wari
Huarina, Battle of, 121
Huaynaputina, 20; eruption of, 13–14, 15, 188, 217; volcanic ash from, 14, 15, 39, 63, 79, 110, 186. *See also individual sites and towns*
Hurin (-saya, -suyu), 8, 54n8; in Chucuito, 66; in Cusco, 43; and Moquegua, 48; in Tawantinsuyu, 43–44; and Torata, 66, 77, 83, 102, 162
Hurtado de Mendoza, Viceroy, 80, 121
Hurtado Zapata y Echagoyen, Capt. Don José, 196

Ilo, 24, 29, 40, 65; in encomienda, 81; modern province of, 85, 86; and Moquegua's wine, 216. *See also* Colesuyo
Inga Pari, 102, *103*
Inka(s), 7, 8; and ancestors' journey, 46; and boundaries, 45, 46; and landscape cognition, 42, 44; origin myths of, 48, 54n9; use of stone, 46, 52
Inka-Lupaqa alliance, 13, 32, 47; and encomiendas, 119; formation of, 49, 50, 59; and Moquegua, 67

Inka Polychrome, 156, 285, 299
Inka spatial strategies, 65–66, 67; production enclaves, 66; resettlement, 32, 53, 160–161; site planning, 12; spatial order, 52. *See also* Moquegua valley, Inkas in
Inquisition: in Lima, 204, 319n1; in Spain, 237, 319n1
Isabel, Queen. *See* Ferdinand and Isabela
Isabela Polychrome, 240, 290
Isabel Palla (Chimpu Ocllo of Cusco), 56–57, 126
Isabel Palla (of Nasca), 126

Jesuits, 107, 109; in Arequipa, 172, 204; in Cusco, 204; expulsion from Peru, 205; heredad of, 197–108; in Moquegua, 204, 208; and Yaravico, 172m 196
Jones, John, 193, 194
Julien, Catherine, 52

Kallanka: at Sabaya, 62, *63*, 66, 67; at Torata Alta, 67, 134–135
Kallawaya, 17n2, 43, 53n4, 71. *See also* Umasuyu
Kancha, 12, 62, 132, *134*, 160, 161, 166n2
Kero, 38, 163, 222n5, 266, 299, 315
Khipu, 42
Kiln, 109; at Chincha, 110; at Locumbilla, 182–184, 194
Koli: language, 33, 39, 70, 72, 75, 86; personality traits, 48, 72
Kubler, George, 12
Kuraka, 8, 98; duties of, 45; in encomienda, 118; and horses, 220; legitimacy of, 102

Lagar, 108, 116n7
La Gasca, Gov. Pedro, 121
Lake Suches, 67
Lake Titicaca (basin), 15, 20, 31, 219; Aymara señoríos in, *74*; and Copacabana, 207, 218; and Inka origins, 48; and Inka re-spatialization, 52–53, 61; and Moquegua's wine, 216; sediment core from, 37; post-Tiwanaku, 47. *See also* Aymara; Collao; Lupaqas; Qollas; Tiwanaku
La Matriz, 172, 208–209, 210, 216. *See also* Santa Catalina de Alejandría, Iglesia de
Landscape, 5, 6, 16n1; colonized, 31; cultural, 6; embodied, 42–43; Inka cognition of, 42, 44; of Moquegua, 6, 7, 19–20

Late Horizon, 7, 14, 32, 40–42. *See also* Collao; Inka(s); Inka spatial strategies; *individual Inka rulers*
Late Intermediate Period (LIP), 7, 31; polity in southwestern Peru, 39, 50, 73, 82; settlement in Moquegua, 37–40; settlement in Torata valley, 67
Laws of Burgos, 118
Lechtman, Heather, 53n5
Lefebvre, Henri, 311, 313
Lima: archdiocese of, 100, *101*; audiencia of, 99, 101; Councils of, 204, 205. *See also* Callao
Limpieza de sangre, 57, 91, 93
Lister, Florence and Robert, 251, 252, 256, 295; and green decoration, 273–274, 276, 289, 290, 306; and Panama pottery, 258, 305
Little Ice Age, 28
Lloque Yupanki (Inka), 49, 50, 55, 58
Lockhart, James, 245
Locumbilla bodega/heredad, 11, 106, 112, *177*, 184–186, 195–196; adobes at, 180, 182, 190, 197n4; archaeofauna at, 192; earthquake damage to, 197n3; grape seed deposits at, *181*, 185, 186, 188, *189*; hospital at, 195; Jesuit school at, 196; owners of, *196*; radiocarbon dates from, 13, 184, 186; volcanic ash at, 186–188, 191. *See also* Yaravico heredad
Locumbilla bodega structures: brick floors, 190; chapel, 189–190, 211; falca, 16, 182, *184*; fermentation bodegas, 178, 180; kiln, 182–184, 194; lagars, 178, 180, 187; late eighteenth-century construction, 181–182, 178, 196; plan of, *175*, *176*, *177*; residential sector, 189–191; sixteenth-century construction, 186–*187*
Locumbilla ceramics: botijas, 183; Indigenous polychrome, 65, 188; Pearlware, 178, 182; tinajas, 181–182; tin-enameled ware, 191, 281–282 (*see also* Mas Alla Polychrome); whitewares, 191. *See also* Mechero Plain
Locumbilla (land), 122, 172, 176, 188. *See also* Vizcarra, Alonso de
Loza, 191, 224, 227, 255; and class, 277; New World production spheres of, 267, *268–271*, 282, 300, 304–305, 306, 317, 319. *See also* Majolica; Tin-enameled ware
Lupaqas, 13, 31; colonists in Moquegua, 14, 32, 33, 39, 61, 70, 71, 72; and conquest of Collao, 49–52; hanansaya moiety of, 51, 59; polity, 47. *See also* Chucuito

Luster ware, 230, 233, 238, 241, 246n2, 298; in colonies, 247n14; production technology of, 250. *See also* Málaga; Valencia

Magdalena de Cao Viejo, 139, 142
Majolica, 223; etymology, 227; Hispano-Moresque ware, 232, 270 (*see also* Morisco ware; Mudéjar pottery; Verde y morado, in Spain); imports in northern Europe, 235, 236–237; Italianate (Renaissance) style, 233–235, 242, 289, 295, 300, 305, 307, 315 (*see also* Sevilla; Talavera de la Reina); tiles, 241; at Torata Alta, 136, 156, 307. *See also* Loza; Tin-enameled ware
Málaga, majolica production in, 227, 229, 233, 246n2. *See also* Luster ware
Malata, 166n5. *See also* Colca valley
Manco Capac (Inka), 43, 51
Manises, majolica production in, 231, 232, 233, 238, 246n2, 250–251
Marianism: in Peru, 207; in Spain, 200–201, 202; and tinajas, 216; and wine, 222n7
Martínez Vegaso, Lucas: business success of, 125, 127; and Carumas encomienda, 123, 124, 125; coastal encomienda of, 75, 80, 81, 125, 126; and Convento de San Francisco (Arequipa), 204. *See also* Dávalos de Ribera, María; Tarapacá (Viejo)
Mas Alla Polychrome, 263, *264*, 282; and HDSA, 287, 289, 292, 295, 297, 298, 301; at Locumbilla, 191, 263; at Torata Alta, 156
Mayta Capac (Qhapaq), 55, 58–59
Mazuelo family, 122
Mechero Plain, 184, 185–186, 188, 194
Mercedarian order, 99, 203, 204; in Arequipa, 107; in Moquegua, 107, 204, 210 (*see also* Cupina toponymic zone)
Mexico City loza: blue decoration of, 267; clays for, 256; colors of, 290; decorative motifs on 295–296; green decoration of, 224, 273–274, 306; and production, 241–242, 255–257
Middle Horizon, 7, 35. *See also* Tiwanaku; Wari
Migration, 242–244, 276; to Mexico, 243; to Peru, 243; of potters and painters, 304–305
Milky Way, 43, 161
Misogyny, Spanish, 98, 200–201
Moiety, 8, 43–44; in nested regional model, 83. *See also* Dual organization; Hanan; Hurin; Parcialidad; Tawantinsuyu

Mojon, 45, 53n6; and encomiendas, 118; and Inka labor responsibilities, 80–81; in Moquegua, 80, 106, 124. *See also* Boundary(~ies)
Molle (*Schinus molle*), 29, 36; at Locumbilla, *193*, 194, 195. *See also* Chicha
Montalvo: bodega, 172, 197n2; family, 122, 172
Moquegua, Department of, *2*, 19; geology of, 20–22; modern provinces of, *85*, 86, 314; moiety (hanan), 67, 77, 84, 102; physical environment of, 19; respatializations of, 318; river systems of, 22–24 (*see also* Río Osmore; Río Tambo); weather of, 27–29
Moquegua Bodegas Project, 9, 11, 17n3, 78,211; at Locumbilla, 112, 177; at Yahuay, 114–115; at Yaravico Viejo, 112. *See also* Torata Alta fieldwork
Moquegua valley, *10*, 11, 23–24; and corregimiento, 81; dispute with Escapagua, 100, 101, 208, 314; no encomienda in, 117, 128n2; first Spaniards in, 123–124; Inkas in, 53, 55–56, 59, 60, 62, 64–65, 311 (*see also* Inka spatial strategies; Moquehua); and irrigation water rights, 120, 312; population decline in, 102; soils of, 25–26, 30, *105*; Spanish respatialization of, 102, 130, 313. *See also* Frontier, Moquegua as; Osmore valley; Periphery, Moquegua as; Villa Santa Catalina de Guadalcázar; Wine
Moquehua (Inka town), 56, 60, 64, 65, 67, 126, 312
Moquiguaya, 119
Moquingoa, 87n3
Morisco(s), 224, 230, 237; artisans in New World, 225, 243, 276–277 (*see also* Migration; Mudéjar style); in Mexico, 245, 248n21; in Peru, 245, 248n20, 276
Morisco ware, 240, 262, 272, 290 (*see also* Sevilla, majolica production in)
Moseley, Michael, 9
Mudéjar pottery, 231, 232, 243, 246n4, 246n7; and calcareous clays, 252; decorative style of, 300 (*see also* HDSA); of Muel, 238, 250, 282, 301, 305; of Teruel, 232, 238, 282, 301. *See also* Aragón; HDSA, and Muel/Teruel; Luster ware; Majolica; Málaga; Valencia; Verde y morado in Spain; Zaragoza
Mudéjar style, 224, 230–231; in Andean architecture, 206–207, 239–240; in architecture, 231, 245; in pottery, 224 (*see also* Verde y morado in Spain); in Sevillan architecture, 235
Murra, John, 12, 52, 164
Muslim persecutions, 237–*238*, 247n10, 304; exiling, 237; expulsion from Sevilla, 230; forcible baptism, 237. *See also* Alpujarras rebellion; Migration

Nasrid dynasty in Spain, 230
Natt, Wendy, 283, 284
Nested regional model. *See* Southwest Peru region, and nested model
New Laws of the Indies, 118
Nicoluso, Francisco, 234, 247n16
Nieto, Mariscal don Domingo, 86
Noguerol de Ulloa, Francisco, 80
Nueva Castilla, 94, *95*, 96

Ocelocalco, 219, 271–272
Ocolla, 71; toponymic zone, *105*
Olive jar. *See* Botija
Omasuyos, 47, 74, 75
Omate, 75; on Inka road, 119; in nested regional model, 83
Omo, 77; Carumas lands in, 124; Middle Horizon site, 37, 65; toponymic zone, 106, 182. *See also* Tiwanaku
Orcosuyu, 74, 75
Osmore valley: archaeological sites in, 9 (*see also* Programa Contisuyo); Indigenous colonization of, 3, 33, 35, 37, 39; Inkas in, 55–56, 61; ritual landscape of, 79; soils of, 7, 24–26; vegetation of, 29. *See also* Moquegua valley; Río Osmore
Otora, 130. *See also* Río Otora
Oviedo, 244
Ovina. *See* Ubinas

Pacajes (polity), 47, 52, 61, 154, 163; Moquegua colonists from, 70, 72, 116n9
Pacariqtambo, 48, 49
Pacaxa, Carlos, 102, *103*
Pachacuti (Inka), 56; and conquest of Collao, 49, 50–51, 52; and conquest of Moquegua, 58
Pacific Copper Belt, 21
Pacific War, 11
Panama Blue-on-white, 258, 290; decoration on, 291, 297, 298–299

INDEX 373

Panamá La Vieja, as shipping hub, 239, 258
Panamá La Vieja, pottery of, 258, 290; and cobalt, 269, 304; and HDSA, 290–291, 293, 296–297; and kilns, 258, 262, 271; and New World production spheres, 304; and tin-enameled ware, 224, 251, 257–258, 259, 282, 305. *See also* Feldspar-inlaid ware; Panama Blue-on-white; Panama Polychrome
Panama Polychrome, 258, 271, 289, 291, 299, 305; lacy decoration of, 273, 297; in Lima, 262; and verde y morado, 271, 279n13, 301
Parcialidad, 8, 82. *See also* Moiety
Paterna, majolica production in, 231, 232, 236, 273, 282, 297, 301
Patronato real, 100, 115n2
Paucarcolla, 49, 50
Pease G., Franklin, 75
Period, 7. *See also* Late Intermediate Period
Periphery, 7, 15; Moquegua as, 81, 309, 311, 318; and styles, 206
Persia, early trade with China, 228
Peru loza, 243; and blue pigment, 261, 270, 272; and colors used, 260, 262, 263, 266, 267; in Cusco, 243, 259, 262–263, 266, 274, 275, 276, 289, 292; and green and black decoration, 261, 263–266, 274–275, 305, 306, 315, 316–317, 319 (*see also* Mas Alla Polychrome; Escapalaque Yellow Polychrome); in Lima, 243, 259, 261–262; and morisco/mudéjar influence, 282; in Titicaca basin, 261, 263, 265, 273, 292 (*see also* False majolica). *See also* HDSA; Loza, New World production spheres of; Verde y morado in New World
Pisco, 16, 29, 104, 108, 195, 216
Pizarro, Francisco, 54; and early explorations, 94, 99, 117; encomienda awards of, 117, 119–120, 125; expedition to the Collao, 119, 121; recruitment of southwest settlers, 119
Pizarro, Hernando, and defeat of Aymara, 51
Pizarro, Gonzalo, 121, 204
Pizarro, Juan, first encomienda awards of, 119, 123, 125
Pizarro, Pedro, encomienda of, 81, 120
Place(s), 5, 6; defined by Inkas vs. Spaniards, 160–161; naming of, 69 (*see also* Toponymy)
Pocsi (San Francisco de), 75, 130
Poison, 61
Policía cristiana, 97
Polvorín, 61, 67, 167n11

Poma, Ana, 171
Poma, Francisco, *103*
Porcelain, 246n5, 270, 278n2, 292; in Peru, 271, 157; at Torata Alta, 136, 149
Portobelo, 239, 258, 272
Potosí, 15, 99; and Moquegua's wine, 216
Presidio. *See* Garrison; Torata Alta site, as presidio
Programa Contisuyo, 9, 12, 39, 135
Pucara (fortification), 47, 60
Pucará (town), 50
Puebla (Mexico) loza, 273, 296, 298; and cobalt pigment, 268–269; colors of, 290; in Lima, 262; production of, 224, 256
Pukina. *See* Puquina
Puquina (encomienda, town), 71, 75, 130
Puquina (language), 33, 48, 77; in Moquegua, 70, 71, 72; in Titicaca basin, 86–87n11

Qari, 49, 51, 59; don Martín, 118, 165
Qollahuayas. *See* Kallawaya
Qollas, 31, 154; colonists in Moquegua, 33, 39, 59, 61, 70, 71, 72, 312 (*see also* Ocolla); and conquest of Collao, 49–52, 58; control over southwestern Peru, 39, 50, 73, 82; polity, 47; at Sabaya, 63. *See also* Hatunqolla
Quadripartition: of Inka space, 43–44, 46. *See also* HDSA, and quadripartition
Quechua, 33, 48; toponyms, 71–72
Quelccaya ice cap, 28, 37
Quinistaca, 75
Quinoestacas, 77, 119

Ramírez, Susan, 40, 53n6
Reconquest/Reconquista, 70, 91, 93, 199, 224, 228
Reducción, 97, 129–130, 204. *See also* Congregación
Region, 1, 82
Requerimiento, 54n10, 96
Restall, Matthew, 242, 247n17, 315
Ribera, Nicolás de, 126
Ricinus comunis, 115, 194–195, 197n6
Rinconada toponymic zone, 107
Ring Site, 31
Río Capillune, 23, 26, 130
Río Caplina, 24
Río Coscori, 23, 130
Río Huaracane, 23, 24, 39, 130

Río Ilo, 24, 74. *See also* Ilo
Río Locumba, 24, 81, 87n8, 104, 116n5
Río Osmore, 20, 22; flooding of, 28, 29; flow of, 27; as jurisdictional boundary, 99; lacking name, 77; in nested regional model, 83–84; and Spanish settlement, 100; tributaries of, 22, 23 (*see also tributaries' names*). *See also* Moquegua valley; Osmore valley
Río Osmore confluence area, 25, 26, 64; soils in, 60; Spanish settlement in, 100; toponymic zones in, 105–106. *See also* Cochuna; Moquehua; Yaravico
Río Otora, 23, 26, 39, 61, 67
Río Quilancha, 23
Río Sama, 24, 81, 87n8
Río Tajo (Spain), 91, 92
Río Tambo, 13; encomiendas in, 120, 123, 125; in nested regional model, 83–84; tributaries of, 22. *See also* Carumas; Ubinas
Río Torata, 12, 23, 24, 60, 71; sites along, *36. See also* Torata valley
Río Tumilaca, 23, 24, 25; as boundary of Cochuna, 77, 101; as boundary of Lima audiencia, 99; and city of Moquegua, 64, 77, 99, 101; flooding of, 29; and reduction, 130; and Spanish settlement, 100; tree crops in, 30
Roads: camino real, 172; coastal, 67, 75, 119; Cochuna, 66, 77; Collasuyu, 66, 77; Inka, 40, 61, 64, 73, 161; in Moquegua valley, *26, 68*n5, 119; in Ubinas, 83
Rodman, Margaret, 314
Rodríguez de Huelva, Hernán, 123
Rodríguez de Ves, Juan, 174
Rostworowski, María, 74, 87n5
Rovira, Beatriz, 272
Rowe, John, 51
Rufford Company (brick), 110

Saavedra y Vasco, doña Mariana de, 122
Sabaya, 62–*63*, 65, 71, 126, 166n9, 222n10, 167n12; in Cochuna, 125; as Inka administrative center, 66, 67, 160; volcano, 87n2
Sacata toponymic zone, 107
Saint James the Greater (apostle), 93, 220
Saint Joseph, 196, 197n7
Saints: in early Europe, 200, 201; names on Moquegua tinajas, 212–216; Peruvian, 205. *See individual saints*

Salinas, Battle of, 121
Samegua, 30, 77, 106, 124
San Agustín de Torata, 166
San Antonio (saint), 203
San Antonio (site), 38, 63, 67; as Cochuna fortification, 60, 62, 64; possible Late Horizon occupation at, 39, 66; name of, 87n7; as Qolla settlement, 39, 71; setting of, *131, 132*
San Antonio de Padua (hospital), 195, 208, 209
San Bernabé, 209, 212
San Blas, 203
San Isidro Labrador, 114
San Juan, Juan de, 126
San Martín de Porua (Porres), 205, 209
San Roque, 203
San Sebastián (community), 99, 101; founding of, 124, 208. *See also* Escapagua Villa; San Francisco de Esquilache
San Sebastian (saint), 208
Santa Catalina de Alejandria, 208; Iglesia de, 208–209. *See also* La Matriz
Santa Catalina de Siena, 205
Santa Fortunata, 210
Santa Rosa, 205, 208
Santiago, Order of (Saint James of the Sword), 92–93
Santo Domingo (bodega site), 196
Santo Domingo Blue-on-white, 240, 290
San Toribio Mogrovejo, 205
Sapindus saponaria, 115, 194–195, 197n6
Sarmiento de Gamboa, Pedro de, 39, 48, 58; on Inka conquest of Collao, 49, 50–51; on Qolla LIP polity in southwest Peru, 73
Sempat Assadourian, Carlos, xvi, xvii
Sevilla, majolica production in, 229, 234–236; clay used, 252; decoration of, 289, 295; and Morisco ware, 290; potters' barrios in, 235 (*see also* Triana)
Sgrafitto ware, 272–273
Sibaja, 125. *See also* Sabaya
Sillustani pottery, 65, 149, 154, *155*, 163
Silva, Hernando de, and Carumas encomienda, 123, 126
Smith, Greg, 110, 115
Solar cycles, 79; winter solstice, 38
Sorcery. *See* Witchcraft
Southern Oscillation. *See* ENSO events
Southwestern Peru region: Cieza de León on, 73; Inka annexation of, 162; and nested

INDEX 375

model, 83–84; Qolla LIP polity of, 39, 50, 73, 82, 162
Space(s), 4, 160; espacio Moqueguano, xvi, 309; espacio Peruano, xvi
Spanish colonial administrative institutions: Medieval roots of, 93, 94, 97; and re-spatialization, 94. *See* Audiencia; Corregimiento; Encomienda; Limpieza de sangre; Reducción
Spatialization, 4, 6, 31; hybrid colonial, 81; of pottery decoration (*see* HDSA); and respatialization, 32. *See also* Inka spatial strategies; Quadripartition; Space(s)
Stanish, Charles, 71
Stone, 44: and adobe construction, 139; bedrock outcrop of, 135; and pirca construction, 62, 134, 139; veneration of, 218
Suañalay, 103, 115–116n4
Sugar, 173
Suhuba, 77. *See also* Sabaya
Suhubaya, 126, 160. *See also* Sabaya
Sujabaya, 128n8. *See also* Sabaya

Tacasi, 102, *103*
Tacna, 21, 22, 26; and coastal road, 75, 119; in nested regional model, 83; San Pedro de, 130
Taking possession, 90, 96
Taki Onkoy, 98, 312
Talavera de la Reina, majolica production in, 234, 236, 238, 241, 242, 289, 297, 298
Tambo, 40, 64. *See also* Camata, Tambo
T'ang dynasty, pottery of, 228, 249
Tarapacá (Viejo), 74, 75, 80, 119, 197n6, 166n3, 166n9; and encomienda, 125, 130; plan of, 161–162; silver mine, 125. *See also* Martínez Vegaso, Lucas
Tarata, 72, 82, 125; in nested regional model, 83
Tawantinsuyu, 40, *41*, 42, 46, 73; moieties in, 43, 48. *See also* Antisuyu; Chinchaysuyu; Collasuyu; Contisuyu
Tiahuanaco. *See* Tiwanaku
Tinaja(s), 9, 109; inscriptions on, 109, 116n11, 211–217; Moquegua's oldest, 112 (*see also* Yaravico Viejo bodega)
Tin: as opacifier, 228, 249; in Peru, 257, 263; source of, in Mexico, 257; source of, for Spain, 253, 257
Tin-enameled ware, 64; in Andes, 251, 256 (*see also* Peru loza); beginnings of, 228–229;

clay used for, 251–252; in Ecuador, 261, 271, 289; glazes of, 253–254; in Mexico, 241, 243, 255–257 (*see also* Mexico City loza; Puebla [Mexico] loza); stylistic analysis of, 302 (*see also* HDSA); and tiles, 261; at Torata Alta, 156. *See also* Loza; Panamá La Vieja
Tiwanaku, 7, 14; colonies in Moquegua, 33, 37, 65, 311 (*see also* Omo); fall of, 31, 47, 49; Gateway God, 46; language of, 33, 71; and walled compounds, 45
Toledo, Viceroy Francisco de, 58; reforms of, 98, 128n4
Topa Yupanki (Inka), 45, 56; and conquest of Collao, 49, 50, 51, 52, 61; and conquest of Moquegua, 58
Toponym, 6–7, 69–70; and landscape construction, 312–313; religious, 210
Toponymic zones, 78, 105–107
Torata (town), 22; church at, 100, 166; as Cochuna, 77; etymology of, 72; lands in Moquegua, 104, 106
Torata Alta (site), 12, 125, 312; abandonment of, 136, 147, 165–166; architecture of, 133–134 (*see also* Torata Alta structures); beer production at, 153, 163; as Cochuna, 62 (*see also* Cochuna valley); as congregación, 12–13, 15, 102, 129, 130, 160, 312; eastern sector of, 135–136, 137–138, 162, 163; and feasting, 164; horseshoes at, 149, 218–219, 220, 149; as Inka administrative center, 14, 63–64, 66, 67, 135, 136, 160; and Lupaqas, 14–15, 126, 131, 312; map of, *134*; and Middle Horizon, 37; and moiety organization, 162; plazas at, 134, 135, 161, 164; as presidio, 136, 160 (*see also* Garrison); resistance at, 218, 221, 312; setting of, *131*, *132*; textile production at, 152–153; western sector of, 135, 136
Torata Alta fieldwork, 12, 132; and artifacts, 146, 147, 149, 152–157, 167n13; and botanical remains, 157–*158*; and ceramics, 136, *147*, 149, 150, 153, *154–155*, 163, 163–164; in church, 139–143; and faunal remains, 158–*159*; and periodization, *133*; and radiocarbon dates, 13, 137–138; and stratigraphy, 14–15, 133, 139; and volcanic ash, 15, 133, 136, 137, 139, 146, 147, 149, *151*, 219, 165
Torata Alta structures: church, *138*–143, 165, 166n7; domestic, 148–152; elite residence, 164; and food preparation, 146–148, 163;

kallanka, 67, 134–135, 166n7; kanchas, 161; modern shrine, 141, *144*; possible aqllawasi, 165; possible friary, 145–146; sizes of, 136, *137*, 163; types of, 136

Torata valley, *132*; and hanan, 162; as hurin, 66, 77, 83, 102, 162; and Inkas 55–56, 62, 65, 66; kuraka of, 102, *103*; population decline in, 102; Qolla colonists in, 160; road through, 66; soils of, 25–26, 60. *See also* Cochuna (valley)

Tordoya Várgas, Gómez de, 123

Treaty of Tordesillas, 115n1

Trelles Aréstegui, Efraín, 124

Trent, Council of, 98, 202, 203

Triana, 235, 237, 240

Tribute goods, 120

Tschopik, Harry, 49, 51, 61

Tumilaca, 71, 130; and doctrina, 100

Tupu, 63, 147, 163

Ubinas (San Felipe de), 22, 75, 77, 82, 130; corregimiento of, 81, 101; encomienda, 80, 125, 126; in nested regional model, 83

Umasuyu, 47, 71. *See also* Omasuyos

Umate, Umati. *See* Omate

Umayyid dynasty, 223; in Spain, 229

Upton, Dell, 6

Urcosuyu, 47. *See also* Orcosuyu

Urton, Gary, 46

Usnu, 62, 68n3, 135

Vaca de Castro, Gov. Cristóbal, 121, 123, 126

Valdivia, Pedro de, 125; and conquest of Chile, 128n2, 204

Valencia, majolica production in, 231, 237, 238, 246n2, 282, 298, 301 (*see also* Manises; Paterna)

Van Buren, Mary, 165, 167n13

Vásquez de Espinosa, Antonio, 165

Vecino, 120

Verde y morado in New World, 270, 272, 273, 276–277, 319; in Andes, 261, 263–266, 274–275, 305, 306, 315, 316–317, 319; comparing Spain with Peru, 301–302; in Mexico, 224, 273–274, 306. *See also* Loza, New World production spheres of; Mas Alla Polychrome

Verde y morado in Spain, 232, 250, 270, 316; in Paterna, 232; spread of, 229. *See also* Mudéjar pottery

Vertical archipelago model, 12

Viceroyalty of Peru, xvii, 15, 99

Villa San Francisco de Esquilache, 78, 101

Villa Santa Catalina de Guadalcázar, 78, 101

Vineyards, 15, 29, 30, 116n5, 120; and glaze ingredients, 253; in Moquegua valley, 104, 106, 164, 171, 318; patron saints of, 208, 209, 212, 222n8; and Virgin Mary, 222n7; Yaravico, 96. *See also* Wine

Viracocha (Inka), 49, 51

Visita, 102, 115n3, 130

Vizcarra, Alonso de, 122, 172, 176. *See also* Locumbilla

Vizcarra y Bueno de Arana, doña Isabel de, 122, 172, 173. *See also* Fernández Maldonado, don Diego

Vizcarra y Estrada, don Diego de, 122. *See also* Estrada y Vizcarra, Capt. Alonso de

Volcanos, 20, 22, 222n9; ash from, 21, 63. *See also* Huaynaputina

Waka, 44, 98, 218; absence in Moquegua, 67, 79; as boundary, 46

Waranga, 82

Wari, 7; colonists in Moquegua, 33, 35, 37, 311 (*see also* Cerro Baúl); roads, 40, 68n5; and walled compounds, 45

Wayna Qhapaq, 50, 56–57, 102

White undercoating, 224. *See also* False majolica

Wine, 9, 14; agro-industry in Moquegua, 15–16, 94, 104, 210, 216, 318; for church use, 100; and saints, 222n8; and weather, 27, 29; at Yaravico, 173, 174. *See also* Pisco; Vineyards

Witchcraft, 61, 79, 221

World system, 15, 40

Yacango, 100, 130

Yahuay bodega, 11, 105, 114–115, 210; chapel, 114; plan, *114*. *See also* Dominican order

Yaracachi, 77, 124; bodega, 106, 169

Yaravico heredad, 96; boundaries of, 172; and Buenos, 122, 169, 195; Guerrero sale of, 173–174; Jesuit sale of, 96, 109, 172, 173, 196; soils of, 174

Yaravico toponymic zone, *105*, 106, 112, 169, *170*, 185; bodegas and industrial facilities in, *171* (*see also* Locumbilla)

Yaravico Viejo bodega, 112–114, 170, 171; early tinaja at, 112, 181, 216–217; plan of, *113*
Yayal Blue-on-white, 240, 290
YB inscription, 182, 183, 217
Yungas, 47–48
Yunguyu: in altiplano, 52, 72; in Moquegua, 72

Zaragoza, majolica production in, 229; glazing of, 253–*254*, 278n8, 301
Zori, Colleen, 53n5
Zuidema, Tom, 43, 54n8, 73
Zunilata, San Mateo de, 102, 115n4, 130

www.ingramcontent.com/pod-product-compliance
Lightning Source LLC
Chambersburg PA
CBHW052130070526
44585CB00017B/1773